UNDUE
INFLUENCE

UNDUE INFLUENCE

THE EPIC BATTLE FOR THE
JOHNSON & JOHNSON FORTUNE

DAVID MARGOLICK

WILLIAM MORROW AND COMPANY, INC.

NEW YORK

It is the policy of William Morrow and Company, Inc., and its imprints and affiliates, recognizing the importance of preserving what has been written, to print the books we publish on acid-free paper, and we exert our best efforts to that end.

Margolick, David.
    Undue influence : the epic battle for the Johnson & Johnson fortune / by David Margolick.
      p. cm.
    Includes index.
    ISBN 0-688-06425-6
    1. Johnson, J. Seward d. 1983—Will.   2. Johnson, Barbara
Piasecka—Trials, litigation, etc. I. Title.
KF759.J64M37   1993
338.7'616151'0973—dc20   92-27521
                                                  CIP

Printed in the United States of America

First Edition

1 2 3 4 5 6 7 8 9 10

BOOK DESIGN BY MICHAEL MENDELSOHN

To my parents

ACKNOWLEDGMENTS

It is difficult to remember all of the friends and colleagues who blessed me with their kindness, encouragement, and criticism during this book's long and difficult gestation. I'd like, nonetheless, to try.

At *The New York Times*, Peter Millones, Dennis Stern, Anna Quindlen, Abe Rosenthal, John Lee, Jonathan Landman, and Soma Golden either encouraged me to write about the Johnson case initially, supported me when the project evolved into a book, or waited patiently for the undertaking to be done. Several people at William Morrow, including Sherry Arden, Howard Kaminsky, and Larry Hughes, showed similar enthusiasm and endurance. Early on, when competitive pressures threatened to truncate this project, Larry urged his associates to, as he put it, "Let David write his book." That I have tried to do, and I hope I have justified his faith in me.

At Morrow and beyond, Douglas Stumpf has been this book's most consistent champion. When his official duties changed, Liza Dawson inherited them ably. I'm grateful, too, to others at Morrow who shepherded this book along, including Susan Halligan, Wendy Bellermann, Deborah Weiss Geline, and Joan Marlow. Then there are the faithful and persistent readers who slogged through the manuscript at various stages of bulk and coherence. They include Norman Bloch, June Gardner, Doug Lavine, Irv Lipner, Marian Mass, David Ostwald, Ludwik Seidenman, Richard Shapiro, Rorie Sherman, and Jonathan Winer. Others who helped me in a variety of ways include Julian Bach, Karin Bornstein, Elizabeth Cohen, R. K. Chaffin, Neil Hoos, Michael Mendelsohn, Barbara Oliver, Frank Prial, Richard F. Shepard, Suzy Stein, Matthew Wald, Nathaniel Weiss, and the anonymous geniuses behind (or inside) the Tandy TRS-80 and the Leading Edge Model D.

For little more than a photograph of her beloved Ted Williams, Esther Newberg has worked energetically for this book. From my start at the *National Law Journal*, Jimmy Finkelstein has spurred me on. So has my cousin, Lionel Margolick. Lucjan and Felicja Dobroszyski have been steady sources of love, wit, and wise counsel. I am saddened that three others—Arnold Bauman, Cleave Ferguson, and Izzy Halpern— did not live to see what is in part the product of their constant encouragement. Finally, there are the hundreds of people who granted me interviews, often repeatedly. Many of their names appear in the book; many more do not. I hope they feel I have honored their confidences and warranted their time.

David Margolick
New York

CONTENTS

PRELUDE

The date was May 25, 1989, the occasion the annual Corpus Christi procession in Gdańsk, Poland, birthplace and home of Solidarity. Twenty-five thousand marchers made their way through the medieval city, many carrying pictures of their most famous countryman, Pope John Paul II. Leading them was perhaps the second-most-famous Pole in the world, a man who, with his beefy build and bushy mustache, was very nearly as recognizable: Lech Wałęsa. And at his side was a woman who, while neither as famous nor as powerful a Pole, could claim another superlative: She was undoubtedly the wealthiest.

Barbara Piasecka "Basia" (pronounced BAH-sha) Johnson was a radiant blonde, with a freshness and energy that made her look younger than her fifty-two years. Her smiling face, with its high cheekbones and flattened Slavic features, was unmistakably at home in this crowd. Yet with her understated but elegant clothes, so conspicuous in the sea of shabby Eastern bloc fabrics all around her, it was equally clear that Basia Johnson had long since escaped this place, and was making a triumphant return. Actually, given her regal air, one wondered whether Basia really believed she belonged to this world at all, or, instead, had been ordained to float above it, reaching down occasionally to lend mere mortals a helping hand.

Like most of his countrymen, Wałęsa knew the bare outlines of Basia's remarkable story, even though the Polish Communist regime, apparently intent upon neutralizing one of its wealthiest—and, therefore, its most dangerous—critics, had allowed little of it to seep into the official press. He undoubtedly knew how Basia had left Poland for the United States only twenty years before, with two hundred dollars in her pocket, and taken a job as a maid in the household of J. Seward Johnson, Sr., the Band-Aid and baby-powder heir. To an unhappily married and perpetually libidinous fellow like Seward Johnson, who'd had WASP wives all his long life and was far more interested in sex and sailboats than in sutures or suppositories, the passionate and kinetic Basia, forty-two years his junior, had been a godsend. She captivated

11

and captured the old man, moving within three years from maid to mate. Seward and his youthful Eastern European bride were, as their acquaintance Gregory Peck once put it, "obviously a somewhat bizarre couple." But they spent twelve years together, traveling, collecting art, building fabulous homes and, at the end, suffering. When Seward died in May 1983, he left her virtually all of his $400 million fortune, but she secured it only after battling her six stepchildren, the bitter fruits of the old man's two prior marriages.

Seward had made all his children millionaires many times over during his lifetime, but for them that had never been enough. Not content to follow the example of the disinherited Pullman heir, who brought his dog with him whenever he visited his father's grave, they claimed Seward's last will had been the product of either his dementia or Basia's coercion. As the eldest daughter, Mary Lea Johnson Ryan D'Arc Richards, once put it, Basia had treated her father "like a prize animal going to slaughter." Assisting Basia, the Johnson children charged, was Nina Zagat (pronounced za-GATT), an associate at the prestigious New York law firm of Shearman & Sterling who stood to receive as much as $30 million in fees and commissions for what they claimed was translating Basia's grand conspiracy to steal Seward's estate into legalese. The children set out to depict Nina not as Seward's lawyer but Basia's, and as her flunky, toady, shadow, henchperson, and "do-everythinger" as well. The Johnson children insisted that their motives were altruistic. They sought nothing for themselves, they said; it was for their father's favorite charity, also disinherited, that they were fighting. Not everyone was buying. "The money means nothing to you?" a skeptical reporter once asked Mary Lea Richards. To this, Mary Lea, a childlike woman who seemed to symbolize the fiscal and psychological poverty of an entire family, ingenuously replied, "Anyone can use it."

The will contest that followed was the largest, costliest, ugliest, most spectacular, and most conspicuous in American history. There was a huge set of players: lawyers from several of New York's most illustrious law firms, witnesses, family members, jurors, a judge who was self-made, street-smart, and almost entirely out-of-control. The cornucopia of characters included a Corn and a Berry, a Peach and a Plum. Seward Johnson, a man obsessed with privacy his entire life, had been publicly dissected. In many ways the contest was less between Johnsons than between the people, variously strong-willed, determined, or opportunistic, who had annexed themselves through marriage to their fortunes and the lawyers who had annexed themselves to *them*. Faced with a series of unfriendly wills spanning more than twenty years, the aggres-

sive, ruthless lawyers Seward's offspring and their spouses hired set out
to make the experience so traumatic, so embarrassing, so humiliating,
for Basia that she would cry "uncle" to her stepchildren and pay them,
and handsomely, just to go away.

The Basia that emerged from the case was alternately compassionate
and cruel, cunning and naive, loyal and fickle, generous and selfish,
explosive and meek, articulate and tongue-tied, helpmate and tormentor, cheerful country girl and urbane shrew, someone who spent her
husband's final weeks either wiping his rectum or circling in auction-
house catalogs the antiques she'd soon buy with his money. But Basia
survived what she called her "American hell," and when she walked
out of Surrogate's Court in June 1986, nearly three years after the battle
began, her fingers raised in the sign of victory, she was one of the
world's wealthiest women, a person whose fortune and good fortune
seemed to guarantee her a life of nearly limitless possibilities.

It was a story that astonished everyone—everyone, that is, except
Basia herself. When Basia had been a young girl in Wrocław, a Gypsy
told her she would become wealthy and famous. When she left Poland
in 1967, Basia herself was bold enough to predict she would return one
day in a chauffeur-driven Rolls-Royce. "What do you think will happen
to me?" she asked someone, in a rare moment of uncertainty, upon
arriving in America. "Miss Basia, don't worry about your future," he
replied. "With your smile you will conquer everything."

Sure enough, that had come to pass; and by now she'd grown blasé,
even a bit bored, by her story. It was the nonchalance of the Chosen:
someone convinced she was psychic and could commune with animals
and flowers; who considered Saint Francis a soul mate; who thought
she could cure any living thing, be it animal or employee or lawyer,
merely by laying her magical hands on it. But for all of her solicitude,
her world had room for almost no one else. In lieu of the children she
never had, the family members she tyrannized, and the friends she
picked up only to discard, there were sycophants, opportunists, and
dachshunds. Basia was someone who treated some dogs like people and
some people like dogs.

Wałęsa did not know this tortured side of Basia's tale. He did not
know that for this restless and mercurial woman, everything—her
homes, her artwork, her extracurricular interests, her associates, her
employees—was in a constant state of flux; that her life was a succession
of battles, many of her own making; that Seward's death and the vast
new wealth it brought her released the kind of explosive, erratic behavior that straitened circumstances had previously forced her to hold

in check. Instead, he appeared to fall hopelessly in love with her, won over by the same combination of charm and dynamism, sunniness and sensuality, with which she'd snared Seward. Basia was not, as Wałęsa had feared, one of those affected, pampered princesses who walked around surrounded by cats and dogs and toadies. Instead, she struck him as simple, pretty, unpretentious—"grand in her simplicity" was how he put it. As two obscure Poles whom fortune had placed in extraordinary positions, they had much in common; and the bond between them only deepened as Wałęsa described to Basia the travails of the nearby Lenin Shipyard, the birthplace of Solidarity, which the Communists now proposed to close, ostensibly because of its unprofitability. To keep it open required a miracle. Basia knew next to nothing about ships, save for her late husband's pleasure crafts. But she did know something about miracles. "I will help," she told Wałęsa without skipping a step. "I'm taking it." Within hours, she had committed up to $100 million of Seward's fortune to purchase it.

Poland always had been a place where women worked wonders: The national icon was the Black Madonna of Częstochowa, who pious Poles believed had helped rout the Swedes in the seventeenth century. Now, the country had found its latest heroine. Basia found herself showered with the kind of acceptance and adulation she'd never found in America. There, she would always be a "former chambermaid." Here, she had instantly become a queen, a saint, a savior. Conversely, the Poles had given Basia something, too: a cause, one that united her with her homeland.

Basia had always trusted her instincts, an easy thing to do when one had friends in high places. "I'm fortunate to be in a position to do this," she told an interviewer. "I'm very grateful to God that He chose me to do these things." Still, those who knew Basia Johnson doubted that this new and dramatic deal would ever come to pass. One had, they explained, only to consider her history.

PART ONE

THE
FAMILY

I

One day in the Indian summer of 1968, Esther Underwood "Essie" Johnson, the second wife of J. Seward Johnson, Sr., stood in the kitchen of her Oldwick, New Jersey, home, getting ready to interview a prospective cook. The job requirements, like the house itself, were surprisingly simple for people of such enormous wealth. Long before it became fashionable, she and Seward favored lean, no-frills cuisine. That was why, when the old cook quit, Essie had simply asked her maid, Zofia Koverdan, to find her a replacement, perhaps even another Polish girl so that the two employees could talk on the job. Koverdan had come up with a candidate, someone who'd arrived in America only a few weeks earlier. Essie promptly dispatched her chauffeur to Perth Amboy, an hour or so to the north, to fetch her.

When the limousine returned to the Johnson home, a young woman, wearing a brown suede dress and multicolored scarf, emerged. She was not innately beautiful. Though still youthful, she had lost the lithe, airbrushed perfection of adolescence. She was not heavy, but a bit lumpy; her high cheekbones made her face seem a bit squished. Still, there was a spirit to her—a freshness, a sunniness—that made her more appealing than anything purely physical ever could have. More than anything else, it was her smile. Somehow, it resonated both an earthy, European wholesomeness—a Polish noblewoman once said that it conjured up for her the fields of her native land—and an unalloyed sexuality. It lit up everything around it. For a man, it was the kind of smile that promised to envelop with every kiss. The young woman was ushered into the dining room. Then, with Koverdan acting as interpreter, Essie introduced herself, and the two women shook hands. What appeared at the time to be an ordinary job interview was in fact a historic moment in the bizarre and unpredictable saga of one of America's wealthiest families. The second Mrs. J. Seward Johnson, Sr., had just met the third.

*   *   *

17

Only a few weeks earlier, late on the afternoon of Labor Day 1968, Basia Piasecka first set foot in the United States. She had two hundred dollars to her name, scarcely more in inflationary times than the handful of kopeks brought over by an earlier generation of greenhorns. Her first American night was spent in a ten-dollar-a-night fleabag hotel in midtown Manhattan. The first natives she saw there were two women, curlers in their hair, sitting at a soda fountain—something, she thought disgustedly, that no well-bred Polish woman would ever have done. She slept fitfully and awoke early, pulled open the blinds, and surveyed the scene. Some drunks had gathered on the street below, and in the building across the way stood a surreal ensemble of manikins. It felt more like Mars than the America she'd heard so much about from half a world away. But Basia knew it was only temporary. Besides, she'd seen a lot worse.

Barbara Piasecka was born on February 25, 1937, in Staniewicze-Kuty, a hamlet in what was then the eastern portion of Poland. She was the fourth and final child—and only daughter—of Wojciech Piasecki, a farmer of modest means and his wife, Pelagia. Like those of millions of Poles of her generation, Basia's earliest sensations were of flight and fear. She was barely two when the Germans and Russians marched into Poland from opposite directions and divvied it up. Fleeing what they deemed the greater evil, the family headed west, to Warsaw. Basia later said her first memory was of being grabbed from her father's arms by a Soviet soldier, an experience that helped explain her rabid and lifelong Russophobia. The Piaseckis remained in Warsaw for the next year, staying in a succession of shelters. They eventually settled on the right bank of the Vistula, where her father and brothers spent the rest of the war working in a peat mine. Once the fighting ended, the family moved again, this time to a farm near Poznán. But when the Polish Communists collectivized agriculture shortly after World War II, her family was stripped of their property. In 1950 the Piaseckis moved to Wrocław, where Basia's father took one of those anonymous bureaucratic jobs so common in Eastern bloc countries of that era. At the same time he maintained a small farm.

Basia graduated from grade school and high school in Wrocław, and, in 1957, took courses at the local agricultural school before dropping out, presumably to help her family make ends meet. For the next couple of years she remained at home. Though neither brilliant nor original, Basia was diligent, and managed to get further in her studies than any of her brothers. Indeed, in a reversal of the usual sexual equation, her education was largely the product of their collective labors. Still, her home life was not without its traumas. Basia's mother had a history of mental illness, and at times had been institutionalized. She was given to hallucinations, paranoia, and severe tantrums that she often directed at her daughter, who had been, she regularly reminded the girl, an unwanted child. Basia loved her father as much as she loathed her mother, and lived in fear that in one of her rages, her mother might hurt him. (All her life, she was to prefer the company of older men, largely because they made her think of him.) In such an environment friends were an escape, and Basia made them easily.

In 1959, she entered Wrocław University, where she was to spend the next five years studying art history and philosophy—a path, oddly enough, which probably would have been closed to someone of her humble origins before the dreaded Communists came. After earning her master's degree in 1965 for her thesis on a Polish landscape painter named Jan Stanisławski (for which she received a "*Dobry,*" or "Good"), Basia worked briefly at the National Museum in Wrocław. She then enrolled in a doctoral program in art history at the Jagiellonian University in Cracow.

Basia had a natural beauty that needed no embellishment, and she knew it. Her dress was neat, simple, and modest. She wore no makeup, nor did she smoke or drink. From the age of twelve on, she had boys buzzing around her: There was Lech, a dissident who became a Communist; Richard, a boy from Lwów who brought her chocolates and flowers; Zbigniew the Bulgarian; Tadeusz, who taught at the Polytechnic; Witold, an assistant to her philosophy professor; Dariusz, the first boy with whom she had sex; Janek, a geologist she'd met through a friend of her brother during a trip to Ghana. Basia called all her boyfriends "fiancés," but for her the distinction between "fiancé" and "friend" was blurred. She found she preferred the company of older, more worldly men, men more like her father. While her contemporaries married and had children, Basia remained single.

A job in an art museum paying her a thousand złotys a month was not enough to satisfy a woman of Basia's ambitions. In 1967 she left Poland again, this time for Rome. Her worldly fortune was on her finger, in a ring her brother and a family friend had given her, which she sold en route to Italy. She went there, she later said, to pursue a scholarship from the Vatican to study art history. It was a claim no one was ever able to substantiate; Basia herself was always fuzzy on the details. She stayed in Rome for ten months, in a pensione run by some relatives of Stefan Cardinal Wyszynski, the Roman Catholic primate of Poland. Again displaying her lifelong ability to make people want to help her, Basia had her hosts finagle political asylum for her, then a visa for the United States.

Now, she found herself ensconced in the dingy Hotel Wolcott. In an era of international homogenization, elevators, like toilets, still vary from culture to culture. When, during her first morning in America, she boarded the elevator, she pressed the wrong button and found herself in the bowels of the building, where she encountered a Polish-born janitor. Over breakfast in a nearby café, he discouraged her from seeking work in a museum or on a Polish-language newspaper, as she had planned. Far better, he said, was a job as a domestic; with free room and board, one could save enough money for English classes. Together, they reviewed the classifieds. Later Basia explored the neighborhood, and spent the first of her few dollars on some shampoo and bandages. Both, she later recalled, were made by a company she had never heard of before: Johnson & Johnson.

Basia stayed at the New York hotel for a few days without mishap. But as she prepared for bed one night, she saw a man's hand coming through the curtains. Her screams frightened the intruder away. The following day she recounted her experience to Heronim Wyszynski of the Polish Immigration Committee in New York. He took pity on the pretty girl, and asked her to move in with him and his wife in nearby Perth Amboy until she could find a place of her own. Wyszynski dispatched his wife, Danuta, to the local train station with directions to look for a "typical Polish beauty" disembarking from the New York train. She had no trouble recognizing Basia.

Shortly thereafter, Basia accompanied the Wyszynskis to a party given by some friends. Among the guests was Zofia Koverdan, still carrying Essie Johnson's instructions to find a new cook. When Danuta suggested Basia, Koverdan hesitated; with her flowing light brown hair, blue eyes, and long lashes, the new arrival seemed too fine to spend her days toiling over an oven. Indeed, when Basia discussed her future with Koverdan, she talked of becoming an actress, meeting a rich man, leading a good life. But Koverdan liked her instantly, and encouraged her to seek the job. She assured Basia that in the Johnson household, limited cooking experience would not necessarily be a handicap. "They eat very simply," she explained. "They're always on a diet."

A few days later an apprehensive Basia, wearing her best Polish clothes, journeyed to Oldwick, an elegant community in New Jersey horse country an hour from New York. She was ushered into the room where the help ate their meals, and awaited Essie Johnson. A few moments later the chatelaine, an elegant older woman of an athletic,

Katharine Hepburnesque cast, more handsome than pretty, entered and introduced herself. Essie asked Basia if she could cook, and Basia assured her in her halting English that she could. What could she cook best? "Hors d'oeuvres," Basia replied. Sensing that her new friend was already foundering, the motherly Koverdan stepped in. "If she can cook fancy stuff, she can certainly cook a regular meal," she assured Essie. The ploy worked. Shortly thereafter, carrying the small suitcase that contained all her worldly belongings, Basia joined the Johnson household.

Basia did not catch her first glimpse of J. Seward Johnson, Sr., until she'd been on the job for nearly a week. One morning, a trim man with an immaculate white goatee took a detour through the kitchen en route to the garage. Seward Johnson was seventy-three years old, but walked and talked with the vigor of a much younger man. His blue eyes had a youthful sparkle, the result of both his joie de vivre and some malfunctioning tear ducts. Though he was heading toward his office, he was wearing the casual tweeds of a country gentleman rather than the conformist gray flannels of a Johnson & Johnson executive. The clothes were apt, for Seward's official responsibilities were few. "My wife told me we have a pretty cook," he said to her pleasantly, as Essie stood not far away. "I'm Mr. Johnson. I hope you will be happy here." Basia, flustered, simply smiled, then watched him bound out the door. She could not explain it, but she was struck by an odd feeling—that somehow, somewhere, she had seen this man before.

II

Just who was John Seward Johnson, Sr.? According to the corporate publicists at Johnson & Johnson, he was not your ordinary executive, but the patrician, paternalistic type—one of that rare breed of chieftains, like Ford or Kaiser, who not only ran a giant corporation but had his name emblazoned on it. In 1968, around the time that Basia carried her tiny suitcase into Oldwick, the cover of the Johnson & Johnson employees' bulletin featured Seward's smiling countenance upon it. Inside was a profile of the company's "finance chairman," whose job it was, it said, "to keep Johnson & Johnson's money moving." His appeared to be an awesome task, requiring work from dawn to dusk in the office, then homework far into the night. The written account was curiously vague about precisely what those tasks were. But by noon each workday, it stated, "Mr. Johnson would have made decisions that triggered financial transactions involving millions of dollars."

The article described Seward's beginnings at J&J in 1916, his roles there after World War I in corporate planning and promotion, his travels with his older brother, Robert Wood Johnson, in search of foreign markets. It reported how, by 1930, the thirty-five-year-old Seward had risen to vice president and treasurer of the company. And then, once more, the report grew hazy. In 1937, it related, Seward had resigned "to assume responsibilities in the foreign activities of the company," though his postings, responsibilities, and accomplishments were never enumerated. At some unspecified point he had apparently returned to the United States, serving once again as vice president of J&J and as a member of its board until 1955, when he'd gone into what the authors called "semi-retirement." It was from this that he had emerged, ostensibly at his older brother's request, to take the finance job in 1967.

Surprisingly for what had long been a family-run company, nowhere in the article was there any mention of any wife or children. Instead, there was a picture of Seward the sailor man wearing a floppy white hat and striking a solemn old-man-and-the-sea-type pose. Nearby were two photographs of the *Ocean Pearl*, his beloved sixty-one-foot ketch. There were shots of Seward the gentleman farmer standing alongside one of his prize-winning Holsteins. And Seward the philanthropist, who thirty-odd years earlier had slaughtered some show sheep for the Depression-era hungry, and had ground them up democratically so that no one would get a choicer cut. And Seward the humanitarian, whose concerns included oceanography, conservation, medical care, and, now, in the wake of the assassination of Dr. Martin Luther King, Jr., racial justice. "We are postponing any further expansion of charitable activities in international relations until the problems of our ghettos and cities and race relations are corrected," he declared confidently.

There was Seward at his office desk, reviewing his day's appointments with his secretary, Miss Mary Frances Perree. In what the magazine called his "rich, young, resonant voice," Seward explained Perree's duties: "administering the activities assigned to this office, carrying out my directions, but adding an additional and natural Irish diplomacy which results in getting things done cheerfully." (Years later, Perree listed one further responsibility: to keep away all of the "leeches" after Seward's money.) There was also a picture of Seward climbing into his Porsche—New Jersey license plate ISJ–4—at day's end. Seward Johnson was clearly one mogul who did not let his vast power go to his head, or allow his awesome responsibilities to get him down. "Through all of this," the reporter wrote, "Mr. Johnson's disposition remains cheery, lighthearted and confident. He goes about the preparation for his executive responsibilities with a casual competence." Each morning, for instance, all these executive responsibilities waited while Perree served Seward his ration of three cookies. "With a smile that brightened his rugged, handsome face lined with regular laughter, he chuckled, 'maybe it will improve my disposition,' " the article continued. "With that he broke into easy laughter, and settled comfortably into his black leather chair."

That reclining position, the article neglected to say, came easily to Seward. Other members of his family had seen to that.

The Johnson & Johnson saga began with Seward's grandfather, a Pough-keepsie drug clerk named Robert Wood Johnson, who came to New York in the early 1870s and began manufacturing medicinal plasters. During the celebration of the American centennial in 1876, he heard a lecture by Sir Joseph Lister, one of the men who first recognized that airborne germs—"invisible assassins," he called them—caused infection. From that, Johnson hatched the idea of a new type of surgical dressing: ready-made, individually wrapped, antiseptic. By 1886 he and his two brothers, James Wood Johnson and Edward Mead Johnson, were manufacturing it out of an old wallpaper factory in New Brunswick. The following year, Johnson & Johnson was incorporated. Within a few years J&J products, featuring the company's distinctive red cursive logo and a bright red cross, could be found all over the world.

There followed innumerable innovations—the first first-aid kit, the first sterile bandages, improved sutures. Many were the handiwork of Fred Kilmer, the company's scientific director and father of Joyce Kilmer, the poet who wrote "Trees." In 1894, the year before Seward's birth, Johnson's baby powder was rubbed on the first of billions of buttocks. The Band-Aid came along in 1920, the quaint sexist folklore attributing its creation to a newly married employee whose young bride kept maiming herself in the kitchen. For Johnson & Johnson good citizenship was good business: Through products and propaganda, the company became synonomous with hygiene, health, healing. So, too, for that matter, were death and destruction. The company shipped 80 percent of the surgical supplies used after the 1906 San Francisco earthquake and prospered during World War I, the largest mass infliction of wounds in human history.

In 1897 Edward left to set up the rival pharmaceutical firm of Mead Johnson. Edward's two brothers remained, with Robert Wood in charge. As Robert ran the company, he raised a family. A son, also named Robert Wood, was born in 1893. The hero of our story, christened John Seward but generally referred to by his middle name, came along two years later. He was followed, in 1897, by a daughter, Evangeline. Together, they led pampered but regimented childhoods, the kind filled with pet ponies, governesses, footmen, and phaetons. Everything was done according to routine: luncheon every day in the dining room with their parents, suppers by themselves in the nursery, an audience with Father in the library at five-thirty every afternoon. When it came to imparting his worldly wisdom to his children, time was of the essence; Robert was fifty when the first of them was born. Papa Johnson lived well. He had his salmon shipped in from Canada, his ducks from Georgia, his coffee from Brazil; he amassed so much fine wine that his widow remained amply stocked long after his death, just as his son Seward would do with Basia seventy years later. The Johnsons had two homes in New Brunswick, one for winter use, the other a farm for spring and fall. Summers were for traveling. For instance, young Robert and his mother went to England in 1910 for the coronation of George V.

Robert's oldest son and namesake showed an unusual aptitude for business—far more than his brother, Seward, chose to (or, given the family's patrilineal ways, his sister Evangeline was allowed to) display. Upon the elder Robert Wood's death in 1910, J&J was run by their uncle James, but only until the younger Robert Wood Johnson came of age. The second Robert Wood quickly rose through the ranks, and by 1932 was running the entire company, a perch from which he became a towering figure in American industry. As the company grew, so, too, did the Johnson family's wealth. When the company stock went public in 1944, Robert Wood and Seward each took a third (the rest was placed on the open market), then watched it divide and redivide like cells. Sister Evangeline was given the booby prize: preferred stock that paid comparatively generous dividends but didn't increase in value. A vital, exotic, and beautiful woman, Evangeline cultivated a life of her own, away from the company. She married the conductor Leopold Stokowski, bore him two daughters, and became an art collector, political activist, and aviatrix. In the early 1920s, when she waged a one-woman campaign in Palm Beach to allow more abbreviated bathing suits, she printed up some handbills and dusted the beach with them from the open cockpit of her plane.

Ramrod-straight, imperious, dictatorial, fastidious, Seward's big brother, Robert Wood Johnson, was, in the words of one colleague, "the only person I ever knew who never doubted any decision he made." For decades this man, undeviatingly dressed in a perfectly pressed dark blue suit with a perfectly starched white shirt, was a fixture around the company, around New Brunswick, around New Jersey. He was a chairman in the Mao Zedong mold; his speeches were taped and played throughout his factories, his thoughts collected in books. He was obsessed with cleanliness. He arrived on impromptu inspection tours by helicopter, to make sure nothing was improperly stored on factory roofs; anyone whose office wasn't spit-shined, whose desk wasn't dustless, was summarily fired. Once, he picked up a brick and threw it through a dirty factory window. Even his home would have made Lister proud: One tale had it that he would not permit cars on his driveway, lest the oil from them soil the crushed white paving stones. He was an enlightened industrialist, an apostle of modernization, corporate responsibility, good employee relations, and public-spiritedness. It was he, for instance, who first proposed a "New Jersey Turnpike." Though he officially earned the title of General for his production work during World War II, Robert Wood Johnson in fact played the role all of his life.

The company's in-house histories of its founding family were as scru-

pulously sanitized as its production lines. They never noted the tu-
multuousness of the General's personal life, including his three
marriages, the second to a chorus girl, the third to a ballroom dancer.
The last marriage, to Evelyne Vernon "Evie" Johnson, was his longest
and most public; photographers shot them on the *Queen Mary*, at the
Stork Club, or indulging their passion for ballroom dancing. And compared to fatherhood, marriage had been a breeze. The General's son
and heir, yet another Robert Wood Johnson, tried working his way up
the J&J ladder, but "Bobby" Johnson preferred drinking and card playing
to corporate affairs. Perhaps just as bad, he was overweight, thereby
lacking the discipline his father prized. The General hounded his son,
had him investigated, tapped his telephone, and eventually kicked him
out of the company—placing his personal effects, according to one
story, on the front lawn of the company's offices. Bobby Johnson died
only a few months after his father did.

Seward, two years the General's junior, had been a frail child. He
always seemed to be in bed, sheltered from a hostile, germ-infested
world by a sheet soaked in J&J camphenol. He had curly blond hair
that fell to his shoulders, and looked so much like an angel to his
mother that she would often stand by his crib at night just to make
sure he was still breathing. Seward had a series of private tutors, then
attended the Rutgers Preparatory School, from which he graduated in
1913. Two years later, at age twenty, he headed off to Yale's Sheffield
Scientific School, an appropriate place given his tinkering turn of mind.
But he was never much of a student, and though he always considered
himself a Yalie, he actually left college at the end of his freshman year.
The only degrees he ever won were honorary, invariably from institutions coveting contributions.

Seward worked briefly at Johnson & Johnson, but when the United
States entered World War I, he enlisted in the navy. In September
1917 he became a seaman second class, specializing in sending coded
messages by semaphore and blinker. Eventually, he went overseas, becoming second-in-command of Sub Chaser 255—assigned, as he later
described it, to "bottle up" German and Austrian submarines in the
Mediterranean. By the Armistice he'd become a lieutenant and earned
the nickname "Speedy"—though more, apparently, for sexual exploits
than nautical ones. Indeed, when, a few years later, his brother Bob,
sought Seward's help in setting up a "planning department" for the
company, he tracked him down in Spain, "studying old wine and young
senoritas." Seward worked briefly in promotions, then, in 1922, traveled
with the General and Carter Nicholas, Seward's nephew, lifelong sailing

companion, and fellow philanderer, on an "inspection tour" of the British Empire, France, Egypt, India, Australia, China, and Japan. In all likelihood, Seward's contributions to the endeavor were small. Indeed, while the tough-minded General gave his life to the company, Seward largely went along for the ride. "You can't have two captains of a ship," Seward would say. "My brother's the captain of Johnson & Johnson."

Seward began his marital career with Ruth Dill, whom he met at a garden party in New Brunswick in 1920. He was twenty-five; she was sixteen. Ruth was the daughter of Colonel Thomas Dill, onetime attorney general of Bermuda. (Her younger sister Diana was once married to Kirk Douglas; Michael Douglas was her nephew). Ruth, who was in boarding school at the time, initially found "Johnny" Johnson stuck up, or perhaps shy, and the relationship went nowhere. The two remained in touch, but so unromantic—or obtuse—was the young Seward that when he wrote her from various ports-of-call on his round-the-world junket, he invariably described the women he'd met along the way. But when Ruth sailed to England with her family in 1924, Seward showed up on board. Spurred into action by a foppish competitor, Seward cut in on Ruth in the middle of a fox-trot, and took her out on deck. Lloyd Mayer, biographer of Ruth's father, described what ensued:

> It was a mellow night. The ship rolled slowly, rhythmically, like a contented whale, her masts tracing patterns on the starry sky. Phosphorus gleamed in the pearly ruffle of her wake, the throb of her engines synchronised with the beating of Ruth's heart. For she was excited by the sudden manifestation of an unsuspected dynamism in Johnny. He led her to a sheltered corner of the boat deck, then his arms encircled her and she yielded to his embrace. "I've loved you always, darling," he said. Responding to his kiss left her breathless, a moment later she whispered, "Oh, Johnny—I love you, too."

The next morning, while the old man was shaving, Seward asked Ruth's father for her hand. "My God! You almost made me cut my throat!" he thundered before granting his consent. The two married in London on July 14, 1924, Seward's twenty-ninth birthday, then honeymooned in France and Italy. A family quickly followed. The first to arrive, in August 1926, was Mary Lea, who made her public debut at the age of two on the Johnson & Johnson baby-powder can. Another daughter, Elaine, followed a year later. In 1930 came a son, John Seward Johnson, Jr. Two years later Diana arrived. Ruth was a kindly but somewhat distracted mother: An avid golfer, she once, according to one family story, wrapped young Junior Johnson in a fur coat, placed him on a green momentarily, and forgot to pick him up. The baby spent the night on the links.

To house his growing brood, Seward built a $350,000 stone mansion across the Raritan River from Johnson & Johnson's New Brunswick factory. Ruth named it "Merriewold," a name, she later said, she found "in some book or the other." It was a stately structure, adorned with English oak, Italian marble, and, on the roof, five hundred tons of slate imported from the Cotswolds. Inside was a circular staircase modeled after the one in Philadelphia's city hall. The fireplace in the breakfast room has the signs of the Zodiac under which Seward, Ruth, and Mary Lea were born, and, this being Prohibition, there was a taproom hidden behind the *Encyclopedia Britannica.* Seward installed his own personal landing field in the backyard.

Contemporary press reports painted a romantic picture of the young executive and his "titian-haired Bermuda wife." In his considerable spare time Seward prospered as a sailor. He owned and raced yachts on Long Island Sound, and, in 1933, won the Prince of Wales Cup in Bermuda. The year before, he was one of four Americans honored by King George VI for winning the British-American Cup. (During Prohibition he occasionally directed his sailing skills toward bootlegging, outrunning Coast Guard cutters with shiploads of illegal hooch. "They couldn't touch us," he later boasted.) But life at Merriewold proved problematic. The danger of kidnapping had stalked Seward and his siblings from childhood; once, their father received a scrawled note from "The Black Hand" threatening to kill his children unless he deposited two thousand dollars in a graveyard outside New Brunwick, and the children were shadowed by Pinkerton detectives until the culprits were caught. Early on the morning of March 19, 1932, only two and a half weeks after the Lindbergh baby had been abducted in nearby Hopewell, an intruder tried to break into young Diana Johnson's nursery. Whether it was an attempted kidnapping or a botched burglary was never clear. But the episode fanned Seward's lifelong obsession with security; soon, bars were installed on the windows and barbed wire wrapped around the house. Even these precautions failed to calm Seward, and before long he shipped off his family, complete with a milk cow, to Bermuda for two years. They were to return only briefly to Merriewold before giving it up.

Seward's experiment with monogamy was short-lived. Philandering might have been in his nature, or perhaps had been imposed upon him;

his mother-in-law theorized that Seward had never been normal after young Junior Johnson dropped an iron flowerpot on his father's head. At one point Seward fell for Ruth's nineteen-year-old sister Frances, and stalked off to England when she spurned him. Later he had an affair with the daughter of the Brazilian strongman Getulio Vargas. Johnson & Johnson began distancing itself from its prodigal grandson, announcing that he had resigned as treasurer to "assume responsibilities in the foreign activities of the company." The stoical Ruth had given her wayward husband two years to mend his ways. But Seward persisted, and in October 1937 she went to Reno for a divorce. (There she ran into Seward's sister, Evangeline, whose marriage to Stokowski had also come apart once Greta Garbo had come along.) During the perfunctory proceedings that followed, Ruth's lawyer asked her to describe Seward's attitude toward her. "Extreme indifference," she replied.

Ruth got custody of the four children. She also got a written pledge from Seward to bequeath to them one half of his ever-growing estate. That provided little short-run consolation for youngsters shattered by divorce and a largely neglectful father, but legally at least, was to prove of considerable importance later on. Ruth subsequently married a Boston businessman named Philip Crockett, and moved into what had once been the chauffeur's cottage at Merriewold, whose main house had been sold. There she was to spend the next half-century, living in the shadow of her early opulence.

Seward eventually returned from his peregrinations, and in 1939, after being spurned by the theatrical designer Lucinda Ballard, he married Esther "Essie" Underwood of Boston. The choice was surprising, and not just because friends thought Seward preferred her sister. Essie seemed more refined, progressive, and artistically inclined (Georgia O'Keeffe was a close friend) than the rather rudimentary Seward. She held little appeal sexually for him; years later Basia claimed Seward had told her that on the night he'd married Essie, he'd actually slept with another woman, and that Essie wasn't much interested in men. Be that as it may, Seward the gentleman farmer was soon doing some more breeding. A daughter, Jennifer, was born in 1941, and five years later came a son, James. In a lifetime spent trying to reduce his tax bills, the newest arrivals represented what might have been Seward's only slips; both children were born on January 2, a few hours too late to afford him exemptions for the previous year. Seward's second family, which rarely mixed with his first, spent the school year in Oldwick, summers on Cape Cod, and winters in Hobe Sound, Florida.

During World War II Seward made his modest contribution to the

Arsenal of Democracy, managing a Johnson & Johnson machine shop that had been retooled to manufacture aircraft parts and made an abortive stab at developing a diesel engine for planes. His subordinates saw him as a benevolent but lazy boss, who sauntered in late each morning and took men off war work to make doodads for him. The company ceased operations after V-J Day, and Seward returned to Johnson & Johnson. His title sounded impressive: vice president and member of the board of directors. In fact, his responsibilities were nil. A keen judge of talent, Robert Wood Johnson decided that the Seward who served least served best. In the meantime Seward grew richer: By January 1962 his J&J holdings—the vast bulk of his wealth—were worth nearly $51 million. Five years later they had grown to more than $91 million.

Seward continued to sail, ultimately commissioning the *Ocean Pearl*, a handsome vessel, its keel carved from a single log and finished entirely in teak. The hand-sewn sails were the rust-red color favored by Breton sailors. When he wasn't racing himself, Seward sponsored boats in the America's Cup and, combining his recreational and scientific interests, became involved with the Woods Hole Oceanographic Institute. He also continued his evolution into a country squire. Years earlier a family adviser had happened upon the youngish Seward lying on a couch in a trancelike state, trying, as he explained, "to think like a cow." Seward treated his prize-winning herd of Holstein-Friesian dairy cattle like royalty, feeding them imported oats, providing for them in his will, and as the Cold War raged and nuclear Armageddon loomed, designing a bomb shelter for them—"a Noah's Ark kind of thing," his lawyer at the time later said.

With an older man's wisdom, a younger man's libido, and a connoisseur's eye—though most men appreciated breasts and buttocks, he once explained to a pretty younger woman, he personally favored necks—Seward remained sexually active. "He led a private life, which is not to say that it wasn't hedonistic," a lawyer once said of him. One might have thought Essie hadn't cared; members of the J&J family knew she had women guests at her home in Cape Cod, and that she had little respect for Seward anyway. "She called him all kinds of names in public," one said. "She'd say, 'You're stupid! That's why your brother is running the company and you're not!' " Still, Essie periodically went through his pockets, looking for incriminating evidence; convinced it was perverse for someone of his years still to be chasing skirts, she made him see a psychiatrist at Payne-Whitney. In the J&J executive suite word was that Seward "would screw anything that would move or not move." Assignations aboard the *Ocean Pearl* were simple; Seward's faithful skipper, Raymond Gore, dutifully omitted the names of Seward's companions from the ship's log. On land, however, things could become more complicated. Once, when inclement weather delayed a paramour's departure from Oldwick beyond Essie's scheduled reappearance, the young woman spent the night chez Perree—that is, chez Fran Perree, who like many executive secretaries doubled as accessories after the fact. With loyalty like that, it was small wonder that Seward bestowed shares of J&J stock upon her, bought her a new Mercedes, bequeathed her as much as ninety thousand dollars in various wills, and sang her praises to Johnson & Johnson's in-house hagiographer.

Publicly, Seward made a great show of his devotion to Johnson & Johnson. He banned all suntan lotions from the *Ocean Pearl*—he claimed it hurt the teak—but granted a special exemption for J&J baby oil. Once, he upbraided a passenger who'd brought Curad bandages instead of the house brand on board. Periodically, he descended from his tractor and came into his New Brunswick office, but usually only when rain prevented him from doing any farm work. Sometimes he would come to board meetings in overalls, or, on at least one occasion, in a safari suit and boots. From time to time he sent kibitzing letters to J&J brass. But for the most part Seward's official "semiretirement" in 1955 scarcely altered his routine. Nor was it changed much twelve years later when he was named chairman of J&J's "finance committee," since the finance committee never met. Perhaps, as the J&J article stated, on the average day Seward "made decisions that triggered financial transactions involving millions of dollars," but if so, it was only because he'd sold off a small chunk of his own stock.

For the most part Seward lived simply. The Oldwick house, while tasteful, was nothing fancy. Though he kept abreast of his wealth, religiously checking J&J stock prices in the morning paper, he rarely flaunted it; indeed, he told people he had no idea how much he was actually worth. If he had trouble spending his fortune, he had just as much difficulty giving it away. While Robert Wood Johnson formed the Johnson New Brunswick Foundation, the precursor of the great foundation that now bears his name, Seward's philanthropy was microcosmic, anecdotal: getting someone a job at J&J, paying for a crippled child's operation, grinding those prized sheep into lamb burgers. At times, undoubtedly under Essie's influence, he revealed a progressive streak, at one point creating an organization that made grants to schools to encourage understanding of other lands. But this was the exception. Simply to save taxes, he had to give away a certain amount of money annually; but so bereft of ideas and energy was he that when tax time came, the task fell by default to his lawyer and his secretary. Eventually, he did find himself a pet charity, the construction of a new hospital for Hunterdon County, where Oldwick was located.

Seward loathed confrontation every bit as much as his older brother relished it. Indeed, Seward was the sort who disliked dissonance or discomfort of any kind. He was someone who arranged to take museum tours after hours, when the crowds were gone, who hated using public toilets or public transit, who liked arriving in a place to find freshly laundered clothes awaiting him in the dresser drawer, who had an automatic transmission installed in his 1938 Rolls-Royce so that he could drive in style without having to shift gears. He hated haggling over money and rarely carried any with him, assigning that chore to Captain Gore or some other flunky. Handed a restaurant bill in Paris once, he laughed and said, "I'm not going to check it. I know they're cheating me anyway."

Whenever there was dirty work to be done, he generally imported somebody else to do it. It was a trait he may have inherited from his mother, who would call the governess whenever she had to turn her children down. "I only wish to say 'yes' to my children," she said. Seward, however, rarely said "yes" or "no" to his children. Indeed, he rarely said anything to them at all.

III

Seward Johnson's attitude toward parenthood could be summarized in a few words: Making children was fun; rearing them was not. Apart from a handful of happy memories, just about the only support he gave his two sets of children was financial, and that was more a matter of company policy and legal obligation than an expression of fatherly concern. When Johnson & Johnson went public in 1944, he set up trusts for Mary Lea, Elaine, Junior, Diana, Jennifer, and the "child about to be born"—Jimmy, as it turned out. Each was funded with 15,000 shares of the newly issued stock, worth $471,250 at the time but certain to grow with the company. Kenneth Perry, the J&J lawyer tending to family affairs, called in Mary Lea and Elaine to tell them they were now very wealthy young ladies. "He left the room, my sister and I danced around the table, and that was the end of that," was how Mary Lea later remembered the scene.

Among Seward's major concerns in life was determining how his vast fortune should be distributed upon his death. He became what one lawyer called "a prolific, even almost professional, testator," altering his will to suit changing whims and tax laws. His grand testamentary scheme, as he once put it, was to devote a third of his money to his family, another third to charity, and the third third "to living it up." Seward apparently believed that by setting up the six 1944 trusts, each of which was soon worth tens of millions of dollars, he had satisfied his obligation to his children, as well as his 1937 pledge to Ruth to leave his children half of his estate, for in the thirty-two wills and codicils he signed from 1966 on, he left virtually nothing further to any of them. The 1944 trusts served other functions, too. As "generation skipping" instruments—that is, income from them went to the children, but their principal remained largely off-limits to them and would, as long as they outlived their spouses, end up primarily with his grandchildren—they provided a handy way to dispose of a large portion of his fortune tax-free. And, since the trustees were J&J brass, the trusts kept the stock under company control. The trustees enjoyed "absolute

33

and uncontrolled discretion" over the trusts, including when, if ever, the children could dip into the principal—meaning, effectively, that they controlled the children's lives. Thus, the children's money, though vast and tantalizingly close, was mostly out of reach. The trusts seemed perfectly structured to rob them of any initiative or independence, to make them millionaires, beggars, and loafers simultaneously, to give people with few apparent intellectual gifts and limited ambition and discipline even more incentive to slough off. Though all went through the motions of educating themselves, several were to spend as much of their lives in courtrooms as in classrooms. The trusts also sowed the seeds of intergenerational warfare among Seward's heirs. Every dollar of trust principal the trustees doled out to his children was a dollar taken from his grandchildren, who would become instant millionaires once their parents had the good grace to die. Undeterred, Seward's issue found themselves spouses (or spouses, often of the gold-digging kind, found them), moved to places where they rarely saw their parents or their siblings, and began rearing rivals.

Mary Lea's public career went into a prolonged eclipse following her debut on the baby-powder can. She had a brief stint onstage, touring once in summer stock with Tallulah Bankhead, but it had been a frustrating experience. "I needed applause," she later said. Her theatrical ambitions thwarted, she married William Ryan, a stern and eccentric man and, to Seward's Episcopalian chagrin, a Catholic, who had once toyed with the priesthood. The Ryans moved to a chicken farm in Maryland and, every year from 1952 through 1956, invariably nine months after their annual vacation in the Poconos, Mary Lea begat a child (the first five, Eric, Seward, Roderick, Hillary [another boy], and Alice, had birthdays of September 1, September 4, September 1, October 22, and September 13, respectively. The sixth child, Quentin, was inexplicably born in February of 1958). The elder Ryan dabbled in different careers, from farming to newspaper publishing. He told people he was "in investments," though when asked what her husband did, Mary Lea would reply, "He cuts the grass."

The bland and unremarkable Elaine, Seward's second daughter, was actually the first to wed. In 1949 she married Keith Wold, an ophthalmologist from Minnesota. (Wold's family thereby completed the biggest marital daily double in history: His sister Betty had already bagged cousin Bobby Johnson, the General's son). The Wolds moved to Florida and had a son and a daughter. Wold stopped practicing medicine in 1965—for reasons of health, he maintained—and devoted himself instead to managing Elaine's assets and dabbling in scientific research, including work on a cure for diarrhea. Diana married a fellow horse enthusiast named Richard Stokes, and they had three foals. Jennifer, Seward's daughter by Essie and the most dynamic of his offspring, wed race-car driver Peter Gregg, and had two sons with him. Her younger brother, Jimmy, married Gretchen Wittenborn Snow and adopted her four young children.

Seward watched his children go their respective ways and, for the most part, paid them little mind. Johnson & Johnson management was no more anxious to employ his daughters than to employ him; only Mary Lea ever worked for the company, and only briefly. But for a time Junior, like the General's son Bobby, figured prominently in J&J's plans. Upon turning twenty-one in 1953, he became a trustee of his own and his siblings' trusts, and in 1965 he would gain full voting rights over the huge blocks of stock in each of them, thereby assuming a large voice in corporate affairs.

From the very beginning, however, Junior Johnson wore the family crown uncomfortably. He was only seven when his parents divorced, and was left traumatized by the experience. He bounced from school to school, finally studying poultry husbandry at the University of Maine—not because he especially liked chickens but because, as he later explained it, it required the least effort. He soon landed in the navy and was shipped off to Korea. Following his discharge in 1955, he married Barbara Eisenfuhr Kline, a woman who, though yet to turn thirty, had already been married and divorced three times. She was an exotic, mysterious woman; Junior's immediate predecessor, who had been married to her for four years, later said he was never really sure of her age, or whether she was German, Swiss, or French. A world-famous collector of scrimshaw, she also collected rich heirs she met aboard ship; she ran into Junior, whom various documents suggest was either three or seven years her junior, while cruising to Bermuda in 1956. The two married that September in Virginia City, Nevada. Accompanying Barbara was her seven-year-old son, Bruce, whom Junior subsequently adopted.

Perhaps sensing that trouble lay ahead, Seward tried to dissuade Junior from joining J&J, going so far as to buy him a 375-acre farm, complete with cows. But Junior, a young man with big dreams, was eager to please his father and assume his familial role, no matter how ill-suited for it he might be. He was given a job at Ethicon, J&J's suture manufacturer, but his career there was brief. Before long he was fired, ostensibly for absenteeism, and his involvement in company affairs was reduced to passing along such periodic brainstorms as toilet paper carved into rectangles of varying lengths instead of the usual squares. Other than that, Junior remained unemployed, spending his time designing fantastic Fritz Lang–like buildings, complaining to and about his trustees, dreaming his dreams. Such indolence was too much even for Seward to bear. "At least I have work," he would say to Junior. "I shine my own shoes."

Fearful, perhaps, that Junior's new and more worldly wife could manipulate him and thereby endanger J&J, General Johnson and his minions dispatched detectives throughout the United States and Europe to scour through her past, hoping to find either some dirt—that she was a Nazi, maybe, or short of that, a Jew—or something that would invalidate the marriage. Supervising the effort was Kenneth Perry, J&J's general counsel, whose job consisted in substantial part of cleaning up the family's messes: It was Perry, Junior once said, who arranged abortions for unmarried Johnson women, and once disposed of a young black stable hand with whom one of Seward's daughters had gotten involved. There were clumsy efforts to split Junior and Barbara apart: Once, Junior recalled, he was called down to the company, ostensibly to sign checks, only to be handed two pistols. It was, he surmised, J&J's way of telling him to watch out for his wife.

Much to Junior's frustration, Seward did nothing to hinder the persecution. "My marriage is under threat, my children, should I have any more, are likely to become bastards—because of this, my life is hell," Junior wrote him. "Anyone who takes the course of perpetrating this situation, I must, in fact, consider my REAL enemy. Dad, show me your colors. Do you, as my father, uphold the sanctity of my marriage?" Seward never replied. A few days later Junior also wrote to the General. "I ask you, Uncle Bob, to use reason, not legal mumbo-jumbo and stand by me and demand my interests are protected and insist that I be taken off the knife of inhuman uncertainty," he pleaded. "I call upon your sense of humanity; I call upon your very manhood." (The General, in return, urged Junior to seek psychiatric help.) Seward also did nothing when Junior was fired at J&J; questioned later about it, he claimed not even to know the reason for the discharge. "Honey, you don't know what it's like to talk to someone who is supposed to be your father but who will sell you down the river," Junior later wrote Barbara. "He is so stupid and so weak behind me. To hell with all stupid jerks like my father and Uncle Bob."

Predictably enough, all of the resistance to his marriage only drove Junior closer to his bride. It also drove him, on at least one occasion, to attempt suicide. One snowy afternoon in January 1958, he drove one of his two Edsels to a remote area in Princeton, hooked up a hose to the exhaust pipe, and tried to asphyxiate himself. (He had brought a gun with him, but the ammunition he had purchased for it didn't fit.) "To whom it may concern: this is to certify that I took my own life. J. Seward Johnson, Jr.," he wrote on one note. Another, to his wife, read: "Dear Barbara, I am dying very happy. I love you very much you are as beautiful inside as a saint. I know my father will see that nothing will harm you again and no one will do you injustice because he knows you are good and I love you."

The suicide attempt, like so much of what Junior did, was botched. A man spotted Junior, his face cherry red, hunched over the steering wheel, and summoned a police officer. The officer smashed the window, dragged Junior out of the car, gave him artificial respiration, and rubbed snow on his face and hands. But only when he placed ammonia capsules (Johnson & Johnson, it seems) in each of Junior's nostrils did the young heir come to. (Neither Junior nor any other Johnson ever expressed his appreciation to the officer, Tony Diaforli. "I was out there bare-assed," Diaforli later recalled. "It's a wonder I didn't get pneumonia, and the son of a bitch never said 'thank you,' 'kiss my ass,' nothing.") Seward subsequently admitted that he did not read Junior's suicide note until five years after the fact. As for Barbara, Junior later charged that her only reaction to the episode was to say that next time he tried such a thing, he should do a better job.

Indeed, by now a marriage under siege had begun disintegrating on its own. So demanding was Barbara, Junior later charged in court papers, that she reduced him to the role of glorified hausfrau, spending his life cooking, answering the phone, directing servants. By September 1958, he maintained, Barbara had deemed their marriage salvageable only if she could go back to Europe—alone—to mull things over. But the plan backfired; upon her return, the same documents state, Junior claimed in the petition, an elated Barbara bragged about her latest sexual conquests at sea, particularly with a man named David Proudlove. She continued to see Proudlove when she returned, and by December he'd moved into Junior's house and, for all practical purposes, his bed. In his plea for divorce Junior listed some of her offenses:

- "She permitted herself to appear scantily clad and in compromising positions with Proudlove.
- "She frequently permitted Proudlove to embrace and fondle her amorously, and to kiss her lips, legs, thighs, and other parts of her body.
- "She received from Proudlove many intimate notes and love poems.

- "She committed adultery with Proudlove.
- "She frequently carried on conversations with Proudlove in her bed-room as though he were her husband.
- "She relegated [Junior] to such menial duties as serving her breakfast in bed, cooking for the household, including Proudlove, acting as babysitter, chauffeur, and errand boy."

Junior's life became, by his own description, "one of constant misery, strain, pressure, and humiliation." The marriage nonetheless survived, and in 1961 Barbara gave birth to a girl. But by the following year it was once more on the rocks. It was then that Junior sued for divorce, submitting what remains arguably the most bizarre and self-destructive document ever filed in a court of law. What followed, as one family attorney put it with lawyerly understatement, was "very, very extended, very acrimonious, and quite lurid."

Junior's motion reviewed his wife's long marital history, dating back to the mid-1940s. He used not only the dirt the J&J investigators had found on Barbara but the company's party line: that because the first of Barbara's divorces was fraudulent, all her subsequent marriages were null and void. Junior now charged that a new boyfriend, an aspiring artist named Darby Bannard, had picked up where Proudlove had left off: kissing Barbara, fondling Barbara, dressing and undressing Barbara, watching Barbara bathe or void, sleeping with Barbara, and, had Barbara had her way, joining Junior and Barbara to create a "cozy" threesome in bed ("Plaintiff refused such a tri-partite arrangement," the divorce complaint states). Despite "frequent requests and entreaties," Junior charged, he and his wife had made love only three times in the prior three years—once with Bannard sitting in the adjoining bedroom.

Both Barbara and Bannard denied the charges. "He would go into fantasy land with his lawyers, and they would write it down," Bannard later said. But intent on proving his point and on extricating himself from the marriage cheaply, Junior moved to catch the alleged lovers *in flagrante delicto.* For the modest fee of one thousand dollars, he and his lawyers hired eight men familiar with three fine arts: breaking, entering, and picture-taking. The ringleader, a private eye named Harry Purcell, repeatedly and surreptitiously cased the Johnson joint. Once, after a boulder on the lawn appeared to move, he ran away, terrified; he could not have known that it was only George, Barbara's century-old pet turtle.

D-Night—the wee hours of ice-cold February 8, 1963—arrived. While Junior and the lawyers remained in their car along the road, the raiders entered through the back of the house. The noise awakened Barbara's pugnacious bulldog, Ebenezer, but Purcell was prepared; a squirt of ammonia onto the pooch's nose from a snub-nosed Woolworth .45 water pistol put Ebenezer temporarily out of commission. The posse then split in two, with each half climbing a different staircase to the bedroom. They opened the doors and snapped on the lights; the photographer took out his Speed Graphic and started clicking away.

Alas, his would not be the only shots that night. Barbara, who had been in bed—alone—had long feared Junior. Once, he had boasted to her that it was "very easy to have someone disappear—and very cheap." She reached for the .22 Colt target pistol she kept in her bedside table, which her father, a champion trap-shooter, had taught her to use, and when one of the raiders, fifty-year-old Harvey Blount, approached her, she shot, and shot, and shot. He fell in a pool of blood. Aroused by the ruckus, Bannard and another man staying elsewhere in the house that night entered the bedroom, where they were immediately roughed up by the detectives. Amid the ensuing confusion Barbara jumped from the window and fled to a neighbor's house, where she telephoned the police. Meanwhile Junior and his lawyers sped away.

In Princeton, a city where indiscretions are normally private, the shooting caused a sensation. Charges and countercharges flew, involving Barbara, Junior, Bannard, Blount, Purcell, and the Princeton chapter of the Society for the Prevention of Cruelty to Animals, which, in an early blow for animal rights, filed a complaint on behalf of Ebenezer (there was testimony that the dog had suffered trauma to his eyes and his psyche, and had stopped wagging his tail). All charges against Junior and Barbara were eventually dropped. The only party to suffer any lasting physical harm was Blount, who lost an eye; he eventually procured a token settlement from the Johnsons for his troubles. As for legal consequences, the only victim was Purcell, who lost his detective's license. In a vain attempt to retrieve it, he sent a handwritten entreaty to Seward, to which the old man, characteristically, never replied. Purcell's wife finally reached Seward by telephone, but their conversation was brief. "Let him go get a job pumping gas!" Seward snapped before hanging up on her.

As the imbroglio died down, the divorce heated up, legally and rhetorically. In December, only a few days after John F. Kennedy had been shot, Barbara's lawyer invoked Lee Harvey Oswald to suggest just how dangerous Junior was. "Plaintiff's condition today demands psychiatric, psychological, and psychoanalytical assistance," he argued. "The tragic assassination in Dallas shows the lengths to which an af-

flicted mind can go." Around the same time the General, having reviewed what he called the "massive peregrinations" of the case, outlined
five "general impressions" he had reached:

"1) The two persons involved are abnormal.
"2) The miscellaneous legal associates of Seward Johnson and Barbara
Johnson have changed frequently and added to the difficulties.
"3) Any reasonable price that will extricate Seward Jr. from these
complex problems should be paid.
"4) He is wise to resign from various trusts at this time.
"5) I hope that he can be given a chance to lead a new life and will
do so successfully."

During the legal skirmishing the various parties gave depositions,
Seward among them. At one point he was asked whether his initially
favorable impressions of his daughter-in-law had changed since he'd
first met her. "I didn't have any impression then. I didn't change my
impression. By that time, I had an unfavorable impression, yes," he
replied. A subsequent colloquy between Seward and his interrogator
revealed some dimensions to Junior's marriage.

Q: "Did not Barbara tell you that Seward [Jr.] was in need of psy-
chiatric treatment for some very unusual tendencies which he had?"
A: "I don't know."
Q: "Do you remember in that conversation the word 'masturbation'
being used?"
A: "I remember she mentioned that, but I don't know when."
Q: "Do you not remember that it was on that particular occasion that
she said to you, 'He requires psychiatric treatment because it is unusual
for a married man to indulge in such excesses'?"
A: "Yes, I think I do remember her saying that."
Q: "Now, do you remember what your response to Barbara was when
she mentioned these tendencies of Seward, Jr.?"
A: "It seems to me that I rather questioned the whole thing."
Q: "Do you not remember saying to Barbara, 'If that's the way he
derives his pleasure, that's for him to determine'?"
A: "No, I don't remember that at all."
Q: "Perhaps I can assist you: Do you remember saying to Barbara that
Dr. Kinsey said that such an attitude was normal?"
A: "I think I mentioned Dr. Kinsey, yes. I thought of that report,
yes. But I don't know that I said it was normal, no."

The divorce case went to trial in late 1964. Seeking to prove either
that his wife had not been divorced when he married her or had been

adulterous afterward, Junior produced a series of witnesses, including a maid who described seeing Bannard in Barbara's bedroom and bathroom (she also mentioned her surprise upon first spotting Junior, who was thinner than in newspaper photographs. "I was under the impression he was a big, fat man drinking Metrecal to stay in shape," she testified). In the meantime J&J offered Junior a deal: He could collapse his trust, and thereby gain funds for his divorce as well as a measure of financial independence for himself, but only if he resigned as trustee of his siblings' trusts and thereby relinquished his remaining influence at Johnson & Johnson. Junior resigned. Apparently upset to lose their only pliable trustee, two of Junior's sisters, Mary Lea and Diana, promptly went to court to block the deal. That was enough to rouse even Seward. In a rare, handwritten note he called Mary Lea "a troublemaker beyond my imagination," and expressed regret that he had created a trust for her in the first place. "Under the circumstances," he concluded, "I will not include you or your family in any further estate planning." The girls quickly smartened up and dropped their lawsuit.

Shortly after his divorce, Junior wed a woman named Joyce Horton. Barbara remained in Princeton, in the same house where the raid had taken place. Her son, Bruce, whom Junior had adopted but from whom he grew estranged following the divorce, graduated from Wesleyan University and soon headed the Museum of American Folk Art in New York. But in 1976, at the age of twenty-seven, he died in a motorcycle crash in upstate New York. Junior did not attend his son's funeral. Junior's mother, Ruth Crockett, did, causing a rupture in their relationship that was to last for several years.

By the mid-1960s the joylessness of Seward's family life was apparent. He had given his children little but money, and they had brought him little but embarrassment. His eldest son, creative but erratic, would have an even more minimal role at Johnson & Johnson than he. Seward told a friend that Mary Lea, his eldest daughter, "was not worth the time to talk about" and that his other daughters were "whores." He also complained that his own marriage was moribund, for Essie, apart from holding little attraction sexually for him, shared none of his interests. Once, he brought her a hawkbill turtle, a souvenir of one of his periodic Caribbean underwater expeditions, only to have her say she "didn't want anything dead hanging on my wall." Increasingly, Seward was chasing more than sharks on these oceanographic jaunts, with mixed success. A young woman he'd once brought along, ostensibly as a radio operator, was promptly shipped back home after Seward found her in bed with one of his shipmates. And he made a play for Joyce Grob, who held the women's scuba deep-diving record and had done stunts in the James Bond movie *Thunderball.* He told her how he craved a companion, someone to dive and sail with him and keep him company aboard the *Ocean Pearl,* and how he could set her up financially for life if she'd agree. Grob, who loved Seward but sought marriage and children with a younger man, declined.

In January 1968 Seward suffered another setback: the death, from cancer, of his older brother. THE GENERAL IS DEAD, the *New Brunswick Home News* declared solemnly, in type bigger than it used to announce the Tet Offensive of the same month. As the flag atop Johnson & Johnson's Johnson Hall flew at half-staff and its factories sat idle, Seward joined hundreds of others, including three governors of New Jersey, in bidding him good-bye. Apart from a few modest bequests, the General left his entire estate, including more than 10 million shares of company stock, to the foundation bearing his name. "He was born with opportunity, which has a tendency to spoil a man," the rector said at his funeral. "Instead, he used it to enrich his own life and the lives of an untold number of people." The same words, or at least the first thirteen of them, could also be applied to Seward. Now nearly seventy-three and robust, he still had time enough to write the second half of his own epitaph.

The General's will contained one last bow to corporate mythology. "I am confident in the future of Johnson & Johnson and that the success of the efforts of two generations of family leadership and enterprise will be continued under the leadership of my brother," he wrote, knowing full well that by his own design neither Seward nor any other Johnson would ever run Johnson & Johnson again. Seward assumed his ceremonial post with the finance committee. It was at this point that the corporate propagandists unveiled the new-and-improved Seward in the company magazine.

There was in fact a new Seward, though hardly the one portrayed in the article. Instead, it was one who could have emerged only after the General's restraining hand had finally been lifted. Visiting his father one day, Junior happened upon a bizarre scene, like one of those children's pictures in which fifty different things are awry. Seward Johnson, normally a decorous man, was leaning back in his chair, feet up on his desk. Seward, who hated tobacco long before "passive smoke" entered the lexicon, was holding a cigar. And Seward, who normally got sick on anything stronger than wine, had a bottle of liquor—brandy or bourbon, Junior could not recall which—in front of him. Savoring his son's disbelief, Seward poured two stiff drinks, then made his declaration of independence: from his late brother, from his wife, from responsibility. "I'm going to take on a mistress," he said.

Who this mistress was and whether he had yet selected her the old man did not say. "I, with some trepidation, lifted my glass in response and took a healthy swallow," Junior said later. "I think we sat there and both drank the drink, and I don't think either one of us was used to drinking it straight, so we sat there in silence. He had thrown off all of his feelings of constraint, and so I was wondering what else he was throwing off."

That a lifelong womanizer would think his philandering noteworthy or bother announcing it is only one of the things that makes Junior's account sound farfetched. But it was undeniable that after a lifetime spent under his older brother's thumb, Seward Johnson was suddenly, dizzyingly free. The mistress he found shortly thereafter wasn't nearly as ready-made as Joyce Grob, the scuba diver. But what she lacked in compatibility, she more than made up for in convenience. She lived, quite literally, under the same roof.

IV

I t did not take long for Basia's inexperience in the kitchen to show.
She pored over the Johnsons' cookbooks, but her English was not
up to the recipes. Nor was her timing up to the standards of the
ever-punctual Johnsons. Lunches called for one o'clock weren't ready
until three, and were invariably undercooked or overcooked. Her turkey
turned out raw, her rice like mud. After about a week an anguished
Essie approached Koverdan. "She isn't working out," she said. "I'm
going to have to fire her." "Oh, Mrs. Johnson, give her another
chance," Koverdan pleaded. "She might be nervous." In the meantime
the loyal Zofia vowed to make haste with her cleaning chores so she
could rescue Basia in the kitchen. Even that wasn't enough, and a few
weeks later Basia was once more on the brink. Koverdan proposed a
solution: They would trade jobs. She would cook, while Basia would
become the upstairs maid, responsible for making the beds and cleaning
the bathrooms.

Basia continued to spend her spare time with the Wyszynskis in Perth
Amboy. Through them, in January 1969, she met a dashing Polish
sailor named Piotr Ejsmont, who had recently escaped from Poland with
his twin brother. Together they had sailed their twenty-three-foot boat
from Denmark to America, and now the two glamorous, bearded men,
distinguishable only by the silver crown on Piotr's front tooth, were to
embark upon a yearlong sail around the world. Two months after Basia
and her sailor man met, they announced they would wed after the
voyage. The Ejsmonts set off in June; Basia, who had accompanied the
Johnsons to their summer home in Chatham, returned to New York to
bid them good-bye. She looked on as a priest blessed the boat, very
nearly tipping it over as he boarded. If the craft couldn't withstand his
weight, a few onlookers wondered, how would it ever circumnavigate
the globe?

Basia had planned to work for the Johnsons only until she'd saved
enough money for English classes. Even at a salary of a hundred dollars
a week, by the summer of 1969 she'd managed to put aside a few

thousand dollars, and was tempted to quit. Koverdan convinced her to stay a while longer, to make some more money and spend a summer on Cape Cod. It was the best advice Koverdan ever gave her.

Basia could not help but notice that the Johnsons' marriage was strained, and that when it came to Seward's eyes, more than his tear ducts were hyperactive. (It was after she arrived, for instance, that Seward had a fling with a beautiful Scandinavian woman named Grete.) One night, for instance, Basia made her usual trip to the Johnsons' bedroom to turn down the covers. When she knocked on the door, she heard Seward's muffled voice. "Barbara, I'm ready," he said formally, cryptically, alluringly. Puzzled and tickled at the same time, Basia scurried downstairs. But if Essie felt any qualms about having a young and voluptuous woman working right under her husband's nose, she never let on. The man she seemed most worried about wasn't Seward but his son-in-law, Keith Wold, the husband of his daughter Elaine. During one of the Wolds' visits to Oldwick, Keith wandered into the kitchen to chat with the beautiful Polish servant girl. He began by asking about her work and Poland; later he requested a cup of tea. Basia saw nothing predatory in his behavior, but Essie, who had known Wold far longer, evidently did. She chastised him for putting Basia to work after hours, then sent Basia to bed, with instructions to lock her door from the inside.

True, Essie had decreed that Basia not wear any risqué swimwear while at Chatham. Basia got around that particular proscription by hiding the corpus delicti under the orange bathrobe Essie had bought her in Bergdorf's until she reached the beach, well out of Essie's sight. And according to Basia, it was Basia in a bikini more than Basia in her brown maid's uniform who really caught Seward's eye; Seward's daughter Jennifer later told her, she said, that he had very nearly run his boat aground once when he spotted her walking along the shore. In fact, there is evidence that Seward did not wait that long. A friend of Basia's later recalled how, in a letter she'd sent him from Oldwick, she'd related that both Seward and one of his sons were making eyes at her, but that she knew which one to cultivate. Moreover, Seward's longtime secretary, Fran Perree, later said the affair began while Essie was at Cape Cod and Seward had remained behind, ostensibly "to work the farm."

Basia's version of the courtship may not be the most reliable, then, but it is the most detailed, colorful, and in its own way, romantic. She has related how, shortly before she was due to leave the Johnsons' employ and return to New York in August 1969, Seward inquired about her plans, and instructed her to call his secretary when she found a place to live. A few days later Basia bade him farewell. "I hope to see you soon," he said, shaking her hand firmly, just the way her father always did. Then Seward's driver, Andy Potvin, took her to the bus station. "You should marry a very rich man, at least as rich as Mr. Johnson," she said he told her. "You deserve that. And then we'll come and work for you."

By the time Basia reached Perth Amboy, after spending a few days in Boston, Seward had already called twice. She did not return his calls, she says. Instead, she began looking for an apartment in New York, eventually renting a two-hundred-dollar-a-month studio on East Fifty-seventh Street, and started studying English at New York University. But Seward persisted, and when he finally tracked her down, he invited her to his office. "I have something very important to tell you," he said mysteriously. The J&J limousine fetched Basia and brought her to Johnson & Johnson, where she was met by the faithful Fran Perree, keeper of Seward's secrets, procurer of his cookies, guardian of his gate. This time around, according to Basia, Perree's "natural Irish diplomacy" was nowhere to be seen. Instead, Perree appeared angry, as if someone else, younger, prettier, and more eligible than she, were encroaching on her turf. Perree informed her boss that his visitor had arrived. "Bring her in immediately," Seward barked. "Close the door and don't interrupt us. I will call you when I need you."

Seward, according to Basia, came to the point quickly. Basia had impressed him with her hard work, thrift, and determination, he said. That kind of spirit reminded him of the American pioneers, and deserved his support. With that in mind, he made a proposal. All his life, he said, he'd wanted to collect art, but he'd always been afraid; he knew nothing about the stuff, and besides, all art dealers were cheats. He knew of Basia's background in art history, and he wanted her to advise him. As a dry run, he asked what she thought of the three paintings hanging in his office—two by Hans Hoffman, the other by Franz Kline. The Kline was good, she told him, with brushstrokes that were strong, decisive, and expressive. But the Hoffmans had no artistic value at all. As it happened, Seward agreed with everything she said, and offered her a job, as curator of the nascent J. Seward Johnson, Sr., collection. The new post paid twelve thousand dollars per annum.

Having bestowed upon Basia a new vocation, Seward then offered her a new avocation: scuba diving. With that, he explained, she could assist him in his oceanographic research. There was a measure of urgency to his request; in six weeks he would be diving in the Bahamas, and he wanted her to come along. Basia objected; she couldn't very well learn diving and English simultaneously. "Don't worry about that," he replied. "You can go to private tutors." And it was done (the diving instructor, on Long Island, mistook Basia for Seward's daughter). Rather than subject his new curator to a train ride with the hoi polloi, Seward gave Basia two thousand dollars to cover the cost of a rental car. Asked years later how she had reacted to Seward's extraordinary proposals, Basia recalled that she'd been "pleasantly surprised."

Concerned that Basia's immigration status might pose a problem for their upcoming expedition, Seward put his lawyer, Robert Myers, on the case. Seward never told Myers how or where he'd met Basia, but as the relationship grew more intimate and expensive, Myers quickly became Seward's bagman. In the fall of 1969 alone Myers made at least four trips to Basia's New York apartment, bringing her nearly eleven thousand dollars. Through a series of calls to Washington and Nassau, Myers assured Basia's egress and ingress into the United States. But leaving nothing to chance, Seward asked a high official at the Smithsonian Institution, to which he'd given large donations, to cable the Bahamas. The Smithsonian dutifully explained to the authorities there that as "photographer, research assistant and diver," a certain "Miss Piasecka" was a key member of Seward's team and should be treated accordingly.

There was no hint at the time that Seward was out not just to study sharks but to impersonate one. Indeed, if Seward had designs on Basia, she said she didn't discern them while sitting in his office. As she later told the story, he was barely perturbed when she mentioned her engagement to Ejsmont. "He sounds like a great young fellow," Seward said. "Maybe he'd like to work for me when he comes back." But around Christmas, word arrived that the Polish sailors, last heard from in Argentina, had vanished at sea. Basia's bereavement was brief. She continued to see Seward, and in February they were on the road again, first to Rome and then to Brazil, the very place where Seward had romanced the dictator Vargas's daughter thirty years earlier. Basia finally sensed that something was afoot: In Rome Seward had grown upset when she'd smiled at an Italian waiter. But things between them, she later insisted, remained platonic. In Rome they had not done as the Romans did, but slept separately in a suite at the Hassler; there were similar arrangements in Brazil, where, on February 25, 1970—Basia's thirty-third birthday—Seward steered her into a cocktail lounge, took her hand, looked her solemnly in the eye, and began to speak. "I really love you, and I want to marry you," he declared.

Here, Basia's own stories deviate. In one version she flatly turned him down. "Let's just live together and be friends," she suggested. "Why destroy our love affair with a piece of paper?" But Seward, this version goes on, carried on until she relented. "Seward was old-fashioned and insisted he wanted to get married," she said later. "He said I was his future. I was the extension of his dream, his life. His children were his past." (In fact, he rarely mentioned them to her at all; nearly another year was to pass before she learned Junior existed.) In the other version Basia's more pragmatic side emerged. "I really love you, and I want to marry you," Seward still declared. "But how?" this Basia replied. "You're already married!" "Don't worry," Seward reassured her. "That's no problem. You're the greatest love of my life!" And with that, he took out an amethyst ring and placed it on her finger. Basia did not know what was happening, but it was something elemental, visceral, celestial. Seward Johnson loved her, of that there could be no doubt. And what did she think of him? Up to now, she had never really known. But at that precise moment, it dawned on her that she loved Seward Johnson, too, that he was the most handsome and intelligent man she'd ever met. "When I said 'yes' to Ejsmont, it was only 'yes,' " she recalled. "When I said 'yes' to Seward, it was more than 'yes.' It was my soul, my anima, my destiny." Only then, she maintains, did they exchange their first kiss, and it was "as if two comets had met." That night, their two bodyguards guarded a single room, and Basia and Seward made love for the first time. Basia later said that Seward told her she was "terrific—the best I've ever had."

For veteran Seward-watchers, his latest fling was particularly hard to fathom. Basia was hardly the robust, rugged outdoorswoman he typically favored, and given her choppy English, the couple could hardly converse. Then there was the chasm in their ages; Basia was younger than four of Seward's children. "I thought she was his granddaughter," one oceanographic buddy later recalled. Still, Seward had always been a man of few words, and she seemed to make him happy. When the lovebirds returned home, word of their romance quickly spread. One day the cook whom Basia had replaced at Oldwick excitedly told Zofia Koverdan that Basia had "hit the jackpot!" "What jackpot?" Koverdan replied quizzically. "Don't you know?" the cook shrieked. "She's with Mr. Johnson!"

Seward quickly abandoned Oldwick and Old Essie, setting up a pied-à-terre across the street from his office in New Brunswick. Rarely, though, did he sleep there. Instead, he could be found in the suite he'd rented for Basia at the Westbury Hotel, on Madison Avenue and Sixty-ninth Street. Basia assumed her curating responsibilities, as specified in the "employment agreement" Myers had drawn up. It described Basia as "a qualified curator, able and willing to devote to the employer whatever time and effort may be necessary or desirable," and defined her duties as "the acquisition, promotion, displaying, showing, exhibiting, and selling of artistic works."

Myers considered the whole thing a subterfuge, a way to funnel Basia a thousand dollars in cash each month. That may have been true, but an impressive collection did take shape. By January 1971 Seward had spent more than $2 million on paintings by Matisse, Cézanne, Mondrian, Monet, Picasso, Léger, Braque, Chagall, Klee, and perhaps most fittingly, Pissarro, the French painter who'd married his mother's maid. He also purchased sculptures by Henry Moore and Jean Arp. If Basia had played any role at all in buying this artwork, at what turned out to be such bargain-basement prices, she had more than earned her keep as a curator. In any case, they were expenses Seward could amply afford: By April 1971 his J&J stock was worth $286,548,718.50. By that May he had added Courbet, Degas, Rouault, and Vlaminck to the roster. By November there was another Courbet and two more Monets, along with a Brancusi *Bird in Space* purchased for the bargain price of $275,000 from Nelson Rockefeller. (Basia and Seward helicoptered up to Pocantico Hills to see the work, which had been shattered by lightning after Happy Rockefeller had placed it outside. Seward had it pasted together, good as new, with Adaptic, a Johnson & Johnson product used to fill teeth, and that coup seemed to please him as much as or more than the aesthetics of the piece.)

By April 1972 there were works by Renoir, Bonnard, and Maillol, along with a second Braque, a fourth Monet, and fourth and fifth Courbet. Soon, there was another Cézanne, though a Kline, a Kokoschka, and the Hoffmans Basia had ridiculed were gone. In November, Seward bought his first van Gogh, and was also the proud owner of two pieces by Rodin. His artistic tab now totaled nearly $8 million. The commissions went primarily to Harold Diamond, a New York dealer who, along with his wife, Hester, an interior decorator, were to grow wealthy from Seward and Basia over the next few years. To house Seward, his bride-to-be, and at least a fraction of their collection until they built their dream house somewhere in New Jersey, Myers found a cozy two-bedroom apartment at 45 Sutton Place South. By Seward's standards the place was not large, but it felt familiar: situated on the corner of the building, with the East River visible from the living room, it was almost as if he were aboard ship. The purchase money was Seward's, the title, Basia's. Though their May-December relationship was still in its springtime, Myers the lawyer was paid to anticipate stormy weather. He knew that were Seward the legal owner, he might be considered a New York resident, and would be bound by law to give Basia part of his estate in the event of a divorce. Basia set about to renovate the place, a task made much easier by the infrequency of their stays there. Between March and October 1970 they spent one hundred days abroad, traveling back to the Bahamas, to Ireland (twice), and to Canada.

Seward had, to use one of his favorite terms, gone "ga-ga" over Basia Piasecka. Besides all the cash he was lavishing upon her, he set up a $500,000 trust fund for her at a Washington bank and bought her jewelry, furs, and other gewgaws from H. Stern, Tiffany's, Hermès, Gucci, and Bergdorf's. Though Basia showed no particular interest in or aptitude for the sea, he commissioned a new yacht—to be called the *Basia*—from the Hinckley Boatyard in Maine. He bought her a stunning house overlooking the Mediterranean in Ansedonia, Italy, an hour and a half north of Rome. Later, for a bit of *lebensraum* and a place to walk the dogs, he built her another house, complete with an olive grove, up the hill (Basia named it "Villa Beata," after her niece). Essie Johnson, who technically remained married to Seward, was unamused by his conduct. At one point Seward dispatched Myers to Cape Cod, with the unenviable task of telling her to curb her expenditures— this at precisely the time Seward was spending fortunes on his Polish paramour. "Why don't you go back and tell Mr. Johnson to marry that whore?" a disgusted Essie asked.

Members of Seward's first family, who had always considered Essie a cold fish anyway, were generally more tolerant. A few of Seward's children had seen Basia the servant girl at Oldwick, but most met her only after she had become Basia the mistress. In December 1970 Junior and Joyce Horton Johnson, the morose, battle-scarred woman he'd met and married around the time his marriage to Barbara fell apart, stopped by the newly renovated Sutton Place pad before dining with Seward and Basia at Lutèce. As Junior recalled the scene, his father had undergone a renovation of his own. Instead of his usual tweeds, he was sporting a turtleneck, with a large gold medallion around his neck; his old reserve had given way to what Junior called an "almost combative swagger." The visitors had barely caught their breath when the old man began showing them around his love nest. "He marched us into the bedroom for no reason at all, like a teenager might do, and sort of said, 'Look!' " Joyce later recalled. "And there was a large nude over the bed." It was Matisse's *LuLu*. While Basia stood like a nervous schoolgirl—"We are going to get married soon," she said meekly— Seward acted like a schoolboy, with all of a schoolboy's gaucheness. The room, Joyce went on, "looked like a little intimate boudoir, and he marched us in there, and none of us wanted to go, and it seemed to be ... it was like an ego trip ... it wasn't ... it was awkward."

At the time, and for the record, Junior was delighted by the dramatic turn in Seward's life. "It was very nice to see you the other night, and to meet Barbara," he wrote his father a few days later. "I am so happy you have someone you can do so many things you like to do with. Your apartment is very nice, even though you find it difficult to find space for all your Picassos, Pissarros and Cezannes." Later, he professed to have been considerably more ambivalent. Sure, with Uncle Bob gone and Essie going, his father could finally come into his own. But this much? "Before, he seemed to draw strength from relating to nature and leading a quiet life," Junior later said, "and all of a sudden he seemed to be tripping the light fantastic." (Basia had misgivings about Junior, too: With all his obsequiousness toward his father, he struck her as more servant than son.) At a family wedding Junior approached his stepmother-to-be with all the butterflies of a young beau at a prep-school mixer. "I asked Basia to dance as an expression of family endorsement, feeling inside me at the same time, I was in the process of jumping off some sort of cliff," he said later. But if he and his siblings were worried about their father, they didn't show it. Junior himself found Basia "full of life"—and a very good dancer to boot.

In the meantime Seward had to introduce, and explain, Basia to his old cronies. Anyone asking Seward how they'd met could sense he'd ventured onto thin ice. "Basia was around Oldwick," Seward might say. He gave some people the impression he'd met Basia in some Polish library—surely the first library Seward had entered since his Rutgers Prep days—and had brought her over to sponsor her education. (Basia, too, would never tell Polish friends she'd been his maid, only that she had "worked for" him.) Around Johnson & Johnson, officials followed the developments with a mixture of envy and bemusement, condescension and apprehensiveness. Aware of Seward's track record, they did not expect the affair to last, but in case it did, J&J investigators checked out Seward's European-born Barbara as they once had Junior's. The first executive to acknowledge the affair was Philip Hofmann, the company's chairman, who invited Seward and Basia to a horse show

together. Any priggishness or prudery Hofmann might have felt had to
yield to pragmatism; the old man, after all, was J&J's largest single
shareholder. Besides, Essie had never been such a bargain. An avid
antivivisectionist, she'd once accused J&J of torturing animals in its
experiments; another time, Hofmann later recalled, she "ate my ass
out" over the embarrassingly low salary—$25,000 per year—that Se-
ward collected at J&J, a figure listed for all to see in the company's
annual report. Hofmann promptly gave the old man a $50,000 raise
just to get Essie off his back, and keep Seward's proxies in place. Seward
officially unveiled Basia at New York's "21," during a retirement party
for one J&J executive, and Basia thought she'd been warmly received.
Behind her back, though, the comments were not always so kind. Once,
as Seward and Basia shared a bed and blanket on the J&J corporate
plane en route to Europe, one executive pulled another aside. "The
screwing that he's getting now is nothing compared to the screwing
he's gonna get," he predicted. Others started calling Basia "Alaska"—
to the more historically inclined, the place once known as "Seward's
Folly."

By the fall of 1970, Seward had bestowed so much money on Basia
that she needed a will—and a lawyer—of her own. He asked his lawyer-
nephew-friend-and-frequent-fellow-philanderer, Carter Nicholas, for
help finding one. Nicholas in turn turned to Thomas P. Ford, head of
the individual clients department at Shearman & Sterling, one of New
York's oldest, largest, toniest, and stuffiest law firms. Ford delegated
what looked like the relatively simple, one-shot task to one of his junior
attorneys, a twenty-eight-year-old recent Yale Law School graduate
named Nina Zagat. Bumping Robert Myers aside, at least for the moment, Seward retained Shearman & Sterling on his own behalf as well.
In his latest example of largess, he decided to bequeath Basia some of
his seemingly inexhaustible supply of J&J stock. The firm drafted a
codicil to that effect, leaving the precise number of shares blank. In
mid-January 1971 Seward and Basia came to Nicholas's office in Rockefeller Center and met Nina for the first time. Seward signed the codicil,
which left to Basia—to whom he referred as "my friend, Barbara Z.
Piasecka"—the stock in the holding companies owning his newly purchased art and Italian property. Upon his death, then, all of the artwork
would belong to Basia. As for the shares of J&J stock, Seward wrote
in "9,000," a bequest worth roughly $500,000.

Basia and Seward briefly considered buying a larger place in New
York, including a town house that later became the residence of the
secretary general of the United Nations. But they opted instead to build

a new home near Princeton, and to live in the charming eighteenth-century farmhouse Seward purchased in Skillman, New Jersey, until it was completed. One day Seward arrived for a tour of the temporary quarters, but his inspection was perfunctory. "He was talking land, but he wasn't thinking land," an eyewitness later recalled. "His hands were all over her. He was like a stallion hot for the trot." The Skillman house would require extensive renovations, notably the installation of various DEW-lines for the security-conscious Seward. As they got under way, Basia and Seward flew off to Ansedonia, where Seward first met Basia's parents and brother Gregory. None of Basia's relatives spoke English and hadn't heard, in Polish or any other language, that Basia had worked for Seward, let alone fallen for him. What Basia's mother thought of the match is not clear, though given their strained relationship Basia would probably not have much cared. Her beloved father had some reservations—"Don't you think this man is a little too old for my daughter?" he asked a friend—but he kept them from Basia.

Back in New Jersey lawyers for Seward and Essie began the laborious task of disentanglement. By August 1971 they had hammered out an agreement. "Unhappy marital difficulties have arisen between the husband and wife with the result that the parties have been living separate and apart in different habitations continuously and without interruption since Jan. 15, 1970. . . ." it began. Under it, Essie got $20 million, plus the homes in Hobe Sound and Chatham; Seward retained docking privileges there, though without any guarantees about the kind of reception he'd now receive once on shore. Once the agreement was struck, all that Seward had to do was come to court and sign it. Still, it took hours for his lawyer to convince this congenitally nonconfrontational man to go. Finally, on November 3, 1971, the thirty-two-year-old union, forged while Basia was but a toddler, officially died. Essie never remarried. But Seward's third and final bout with bachelorhood was his briefest.

The next day, Myers sent copies of a prenuptial agreement he'd drafted for Seward and Basia to Carter Nicholas and James Pitney, another in the Johnson family's stable of lawyers. The wedding was set for a week later: Armistice Day, November 11. On the tenth, Seward, Basia, and the lawyers gathered again, this time at Johnson & Johnson's Kilmer House, to review the pact. It marked another quantum financial leap for Basia: Assuming she stayed with Seward until his bitter end, she stood to collect $10 million, plus an art collection worth millions more, plus the properties in Ansedonia. "Both Mr. Johnson and Miss Piasecka arrived in good spirits and briefly discussed the plans for their pending wedding," Myers subsequently wrote in a memorandum. "Miss Perree advised them that the rings to be used in tomorrow's ceremony were to be delivered at any moment by a messenger from Tiffany's." Myers then asked each to disclose his net worth. Seward's at the time stood at $328,575,040. It consisted, for the most part, of Johnson & Johnson stock: 3,381,291 shares of it, then selling for ninety dollars apiece. The *Ocean Pearl* was worth $100,000, the Oldwick farm $800,000. Basia then listed her assets: the $500,000 Seward had given her in trust; the furs, jewelry, and clothing he'd bought her, worth around $50,000; and $359.06 in cash. In all likelihood Seward had given her most of that, too. Basia, not surprisingly, had no questions for the lawyers. Nor did Seward. At three-thirty they signed the document, to which the faithful Perree affixed her notarial seal.

By the time the formalities were over, the packages from Tiffany's had arrived. So had another, larger box, bearing a label from the Kennedy Galleries in New York. Perree, who had already peeked inside, handed it uneasily to Seward and asked him to remove the lid, remarking that she hoped he hadn't ordered what was inside. Seward took the box, lifted off the top, and peered in. It contained a bird's nest—and a broken egg. Was it Essie's parting shot? Or Perree's? Or something else? No one would ever know. "This was completely unexpected as far as Mr. Johnson and Miss Piasecka were concerned, and none of us could understand the reasoning behind the package," Myers wrote.

The nuptials were to take place in the Skillman house, which Basia had festooned for the occasion with orchids and lilies of the valley. Only a select few were invited: Grace Lambert, heiress to another pharmaceutical fortune (Warner-Lambert) and an old friend of Seward's; Carter Nicholas and his wife; Hester and Harold Diamond; Fran Perree, James Pitney and Robert Myers; Lloyd Wescott, the man who'd convinced Seward to help fund the Hunterdon Medical Center, and his wife; and just to make it official, a local justice of the peace who happened to be a J&J lawyer. None of Seward's children were on the guest list. Indeed, the only relative of either spouse on hand was Seward's sister-in-law Evie Johnson, the General's widow.

Shortly after everyone had arrived, the betrothed and their guests gathered by the fireplace in the living room. The thirty-four-year-old bride wore a greenish dress with gold and blue threads, along with a matching green ring Koverdan had lent her for the occasion; the seventy-six-year-old groom wore a tuxedo with a maroon velvet coat and an ecru cummerbund. The ceremony, which Seward himself had composed, was brief, and was followed by toasts. One came from Basia, in her halting English. "Here's to the man who has given me everything and will give me all, if necessary," she said. Hugging her, petting her, holding her hand, Seward seemed inclined to agree.

Basia, too, seemed jubilant, but in her own, very different way. It was not the usual bridal happiness, of a young woman anticipating wifehood and motherhood. "Now is the wedding; maybe next we are going to have a baptism," one guest declared impishly. "Perhaps for the puppies," Basia replied. As far as anyone could tell, neither then nor at any time afterward did Basia ever display the ineffable sadness of a woman who covets the children she would never have. "She was happy, but I couldn't see the love," one eyewitness later recalled. "She was radiating happiness, but it was the happiness of someone getting what she wanted."

V

In early 1972, a few months after they married, Seward and Basia
sailed the Mediterranean with another pair of newlyweds: Joyce
Grob, the scuba-diving champion Seward had courted a few years
earlier, and the man she had married instead, a NASA astronaut named
Scott MacLeod. As they approached a small, seemingly deserted island
near Corfu, something stirred in Seward. He knew this place, he told
his shipmates; a woman he'd met during World War I, on shore leave
from Sub Chaser 255, had once lived here. The two couples landed,
disembarked, and began negotiating the hilly, rocky terrain. They happened upon a farm and its gnarled, toothless proprietess. Sure enough,
the crone was Seward's old lover.

It was another reminder of how youthful, energetic, and well preserved Seward Johnson, at seventy-six, remained. Here was a man who
simply refused to grow old or to act his age. On the same trip, at another
island, he gazed wonderingly through his binoculars as his bride went
ashore to fetch some figs. It was as if he could not believe his good
fortune. "I love that girl!" he told Scott MacLeod.

Seward was revitalized by his marriage. Up to now, he had squandered
his energies and wealth on small-scale, often self-indulgent endeavors.
Now, with the help of his dynamic bride, he harnessed them as never
before; pet projects long delayed or dimly perceived suddenly came to
fruition. In January 1973 he held nearly $396 million in Johnson &
Johnson stock; with intensified charitable giving and a lavish new lifestyle, it was never to reach that level again. Moneys previously earmarked for Woods Hole or the Smithsonian now went to the fledgling
Harbor Branch Foundation, an oceanographic research center he set
up with Edwin Link, inventor of the Link flight simulator and other
technological marvels, in Fort Pierce, a dusty agricultural community
halfway up Florida's Atlantic Coast. Over the next decade Seward
poured more money into the place—$144 million—than anything since
his children's trusts.

Indeed, Harbor Branch became a kind of surrogate child to Seward, an outlet not just for his philanthropic urges but his lifelong love of the sea, intense scientific curiosity, concern for the environment, and taste for tinkering. He peppered and papered scientists there with a steady flow of suggestions—some precocious bordering on visionary, others crackpot. Once, he proposed that Harbor Branch document every scientific phenomenon occurring in the entire coastal zone, an idea that the head of the foundation, Robert Jones, protested would take one thousand times as many scientists as Harbor Branch had one thousand years to do. "Well," Seward replied, "can you do it for a cubic foot of water?" The proposal, like many others, was received politely, then quietly deep-sixed. "Keep those ideas coming," Jones once wrote Seward. "We may hit a jackpot yet." Seward happily obliged. Concerned about another Great Crash, Seward once suggested converting the foundation's endowment from perishable stock certificates into more durable gold bullion, then burying it.

To keep abreast of his foundation, he and Basia built a $2 million hurricane-, bullet-, and bomb-proof home on a snake-and-mosquito-ridden site nearby. The main portion of the home, with sleek teak trim on the outside, was built to resemble the bridge of one of Seward's favorite ships. Another, the *Ocean Pearl*, was docked nearby. In the back was a swimming pool covered by a dome fashioned by the creator of the Unisphere at the 1964 New York World's Fair. The grounds were studded with fruit trees: oranges, tangerines, grapefruit, lemons, limes, bananas, tangelos, figs. (Many were later ripped out when Seward's allergies kicked up.) Seward thrived in the new house, and left to his own devices, would probably have stayed there year-round. He loved driving over to the foundation in his golf cart, either to work in his office, read and comment upon scientific reports, or kibitz with the researchers. Other times, he was content to sit on the porch, watching the boats and the manatees.

Basia made a show of her interest in scientific things but knew little about them and cared less. She loathed Fort Pierce, a crime-ridden, grime-ridden place with few cultural amenities, preferring to spend her time either in New Jersey, Ansedonia, or another link in the Johnsons' growing archipelago of properties: Children's Bay Cay, a remote private island in the Bahamas once owned by Hume Cronyn and Jessica Tandy. The Johnsons also bought a farm in Poland, though more for political than economic or recreational reasons. The farm was located in Szczescie ("good luck" in Polish), a village not far from Wrocław. Though they had no intentions of ever living there—it would be managed by Basia's brother Gregory—Seward pumped hundreds of thousands of dollars into it, all to prove the superiority of capitalist agricultural methods. Gregory Piasecki also presided over another of the new Seward's pet projects: the conversion, in the Baltic port of Szczecin, of a 119-foot Polish fishing trawler into a luxury yacht large enough to accommodate six guests. The craft itself cost Seward only $260,000, but he spent nearly ten times that on renovations. The boat was christened *Mazurka*—so named, Basia later claimed, because Seward, who had never previously evidenced much of an interest in classical music, had developed a taste for Chopin.

Furnishing their far-flung properties required some serious shopping. Years later the clerks at Bamberger's in Princeton could still recall Basia and her entourage arriving there one day, checklists in hand, ordering three of everything—pillows, sheets, towels—barking orders like "Give me two sets of every color you have!" "This is the young maid who married the dirty old Seward Johnson!" the girls giggled. The next day a van arrived to haul the haul away. Basia's relationship with so resolutely middle class a store was brief; soon, she was buying her bedding at Leron, the exclusive Madison Avenue boutique.

Supervising the estates kept the Johnsons constantly on the go. Their longtime pilot, Dan Malick, later estimated that between 1971 and 1983 he spent four thousand hours ferrying Seward, Basia, and their various dogs in their ever-changing fleet of aircraft: a Beechcraft King-Air, a Swearingen Merlin III, a Grumman Goose, two Grumman Gulfstream IIs, and a Westwind. (Getting in and out of the country was no longer a problem for Basia: In December 1971 she'd become an American citizen. Basia later said it was the happiest day of her life; Seward predicted that great things would flow to the United States from her new status.) On terra firma the Johnsons had another luxurious fleet at their disposal, consisting of Rolls-Royces, Bentleys, and Porsches. The fancy cars were only for special occasions, though; obsessed as he was with security, for everyday use Seward favored what he described as "several inconspicuous Buicks."

But all of the Johnsons' purchases—residential, naval, automotive—paled beside their most colossal undertaking. This was Jasna Polana, their simple "summer home" in Princeton.

"Hilltop," a 140-acre property on the Princeton-Lawrenceville Road, was one of the last great estates in the area. It belonged in 1970 to Mrs. Ferdinand White, Sr., whose grandfather, John Roebling, designed the Brooklyn Bridge. Though her property contained many buildings—a charming Georgian home, along with stables and barns, in one of which, it was said, the blood of Continental soldiers could still be seen in the floorboards—what distinguished it most was its bucolic grounds: Its meadows, brooks, and bridle paths, its azaleas and rhododendrons. When Mrs. White died in 1971, her son decided to sell the place. He set the asking price at $1 million, a fortune in what was still a sleepy college town.

Though they liked living at Skillman, Seward and Basia coveted a place of their own design and inspiration, large enough to accommodate their growing art collection, with enough land left over for a working farm. Robert Myers spent several months in early 1971 canvassing the Princeton area for possible sites, often on harrowing rides aboard the Johnson & Johnson helicopter. When he recommended the White estate, Seward bought it on the spot; a check for $100,000 sealed the deal. On November 24 the *Princeton Packet* (which had reported nothing about the Johnson Piasecka nuptials two weeks earlier) broke the news. "J. SEWARD JOHNSON, SR. SET TO BUY $1 MILLION 'HILLTOP,' " it declared.

Almost overnight, the estate, which had never been fenced off to either deer, horses, or humans, was surrounded by four and a half miles' worth of walls. And, as in Berlin, the barriers grew more ominous and sophisticated with time: An innocuous snow fence gave way to the chain-link variety, the kind adorned with ringlets of razors. A cadre of security men appeared. A guardhouse sprang up on Provinceline Road, and the entrance along Route 206 was also patrolled. Further adding to the military flavor, the Johnsons made periodic inspection tours by low-flying helicopter, shaking up neighbors and prompting threats of retribution. One resident telephoned Seward to complain, only to be told that Mr. Johnson did not take calls. "Tell him his next-door neighbor is about to shoot down his fucking helicopters!" the neighbor exclaimed.

Quickly, speculation arose about the house rising behind the local Iron Curtain. Princeton had always been one of those affluent, enlightened towns where conspicuous consumption was déclassé, where millionaires drove Volkswagens, where the most public signs of excess were all the empty bottles of expensive liquor found in local garbage cans every Monday morning. The townspeople's imaginations ran wild. But even the most fanciful among them could not have envisioned what was to occur. As Basia's personality emerged, the notion of a "simple country house" evolved into what she called "the biggest and best house in the world." And, she might have added, perhaps the most expensive. No one who worked on the project ever forgot the experience. "They talked about it the way survivors talk about battling the Great White, observers about seeing the Loch Ness monster, or veterans about the rigors of war," a reporter named Shawn Tully later wrote. "The experience was as much a part of them as a tattoo."

To design the house, Seward recruited an old navy buddy from World War I, Wallace K. Harrison. Rich patrons were nothing new for Harrison; he had spent much of his career as in-house architect for the Rockefellers, working on Rockefeller Center, the United Nations, Lincoln Center, and the Albany Mall. Even so, it was an odd choice. Though Harrison had done homes for Nelson Rockefeller and J. Robert Oppenheimer, his forte was not residences; indeed, if his experience with the Johnsons was any indication, some of his residences were forts. Furthermore, for Harrison as for the toothless woman near Corfu, the years had not been quite so kind as they had been to Seward; his hearing and heart were giving out. Harrison knew he couldn't make any money off an old friend, and given that friend's insatiable sexual appetites, he had doubts about the most important of the foundations upon which the new home would rest. But loyalty prevailed, and Harrison took the job. Harrison told his associates only that they'd be working for a wealthy industrialist named Johnson, leaving them unsure whether that wealth came from Band-Aids or outboard engines or floor wax or ice cream.

Seward and Harrison agreed where the house should be located— far enough off the highway to screen out all sounds and snoops—but disagreed on the design. Harrison, father of the famous Trylon and Perisphere at the 1939 New York World's Fair, had always been a modernist, and envisioned a contemporary building. Seward was more of a traditionalist. During an early meeting with the architects, he pulled from his pocket a crumpled piece of scratch paper containing a crude pencil sketch of what he wanted: something he called an "Irish country house." It was a pedestrian design, resembling one of those red plastic hotels found on Boardwalk or Marvin Gardens more than a great manse. But the piece of paper became a kind of blueprint, one that Harrison glued to his office wall. Seward directed that the entrance hall be fifty feet wide and that the rooms downstairs be big enough to display works of art. He also decreed where the bedrooms, spa, and fountain were to go, and that there would be separate wings for servants and guests. On one point he was especially adamant: There would be no excess ornamentation—or, as he contemptuously called it, "gingerbread." Basia did not attend the first meeting with the architects. When Seward finally unveiled her, she seemed to understand little, said less, blushed constantly, and smiled shyly at anyone looking her way. Years later, however, a secretary could still recall how Basia dropped her sable coat on the floor that day, how the brittle but still gentlemanly Harrison bent over to pick it up, and how, after the old man had handed it to her, she neglected to thank him for the gesture.

Building mansions was nothing new for Seward; he'd been through it all ten years before Basia had even been born. But in scale and extravagance the new project dwarfed Merriewold, the home he'd built with Ruth Dill. With its 53,173 square feet, the as-yet-unnamed house would undoubtedly be (if you didn't count the guest and servants' quarters) the largest two-bedroom structure in history. Simply to trace the shape of the building on the site took two hundred balls of string. It would include thirty-two toilets, twelve bidets, twelve lavatories, eighteen sinks, nineteen bathtubs, thirteen shower stalls, two elevators, and two vaults—one for art, the other for the seven thousand bottles in Seward's private wine cellar. Apart from the main event, there would be an enclosed swimming pool, an orchid house, a combined "breakfast pavilion" and doghouse, and a covered tennis court. Lewis C. Bowers & Sons of Princeton, whom Harrison hired as general contractors, estimated the house would cost $4.5 million and take two years to build. Harrison feared even those estimates were low, and proposed some money-saving ideas. "We're not going to do any of that," Seward snapped. "And please excuse me. I have to meet my wife to go shopping."

Who was the prime mover behind this monumental endeavor? It quickly became clear that it wasn't Harrison or Seward, but Basia. Many people, particularly Seward's old cronies and his new wife's childhood friends from Poland, noticed the same thing: Basia's sudden and unimaginable wealth unleashed something in her. When it came to living and acting like a millionairess, she needed no apprenticeship. It was as if she'd known opulence in a prior incarnation, so that she was not starting from scratch so much as making up for lost time. Almost overnight, she leapfrogged from awkwardness to comfort to dominance to abusiveness, or, as one eyewitness put it, from "mousy little maid to conniving little witch." And from the claustrophobia of a studio apartment in Manhattan to country living in Princeton. The new house would be a monument to her megalomania. Only the dollars would be Seward's, and this, to all appearances, was just how he wanted it to be. "The golden rule is made by the man who has the gold," he liked to say. And now, the man with the gold wanted to spend it on his bride. "This is your house," he once told Basia as they viewed an elaborate scale model of the estate. "You can do what you want with it."

When Seward spoke of the house-to-be, it was in relatively modest terms. He was thinking of posterity as much as current creature comforts; eventually, he suggested, the property would be donated to the town of Princeton. For Basia, the goal and the rhetoric were very different, as a tour guide at Wilanów, the seventeenth-century summer palace of Poland's King John III in Warsaw, learned once when he showed Basia around. The estate is one of the loveliest in the country, yet Basia was singularly unimpressed. "This is not a palace compared to what I'm building," she declared. As the tour ended, she handed the guide her card. "If you are ever in America and want to see a *real* palace, I'll show you one," she said.

Basia's fingerprints were on the blueprints from the outset. One could see them in the Polish name she gave the estate: "Jasna Polana." It had no precise English equivalent; the usual translation was "bright meadow" or "bright glade." In Princeton, where homes are dubbed "Drumthwacket" or "Morven," so Slavic-sounding a name was taken as a sure sign that Seward was not the real master of the realm, even though Basia later claimed it was he, not she, who'd insisted on something Polish. (Years later, when one of his secretaries asked him why he had never learned Polish, Seward replied that he didn't have the slightest interest in the language.) There was one small problem with the selection. "Jasna Polana" had already been taken—by Tolstoy, who'd called his country home "Yasnaya Polanya," which meant the same thing in Russian. Basia later insisted that any resemblance was coincidental, and her denial is plausible. For one thing, it was unlikely that someone as Sovietophobic as she would have named a monument to herself after anything Russian. Nor is there anything to suggest that Basia ever read any Tolstoy or studied his life; had she, she might have hesitated. After all, Tolstoy had been so miserable at Yasnaya Polanya—largely due to his hectoring wife—that he'd eventually fled the place.

By May 1972 Bowers had assembled an all-star cast of subcontractors for the project. The engineers were from Syska & Hennessy of New York, which had worked on Lincoln Center and the latest incarnation of Madison Square Garden. The landscaping went to Clarke & Rapuano, a firm long associated with the megaprojects of Robert Moses. For the masonry he brought in Bergen Bluestone, which had done the facade of the Lincoln Tunnel. Friedman Marble, suppliers of the stone for the Ford Foundation, Regency Hotel, and many other buildings, would do the same for the Johnsons. Other distinguished firms were retained to handle the plumbing, roofing, and flooring. There were so many players, in fact, that an elaborate chart was prepared so that Seward could keep them all straight. They began the project with the same sense of anticipation that Michael Rapuano, the landscaper, imparted to his men: They were, he told them, about to work on what would become "the most talked-about house in the country."

It was Rapuano, who'd helped design the Henry Hudson, Palisades, Garden State, and Hutchinson River parkways as well as the promenade in Brooklyn Heights, who got things under way by laying out the access roads and bridges. At Jasna Polana as in his other projects, the principle was the same: Adapt the roads to the contours of the land rather than the other way around. Basia and Seward spent hours walking around the virginal property with Rapuano, an older man nearing retirement himself. When the roads were functional, ground was officially broken on the Big House. It was a modest ceremony, attended only by the Johnsons, Rapuano, Harrison, and a few others; each dug out a few ceremonial spadefuls of earth with a shovel spray-painted gold for the occasion. There was no time to waste: In a few months Seward Johnson would be seventy-seven years old.

VI

For the next five years the finest materials from all over the world converged on the construction site. Basia had hoped to import the stone for the house from Poland, but the quarry she had selected was closed, and even were it started up again, it was simply too costly and inconvenient to ship a rock pile across the Atlantic. She settled instead for Laurel Hill sandstone, extracted from a long-dormant quarry near Scranton. Basia wanted every single block "hand-dressed"—that is, cut by hammer and chisel rather than by saw. Before long, she'd put very nearly every mason in the area to work. The stone used for the door trim came from Minnesota; the central courtyard from New Hampshire; the walkways from upstate New York. The marble for the monumental central staircase, whose two serpentine strands would curve, converge, then double back, was Yugoslavian travertine, shaped in Italy and sent over in numbered slabs. For the roof the Johnsons imported twenty-four thousand square feet of English hand-sawed slate. Six tons of copper domes and gutters came from Germany.

For the interior Hester Diamond, wife of the Johnsons' favorite art dealer, went on a prolonged European shopping spree, stuffing a Trenton warehouse, and her own pocketbook, in the process. (So jam-packed with artifacts did the warehouse become that when workmen went there to fetch a Henry Moore piece, it took them a day just to find it.) Diamond bought Basia fifteen antique fireplaces and eleven eighteenth-century mantels, culled largely from derelict French châteaux. The library on the second floor was built in Scotland, then disassembled and shipped. The parquet floor in the entrance hall was also antique French, sent over from Paris in blocks to preserve the original grouting, and complete with the handiwork of generations of French termites. An antique boudoir, complete with peephole, also came from France, to be installed outside Basia's bedroom. Seward told people it was where Marie Antoinette had had her assignations. Diamond's shopping list also included tapestries; at least twenty-six Aubusson rugs and carpets; chandeliers costing at least $200,000; mirrors running another $65,000;

a $68,000 suite of George II–style furniture, plus assorted urns, arm-chairs, stools, wine coolers, coal buckets, candelabras, daybeds, sofas, tables, and chests. Meanwhile the art purchases continued. In early 1973 Seward and Basia bought themselves their first Modigliani (*La Rêveuse*) for $1,925,000; another Picasso (*Woman with Mandolin*) for $1,100,000; and a Kandinsky, for $400,000.

On the grounds were installed imported antiques of a different kind. Alas, one of the few things Seward's millions could not buy him was time enough to watch mighty oaks from little acorns grow, so the landscapers looked for ready-made models instead. They located five blue atlas cedars, each forty-five to fifty feet tall and one hundred years old, in Pennington, New Jersey, uprooted them, packed them lovingly onto separate trailers, and brought them to the estate, where they had to be lifted over the skeleton of the house with the help of twelve men and a hundred-ton crane. When Grace Lambert, the Listerine heiress next door, complained she could see the rising Jasna Polana from her window, Seward had a row of mature white pine helicoptered in to block her view. Around the orchid house, for which Seward bought an entire nursery in Florida, five thousand plants in all, went a group of honey locust trees, as tall as the cedars. All told, the Johnsons installed 150 to 200 mature trees—birches and junipers, dogwoods and pin oaks. As for vegetation, Rapuano found boxwoods and magnolias in Maryland, azaleas in Virginia, roses in Pennsylvania. For the outdoor bowling green, he brought in fifteen thousand square feet of Connecti-cut sod.

Many of Jasna Polana's most dramatic features were, like its name and guiding spirit, imported from Poland. Convinced her homeland was insufficiently respected in the land of the Polish joke, Basia turned the estate into a showcase of Polish craftsmanship. Doing so called for repeated trips back home, during which this symbol of malapportioned wealth was met by fawning, flower-bearing flunkies from Poland's os-tensibly egalitarian Communist regime. Basia particularly prized the decorative ironwork, the gates and grilles and lanterns, that adorned Poland's castles, monuments, and public places. Fabricating these works by hand was an old, proud Polish tradition, one that had prospered as artisans reproduced what the Nazis had obliterated. Now, the men who rebuilt Warsaw after the Uprising would build pieces of Jasna Polana. Basia traipsed regally through Poland's most historic cities, her entou-rage of artists, architects, and apparatchiks in tow, pointing out what she wanted. And, abracadabra, drawings would be made and replicas fashioned. The fence around the statue of the great Polish poet Adam

Mickiewicz in Warsaw became the model for the fence around the breakfast pavilion. Four gates from the Cathedral of Gniezno would be installed around the estate. The gate bestriding Warsaw's Potocki Palace would be reproduced for the epic main entrance. The front door would be a hand-hammered facsimile from a building on Krakowskie Przed-miéscie, Warsaw's main street. Thirty-eight lamps like the ones over-hanging Warsaw's old city would ring the estate. The decorative grillwork under the windows mimicked some in Gdańsk, while the doorknobs and hinges came from the Wawel Castle in Cracow. Other features derived from Wilanów, the Warsaw palace Basia had vowed to outdo but in this instance was content to mimic.

Another group of Polish artisans worked on the breakfast pavilion, a two-story antique gazebolike structure (Junior called it "the pagoda affair") Basia found in Poland and had transplanted to the rear of the main house. Made of Carpathian larch wood, it was disassembled and shipped in forty-five hundred separate pieces; inlaid in its floor was a star-shaped pattern of birch, walnut, mahogany, ebony, rosewood, and oak. With its warm wood tones and floor-to-ceiling glass (bulletproof in its Americanized, Johnsonized incarnation), the heptagonal room would be Jasna Polana's coziest space. Built above it was the doghouse, where the Johnsons' growing brood would reign supreme. The king of the canine castle was Princey, a boxer Basia's brother Gregory had given them, whom Seward impishly had named after his sister Evange-line's second husband, a fellow of obscure royal lineage calling himself Prince Zalstem-Zalesky. Also resident would be Clara, a mastiff. The dogs' digs included a stove, refrigerator, stainless-steel sinks, and cus-tom-built beds with custom-made mattresses, kept warm by hot-water pipes beneath them. The place would be air-conditioned in the summer and heated in the winter; also heated was the bronze stairway leading up to it, so that even in the most inclement weather paws could remain dry and toasty. From their second-story perch, the dogs had one of the best views of the estate, as well as direct access to Basia's bedroom. Anyone believing in reincarnation could scarcely have done better than to have returned as Princey or Clara.

To install what their countrymen had made, teams of Polish workmen flew into Kennedy Airport, carrying their primitive implements with them, and were trucked to a motel the Johnsons took over near Prince-ton. The Johnsons not only housed the workers but fed them, clothed them, entertained them, and gave them spiritual succor, providing field trips to places like the shrine of Our Lady of Czestochowa in Doyles-town, Pennsylvania. Their tenure was not altogether smooth. Times were tough in construction, and local unions threatened to halt work unless one American was hired for every import. Moreover, the task of reconciling the English and metric systems was compounded by a babel of languages on the work site. Basia needed someone to act as translator and liaison to the Polish workers, and brought on a man named John Stroczynski. It was repaying an old debt, for he was the brother-in-law of Danuta Wyszynski, Basia's benefactress from Perth Amboy.

Jasna Polana might have been derivative architecturally, but it was an incubator technologically. A whole set of taxing problems arose from Seward's desire to have a saltwater swimming pool. Where was the brine to come from? Rumors that the Johnsons planned to pipe it in from the Atlantic Ocean sixty miles away were unfounded, though at one point Seward suggested tank-trucking it in. Engineers opted instead for on-site salinization, and developed sophisticated stainless-steel duct-work to hold the water. Disposing of it after Seward's dips proved more problematical, however, and the idea was eventually abandoned. Later, someone asked Seward what he planned to do with the four tons of salt he'd bought for the aborted project. "Take it down to Florida bag by bag and use it on the dinner table," he replied.

The tennis pavilion, for which Seward wanted a retractable roof, offered further mechanical challenges. As designed, it took four men two weeks to raise and five days to lower. In fact, it took three months to put up and never did come down, at least not until a snowstorm knocked it out of commission permanently. The playing surface was state-of-the-art "Elastroturf," selected only after interviewing the comedian Alan King and others already using it. The surface was especially formulated for Seward's game, which he described as follows: "Well, I like to lob a lot." When Seward decided to add an indoor bowling green, the turf had to be reformulated. Then, when condensation from the roof dripped onto it, the Johnsons had to buy a special vacuum cleaner. Then, when glare from the ceiling proved bothersome, the lighting had to be changed.

The plumbing contractor created an elaborate heating system for the towel racks. Engineering experts in Chicago devised special mechanisms for the orchid house, where an alarm went off whenever the room temperature left its prescribed range. The wine cellar, with its seven thousand felt-lined terra cotta flues, also had elaborate temperature and humidity controls. The main gate to the inner courtyard was opened and shut through an underground, noiseless system sensitive to the touch, so that it wouldn't crush anyone who happened to be in its path.

Some of the niftiest notions never made it off the drawing board. One was a transparent plastic chute, in which the dogs could descend smoothly from their penthouse to the estate grounds. Also unrealized was Jasna Polana's electronic massage table, even though it was surely the most expensive of its kind ever, built or unbuilt. Not wanting any old apparatus, the Johnsons directed Syska & Hennessy to create one that operated noiselessly and didn't look too institutional. The task was farmed out to Olaf Soot, designer of the movable equipment at the Metropolitan Opera, Juilliard School, and Kennedy Center as well as the General Electric "Carousel of Progress" at the 1964 New York World's Fair. Seward approved Soot's proposal, but Basia did not; instead, she called Soot "incompetent" and complained his design was a breeding ground for bacteria. By the time Soot submitted his second version, design costs alone had risen to $16,797.41. By his estimate construction would cost another $20,202.00. A $37,000 massage table was too much for even Seward to stomach, and it was never made.

But Jasna Polana's greatest technical contributions to mankind were undoubtedly in security. Forty years after the attempted kidnapping of his daughter Diana at Merriewold, Seward remained fixated on safety. He was the sort who booked appointments, then made last-minute schedule changes to foil anyone who had somehow become privy to his plans. Now, in an era of international, highly personalized lawlessness, when thugs spirited away Bronfmans and Hearsts and demanded millions for their return, his paranoia peaked. Having an active and occasionally undisciplined wife, who from time to time would wander off the estate unescorted, didn't help. (In one such detour Basia totaled the twenty-five-thousand-dollar birthday Mercedes he'd just given her; he promptly bought her another.) As a result, Jasna Polana was less a home than a vault with beds. "I have so much security, I can't go out and take a pee without setting off an alarm," Seward once observed.

The first line of defense was human. Early on, Basia talked about bringing in mounted Texans, accompanied by wolves, to patrol the grounds, an idea she apparently picked up from the tobacco heiress Doris Duke. At another point she spoke of enlisting the Mafia. In the end the Johnsons recruited their security force largely from local police departments. As they patrolled the grounds, they wore uniforms with special patches on their sleeves: a yellow oak leaf with a cluster of acorns, on a field of red and white, with JASNA POLANA SECURITY stitched in. The design was a security man's, the iconography, Basia's; the oak, she explained, was the strongest tree of all, while red and white were Poland's national colors.

Where the animate security left off, the inanimate began. Working jointly, Honeywell, Inc., and Syska & Hennessy designed an elaborate set of contraptions. The system was, itself, top secret: Terms like "Johnson mansion" or "Jasna Polana" never appeared on the plans, which referred only to the "N-490" project. For aesthetics as well as security, all devices were designed to be invisible. The quaint eighteenth century Polish lanterns that ringed the house were fitted with twenty-first-century electronic sensors, developed by a company that had previously worked for the National Bureau of Prisons, thereby surrounding Jasna Polana with an invisible electronic shield. Anyone climbing the wall—or, until various adjustments were made, any bird flying over it—was instantly detectable. And, with underground sensors, so, too, was anyone walking on certain patches of ground, or, for a time, any raindrop falling on it. Anyone managing to slip through the perimeter faced more daunting obstacles in the house itself. All of its inside doors were wired, so that openings and closings could be monitored in the security center, located beneath the servants' wing. The windows, made of bulletproof glass, were rigged so that they could not be opened more than six inches without setting off an alarm. Were any of the gates ajar, a green light next to Seward's bed went on. There was also a panic button in the wall, and portable panic buttons, similar to garage-door openers, for use outside the house, just in case kidnappers arrived by helicopter during any of the Johnsons' perambulations.

To discourage subterranean infiltration, all drainpipes on the premises were sealed, with bars placed over them. A sophisticated sensor screened every letter arriving on the estate. Lest anyone use it as a road map, Seward had the intricate scale model of the estate (which had been insured for ten thousand dollars) smashed into smithereens when work was complete. A hidden staircase—tucked behind shelves of fake books in the library—allowed him to go undetected from one floor to another should the need ever arise. The wine cellar was enclosed by a Mosler bank-vault door. As security chiefs came and went, the system was further refined and embellished, with the latest hidden cameras, sensors, and other Vietnam-era innovations brought in. Still, when all was said and done, Seward had more faith in Princey and Clara than in the fanciest doodads. "No matter what you give me for security, I put my trust in my dogs," he said once. "When there's someone out there, they bark."

Even without the star-crossed massage table, costs soared beyond the most pessimistic—or, for the contractors, the most optimistic—projections. By late 1975, they hovered around $18,000,000; the tab included architects' fees ($1,330,000); landscaping ($2,065,000); the tennis court ($200,000) and surface ($16,000); wine cellar ($40,000); purchase and installation of the cedars ($35,000); manufacture, importation, and installation of ironwork ($1,200,000); light dimmers ($61,000); antique parquet floor ($100,000); and orchid house ($78,000). So, too, did the level of pain. Most of those erecting Jasna Polana were used to working for wealthy, difficult clients. But nothing prepared them for Basia Johnson.

To most of the workers, Seward was a model employer, a benevolent and occasionally befuddled old man. Jasna Polana was clearly not his baby; Harbor Branch, he told visitors, was "ten times more important" to him. His direct involvement in the project related primarily to creature comforts—like his insistence that the heating and air-conditioning be absolutely silent so as not to interfere with his post-prandial naps. Though there were exceptions—the private eye Junior had hired for his ill-fated raid was one—Seward generally appreciated working people; he was the type to tip a cleaning lady ten dollars, even if he had to borrow the cash to do so. More than that, he genuinely liked their company, certainly more than that of stuffed-shirted J&J executives. Sometimes he would share surprisingly intimate thoughts with them. "You know, I made over half a million dollars today," he told one worker who wouldn't make that much in a lifetime. "I make more damn money than I know how to spend. And I did nothing to earn it. They tell me to stay away from the office, and yet they keep paying me."

If Seward had never been in the workaday world, Basia had just escaped from it. Despite, or because of, that, she strutted around the construction site like a camp commandant, hurling abuses, insults, complaints, epithets, orders, objections, and objects at anyone incurring her wrath. Her conspicuous solicitude for living things—to move rather than cut down trees, to nurse wounded deer or birds back to health, to pamper her dogs—stopped mysteriously at human beings, particularly human beings working for her. And that tendency became more pronounced as her English improved, her hegemony grew, and any need to rein in her impulses diminished. "To err is human, to forgive divine. Neither is the policy of Mrs. Johnson," an employee once remarked.

Basia's most famous tirades concerned Jasna Polana's most basic feature—its stone—and questions over its color, shape, pattern, surface texture, and bonding. Repeatedly, masons erected sample walls for her, and just as repeatedly Basia condemned them, usually by slashing an

X on them with a piece of chalk or crying "No! No! No!" It would then be dutifully demolished and rebuilt with some slight variation. One of the glories of the quarry the Johnsons selected was its rich range of colors; gradually, Basia eliminated all the greens and reds, insisting that only pinks and tans be used. Once that was settled, there was the thickness of the joints to consider. The standard width is three quarters of an inch to an inch; Basia wanted half that. Furthermore, she wanted all to be exactly the same size. By one man's count eleven walls were raised and razed before one met her exacting specifications. Changes in the stonework alone added $284,000 to the cost of the house.

Inside, Basia insisted that Jasna Polana's monumental stairway look as though it had been carved out of a single piece of travertine; workers had to camouflage all joints with a mixture of marble dust and epoxy. ("Take it up! I don't want to see the seams," she told the workman who had laid down the first couple of steps. "I'm not a tailor!" he replied as he packed up his tools.) Eyes closed, she ran her fingernails across countertops in search of imperfections, then screamed "Horrible workmanship!" when she felt one or thought she had. Antique fireplaces that took weeks to reconstruct were systematically disassembled and reassembled until they met her exacting specifications.

Basia moved newly installed walls, windows, doors, switches, and trees with abandon, sometimes feet, sometimes fractions of an inch. Altering the size and location of the windows in the wings cost an additional $180,000. Changes in chimney stone added $64,000 more. Virtually overnight, Basia had four porcelain bathtubs ripped out and replaced by four other basins, each scooped out of a solid block of marble like softened vanilla ice cream from a virgin bucket. The cost of the new two-ton tubs, complete with gold-plated fittings: $20,000 apiece, plus an additional $11,000 to install. What was to have been Seward's saltwater bath became a reflecting pool, painted progressively darker shades until it pleased her. Thousands of dollars' worth of sod was ripped up when Basia determined it looked artificially immaculate. Later, Basia was to say she changed only "small things." In fact, during Jasna Polana's construction there were a total of 330 change orders, raising the cost of the place astronomically. One change, though, came free. Whether out of deference, shame, or pique, Harrison removed his name from all drawings of the house, attributing its design to "Mr. and Mrs. J. Seward Johnson, Sr.," instead. (After Jasna Polana was finished, Basia sought to honor the architect by erecting a Wallace K. Harrison Pavilion at Lincoln Center. The plan was well under way—

Harrison had drawn designs, while Nina Zagat had met several times with the restaurateur Joe Baum and Metropolitan Opera officials— before Basia lost interest in the project.)

Some of Basia's changes made aesthetic sense; at times her eye was keener than that of the "experts" she had hired. But it hurt too much for anyone to say so. "Stupid Americans!" she might shriek at them. "No Good" ("NG" for short), she might write on their handiwork. As workmen looked on, half-horrified, half hoping she would electrocute herself, Basia would take a hammer claw or screwdriver to some light switch or thermostat or doorbell that displeased her, and rip it out. She became known as "the Tiger" or simply "the Bitch." Only the Polish workmen seemed exempt from Basia's fury. Their sole enemies were the elements; once, after spending their lunch hour lying in a lush bed of greens, they broke out in poison-ivy rashes (Basia blamed her American help for the epidemic, claiming they had overchlorinated the swimming pool). The general contractor found that the surest way to keep his own men contented was to ply them with fresh Polish jokes, and he constantly pumped friends to replenish his supply.

Ordinarily, one might have thought Basia would have empathized with working men and women, having just emerged from that class herself. As if by habit, she still manifested some of their frugality, saving bread crusts for the birds, advising women working for her to buy good underwear because it lasted forever, continuing to purchase lottery tickets. Instead, it was the other way around. What could account for her contempt? Perhaps it was that feeling, common among the nouveau riche, that people were forever trying to hoodwink her. Perhaps it reflected the hypersensitivity of a proud Pole in a land in which her countrymen were often disparaged. Or perhaps it was simply the arrogance of someone who is suddenly, magically, freed from any need for restraint. In any case, Basia was an equal-opportunity abuser. While she specialized in underlings, at one time or another she took on the three men most responsible for her dream house: Harrison, Rapuano, and Seward himself. Once, after she'd called Harrison "a stupid old man," he'd begun to tremble, and Seward had to go over and comfort him. "I'm not going to take this bullshit anymore," the normally courtly Harrison remarked after a bout of Basia's abuse. Another time, she gave Rapuano a wicked tongue-lashing; the following day he had a heart attack and died, and many of Rapuano's associates blamed Basia for it. Seward, too, took his licks. At various times she called him "an old fool" or a "senile old man." Once, as a workman looked on, Seward made the mistake of suggesting where some furniture should go. "Go to bed, you old fool, you're nothing!" she told him.

And yet, to Seward at least, it didn't seem to matter. Sure, on occasion she'd treat him like a mutt, but he'd still act like a puppy. "He would fall all to pieces like a jerk," one worker recalled. "He idolized her, he adored her, for whatever reason I never knew. With his money I would have done better than that." Seward knew that Basia was volatile, but he found her incandescent, too. As they walked around the estate, he would hold her hand; when he thought people weren't watching, or maybe even because they were, he would pinch her behind. "Mr. Johnson would never contradict her," one contractor said. "He told us quietly, 'Just let her have what she wants.' "

As Jasna Polana rose, Basia, in the time-honored manner of successor spouses everywhere, purged those whose ties to Seward predated hers. Among the first to go was Seward's longtime secretary, Fran Perree. Basia had neither forgotten nor forgiven what she'd considered Perree's snootiness the day Seward had summoned her to J&J, and not long into the marriage she picked a fight with her over some clerical matter. And some fight it must have been. "In my 43 years I have never been talked to or screamed at in this manner, and, quite frankly, I am not emotionally geared to accepting such unjustified abuse," Perree subsequently wrote Seward. Before long, Basia delivered an ultimatum to Seward: Either Perree goes, or she would. And go Basia did. Seward might have been able to treat his other "dumb blonde" wives with disrespect, she later told someone, but not her. She fled to New York, pointedly opting to go there by bus rather than use Seward's chauffeur. Seward, thunderstruck, did not know what to do; several times he called Philip Hofmann, J&J's chairman, for guidance. But with Koverdan playing Kissinger, after a few days she agreed to return—by limousine. Perree, however, never did.

Robert Myers's days as Seward's lawyer were also numbered. With all the changes wrought by Seward's third marriage, Myers's Johnson business was briefly brisk. In June 1972 Seward revised his will to increase Basia's trust to $50 million, and to leave her the *Ocean Pearl* as well; the bulk of his estate went to Harbor Branch. The following January he enlarged the trust again—this time to $100 million, with Basia authorized to dispose of the corpus as she wished at her death. Only a few days later Seward changed his mind, and his will, once more. Now, Basia would get half his estate: $100 million in trust, the rest outright. To Myers, Seward's objective was consistent and clear: to get as much money to Basia as he could without adding to his own tax liability.

But when Seward decided to make further testamentary changes in April 1973, he circumvented Myers and returned to Tom Ford and Nina Zagat, the Shearman & Sterling lawyers who had handled his November 1971 codicil. As Ford later explained it, Seward asked them "to basically represent Mrs. Johnson's interests in the drafting of Mr. Johnson's will," and that it surely did; the resulting document included several changes that would accrue mightily to Basia's benefit were Seward suddenly to die. Availing themselves of a recent IRS ruling, the Shearman & Sterling lawyers included the value of Seward's foundations in his estate, thereby increasing the size of the half that Basia, as Seward's wife, could take tax-free. The will they drew up also allowed Basia to withdraw principal from the $100 million trust, effectively turning it into a bequest. Myers knew nothing about the new will until a copy of it arrived one day in the morning mail. Immediately, he told Seward about its drawbacks: Because New Jersey had no marital deduction, it would add $43 million to his tax bill and would give the impressionable, impulsive Basia unprecedented discretion over his fortune. Seward's lawyers, old and new, promptly huddled, and the changes were undone, at least for the time being. Even so, as of May 1973, ten years before Seward's death, Basia already stood to inherit half his $370 million estate. Some $100 million of that would be in a trust; another $60 million would be in cash. Most of what remained would go to charities of Basia's choice. His children inherited nothing, but that was nothing new; they hadn't been in his wills since the mid-1960s.

Myers won the battle but lost the war. Seward had apparently decided his interests and Basia's were identical, and that Basia's lawyers should be his as well. He conjured up some grievances against Myers, and the two men parted company. To sweeten Myers's departure, Seward arranged for him to remain a "tax adviser" to Harbor Branch and counsel to the Robert Wood Johnson Foundation, and to receive $150,000 in severance pay. Myers never saw—or even talked to—Seward again. In July 1973 Seward handed his legal portfolio to Nina Zagat. Suddenly, a sixth-year associate, whose own professional prospects were otherwise comparatively modest, had landed the wealthiest individual client in the firm's individual-clients department.

From the outset the Johnsons liked the woman Seward affectionately called "his expensive lawyer." Nina Zagat was a plain woman with dark brown hair, given a bit to chunky matronliness even before she had children. In intellect as in appearance, there was nothing fancy or chic, sharp or slick, about her. In her work at Shearman & Sterling, which she had done for the Dillons and a few minor Rockefellers before she began concentrating on the Johnsons, she was cautious, deliberate, and meticulous—so meticulous as to strike some as either plodding or calculating, cold or aloof. But after all the glib lawyers he had encountered over the years, Seward found Nina's very ordinariness, her air of earnest innocence, her lack of cynicism, refreshing. Sure, she lacked the snap, crackle, and pop of some other lawyers, but she would serve him doggedly, unselfishly, competently if not dazzlingly. Most important, he felt she was honest with him. She gave him straight talk rather than lawyerly gibberish, and if she didn't know the answer to something, she said so. Furthermore, she was roughly Basia's contemporary, and was kind and unthreatening enough to keep her company without crowding or upstaging her. For the next decade, then, Nina's practice came to consist increasingly of the legal care and feeding of one of America's most eccentric and extravagant couples, an assignment for which no course at even the fanciest law school could possibly have equipped her.

Nina Safronoff—she was named after the Greta Garbo character in the film *Ninotchka*—was born in New York in 1942 and grew up on Long Island, where her father practiced law. Samuel Safronoff left Nina's life early and suddenly; one night when she was sixteen years old, her mother awakened her to say that her father, still in his forties, had had a heart attack, and was lying dead in the next room. The trauma anesthetized her against lesser setbacks; events that excited or angered others left Nina almost unnaturally unperturbed. After her father's death she fended largely for herself, first at a public high school, then at Vassar and Yale Law School, where she was one of only 12 women in a class of 167. Mild-mannered, soft-spoken, without the hard edge that members of embattled minorities often acquire, she was nonetheless a pioneer—a woman intent upon practicing law without scuttling her personal life. She was a good student, but neither a scintillating nor conspicuous one, and she became even less visible after her marriage, in the spring of her second year, to a classmate named Eugene H. "Tim" Zagat, Jr. As graduation neared, both Zagats applied for jobs at prestigious New York firms. Nina's grades were better, but typically for that time, it was Tim who got the better offers. Hell, hiring partners guffawed, if you let women in, how could you ever tell dirty jokes? Tim headed for Hughes, Hubbard & Reed; Nina landed in the individual-clients department of Shearman & Sterling.

Through no fault of her own, Nina's long-term prospects there were nil. In the hundred years that had passed since Thomas Gaskell Shearman met John W. Sterling, the firm had never named a woman partner.

Indeed, when Nina arrived, there were still some S&S lawyers who refused to work with women—one of the partners in Nina's department complained that they made him feel "uncomfortable"—and "girls" were still barred from the firm's annual summer outing. Another Yale-trained woman, Margaret Smith, had long languished at Shearman & Sterling even though she handled the bulk of the Dillon family's legal work, work that would have netted any man a partnership. "Never, ever get it in your mind that you'll become a partner in this firm," she warned Nina shortly after her arrival in October 1967. "And if you know how to type, don't let anyone know." Increasing the odds still further, at Shearman & Sterling as at most large firms, the individual-clients group was a loss leader, a service the firm extended to plutocratic executives, but a gilded graveyard for those lawyers—eccentrics, aristocrats, gays, fops, women—who traditionally congregated in them. Not that this mattered much to Nina. She and her husband were planning a family, a choice that at the time would probably make partnership unmanageable as well as unrealistic.

In 1968 the Zagats began two-year stints in their firms' Paris offices, where they honed their taste for French culture and cuisine. It was a year after their return that Tom Ford informed Nina that the Band-Aid heir Seward Johnson "had himself a babe" in need of a will. Before long Nina met her newest client, a shy woman five years her senior in a wide-brimmed hat, and her aged but still vital boyfriend. Three years and another will later, a month shy of Nina's thirty-first birthday, Seward requested her services permanently. It was a package deal, for with the Johnsons and the host of legal work they would generate came their foundations and the holding companies for their properties and artworks. All of this meant hefty fees for Shearman & Sterling, which Ford liked to describe as "a Tiffany law firm that charges Tiffany prices." Nina proudly informed Ford of Seward's desires. "I know the firm rules are that I'm not supposed to take on any new clients without approval, but I didn't think you'd mind," she joked. She was right.

Entrusting so valuable a commodity to a junior associate was unusual, but Ford knew his clientele. "Any man who's been married three times has no loyalties," he was fond of saying; without Nina, he reasoned, Seward might just take his business somewhere else. For the next decade Ford watched over Nina, but only sporadically, and without bothering to remember much of what he saw. What his departmental deputy, Henry Ziegler, wrote on Nina's evaluation years later had in fact been true from the beginning: "As long as she keeps the Johnsons happy, that keeps us happy."

VII

From the outset, the Jasna Polana project was shrouded in secrecy. All workers were warned against speaking to the press. True, nothing could be done to stop the helicopters from buzzing over the site periodically, but Jasna Polana's security force kept all earth-bound snoops, voyeurs, and busybodies away. To fill the informational void, fantastic rumors began circulating. One had Seward installing a special machine in his swimming pool to simulate surf. Another had Jasna Polana's indoor tennis court heated by four fireplaces, one in each corner. Still another had Basia stopping by a nearby orchard one Sunday for a few dozen apples, and going home with a few dozen apple trees instead.

For the most part the neighbors just sat and watched and listened unhappily to the grinding sound of earthmovers. But upon learning that the Johnsons had applied to build a heliport on the estate—in order, rumor had it, to faciliate Basia's shopping trips to New York—they mobilized, retaining a lawyer, circulating a petition, and, eventually, convincing the Johnsons to drop the idea. Occasionally, some news emerged. In May 1973 Seward and Basia granted an interview to the *Trenton Times*. NEW HOME FOR JOHNSONS WON'T HAVE GINGER-BREAD, its headline read. "It won't be a tremendous social center," said Seward of the new house. "We don't like crowds. That's why I don't go to football games." Both Johnsons insisted their home would be "plain and simple," and grew impatient over rumors that the place could run $2 million or more. "Speculation is just speculation," Seward snapped. "We don't yet know what it will cost."

In another interview a year later—to the daughter of J&J's general counsel—Seward was a bit more forthcoming. "Well, you could say five or ten million, give or take a million," he said. (The most accurate estimate came from the *Princeton Packet*, which in November 1974 floated a figure of $17 million.) Whatever the price tag, Seward suggested, the estate was well worth the investment. "Without something this size, privacy is lost, and perhaps a certain amount of security," he said. "My wife and I are building this house primarily to avoid the dangers that have become apparent to people of wealth from extortioners, kidnappers and thieves."

The most lyrical account of the project appeared in the New York *Daily News*. The Johnsons refused to speak with the reporter, Bruce Chadwick, and ordered everyone to avoid him. But, as Chadwick wrote in December 1974, "it's hard to hide a house that looks like the seat of a national government." He described the "finely-carved mountain of stone" rising off Route 206 and predicted that one day Jasna Polana would prompt comments like George Bernard Shaw's wisecrack about Hearst's castle: "This is the kind of house God would build, if He had the money." The entire place, Chadwick wrote wonderingly, would house only the Johnsons—"all two of them." "With 36,000 square feet to ramble around in, they shouldn't be getting in each other's way often," he declared. "There will also be a forest of trees to separate the estate from the merely rich." An accompanying centerfold was headed EVEN GREATER THAN GATSBY. "Not far from the spires and gargoyles of Old Nassau is growing an estate that might boggle the imagination of that prominent Princetonian, F. Scott Fitzgerald," it said. "See if you can find, in the air view, the amphitheater, the swimming pool in which you could keep a herd of whales." Other captions described "a croquet field where giants could play" and "not your run-of-the-mill swimming pool. This one has continental shelves."

In a column headlined THAT'S A LOT OF BAND-AIDS, The *Daily News's* "Suzy" revealed more tidbits about the "mind-blowing edifice," with its "nearby mini-mansion" for servants and "a swimming pool big enough to keep a herd of porpoises very, very happy." Her article, appearing in January 1975, also marked the debut in the national press of Basia, whom Suzy described as "a pleasant-looking, Polish-born former art student." Suzy encapsulated Seward's first two marriages and the circumstances of the third. "Barbara applied to come to the United States as a domestic," she wrote. "As luck would have it (I'll say) she landed a job on the Johnsons' household staff and ended up inheriting the boss." As for Seward's children, "Each have [sic] close to $50 million, so there's no point in worrying about them," she wrote.

In March 1975 *People* magazine, which had broken into print around the time the Johnsons had broken ground, weighed in with its own report, entitled "The Mysterious Band-Aid Baron Puts Up a $12 Million Pleasure Dome." "Amazingly, all of this princely grandeur is for one mystery man—the reclusive Band-Aid baron Seward Johnson," the author of the piece, Richard Rein, declared. To learn more, he called

Fort Pierce, where the old man himself answered the phone. Rein asked him whether this "modern-day Versailles" would one day become a museum. "I don't care much about museums," Seward snapped back. "I just want to live with some pictures, that's all. Whatever I have, I want to live with—privately."

"If little is known about Johnson, even less is known about his third wife, Barbara," Rein continued. "He is said to have met her while browsing through a Warsaw library five years ago and later arranged for her to come to the United States—as a domestic. Today an aloof chatelaine who has few friends, she is photographed even less frequently than her husband." Around the construction site, he continued, word was that Basia had "all but taken over the duties of head foreman," and that "whenever something displeased her she merely had it torn out and redone." "A jackhammer comes in handy around here," one harried workman told Rein. Another noted how Seward had given them one bit of advice for dealing with his wife: "Don't cross her."

Coverage like this gave Seward a public prominence he'd never previously had, and made him fair game for a variety of aggressive and resourceful panhandlers. "I am sorry to advise you that Mr. Johnson has no spare cars to give away," Seward's J&J secretary, Joan Kelsey, wrote one of the many supplicants who now came calling. To another, who asked twice for help building her own mini–Jasna Polana, Kelsey wasn't so polite. "You are obviously under some delusion that Mr. Johnson, or anyone else, would just give $100,000 to someone to build a new home," she wrote. "It would appear you would like to go from rags to riches in one shot."

By far the most eye-opening piece on Jasna Polana—"America's Last Palace" or "Who Ever Said It Was Easy to Build a Simple $21 Million Country House with a Swimming Pool?"—appeared in *New Jersey Monthly* in May 1977. By now, the Johnsons had moved in to Jasna Polana; the Maillols were around the goldfish pool and Rodin's "Three Graces" was by the front fountain. The author of the article, Shawn Tully, spent three months chasing down false leads and reluctant witnesses. Construction workers either honored their vows of silence, or were unwilling to relive so unpleasant an experience; one said he hoped to "make a million bucks" writing his own book on the subject. Tully's attempt to speak to Seward by phone was no more successful. "An impersonal dial tone interrupted my protestations," he wrote. Later, Tully received a registered letter, signed by Seward, drafted by Nina Zagat.

"We do not authorize you to publish your proposed article and in fact, we specifically oppose any publication of information concerning our lives and/or our house in *New Jersey Monthly*," it stated. "If you proceed with publication, you do so against our express wishes and instructions, and we will be compelled to take appropriate action." It sounded intimidating. In fact, with little legal recourse, Seward tried pressure tactics, convincing Johnson & Johnson to pull its advertising from the impoverished magazine. Photographing Jasna Polana proved just as tricky; in a daring daytime raid, two photographers who penetrated the estate and took pictures of the house eventually turned themselves and their film into the gun- and walkie-talkie-toting security men blocking their exit. "I didn't know how sane they were," one of the infiltrators later explained. "And I didn't want a bullet in the back of my head for pulling this stunt."

The article contained the first reported references to the solid marble tubs, the air-conditioned doghouse, the heated, gold-plated towel racks. By now, the estimated price tag had reached $30 million—more, when adjusted for inflation, than any American house except Hearst's San Simeon. But if Jasna Polana yielded a few of its secrets, its occupants did not. Seward's public persona, a frustrated Tully wrote, was "Howard Hughesian." "Except for an occasional listing in Who's Who and an outdated photograph in an annual report, not much has ever been published about the slight, jaunty fellow who served as vice president of Johnson & Johnson for over fifty years," he wrote.

"Barbara's background is an even greater mystery," Tully continued. "The only photographs of the Polish brunette are privately-owned snapshots, and while it is thought that she is in her mid-thirties, the rest of the information depends on to whom you speak. Some say she received several art degrees—others swear they were scholarships—before immigrating; most prefer to repeat that they heard from a friend of a friend that she was a domestic in Seward's Oldwick mansion. Neither version has ever been confirmed." In an attempt to find out, Tully drove to the Skillman house, where he approached a man working in the barn. "Can you tell me whether Mrs. Johnson was once the family maid?" he asked. "Son, I can tell you just one thing," the man replied. "Get in your car and get out of here as fast as you can." One thing, however, was clear: In what Tully called "the great drama of Jasna Polana," Basia was the star. "She ultimately would end up rewriting the script and establishing herself as auteur of the estate," he wrote. "The fact that fooling with Wallace Harrison's plans is in the same class with telling Frank Lloyd Wright you don't like his sense of proportion didn't deter Mrs. Johnson."

Seward probably never saw the article; his secretary had standing instructions to withhold from him anything in which his name appeared. But Tully's tale brought reactions from at least two readers. One noted the irony of the estate's name, given Tolstoy's abhorrence of materialism and greed. Another said he'd found the account so disgusting that he'd vowed to boycott Johnson & Johnson. Tully, he wrote, "could not be more revealing on how to waste personal wealth, especially to satisfy the whims of eccentric and medieval J. Seward Johnson and his ensconced female." "We want more of this superb reporting," this reader wrote. "Reveal more about what fools some mortals be!"

Two months later, in fact, New Jersey Monthly revealed one more fact about Seward Johnson: He was the wealthiest man in the state. With a fortune it placed at $350 million, it said Seward far outstripped the Dillons, the Bradys, Doris Duke, Fairleigh Dickinson, and Malcolm Forbes. The magazine paid a former Johnson employee $150 for a picture of the old man, which landed on the cover. But if Johnson photographs had been baseball cards, a Basia was even more valuable: The same source was offered $500 for one of her.

While Basia was laying low among her new countrymen, she was surfacing more publicly among her old ones. True, she'd feuded with and abandoned childhood friends who had also come to the United States. But rather than cast about for replacements in the wider American society, it was among the Polish and Polish expatriate gentry that she now looked for companionship and respectability.

In 1975, for instance, she and Seward sponsored the Chopin Piano Competition in Warsaw. Through that they befriended not only the eventual winner, a young musician named Krystian Zimerman, but also Witold Malcuzynski, the famous Polish-born pianist. Malcuzynski, a dashing man of sixty with a mane of silvery hair and a patrician manner, cast a spell over people ("Tall, thin and distinguished, erect yet flexible as a rapier, designed to wear white tie and tails, he would remind one of an old-world engraving did not the nobility of his face and the energy contained in his eyes endow him with a genuinely regal bearing," one such admirer wrote. "His vast, thoughtful forehead, his aristocratic lips, his pale eyes filled with all the dreams of his forebears, reproduce our imaginary picture of Chopin himself"). Unsurprisingly, he mesmerized Basia, too. She'd always had a weakness for elegant older men; this one was a Polish patriot, a musical legend, a student of Paderewski's, who was charming to boot. She became his great champion, hounding

him to practice, touting him as better than Rubinstein. In what was
her surest sign of esteem, she took to comparing him to her own holy
trinity of men: her father, Seward, and Jesus Christ. Basia seemed
smitten with the old pianist, and he, in turn, seemed dazzled by this
young Polish dynamo—"my Basia," he called her. Often, Malcuzynski
stayed with the Johnsons, who stocked their homes in Princeton and
Italy with Steinways for him.

Malcuzynski paved the way for Basia's debut in the Polish-American ar-
istocracy. He introduced her to Halina Rodzinski, widow of the late conductor of the New York Philharmonic and a leader of various Polish
charities. (Basia promptly bought fifty copies of Mrs. Rodzinski's recently
published autobiography at Scribner's bookstore on Fifth Avenue. "Bring
us more people like her!" the store manager told the author.) As Artur
Rubinstein's wife, Nella, said at the time, Basia was "drunk with money,"
and it was Malcuzynski's hope that Rodzinski would take this infinitely
wealthy and promising young Pole under her elegant wing.

It was also through Malcuzynski that the Johnsons met Princess Sofia
Zdziechowska, a member of Poland's aristocratic Radziwill family and
an official of the Biblioteka Polska in Paris, the famous but down-at-
the-heels center of Polish emigré culture once frequented by Mickiewicz
and Chopin. Basia took an instant interest, spiritual and financial, in
the place, thereby gaining entrée into the Polish elite of France as well.
The Johnsons also met Jan Waligura,* a Polish-born psychiatrist three
years Basia's junior who had emigrated to the United States shortly
before she had. Basia quickly came to like the gentle, soft-spoken
doctor, and soon Seward—who had always enjoyed the company (and,
given his hint of hypochondria, the close proximity) of doctors—became extremely fond of him, too. Many were the years when Waligura
would spend Seward's birthday and Father's Day with the old man,
while Seward's own children were nowhere to be seen.

Alas, the beloved Witold died in 1977 in Majorca, an event Basia felt
she had sensed thousands of miles away when the frog outside her window
at Jasna Polana suddenly and inexplicably stopped chirping at her. Grief-
stricken, she dispatched her private jet to Paris, where it was filled with
flowers, then sent it to fetch Malcuzynski's body and return it to Warsaw
for the funeral. Accompanied by Rodzinski, Zdziechowska, and Waligura, Basia attended the funeral, dressed in a widow's black cape and hat
from Dior. The guest room in which Malcuzynski had always stayed during

*For reasons of privacy, a pseudonym has been used.

visits to Jasna Polana was turned into a kind of shrine, complete with piano, photograph of the saintly musician, and a king-sized bed, in which only the most honored visitors ever got to sleep.

By the time of Witold's death the total tab of Jasna Polana could finally be calculated: around $25 million. What was the house actually worth? It was a question the Johnsons, the courts, and the town of Princeton were to struggle over for many years. Everyone agreed it was a white elephant, whose resale value was but a fraction of its cost; only the denominator of that fraction was in dispute. The township appraised the property at $7,435,500, the Johnsons at a third of that. To consider its value, expert witnesses in the dispute compared it to the mansions of the Bronfmans, Don Kirshner, John De Lorean, Diana Ross, and Leona and Harry Helmsley.

And what did it look like? While Jasna Polana the estate was gorgeous, Jasna Polana the edifice was heavy, solemn, uninviting, self-important. More than that, it was dishonest: a new house, built with all the most sophisticated construction techniques and accoutrements, masquerading as something old and venerable. The dark, cavernous rooms on the ground floor were the somber brownish-green hue of the Rembrandt Basia would one day hang by the entryway, with all of Rembrandt's melancholia but none of his profundity. On the inside "Bright Glade" had all the "brightness" of a fifteen watt bulb. Though it was not on the itineraries of most visitors, the doghouse was undoubtedly brighter than anything designed for people. Indeed, the only human space that actually felt human was the niche directly below it, the breakfast room imported from Poland. Everywhere else, one half expected to see velvet ropes by the doors. The quality was captured perfectly by a Polish gentleman who, while touring the place, turned at one point to a fellow visitor. "*Straszny Dwor!*" he whispered. It was the name of a famous Polish opera, for which the closest English translation was "Haunted House."

Finally, Basia could begin the serious business of running her château. To assist her, she hired some sixty people: security personnel, maintenance men, groundskeepers, domestics, farmers. The new estate manager would be John Stroczynski, the man brought in a few years earlier as liaison to the Polish workers. Reliable, loyal, ever mindful that she had elevated him from a drone to an executive, he evinced precisely the kind of dogged, doglike subservience Basia prized. "If she had asked him to murder a couple of people, he would have done it without a moment's thought," a co-worker once said. So lavishly was Basia staffing the place—by late 1977 the employee roll had swollen to ninety—that Nina Zagat, warned Basia that she was exceeding her budget and should promptly launch an austerity campaign.

Basia Johnson finally had her Polish palace, but one thing was still missing: Polish nobility. As luck would have it, Basia wanted someone to help manage her personal affairs, and Madame Zdziechowska nominated Countess Maria Krasinski, a Polish emigrée then living in England. The countess came from impressive stock; her father had been the governor general of Bessarabia and chamberlain to Czar Nicholas II. Moreover, she'd married Count Stanislaw Krasinski, scion of one of Poland's most illustrious families. One of the count's ancestors, Zygmunt Krasinski, had been among Poland's greatest poets; his family's estate in Warsaw had become the Polish national museum. Between the physical leveling of Poland during World War II and the social leveling in the Communist era afterward, the Krasinskis lost just about everything. They'd washed ashore in England, where he worked as a gardener and she as a housekeeper on some famous estates. Eventually, they opened their own gardening business, but their earnings were modest, and when their old friend Zdziechowska mentioned posts at the fabulous new Johnson estate, the Krasinskis were receptive.

In February 1977 Basia flew them over for interviews and promptly hired them—she as "personal secretary and assistant" and "manageress of the household"; he as head gardener. At one point Count Krasinski interjected something about a contract, only to have Nina brush such concerns aside. "The Johnsons' word is worth more than any contract," they said she assured them. Suddenly, gloriously, after years of tumult and penury, the count, sixty-two years old, and countess, fifty-seven, had jobs for life.

The prospect of having two fallen patricians groveling before her probably didn't displease Basia. "The scenery was very touching," she later said of the interview, in the charmingly choppy English that she always spoke. "He was so happy, he kissed my hands, tears show in his eyes. He make move like he want to kiss my feet." Hiring them, she was convinced, was not only wise administratively; it was an act of Polish patriotism. Count Krasinski sold his small gardening business, and that July he and his wife began working at Ansedonia.

Those who saw Basia and the Krasinskis together foresaw that their relationship was probably doomed. The mix, of their high origins and low status and Basia's low origins and high status, was simply too combustible. And sure enough, the perfectionistic Basia, who was perhaps too newly rich ever to learn the fine art of delegating, soon began collecting grievances, most of them either picayune, blown way out of proportion, or altogether trumped up. She sent them to Rome to buy cheapo china for the kitchen; instead, they shopped at Ginori on Rome's Via Condotti—"the most expensive street in the world," Basia lamented (the Krasinskis insisted they'd gone there because they'd been warned Basia wouldn't want anything second-rate). Basia requested that a car be waiting for her when she returned from Malcuzynski's funeral; the Krasinskis supposedly failed to arrange for one. The Krasinskis' mealtime discussions, in Polish, so annoyed Seward that he took to eating in his bedroom. Basia spent twenty thousand dollars on olive trees for the count to plant, but most of them died from the heat. And she was getting stuck with the Krasinskis' food bills, which, she thought she had made clear at the outset, were their responsibility.

When the Krasinskis arrived at Jasna Polana that fall, they nonetheless received a tumultuous welcome. The entire household staff lined up outside the door to greet them, and a festive meal was served in their honor. But things didn't improve. Basia now complained that they dumped too much of their own laundry on the maid, sent doggie bags around the estate on five-thousand-dollar Meissen plates—and were still sticking her with their food bills. To make matters worse, when Basia's austerity drive began, Count Krasinski balked at handing out all of those pink slips. "Oh, Mr. Krasinski, you are just like Saint Francis!" said Basia, who dismissed him as "a soft-boiled egg." There was more. The clematis the count planted allegedly choked the crab-apple trees; he allegedly failed to remove dead branches from the box-woods and allegedly let weeds grow three and four feet high around the house; he allegedly contaminated the rose garden by planting flowers other than roses. And he allegedly failed to follow directions, allegedly talked back, allegedly wasted work hours writing poetry and reminiscing about his days in the Polish Home Army. And Countess Krasinski was allegedly too sick too often. The Krasinskis, of course, saw all of these things differently. And it didn't help for them to hear such complaints from a commoner, someone whose mother spoke peasant Polish and walked around the estate in a mink stole and wooden clogs. Nor did it help when that commoner started hurling flowerpots at them.

VIII

One task remained before Jasna Polana could be considered complete, and that was to find a fittingly colossal way to inaugurate it. As 1978 began, Basia began planning an opening gala, to be held sometime in May.

How epic an event was Basia anticipating? One got a pretty good idea from her list of invitees. Even though Seward felt his performance in the White House unworthy of a fellow navy man, "President and Mrs. J. Carter" topped the list, followed by Vice President and Mrs. W. Mondale. Representing the Cabinet were Secretary of State and Mrs. Cyrus Vance, Energy Secretary and Mrs. James Schlesinger, and National Security Adviser and Mrs. Zbigniew Brzezinski. On the local scene, Basia invited Senator and Mrs. Clifford Case, Governor and Mrs. Brendan Byrne, and Representative Millicent Fenwick. From the media there were Mr. and Mrs. Walter Cronkite, while the literary establishment would be represented by Mrs. Anne Morrow Lindbergh and Mr. and Mrs. Aleksandr Solzhenitsyn. Had he come, he would have to hobnob with the various Polish Communist party functionaries Basia had also invited: Ambassador (from Warsaw to Washington) and Mrs. Romuald Spasowski; Mr. (of the Central Committee) and Mrs. Bogumil Sujka; and Deputy Minister (of Culture and Arts Affairs) and Mrs. Wiktor Zin. Completing this incongruous mix were Messrs. and Mrses. John D. III, David, and Nelson Rockefeller. "Of course, for me they'll come," Basia said confidently of her selections. Ultimately, almost none of them actually did. In fact, so many people sent their regrets that Basia had to hastily find others to invite.

Oddly enough, among the first steps Basia took to ready the new house was to destroy part of it. Because Jasna Polana's dining room could not accommodate 150 to 200 people, she decided to redo—or, as Countess Krasinski later put it, to "abolish"—Jasna Polana's servants' wing. Only a few years earlier, Seward had talked of how he and Basia had made these rooms special so as to entice what he called "the upper classes of the profession." Now, three newly completed rooms and

86

everything in them fell under the wrecker's ball. Thousands of dollars'
worth of pipes, lights, sinks, tubs, and time went tumbling into one of
two Dumpsters in Jasna Polana's monumental courtyard.

To cook the festive meal, Basia had originally considered some local
caterers—the types, Nina later said dismissively, more accustomed to
working bar mitzvahs in Trenton than open houses at America's newest
and greatest mansion. Nina offered a counterproposal: Paul Bocuse, the
man Craig Claiborne called "indisputably the most famous chef in the
world." Never before had Bocuse, who ran a three-star restaurant in
Lyons, cooked in a private American home. But he agreed to take the
job under two conditions: First, he would not cook for more than 150
people, and second, he needed the proper equipment, which he would
determine upon studying the design of Jasna Polana's kitchen. Bocuse's
fee: eight thousand dollars, plus one hundred dollars a head. All told,
the tab promised to be tens of thousands of dollars.

Bocuse came to Princeton in March, and hit it off famously with the
Johnsons. An uncharacteristically nervous Seward carved the roast beef
that day, impressing Bocuse immensely with his graciousness. Together
they discussed the menu for the party, which would be almost entirely
of Bocuse's design, though with a couple of exceptions. For Seward,
there would be something with eggplant, his favorite vegetable. And
for Basia, there would be something on a Polish theme. The chef
planned to bring most of the fixings from France. As for the wine, they
need look no further than Seward's vault, which awed even Bocuse.
Bocuse and Seward spent some memorable moments together there,
sampling possibilities. They selected Chassagne-Montrachet 1976, one
of the superlative white wines of Burgundy, followed by Château Haut-
Brion 1964, a fine vintage of one of France's greatest Bordeaux. (Seward
had once ordered sixty-six cases of the stuff.) Then came Chambertin
1966 Camus Père et Fils, one of the finest red wines from Burgundy.
Seward himself thought his Chambertin a bit over the hill, but after
swishing it around a bit, Bocuse most emphatically disagreed. "C'est
formidable!" he exclaimed. "Le goût de terroir!" (A good Burgundy, he
explained, should always smell like chicken shit.) When Junior called
Jasna Polana that afternoon, his father picked up the extension in the
wine vault and offered his findings: Each bottle was tasting better and
better.

As Bocuse envisioned it, the dinner would be a sumptuous, plenteous
affair. It would begin with caviar and eggs served in the shell, a traditional appetizer at a luxury meal. Next was Bocuse's signature dish,
"soupe de truffes V.G.E."—the same colossally expensive concoction

(made of truffles and strong consommé and served in a special crock with a pastry crust) he'd prepared three years earlier when Valéry Giscard D'Estaing ("V.G.E.") awarded him the French Legion of Honor. *Newsweek* once called the soup "orgiastic"; with truffles selling for sixty dollars a pound, Claiborne wrote, "it almost goes without saying that a soup as costly as this is only for a once-in-a-lifetime occasion." After that would be lobster terrine with a watercress sauce, then some grapefruit sorbet. The main course would be "*suprême de volaille en vessie Basia*" or chicken cooked in a pig's bladder, an old rustic recipe from Bocuse's home region of Burgundy. On the side, in lieu of the usual mixed vegetables, would come Seward's beloved eggplant. Then came foie gras, a salad of artichoke hearts, string beans, and diced tomato with a vinaigrette dressing, then cheese and assorted desserts prepared by another member of Bocuse's entourage, Jenny Jacque of Le Nôtre, baker to Georges Pompidou.

Basia had the entire menu printed up in folio form, complete with tassels of red and white, the Polish national colors. On the cover the words "Jasna Polana" appeared in cursive script, and beneath them was a photograph of Basia taken by Halina Rodzinski during a visit to the estate a few months earlier. Basia, filled with good food and drink that day, had been in an ebullient mood—"I'm the happiest woman in the world. I have the nicest house in the world, a wonderful husband, friends," she had said—and the photograph, showing her in a white blouse, peasant skirt, and blue headdress, her arms raised jauntily in front of her as-yet unfinished château as if acknowledging tumultuous applause, captured a woman who'd expected everything from life, and gotten it.

The Johnsons were opening up their world, at least momentarily. Still, some of the usual paranoia obtained. The estate's new "director of security services," John Pellegrini, laid out an elaborate game plan for the evening. A total of twenty-six guards would be working; those in the house were to wear tuxedos, with inspection of the troops to take place three hours before the guests arrived. Unless Walter Cronkite showed up—he did not—no reporters or photographers were to be allowed on the estate without Basia's specific authorization.

Bocuse and his entourage of eight flew into Kennedy Airport the day before the party, bearing sturgeon caviar and foie gras canned the previous night; fresh string beans; huge chunks of French cheeses and butter and gallons of *crème fraîche*; *tuiles* and macaroons and other assorted sweets; boneless breasts of chickens, already sliced and stuffed with truffles. Whatever he needed locally he bought with André Soltner of Lutèce, the famed French restaurant in New York. Indeed, just about the only thing he didn't bring were chervil and fresh raspberries; for that, he had Richard Grausman (a friend of Nina Zagat's and a chef himself) scour the gourmet marts of Manhattan. Much of what Bocuse carried was packed in Styrofoam tubs marked AMBASSADE DE FRANCE. In case the diplomatic ruse wasn't enough, Bocuse suggested to his assistant, Yanou Collart, that they seek out the fattest customs agent available, surmising that he'd construe any bans against imported food more leniently. "Would you like to meet the greatest chef in the world?" Collart said to the man she selected. The official let the food pass, and got himself and his family an invitation to eat on the house at Bocuse's restaurant as baksheesh. Bocuse's entourage was met by a convoy of vehicles from Jasna Polana, including a refrigerated van. When he arrived at the estate, Bocuse found a specially outfitted kitchen, complete with newly installed Blodgett ovens and a flame for the pot-au-feu. In his bedroom, the towels had PAUL BOCUSE stitched into them.

This time, at least, the gods were unkind to the Johnsons. When the magic night arrived, it came with torrential rains, scotching any idea of using Jasna Polana's splendid grounds. But the private jets still made it into Mercer Airport; fleets of limousines still wended their way to the Big House, and a butler still met guests at the door, with a radiant Basia hovering nearby. She'd been with Seward eight years now, but two more would have to pass before she was even half his age. "She was so young and vital and with it, and Mr. Johnson was doddering around like a doge," one eyewitness later recalled. The festivities began with a short concert in the drawing room, performed by some Polish musicians. Then, the guests moved down the hall to the newly created dining room, where only a few months earlier servants had briefly slept. Each of thirteen tables was set with black-and-white cloths, matching the Franz Klines hanging on the wall. On each table sat an Alvar Aalto vase with anemones, either purple with a single red or red with a single purple. Rumor had it that the florist's bill alone that night reached seventeen thousand dollars.

Seward and Basia presided over separate tables. Seward was flanked by his former sister-in-law, Lady Dill of Bermuda, and Mrs. Brendan Byrne, with J&J's James Burke, Mrs. Wallace Harrison, and Ed Link, his Harbor Branch compatriot, nearby. At Basia's table were Governor Byrne and Wallace Harrison. Looking around the room, one could spot Mr. and Mrs. Nicola Bulgari of jewelry fame; Scott and Joyce Grob MacLeod, the Johnsons' friends and Mediterranean sailing companions; and Mrs. John D. Rockefeller. Not far from Mrs. J. Seward Johnson,

Sr., III was Mrs. J. Seward Johnson, Sr., I; Mrs. J. Seward Johnson, Sr., II, had not been invited, though Mrs. J. Seward Johnson, Jr., II, had been. Junior Johnson himself sat near the Metropolitan Opera's Anthony Bliss; Tiffany chief designer John Loring, who spoke no Polish, was alongside Basia's brother Gregory, who spoke little English.

As the assembled guests blithely made conversation, there were assorted crises in the kitchen. Bocuse had choreographed everything like a Balanchine, but acts of God intervened. Service was to be "à l'assiette"—that is, by the plate rather than from platters. But the rented dishware did not arrive; the supplier's trucks had been caught in the monsoon. Basia reluctantly agreed to bring out her own luxurious china. "We will use the Queen Anne plates," she declared. "Please explain to the waiters that these are not 'Queen Anne-era' plates. These belonged to Queen Anne." There was a second fright over the sorbet: It was melting prematurely. A Jasna Polana electrician paid an emergency house call to the freezer, and stabilized the situation. Outside, there were problems of a different sort. Like her husband, Basia was a passionate antismoker (even her own brother had to sneak cigarettes like a schoolboy whenever she was in the vicinity) and in case she had not made her attitude sufficiently clear, there were no ashtrays anywhere. A series of collective nicotine fits ensued, with guests springing up between courses and heading for the bathrooms. "It was like intermission at the opera," one recalled.

As the meal progressed, piles of food started coming back to the kitchen, not because it wasn't spectacular, but because there was far too much of it. One story had it that some of Basia's relatives mistook the palate-clearing sorbet for dessert and thought the meal was over after it was served. Dozens of bottles of expensive wine lay uncorked and untouched. The foie gras returned almost untouched. Bocuse was devastated. Only when, wearing a clean apron, hat, and his various medallions, he took a bow at the end of the meal, were his spirits revived. "The great Paul Bocuse came to Jasna Polana and conquered our hearts with his presence and his marvelous food," Seward wrote on Bocuse's own ceremonial menu. Meanwhile, hordes of beefy bodyguards relegated to the tennis pavilion for the duration of the party were ravenous. No one, it seemed, had thought to feed them, even though there were ample leftovers. Eventually, one abandoned his watch, headed off to a nearby diner, and fetched some sandwiches.

It was all peculiarly fitting. Measured simply by its ingredients, the meal, like the mansion, was impeccable; taken together, it was a monument to excess. By the time it was over, no one had much energy for anything, including dancing to the music of Michael Carney's orchestra. So many people left so early that at one point Basia locked the living-room doors to prevent further escapes. Later, when departures were allowed, each guest was given one of the crockery bowls in which the truffle soup had been served, with "Jasna Polana, May 24, 1978" painted on it; by now they'd been scoured, dried, and filled with chocolates made by Bocuse's son-in-law. The local help left less ceremoniously. It seemed that Evie Johnson, the General's widow, had misplaced her jewelry-studded facial kit, and the waiters and others brought in for the night were frisked on their way out. The bauble was eventually found in the game room.

The opening party was a rousing success, but it had one sad footnote. Or two.

So hard had she worked planning the festivities that Countess Kra-sinski, who'd always suffered from low blood pressure, landed in the hospital with high blood pressure instead, along with headaches, fever, and exhaustion. And Count Krasinski developed high blood pressure for the first time. Basia, already dissatisfied with the noble duo, placed the countess on a six-month unpaid leave, and stripped the two of their apartment and car. The count remained on the payroll, but only "on probation," at least until after a tea party Basia was planning for July.

Shortly before that party, a far more modest affair than the opening dinner, was to be held, Basia grew concerned about some yellowed grass in the sculpture garden, and directed the count to water it. Nothing happened, and she asked again. And sure enough, shortly before the party, Basia noted that the grass had suddenly, miraculously, turned a verdant green. The miracle quite literally wore off, however, when Basia walked through the grass, and discovered her white shoes were suddenly green as well, and not the green of chlorophyll but of paint. Count Krasinski later insisted he hadn't "painted" anything, but applied a grass conditioner routinely used to spruce up golf courses and ceme-teries. But the details didn't matter. He was fired. The Krasinskis fled their "lifetime" jobs in Princeton after only a few months, eventually landing on the East Hampton estate of Dina Merrill and Cliff Robertson.

They had not heard the last of Basia, though. That fall, John Stroc-zynski, the estate manager, ordered them to remove their belongings from Ansedonia at their own expense. ("Nothing will be send [sic] before we receive money from you," he wrote. "Mrs. Johnson do this because according to agreement, you should have covered your food expenses during your staying at Villa Beata, which you didn't do?" It was signed "Best regards.") Conversely, Basia had not heard the last of the Krasinskis. In 1980 they filed a $300,000 breach of contract suit against her and Seward. The case moldered for two years before it finally went to trial in Trenton. Seward was invisible throughout; for Basia, though, the trial was a kind of public debut, and a happy one at that. Her lawyer, James J. Shrager of Newark, portrayed her not just as the real victim in the case—a "target defendant," he called her, the type routinely preyed upon by litigants out for a fast buck—but the underdog, too. Pointedly calling the Krasinskis "Count" and "Countess," Shrager painted the plaintiffs as snobs unable to submit to a social inferior.

Whether by native instinct or good coaching, Basia aided her own cause. She made no grand entrances, dressed modestly, displayed a pleasant, almost demure expression in court, and was disarming on the stand. The Krasinskis' lawyer, William Stackpole of Princeton, had resolved to arouse Basia, to let the jury see her, as he put it, "with fangs bared." But she held her temper in check. His efforts to depict Jasna Polana's revolving door—"I would like to show that the turnover is amazing, and people are fired right and left all the time," he told the court—made little impression. How, the jurors might well have asked themselves, could such an unaffected, decent, down-to-earth girl ever hurt anyone? The Krasinskis, Basia testified, were not just incompetent, insubordinate subordinates, but stuck-up, too. "He was absolutely jealous what I have and he has to work for me," she said of the count. "He was very unhappy because here I am, commoner, and he has to work for me." She recalled how the count once suggested installing the Piasecki coat of arms in Jasna Polana's courtyard. "You push me to be a snob, and I don't need to be a snob!" she said she remonstrated. "I am just a real person, and commoner!" Why hadn't she fired them earlier? "Well, I think I was patient as a saint," she replied.

Before long the jury got to hear about the magical metamorphosis of the painted grass. "So I went there, and walk on this grass, and it is green," Basia told the court. "I said, 'What happened here? It was yellow. Suddenly it is green. What did you do, Mr. Krasinski?' "

"What happened when you walked on the grass?" Shrager asked.

"Well, my shoes were green," Basia replied. "That was two o'clock. And four o'clock was party. So I said 'What did you do? I told you to water that grass a week or ten days ago. Why didn't you do that?' And he said, 'You don't know anything! You shut up!' Well, I think I turned green, like the grass." The jury broke into laughter, as did the judge.

Even a guest appearance by Dina Merrill didn't help the Krasinskis' noble cause. Under the Krasinski regime, she testified, her own gardens had "never looked so beautiful." But her testimony was undermined by a small bit of cross-examination.

> SHRAGER: "Does he keep the grass watered?"
> MERRILL: "No, we have an underground watering system."
> SHRAGER: "Has the grass been green in your experience?"
> MERRILL: "Oh, yes."
> SHRAGER: "Has Count Krasinski ever painted your grass green?"
> MERRILL: "No."
> STACKPOLE: "Your Honor, I object!"
> SHRAGER: "I have nothing further."

"A Hutton may have spoken, but the jury didn't listen," *People* magazine later reported. After deliberating just long enough to enjoy lunch courtesy of the state of New Jersey, the jury came back for Basia. She'd been a smashing success. Along with her other triumphs, she proved she could conquer a courtroom. It was nice to know, given what was to become her penchant for winding up in them.

Not long after the Krasinskis were fired, Basia had a falling-out with their sponsor, her onetime "closest friend" Sofia Zdziechowska, the Polish noblewoman she'd met through Witold Malcuzynski. Basia had agreed to help bail out the impoverished Biblioteka Polska in Paris, but only on one condition: that it come under the control of the Barbara Piasecka Johnson Foundation. The arrangement, suggested by Nina, was made principally for tax reasons. But to Zdziechowska, it was an affront to the Polish nation. "No Pole would have agreed to such a thing!" she later said. The two exchanged bitter words—"I have lifted you out of the dirt, and I'll put you back there!" Basia told her; "I don't need your money and I won't take such abuse from a peasant like you!" the Polish noblewoman replied—then never spoke again. Zdziechowska later said she was convinced Basia was either extremely cunning or mentally ill.

Around Jasna Polana—which, Basia once boasted, she "ran from scream to scream"—some would have seconded Zdziechowska's diagnosis. Basia periodically exploded, invariably over minutiae, and when she did, she was like a water fountain gone berserk. Once, she threw an improperly cut grapefruit against the wall. She grew apoplectic when someone hung a roll of paper towels improperly, or when one foreign-born butler misunderstood her English and brought her paper instead of pepper. People arrived on the estate, committed a faux pas or two, and were gone. "Now, Basia, you can't expect perfection out of servants who've been here only three days," Seward said to her after a tiff over a coffeepot. A cook was canned because he failed to slice meat to Basia's liking. A gardener fled for his life when some tulips he'd planted came up the wrong color. Even Zofia Koverdan, who'd secured and saved Basia's job at Oldwick, thereby setting her whole odyssey in motion, was not immune. In the fall of 1980 the two women were reunited, when Basia hired her to work at Jasna Polana. Her second tour of duty lasted but six months. Once, Basia screamed at her old friend for an hour and a half over some errant fruit. Koverdan quit, this time for good. Jasna Polana security men hovered nearby as she packed her bags, apparently to make sure she stole nothing when she left.

Among estate workers a pseudoscientific seismology developed, designed to discern the fault lines in Basia's personality, ascertain what was responsible for them, and anticipate the next quake. None knew of her mother's psychological problems, though some surmised that the underlying cause was mental. Others said it followed Basia's menstrual cycle—a subject on which Basia regularly kept her associates apprised— or the phases of the moon. Workers kept tabs of such things on their office calendars. There were different theories, too, about how best to cope with her rages. One employee, having discovered that Basia's fury only worsened with his every interjection, learned to say nothing and focus with Zenlike concentration on the freckle between her breasts until the eruption subsided.

Seward's children played little or no role in the Jasna Polana saga. One key contractor later recalled that in his five years on the site, he never saw any of them. If anything, Seward's new nephew, born in May 1975 to Gregory and Lucyna Piasecki, meant more to him than his own offspring. As Basia later described it—attributing, as she often did, near-mystical powers to her husband—Seward virtually had ordained the birth: There came a time, he told Gregory in quasi-biblical fashion, when one life must replace another; Basia's beloved father had recently died, and it was time for another male Piasecki to take his place. And so Gregory and Lucyna went to work. Seward traveled to Poland for the christening of the lad, who was named, appropriately enough, Seward Wojciech Piasecki. Shortly thereafter, the boy moved to Jasna Polana with his parents (Basia's other brothers, Piotr and Roch, remained in Poland). Judging from Seward's subsequent wills, Seward Piasecki mattered as much or more to J. Seward Johnson, Sr. (referred to by some family members as "Seward the Great"), than either

J. Seward Johnson, Jr. (known as "Seward the Lesser"), J. Seward Johnson III (Junior's son), or Seward Johnson Ryan (Mary Lea's son, and known as "Seward the Least").

Still, thanks largely to Basia, the fractious Johnsons were seeing more of one another. As her marriage to Seward matured, Basia became an increasingly dominant—and accepted—member of the family, another can-do in-law in a clan awash in ineffectuality. Once, Basia invited her predecessor, Essie Johnson, to spend a day at Jasna Polana, and the visit went so well that the two Mrs. Johnsons even took a Jacuzzi together. (Essie still called Basia "Basia," while Basia still called Essie "Mrs. Johnson.") Afterward, Essie thanked both Basia and Seward for her "wonderful day" on their "beautiful" estate. "Please come to Hobe Sound some time for lunch and a swim," she added. Seward himself mended some familial fences in September 1977, when he officiated at the wedding of his widowed sister, Evangeline (who had never forgiven him for shortchanging her on J&J stock) to Charles Merrill, a magazine editor, painter, and sculptor several decades her junior.

Over the years Junior was really the only one of Seward's children to keep in touch with him regularly. As if to leave his disastrous divorce behind him, he moved to Boston in the late 1960s, where he began a second family with his new wife, Joyce Horton. He also tried his hand at sculpting. His oeuvre, usually manikinlike representations of people in everyday scenes, befitted someone short on technical skills and artistic vision but long on aspirations and whimsy. Junior, forever trying to improve a relationship he once described as "affectionate but formal," kept his father apprised of his artistic progress whether Seward wanted it or not. In 1974 he began making a bust of his old man. "I *want* every criticism *possible*—it could only make it better—and I want the best," he wrote Seward. (Apparently unsatisfied with the results, Basia and Seward commissioned the Italian sculptor Giacomo Manzu to make separate busts of them. In the completed works, Seward ended up looking like a New England preacher, Basia like a farm girl.) "We were also disappointed that you could not make it over to Paris and catch us trying to effect a change in our personalities (for the better we hope)," Junior wrote his father in another characteristically fawning letter. Eventually, Junior found the surest way toward his father's heart: Though he had little aptitude or interest in anything nautical—in fact, he was prone to seasickness—he became active at Harbor Branch.

The other Johnson children went their own unremarkable ways. The reclusive Jimmy dabbled in painting and farming in New Jersey. Jennifer divorced race-car driver Peter Gregg (who subsequently remarried and committed suicide in rapid succession) and dabbled in the arts in Jacksonville. Elaine, Seward's second daughter, continued to live a dilettantish life in Boca Raton, where she and her ophthalmologist husband, Keith Wold, moved with their two children after his early retirement. Diana's marriage to Richard Stokes fell apart after they, too, had two children, and she quickly wed a fellow horse enthusiast named Bertram Firestone. With a last name like his, many thought Firestone himself was heir to a famous fortune; in its article on the Jasna Polana opening, *Jours de France* referred to him as "M. Firestone, *des pneus*"—"Mr. Firestone of the tires." In fact, he had been born "Fierstein" and merely married heiresses; one of his two previous wives was from the Avon cosmetics family. In racing circles the joke was that he kept marrying up by a factor of ten. What he lacked in lineage he made up for in comportment, affecting the life of a country squire.

Basia considered her stepchildren a weak-willed, dim-witted lot. It was hard for her to comprehend how they shared Seward's genes. But her familial instincts were strong, and she made periodic pitches for unity. She encouraged Seward to stock the foundation's board with relatives, and soon Jimmy and Jennifer were also on it. She spent time with Elaine and Diana, usually at Maine Chance, Elizabeth Arden's fancy fat farm near Phoenix (if Elaine could be said to have a "career," it lay in watching her weight). In 1979 Basia held a wedding reception at Jasna Polana for Elaine's daughter Diana (aka "Dindy"). ("Dearest Basia and Dad," Elaine wrote afterward. "There are no words to thank you enough for the wonderful gathering of family and friends for this beautiful celebration party.") The following year Seward and Basia, along with the Zagats, joined the Wolds and Firestones for Ascot Week in London. Keith and Diana Wold even purchased an excess Pissarro from Seward and Basia for $160,000. Seward wanted to make a profit on the painting; it was Basia who insisted he sell it at cost.

At least some of Seward's descendants acknowledged the role Basia was playing in reuniting the family. Like his five siblings, Mary Lea's second son, the twenty-seven-year-old Seward Johnson Ryan, had never seen much of his grandfather until Basia came along. He said so in a bittersweet confession sent to his grandfather and stepgrandmother in November 1979.

Dear Granfather [sic] and Basia,
    I greatly appreciate having had the opportunity to get to know you two somewhat in the brief time we have spent in each others [sic] com-

pany recently. I have always been very proud of my family, and it is satisfying to get a glimpse of the fine reality that what was before perhaps a wishful pride. Speaking with you, Grandfather, however briefly, made me realize the great stuff from which I come.

I wish I had had the means to know you earlier in life and look foward [sic] to our next meeting. Basia, of course I think you know I think the world of you, with your very special lust for life. Its too bad about all this Goddamned money—If it were not there maybee [sic] we could be a closer family.

I will look forward to seeing you the next time I can and sincerely wish the very best to all at Jasna Polana (that includes you, Prince, Clara, Julie and Cleo).

With my highest regards
Your Grandson
Seward[3]

The next time Seward[3] wrote to Seward[1], his words were even more plaintive. It happened in October 1981, and carried two bits of news: (1) that he was in the Hazelden Foundation, trying to lick ten years of drug abuse ("they call it chemical dependency out here, which is really just a nicer name for the same thing"); and (2) that Seward Johnson was now the great-grandfather of a baby girl "who was, unfortunately, born out of wedlock." "I have the feeling that you may have found my letter in some way offensive," Seward Ryan wrote, though there was no evidence to suggest that the old man had particularly cared about it one way or another. "I am sorry for that. It's just that it is difficult to write you seeing as how we've never been particularly close or anything. I was in an altered state of mind when I wrote that letter, anyway, and I am sorry if you found it distasteful."

If Seward's children had any reservations about Basia and the effect she was having on their father, they remained mum. In fact, as time passed, Junior grew more complimentary. In a "vice presidential critique" of Harbor Branch brass he wrote for his father in early 1978, he summarized his stepmother's personality. "Believes that if you have an opinion it should be a strong one, and if someone else has a different opinion they better be able to acquit themselves loudly and clearly," he wrote. "Basia has very good instincts and she also respects others who she instinctively feels know a particular subject better than she. And, conversely, demands the same courtesy in return. Her fault is that Basia sometimes likes to reduce things to all black and white or the best and the unacceptable."

In a letter he sent Basia and Seward in September 1979, Junior praised his stepmother more directly, extolling not only the "delicious spaghetti" she had fed him but her familial fence-mending. "Basia has been making a very nice effort to pull the family together," he wrote before closing: "Please send my love to Basia the cook and Basia the peacemaker." Mary Lea also gave Basia good grades. "People have snickered about the May-December liaison, but not Mary Lea Johnson," a New Jersey reporter wrote in 1976. " 'She seems like a nice girl,' she says. 'My father is a happy man.' "

The same could not always be said for Mary Lea, whose own love life—particularly her choice of mates—would also play a role in the unfolding Johnson saga.

IX

Mary Lea had kept a low profile following her fight with Seward in the mid-1960s, when he had branded her "a troublemaker beyond my imagination." Much of that time she'd spent rearing chickens, and, with considerably less success, children. Whatever time she might have had for creative pursuits was either consumed by her pregnancies or stifled by her tyrannical husband, William Ryan. To escape the debris from Junior's divorce, she briefly fled with her family to Europe. Upon their return the Ryans settled near Oldwick. Gentle, kindly, grasping tenuously to reality, Mary Lea was too pathologically distracted to raise children, however childlike she might have been herself. Now, physical problems—a bad back required repeated surgery, accompanied by bouts of drug dependency and obesity—eroded her already limited instincts for motherhood. Her life entered an even more tumultuous phase in the early 1970s, as her loveless marriage to Ryan disintegrated and other pretenders entered the picture.

The first was Dr. Victor D'Arc, a psychiatrist on the staff of St. Luke's Hospital in New York. D'Arc, born D'Arcangelo in New Orleans, was a suave, somewhat exotic man, himself recently separated, who had been treating two of Mary Lea's sons for their drug problems. Soon D'Arc and Mary Lea began romancing one another. Mary Lea plied him with theater tickets, limousines, financial statements (one pegged her worth at $56 million), and promises to lose weight. D'Arc, a man with two daughters in private school, a yen for the arts, and a general attraction to wealth, found the pitch appealing, and they married in July 1972. Mary Lea, like Seward, had six children; and Mary Lea, like Seward eight months earlier, invited none of them to her wedding. Shortly thereafter, as if following the precedent set by his new brother-in-law, Keith Wold, D'Arc quit his medical practice, ostensibly to "manage" his wife's portfolio.

The art fetish that already had hit Seward and Basia soon spread to the D'Arcs. Mary Lea and Victor established their own gallery, housed in the $1.6 million mansion they bought in Far Hills, New Jersey. They spent millions more renovating the place, which Mary Lea named, after her childhood home, "Merriewold West." Before long she had exhausted her savings and, with her trustees' consent, dug into her trust.

Almost overnight, she and Victor had become what one reporter called "supreme patrons of the arts." The D'Arcs opened up their home for shows featuring tapestries, outdoor sculptures, and paintings; Mary Lea, a woman starved for applause since her aborted acting career, finally got some curtain calls. "Art-loving Dr. Victor and Mary Lea D'Arc prove they aren't idle rich," stated one story. "For the art lover a trip to Merriewold West will be rather like being a six-year-old on a particularly bountiful Christmas morning," went another. So excited was Mary Lea by all the attention and approbation that she embellished things a bit. "We had collected so much over the years it was just stacked in warehouses where no one could see it," she boasted only a few months into her second marriage and a few years removed from her chicken coops. Referring to her Cybis porcelains, she purred, "They've turned out to be an excellent investment, and so much prettier to look at than stocks."

D'Arc shows featured works by Chagall, Matisse, Calder, Liberman, Nevelson, Noguchi, and David Smith. But it was the sculpture on display along the drive leading to Merriewold West that proved most fitting: Magritte's *Delusions of Grandeur*. Quickly, the D'Arcs fell into the red. "People in the suburbs come to look, not to buy," Mary Lea lamented. Soon, they shifted operations to New York, where they opened the "M. L. D'Arc Gallery" on Fifty-seventh Street and Fifth Avenue. There, "post-conceptual" artists like Les Levine, Allan Kaprow, Dennis Oppenheim, Eleanor Antin, and Roger Welch were guaranteed an annual stipend, whether or not their works sold. It was a visionary venture, one for which the normally docile, dazed Mary Lea had much enthusiasm but little aptitude or knowledge. As her lawyer, the dour, superstraight Phillip Broughton of Thacher, Proffitt & Wood, watched warily, she pumped a fortune into the enterprise. The gallery soon foundered anyway. Then again, so, too, did the D'Arcs' marriage.

One bone of contention was Mary Lea's children, victims of a lifetime of maternal neglect punctuated by interludes of shockingly irresponsible indulgence. As they grew up, Mary Lea remained too self-involved to pay them much motherly mind; once, she handed a charge card to one of her sons, age fourteen, and told him to go buy some clothes for himself. She let them puff on her cigarettes, and when more serious drugs made their debut, she was just as generous.

None of the Ryan children went the catastrophic way of cousin Keith

Wold Johnson, a grandson of the General, who in 1975 was found dead in a Palm Beach hotel room, a belt wound tightly around an arm containing at least eleven fresh needle marks. But young Keith had learned about drugs from the Ryan boys—"I gave him his wings," one of them noted sadly at his funeral—and they in turn had studied at their mother's feet. One son recalled how, during his twelfth birthday party, Mary Lea "got so bombed on pain killers and Scotch" that she fell down the stairs. The same son recalled how, during one long train trip, she gave each child a shot of whiskey and a sleeping pill "to knock us out so we would not bother her." When another was in a serious car accident, Mary Lea brought him cases of vodka and told him to drink it with his pills to ease the pain. Mary Lea gave her children cocaine for Christmas and marijuana for use year-round. Sometimes, she shared marijuana, opiated hashish, and "angel dust" with them. For a change of pace, they took a sampler from her well-stocked medicine chest. Roderick and Seward Ryan were repeatedly arrested for drug possession. Seward Ryan's bout with drug abuse eventually led him to hold up a cabdriver and to father two illegitimate children (one of whom he named Mary Lea) before reaching Hazelden. D'Arc later charged that Seward and Roderick planned to blow up the Far Hills police station to regain incriminating evidence the authorities had obtained about them. He also accused Roderick of injecting the family poodle with heroin. (The Ryan children later maintained all they had done was give the dog the very pills Victor was feeding their mother, to demonstrate the effect such an array of drugs had on living creatures.)

But the real problem in the D'Arcs' marriage appeared to stem from their own confused sexual identities. Victor had always known Mary Lea was a woman of kinky tastes. She regaled him—and others, for she was not particularly selective in her audiences—with stories of her sexual adventures, none of which anyone could ever be sure were real or simply the product of her fantastic imagination: the time her uncle in Bermuda took her out in a boat and forced her to have sex with a black man; the time she said she made love with another uncle, Kirk Douglas; her various experiences with various sexual deviants. Soon Victor began to see some sexual eccentricity firsthand. Mary Lea, he later charged, was forever haranguing him either to engage in a ménage à trois with men and women, or to accompany her to live sex shows featuring lesbians and transvestites, or to allow her to have lesbian affairs of her own. Mary Lea in turn was to charge that Victor pressed her into having sex with various men as he watched, and preferred the company of men himself. "Did there come a time during your marriage when you learned that your husband had homosexual propensities?" a lawyer asked during their divorce proceedings. "About six months after we married," she replied. "He asked me to perform fellatio and made a remark that 'men could perform this act a lot better than women,' that 'any man that's done this to me does a better job than you do.' "

It was against this most unpromising domestic backdrop that the D'Arcs exchanged the world of art for films. Their entrée into the movie business was John Fino, a Bronx-born ex-marine who'd met Victor in the early years of his marriage to Mary Lea. Over time Fino became a de facto member of the D'Arc household, a combination handyman, chauffeur, adviser, gigolo, and friend. With his primitive ways and profane patois, Fino was an oddball in the artsy world of Merriewold West. But despite some brushes with the law, he was a gentle, ingenuous, and loyal soul with the sweetness and look of the young DeNiro—"a kid in a man's body," someone once said. He was also, as a former lover of his once put it, the "best hung" man she'd ever seen, and he kept company with the D'Arcs, jointly and severally, socially and sexually. Mary Lea and Fino became a superannuated Jack and Jill, journeying together to Fino's old turf in the Bronx, stopping by his favorite bar, stalking the garbage trucks manned by Fino's friends. Once, on Bruckner Boulevard, Mary Lea proposed marriage to him. "When I die, Victor inherits a lot of money, and you could inherit it," she said. "You and I could take off together. We could have so much fun." The ever-loyal Fino told D'Arc that Mary Lea was making passes at him, and that maybe he shouldn't keep coming around. D'Arc was unconcerned. "Our marriage is just for convenience," he replied. "If you want to give her a good humping, go ahead."

Fino was a frustrated actor who'd landed bit parts in films like *Crazy Joe Gallo* and *Godfather II,* and he was convinced that Mary Lea's fortune could make him a star if he could find the D'Arcs the right deal. He promptly introduced them to his closest connection to Hollywood: a small-time casting director and Double-A impresario named Martin Richards.

Marty Richards was one of those types always found at the fringes of show business, a character out of *Broadway Danny Rose.* For decades he had survived on his wits and his charm, hustling jobs, eking out an existence, living beyond his means, plotting his next move, dreaming of big breaks. Richards might take you for a ride, but would do it so solicitously you couldn't remain mad at him for very long. He had begun life as Morton Richard Klein—like Fino, a poor kid from the Bronx, the son of a goulash-parlor operator and small-time stockbroker.

Born with a sweet face and angelic voice, he performed for the USO, sang on Ted Mack's *Original Amateur Hour*, and made his Broadway debut at the age of eleven in *Mexican Hayride*. He had flings with radio and television, hawking Tootsie Rolls on the Paul Whiteman show, making the nightclub circuits in Las Vegas and New York. Periodically, the press took notice, though always briefly and at the back of the book. In 1956 the *Daily News* wrote of "Mart Richards," an "up-and-coming young baritone" and "teen-age sensation." Four years later *Radio Daily–Television Daily* declared, "We caught a handsome young singer at 'The International' by the name of Marty Richards, and ya-wanna-no-sompin this guy is great." The *Journal-American* reprinted one of his assortment of publicity pictures, depicting him either as the boyish heartthrob with a ducktail; the dashing roué, trench coat over his arm, lighting a cigarette; a menacing young tough of the *West Side Story* school; or a sensitive, soulful youth with dreamy eyes and the luscious lips of a Caravaggio character.

Richards cut a few records, songs with names like "What Makes One Fall in Love?" and "*Bella Bambina.*" Years later, he claimed that Ed Sullivan booked him for a couple of shows and called him "the next Robert Goulet." (Robert Precht, Sullivan's son-in-law and producer, could not recall those appearances.) Instead, he was more like the last Al Martino. His Italo-romantic shtick was hopelessly dated; or, as he once put it, he woke up one Las Vegas morning "singing Vic Damone when Elvis Presley was in." As his singing career fizzled, he took a shot at acting, with minor roles, he later said, in films like *The Hustler* and television shows like *The Defenders* and *Playhouse 90*. He also did summer stock, including a production of *The Fantastiks* directed by Mervyn Nelson, a man of the theater and acting teacher many years Richards's senior. Though he had been married briefly to the daughter of an oil executive, Richards preferred the company of men, particularly Nelson. The two men became close confidants, and lived together for a time. "They were always plotting and planning something," one friend later recalled. "Marty always had a sense of style, but Mervyn had the brains. I liked them, but I didn't trust them." Between gigs Marty had flings at hairdressing and as an elevator operator in the Sherry Netherlands Hotel. He was usually broke, but never did he show it. "He was always dressed impeccably," a friend recalled. "No one ever knew he didn't have a dime in his pocket." Eventually, he landed a job casting extras. Richards also played minimogul in two films Nelson wrote and directed: a *Boys in the Band* knockoff called *Some of My Best Friends Are*, starring Sylvia Syms, Rue McClanahan, and Fannie Flagg, and *Fun and Games*, an X-rated romp in which a staid New Jersey couple tours New York's sadomasochistic scene.

When Fino, one of those extras Marty Richards had cast, sought someone who could unite D'Arc dollars to his own acting talents, it was to Richards that he turned. In exchange for Fino's introducing Richards to the D'Arcs, Richards promised to come up with a marketable script, one containing a large role for Fino himself. Together, Richards and Fino devised one promising possibility: the story of an embattled police precinct that would one day become *Fort Apache, the Bronx.* It was Fino, in fact, who knew the two policemen on whom the film was based.

A homely, love-starved, and rich rube, her marriage to another show-biz ingenue very nearly on the rocks, in search of someone to show her Hollywood: for Marty Richards, ever manipulating, ever strapped for cash, it was all too fantastic to be true. "Give me an open door with this woman, and I'll make you a star!" Richards told Fino. Fino, driving Mary Lea's Mercedes, picked up Richards and a business associate, Gil Champion, and brought them to Merriewold West. "It was like walking into a fairy tale," Richards later said. "I mean, it was an incredible house and Mary Lea reminded me of Jane Eyre. Here was a lady who seemed to have everything and was extremely sophisticated and, in my eyes, very, very attractive." No one had ever accused Mary Lea of that before, but for Richards, whom a reporter once described diplomatically as "not the marrying kind," the attraction was clearly more fiscal than physical. (In another version of the story, offered by a longtime Richards loyalist, Marty first laid eyes on Mary Lea during an extravagant party she threw. "I'm going to marry her!" Marty told this friend. "What are you talking about? Look what she looks like!" the friend replied, pointing to the heiress in her tentlike muumuu. "Never mind," Richards told her. "Look what's going on here!") The D'Arcs and Richards agreed to form a production company, with Richards getting twenty-five thousand dollars up front for his work. The deal was struck. They toasted to show business.

Quickly, however, business became romance. Richards and his friends became regulars at the M.L. D'Arc Gallery. Even when Richards was off talking to someone else, his surrogates surrounded Mary Lea, flattering her, fussing over her, smothering her with solicitude, killing her with kindness. Soon it became clear that Richards was the latest in the long line of opportunists to glom onto the Johnsons. He dined with her, accompanied her on shopping trips, picked out her clothes, told her how beautiful she looked in them. "Marty Richards acted as

if he just worshiped her," one friend recalled. Not surprisingly, Mary
Lea found Richards charming, and his Broadway world far more fun
than artwork she had never understood anyway. Mary Lea actually
started looking and acting like Marty. "She lost the look of a gallery
owner, and got the Liza Minnelli look," an associate later said. Before
long Marty and Mary Lea were living together, and telling people they
were in love.

And if love means sating another's lifelong need, perhaps what they
said was true. Mary Lea Johnson Ryan D'Arc couldn't give Marty Richards the kind of sexual companionship he craved; all she had to offer
was her money, which was precisely what Richards coveted. Conversely,
the only things the impoverished Richards had to give Mary Lea were
the only things she had always lacked: attention, kindness, a bit of
glamour. "All she needs are strokes," an observer said at the time.
Marty and his entourage continued to dote on her wildly—applauding,
for instance, whenever she entered a room. Whether such gestures were
genuine or synthetic didn't really matter. Richards proceeded with a
most unusual courtship—unusual in that Mary Lea bankrolled most of
it. Devising one of the wisest loss leaders ever, he spent $14,000 of the
$25,000 the D'Arcs had given him at Buccellati's on jewelry for Mary
Lea. "She opened up a new life to me, and I felt that no one else had
given her anything," he explained. In the lower left-hand corner of
the check he gave the store, he wrote two words: "Engagement Ring."
It was preposterous. It was also prophetic.

While he was lavishing his attentions on Mary Lea, Richards neglected John Fino; the Fort Apache project languished, and he hadn't
taught Fino a thing about filmmaking. Frustrated, feeling betrayed, Fino
warned Victor D'Arc that Richards was about to take him "for everything he had—including his wife." D'Arc laughed. But before long a
distraught D'Arc told Fino that his dire prediction had come to pass.
The doctor also said, in effect, that having made this mess by bringing
Richards into their lives to begin with, Fino had to help him clean it
up. D'Arc asked Fino to rough Richards up, or find someone else to do
it. Fino in fact found a hired hand, and the three headed for Richards's
West Side apartment. But the deal fizzled, Fino later said, when he
learned that D'Arc's real objective was not to intimidate Richards but
to kill Mary Lea.

Later, according to Fino, D'Arc revisited the subject. He offered
Fino $2.5 million—enough, he said, to buy him biplanes, yachts, Fer-
raris, and Hollywood stardom—for killing Mary Lea. "He said it was
the opportunity of a lifetime," Fino later testified. Were Fino to say

no, the doctor warned, he would simply find himself another hit man. Fino was in a fix: Somehow he had to warn Mary Lea of the doctor's diabolical plot, but without either implicating Victor, to whom he remained loyal, or helping out the dastardly Richards. His solution was to alert Mary Lea there was danger lurking, then have his own father, posing as an unnamed contract killer, "negotiate" the terms of the hit with D'Arc over the telephone, tape recorder running. The younger Fino would then inform D'Arc of the incriminating tape, and threaten to hand it over to the police if the plot proceeded. It was a neat trick: Mary Lea would be saved; D'Arc would be checkmated but unharmed; Richards would remain where he was; the *Fort Apache* project could resume. In other words, things could return to their normal bizarre state.

The Finos went to work. Fino the elder, identifying himself only as "Teddy," spoke by telephone to D'Arc on at least seven occasions. He told the doctor he'd found someone to ice Mary Lea for ten thousand dollars, but that for so cut a rate, there could be no "fancy stuff"; it had to be "just one of them 'Ping-Pong and it's over with' "–type rubouts.

"He can make it look like a mugging, can't he?" D'Arc interjected, according to a transcript of their conversation. "He can take her purse or something like that?"

"Well, uh, I don't know if he, you know, I got to tell him that because he said if it's a mugging, it's got to be a girl or something involved in it, you know," Teddy replied. "You know what he said, 'cause a guy can't walk into a woman's shit house."

"Yeah, well, can he arrange that?" D'Arc asked.

"Well, yeah," Fino replied, "I can talk to him, but, uh, I don't know if it would be the same amount."

"Well, what do you think it would be now? What's he talking about, just shooting down in the street?"

"Yeah, yeah."

"Oh, but that's ridiculous. Can't he do a mugging at least, take her purse or something?"

"Well, then I'll find out. Is she with that other guy or alone?" The reference, apparently, was to Richards.

"Well, during the day, she's apt to be alone because he's busy with other things," D'Arc replied.

"Oh, and no way of catching up with him, right?"

"Well, that'll have to come later, Teddy. I think the most important thing now is to reach . . . is to get her out of the way. 'Cause I don't want any changes to be made, you know, economically." Once again, D'Arc urged Fino to make it look like a mugging. "And if it comes up and costs a couple of thousand more, okay," he added. "My deal with you still goes, Teddy. I'll give you fifty thousand dollars over the next year after the operation. And that's a promise." Negotiations continued, with D'Arc pressing for what he called "a neat, uh, operation," to take place preferably when D'Arc himself was out of town. But as D'Arc realized over time that John Fino had tipped off others to the scheme, he dropped the whole cockamamie idea.

The plot would not die, however, particularly after John Fino played the tape for Mary Lea and Marty. Hearing her husband and a man with a raspy Bronx accent discuss her murder, Fino later recalled, was enough to make Mary Lea fall on the floor in shock. ("She had a little of that actress shit in her," he later explained.) Richards saw something different: a tailor-made chance to "rescue" the helpless, guileless, witless, loveless heiress and dispose of his rival simultaneously. He begged Fino for the tape, offering him $50,000, then $100,000, for it. "His veins started popping out," Fino recalled. Fino refused. But Richards somehow obtained a copy of it anyway. In June 1976 Marty, Mary Lea, and a bodyguard named Anthony Maffatone journeyed to the Bronx, where they presented the evidence to Mario Merola, the legendary district attorney. "It appeared he had one goal in mind: to get Victor D'Arc out of circulation. And he thought a little discomfort from law enforcement might do the trick," a lawyer in Merola's office recalled.

Even in the Bronx, where the authorities had seen just about everything, the case of a jilted bisexual psychiatrist hiring a double-dealing father-and-son team to bump off his portly heiress wife, as told by a fast-talking gay casting director, seemed too outlandish to believe. As one lawyer, who later tried to sell the story to a literary agent, put it, "*Forty-second Street* had come to the Grand Concourse." Merola, too, was wary. "Why should I give a shit about these goofy people, a faggot and a fat broad?" he asked. But an investigation was launched. Investigators wired both Mary Lea and her eldest son, Eric Ryan, and sent them out—Mary Lea to talk with John Fino, Eric to see D'Arc.

With two officers at the next table and policemen outside monitoring the conversation, Eric broke bread with D'Arc at a Manhattan restaurant called the Spaghetti Factory. But instead of saying anything incriminating, D'Arc merely lambasted Richards. "He said that he [Richards] was a homosexual, that obviously he had no actual sexual desire for my mother, and that he had a long reputation as a liar and a cheat," Ryan later testified. "He went on to warn me that Mr. Richards

was only interested in my mother's money, and that he would see that
we were all cut off." D'Arc also urged his stepson to convince Mary
Lea's trustees to cut her allowance on the grounds of incompetency.

Around the same time, a Nagra tape recorder and a transmitter
nestled into her ample person, Mary Lea dined with Fino at a restaurant
on First Avenue. As their orders were taken, she pumped him for
information about the murder plot. Fino had not been fooled; his lawyer
had warned him that Mary Lea might be wired, and Fino made a point
of smiling periodically at the policemen sitting nearby. Here, too, the
conversation, later transcribed by the police, centered on Richards.

"He is a doll. He is really the kindest person," Mary Lea said.

Fino, who by this point was calling Marty as often as fifteen times
a day to reignite the *Fort Apache* project, was too disillusioned with
Richards, whom he called the "little conniver," to buy that. "I took
him out of the street," he lamented. "He was on Tenth Avenue doing
stag films. I introduced him to you. Now he's in and I'm out.

"They're after your bread," Fino continued. "I think this guy Marty
is after your money. I don't care how much they like you. And how
much you like them. You're gonna find this out in the future time.
Marty wouldn't give a damn whatever happened to you. Don't you
think if you married Marty, that he'd get rid of you and beat it off in
the sunset with some fag? Come on, baby, use your head. Just keep
your bank account well protected.

"Don't even think of marrying him," he went on. "I don't care how
much you love him. He never met anybody like you before in his life.
And he thinks he's making a big score. And, uh, I think you're a little
bit off the wall for falling in love with a guy that likes to suck on guys.
'Cause he's always gonna do that. He's just after your bread. And if
you want to find out the truth about it, marry him, and see how long
it would last.

"Marty was telling me . . . all through this whole thing . . . and I swear
on my dead sister he says, 'John, leave me alone with this woman, and
we'll all be rich,' " Fino continued. " 'Give me a free road with Mary
Lea. We'll all be rich.' He was telling me that. And I'll swear to it.
I'll take a lie-detector test. I said, 'She's a friend of mine. I don't want
to see her hurt.' He said, 'Well, Johnny, just stay out of it. Until I get
things set up.' And bang! He got things set up."

Fino then began grilling Mary Lea about the relationship. "You got
a boyfriend now?" he asked.

"Marty," she replied.

"Ah, come on!"

"I love him!"

"Ah, come on! You got to be kidding!"

"I'm not kidding you. I really do."

"He fool around with girls?"

"No."

"Do you think he fools around with guys?"

"No."

"I could prove you wrong. . . ."

"You can?"

"I certainly can."

"Uhm . . . I know he has . . . in the past."

"I could prove that within the last month and a half . . . I could name . . . three guys that he's seeing."

But Mary Lea stood steadfastly by her man.

The Bronx prosecutors came to consider Richards a troublemaker, busy-body, and all-around buttinsky. "We should have indicted that guy; he's fucking up our investigation!" a frustrated Merola once declared. The authorities remained convinced the murder plot, however weird, was real. But with Fino refusing to cooperate—doing so, he was con-vinced, would only help Richards—the case was dropped for lack of evidence. The only charge ever brought in the saga was against Fino, for contempt of court. When he went on trial in June 1977, the sordid saga hit the airwaves and the tabloids. "TELL OF PLOT TO SLAY BAND-AID HEIRESS," the *Daily News* screamed. D'Arc dismissed the allegations as "ridiculous," the product of the gold diggers around Mary Lea and her own "menopausal problem." He complained of receiving threat-ening phone calls and "a voodoo-type doll with pins sticking in it." Those who had watched D'Arc and Richards fight over Mary Lea dis-missed the notion of a murder plot. "Victor was too quiet, too timid, too uncreative, and too lazy," one said. "To be decadent, you need more guts." Another added, "I don't know anybody who believed it. On the other hand, this was the weirdest family in history."

D'Arc returned to his psychiatry practice, but he did not emerge scot-free. When, in August 1977, a New Jersey judge had to divide the D'Arcs' assets, Mary Lea's lawyers brought up the tapes anew, arguing that the doctor came to court with hands that were not only unclean but very nearly bloody. When the doctor was asked whether he had discussed "eliminating your wife by way of murder" with Ted Fino, Victor D'Arc's lawyer objected, on the grounds of relevance. "Do you mean if a party to a marriage is seeking divorce on the grounds of extreme cruelty, it is not relevant whether he made an effort to murder the other party?" the amazed judge asked.

Not surprisingly, D'Arc got little of Mary Lea's money. Meantime, the hapless Fino went off to jail. "I did a total of twenty-six months locked in a cage because of your games to control Mary Lea Johnson," he later wrote Richards. As for Richards himself, he lived happily and wealthily ever after. People who had known him during his down-and-out days witnessed a startling transformation. A man who wore scuffed Thom McAns was now buying half a dozen pairs of expensive shoes and handfuls of fifteen-hundred-dollar suits at once, racking up mammoth dry-cleaning bills, and insisting Mary Lea's chauffeur wear a hat so that passersby could see him alighting from her Rolls-Royce in style. Marty soon moved in with Mary Lea—it cut down on the cost of bodyguards, she explained—first in New York, later in a home they rented in Malibu from the film director Franklin Schaffner. The California arrangement was a kind of package deal, for Schaffner was to direct *The Boys from Brazil*, a film to be funded by the Producer Circle— the company, created with Mary Lea's money, which Marty and a few partners opened up on Sunset Boulevard. Meantime, Marty's conspicuous courtship continued, his whole entourage smothering Mary Lea with glitz. "Everyone was hanging from her tits," an eyewitness later recalled. "Marty was like a Jewish mother." In fact, they would soon be related. They announced plans to wed.

The relationship had its skeptics. One of Mary Lea's children asked why she was involved with someone who was so "obviously a sissy." "Marty is a man of many experiences," she replied. "Some friends say that she and Richards are an odd couple," a *Daily News* reporter wrote. "He is a 46-year-old show business veteran. She is four years older, overweight and matronly, and a shy newcomer. But she seems as thrilled as a teenager with her new relationship and is spending a small fortune decorating Al Jolson's former home in Beverly Hills, where they will live." In June 1978, after cruising from Los Angeles to Santa Barbara in a stretch Cadillac, Mary Lea and Marty were married in a lawyer's office, hastily festooned with a few flowers. Three guests—the lawyer officiating and another couple—attended. By now Marty, who had been a nervous wreck en route, had regained his old ardor. "You never have to worry: I will take care of you and protect you for the rest of your life!" he told his new wife, who was her characteristically distracted self throughout the makeshift ceremony. "She wasn't there," one of the eyewitnesses later said. Neither were any of Mary Lea's children.

In fact, they didn't learn of the marriage for several weeks.

Even those wariest of Richards and his shenanigans had to concede that whatever else he gave Mary Lea and however much he took in return, he made a perpetually unloved, unsung woman feel very special. He treated her unctuously, played escort to perfection, put her on the map in whatever way he could; an eyewitness recalled Marty waving the *Daily News* article on the D'Arc murder plot and declaring, "Look, Mary Lea, you're famous!" Through the Producer Circle, he introduced her to the glittery worlds of Hollywood and Broadway. A succession of reporters interviewed the happy couple, with Marty talking nonstop as Mary Lea sat by beamingly. Mary Lea told one that Marty had married her in spite of her wealth rather than because of it, since such unions could be "emasculating." Marty, unsurprisingly, concurred. "It's been one of our major problems," he said. Somehow, he managed. So frequently did he drop familial references—"my father-in-law this," "my sister-in-law that"—that it seemed even Richards couldn't quite believe the magical turn his life had taken. At long last, his ship had come in. It was the *Queen Mary Lea.*

X

A
mid the public cooing Mary Lea's six children watched her amorous adventures apprehensively. True, even Mary Lea Richards would be hard-pressed to squander the $50 million or $60 million still in her trust, which was controlled by her trustees. But she was also free to bequeath the principal to her spouse. To the Ryan children, then, Mary Lea's love life was far more dangerous than her extravagance. They had survived the D'Arc age. But now, the Ryans watched with horror as another, far more clever, fortune hunter entered the picture, and isolated them from their mother more than ever. Convinced he could be denied Mary Lea's millions only if discredited, they scoured Marty Richards's background for anything damaging. Hillary Ryan came up with an all-encompassing epithet for Marty: "Broadway Jew fag." It was hard to know which of those terms was, to him, the most damning. They had another term for him, too. Marty Richards was their Basia.

In fact, Marty and Basia hit it off from the beginning, and was that really so surprising? Both were ethnic types who married into the same WASPy family; both were flamboyant dynamos who energized and reinvigorated their spouses; both were halves of incongruous matches that raised eyebrows and sneers and charges of gold-digging; both could feel the watchful stares of wary family members ever upon them. In December 1978, when the Richardses held a belated wedding reception for themselves at the Stork Club, it had been Basia who prevailed upon a reluctant Seward to attend. For Mary Lea, it was a dream come true. "When he walked into the reception, she started crying something terrible because she wanted him there so badly," Marty later said. For him, too, it was "a dramatic moment." "I was meeting the great Seward Johnson," he said. "I was very impressed."

Over the next few years Basia was to spend a great deal of time with the Richardses, in New York, California, and Italy. In 1979 they visited her and Seward at Jasna Polana. "Thank you for a marvelous two-day visit!" Mary Lea wrote, with "love and MANY kisses" afterward. "Your home is the most beautiful we have ever seen and we wish you a long and happy life together." If Basia played host to them in Italy, the Richardses invited her to New York's Black and White Ball. When Marty's father died in 1980, Basia attended his funeral. In 1982 the Richardses accompanied Basia and Nina to the annual Bal Polonaise in New York, where Basia met another storied bride, Princess Grace of Monaco. "You bring much love and glamour into our lives," Richards wrote once in a "Dear Basia" and "Love, Marty" letter. So close did the two of them grow that at one point a jealous Mary Lea considered leaving him; at another, Basia discussed producing a picture with Marty.

Instead, the two teamed up on a very different sort of production. Along with Rock Hudson, the transvestite comedian Lynn Carter, and Seward's sister-in-law, Evie Johnson, Basia had attended the ceremony in May 1979 when Marty Richards had become a Knight of Malta. Joining the ancient Catholic fraternal organization might have seemed an odd step for a man named Klein; in fact, this particular chapter had previously had no Jewish members. But ever eager for respectability, Richards pressed to be admitted. "The word 'no' is not in his vocabulary," said Kenneth Rooney, a Knight and old friend of Richards's from his show-biz days, in his nominating speech.

Perhaps because of her own religious roots, perhaps because Marty received a photograph of the new Polish pope, Basia was extremely moved by the solemn medieval ceremony. She asked Richards whether Seward could be similarly honored, and Marty promptly obtained an application. The old man, who had little use for religion and spent a lifetime deflecting attention from himself, could not have been terribly interested in such a spectacle. But he was a good sport about it all; under "profession," he wrote "oceanographer," and under "education," he put "experience." The archbishop of the New York chapter, Lorenzo Michel de Valitch, approved the nomination, as did his "Supreme Council." The ceremony was set for June 14, 1980, a month shy of Seward's eighty-fifth birthday. Before then, Seward had to read up on the history of the order. Marty Richards, too, had some homework to do, for it was he who would extol his father-in-law at the ceremony. For a Seward primer he turned to Larry Foster, the J&J publicist, who had already gathered materials for Seward's obituary. In a sense the ceremony would be a double-ring investiture: Seward would be joining the Knights of Malta, and Marty would be joining the Johnsons.

Basia now had to plan another Jasna Polana extravaganza, only two years after the first. But by now the drill was established. Paul Bocuse would again cater the affair, at least for the most important guests inside; the rest, including Basia's relatives, would eat the lesser food of the noted New York caterer Donald Bruce White in a tent on the grounds. (Basia later refused to pay White's three-thousand-dollar tab, ostensibly because he had failed to serve the proper dessert. The matter ended up in court, and White eventually got paid.) Once more, there would be renovations: the dining room ceiling had to be raised three meters to accommodate the new Baccarat chandeliers Basia had bought. This time, though, there'd be no problems with rented plates. Everyone would eat off $250,000 worth of custom-made Lenox china emblazoned with the Johnson family rooster—or, as one guest described it, "Seward's cock." Peter Duchin, whose father, Eddy, had known Seward from Hobe Sound, would supply the music. The Knights would bring much of the paraphernalia for the ceremony, the flags and scrolls and robes. Basia had Seward measured for the cardinal-red cape he would wear, and ordered a special two-handled sword with Seward's name engraved on it for the knighting, which was to take place on a specially designed altar located in front of the main stairway. The rite would be followed by a short piano recital, then cocktails and dinner.

The night of the Knights arrived, and this time the weather proved cooperative. Upstairs, Chevalier Rooney and Huey Spratt, the Richardses' driver, helped Seward dress, putting on his vest, his coat, and his cuff links, tying and adjusting his bow tie. The guests—pretty much the same as the last time around, though supplemented by Gregory Peck, I. M. Pei, and Barbara Sinatra—began arriving, having driven past the torches that lined both sides of the road to the house. Security was tight: Besides the usual complement of bodyguards, seventeen off-duty police officers were on hand, all wearing rented tuxedos with red carnations. The house was filled with thousands of orchids. From the garden came the sounds of Chopin. At the appointed moment the guests went inside, and the ceremony began. Each was handed an ornate multipage printed program, with SOVEREIGN MILITARY ORDER OF SAINT JOHN OF JERUSALEM, KNIGHTS OF MALTA and PRIORATE OF THE MOST HOLY TRINITY OF VILLEDIEU: INVESTITURE OF JOHN SEWARD JOHNSON AS A KNIGHT COMMANDER OF GRACE on the cover. Inside was a brief history of the order, the text of the proceeding, an explanation of the Maltese cross, and an essay on knighthood.

The crowd assembled expectantly. To the right of the altar sat Seward Johnson, resplendent in tuxedo and the "Star of Peace" sash he'd received two weeks earlier. Also seated, at the foot of the altar, were Basia and Mary Lea, each wearing cardinal-red gowns of their own. In between stood the assembled guests. Chevalier Rooney, master of ceremonies, a large and muscular man with a robust voice, rose to welcome everyone, then turned to his old friend and fellow Knight. "I present Chevalier Marty Richards, who will say a few words about the postulant, J. Seward Johnson," he declared solemnly. Chevalier Marty took his place at the microphone. He was immaculate as always in his tuxedo, with his own magenta Knights of Malta ring displayed prominently on his right hand. Nearing fifty, he still retained his sweet mien and boyish build. His face had its perpetual tan; his hair, graying now at the temples, was neatly coiffed to hide his incipient bald spot. Only two days earlier his father had died, and his eyes were still red from crying. Very little else could have induced him to leave the *shiva,* he later said. But while he'd lost a father, he'd gained a father-in-law, and the chance to extol him was not to be missed. He fingered the file cards on which he'd written out his remarks. They represented only a portion of what he'd wanted to say; Rooney told him the speech shouldn't exceed five minutes, and Richards, full of newly excavated encomiums, had reluctantly complied. What star, after all, willingly yields time on the stage? Then, in his fragile but mellifluous radio baritone, he began to speak.

"On behalf of Basia and Seward, may I extend to you a warm welcome to Jasna Polana," he said. "This is a memorable and a happy occasion for the family and friends gathered here to honor Seward, the patriarch of the Johnson family. It is memorable because it gives us a rare opportunity to pay tribute to Seward Johnson, who all his life has chosen to avoid the limelight, even though he has deserved it many times before. It is also a happy evening because Basia made it that way—as only Basia can." Basia, sitting nearby on her throne, beamed. Chevalier Marty listed Seward's contributions to oceanography, animal husbandry, medical research and care. He saluted his "loyalty to the arts," which accounted, he said, for "the Johnson family success in the theater, music, and in art." And, he went on, "certainly Jasna Polana is a tribute to Seward and Basia's love of the cultural world." Sooner or later in his long life, Richards said, the self-effacing Seward would have to take a bow. "That happy and memorable occasion is tonight, and all of us are privileged to be a part of it.

"Perhaps the best honor of all that a man or woman can receive is to earn the respect and affection of his family and friends," continued Chevalier Marty, who described himself as "a new and very proud member of the family." "That Seward has, and your presence tonight is further tribute to him. It is my great pleasure on behalf of the Sovereign Military Order of Saint John of Jerusalem, Knights of Malta, to present to Seward the distinguished Maltese cross, in recognition of his service to his fellow man."

The audience broke out into applause, which was cut short by Chevalier Rooney. "Would the postulant, J. Seward Johnson, please come forward!" he declared. Then Seward, accompanied by two Knights, went up to the altar, shook hands with Archbishop de Valitch, and genuflected on the red cushion with the Maltese cross. As usual, little daylight entered Jasna Polana's monumental, gloomy main hall; but for once, with the ancient ceremony under way, the funereal sepia setting seemed apt.

"What do you seek?" the archbishop asked Seward, reading from the printed program.

"To receive investiture as a Knight of the Sovereign Order of Saint John of Jerusalem," Seward replied. Even at his advanced age, he could still read without glasses.

"Do you promise to be faithful to the noble purposes of the order, participate in its services, and live as an exemplary person and a true knight under the code of chivalry?"

"I do," said Seward.

The archbishop read the Ten Commandments of Chivalry. Then a kneeling Seward placed his right hand on the Bible and swore "to observe what is asked of me." As Seward stood up, another Knight read a papal blessing printed on a scroll. Seward obligingly knelt again, and the archbishop placed his hands atop Seward's head. "Be a loyal, trustworthy, intelligent, and a valiant knight in the service of Saint John," several Knights intoned together. The archbishop handed Seward a replica of an old crusader's sword. "I like guns myself," Seward quipped quietly, departing momentarily from the text. But he took the sword, kissed it, and handed it back to the archbishop, who touched him with it three times, signifying his commitment to fighting evil and upholding goodness. "In virtue of the decree received, and by the authority invested in me, we confer upon you the honor of knighthood in the Order of Malta," the archbishop said. With that, he blessed the Maltese cross and placed it around Seward's neck. Chevalier Marty approached Chevalier Seward and placed a bright red cape on his shoulders. As Basia mounted the platform—a breach in the sexist protocol permitted this one time—the newest Knight kissed his archbishop's ring. Then Basia handed her husband some diamond-and-ruby cuff links containing the Maltese cross.

Simply by reading his script, Seward had said more in public than at just about any other time in his life. But he wasn't finished. As Chevalier Rooney twirled him around to display him to the audience, he grumbled good-naturedly, "You're making me feel like a ballet dancer." The audience broke out into hearty applause. As a photographer documented the occasion, Chevalier Marty kissed Chevalier Seward. The guests came up to congratulate Seward. To each of the women he handed a red rose, symbolizing the blood of Christ.

It was a glorious occasion, marred only by the theft of Seward's Maltese cuff links. After the ceremony Seward milled with guests and family, then drank wine in the kitchen with the archbishop. Later, he danced in the tent. He stayed up late, at least late for him, not getting to bed until sometime after ten.

In his benediction that night the archbishop spoke optimistically of the future. "In the name of Saint John the Baptist we are now and will always be with God and in peace," he declared. "Chevalier Seward, may it please God your fame and success increase and continue to do so. May God also protect you and your family and may they always be in good health." But even with everything he had to do in the kitchen, Paul Bocuse hadn't been too busy to notice that in the two years since he'd last seen Seward, the old man had changed. He'd grown older, frailer, paler. He would never see the old man again. The next time Seward and his family would gather together would be under sadder circumstances. It would be at his funeral.

XI

Jasna Polana was a surprisingly self-sufficient place. One could eat Jasna Polana lamb from Jasna Polana sheep, garnished with Jasna Polana vegetables and Jasna Polana herbs, with a Jasna Polana salad (topped with Ansedonia extra-virgin olive oil) and Jasna Polana bread spread with Jasna Polana butter and Jasna Polana preserves. But for all that, Jasna Polana was not yet complete. It did not yet have a chapel.

Basia had never been especially religious, particularly by Polish standards. Catholicism called for altogether too much abnegation and deference to others for that. For her, religion consisted largely of hobnobbing with important priests, including her countryman Pope John Paul II, whom she saw once at the Vatican. It was not a private audience, but, as she liked to point out, he seemed to wait until the riffraff had departed, then held her firmly by the wrist and looked her in the eye, as if there were some sort of secret understanding between the two.

By the late 1970s, it is true, Basia had begun trading in her later secular works for religious paintings from the Renaissance; the bright colors and themes of Fauvism and French Impressionism gave way to gloomier religious motifs better suited to her lugubrious home. In a three-way deal involving the art dealer Colnaghi's and perfume heir Ronald Lauder, she traded a Kandinsky for a Botticelli (plus a sampler of Estée Lauder products). A Degas went for a Cranach; a Monet and a van Gogh for a Tintoretto; another Monet and a Braque for a Velázquez. She unloaded seven Picassos, seventeen works by Dutch and Flemish masters, two Renoirs, one Cézanne, four Courbets, and even a Franz Kline, whose bold brushstrokes she had so admired that afternoon in Seward's J&J office; with the proceeds, she bought works like Giorgione's *Dead Christ Supported by an Angel* and Bellini's *Madonna and Child with a Donor*.

If, as Basia once said, her paintings were her children, she abandoned them with surprising ease. Art dealers flocked obsequiously around her, indulging her every change in taste. "Every single person whom you

118

have met has fallen under your spell and responds to your love and understanding for works of art," Jacob Rothschild of Colnaghi's wrote her in 1979. (Relations with Rothschild were not always so sweet. Once, Basia bought two paintings from him for several million dollars, only to learn later that their authenticity had been disputed. Basia demanded a rebate and an apology. But when Nina read her what Rothschild had written, Basia deemed it insufficiently contrite. "Tell him to wipe his ass with it!" she told Nina.) Basia didn't so much worship Jesus Christ, Saint Sebastian, Saint Francis, and some of the other religious figures depicted in her new paintings as she identified with them. She was, in essence, buying paintings of her peers. Moreover, she believed religious art was underpriced, and therefore a good investment.

Whatever mixture of conventional piety and self-worship it represented, the chapel project greatly animated Basia. For guidance, she and Seward looked at photographs of other famous chapels by Bernini, Borromini, and Vignola. The Johnsons' version would rise a few hundred yards from the main house and, as they envisioned it, fill many functions. It would be a gallery of religious art. It would be available for various womb-to-tomb rituals: baptisms, weddings, memorial services. It would be a place for contemplation, one in which, as Basia once told the visiting Polish tennis player Wojtek Fibak, "people will be able to appreciate the beauty of God's creatures." Should the need arise, it would serve as the Johnsons' refuge from nuclear war. So saith Seward at the ground-breaking ceremony in 1980. Jesus said unto Saint Peter, "Upon this rock I will build my church." "This is the place!" Brigham Young declared on first setting his eyes on the Great Salt Lake. And verily Seward Johnson said unto John Stroczynski, "In the basement we will have a fallout shelter, because sooner or later, the Russians will attack us."

True, a chapel atop a fallout shelter was an odd notion; perhaps the Johnsons were just hedging their bets. But when Seward expounded upon the idea a bit, it took on an even more apocalyptic ring. The shelter he envisioned would be part time capsule, part Noah's Ark. It would house not only some animals—a throwback, really, to the cow shelter he'd discussed years earlier—but also art objects, books, and other indicia of human achievement. And like a latter-day Noah, Seward decreed that everything be installed in twos: two furnaces, two generators, etc., so that if one failed there would be a spare. He also directed that the larder be amply stocked. First and foremost, though, the chapel would be the final resting place for Basia, Seward, and their dogs, and therein lay the real genius to this split-level arrangement: Come atomic Armageddon or the resurrection, there would be plenty of canned goods nearby. What was eventually built was large enough for fifty people, and came complete with telephones, maids' quarters, and a crematorium to dispose of anyone who died while inside.

Exactly who was to go where in the crypt upstairs remained unclear, as Stroczynski discovered one day upon seeing Seward and Basia pore over blueprints. Seward insisted he be interred in one corner, but Basia also coveted that side, whose wall would be large enough to accommodate the painting of Saint Francis she wanted hanging over her remains. At this point the loyal Stroczynski offered the ideal solution. "Mr. Johnson," he said, "what about if you build a tunnel so you can go to each other?" With or without tunnels, there would be nothing chintzy about this chapel. Its twelve exterior marble columns were to cost forty-five thousand dollars each. The interior would include candelabras, artworks (including a Castiglione of God creating the animals) and a plaque commemorating Solidarity—like the *Mazurka* and the name Jasna Polana, Basia later maintained against all available evidence that this was Seward's idea. Atop would be a silver bell, which Basia commissioned from London's Gravesend Foundry.

Such explicit acknowledgments of mortality were rare for Seward. He seldom talked about death, opting for euphemisms like "retirement" instead. He had trouble confronting the demise of others; when Carter Nicholas was dying of cancer, for instance, Seward couldn't bear bidding him good-bye. He could not be blamed for thinking that normal actuarial rules did not apply to him; all those years of polyunsaturated eating had clearly paid off. He might describe some of the older Harbor Branch scientists as "fairly much over the hill," but that was not how he thought of himself. Nor had his sexual drive dried up, though on that score all indications were that Basia had sated the savage beast. Never were there any signs that he had ever grown disenchanted or bored or fed up with her, or craved any extramarital companionship. Older men had strange sexual tastes, Basia once told a friend, but she had always done her best to accommodate Seward's. That satisfaction could be seen in his single acknowledgment of mortality: his wills.

Once the Johnsons settled into marriage, things were largely quiet on the testamentary front. Instead, Nina was left free to concentrate on legal chores arising out of their multifarious activities: managing Seward's assets; building and maintaining Jasna Polana; constructing and, before too long, disposing of the *Mazurka*; authenticating, buying, selling, importing, and exporting over $100 million in art and sculpture;

structuring Seward's foundations and protecting their tax-exempt status. Nina handled the purchase of Children's Bay Cay and the Johnsons' New York pied-à-terre, in the same Central Park West apartment building in which the Zagats themselves lived. She devoted large chunks of time to a lawsuit Seward brought against the Smithsonian Institution over the uses to which it had put a $10 million trust he had created on its behalf for underwater oceanography. There were immigration problems with workers to tend to. And extricating one of Basia's bodyguards from charges that he had carried firearms illegally across state lines. And effecting Seward's decision to give his Oldwick home to Jimmy, and handling Basia's negotiations with the Biblioteka Polska in Paris. And, on occasion, doing legal work for Junior, and, at Seward's request, legal favors for Diana, Elaine, and Jimmy. The job had its perquisites, including plenty of fine dining, first-class accommodations, and travel (Nina was on board for the *Mazurka*'s disastrous shakedown cruise in Poland, in which errant sewer gas had everyone on board, including Nina, vomiting over the side of the boat. "Next time, check the wind direction first," Seward told Nina afterward. The trip had even Tom Ford, a former navy man, turning green.) But for all its cushiness, Nina's job had its drawbacks. Whether at home or at her hairdresser or the hospital or on vacation, whether early in the morning or at night or on weekends, she remained always at her clients' beck and call. Even the birth of two sons, in February 1975 and August 1977, gave her only temporary relief.

In early 1976 Seward began fiddling around with his estate plan once more. First, he provided that were Basia to die before him, a $20 million trust was to be created for their newly born nephew, Seward Piasecki. Seward officially moved to Florida—registering to vote there, obtaining a Florida driver's license—thereby saving himself tens of millions of dollars in estate taxes. That done, he once more included his foundations in his estate, thus increasing the size of the half Basia could inherit free of taxes. And though he already had three executors— Basia, Junior, and Jennifer—he resolved to add another: his lawyer, continuing a practice he had begun with Kenneth Perry and continued through Robert Myers and Carter Nicholas. Indeed, Nina prospered with Basia & Seward as she never had with Shearman & Sterling. Nina had come up for partnership in 1975. That was eight years after her arrival, the normal apprenticeship at such establishments. When the firm announced new partners that year, her name was not on the list; that constituted the only official rejection she ever received. "Nina is a fine lawyer and a very intelligent person, but I did not think she had the indefinable extra something that makes a partner," Ford's deputy, Henry Steinway Ziegler, later explained. (Of course, three such "indefinable extra something"s were a pair of testicles and a middle name like Steinway.) Had she been working anywhere else in the firm, she would have had to leave; trusts and estates lawyers, however, had the option of becoming "permanent associates." It was a lucrative but somewhat degrading status, with no prospect other than of becoming an ever more senior junior lawyer. Undeterred by such a snub, Seward handwrote her name into the document. "Well, I hope this will be helpful to you," he said. Seward never explained to Nina why he was making her an executor, and Nina had not asked. But suddenly, she stood to collect a $375,000 windfall at his death, plus thousands in trustee's fees annually—money that, as an associate, she got to keep rather than kick back into the firm kitty. This new will was to be Seward's last for five years. In the meantime Nina resumed her customary legal chores. And in her leisure hours she and her husband began compiling a survey rating New York restaurants—a homemade, mimeographed, high-calorie labor of love similar to one they had compiled during their Paris years.

As Seward's estate grew with every jump in the price of J&J stock, so, too, did his bequests to Basia, particularly as tax laws came to allow larger marital deductions. Though Seward rarely discussed his estate with anyone, in 1981 he told Jan Waligura, the Polish-born doctor of whom he had grown so fond, that he was thinking of leaving Basia his entire estate. She would receive it in trust, though Seward gradually gave her greater discretion over the fate of those trusts—specifically, the power to choose the charities to which the trust principal would go upon her death. Bequests to the foundation Seward had set up for Basia in the mid-1970s, which she used primarily to fund fellowships for Polish artist and writers, grew at the expense of Harbor Branch, largely because Seward had already funneled tens of millions to oceanographic research. Apart from a token gift to Jimmy—Seward's remaining property in Chatham, Massachusetts—the children remained disinherited, just as they had been even before Basia came along. This, too, he discussed with someone else: characteristically enough, with one of Jasna Polana's groundskeepers. The man was out haying one day when Seward pulled up in his Bentley and asked him to jump in. Surely, the workman thought, the old guy was either about to dress him down for something or repeat some yarn from his navy days. Instead, Seward got personal, asking the worker how many children he had. Two, the perplexed employee replied. "I hope you have better luck than I did,"

Seward continued. "If I had it to do all over again, I wouldn't have any." Of them all, he went on, only one—a son—was any good. (That, the worker knew from prior conversations, was Jimmy.) "The others," Seward went on, "aren't worth shit." The conversation resumed the next day, as Seward and the worker drove around Jasna Polana by truck. A report on Seward's wealth had just come over the radio, and Seward awkwardly insisted he hadn't realized he was worth so much. But none of that money, he said, would end up with his children. "My children have nothing to worry about for the rest of their lives," Seward said. "It's all settled. They're all taken care of."

To Nina, Seward never had appeared all that interested in his children. But foreseeing problems down the road, on several occasions she asked him whether they knew they would receive nothing upon his death. Always, Seward assured her that they did, and were reconciled to it. "The only one who would create any problem might be Keith Wold, but I don't think Elaine would ever let him do that," he said. Once, he directed Nina to ask each of them how much their 1944 trusts were now worth, only to have second thoughts. "Nobody is expecting anything, and if you start asking questions, maybe they will get the wrong idea," he said.

Even before Nina was named an executor and trustee, Ford thought Seward should consider changing the way in which administrative costs were to be calculated. As things stood, the executors determined who among them got what, a formula that almost guaranteed strife; moreover, that figure, taken with legal fees, could not exceed 1.5 percent of the estate, raising the danger that there would be too little left over for the lawyers. In May 1979 Nina described to Seward the deficiencies of that arrangement and suggested he follow the New York statute, which included its own formula, one that provided that up to 2 percent of an estate could be given to each executor, with a separate fund for the lawyers. Based on a $160 million estate, that would mean a maximum of $3.2 million for each of the three executors. With projected legal fees, administrative costs could run up to $11 million, more than four times what they'd have been under the former arrangement. In October 1980 Seward told Nina he wanted Junior to be given the maximum percentage, and for everyone else, including her, to receive the same. The following year she presented Seward with a draft codicil with the revised language. And only on May 19, 1981, as Seward's health took an ominous turn and wills no longer seemed like such exercises in irrelevancy, did she present him with something he could sign.

As early as the beginning of 1979 Seward, now eighty-three, found he was tiring more easily. His voice was persistently hoarse, his nose runny. He was also having difficulty getting and sustaining erections— or, as he tastefully told one doctor, was experiencing "a persistent loss of muscular tone." The Johnsons didn't talk much about their sex life, but all indications were that it had always been active and satisfying; for the hypersexual Seward, no problem could be as disturbing. A year passed, and things got worse. Food, even food on the television screen, made him sick. In his first three months as a Knight of Malta, he lost twelve pounds. In October 1980, while Basia was in Europe, Seward checked himself into the Brigham and Women's Hospital in Boston. Tests revealed no systemic problems, though given what one doctor called his "persistent libido," Seward was told to consider a prosthesis. Three days after he arrived, Seward checked out—"in excellent health," the discharge summary said. But in the first half of 1981 his appetite continued to ebb, his weight to drop, his bones to ache. At night he sweated profusely; by that May he began running a fever. It was then, while massaging Seward's arthritic shoulders, that Basia detected a lump above his left collarbone. A doctor confirmed her finding and arranged to have him examined immediately at the Princeton Medical Center. It was then that Basia called Nina, suggesting that the new codicil be signed.

On the morning of May 19, only a few hours before Seward was to be hospitalized, Nina and Jay Gunther, her longtime teammate from Shearman & Sterling's probate department, brought the document to Jasna Polana. Sitting in Seward's bedroom, Nina twice more asked Seward whether he wanted to keep the commissions at the maximum rate allowed by law or set them lower. "Well, the executors and trustees are Basia and Seward, Jr., and you; no, I want to keep it that way," he told her. By now, the estate was worth around $200 million; Nina, along with Basia and Junior, now stood to collect $4 million each as executors, plus $500,000 annually for the rest of Basia's life for managing her two trusts.

The money didn't matter to Basia, who stood to receive it by inheritance anyway. By normal standards Junior, as beneficiary of one of the 1944 trusts, wouldn't have needed it either. But Junior was forever living beyond his means, pleading poverty to his trustees, and lobbying his father to leave him more than his siblings. That, he explained, would help make up for his costly divorce, which had drained his trust considerably and thereby threatened to make his two children, as he put it, "the poorest cousins." Actually, Seward had already provided for them, too, in a pair of trusts, worth tens of millions of dollars, he created for his grandchildren in the early 1960's. But for Nina, whose salary had yet to break into six figures, it was an altogether staggering sum—even if she was, as Seward had called her during the Knights of Malta soiree, "the best trusts and estates lawyer in New York," even if, as the old man slowed down, Nina had gone from being merely Seward's lawyer to Basia's steadiest companion and maybe her best friend.

Apart from the fact that each had once been a Girl Scout, the two women—the impulsive, tempestuous Pole and the unexcitable, hyper-methodical American—had almost nothing in common. But like Seward and Basia, or Marty and Mary Lea, Basia and Nina were both incongruous and symbiotic. The Johnsons gave Nina all the glamour and excitement money could buy, a world far removed from the quotidian life of a Wall Street associate. Someone who saw Nina and Tim Zagat in that world once said they were like "children in a candy store." The Johnsons also gave her interesting legal work and the autonomy to set her own schedule, one well-suited to raising her young family. Conversely, Nina served the Johnsons loyally, reliably, honestly, uncomplainingly. Moreover, Nina offered Basia just about the only things she could not buy: friendship, understanding, tolerance, and companionship, even if they all came with a quarterly Shearman & Sterling statement attached.

Things between the two women were not always smooth. At times Basia, as recklessly impulsive as Nina could be plodding, grew exasperated with Nina's pace, dubbing her "the Queen of Delay." Frustrated by how long it was taking to obtain construction permits for the new chapel, in the fall of 1982 Basia exploded at Nina, leading the Johnsons to consider replacing her and Nina to flirt with quitting. (When the contretemps had blown over, both Junior and Mary Lea told Nina how happy they were she'd survived.) To the world at large, though, they seemed a team. Like her husband, Basia liked to delegate dirty tasks, and to Nina fell such chores as handling sensitive employee matters or extricating Basia from some rashly made pledge or purchase. Those who resented Basia came to resent Nina at least as much, viewing her as Basia's enforcer, her apologist, her henchman, her heavy. Nina exacerbated things by appearing to have absorbed some of Basia's imperiousness.

Why would Seward have provided for Nina so munificently? How to explain the extravagance of someone who had spent a lifetime pinching pennies, at least those pennies earmarked for taxes or legal fees?

Perhaps he didn't understand what he was doing, though given his familiarity with wills and trusts—he'd signed dozens of the former, set up at least a dozen of the latter, and served as the executor and trustee of the General's estate—that was highly implausible. Perhaps Nina, with or without Basia's connivance, had deliberately deceived him, though so bald and colossal a heist seemed utterly beyond her personality, character, will, or imagination to try. Perhaps it was out of affection for Nina, but $24 million worth of affection? That seemed implausible, too. Most likely, it was because he feared that once he was gone, opportunists galore would buzz around Basia, and Basia, mercurial and manipulable, could prove easy prey. (Seward had acknowledged as much during a visit to Shearman & Sterling in May 1979, when he told Nina he worried about Basia's periodic flare-ups, and how they could well grow worse as his wife, now forty-two, approached menopause.)

That, presumably, was why he had chosen to leave Basia his money in trust, with Nina as trustee. Nina would be Basia's best, and perhaps her only, defender. And though Seward liked Nina, Nina was human, and he might have surmised that the best way to keep her loyal was to give her so much money that she couldn't conceivably want more. The arrangement was not without precedent. Seward had always given a flat 10 percent commission to his art dealer, Harold Diamond, even though he undoubtedly could have negotiated better terms for more expensive items. This way, he reasoned, Diamond always had an incentive to do his very best. Seward could be penny-pinching, but for things he deemed important he was willing to pay top dollar.

But what Seward wanted posed some dangers. Simply stated, it looked bad for a lawyer to receive so much money from a will that she herself had written. "Attorneys for clients who intend to leave them a bequest would do well to have the will drawn by some other lawyer," one classic court decision stated. "Any suspicion of improper influence used under the cover of the confidential relationship may thus be avoided." Nina would collect her windfall in fees and commissions rather than by bequest, so that case wasn't precisely on point. Still, she stood to profit enormously from a document she drafted for someone else, and that someone was eighty-five years old and ill. It behooved her to make clear, in whatever way she could, that she was carrying out her client's wishes rather than lining her own pockets.

And yet, for a variety of reasons, she never pressed Seward to explain the arrangement, or, better yet, to create a record that would be available after he was gone. For one thing, Nina was not terribly curious or aggressive. If this was what Seward wanted, who was she to ask questions, to appear to be challenging or second-guessing him? For another, she was a bit naive, even innocent, with little strategic sense—something her legal career, spent almost entirely in the cushy world of a single, fabulously wealthy couple, had done little to change. Her universe did not include people who would try to pervert Seward's clear intent, and so she did not protect against them. Nina was a straight arrow, the type to do everything by the book, to think that everyone else does everything by the book, and that doing things by the book is all you have to do. Mostly, she was complacent, in large part because her bosses were; if the arrangement set off any alarm bells among her Shearman & Sterling superiors, they were inaudible. Finally, she was unexcitable. Other multimillionaires in the making, salivating over the fortune in their future, would have thought constantly about protecting themselves. But Nina was a placid, almost stolid sort. A lot of things could happen. Seward could always change his mind. Because she was not one to count her chickens, she did not think to protect her nest.

Shortly after Nina and Gunther checked out of Jasna Polana, Seward checked into the Princeton Medical Center. The biopsy confirmed the worst: cancer. Another test, performed three days later, revealed that the tumor had metastasized from his prostate. Already, it had spread beyond the pelvic area and into the bones. Basia was told that her husband was dying, and that were nothing done soon, he would succumb quickly and wretchedly. The best way to retard the process was to remove his testicles, which produced the hormone that helped the cancer spread. With that, Seward's prognosis grew to eighteen to twenty-four months, possibly more. Basia could see the terror in Seward's eyes as the doctor spoke. But everyone, Seward included, knew there was no choice. "Let's get it over with," he told a nurse. It was Friday. The doctor suggested surgery Monday. At Basia's insistence, the operation was set for Saturday.

On the morning of May 23, Seward, who'd been given a mild sedative beforehand, was wheeled into the operating room. He was placed on a table in a supine position, and an anesthesiologist hooked up his arm to an intravenous line carrying small dosages of Valium and morphine. A nurse shaved his scrotum and cleaned it with Betadine, and then draped everything but the doomed organ in sterile cloth. Some Xylocaine was injected into the area, and within a few minutes, Dr. James Varney had removed Seward's testicles, placed them in a jar, and sent them to the lab. A bandage was placed over the incision, and a jock

strap over that. The entire procedure took only a few minutes. Seward
remained awake through it all. Anxious to calm Seward's fears, Basia
downplayed the entire episode. "No tears!" she told all visitors.

Things were not quite so smooth postoperatively. Without the doctor's authorization, Basia gave Seward some Tylenol to ease his pain.
Later she chewed out Varney for estimating Seward's life expectancy,
which she considered improper. (Varney was equally exasperated with
Junior, whom he called "Seward, Jr., or Seward III or IV or V, whatever
his name is," and described as "a big horse's ass trying to interfere.")
Basia warned another internist that unless he shaped up, "he was going
to have *his*, not off the record, balls removed." But within four days
Seward went home, and before long he'd regained his strength and
spirits. There were setbacks: That September Ed Link, cofounder of
Harbor Branch, died of prostate cancer. During a visit to Florida on
Election Day, intended as much to strengthen his residency claim as
to do his patriotic duty, Seward was hospitalized briefly for vertigo and
double vision. But tests taken a year after the operation showed his
cancer in remission. Seward and Basia, joined by Jan Waligura and
Nina, celebrated over lunch at the Four Seasons. In June, Seward,
describing himself as "a youngish eighty-six-year-old," wrote a long
letter on defense policy to Ronald Reagan. In it the old man, who had
recently joined a group called "Friends of the President," praised Reagan
for the "masterful job" he'd done reducing inflation, declared his readiness "as a person of considerable means" to support pet Reagan candidates, and urged that fleets of low-cost "tank killers" could both
enhance America's security and cut its budget deficit. In his reply a
month later Reagan gratefully assured Seward that he would forward
his suggestions to the secretary of defense.

Seward's improved state, her resounding triumph in the Krasinski
case, the upcoming summer season in Ansedonia—everything seemed
to be breaking Basia's way as 1982 progressed. In Italy Basia and Seward
received Amintore and Maria Pia Fanfani, the Italian political leader
and his wife; the Maurizio Bufalinis (he was supplying the marble for
Jasna Polana's chapel); and Waligura. But in August Seward's condition
suddenly worsened, and he hastily returned to Jasna Polana. In September he began receiving chemotherapy around his hips and pelvis
and using a cane. In a brief sketch in *Forbes* magazine—which claimed
that Seward was the 180th richest man in America—his sense of humor
was described as "rye [*sic*]." He was feeling anything but that now.
Seward socialized some that fall. The Johnsons visited William Burks,
one of the doctors who'd treated him at the Princeton hospital, and

hosted P. James Roosevelt of New York's Seawanhaka Yacht Club, who sought to learn more about Seward's sailing career. But shortly after returning from another voting trip to Florida, Seward collapsed while trying to get out of bed. He eventually reached a telephone and summoned help. By the next morning, however, he was alert.

Alas, Seward was not the only Johnson feeling the twin ravages of cancer and old age. So, too was Princey, their beloved boxer—Princey, who always accompanied Seward in his perambulations around the estate; Princey, who shared champagne and pancakes at the Johnsons' Sunday morning breakfast table; Princey, who on occasion was given communion wafers; Princey, who accompanied the Johnsons on their world travels; Princey, whose portrait hung, alongside one of Basia, in the Fort Pierce house; Princey, whom Basia had trained to bark ferociously whenever she whispered "Brezhnev!"

At the usual ratio of seven years to one, by the fall of 1982 Princey and Seward were about the same age, and in about the same shape. As Seward and Basia flew to Florida to vote, Gregory Piasecki loaded Princey into the Johnsons' camper and drove him up to Ithaca, home of the New York State College of Veterinary Medicine. Doctors diagnosed abdominal cancer, which had already spread throughout the dog's body. Princey had but a few weeks to live. "All of us extend our deepest sympathy at your loss," the hospital's report to the Johnsons stated. Word of Princey's prognosis reached Seward at the Princeton Hospital, where he'd gone briefly after falling in his bedroom, and he was devastated. The feelings were mutual: When the dog returned from Ithaca, stitched-up belly and all, he ran up Jasna Polana's monumental staircase looking fruitlessly for Seward. There were some last-minute blood transfusions, but to no avail. On November 18, after a long vigil, Princey passed away. That night the Johnsons slept alongside their dead dog. Princey, Mary Lea later said, "was, well, almost a human being as far as Dad was concerned." Basia went one step further. "He was our son," she declared.

A pall fell over Jasna Polana as preparations were made for the dog's funeral. Seward directed Gregory to fetch his favorite spotted fur blanket and place Princey atop it on a table in front of the grand staircase. There, the dog would lie in state, and people could pay their last respects. Stroczynski took measurements for Princey's custom-made coffin. Seward wanted it to be airtight, so that when archeologists discovered it a few millennia hence, the remains would be sufficiently intact for scientific research.

All of Jasna Polana turned out for the solemn ceremony, along with

select invitees: Harry Bailey, the art dealer with whom Basia had become
friendly; Jan Waligura; Nina; Junior. (The Richardses could not attend,
but sent flowers.) Basia wore black. Together, as the guests stood solemnly in the hallway and some of the household staff snickered behind
them, Gregory lifted the canine corpse and placed it in the wooden
box. Lining the container were the brightly colored autumn leaves
Seward had asked the workmen to collect from the woods in which
Princey had so loved to romp. Then, four Jasna Polana workmen,
doubling as paw-bearers, carried the casket out the front door and down
the steps. There, they inserted it into a larger metal box and soldered
it shut. It was then time to take Princey to his temporary resting place
near the theater garden—temporary because a crypt was already reserved
for him in the incipient chapel, beneath a plaque that would one day
read PRINCE OF JASNA POLANA.

The procession wound its way to the grave site, where a hole had
already been dug and where some fifteenth-century ironwork Basia had
bought at Sotheby's would be placed. Princey's remains were laid gently
in the good earth whence he had come. As Seward watched, could he
not have been thinking that he would shortly follow?

XII

T hey say death comes in threes. On December 4, Basia's aged mother took ill and had to be hospitalized. And then, on the twelfth, Seward collapsed again. The doctor summoned to the house found him very weak, a bit disoriented, sweating, and slurring his speech. He was taken by ambulance to the Princeton Medical Center, where doctors determined that medication and chemotherapy had reduced both Seward's electrolyte and blood count, leaving him light-headed and weak. A transfusion improved his condition dramatically, as it would on several subsequent occasions when he exhibited the same symptoms. He was discharged on the twenty-first, feeling "tremendously better," he said. As 1983 began, Seward seemed stable. He had also lived seventeen of the twenty-four months he'd been allotted at the time of his operation.

Aside from periodic setbacks—there was another transient spell of weakness in early January—Seward conducted business as usual. So did his children. On January 21, Junior and another Harbor Branch official came to Jasna Polana to discuss foundation business, including a proposal to build a new $10 million research vessel. Basia, praising Junior's handling of the foundation's portfolio, persuaded Seward to forgive a $1 million loan he'd made to Junior for the atelier he'd built to make his sculptures. Apparently unperturbed by Seward's state, in mid-January the Richardses and Wolds left for a three-month $20,000-a-couple Pacific cruise on the QE 2. Diana and Bert Firestone did check in on Seward around the same time, but it was the precarious state of their own finances rather than of Seward's health they had called to discuss.

Largely with Diana's money, the Firestones had plunged into horse-flesh as never before. But when the income from Diana's trust—by 1981, nearly $3.5 million annually—proved insufficient, they borrowed from principal, too. All told, between 1972 and 1981 they received $30.4 million from the trust, and still, they were broke; in February 1981 the trustees lent Diana nearly $4 million more. One trustee,

131

Nicholas Brady, president of the Jockey Club, chairman of Dillon Read & Company and, later, George Bush's treasury secretary, was particularly disgusted. "The horse game is largely a tax game," he complained. Diana complained that her trustees didn't understand her devotion to horses and were unfair to Bert, whom they had pegged as a fortune hunter.

By February 1982 the Firestones, their debt hovering somewhere between $25 and $35 million, were once again before the trustees, cup in hand, soliciting $6 million more. When the trustees refused, Diana turned to Seward for support, financial and familial. In June, Seward agreed to back a $2 million loan, and, according to Diana, suggested that with Brady about to be named to the United States Senate, she push for Junior to take his place—the place he had relinquished as part of his divorce deal seventeen years earlier. Diana did just that, assuring her trustees that because she and Junior really didn't know one another all that well, he'd extend her no favors. Unconvinced, the trustees named another pharmaceutical heir, Albert W. Merck, to the post. It was Merck's appointment that the Firestones came to Jasna Polana to discuss.

During his December hospitalization Basia had hired some nuns to tend to Seward, and even after he'd returned home, he had round-the-clock nursing care. Like others in Basia's employ, the nurses did not have an easy time of it. On January 7, the day Basia's mother died, the nurse on duty, one Judith Abramowitz, gave Seward some papaya juice Basia deemed too old. "Mrs. Johnson hysterical," the nurse wrote in her notes. "Absolute rage ensued." Later that month Basia opted for more unorthodox treatment for Seward. She brought in Clive Harris, the world-famous faith healer.

Basia was a student of faith healing, in part because she believed her own hands were endowed with magic, medicinal heat. She was convinced, for instance, that simply by holding in them the crumpled hummingbirds that crashed periodically into the swimming pavilion, she could help them once again to fly. It was not surprising that she'd heard of Harris, a slim, balding Englishman whose fingers were said to emit a therapeutic electrical charge; most Poles had. During Harris's regular visits to Poland hundreds of thousands of Poles, from the lowliest peasants to the most pious priests to the loftiest Communists, waited hours for a few seconds of his time, during which he would lay his hands on their heart or throat or whatever else ailed them.

Like most modern medicine men, Harris didn't make many house calls. But like Paul Bocuse before him, Harris made an exception for the Johnsons. Surely, Shearman & Sterling's London office, which arranged for him to visit Jasna Polana, never had handled a more unusual assignment. And surely even Jasna Polana had never entertained a stranger guest. Harris, a gnomelike man who looked like E. T., would not eat or sleep at regular times and spent hours regaling listeners with his tales: how his healing powers were first discovered (during a childhood hospitalization, when he cured the other children in his ward); how he battled witch doctors; how, with a submachine gun sticking in his gut, he healed one African potentate. As long as he was around, other Johnsons availed themselves of his services; he treated Joyce Johnson's bad back and, she believed, eased a tremor in her hand.

Seward reacted warily to Harris's arrival, and from someone who'd made his fortune in pharmaceuticals, who fancied himself a scientist, such skepticism was understandable. But desparation does strange things to even the most rational people, and Harris made a believer out of Seward. "I feel so much stronger, and it's all due to Mr. Harris," he told one nurse. And for that, Basia was grateful, offering Harris $100,000 for his eight-day stay. (Angry, perhaps over Seward's ultimate fate, Basia subsequently stiffed him. At her insistence Shearman & Sterling hired a British investigator, named Drake, to check out Harris's bona fides with the National Association of Spiritual Healers, then paid Harris a small fraction of his fee.) How were the Johnsons to work with? Years later, when a reporter came calling, Harris, citing what was apparently the faith-healer/patient privilege, would not discuss his experience.

Seward was about to make his annual pilgrimage to Florida in mid-January when he once again awoke weak and dehydrated. Once more he was whisked off to the hospital. But Basia knew that for Seward, simply anticipating a trip to Fort Pierce was a great tonic. And sure enough, the next morning he was again raring to go. At Basia's insistence and over the doctor's objections, Seward checked out. Then, accompanied by Basia and Harris, he flew to Fort Pierce. Seward arrived—pale, weak, stiff, but cheerful—and walked from the plane to the car unassisted.

The task of preparing the Florida home for the convalescing Seward had fallen, appropriately, to John Peach. Peach, a prematurely balding man in his mid-thirties, was another of those people, like Captain Gore of the *Ocean Pearl* and James Pitney, the family's New Jersey lawyer, who lived well tending to the Johnsons. He had met Seward in the 1960s, was Harbor Branch's first official employee, and had been the Johnsons' eyes and ears during the construction of the Fort Pierce house.

Now, he adapted the place to the old man's new needs. So that he needn't climb stairs, the spare room on the ground floor was converted to a bedroom. To ferry him upstairs, an elevator chair of the sort seen alongside the summer-camp ads in the Sunday supplements had been installed. Peach had also lined up nurses, a pharmacy, and suppliers of oxygen and hospital equipment.

For his primary medical care, one of Seward's Princeton doctors had recommended Fred Schilling, a cardiologist in Boca Raton who agreed to see Seward at his office or, if necessary, fly up to Fort Pierce by helicopter. Schilling, who hailed from New York and had followed his aging patients southward, took his maiden flight to Fort Pierce four days after Seward's arrival. For him millionaire patients were nothing new, and that these were the Johnson & Johnson Johnsons neither impressed nor intimidated him. Little did, for Schilling was a man of certitude, someone who ruled everyone—patients, nurses, secretaries, his seven children—like a patriarch. Still, he quickly realized that tending to the Johnsons would be unlike anything he'd done in forty-one years of practice. Seward himself would be no problem; despite his debilitating illness, the old man struck him as dignified and proud, alert and intelligent, a man of a few well-chosen words. Moreover, he had blind confidence in Schilling, precisely the kind of patient doctors recommend most. But Basia was a thornier proposition. Schilling could feel her measuring him up and down, making sure he was up to the job. Worse, she had her own psychoceramic ideas about health care, as was apparent from the whole apothecary of pills and vitamins, quack remedies and Old World potions, to be found in Seward's bedroom.

Before long, Schilling had reviewed Seward's situation and apprised Basia and Peach of his findings. Seward's ribs, he reported, were riddled with cancer. Alert Seward might be, but disease was eating him alive. His condition was terminal; whether that meant he would last several months or only a few days was impossible to say. Basia told Peach to fetch Junior, who was on one of his periodic inspection tours of Harbor Branch, so that she could tell him of Schilling's diagnosis. "This better be important!" huffed Junior, anxious as ever not to seem to be under Basia's thumb. Over the next few months Junior often watched awkwardly from the sidelines as Peach, far more than he, the eldest son, helped Seward to die.

There was little to do but wait. For Basia, this meant making Seward as comfortable as possible as long as possible. To her, and therefore, to everyone working for her, it also meant pretending that nothing catastrophic was afoot. The word "death" was stricken from the vernacular. For Basia, it was part delicacy, part avoidance, part hope; every time she heard talk of some new cancer cure, she clamored to learn more about it. Whether out of stoicism, ignorance, disbelief, denial, or politeness, Seward played along with the ruse. He talked animatedly and convincingly about going up to Jacksonville to watch Harbor Branch's new boat being constructed, of boarding it via the special wheelchair ramp being installed for him, of staying in his personal cabin—even though such things were months, even years, away. He never asked Schilling his prognosis, and that was fine with the doctor, who had little use for such newfangled notions as confronting patients who already knew the jig was up with reminders of their own mortality.

The world Basia and Peach had created, the world Schilling discovered—the world of J. Seward Johnson, invalid—was compact and intricate. It consisted principally of his bedroom, much of which was swallowed up by the hospital bed Peach had bought for it. At its far end a sliding glass door opened up to a small courtyard. Hard by the bed was a private lavatory, the new, windowless kind found in Holiday Inns and modern New York luxury apartments. At the foot of the bed was a table for equipment, medications, and the nurses' notebooks; nearby was the chair in which the nurses sat. As time passed, the room was further adapted to Seward's special needs and neuroses. Annoyed that his Kleenexes were always getting lost in his covers, he had a shelf installed on the side rail to hold them. On his bedside table were his glasses (the ones for watching television in the black case, the ones for reading in the brown), a container for his hearing aids, and a phone. Taped to the lamp   and placed strategically throughout the house—were the numbers of various doctors, nurses, and helicopter services. There were also buttons for ringing Basia, the nurse on duty, or any other room in the house, as well as a remote-control device for the television.

At first Seward took regular excursions from his room. Some were as modest as the mealtime walk to the living room. Peach, who stopped by the house several times daily, occasionally took him for short rides on the golf cart, or Captain Gore might take him out on the *Ocean Pearl*. Then it was back to bed for a nap. Around teatime at four Seward might go outside again, dressed in pajama bottoms, a small scarf, slippers, and a sweater. But to the extent possible, the world was brought to Seward. Every morning someone would drive to Vero Beach for his newspapers: *The New York Times, The Wall Street Journal, The Miami Herald*. Sometimes only the *Herald* had come in, and that would make him unhappy. "Where are my New York papers?" he'd grumble. "I'm tired of reading all about the Cubans!" In fact, his reading was pretty much confined to the stock listings, where he'd check not just J&J but IBM and John Deere, whose tractors he had always liked. A web of wires linked Seward to a television, a radio, and a videocassette recorder, which he used to watch Harbor Branch promotional films and movies. (He liked *On Golden Pond* but not *Oh! Calcutta!*). When reception for the Super Bowl was poor, Peach installed a satellite dish. Seward's taste was eclectic: He liked watching the weather reports and an occasional game show, as well as Jim and Tammy Faye Bakker, to whom he sent a contribution. At six-thirty the news came on, and at seven-thirty there was *Crossfire.* Sometimes he'd watch it all with the sound off. But all these gizmos gave Seward less pleasure than the picture hanging above them. Indeed, that painting, fashioned by some obscure marine artist in Jacksonville and costing only a few hundred dollars, excited him far more than all the Giorgiones and Botticellis Basia had bought with his money for millions more. It was a rendition of Harbor Branch's new ship. Originally, it was to have been christened the *"R/V* (Research Vessel) *Johnson,"* but that wouldn't work; it looked too much like "R.W. Johnson," thereby thrusting Seward into the General's shadow yet again. Hence the name *"R/V Seward Johnson,"* which could be seen on the ship's bow in the drawing. Cruising alongside it, with its distinctive red sails, was the *Ocean Pearl.*

Seward's compulsiveness grew along with his illness, forcing his nurses to learn an elaborate code of conduct. He hated having his television viewing interrupted; medications were to be administered only during commercials. He liked his coffee served at a certain temperature and took it with honey, not sugar. He liked his spoon placed in a certain way on his saucer. Anyone putting ointment or powder on his feet always had to start with the big toe. The slightest sounds or motions disturbed him; he would expel any nurse who turned pages too loudly. He cherished his independence, fumbling around for things, knocking them off the table sometimes, before he would let anyone else help him. He was territorial. "Get away!" or "Get out of here!" or "Don't touch that!" he snapped at trespassers. He hated being helped, as a new nurse named Bonnie Weisser learned when she innocently lifted a glass of orange juice to his mouth. "Basia! She's trying to choke me!" he screamed.

To keep the unpleasantness to a minimum, Weisser, who came to head the entire nursing operation, began compiling a list of Seward's "likes & dislikes." He liked his Kleenexes popped up in the box. He liked to let his Metamucil sit for five or ten minutes before taking it. He called urinals "bidets." He liked his "Liqui-Doss" served in a short glass of plaid design, mixed with three parts fresh orange juice, and with a large saucer underneath it. He liked to place his head on the corner of the pillow. Wherever possible, only Johnson & Johnson products would do; Johnson's baby powder (unmedicated) was to go on the seat of his commode, for instance, while only Johnson's baby shampoo, dissolved in warm water, could be used to clean his rectum. Most of all, he liked to know what was happening. "Always try to explain to Mr. Johnson what or how you would like to do something and *ask* his permission," she wrote on the nurses' manual. "He cooperates much better when he understands (Don't we all!!!)."

Notwithstanding Weisser's helpful hints, the turnover of nurses was considerable. The most notable victim was one Sheril Bennett. She had originally turned down the Johnson job after hearing that Basia had thrown a lamp at one of her predecessors; on her sixth day of duty, she was in Seward's bedroom when Basia barged in, got a whiff of Bennett's perfume, and immediately opened the sliding door. "It stinks in here! You stink! You stink! I can't stand the smell!" she shrieked. "You smell like a whore!" When she ordered Bennett to take a shower, the nurse quit. "Mrs. Johnson could make you want to commit murder," Bennett later said.

In late February Basia, who complained that while in Fort Pierce she felt "like a duck in a cage," headed north for a few days, leaving Seward in Junior's hands. When Seward weakened once more, Junior panicked, and arranged to take him to Boca Raton by helicopter. By the time they were airborne, Seward was receiving a transfusion and bouncing back; it was Junior, who was petrified of flying, who needed the comforting. Junior ended up spending the night at his father's bedside in the hospital; as Seward lay tethered to an intravenous machine, father and son talked and talked and talked some more, as they had not talked for years—about Diana's trust, about the new ship, about foundation affairs, the stock market, trips they'd taken together long ago.

Anyone entering the hospital room that night would have thought these two Seward Johnsons an unlikely pair, sharing nothing but a name. They did not look like one another. Even in his twilight years Seward the elder was trim, dapper, and handsome, while the younger Seward was porcine and jowly. (So concerned had Seward grown about Junior's girth that a few months earlier he'd sent him a health-food cookbook called *Jack Sprat's Legacy* and a scrapbook of low-fat recipes.) Seward, Sr., was a man of few words; Seward, Jr., babbled. Seward,

Sr., had a scientific, technical bent, with little appreciation for the arts; Seward, Jr., had little aptitude for science and spent his time making his sculptures. Senior loved planes; Junior had a pathological fear of flying. Senior loved boats; Junior got seasick. Senior loathed tobacco; Junior chained-smoked Pall Malls. Senior was an epicure and an oeneophile; Junior ordered wine bottles by the number. Over the years their relationship had evolved from affection to antipathy to estrangement to resentment to indifference to occasional concern to an awkward kind of love. For the past eight years they'd lived roughly two miles from one another, and in all that time Seward had been to Junior's home twice. And yet, in the time-honored manner of a spurned son, Junior persevered, ever importuning, experimenting, pushing for acknowledgment and approval. He wrote many letters. (He usually addressed the old man as "Dad" though he'd experimented with "Seward" for a time.) In them he'd update his father on things Seward had never asked about, or pass along friendly, unsolicited bits of advice that invariably went ignored. "I would like to remind you that you always wanted a bathroom with a fireplace. I might suggest a polar bear rug for the finishing touch," he wrote when Seward and Basia were planning their house in Ansedonia. "I have sort of missed you, and have a longing to re-know you—because I am always delighted to be surprised by finding new facets in someone I have known and loved," he wrote in 1970.

The letters usually went unanswered—or, worse, something oddly impersonal would arrive in return, like Seward, Sr.'s letter to Seward, Jr., of July 25, 1979:

Dear Seward,

All of my life I have deplored the fact that the United States economy requires the stimulant that comes with a war to prevent the development of economic recession, and the lowering of the buying power of the dollar called inflation. It is obvious that the buying power of the dollar is increased when supply is greater than demand. Demand is fed by increasing wealth. Basically, wealth is produced by production of natural resources, especially by Agriculture, Fishing, Transportation, Water Power, Lumbering, Ranching, Teaching, Learning, Research, and Wisdom. Incentive! God gave us incentive as part of the capitalistic system. One grain of wheat, when planted, produces 30 grains or more. The animals in our fields reproduce abundantly. These are the laws of nature. Hopefully, our government will discontinue the impediments they have imposed on wise capitalists.

Love,
Seward

c.c. Basia.

When it came to earning recognition, Junior was more successful as a sculptor than as a son. Around this time Junior began receiving national publicity, as well as flak, for his "hyper-real" creations—essentially manikins cast in bronze and affecting everyday, often whimsical poses. The decision in May 1982 to place four of his figures outside Trenton's new courthouse prompted complaints from serious students of art, who considered them cheap, ugly kitsch. "Many in the art community may not see Seward Johnson as an artist, but what's their measure?" asked one of those who commissioned Junior for the job. "The workmen who see the first piece, already installed, enjoy it there every day. If human beings and taxpayers are going to enjoy it, that's my measure of art." Another of Junior's pieces, showing three boys drooling over a *Playboy* centerfold, had to be removed from a New Haven park after offending Catholics and feminists alike. Later, a statue depicting a black youth carrying a large radio (what Junior called a "Third World briefcase") angered the New Haven chapter of the NAACP. The attendant publicity earned Junior a profile in *People* magazine. Seward hadn't bothered going to Junior's first opening; on the other hand, Junior sensed his father liked his gargantuan statue of King Lear, which was displayed for a time at Jasna Polana.

Basia returned to Fort Pierce in time for her forty-sixth birthday on February 25, which Seward, the Zagats, Gregory Piasecki, and Jan Waliguru helped her celebrate. It was really a double celebration: Tim Zagat had just lost thirty pounds on one of his periodic crash diets, a fact that so impressed Junior that he asked Nina to send him some information on it. The evening's entertainment was a video of *La Cage aux Folles*, which Tim had selected partly because the Richardses were planning to produce a musical based on it. But the adventures of a gay French couple didn't appeal much to Seward. "This isn't very funny at all!" he complained. "If you can't get me a good western, I'm going!"

XIII

Nina had not come to Florida simply to watch films. Just before heading South himself, Seward had told her he wanted to leave his Cape Cod property to Junior rather than to Jimmy, to give Basia $1 million in mad money, and make some other technical changes in his will. On February 18 she and Gunther flew down to Fort Pierce with a codicil effecting what Seward had requested. (During the same visit, Seward showed Nina a letter he'd recently sent to James Burke, chairman of J&J, congratulating him on his handling of the Tylenol tamperings.) Still, Seward was not finished. A week later, when Nina arrived for Basia's birthday, he gave her further instructions. Prompted, perhaps, by their cozy night together at the hospital in Boca Raton, he now wanted to leave Junior $1 million outright in addition to the fees he stood to collect as executor and trustee. Three years earlier, Seward had arranged for Junior to succeed him as the power at Harbor Branch; now, he wanted Nina to draft a letter to Junior, urging him to consult Basia on all important foundation matters. He also wanted to even off the amounts going to Basia and her foundation, on the one hand, and Harbor Branch on the other, which Shearman & Sterling proposed to do by setting up a second trust. This new, so-called Q-TIP trust, would produce income for Basia, but upon her death, its principal would go to Harbor Branch rather than to whomever she chose.

By March 10 Nina and Gunther were back in Fort Pierce, with a newly revised will. Perhaps anticipating the holiday a week away, Gunther wore Kelly-green pants, which prompted such ridicule that he'd gone upstairs and changed. After lunch—a torturous affair for Gunther, a dog lover whose stomach nonetheless knotted up from watching the Johnsons' new dachshunds eat off Basia's plate—Nina went over the latest changes with Seward. Then he signed his latest will. Yet there were still more things on his mind, like Jasna Polana's chapel. Concerned that Basia might not have enough cash to complete it, he directed Nina to draft a letter to her trustees, asking them to be generous with additional funds. Then, with no apparent prompting, he raised a more sensitive subject. Would it be possible, he asked Nina, for any of his children to contest his will?

It was hardly an outlandish thought. Many of the pieces for a will contest were already in place: a fabulous fortune, a much-disliked step-spouse destined to inherit virtually everything, a group of love-starved and financially strapped children who craved more but could easily wage war with what they already had. But what prompted Seward to raise this issue now? Perhaps it was his way of acknowledging that no longer could he play the king in his countinghouse. He knew he would die soon; whatever he wrote now could be for keeps.

Nina proceeded to recite for Seward something that sounded like *The Golden Book of Will Contests*. A will, she explained, could be challenged on several grounds. One was that it had been not been properly executed. Clearly, such a claim could never prevail; she and Jay Gunther had been through the drill innumerable times. Another was lack of competence; the children could say Seward had not known what he was doing when he'd signed the will. But the mere fact they were conversing intelligently now took care of that, Nina reassured him; one had almost to be deranged to be considered incompetent. Finally, the children could claim Basia had coerced Seward into doing what he did. But claims of "undue influence," like claims of incompetence, rarely held up in court, particularly against a wife. In short, the children wouldn't have a leg to stand on. That taken care of, Nina presented to Seward the letter he'd asked her to write to Junior, urging him to consult Basia on foundation matters and "consider her judgments as you would my own." Seward liked Nina's language, but was unsure how to sign it. "Love, Dad," she suggested. Nina's business, at least in Fort Pierce, was completed, and she walked to her car with Basia. "I think this will is much better for me," Basia said. Nina asked what she meant. "I always knew that Seward would want me to support Harbor Branch, and now I know what amount of support he would want," she said.

Seward Johnson had already exceeded his biblically allotted life by six years when Nina began working for him. She had spent most of her professional time since then thinking of little but his affairs. And yet, up to this time she had never taken the threat of a will contest seriously, in part because Seward himself hadn't. Once she'd gotten back to New York, Nina hastily huddled with her Shearman & Sterling colleagues to devise additional ways to safeguard what was by any standard the most important will in the firm's vault. One suggested the inclusion of an "*in terrorem*" clause. Under it, Seward would leave each child a pittance—say, a mere million or two—then threaten to take away even that if they contested things. Nina and Ford rejected that idea because Seward already had; he refused to give them anything, even to buy peace posthumously. Sensing that what they craved still more than money was paternal approval, Nina suggested killing the children with kindness. Up to now, the wills said little about them except, in so many words, that they were being left out of it. Henceforth, they would contain the following words of synthetic solace: "It was my wish to provide my children with financial independence at an early age, and, accordingly, I created a substantial trust for each of them during my lifetime. It has been a source of pleasure to me to see my children pursue their interests independent of me and in a way that would not have been possible if I had not provided for them in this way." It was a polite, legalistic way of saying "You've already gotten yours. Get lost."

The statement was out of character for Seward, an undemonstrative, unreflective, unsentimental, and uncommunicative man. In fact, it represented an amalgam of scraps Nina had picked up over the years, as polished by Gunther and reviewed by Ford. Nina was torn: She wanted whatever words she attributed to Seward to sound real, but she also wanted them to be true. So she combed her memory. She'd once heard Seward praise Diana's horse-breeding business. He'd said nice things about Junior's sculptures. He'd said Mary Lea could never have produced her plays without his money. Those were the easy ones; with Elaine, Jennifer, and Jimmy, Nina really had to stretch. But she knew Seward shared Elaine's concern for physical fitness and Jimmy's interest in farming. And just maybe he had mentioned Jennifer's photography to her once.

Nina worked on the changes, coming up with a product that was to win praise in the industry. SMART WILL DRAFTING WILL CHILL WILL CONTEST, a trade publication declared in what was to become the probate press's version of DEWEY BEATS TRUMAN. Meanwhile, Seward had more visitors in Florida. On March 11 Junior came with his family. The next day Seward discussed funding the new R/V *Seward Johnson* with Junior and David Clare, president of J&J and a trustee of Seward's charitable trusts. "What you have just seen is my life's work," Seward told Clare after he'd been given a tour of the Harbor Branch facility. At times Seward felt chipper. More often, he was plagued by aches and pains, for which he took a regimen of Extra Strength Tylenol, Tagamet, and Metamucil. But late on the night of March 17 he declined sharply. When the nurse, a devout Catholic named Judy Smith, arrived for work, even her roseate faith couldn't blind her to the change. "Much weaker tonight," she wrote.

Things were even worse the next morning. Seward told Basia he felt drained and begged her to do something. When Peach arrived around nine, Seward mistook him for Junior. Basia called Schilling in Boca Raton, then went into Seward's bedroom. When she emerged moments later, she told Peach to get a priest; she wanted Seward to be given last rites. "I know he is dying!" she exclaimed. "He is completely—he doesn't know what is going on. He can't speak. He doesn't know anything. He is not going to last until dinner. He is dying! He is dying! He is dying! He is dying! He is dying! He is dying! He is dying! He is dying! He is dying! He is dying!" Basia begged Junior and Joyce to cancel the Caribbean cruise they were to begin the next day, which would have left three of the Johnsons plying the seas while their father faded. "Don't go on it!" she'd pleaded. "You have to stay here! Seward is dying!"

Seward liked reading the Bible, but in all his years with the old man, Peach had never heard him talk about religion. Nor did Peach have much truck with priests personally. But accustomed to carrying out odd orders uncomplainingly, he started searching for one. Sensing instinctively that a Fort Pierce priest wouldn't be fancy enough for Basia, he looked under "churches" in the Vero Beach Yellow Pages and, as he later put it, "got some turkey on the phone." In the meantime, Schilling arrived, and diagnosed another electrolyte imbalance. An IV was set up, Seward bounced back quickly, and the priest was called off. Schilling and Basia agreed, however, that when the old man's time came, no heroic measures would be taken. Still, the scare convinced Basia to keep a doctor around at all times, and Peach arranged to ferry them in by helicopter. The pilots were instructed to come at odd hours and land as far from the house as possible, so that Seward wouldn't know anything was afoot; if he asked, he was to be told the men in white coats he saw traipsing around were technicians. When they weren't attending the patient, the doctors would be confined to the guest cottage, out of Seward's sight.

All this secrecy galled one of the new doctors, a transplanted Philadelphian named Jonathan Wideroff. Wideroff, in his early thirties, took the job because Schilling had assured him it would be interesting and easy, and besides, business was slow. But because of all the subterfuge, he couldn't lie on the grass, read a book, get a tan. Instead, he had to rot away inside, watching game shows, rereading old *National*

Geographics. To make matters worse, Basia forced him to carry a bulky portable telephone with him at all times, even though he never strayed more than two hundred feet from the house. Once, he had just stepped into the shower when she called, and she still blew up at him for taking so long to respond. She was, he concluded, a pain. Word was she had once been pretty, but to his way of thinking, she had turned into a hag. The whole setup was unreal to Wideroff: Had Seward Johnson been your garden-variety Florida retiree—as the doctor put it, "your average retired elevator operator from the Bronx"—he would have made do with a visiting nurse. Instead, he had his own personal M.A.S.H. unit.

Still, the job had its good points. One was the money, which Wideroff collected in cash, thousands of dollars in all. He liked Seward, who had what he called "a sharp mind in a dying body." And there were other interesting characters around: "Chopper Don" Chasen, the mad helicopter pilot who pointed out alligators and drug dealers and wild boars along the way up; and Ray Gore, the embittered skipper of the *Ocean Pearl.* Over leisurely dinners in the ship's hold, the two men exchanged gripes; Wideroff complained of "baby-sitting a dead man," while Gore bitched about Basia. He acted, Wideroff thought, like a jilted lover: He'd lived a good life with Seward all these years, then Basia had come along and spoiled everything. Gore struck Wideroff as a seething, raging, repressed man, the type to climb atop a Harbor Branch building one day and start spraying passersby with an AK-47. Junior Johnson struck Wideroff as a pompous goon—gross, affected, patronizing, off somewhere in the ozone. The old man seemed to ignore his son, and no wonder. Someday, Wideroff thought, he'd have to get his wife, who was also a doctor, to come up and survey the whole unbelievable scene.

Nina returned on March 22 with the revised will. To witness it, she brought not only Gunther but James Hoch, another associate in Shearman & Sterling's individual-clients group. It was one of Nina's new precautions; under the law, since she was no longer a witness the children could not question her now unless they formally attacked the will. Ideally, one wouldn't want two associates, one of them quite junior, witnessing a will of such magnitude and portent. But Ford hadn't offered to go himself, and his second-in-command, Henry Ziegler, had vetoed Nina's request to bring along a more senior associate. Seward approved of Nina's new, more disinherited-friendly language, and signed the will, with a pen chosen from the two boxes of his favorite Uni-

Balls Nina brought him. It was a most peculiar gift, for it was clear from his shaky signature that Seward wasn't doing a lot of writing these days. "You gentlemen slipped in under the line on this one," he told the attesting lawyers afterward.

No one mentioned anything to Nina about Seward's ordeal a few days earlier. But now that she'd disposed of Seward's property, the time had come for her to think about disposing of Seward, too. Like much of his posthumous planning, Seward had had several changes of heart on this subject over the years. He had made it clear long ago that he didn't want to be buried in the family crypt in New Brunswick, where even in death he would be in the General's shadow. For a time he talked about donating his body to the Hunterdon Medical Center; that way, science could benefit from the Johnson family immediately, rather than have to wait the millennium or two it could take until someone stumbled upon Princey. He had provided for cremation until Basia objected. He'd even instructed Captain Gore once to strap him to the galley of the *Ocean Pearl* and bury him at sea with his beloved boat. Then the Jasna Polana chapel came along and settled everything. But while that was to be Seward's ultimate resting place, it could not be his first one, and not just because it remained incomplete. To shore up his fragile legal ties to Florida, it made sense to let him bask in the Sunshine State, at least for a while.

On the morning of March 23 Nina and Peach met with Bill Nixon, czar of the Hillcrest Memorial Gardens. The facility, which billed itself as "a place of beauty, with broad unbroken vistas enhanced by well-planned landscaping," was just a stone's throw up Old Dixie Highway from Harbor Branch. Nina and Peach spurned the Gardens of Faith, Prayer, Memories, Devotion, and the Madonna, and bought Seward a niche in row six of the above-ground mausoleum, "Florida's most beautiful," built of "ageless European marble" of the sort that might ease the transition from Jasna Polana. Seward's top-row perch was eighteen feet high and faced east, guaranteeing that he could still oversee his beloved foundation. Nina didn't say for whom she was buying the niche, but specified that it was to remain unmarked, thereby assuring Seward the same privacy in death he'd always sought in life. (When Nixon found out the new resident's identity, it was a bit of a thrill: Vaughn Monroe was buried in nearby Stuart, and Perry Como had bought a plot in Jupiter, but Seward would be Hillcrest's first celebrity tenant.) The vault contained space for Basia, too; Nina thought it unseemly to buy a slot for just one of them, and besides, it wasn't all that much extra. History does not record whether she opted for Hillside's "Side by Side" plan or "True Companion," in which the coffins are placed head to toe.

Nina invited Junior to come over and check things out, but no more anxious to face such things than his father was, he declined. She also showed him the canned obituary of Seward that Larry Foster, Johnson & Johnson's public-relations chief, had prepared. Junior suggested it be accompanied by a photograph of Seward in a white sailor's hat, looking very much like the old man and the sea, which he kept in his living room in Princeton. (Junior thought his sister Jennifer had taken it; it turned out that for all the pictures she had taken, she had never photographed her father.) Peach and Nina also asked Junior if, when the time came, he would speak at Seward's funeral. Junior agreed to—provided, he said, he wasn't too upset. Nina and Junior then went back to dine with the man whose death they had spent so much of their morning anticipating. Nina always clammed up awkwardly whenever anyone asked her about anything off-limits; fortunately for her, Seward did not inquire into what she'd been up to. On the menu was Basia's delicious spaghetti, Junior's favorite; but his wife, Joyce, a woman who agonized over many things, seemed paralyzed by all the options on the platter. "Perhaps you can serve someone next who doesn't have so much trouble deciding which meatballs they want," Seward grumbled. There was still some life in the old man.

With Seward's cancerous bones unable to produce enough blood, transfusions became increasingly important. Between them he would gradually wilt, becoming lethargic and momentarily confused. But with a fresh supply of blood, it was like the dying swan played in reverse. When a nurse named Mary Banks assayed Seward on March 30, two and a half weeks after his last fix, he was frail and shaky. But after a transfusion in Boca Raton the next day, she wrote that he was "alert and awake, sitting up watching TV, had a sparkle in his eye."

En route to the hospital that day, as Seward and Basia sat in the back of the van, Junior told Peach to kill some time once they'd checked in; he wanted to talk to his father alone. What was gnawing at him was his future at Harbor Branch. Junior had little aptitude for oceanography; asked once how knowledgeable the heir apparent was about boats, a diplomatic Harbor Branch official replied, "Let me say that he is very interested in becoming more knowledgeable all the time." But with his erratic past, the prospect of heading an institution his father founded and cherished meant a lot to Junior. That was why he had been laboring to understand the place and act "presidential." He'd recently concluded, for instance, that Harbor Branch wasn't serving mankind sufficiently—that it was spending too much time "counting the spots on fishes and seeing which way they traveled" rather than on more practical things—and decreed that all scientists must prove themselves useful by 1985 or be out. A Harbor Branch geologist came up with one scheme Junior liked: cultivating mollusks capable of developing stainless-steel teeth biologically. Here, Junior thought, was something that could both benefit mankind and make money. He excitedly told his father of the magical metallic mollusks, only to meet a deflating response. His father looked at him as if he were crazy, then smiled and shook his head. "Well, I don't know," he said. "It seems incredible to me."

Junior's succession at Harbor Branch seemed as ironclad as those molluskular teeth. Seward had designated him heir in 1980, and, at Junior's insistence, made the appointment irrevocable the next year. Still, Junior worried. His father, as he later expressed it, "was getting on in years, might become senile—the word he used was 'ga-ga.' " Moreover, Junior didn't trust Nina, who'd drafted the succession documents. Her loyalties, he feared, really lay with Basia, and maybe she'd conveniently left in some loophole to trip up the transition. Just to be sure, Junior sent the papers to his lawyer in Princeton. Sometimes lawyers spot nonexistent problems just to say they solved them. Under Harbor Branch's bylaws, the lawyer said, Seward's appointments could not be irrevocable. If Junior wanted to sleep more easily, he could either ask his father to call a meeting to change those bylaws (an unrealistic option given Seward's condition) or ask him to step down immediately.

It was bad enough for a son to ask his dying father to forsake the very post that was helping to keep him alive. But Junior compounded his lawyer's bad judgment with his own spectacularly bad timing; he raised the subject as the old man lay supine at the Boca Raton Hospital, a needle carrying fresh nutrients into his depleted body. Junior was not just twisting Seward's arm, but doing so while an intravenous line was stuck in it. Predictably enough, Seward balked. "I don't know whether he felt resigning was giving up life, or that it really was too much for him to consider it at that moment," Junior later recalled. "I think he was also saying to me: 'This is a hell of a time to be bringing this up.' " Their encounter ended acrimoniously.

Dejected by his failure, worried about his future, angered by his own ineptitude and his father's inflexibility, Junior stumbled out of the room for some coffee and a smoke. Suddenly, his most important accomplishments of the past few years—reestablishing ties with his father, securing a place at Harbor Branch—seemed jeopardized. He ran into Peach in the hallway. "He wouldn't sign it!" Junior told Peach. "The old son of a bitch wouldn't sign it!" When Peach entered the hospital room, he found Seward seething. "Where's Basia?" the old man snapped. Peach told him a doctor was examining her. "Well, get her!" Seward ordered. He wanted to go home.

Junior and Basia did not agree on all Harbor Branch matters. The point of contention was invariably what she saw as Communist infiltration of the foundation, an odd thought until one realized Basia's passions on the subject; here was someone, after all, who once thought that a particularly rude customs officer had to be a closet Bolshevist. Basia had vehemently objected to a proposed Harbor Branch mission to Cuba, an idea eventually scuttled anyway for fear it would lead indignant Cuban exiles to mount a Bay of Pigs–type assault on the foundation's facility. More recently, she'd very nearly gone berserk over a proposed expedition to the Soviet Union. Junior confessed to naïveté. "Frankly, I am shocked at my own lack of awareness of how each particular instance of technology transfer is adding up to such a massive robbery," he wrote to her. Now, Basia berated Junior for trying to push Seward aside at so inopportune a time, particularly since his succession was never in doubt. Even so, she agreed to plead Junior's case with Seward. The next day she did, and Seward agreed to step down. Junior promptly took out some paper marked "Memorandum from J. Seward Johnson" and wrote out two letters of resignation, one for Harbor Branch and one for the Atlantic Foundation, the entity Seward had created to fund it. The language was straightforward enough. But the handwriting was barely legible, the punctuation worse, and the spelling downright embarrassing: e.g. "Harbour" for "Harbor." Junior presented the papers to Seward, who wrote "John Seward Johnson" on each. Then Junior signed them, too, in his own electrocardiogramlike script. Basia acted as attesting witness. Seward, she noticed, seemed very angry. The torch had been passed—reluctantly, resentfully.

When Junior returned to Princeton, he placed the letters in a vault. As for Seward, he spoke of the episode only to Basia. As she recounted their conversation, he laced into Junior, calling him egotistical, untrustworthy, and ghoulish. Junior, he told Basia, couldn't wait for him to die. And he was going to destroy Harbor Branch; he should have listened to Ed Link, who warned him about his son's incompetence. No longer, he said, did he want the $75 million in the newly established trust to go automatically to the foundation when Basia died; she should have the option of giving it to whomever she wished. Basia later insisted she advised her husband to leave well enough alone, but that Seward was adamant; he wanted to see Nina. As luck would have it, the Zagats had just left for a few days at the Johnsons' house on Children's Bay Cay, a place notoriously inaccessible by phone. Frustrated by his inability to reach her, Seward asked Peach to try. His luck was no better. But on April 3 Nina checked in with Peach, who told her of Seward's eagerness to talk with her upon her return. Once back in New York Nina spoke to Basia about the change Seward wanted. Rather than calling Seward to discuss the matter with him over the phone, she began preparing a draft and planning a return trip to Florida; Seward, she knew, always preferred talking things over in person.

XIV

By early April Seward, this rechargeable toy of a man, was once more running down. On the fourth, when Jimmy and Gretchen stopped by, he was noticeably weaker and losing his balance— though, judging from the "Dear Seward and Basha" note Gretchen sent afterward, he'd been the liveliest wire in the bunch ("Seward, your off- hand 'See you around some day' departure was a cute and endearing reminder that we were being a bit dull," she wrote.) The nurse on duty that evening, Mary Banks, noted "slight confusion" around midnight. By the morning of the fifth Seward was weaker still, and complained of a drowning sensation. When Schilling arrived that afternoon, he diagnosed another electrolyte imbalance, and altered Seward's fluid intake and medication accordingly. This time Seward didn't bounce back so quickly. Seward had always made light of his physical difficulties. Franklin Roosevelt, he liked to note, had run the country from a wheelchair; what was important was his mind. But increasingly, there were signs that it, too, was slipping. Over the next two days several nurses noted his confusion. Seward asked one of them for a drink, only to shoo her away when she brought it. Later he declared, "Now I can see better," when she turned out his bedroom light.

On the morning of April 7 the pendulum continued to swing between rationality and irrationality. Seward was looking for things that weren't there, picking nonexistent items out of the air. "Living in the past for short periods," a nurse named Lorene Chavis wrote. But other times, most times, he was sharp. Schilling's daughter Lisa, a physician's as- sistant, detected no problems, though she recorded what the night nurse had told her: "Some confusion noted—illusions of war 'c' Russia etc.— yet recog. me, wife, & Mr. Peach." He grew stronger throughout her shift and the ones that followed. The following morning, he once again appeared momentarily confused—"I don't think I'm getting enough radiation for my blood," he said. "Do you think the Tylenol Company could do a better job for me?"—but within minutes had rebounded.

Nearly three months had now passed since Basia and Seward had arrived in Florida. For most of that time, the Marty Richardses and the Keith Wolds frolicked aboard on the *QE2*. For them as for Seward, it had not all been smooth sailing. In China the hotels were filthy and, they were convinced, had fed them dog, cat, and rat. Neither Mary Lea nor Elaine had ever told Seward they were going on the cruise, nor had they called to say good-bye. But the travelers, particularly Keith Wold, checked in regularly on him from aboard ship. Wold's sudden interest was surprising; he had neither seen nor spoken to Seward since the Knights of Malta ceremony three years earlier, nor had he done anything to smooth Seward's way at the Boca Raton Hospital, where he had once been a director. Nor, though he knew Schilling socially, had Wold ever asked him about his father-in-law, or tried to dissuade Basia from hiring a doctor whom he considered "highly overrated." But something in the salt air seemed to rekindle Wold's interest in the old man. At first Wold's solicitude impressed Schilling. But as the calls kept coming and coming, and as he heard Wold refer to Seward as "a senile old man" or make comments like "He's sure hanging on!" Schilling sensed something else at work: As far as Wold was concerned, Seward wasn't dying fast enough.

In early April, as the vessel steamed toward Acapulco, Junior told the voyagers that Seward's condition had worsened. "If you want to see your father alive, you better come quickly," he told them. According to Wold, Schilling agreed. "The gist was that we should come home because he felt that he would not live a long time, and that if we delayed any longer he would not recognize anybody," Wold later said. (Schilling later denied ever saying or thinking such things.) Thus, in the wee hours of April 9 (the timing was auspicious for the numerologist Marty, for nine and ten were his lucky numbers), as the mighty ocean liner wended its way through the Panama Canal, the two couples descended into a smaller boat alongside. It was a dramatic moment; many passengers photographed the portly Mary Lea as she climbed overboard. The couples left most of their luggage aboard for flunkies to pick up later in St. Thomas.

The Wolds' plane was on hand to fetch the weary travelers, who arrived in Fort Pierce early that afternoon. Though Seward was sleeping when they walked in, Mary Lea, Elaine, and Marty poked their heads into his bedroom; only Keith Wold was insufficiently curious, waiting until Basia's brother Gregory—"the attendant," Wold called him— wheeled him out. Basia banned any and all talk about what had prompted their hasty exit from the *QE2*. Instead, the conversation revolved around the new ship.

Descriptions of Seward's condition that afternoon varied. Basia and John Peach remembered a loquacious Seward, talking enthusiastically about the new ship and his navy days. Basia recalled the session lasting a couple of hours, and the nurse's notes corroborate her account. Mary Lea, Marty, and Elaine depicted a frailer man, though one able to recognize them and converse intelligently for twenty minutes or so before going back to bed. Once more, Keith Wold is the odd man out. He insisted that Seward hadn't recognized him, fell asleep in midconversation, and "didn't seem to be with it mentally." "He was in the later stages of senility," he later testified. "He was not clear, he was clouded, he had all of the classic signs of senility." Then, as on several subsequent occasions, Wold exhibited all the classic signs of something else: dishonesty.

Peach stayed with the group only briefly, then walked out by the pool to await Schilling's helicopter. After a few minutes Marty Richards walked up and introduced himself. Peach had assumed the diminutive, deferential Richards was the Wolds' chauffeur, hanging around for the return trip or tip; he was startled to learn that this strange man was actually Mary Lea's husband. Richards was the type who could not keep a secret; he'd already confided to one friend that the Johnsons were out to get the goods on Basia—thereby weakening her legal position following Seward's death—by somehow documenting her infidelity. Now, Richards began speaking to Peach, in a chatty, catty, cryptic, and conspiratorial tone. "I understand that if things don't go right, there are going to be problems," he said. "Of course, my wife probably won't be involved in that." Peach could sense Richards was dying to elaborate, and that the surest way to get him to was to say nothing. "Of course, I'm talking about the will!" Richards finally blurted out. Suddenly, it dawned on Peach: So this was what the Richardses and Wolds had talked about all that time at sea.

The Wolds left Fort Pierce quickly, their interest in the dying Seward having dropped precipitously once they had come ashore. This did not surprise Schilling; in his view, of all Seward's children only Junior truly cared about the old man. As for the others, he'd seen their sort before—absentee offspring who came crawling out of the ground only as their wealthy parents were about to go into it. If Seward Johnson had depended on them, Schilling was convinced, he'd have died long ago. Wideroff felt the same way, particularly about Wold, who walked around the place with the most extraordinarily hard, cold stare and never, ever, inquired about Seward's health. This was a death vigil, and Wold was treating it like a business deal, Elaine and Mary Lea like a party, and

Junior . . . well, to Wideroff he simply seemed spaced out. Among the entire group, he thought, only Basia acted as if she didn't want Seward to expire immediately. Between post times at Hialeah Diana squeezed in a brief visit—and another conversation about her trust troubles—with Seward. As for Elaine Wold, Basia thought her more interested in Allush, the alligator who lived in the nearby lagoon, than in her own father.

Even in their short stay, the Richardses saw some deterioration in Seward's condition; Marty claimed that at one point his father-in-law had begun to hallucinate about Nazi submarines. But the nurses saw things differently. "No signs of confusion while awake," one wrote on April 8. "I feel much better; I feel like something more than oatmeal today," another heard him say. "Family here to visit (two daughters and their husbands). Mr. Johnson is alert; color good; seems stronger today. Attentive to family conversation," Bonnie Weisser wrote on the afternoon of the ninth. True, there were jarring interludes, like the time Seward tried exposing his aching hip to the high-pressure system he'd just heard the television weatherman talking about. But by and large Seward seemed to know what he wanted. And didn't want, as Lisa Schilling learned when she told him someone in the Richards-Wold party wished to come into his bedroom and say hello. "Tell them I'm asleep," he mumbled. Indeed, Junior respected his father's remaining capabilities enough to ask Peach not to show him Harbor Branch's most recent portfolio summary, which detailed hefty losses.

Back in New York, Nina worked on the next will. At Ziegler's suggestion, the revised version gave Basia the option of bequeathing the money in the new Q-TIP trust not only to charities of her choice, as Seward had wanted, but to Seward's descendants as well; that way they'd have a $75 million inducement to behave themselves. At Ford's suggestion, Nina and Gunther drafted two additional documents: an affidavit, for Schilling to sign, attesting to the soundness of Seward's mind; and a declaration from Seward that his 1971 prenuptial agreement with Basia, which had long since been nullified by subsequent wills, had officially been revoked. On the evening of April 13 Nina, Gunther, and Hoch flew to Florida. They retired early, the better to be rested for the events the next day. So did Seward; lights were out by eight o'clock, and by eight-thirty he was sound asleep. He slept well that night, at least for someone who had to get up and urinate seven times. As she completed her shift, the night nurse, Judy Smith, made some notes about Seward. "He responds to TLC," she wrote. "He has been pleasant and cooperative. He is a very intelligent man." After some digressions she continued, "He is usually alert in mind and his body is very weak. He has periods of S[hortness] o[f] B[reath] and occasional confusion recently. His lytes were way off but now pretty well controlled so that he usually was alert. Dr. Schilling said he could live a day, six weeks, or a year."

On Thursday, April 14, 1983, Seward Johnson woke up around seven o'clock. A few minutes later Basia entered his bedroom and, following her daily routine, bade him good morning, kissed him, told him she loved him, heard him say he loved her, and asked whether he wanted his coffee now or later. Peach arrived, and Seward asked him if there was any news about Harbor Branch or the new ship. Told there was not, he dismissed Peach with a curt thank you; he had a busy day ahead, he explained. At 7:40 Wideroff went into Seward's bedroom and began drawing blood. The tests showed a drop in Seward's hemoglobin level; it was time for another transfusion. Having been told nothing about a will signing, Wideroff blithely set one up for the next day. And because she never read the nursing notes—she thought it both intrusive and unnecessary; if Seward had been having problems, surely someone would have told her— Nina knew neither that Seward always ebbed between transfusions or that, as things now stood, he would sign his will at low tide.

At 8:10 Seward dozed off again. He awoke fifteen minutes later. On duty was a nurse named Patricia Reid, a sullen and opinionated woman who had never had things easy and who seemed to resent those who had. She'd taken an instant dislike to Basia and found Seward a bit weird. This morning, her fourth, the old man seemed especially off. "Some what [sic] confused for a few minutes," she wrote. At eight-thirty Basia brought him some honey and water, along with oatmeal and bananas, but ten minutes later, Reid thought Seward was still acting peculiarly. By ten, though, he was looking at his newspaper. Meantime Nina had breakfast with Basia. The talk was of the marmalade Nina and Jay Gunther had made from the oranges outside and whose was better. Nina described her recent Caribbean trip. Basia, with Sotheby's and Christie's catalogs in hand, spoke of some purchases she was considering.

Around eleven Seward had his back and neck rubbed with Johnson's baby oil, then had some broth and thirty minutes of oxygen. An hour later Nina walked into his bedroom, carrying legal papers and a pad, and closed the door behind her. Seward was sitting up in bed, his favorite robe on his lap. They hugged and kissed one another. Seward asked about her time at Children's Bay Cay, and whether Mavis and Bill, the caretakers there, had treated her well. He then asked whether, as Junior had claimed, there was a cloud over his succession at Harbor Branch. She assured him there was not, and Seward seemed upset to have had his suspicions confirmed. After a brief discussion about SeaPharms—Junior's pet project at Harbor Branch, designed to produce drugs from underseas substances, about which Seward was skeptical—the two got down to testamentary business. Nina reviewed the changes she'd made in his will. Only the provision allowing Basia to bequeath the remainder of the Q-TIP trust to his descendants bothered him; he agreed to leave it in, but only as long as Basia knew how he felt. Nina then reviewed the forty-eight-page will with Seward, piece by piece but perfunctorily; the document was basically boilerplate, and for the most part was identical to its predecessors. Seward's responses were equally cursory: a "yes" here, an "all right" there, a simple nod of the head. Now, Harbor Branch would not get anything unless Basia said so. Still, Nina thought Seward might like to write something hortatory, urging Basia to consider Harbor Branch in her own testamentary planning. Seward summarily brushed off the idea. "That will only end up with a lot of lawyers," he said.

He then told Nina to fetch Basia, who was in the living room. They both signed the revocation of the antenuptial agreement, then Nina explained to her the additional power she would enjoy under the new will. Seward reminded Basia she needn't leave his family anything. Nor, he said, was there any reason to state even informally that he wanted his money to end up with Harbor Branch. "I want to leave this up to you," he said. "Seward, it's your will," she replied. "Whatever you want."

It was already past lunchtime, and the formal signing was put off until everyone had eaten. Then, suddenly, Basia had a brainstorm. Since everyone was writing letters to one another these days—Seward was writing Junior; Junior had written Seward—she would send one to Seward, reiterating her commitment to Harbor Branch. In it she would pledge to ignore the very power Seward had just given her, so that the money in the Q-TIP trust would end up with the foundation anyway. The letter, while not binding, would show her husband that while Junior might not take proper care of Harbor Branch, he could always count on her. With her reflexive lawyer's wariness of the written word, Nina didn't like the idea, even though it seemed innocuous enough. She knew that documents, whatever their provenance or original intent, can take on lives of their own. It might be better, she told Basia, just to tell Seward what she was thinking. But Basia thought this insufficiently ardent and demonstrative. Nina asked Gunther to run the idea past Ford, hoping he would veto it. Instead, with characteristic nonchalance, Ford gave his okay. Gunther went to work composing something. Not surprisingly, what he came up with had a distinctly legalistic ring to it; to restore some humanity, Basia wrote out by hand on her personal stock—cream-colored paper from Dempsey & Carroll, the elegant New York stationer, with a cursive "Barbara P. Johnson" in the corner—what was surely the most unromantic love letter ever.

"Dearest Seward," it began. "Under certain circumstances—in Paragraph A(2) of Subdivision I of Article NINTH of Part I of the Will you signed to-day you have given me a limited testamentary power of appointment among your descendants and charitable organizations. To the extent that I do not exercise this power of appointment, the property subject to it at the time of my death will automatically go to Harbor Branch Foundation Inc. I hereby agree not to exercise said limited testamentary power of appointment in my will so that the property subject to it will go to Harbor Branch Foundation Inc. at the time of my death." Translated, it meant that the $75 million would eventually end up with Harbor Branch after all, though by Basia's choice rather than Seward's command.

Seward had his lunch. To drink, he had some Gatorade and, at Basia's insistence, a few sips of wine, served in a huge goblet. By two-fifteen he had dozed off. When Bonnie Weisser relieved Patricia Reid around three, he was watching television. At four, after Basia rubbed Seward's back with Johnson's baby powder, Gregory wheeled him out to the living room. For Nina, it was a shock; never before had she seen the indomitable old man in a wheelchair. Hoch and Gunther came in from the pool area, and Seward shook their hands. The time had come once more to execute a will.

Nina began reviewing the document again. It left Basia almost everything tangible: the artwork, the airplane, the houses, Seward's clothing and personal effects, jewelry, automobiles, boats, silverware, china, livestock, and farm implements. Some $225 million went to the Barbara P. Johnson Trust, from which she could draw the income, plus up to $1 million annually of principal for herself, plus up to $20 million during her lifetime for her relatives (but only, Seward specified, if they no longer lived in a Marxist state). The will authorized Basia's trustees— Basia herself, plus Junior and Nina—to withdraw whatever they deemed appropriate for her welfare. Junior got Seward's house in Chatham plus $1 million; the other children got nothing except the solace of Nina's new, more friendly disinheritance language. Anyone who'd worked for the Johnsons between five and ten years collected five thousand dollars; ten-year veterans got twice that. The rest—approximately $75 million—would be in the separate Q-TIP trust, whose interest went to Basia for life, then, depending on how she felt at the time, either to charity, Harbor Branch, or Seward's kith and kin.

Once again Seward said "yes" or "that's correct" or "good" or simply nodded as Nina reviewed the will. When she finished, she asked Seward whether it reflected his wishes, and he said it did. She then yielded to Gunther, who turned to its last page. The document had the crisp, grainy, quality-bond feel of a newly minted dollar bill. But whoever cranked it out of Shearman & Sterling's word processor had neglected to change the "March" left over from the previous will to "April." "Can we all agree that it is April fourteenth?" Gunther asked. They did. Seward fumbled with the pen Nina had given him, then asked Basia for another, the one with which he sometimes practiced signing his name in the tablet he kept by his bed. Where the blank in "IN WITNESS WHEREOF, I have hereunto set my hand and seal this _____ day of March, 1983" appeared, Seward wrote "14," his 1 wavy and perilously close to the preceding s. Then, with two strokes of his pen, he scratched out "March" and wrote "April" on top of it. Had it appeared elsewhere, it would have been barely legible, the A broken in two and the i endowed with an extra loop; in context, it was the crabbed but comprehensible script of a very old man. Gunther asked Seward to sign the will, and it became clear that all Seward's practicing hadn't helped. He started vigorously, with a robust "JSJ . . ." then trailed off asymptotically over the course of "ohnson."

"Mr. Johnson, do you declare this to be your will?" Gunther asked.

"Yes, this is my will," Seward replied.

"Do you ask the two of us to sign as witnesses?" Gunther continued. "And do you ask us to do an affidavit saying that we have done all these things?"

"Yes," Seward replied, "would you be so kind?"

Gunther and Hoch signed their names and addresses, thereby vouching for the soundness of Seward's mind and the propriety of the procedure. Seward sat back in his wheelchair. "That will solve a lot of problems," he said. It was unclear just what he meant by that, and no one pressed him to explain.

Up to now, there'd been no deviations from the usual script. Then Nina told Seward about Basia's surprise letter. "Basia, you don't have to do that," Seward said to her.

"Seward, I want to," she replied.

The letter, Nina insisted, would not be binding. "That doesn't make any difference," Seward replied. "That is very sweet of her."

Basia then looked at the letter, as yet unsigned. "Can I sign it 'Love, Basia'?" she asked Nina. It was a funny thing about the Johnsons: They were forever sending letters to one another, but never knew how to end them. "Sure," replied Nina, the usual arbiter of such things, as the others laughed. Basia handed the letter to her husband, and asked him to sign it, too. It was, she thought, the only way she'd ever get him to read it. Then, betraying the infatuation with formality that people as yet unbloodied by lawsuits often retain, she asked Nina and Gunther to "witness" the document. The additional signatures made the document look as legalistic as it sounded.

There was tea and cheesecake for all. There being no further business for them to transact, Gunther and Hoch left to buy some oranges and grapefruit to take back to New York. Soon the sound of Schilling's helicopter could be heard. The doctor greeted Seward by the poolside, then examined him in the bedroom. He asked the old man the usual questions: how he felt, how his night had been, how his bowels were doing. It was a routine examination, over in twenty or twenty-five minutes. "Past two days—weaker," the doctor wrote in his log book. "Today more active and alert." When Schilling completed his examination, Nina approached him in the hallway and handed him the form she'd prepared, in which he'd certify that Seward was "of sound mind and memory and aware of his acts." Schilling, who had never been asked to do anything like that before, perused it quickly, remarked that Seward's mental condition was "first-rate," and signed it. It required no deliberation; sure, there were fancier ways to test a person's mental capacity—having him count backward or to name the president of the United States—but those were used only when one had doubts, and he had none.

The witnesses returned with their bags of fruit, then bade Seward good-bye. Gunther subsequently placed the will in the Shearman & Sterling vault, along with Basia's "letter," and prepared an affidavit recounting the events in Fort Pierce. "During our discussion with Mr. Johnson it was clear to both Mr. Hoch and myself that he was in relatively good physical condition and totally alert and aware of what he was doing," Gunther wrote. After the guests had left, Seward told Bonnie Weisser he felt "much stronger." That sounded right to her. "No confusion noted this shift," she wrote. Then she went home for the night.

XV

Seward continued to ebb. He fell asleep reading newspapers, watching television, taking baths, conversing. At times he was too tired even to lift pills to his mouth. His blood pressure began to fall, and his breathing grew more labored. His already constricted universe shrank still more as he went from walking unassisted to using a cane to a walker to a wheelchair. Mealtime visits to the dining room, afternoons on the front porch, excursions on the *Ocean Pearl*—all became more arduous and less frequent. Seward's beloved boat grew ragged through lack of use, as if in anticipation of his death.

More and more, Seward stayed in bed. There, he ate meals, took tea, had baths and bowel movements—now, increasingly, involuntarily. For one who'd spent years worrying about irregularity, incontinence was the ultimate irony; more than that, for someone so immaculate and proud, it was the ultimate indignity. Eventually, he needed assistance even to change positions in bed. Every day Seward grew more tender to the touch, more difficult to move. The nurses religiously recorded everything that went into or came out of him, right down to the burps and farts and, more rarely, comments. Weisser had only two real conversations with him (in one, he boasted of having imported the first Porsche ever into the United States).

Seward had frequent nightmares, from which he would awaken agitated and bewildered. There were hallucinations, too, though they continued to follow a pattern heretofore undocumented in the medical and legal literature; that is, they seemed to occur only when a soon-to-be-disinherited heir or her spouse was around to witness it. On the morning of April 24, for instance, Mary Lea (who was about to ask her trustees for an additional $100,000 to cover her trips to Fort Pierce) claimed to have heard her father talk as if he were riding in a carriage with his mother in Sicily. Notwithstanding this, Mary Lea and her siblings continued carrying on, both in and out of Seward's presence, as if things were quite normal. Junior called his father at least five times in the first week of May, once to inaugurate a new speakerphone,

159

another time to calm down Seward about the poor performance of Harbor Branch's portfolio. Diana Firestone called from Nassau on May 10, and spoke with Seward about the Kentucky Derby. The Wolds did not visit; they were too busy throwing themselves a "welcome home" party at the Boca Raton Beach Club, though only after getting a green light. "Two days before the party I learned that it would be all right to go ahead, that he was not going to die," Elaine later explained.

Meantime, Seward went about his tasks. The day after he signed his will, for instance, he again took pen in hand, this time to help an old family friend named Larry Hopp. When Jimmy Johnson had been about to flunk out of St. Lawrence College, it was Hopp who had gotten him into Upsala College; later, at Seward's request, Hopp helped Jimmy get a deferment during the Vietnam War. But Hopp had fallen on hard times, and sent Seward a plea for a loan. On the top of Hopp's note, Seward scratched out his reply. It looked like something off an Etch-a-Sketch—the spelling was poor and the grammar worse, but it was intelligible. "Dear Nina," it stated. "I feel obligated lary Hopp Basia agrees with me, please send $30,000. and to help, and advisce me. Seward." Three days later Nina mailed the money. Shortly after that, Seward watched a Harbor Branch promotional film, expressed his wish that American rather than Japanese steel be used in the new ship, and approved a proposal to add "Oceanographic" to Harbor Branch's name so that it would no longer be mistaken for a bank ("I like this. Seward," he wrote atop the proposal). Scott and Joyce Grob MacLeod, Seward's friends from the pre-Basia era, stopped by for a visit. But the most frequent visitor of all was Waligura, the Polish-born doctor the Johnsons had befriended. So grateful was Seward for his company that when the doctor began having legal problems at Sloan-Kettering (some questions had been raised about his supervision of student research), Seward placed Nina at his disposal.

One can wonder whether it was love or lust, fear or force of habit, that bound Seward to Basia through twelve tempestuous years of tantrums and extravagances. But in Fort Pierce another inducement was amply on display: her devotion. It was not as if Basia had suddenly revealed a newer, softer self. In fact, her behavior during Seward's final illness was quite characteristic. The quotidian was never enough to sustain Basia. She always needed something—a project, a campaign, a cause, a crisis, a vendetta—to keep her going. Now, the same relentless energy she'd poured into building buildings or buying art she channeled into Seward's care. She simply knew no other way.

Basia massaged Seward. She gave him ice packs and heating pads where he ached. She salted his broth and prepared him her special herbal tea, made with equal amounts of lavender, hawthorn flowers, yarrow herb, lemon balm, and chamomile, and a half-measure of valerian root. She read to him, bathed him, cut his nails, combed his hair, trimmed his beard, put on his clothes, wiped his forehead. She helped him walk, and when he could no longer lift up his hand, she could almost telepathically pinpoint his pain. When his lips dried out, she rubbed them with gauze dipped in lemon water. She wiped his rectum, uncomplainingly. She made herself available to him twenty-four hours a day; the nurses were instructed to push A on the intercom or knock on her door if they needed her or he wanted her. Often, Seward asked the nurses to fetch her, so that she could hold his hand or keep him company. "I couldn't figure out why she wanted an R.N. when she would always do everything for him," one nurse said.

Mornings, Seward was always anxious to see her. He grew flustered whenever she left him, though she rarely strayed far or for long. Seward's children flitted in and out; Basia was almost perpetually by his side. When she wasn't there, he kept a photograph of the two of them kissing, taken in Italy the previous summer, nearby. "Let me tell you, she is *some* lady," he once boasted. She tried inspiring him. "Basia, why should I take all this medicine?" he asked her once. "I know I'm not long for this world." It was the first time he'd ever mentioned dying to her, and she was taken aback. "Seward! If someone, even a healthy person, wants to die, he will die," she said, in as strong a voice as she could summon. With that, he promised to carry on, and never raised the subject again.

Unbeknown to him, there were times now when even Basia despaired. Only a few weeks earlier she'd bragged to a nurse that she never worried about money: No matter how much of it she spent, there would always be more. Despite her travails, at a Sotheby's sale in early May she bought a Louis XIV table-desk for $935,000 (more than double the previous record for French furniture sold at auction), along with four Louis XVI cabinets ($264,000); a pair of Louis XV armchairs ($203,500), and a Regence table-desk ($198,000). Under the circumstances the shopping spree seemed perverse. But it was a testament to Basia's extraordinary energy that spending a million and a half dollars on furniture did not distract her from her principal mission. Seward's condition now gave Basia a bit of perspective, as well as a fleeting sense of her own impotence. "I can buy or do or have anything I want, and yet my husband's in there dying, and there's nothing I can do," she once lamented.

Perhaps Basia's behavior did not reflect love. It could have stemmed from her European-style devotion to family, or displaced veneration for her father, or simple compulsiveness. But no one who saw her in Fort Pierce could possibly have thought she was faking it or putting on a show or building a record. She was honoring her wedding vows, and Seward was grateful for it. During one of Peach's visits Seward suddenly took his hand and looked him in the eye. "I want you to help Basia," he said. Peach, taken aback, mumbled a reply. "I want you to help Basia," Seward said again. Once again Peach groped for the right words. "I want you to help Basia," Seward reiterated.

With all the new precautions built into it, Nina considered Seward's April 14 will secure enough to withstand any attack. She still doubted the children would challenge it, not because they were above such a thing but because they already knew their fate and had reconciled themselves to it. But on April 28 she had a most unsettling call from Junior. He had phoned ostensibly to talk about John Peach, who was threatening to leave Harbor Branch for a more lucrative job in construction unless the foundation raised his salary. Junior was resistant; giving Peach the additional twenty-five thousand dollars he was demanding would throw Harbor Branch's pay scale out of whack and jeopardize its tax exemption, since anyone caring to investigate could see that Peach was receiving foundation funds for family work. Given the shape Seward was in and the family's dependence on Peach, Junior felt the whole thing smacked of extortion.

But the Peach matter proved to be just a prelude. Junior proceeded to tell Nina he'd been hearing what he called "noises in the underbrush" that two of his sisters—he would not say which—were already planning to contest Seward's will. He said he considered the scheme disgraceful, particularly since neither even knew what the will contained, and he promised to do what he could to squelch the idea. But, he quickly added, he couldn't guarantee how even he would feel if, as he put it, the will "flew in the face of general social practice" and made him and his siblings "look like a bunch of idiots." (Junior later recalled a similar conversation, though he placed it a few months earlier and said he'd used a different metaphor. "I know how I will feel," he said he told Nina, "if it is a cold fish in the face.") One way or the other, Junior worried all that spring how Basia would, as he later put it, "handle" Seward's will—whether she'd do so with "noblesse oblige," and throw the children some bones, or "go for broke." Essie Johnson had no such doubts. She predicted to Jennifer and Jimmy that none of the children would receive anything.

Nina listened to Junior's rambles, all the while doodling fragments of his conversation on small sheets of lined yellow paper. Junior, she knew, could talk, and talk, and talk on just about anything; one time he spent an entire train ride back from Washington describing his various suicide attempts and rambling on about his attraction to his wife's twin sister. Sometimes the only way for her to follow what he was saying was to write it down, then connect the dots. "He doesn[']t exist anymore as his own will—that's been for a while" was one dot; "feels morally badly" another. There was a "53" with a circle around it, presumably a reference to Junior's age. "It's hot air" was surrounded by a rectangle, with "no guts" written in an attached balloon. This constituted the official record of the conversation, since Nina wrote no memorandum afterward.

Peach had never told Nina of his poolside conversation with Marty Richards two weeks earlier, when he, too, hinted that a will contest was brewing. But she quickly reached a series of conclusions: first, that the sisters Junior was talking about were Elaine and Mary Lea; second, that their spouses were really pulling the strings; third, that Marty Richards and Keith Wold had hatched, or at least discussed, the scheme aboard the QE2; and finally, that Junior, too, was now involved. Before she could ponder things too long, however, her phone rang again. And again it was Junior, this time calling to say he regretted calling the first time and hoped Nina wouldn't say anything to Seward or Basia about their conversation. Nina doodled anew. "Sorry I told you." "Basia seems to have taken on a superego." "As of now she is not someone I want to work closely with." "Don't know what will result—felt I owed you and her." "Feel Her need of him and his of her." "Wanted him to carry the flag . . . Don't know if 1 person agitator—Wanted him to hire a lawyer in New Jersey and they were starting something themselves."

Junior had put Nina in a bind. Seward should surely know of any possible challenge to his will; but it was crucial, too, to keep Junior's confidence and thereby encourage him to defuse the situation. So Nina compromised. She promised to say nothing to Seward or Basia, but urged Junior to dampen things as best he could. He promised that he would.

Nina immediately told Ford of her conversations, as well as Gunther, Hoch, and Edward Reilly, another partner in her department. Ford, to use a baseball neologism, nonchalanted the whole thing. It was a good sign that Junior had called, he said; no one in his right mind would have done so unless he planned to help. He urged Nina to relax. Reilly offered some more practical advice. It was all well and good to build safeguards into the will, he said, but if the will was contested anyway, Basia would need cash to live on until the will was probated. Nina immediately thought of what Seward had always called his "anchor to windward": the $9 million in bonds he kept on hand for emergencies. On May Day Nina came into her office and drafted a new trust, built around the bonds, which would spring to life when Seward died. Basia would collect the income and, if the trustee saw fit, dip into the principal. And since the trustee would be Nina herself, that shouldn't pose any problem. As trustee, Nina stood to collect twenty-five thousand dollars per year, but it was money she would have collected anyway from one of the existing trusts; indeed, by shrinking the size of the estate, she was actually reducing what she made as an executor. On May 3 Nina flew back to Fort Pierce, where she walked a tightrope, telling Seward of the new trust but not the impetus for it. Seward summoned Basia and explained Nina's proposal to her. "This may be very helpful to you," he said. He signed the agreement; once again his scrawl crumbled after an initial burst of energy, enough for him to ask Nina if the signature sufficed. She said it did. She was soon off to the airport, with Seward wishing her a nice trip. She would never see—or even talk to—him again.

Within days, Seward's batteries began running down once more. On May 8 he canceled a trip on the *Ocean Pearl*. On the morning of the eleventh, he slept through his bath. By the morning of the thirteenth, his speech had grown garbled. When Peach arrived, Seward did not seem to recognize him. His blood pressure fell, and he complained of feeling smothered. Schilling directed that a Foley catheter be placed in Seward's bladder to control incontinence and prescribed Demerol for Seward's increasingly intense pain. He also called Junior in Princeton to tell him that Seward's time might finally be up. Things were sufficiently grave for Junior to take a plane notwithstanding his pathological fear of flying, and for the superstitious Marty Richards to fly down on Friday the thirteenth.

Once more, Basia ordered a priest. The fellow Peach had spoken to two months earlier was on the golf course; fortunately, Vero Beach had a second Catholic parish priest, Father John O'Hare, whom Peach convinced to come. O'Hare entered the room, and Seward, whose condition had improved slightly in the interim, smiled and raised his arms. Basia held Seward's hand as the priest, who assumed Seward was a Roman Catholic, removed a vial of oil, dipped his thumb in it, and, after reciting a prayer in his Irish brogue, made the sign of the cross on the old man's forehead. "May the Lord who frees you from sin save you and raise you up," he added, before anointing Seward's hands. "Priest came in to give Mr. J. communion," the nurse on duty, Luella Johnson, wrote. Then, perhaps fearful that for her to acknowledge last rites could violate Basia's ban on references to Seward's mortality, she scratched out "communion" and wrote "blessing" instead.

O'Hare prepared to leave. Peach, a religious skeptic himself, did not know the proper priestly protocol. Do you tip priests for administering sacraments? And if so, how much? Fifteen percent of what? Peach quietly consulted Schilling. "If this were an average family you'd give him twenty-five dollars," the doctor said. "But this is not an average family." Still, Peach didn't want to go overboard. "I didn't want to pay the guy two hundred dollars and have the old man whistle me into the room and say, 'How much did you pay for that shit?' " Peach later explained. He settled on a hundred dollars, which he stuffed into an envelope and handed to Father O'Hare as he left. As it turned out, the priest was disgusted by the gesture, and grew even more appalled upon learning that Seward wasn't even Catholic. He was not the only soul who found the encounter upsetting. "I don't need that," Seward grumbled to a nurse after the priest departed. "That isn't my choice."

The visitation nonetheless proved to be good therapy, for Seward quickly rebounded. The situation eased sufficiently for Junior and Marty to head back north—by train—on the sixteenth. For Junior, it was a matter of habit, for Marty, a matter of numbers: the sixteenth of any month was his day for accidents, and, as Mary Lea later explained it, "He would rather have an accident on the train than in the plane." But Junior, too, had numbers on his mind: the numbers in Seward's will. "If I don't get my fair share out of this thing, there is going to be real trouble," Junior told Marty, at least as the driver taking them to the station later recalled. "If I have to, I'll take her to court."

Like Junior, the Shearman & Sterling management committee was anticipating Seward's death. At a meeting on May 17, Ford broached the sticky subject of how much Nina stood to collect as executor of the Johnson estate. Nina's fee had risen in tandem with J&J stock, and she now stood to earn $6 million—money that, as an associate, she got to keep. But for some reason—either because he'd forgotten what Nina told him, hadn't been paying attention, or feared censure for letting so gigantic an estate escape from the firm's grasp—Ford told the committee she would make around $1 million. Unofficially, some committee members half-facetiously suggested that Nina be made a partner on the spot, an offer that Ford, assuming Nina was no fool, declined on her behalf. Officially, the committee authorized Nina to serve as executor and keep the fees, and Ford, on its behalf, sent her a memo to that effect. The committee also authorized Nina to act as trustee of the two trusts that would spring to life upon Seward's death. For that, she would earn another $750,000 a year for the rest of Basia's life. There was no telling what the partnership would have offered her had they realized the true dimension of her windfall.

Back in Fort Pierce, Seward's bouts of confusion and desperation grew more frequent. "Who are you? Are you available to me or to you? What time are we going out?" he asked one nurse. "What did you say to me? You told me to get out of the soup. I'm not in the soup!" The next night he began ripping out all the tubes sticking into him. "I don't care if it bleeds—I'll die!" he declared. "You go away! Help all those others! Help Jesus Christ!" Basia became more frantic and involved, injecting the painkillers herself after a nurse prepared the syringes. She had learned the technique from her sister-in-law and given shots to her mother; Seward, claiming that Basia had "very delicate hands," insisted that only she give him the injections, which went into his hips.

If one thing sustained the sinking Seward, it was thoughts of the new ship. The bidding process on the R/V Seward Johnson had yet to begin, but with its namesake's days dwindling, Harbor Branch decided to stage the nautical equivalent of a groundbreaking: "the striking of the first arc," when the first two pieces of the vessel would be symbolically joined. The ceremony was set for dawn on May 19.

When John Peach arrived in Seward's room around six-fifteen that morning, the old man was already wide awake, watching the sunrise, eager to get things under way. The morning was bright, clear, and cool, marred only by swarms of insects. They bothered Seward, though given his anemic state, any bug biting into him would surely have been disappointed. Around six-thirty a Harbor Branch welder arrived and placed his equipment by the bougainvillea outside Seward's window. With Seward growing increasingly impatient, the bleary-eyed spectators began assembling in his bedroom: Basia, Peach, and Mary Lea; Bob Jones and Roger Cook of Harbor Branch; Captain Gore; the nurse,

Luella Johnson; and Maurizio Bufalini, the Italian marble dealer who was in Fort Pierce to discuss stone for the new chapel. Cook explained to Seward where the pieces of metal would eventually be placed and showed him the bidding materials. Then, with Peach holding the ceremonial steel at a ninety-degree angle and the masked welder manning the torch, a crackling phosphorescent flash filled the air. Seward turned to the nurse. "Do you think that will take care of the mosquitoes?" he asked.

Everyone applauded. Out on the patio Basia produced a bottle of champagne, which she and Mary Lea—two women soon destined to fall on opposite sides of Seward Johnson's will—broke over the newly soldered steel. "Remember now, we don't go out there barefoot," the nurse told Seward jokingly. "No, I will keep my shoes on," he replied before declaring that he had "some mighty good people" working for him. Then, while Seward remained in bed, Basia served drinks by the pool. Seward requested some champagne for himself and the nurse, and the revelers returned to the bedroom and toasted Seward. Holding the glass in childlike fashion with both hands, he finished one and started another. He went to sleep clutching his glass. "I don't think he wants to give it back to us," someone joked.

It was an emotional experience for everyone, made more moving by the unmistakable imminence of Seward's death. "The last roar of the lion," was how Bufalini described it. Anxious to capture the moment, Bob Jones of Harbor Branch hurried back to his office to write up, in that distinctive argot, filled with sports imagery, acronyms, and techno-talk favored by soldiers, southerners, and scientist, an account of what he had just witnessed for the foundation's newsletter.

May 19, 1983—0720, Harbor Branch Foundation, at the home of Mr. J.S. Johnson. He was weak and he looked very tired. . . . "I had a rough night last night but I'm very glad to see you all and am anxious to get this ship started." The strength and resolve of this man has never ceased to amaze us.

0738—Production Manager Al Mitchell clamps the metal together and strikes the first arc. Seward has turned his head toward the garden and his face is illuminated with the flicker of the arc. He is wide-eyed and his pleasure and anticipation are evident. He is intent on the arc and the metal angle, oblivious to our presence, lost in a moment of privacy within his own thoughts. None of us will ever know what he was thinking, but from what seemed to be far away he was saying over and over. . . . "Oh, oh, oh!"

Al completes the weld and throws back his face shield to end the event. Seward is smiling, his mind is back with us and he is looking around the room. He lifts both of his arms and reaches out to us. We all respond in turn by grasping his hands, he looks directly at Al and says . . . "We have wonderful people here, don't we?" Al smiles back and says . . . "Yes sir, we sure do!" There were tears in the eyes of some big tough men in that room. Their admiration and respect for the frail man lying in his bed was impossible to conceal.

It was only after the two pieces of steel were joined that Seward himself fell apart. Though the house was stocked for the long haul— Basia had brought in months' worth of Pampers and syringes—it was increasingly clear they would not be needed. As Seward's pain intensified, Schilling directed that he be given Demerol every two to three hours if necessary. And as Seward's agony grew, so did Basia's panic. She ordered the nurses to increase his dosage and grew abusive when the nurses balked, calling them "stupid" for letting Seward suffer, accusing them of going through the motions for the money. When she gave the injections herself, she failed to measure out the medicine properly, and the nurses threatened to quit. Peach turned to Marty Richards for help calming Basia. But Richards was a weak reed; he'd watched his own beloved mother die of cancer, and Seward's agony made him hysterical. "It's exactly like my mother!" he cried. "I can't take it anymore! Do something for this man! Why aren't doctors doing more?"

Marty finally took Basia out to the canal in front of the house and tried reasoning with her. But his concerns, oddly enough, were primarily for appearances. Above all, he urged, let the nurses give Seward his shots. Think of yourself, he said: Look at what had happened to Claus von Bulow. Did she, too, want to be accused of bumping off her spouse by injection? "You are not a normal lady married to a normal man," he said. "This kind of thing can be misinterpreted." As Basia later remembered things, Richards made one additional point. As if to stress his sincerity, he told her that what he was saying cut against his own economic interests. And when she stared at him uncomprehendingly, he declared, "Don't you understand what I mean? What I have in mind is Seward's will!"

Blessedly, perhaps, Seward's mind grew more clouded. "I have something very bad to tell you," he told Mary Lea at one point. "There has been a terrible train wreck. There are many people who are suffering, and I must go there immediately to help them." Other times, though, he was lucid. As she prepared to leave one evening, Bonnie Weisser felt the normally undemonstrative Seward take her hand and squeeze it as firmly as his failing strength allowed. "I want to thank you for everything you've done," he told her. When Luella Johnson told him how important it was to be at peace with God, he replied that in that respect, his house "had been in order for some time." He should relax, she went on, because Jesus, too, had died. "I don't want to let go," he replied. A young delivery girl came by with some flowers. "She was beautiful, wasn't she!" Seward said after she left. At another point Peach tried to introduce Seward to Wideroff's wife, a doctor herself. "I don't want to meet any doctor," Seward grumbled. "Mr. Johnson, this is a female doctor," Peach added. Seward then turned over, fixed his glasses, looked up at her, and said, "Oh, my, you are much more attractive than any other doctor who has been around here."

On May 21 the nurses detected Cheyne-Stokes respiration, a pattern of rapid but sporadic breathing that is often a precursor of death. By the next afternoon thirty seconds or more now passed between breaths. At two-fifteen he called out, "Oh, Jesus, help!" He thrashed about in bed, attempting to pull off his pajama tops and rip out his oxygen tube. By dinnertime, with a sedated and eerily quiet Seward lying dying in the next room, Basia, Peach, the Richardses, and a young internist named John Christakis sat down for a light meal—a last supper of sorts. Afterward, Basia went back into Seward's bedroom. His bladder wasn't draining properly, and the pressure was hurting him. "Basia, help me! Help me!" he cried. She put her hands on him. "Basia, I love you. I love you," he said. When she returned to his room around ten, shortly before going up to bed herself, he was sleeping. She watched him silently for a few moments, then walked the short distance to the stairs. Up to now, she had been almost indignant at Seward's predicament, taking it almost as a personal affront. But as she met Peach by the stairway, fury had given way to disbelief. "Seward Johnson will never die, will he?" she asked. Before Peach could respond, she turned and went upstairs in tears.

Fran Cioffi came in at eleven that evening. It was her fifth straight night on the job, but she could feel this was not an ordinary shift change. Seward's vital signs continued to ebb. His pulse was scarcely detectable. The flow of cloudy yellow urine that migrated through the catheter into the plastic bag alongside his bed had dwindled to a trickle; his kidneys were shutting down. A patient had never died on her before, and Cioffi was scared. Christakis gave Seward one last injection of Demerol, then joined Peach in the living room and tried to get some sleep. They instructed Cioffi to wake them if—or, more likely, when—anything happened.

For the next two hours Cioffi moved Seward, applied Vaseline to his chapped lips and nostrils and baby powder to his back, placed his hands under the covers so he couldn't tear out his tubes. So often was she taking his blood pressure that she left the Velcro cuff on his arm. By one o'clock Seward's blood pressure was still dropping and had grown barely audible. He'd stopped stirring so much, and now lay on his right side, his eyes half-closed. Around 2:25 he began moaning. His rectal temperature continued to rise, and the intervals between breaths were now as long as forty seconds. Each gasp seemed like his last. By 3:50 his breathing grew more noisy and rattling. Half an hour later the urine had stopped draining almost entirely, and what was in the catheter seemed thicker than usual. As she sat alone in the dark, Cioffi wondered what, if anything, was going through Seward Johnson's head. She thought, too, about the gilded, privileged life he was leaving, and how hard it must be for him to let go.

By 4:40 Cioffi instinctively sensed that Seward's sands were finally running out, and she awakened Peach and Christakis. "I think you'd better come in," she said. "Mr. Johnson is slipping quickly." Christakis then entered the bedroom, while Peach summoned Basia, who lay wide awake in her bed. "I think it's time," he told her. She entered Seward's bedroom and looked at him with puzzlement and disbelief, touching his face, then grabbing his hands and bending over until their faces were very close. "Seward, I love you, I love you," she said. Both Christakis and Cioffi placed their stethoscopes on Seward's chest. The doctor took his out of his ears, pulled out his penlight, and shined it into Seward's eyes. "Okay, Fran," he said, looking at his watch. "It's four forty-six." Cioffi picked up the nursing log. "M.D. officially declared Mr. J. dead," she wrote. Still, she wasn't quite so sure. She had not put down her own stethoscope so quickly, and she thought Seward's heart had still been beating, faintly, faintly, when the doctor made his pronouncement. She was struck by the strangest of thoughts. On some bare level of consciousness Seward may have had that rarest of human experiences: He may have heard himself declared dead. Christakis reached down to Seward's face, placed his fingers on the old man's eyelids, and pulled them down like tiny window shades. He turned to Basia and took her hands. "He's passed away," he said. "He's resting quietly now." Basia thanked him, then bent down to Seward and kissed his forehead.

The nurse helped Basia reposition Seward's body so that it lay flat on the bed and pulled the blanket up to his chest. Then she disconnected him from all of the wires and tubes running in and out of his body. His jaw was already closed. Peach offered to call the undertaker. No, said Basia, not just yet; she wanted to spend a few more moments with her husband. And for the next twenty minutes Basia and Seward remained alone together.

It was still dark when Charlie Gifford, the undertaker from Vero Beach, drove up in an unmarked station wagon. Peach went into Seward's bedroom to tell Basia, who had been joined by her brother Gregory. The undertaker would have to wait, Basia said. She proceeded to wash Seward's face, while Gregory gave him his last shave. Then she reached for the scissors and began trimming his beard, as she had promised him she would do the week before but had never gotten around to doing. She gave Seward one last kiss on the cheek and returned to the living room, taking care not to look behind as Gifford and his assistants carried Seward out to the hearse. Seward's coffin, unlike Princey's, would not be homemade; from one of Gifford's catalogs Basia had previously selected a stainless-steel model, one suitable for shipment north at some unspecified future time.

The casket cost four thousand dollars, but it was something she could afford. After all, she now stood to inherit virtually all of Seward Johnson's estate. And at the precise moment of his death, Seward Johnson was worth $402,824,971.59.

XVI

Seward's end triggered that peculiar combination of grief and pragmatism that follows most deaths. One must bid good-bye, but one must also tend to a thousand details. At Basia's insistence the minihospital in his bedroom, the one that took months to assemble, was almost instantaneously struck. The hospital bed vanished quickly, replaced by the old, conventional twin beds that had preceded it. Within hours, any semblance of Seward's presence there had been expunged, and the room reverted to its former soulless self.

In Newark Nina boarded the *Westwind*—the Pierre Cardin–designed plane, with black and white and red stripes running down its side, that the Johnsons had bought a few years earlier—and headed for Florida. Earlier, around daybreak, Peach called Larry Foster, the public-relations man at Johnson & Johnson, who released the obituary—J. SEWARD JOHNSON DIES AT 87; SERVED 50 YEARS AS A DIRECTOR OF JOHNSON & JOHNSON—along with a statement from J&J chairman James Burke. Both were faithful to the corporate mythology. ("From 1916 to 1971 Seward Johnson made significant contributions to the growth of Johnson & Johnson as a worldwide leader of the health care industry," said Burke, who also saluted Seward's "outstanding business management skills.") Within the next few days obituaries appeared in *The New York Times*, both Princeton weeklies, as well as in papers from Waco, Texas, to Wichita Falls, Kansas, to Minot, South Dakota, RECLUSE J. SEWARD JOHNSON DIES AT FORT PIERCE HOME, the *Palm Beach Post* declared. Another local paper marked the death of a man "who loved the sea and hated publicity." At Foster's suggestion, a two-part funeral was set for May 25. Walter Waggoner, the veteran *New York Times* reporter who reported Seward's death, stated that the service would be private, and that was an understatement. In fact, it would be a top-secret sunrise affair, open only to family and close friends. Later that morning, once Seward had been filed away into his crypt, there would be a public memorial service on the grounds of Harbor Branch, visible from Seward's new penthouse perch at the mausoleum.

By noon on May 24 many of the key mourners had arrived in Fort Pierce, and after lunch they formed a caravan to the funeral home to view the body. The family appeared united behind the bereaving Basia. En route, Jennifer complained about how cold her own mother, Essie, was and, conversely, how much Basia meant to her. The transformation of Keith Wold was even more miraculous. For years he had not spoken to Basia. Suddenly, he was the picture of solicitude. When they arrived at the funeral home, he took Basia by the arm and escorted her inside. The Richardses invited Basia to recuperate at By-the-Sea, the million-dollar summer home on Gin Lane in Southampton they had recently purchased from New York businessman Jerry Finkelstein and were to redecorate, at mammoth expense, in a style Roy Cohn once described as "Hebrew Imperial." Oddly enough, only Basia's slavishly loyal brother Gregory made trouble for her. Seward lay in his casket, dressed in his tuxedo. But his bow tie wasn't tied to Basia's satisfaction, and she ordered Gregory to fix it. Gregory loved Seward; the night the old man died, Gregory swore he'd awakened to find him sitting at the foot of his bed. Spooked, perhaps, by the memory, he now refused to approach the cadaver, the only time anyone could ever remember in which he'd stood up to his baby sister.

That night, the Richardses and Wolds, Jimmy and Gretchen, Jennifer, Waligura, and some of Mary Lea's children assembled sans Basia for dinner. It was both a reunion and a mixer: Mary Lea's son Quentin, for instance, had never met Uncle Jimmy or Aunt Jennifer before. No one spoke of Seward's will, but the topic hung over everything like a fog. Marty Richards and Keith Wold scuffled briefly and ostentatiously for the bill. Everyone retired early in preparation for the sunrise service. Before going to bed, Basia, Nina, and Waligura sat and talked for a while in the living room, where Peach and Christakis had kept their vigil only two nights earlier. They spoke of Junior, who had been talking grandiloquently, even megalomaniacally, about his future plans for Harbor Branch and the Robert Wood Johnson Foundation. "I think you're going to have problems with him," Waligura said. "He seems to be going bonkers." Basia had not been cowed by her stepchildren's sudden solicitude. "Nina, you'll see," she said at another point. "There's going to be trouble. They will want money." "Why would they?" Nina replied. "It's impossible. They already have enough."

By four-thirty the following morning Basia was up, arranging flowers—roses, gardenias, orchids, cattleyas—for the funeral. (It was, like her healing hands, part of her special rapport with nature: Whatever she liked grew well for her.) Shortly before six, with headlights cutting through the sticky Florida darkness, a motorcade left the Harbor Branch compound and headed for the cemetery. There, the guests found half a dozen chairs set up beneath the niche where Seward would lie; his casket, draped in an American flag, was at the foot of the wall. There was little talk, though plenty of mumbling and grumbling over how early Basia had made everyone get up. The sky gradually grew lighter and multicolored as the crowd stood silently, waiting for the service to begin. Only Junior was missing. Finally, the distant sound of Seward's 1976 Oldsmobile 98 diesel—the one he'd bought in the energy crisis to save on gasoline—could be heard, first starting up, then making its way along Old Dixie Highway and up the hillside. Junior and Joyce parked and alighted. Thus began the ceremony, the Reverend Dr. G. Julius Rice of the Vero Beach Community Church, United Church of Christ, presiding.

As is so often the case in his business, Rice had barely been briefed for the assignment. He'd seen Seward only once, during an organ recital at the church, and never really spoken to him. Peach had asked him several months earlier to give the eulogy, and handed him some background materials on Seward. Rice protested that he preferred meeting those he extolled, only to be told Seward wasn't seeing anyone. Rice had officiated at innumerable funerals, but already, he could see this would be one of the strangest. The people standing around, neither laughing nor crying nor even talking, seemed barely to know one another or have anything in common. Collectively, they looked sinister, almost furtive to him, as if they were doing something they knew they shouldn't be. The only normal one among them was Gifford, the pot-bellied undertaker, and he'd been told to lay low, as if his very presence might offend such hoity-toity company. Rice's instincts were seconded by one of the few non-Johnsons among the mourners. "I didn't see one tear-filled eye in the joint," she later recalled. "They didn't know him. He was a stranger. They were only his family."

Even after Junior's arrival, it remained too dark for Rice to read right away, and he waited until the sky brightened a bit to begin. "We meet here in the early morning to pay our final tribute to Seward Johnson, who has walked with us in life for nearly eighty-eight years," he finally said. The timing was appropriate, he continued, for Seward had been a morning person. "When evening comes to our human bodies, they wear out," he went on. "It is then in God's great providence there is a new morning of the spirit which is eternal. So the evening of life comes, but the morning of eternal life dawns." Rice read the words from "Morning Has Broken," the old English hymn, then uttered a prayer. The flag draping Seward's casket was folded and handed to Basia. The service was over. The sun started peaking up over the horizon, over Harbor Branch. Once the guests drove off, Seward's body was lifted to the top row of the mausoleum and placed behind the unmarked marble slab. In death as in life, Seward had gotten the best seat in the house, and cheaply, too: At Hillcrest Memorial Gardens funerals before three o'clock in the afternoon cost less. Seward would have appreciated the bargain.

The day turned out to be oppressively hot, which only added to everyone's fatigue. But instead of going back to bed, the guests now had to kill time until ten, when the memorial service was to begin. At the Fort Pierce house, breakfast was served. Meanwhile two planeloads of people from New Jersey, including Evie Johnson, James Burke, and other Johnson & Johnson executives, arrived. After breakfast people took guided tours of Harbor Branch, drove around the area, talked among themselves. Some also thought of Seward Johnson's will, and when its contents would be revealed. The speculation, while rife, was mostly private. But among Mary Lea's children, at least, it was open and notorious. Anticipating, even savoring, the old man's demise may not have been very nice, but the Ryan children had never known "Pop-Pop" all that well. Happening upon one of them in his garage at Oldwick once, Seward had very nearly had the young boy arrested; another time, as they urinated alongside one another during a break in the Knights of Malta party, it was apparent to Hillary Ryan that Seward hadn't the foggiest notion who his grandson was.

Seward's fortune already had shaped their lives. With millions lurking somewhere in their future, none had outfitted himself for the present; only the eldest of the five Ryan boys, Eric, and Alice, the only daughter, had college degrees. The rest eked out marginal existences, largely as heavily subsidized entrepreneurs. Together, they watched their cousins make out like bandits (Keith and Elaine Wold once bought their children matching Corvettes), biding their time until some Johnson money rolled their way. Seward Ryan said once that he'd gotten through drug rehabilitation because that great "come and get it" day was in the offing. More than any other family members, they represented what the General had written to Mary Lea twenty years earlier. "It is a historical truth that too many families have gone from 'overalls to overalls' in three generations," he'd said.

Their father, William Ryan, said they'd be lucky to get anything from the old man. And their spouses, all of whom had learned the mixed blessings of marrying into moneyed madness, also had their doubts. "Don't count your cookies before the batter is beaten," one warned. Mary Lea predicted they'd net $5 million each, but was that said out of personal knowledge, or simply to keep them off her back? Soon the guesswork could cease. One encouraging sign was that they'd made it to Fort Pierce intact. They'd flown down together on their mother's rented Learjet, and the thought occurred to several of them that were he so inclined, Marty Richards could have rid himself of all competition for their mother's fortune by arranging for a convenient crash. One balked as he boarded the plane; another crossed himself during takeoff and landing. But they'd survived, and now, as they awaited the memorial service, visions of Seward's sugarplums danced in their heads. They drove along Florida's Gold Coast, pointing out the mansions they could soon afford. But at times like this, everything was an omen. On the way down one had predicted they'd get "a big bagel"—a goose egg, zero, zilch. After the funeral, when the smell of burning bagels wafted over from Basia's kitchen, he sensed how right he'd been.

The Ryans were not alone in their reveries. Two of the in-laws, Jimmy's wife, Gretchen, and Marty, both asked Waligura when the will would be read. "It's not because I'm interested," Richards added hastily. "Keith Wold seems to be very anxious to know about it." To the Reverend Dr. Rice, it all seemed like a scene from *The Godfather:* Everyone appeared preoccupied, as if weighing his next step. As the mourners, their ranks swollen by Harbor Branch employees, made their way toward the foundation grounds, Nina overheard Junior talking to James Burke. "We're going to wait until the dust settles, and then we'll make our moves," he said.

The old *R/V Johnson,* docked nearby, served as a nautical backdrop for the second ceremony. The painting of the *R/V Seward Johnson,* the one that had until two days ago hung in Seward's bedroom, was beside the lectern, a reminder of ships to come. Once everyone else was seated, members and close friends of the family took their places at the front. Leading them was Basia, holding herself erect. The heat was wilting, eased only slightly by a mild sea breeze. "When I go, I hope you're not so cheap that you don't rent a tent," Marilyn Link, Ed Link's half-sister and a Harbor Branch official, whispered to Peach. Junior Johnson, now head of the Johnson family, rose to read what he'd written on the train ride down. "Our father lived in the future," he began, pointing to the painting. "The day before yesterday, my father's future became eternal.

Death had a worthy opponent in my father. He fought back long and hard every inch of the way." Those in the audience plotting a will contest on the grounds of incapacity may have shuddered at what Junior said, but he did not dwell on the point.

"We are here today to celebrate the peace that comes with final surrender," he went on. "We are also here to give death a few second thoughts. It is up to us to re-create his presence in ourselves, in our work, and in our lives. It is up to us—Basia and the rest of the family—to fill that empty place in our beings with the stuff of ourselves that is most like him. It is only through this putting of him into ourselves that we can help him mitigate death's doom."

A trumpeter played the navy hymn. And then it was the Reverend Rice's turn again. He spoke of the need for family solidarity in times of grief. He reviewed Seward's accomplishments—the same litany, real and revisionist, that Marty Richards had gone through at the Knights of Malta ceremony. He described Seward as a dreamer and a visionary, a winner and an achiever. "Truly, Seward Johnson left his mark upon the world," he said. "And now I ask you, if Seward Johnson were standing here this morning, what would he say to each of you? Whatever you think he would say to you, go and do it. That would be the greatest memorial to him, I am sure." Rice then read from Tennyson's "Crossing the Bar." After his benediction, taps was played. Its plaintive notes had scarcely subsided, the mourners had hardly settled back into their seats, when suddenly, two heavy horn blasts cut through the torpid tropical air. It was the *R/V Johnson*. The sound scattered hundreds of sea gulls and lifted everyone momentarily off their chairs. A second later there came a reply—fainter, more delicate, more distant. It was the *Ocean Pearl*, moored in front of the house. Seward's ships were bidding him good-bye.

Basia was sending Seward out in style, something some other women in his life were to recognize. The day after the funeral Seward's first wife, Ruth Crockett, sent Basia her "sincere sympathy." "You have done so much to bring the family together and we all appreciate it," she wrote. "Johnny was a good man and kind and I'm glad he had a good help-mate." Seward's sister, Evangeline, also sent her condolences. "You cared for him selflessly and we should all be grateful to you for your love and devotion," she wrote.

But such elegiac feelings were as ephemeral as the horn blasts. As one of Seward's nurses made her way toward the house after the ceremony, she heard two family members talking. One of them was inquiring into Seward's mental condition in his last few months. The nurse thought it strange, but was too intent upon delivering something to the grieving widow to pay them much mind. When she finally reached her, she stuffed the gift into Basia's hand. It was more appropriate than either of them could have imagined. It was a collection of prayers.

PART TWO

THE
LAWYERS

XVII

C hildren's Bay Cay hadn't been the only place where it had been hard to reach Nina Zagat. The telephone in her apartment on Central Park West hadn't been working properly, and calls weren't always getting through. But within a few hours of Seward's death, Jan Waligura had finally reached her with the sad news from Fort Pierce. Normally, death marks an end. But for Nina, as for any probate lawyer, that was when the real work began. Nina had plenty of things to do, and she had to do them quickly, for Basia wanted her to fly down to Florida that evening, two days before the funeral.

Nina's workday generally didn't begin until after ten, after she sent her two boys off to school. But within minutes of Waligura's call, she was in a cab crossing Central Park, heading toward her office in Citicorp Center. There, she called Larry Foster at Johnson & Johnson, who informed company executives and released Seward's obituary to the press. She opened a new account for Seward's estate—her first official act as co-executor, which placed her in charge of Seward's $300 million stock portfolio (and made her personally liable for any losses). She then retrieved the petition to probate Seward's will, which she and the other two nominated executors, Basia and Junior, had to sign before filing the document in Surrogate's Court. It would officially notify Seward's next of kin that unless anyone objected to it, the will would be deemed valid. The documents certifying Seward's divorces from Ruth and Essie, which had to accompany the petition, were not among Seward's papers. One of her many chores would be to track them down. When Tom Ford, Nina's boss and head of Shearman & Sterling's individual-clients section, arrived, she relayed the news to him. Ford, too, decided to fly to Fort Pierce for the funeral; he, like Nina, would bill the estate for his time. So it was that Seward, a man who'd hated lawyers all his life, ended up paying two of them to mourn for him.

Nina and Ford agreed that once the funeral was behind them, she would review the will with her fellow executors. With Basia, the pro-cedure was strictly pro forma; she quickly signed the probate petition,

181

then left for a few recuperative days in Children's Bay Cay. By contrast, throughout her stay in Florida Nina could feel Junior's hot, smoky breath down her neck. He never actually said the noun "will," but he dropped numerous hints about it, e.g., to catch the northbound Amtrak train, he'd best leave shortly; was there any reason for him to hang around? Nina did not rise to the bait, arranging instead to stop by Junior's house in Princeton two days after the funeral. That would give her a chance to collect her thoughts and plan for the encounter.

As Nina boarded the plane for New Jersey on May 27, she remained convinced Junior would sign the probate petition. Sure, it sounded as though Keith Wold and Marty Richards had been leaning on him to contest the will. But Seward had always assured her that his children knew what was in store for them; surely they would not be surprised. Moreover, both as a confidante and as one of his own armada of lawyers, she had always gotten along well with Junior. After all, wasn't he the one who had warned her about those "noises in the underbrush"? She confidently took out a small yellow pad and assembled an agenda for the upcoming meeting.

"Review will—proponent," she wrote. She would have to explain to Junior that his father had named him executor and trustee, and that he would therefore become a "proponent" of the April 14 will. "Ft. P. house to HB." Basia, who never much liked the place anyhow, wanted to give the Florida property to Harbor Branch as soon as she could under the tax laws; in the meantime Junior should feel free to use it. "Considering CBC to HB + little boats." The foundation might also get the island in the Bahamas plus some of Seward's pleasure crafts. "Seward's personal belongings." Basia had asked Nina to see whether the children wanted any of their father's effects. "MCL." Marilyn Link had been griping to her that Seward's funeral took place too early in the day to garner Harbor Branch any good publicity, and might make the same complaint to Junior. Of course, the hour had been selected in part to keep reporters away—a decision in which Junior had con-curred—and Nina wanted to remind him of that.

A Jasna Polana driver was waiting when Nina landed in Newark. Once she arrived in Princeton, Junior greeted Nina at the door, pecking her perfunctorily on both cheeks in the European manner they'd all picked up from Basia, and they walked inside. Junior had been talking over the telephone to a Harbor Branch official, and their conversation droned on and on—oddly so, Nina thought, since Junior had previously seemed so anxious to hear about the will. Maybe making her wait was his way of asserting his new familial authority, of putting her in her place. She looked around Junior's library. The selections were surprisingly sophisticated. Perhaps she'd always underestimated the guy. Or maybe the books were Joyce's. Junior finally hung up, then plopped himself down on the living-room couch, to Nina's right. Nina proceeded to review the will with him, much as she had with his father six weeks before.

At least as Nina perceived things, the session initially went amicably. Junior appeared touched by Basia's offer of Seward's mementos, and pledged to ask his siblings who wanted what. He also seemed pleased to be inheriting the house in Chatham. The $1 million bequest was a pittance given Seward's googols, but Junior's reaction upon hearing about it confirmed for Nina that Seward had indeed prepared everyone to receive nothing. "That's so generous," Junior said. "He didn't have to do that." He asked whether his father had added the bequest after that touching night they had spent together in the Boca Raton hospital. She said she thought so, and that, too, seemed to please him. At Junior's request, Nina promised to see if there was some way the money could be funneled directly to his children.

Nina then went over what Basia and Harbor Branch stood to collect. She explained that the will would be probated in New York, and that Junior's commissions as executor and trustee would be "generous." She offered to calculate just how generous, but Junior, again surprisingly, didn't seem all that interested, even though he stood to collect $20 million or more for his modest troubles. She offered to go over the will with his brother and sisters, but here, too, Junior was strangely noncommittal. He declined to sign the probate petition, and even Nina's offer to leave him with a copy of the will. Nina agreed not to file the petition until they had spoken again. Then, before Nina could say anything else, Joyce Johnson entered the room and announced it was time for dinner—a dinner to which Nina was apparently not invited. "JSJJr.—Dinner bell," Nina doodled. Monday was Memorial Day; they agreed to talk again Tuesday. On her way out, Junior didn't kiss Nina even once. But Nina was not perturbed; he seemed more hurried than upset.

Junior and Joyce never had their quiet dinner together, at least according to their own very different and less persuasive recollections of events. As the "smooth and impervious" Nina went through the will, Junior later recalled, his mouth "was just dropping open." "I'm in shock, Nina!" he said. "He told me he was going to do something for my children. Where's that?" He said he then expressed embarrassment and chagrin that his siblings stood to collect nothing at all. In twenty years of marriage, Joyce was to testify, she'd almost never seen him so upset. "No one in the family, including all of the grandchildren, are included!" she recalled her husband gasping as he staggered into the dining room. "Basia tried to buy me off for $5 million, and thinks I am going to betray my family!" That night, Joyce said, Junior didn't sleep a wink.

As promised, Nina called Junior on Tuesday, only to find him still equivocating. On Wednesday morning Junior's secretary called Nina's office: Her boss wanted a copy of the will after all. A Shearman & Sterling messenger promptly hand-delivered one to Princeton. When Junior next called Nina a few days later, it was to say he'd have no more contacts with Basia. Nina would thus have to file the probate petition minus Junior's signature, and told him so. As battle lines appeared in Princeton, they also were drawn in Southampton: Marty and Mary Lea promptly revoked the invitation they'd extended to Basia but a few days earlier to recuperate at their summer home, ostensibly because one of their shows was suddenly opening in Boston. But Marty, who wanted to remain well liked even as he conspired, told Nina what was really going on: The family was contemplating a will contest and had been advised by their lawyers to sever all ties to Basia and Nina. "Family up in arms," Nina doodled as Richards blabbed. "Very upset. Better not to discuss until the air clears." Meantime Richards told Waligura that it was Junior who wanted to file suit; he and Mary Lea, he said, were "very much against it."

In the meantime someone had to administer Seward's estate; there were bills to pay and the $25 million loan Seward had taken out—it had been cheaper for Seward to borrow money than to sell off J&J stock—to repay. Nina dispatched Gunther to the Manhattan Surrogate's Court to obtain approval—in legal parlance, the "preliminary letters testamentary"—to handle the estate's finances until the will was admitted to probate.

In most courts this would have been a straightforward bureaucratic proposition. But in Manhattan Surrogate's Court, where all estates matters were heard, one could actually choose between two very different judges, with the official receiving the initial filing quite possibly hearing the rest of the case. There was Marie Lambert, a temperamental former negligence lawyer who was known for taking sides, butting heads, forcing settlements; going with her was risky but usually swift. And there was Renee (pronounced REE-KNEE) Roth. She had been in office only briefly and was still largely unknown; the early line on her was that she was brighter, more knowledgeable, and more level-headed than

Lambert, but slower and less decisive. Shearman & Sterling had to decide, and quickly, whether Gunther would head to the left or the right when he stepped off the elevator onto the fifth floor of Surrogate's Court, where both judges had their chambers. Henry Ziegler wanted Roth. He'd recently heard her say that "no one is going to hold up widows in my courtroom," and that sounded good to him. Furthermore, why inject a wild card like Lambert into an open-and-shut case? On May 31, as Junior continued to weigh his options, Gunther brought the petition to Roth. He requested that the deadline for filing objections be set for August 10. Roth issued the preliminary letters without Junior's signature; he could sign on later, she said. But the judge's law assistant was dubious. "It sounds like a will contest to me," she said. As it did to Nina. "Don't you think we should have someone brief all the undue influence cases reported in N.Y., Florida, N.J. and maybe California?" she wrote Ford. But the notoriously penny-pinching Ford, who would walk places simply to save bus fare, was not about to waste any money, even a client's, on something so frivolous. "Yes—Get summer person," he wrote back.

Before long, three more lawyers were asking Shearman & Sterling for copies of Seward's will. One was Phillip Broughton of New York's Thacher, Proffitt & Wood, longtime counsel for both Diana Firestone and Mary Lea Richards. The second, a small-firm practitioner in New York named John Tommaney, said he was representing Hillary Ryan, one of Mary Lea's sons. The third, and by far the most formidable, entry was Alexander D. Forger of Milbank, Tweed, Hadley & McCloy, who had apparently been retained by the Johnson children. The lawyers at Shearman & Sterling knew Alex Forger, and greeted the news of his involvement with a mixture of dread and disgust.

In fact, just around the time Gunther visited Judge Roth, five of the Johnson children and their spouses—only Jennifer and her new husband, a furniture designer named Joseph Duke, were absent—met at the Metropolitan Club, an elite watering hole on Fifth Avenue and Sixtieth Street, to which Diana's husband, Bert Firestone, belonged. For the Johnsons it was an extraordinary event, the first time in memory they'd assembled for something other than one of Basia's parties or Seward's funeral.

Recollections of the session, which lasted anywhere from one hour to two days depending on who did the recalling, varied considerably (two of the spouses, Gretchen Johnson and Keith Wold, later said they'd entirely forgotten about it afterward). But a few points are not in dispute. It had been a hot day. Photocopies of the recently obtained will were distributed to everyone (though, without a lawyer present, it was hard to imagine anyone making much sense of it). Junior, in his new role of paterfamilias, did much of the talking; Richards, Wold, and their wives said little. There were references to family honor, and how it had been sullied by a document that, as Junior put it, colorfully but inaccurately, left everything to "a bunch of Polish people who he never hardly knew and didn't want around." (The notion that Seward had left piles of money to Basia's relatives, though loony, nonetheless proved persistent. "I read the will briefly, and every page had so many of Basia's relatives on it that I decided I wouldn't read any more," Elaine Wold later said nonsensically.) Most were positive the will did not represent Seward's true wishes, though there were skeptics. If Basia had been so abusive, Gretchen asked at one point, why hadn't anyone spoken up sooner? Junior loved his father too much to say anything, Joyce replied. "How can we be sure that this was not Daddy's wishes?" Jimmy asked. "There is no way we can be certain," Junior replied. "However, do you think your father was not senile?" "No, I think he was senile," Jimmy said. Everyone eventually signed on to the suit, with stalwart declarations of selflessness and family unity. "When we go home tonight, we all have got to search our hearts and really understand why we are doing this, and for the purposes we are doing this— that they are moral purposes and not greedy purposes," Joyce later said she said. Elaine saw another benefit to the undertaking. "You know, this might be a very good thing for all of us," she declared. "It is time we got to know each other better."

All that remained was to hire the lawyers. Each of the children drew up a list of candidates, and one name appeared on three of them: Alexander Forger of Milbank, Tweed, Hadley & McCloy.

Milbank Tweed was one of New York's most venerable law firms, though always considered a notch below the very best, like Cravath, Swaine & Moore; Sullivan & Cromwell; or Davis, Polk & Wardwell. If the Wall Street bar were the Ivy League, Milbank was Cornell. It had been around in various forms for almost a century, though through all its incarnations there ran one key thread: the name "Rockefeller." Milbank lawyers worked on an extraordinary range of Rockefeller enterprises, including the Chase Manhattan Bank; Grand Teton and Great Smokies National Parks; Colonial Williamsburg; Cooper Union; the United Nations; Lincoln Center, and the American Museum of Natural History. In addition, they drafted and administered the wills of the Rockefellers themselves, including twenty for Nelson alone. Milbank maintained a branch office in Rockefeller Center—a place it helped build by devising the means to clear off the speakeasies and whorehouses that had occupied the site—solely to service family members.

By pedigree and politics, Alexander Darrow Forger was not your typical Milbank lawyer. Though he'd gone to Princeton and Yale Law School, he wasn't from old money; his father had been credit manager for a textile concern. But Forger, sixty years old when Junior called him, had risen impressively since arriving at the firm in 1949. Because of the Rockefeller connection, the estates practice at Milbank, where Forger worked, was not the professional dead end it was at most Wall Street firms. Though turf-conscious colleagues saw to it that Forger never worked for the Rockefellers, he still managed to take over the department and, eventually, the firm. And yet, unlike so many other successful lawyers, in selling his services Forger hadn't seemed to sell his soul. He was someone who landed on the public-spirited, enlightened side of nearly every political and professional issue; he'd opposed the war in Vietnam, for instance, and helped integrate Westchester County, where he and his family lived. Moreover, when it came to fighting the parochial, protectionist elements of his profession, he was invariably on the ramparts. He headed the New York Legal Aid Society and defended the Legal Services Corporation against Reagan-era cutbacks. As president of the New York State Bar Association, he'd helped create a fund to reimburse the victims of unscrupulous lawyers. He'd campaigned to overhaul the lawyers' code of ethics and to require all lawyers to donate a bit of their time to the commonweal. Under him, Milbank stopped having partnership meetings at the all-male Down Town Association. He'd spoken out for gay rights before the American Bar Association, despite that group's nastily homophobic element.

Forger not only played the part of the public-spirited patrician to perfection; he looked it. He was tall and stately and trim, with an erect carriage, firm handshake, strong smile, resonant voice, and confident, convivial air. Nature had been good to him. He was one of those who had actually been enhanced by age; rather than thin out or disappear, his hair had turned a distinguished shade of silver, and he'd let it grow long enough to comb it back with a dramatic flourish. His face showed his years, but somehow seemed more engraved than lined. Everything about him, right down to his aviator-type eyeglasses, exuded elegance, boldness, vigor, and strength.

How Forger had come so far was part of the mystery of the man. True, during his apprenticeship many of Wall Street's traditional barriers were coming down. Slowly, family connections, ethnicity, religion, mattered less, merit more. But in trusts and estates the antiquated traditions lived on. Old money wanted old money representing it. Milbank was loaded with Social Register types, who'd gone not only to Ivy League colleges, but to prep schools like St. Paul's or Groton or Hotchkiss before that, whose classmates had become clients. Forger didn't have any of those connections. "His clients were hand-me-downs that no one else wanted," one of his well-heeled contemporaries, who'd fallen by the wayside as Forger prospered, later recalled with amazement. "He didn't know anybody. *He didn't know a soul.*" Far from hiding his differences, though, Forger flaunted them. He was a Stevenson Democrat amid Taft Republicans; while his partners were upstairs bad-mouthing John F. Kennedy during the 1960 presidential campaign, Forger was down on the street, cheering as his motorcade whisked by.

While not exactly cultivating mavericks, Milbank had traditionally tolerated them. The prime example was Forger's mentor, Harrison Tweed, who wore argyle socks, moccasins, and western hats to work, kept a mayonnaise jar filled with whiskey on the ledge outside his office window, and could be seen skinny-dipping with the latest of his wives on his Long Island estate. But Forger came of age later than Tweed, in the conformist 1950s, and his path wasn't so easy. Repeatedly, he tangled with Roy Haberkern, the crusty, conservative southerner who controlled the Chase Bank business, and, perforce, controlled Milbank. Haberkern, who once halted the firm's Christmas show in midperformance because he objected to an irreverent song set to the tune of "Hark, the Herald Angels Sing," did not cotton to Forger's liberal politics or what he once called Forger's "dean of students" personality. These battles impeded Forger's rise and led him on occasion to hunger for something less confining and more public-spirited. In 1970 he ran unsuccessfully for the state senate seat once held by Franklin D. Roosevelt. Two years later he was cochairman of the McGovern campaign in Westchester. Forger never shook the sense that what he did for a living was both socially irresponsible and a poor use of his talents; you could hear it in his acidic references to the "rich old ladies" he represented. But over time he built up his roster of clients, which came to include Mrs. Paul Mellon, and, to the chagrin of the Milbank folks at Rockefeller Center, David Rockefeller himself. He also developed a constituency of younger partners who either admired him, hated Haberkern, or both. Confounding the odds, outmaneuvering or outmuscling or outlasting his detractors, he became head of the firm.

Forger's strength had never lain in the intricacies of wills and estates.

What he sold, and sold dear, was his bedside manner; there were always drones back at the office to crunch numbers or draft documents and, should it prove necessary, there were also pit bulls to litigate. Forger was one of those people who could be dignified and obsequious simultaneously. It was that combination that landed him perhaps the most glamorous client in the world: Jacqueline Kennedy Onassis. She'd come to Milbank's William Parsons, then head of the trusts and estates department, as her marriage to Onassis disintegrated. (Her decision to retain Milbank was a closely held secret; rather than mention her by name, the firm dubbed her file "W.P. Special #2"–the "W.P." designating Parsons.) But Parsons was nearing retirement, and Forger soon got the file.

Aristotle Onassis died in March 1975 in Paris—before he could divorce Jackie and, according to his lawyers at Shearman & Sterling, without a will. Under the laws of many states and foreign countries, widows automatically receive a certain percentage of their husbands' estates. But it was difficult to say which law applied to a man who was born in Greece, traveled with an Argentinian passport, and lived in Monaco and France. After protracted—and, often, heated—negotiations with Shearman & Sterling and Onassis's Greek counsel, Forger struck a multimillion-dollar deal. A few days later, however, an Onassis will that virtually disinherited Jackie surfaced in Athens. Brushing aside complaints that the deal was done and the will gave her nothing new, Forger pushed for more, using the courts as his tool. "I want you to tie up the Onassis shipping interests until they squeak," he instructed underlings. Eventually, the Onassis lawyers caved in, and the widow collected an additional $6 million.

To hear the Shearman & Sterling lawyers tell it, not without their own axes to grind, Forger had dealt in bad faith and extorted money for his client. To Forger, it had simply been aggressive representation. In any case, from that moment on, Jackie called on Forger often. When the photographer Ron Galella kept harassing her despite a court order to keep his distance, Jackie had Forger haul the persistent paparazzo back to court. When Christian Dior ran advertisements featuring a Jackie look-alike, she had Forger sue to stop it. Each time there were court appearances, and when Jackie landed on the front pages of New York's tabloids, Alex Forger could also be seen, standing sternly at her side. Forger guarded his prized client zealously. But he had his vainglorious side, and in his own discreet way he flaunted his ties to Jackie. He spiced his conversations with teasing tidbits about her, and needed little prompting to reach into his briefcase and pull out a picture of his beaming self in a morning suit, flanked by a resplendent bride named Caroline Kennedy Schlossberg and her proud mother.

Around Milbank Forger's charmed legal life was a subject of considerable interest and even some mythology. Most would have attributed his success to the very things Jackie saw: competence, charisma, charm. Others threw in luck. The story, apocryphal though it was, persisted that during World War II he'd saved the life of the son of Milbank's onetime managing partner, and that the old man had gratefully promoted Forger's career ever after. Others threw in an additional ingredient: ruthlessness. It was a side Forger usually managed to hide; when things got nasty, there were always others around to do the dirty work. Eisenhower had his Nixon and Nixon his Agnew; Forger had his litigators to fight mean for him, while he remained elegantly, immaculately, above the fray.

Forger's critics were quiet, for they were going up against conventional wisdom. But to many who had encountered him up close, there was something synthetic and insincere, oleaginous and icy, about him. To them, Forger was one of those people who loved humanity but was contemptuous of people, someone who took an almost sadistic glee in his ability to push folks around without ever breaking into a sweat, losing his cool, or—most important—leaving his fingerprints. Forger appeared to have everything: a compelling personality, a fabulously successful career, an altruistic reputation, a lovely wife and family, one home in Larchmont and another on Cape Cod. And yet, beneath the bonhomie seemed a reservoir of bitterness and rage. Perhaps it stemmed from that gnawing feeling he'd been destined for something more significant. Perhaps it lay in some family tragedy, perhaps something deeper; ultimately Alex Forger was impossible to know. The only thing clear about his shtick was that he had mastered it. He had the peculiar arrogance of someone who knew he could treat people both with contempt and with impunity.

Forger never knew J. Seward Johnson, Sr., though, like any good probate lawyer, he faithfully followed the *Times* obituaries and had read about his death. Nor had he known J. Seward Johnson, Jr., though he'd heard a bit about his sculptures. But when Junior rang, he took the call, then met with him in a Milbank conference room. The two had agreed to speak again once a family summit had been held. Now, after gaining the necessary vote of confidence, Junior summoned him. Forger was in Washington tending to one of his "rich old ladies," Clare Boothe Luce. But upon flying back to New York that evening, he went directly from LaGuardia to 280 Park Avenue, where, in the Board

Room, a private club on the forty-first floor, the strategizing Johnsons had gone for dinner. Accompanied by a young Milbank trusts and estates partner named Jeffrey Brinck, Forger arrived around seven-thirty, just as the Johnsons were finishing their first course. He talked to them about the grounds for contesting a will, then listened intently as the children and their spouses offered fragmentary evidence of Seward's feebleness and Basia's abusiveness. Forger urged them to catalog what they'd seen, for later consideration by Milbank lawyers. Junior, who'd already been represented by so many lawyers he couldn't remember all of them, had just hired himself some more. Milbank also agreed to represent Harbor Branch, which had, not surprisingly, dropped Shearman & Sterling as its counsel.

Why were the Johnsons going to war? All but one were later to insist, with varying degrees of inarticulateness, that what they wanted was not money for themselves but for Harbor Branch. "I took a long walk down the beach by myself, and I came back and I said to myself, 'I can't . . . I felt I couldn't face myself, I couldn't live with myself the rest of my life unless I fought this,' " Mary Lea told Junior's wife, Joyce. Later Mary Lea put it more directly. "Knowing my father's . . . the last quarter of his life was spent on the love of the sea and improving conditions and even supporting, in Washington, groups that would sponsor cleaning up the Atlantic Ocean, [the will] seemed to me a definite slap in the face to him," she said. "It was a unanimous feeling around the table that, for the memory of Dad, and to sort of clear his name, that this was an obligation to do something." All she wanted of her father's, she continued, were a few of his personal effects— presumably the effects Nina, on Basia's behalf, had already offered to Junior. "I can certainly live without his money, but I think that I would have liked to have seen that he remembered all of us and acknowledged our existence in the will, some tangible fact that he had a family, that they all weren't people in Poland he never met," she said, repeating the canard about Basia's kin. Jennifer said Seward's last will "was not what we thought he wanted." Elaine spoke of ensuring that Seward's "dreams are fulfilled."

A few, like Junior, spoke of wanting money for their children; only Diana Firestone admitted that some extra funds would come in handy, and that wasn't so surprising: Two months before the family meeting she'd gone to court to remove Albert Merck, her new and allegedly unsympathetic trustee, and have Junior take his place. Six times between December 1982 and March 1983, she claimed, Seward himself had told her he supported such a switch. *Firestone* v. *Merck,* then, was premised on the claim that Seward had not only been competent in 1983, but bright enough to follow her trust travails and support Diana and Junior every step of the way. Were they to join the will contest, then, Junior and Diana faced a delicate maneuver: to show their father had been competent and incompetent at the same time.

If the children were carrying the banner of Harbor Branch, they were recent converts to the cause. While three of them—Junior, Jimmy, and Jennifer—held various posts at the foundation, only Junior had really been active there. None of them, Junior included, had ever given it any of their own money, though Seward had created special trusts for each of them in the early 1960s to, as he later told a J&J executive, teach them how to make charitable donations intelligently. Only Junior had given it anything at all: four stainless-steel busts, one of them of Seward, that were eventually removed from the lobby and banished to the side of the road leading into the grounds. In point of fact, Harbor Branch really didn't need any more of Seward's money; that was why he had stopped giving it. But just as clearly, several of Seward's children desperately did. These did not include Jimmy or Jennifer, whose trusts were largely intact. Nor did it include Elaine, even after a burglar broke into her home in early 1979, handcuffed her husband, and made off with $1 million in jewelry. But Junior, Mary Lea, and Diana were poor in the way that only the fabulously rich can be.

For many years Junior had been prince and pauper simultaneously. In 1970 he'd asked for, and received, $1 million from his trust, which had already shrunk substantially due to his divorce. Six years later he requested and received $5 million more, and in 1981, he got an additional $3 million. Much of this had been poured into the new home he was building in Princeton, which cost twice the $2 million he'd budgeted. As for Mary Lea, from the time of her first wedding, when the checks she gave her bridesmaids to cover the cost of their gowns bounced, she too, had lived beyond her considerable means. In the 1980s she earned $3 million a year from her trust, but that was never enough. She lost a mint in the D'Arc era, particularly on her art galleries. When, at the end of every month, her creditors came calling, she learned to develop a convenient case of laryngitis. Like her siblings, Mary Lea was too estranged from Seward to ask him to urge her trustees to loosen the reins a bit. Instead, she enlisted John V. Lindsay, the former mayor of New York, to try to break the confounded trust once and for all. His efforts were for naught: The trust, he reported somberly, was "as solid as Fort Knox." So Mary Lea, like Diana, was forced regularly to beg for trust principal. In the fall of 1981 her trustees lent her $800,000 and advanced her another $150,000. The following February they advanced her $735,000 more.

Once Marty Richards and the Producer Circle came along, the losses only accelerated, a process her trustees chronicled in the minutes of their periodic meetings. Between 1976 and 1983 Mary Lea poured $4 million into the enterprise, and though there were some hits—*Sweeney Todd, La Cage aux Folles*—they did not make up for all the *Rockaby Hamlets* and *Foxfires*. Finally, in 1982 the Richardses promised her trustees they would phase out the operation within a year. But the Producer Circle lived, and hemorrhaged, on. Mary Lea's finances were a disaster, the trustees concluded, particularly with Marty Richards around. "The Treasury can't print enough money to make him happy," Mary Lea's lawyer, Phillip Broughton, complained. By August 1982 she owed her own trust $3,513,545.64, and the trustees decreed that every month they would deduct $25,000 from her $155,000 allowance to help pay it off. Even this modest step prompted a "hysterical" phone call to James Pitney, counsel to the trustees and the New Jersey lawyer who'd spent much of his career counseling the Johnsons, defending the Johnsons, bailing out the Johnsons, protecting or divorcing some Johnsons from other Johnsons, profiting handsomely from the Johnsons, and now, keeping Johnson money from the Johnsons. The trustees held firm, demanding evidence that Mary Lea and Marty were "capable of managing their own affairs." It might even be necessary, they noted, "to put Mr. Richards on some sort of a budget."

Mary Lea invoked every imaginable excuse to pry more money from her trustees. But whatever she got was not enough, particularly when compared to her sisters. Diana, she lamented, owned five homes and two jets; even after selling the largest cattle ranch in Florida and a horse farm in Ocala, Elaine lived in four different places every year. "Ms. Johnson professed not to be trying to compete with her sisters, but stressed that she believed her situation was quite inferior," the minutes related. "She complained to her trustees, 'You have never given me what I asked for.'"

Mary Lea had a "total inability to live within any reasonable budget," the minutes for September 7, 1982, noted. But at regular intervals the trustees proved to be pushovers. Eventually, Mary Lea owed $7 million to her trust. "If you keep spending money like this, your kids won't be able to afford bus tickets," one of the trustees warned her. Finally, even Mary Lea's trustees drew the line: They refused to bankroll a will contest, particularly one that seemed an even longer shot than the average Producer Circle production. Citing the case's poor prospects and "open-ended nature," in late 1983 they twice refused to help pay Milbank's bills. Eventually, characteristically, they relented, and forked over $550,000 more.

For several Johnsons, then, obtaining even a modest piece of their father's estate was tempting indeed, particularly since legal fees could be split six ways. And factors like family loyalty, hurt feelings, pressure, spite, and greed could convince the others to come along. But matters like motivation were not Forger's concern. He'd landed some new, deferential, and extremely wealthy clients—the "Billion-Dollar Round Table," he'd called them at the Board Room. True, Milbank hadn't handled a mammoth will contest in decades, since a battle over the estate of Hetty Green. True, too, it was almost impossible to overturn a will, at least unless the testator was either catatonic or in chains. And how likely was it that Shearman & Sterling, one of the city's most reputable law firms, had done something so fraudulent?

Ultimately, however, merit really didn't matter either. This was not one of those fender-bender cases in which lawyers keep a fraction of what they collect; no matter what, Milbank would make its fee. And that was no small thing; with reduced workloads from the Chase and the New York Stock Exchange, business in Milbank's litigation department had been drying up. Moreover, the case would surely generate priceless publicity for a firm anxious in a newly competitive legal marketplace to shed its stuffy nineteenth-century image, to drop its tweediness if not its Tweed.

XVIII

I n one sense, the fate of Seward's estate would rest with the lawyers
handling the case, the jury they selected, the judge presiding. In
another sense, however, it would be people like Cornelius Horn
and Iola Beneway, Abby Strong and Frederick Rollwagen, who would
be calling the shots. All had lived and died in obscurity decades earlier.
Neither Alex Forger nor most probate lawyers in New York had ever
heard of any of them. But all had wills that were challenged by disgruntled and disinherited relatives on the two most commonly cited
grounds: lack of testamentary capacity and undue influence. Cases bearing their names lived on in the law books of New York, and constituted
the rules by which will contests in the state were played.

If a single principle summarized the law of testamentary capacity, it
came from Mrs. Beneway, an eighty-five-year-old widow from Clav-
erack, New York. When she signed her last will in July 1945, her
hearing was gone, her arteries clogged. Her doctor said she was periodically confused and forgetful, senile even. Among the things she
had forgotten were that her own brother had died and that every December there was a holiday called "Christmas." When she left fifteen
thousand dollars to people unrelated to her and five dollars to each of
her nephews and nieces, the next of kin cried "incompetence." But
the court disagreed. "Mere old age, physical weakness and infirmity or
disease or failing memory are not necessarily inconsistent with testamentary capacity," the judge in the case wrote. "Nor," he continued,
"does senile dementia necessarily result in mental incapacity to make
a will; to accomplish that result, there must be such a failure of mind
as will deprive the testator of intelligent action." He concluded with
a phrase often cited in will contests, at least by proponents—that is,
those seeking to have a given will admitted into probate: "The law
looks with tender eyes on the will of an aged person, and in the absence
of the clearest and most convincing proof of invalidity, the courts will
uphold it."

Here was the first, and perhaps the most formidable, obstacle the

Johnson children faced. The common law made common sense. Last wills are generally the work of the elderly, and the elderly aren't always acute. Thus, the law of testamentary capacity consists largely of concessions to the sickness, quirkiness, weakness, forgetfulness, crankiness, listlessness, slovenliness, and childishness of the old. One needs less cognitive ability to sign a will than any other legal document; even someone who has been involuntarily institutionalized can be of sufficiently "sound mind and memory" to bequeath his belongings. Furthermore, swatches of incompetency either before or after a will is signed do not invalidate something executed in between; a single "lucid interval" suffices. Moreover, it matters little if the most erudite experts say someone could not possibly have been competent when eyewitnesses insist he was. "One intelligent and honest witness, testifying that [a testator] was understood and answered, may safely defy all of the learned treatises that can ever be written to show that he could not have been," one old opinion stated. It was an important point to keep in mind in cases in which the objectants to a will were wealthy enough to hire the most persuasive experts available.

Proving undue influence is an even more formidable undertaking. The law recognizes the strong, even extraordinary, hold one person can quite properly have on another, whether out of loyalty, love, gratitude, or consanguinity; only in the most extreme circumstances will any influence be deemed "undue"—only when that power, as one opinion stated, "amounted to a moral coercion, which restrained independent action and destroyed free agency, or which, by importunity which could not be resisted, constrained the testator to do that which was against his free will and desire." "Proof of undue influence," another New York case said, "must be of a substantial nature; it cannot be predicated on fancy, suspicion, or vague assumption."

Thus, it is easy to cry "undue influence!" and objectants invariably do; but only in the rarest of cases do they prevail. This is particularly so when it is a spouse doing the influencing; indeed, this is a point that has prompted unusual passion from those who make it. "The relation of husband and wife is too sacred in its nature, too closely intertwined with all the highest interests of social civilized life, to allow us to bring down their motives and actions to the standard that would exist between mere parties to a contract, or even to that of any other of the nearest relations," one judge wrote. "We are to bear in mind their mutual duty to love and to cherish, in sickness and in health, and the many records of noble devotion which attest how well, in helplessness and weakness, through watchings and through weariness, woman has proved herself the solace and succor of him to whom, in his hour of strength, she clung for support." And this judge was just warming up. A wife, he went on, "has a right to be the first in influence with her husband. Any other doctrine would forget 'the great vow, which did incorporate and make them one,' and would leave her a wife in name, but with limited and abridged attributes. The more truly that relationship is engrossing, the stronger should be, and will be, the influence of one with the other; and the companion of years, the sharer of affliction, the soother of sorrow, the one trusted and unwavering, is to be upheld in exercising, what she cannot but obtain and keep, greater influence, and better, than that of all the world besides."

Still, there are lengths to which, as another judge put it, "even a wife's influence cannot be allowed to go." Those few instances have invariably featured husbands who were aged, decrepit, vulnerable, and kept isolated from old friends by much younger, scheming wives, newly arrived on the scene, who thrust upon them wills that radically departed from previous instruments. Frederick Rollwagen, a butcher in New York City, was one such victim, and he and Seward had certain things in common. In 1871—precisely a century before Seward did likewise— Rollwagen quietly married his youthful housekeeper, Magdalena Herrman. He was sixty-four (twelve years Seward's junior), she was forty-two (eight years Basia's senior). Magdalena, like Basia, cared for her husband loyally but kept him apart from old associates; she, too, fired his trusted employees and built a lavish new home with his money. Unlike Basia, Magdalena selected the lawyer who drafted the fateful will, then purported to translate her husband's every grunt and groan into provisions that were invariably favorable to her. The court held that even in his debilitated state, Rollwagen had been competent. But his last will, it ruled, had been procured through undue influence. This was "not a case where husband and wife had lived together for years after a marriage prompted by mutual affection, which had been increased by years of tender care and a thousand acts of love and kindness, until the husband deemed no bounty he could bestow on his wife too great," the court held. Instead, it was "a case of a scheming woman marrying an old man broken in body and enfeebled in mind."

Milbank could find some solace in the decision, but not much: Rollwagen could barely talk when he got married, and had been married only briefly when he died. Sure, as Gregory Peck put it once, the Seward Johnsons were a "somewhat bizarre couple." But as a general matter, courts knew they had neither the competence nor the right to second-guess marriages, however kinky or unorthodox they might be. For instance, the mere fact that a husband was far older than his wife proved nothing. "A mere discrepancy, however gross, in the age of the spouses seems to me to tolerate no conclusion that there is an absence of affection between them or that one will necessarily overreach the other," one court ruled. "There are some sanctuaries where even the law cannot penetrate, and one is the heart of man or woman, no matter their ages, in and about their individual act of marriage. That it is more natural for the young to mate with the young all sensible people will agree, and that there is a certain lack of dignity in elderly marriages some will readily concede. But the law draws no harsh inferences from acts entirely lawful, no matter how lacking they may be when subjected to a test by the highest canons of good taste."

Thus, it was dubious that Milbank could knock out one will, let alone the long line of them Seward had signed over the years. Forger must have known from the outset that the children could never actually *win* their case; the object had to be settlement. But for that to work, Milbank needed a scorched-earth brand of litigator, someone who could make life so miserable for Basia and Nina that they would eventually have to surrender. The more wretched they could be made to be, the higher the price they'd pay. For this, Forger had his man, the man he'd turned to for several Onassis matters, whom he'd once dubbed "the patron saint of lost causes"—who, he once boasted, "could have gotten Adolf Eichmann off" if he'd taken the case. He had Ed Reilly.

The term "Wall Street litigator" is often an oxymoron. Rarely, if ever, are many "litigators" in New York's old-line law firms actually in a courtroom and on their feet. Mostly, they negotiate, threaten, file motions, take depositions. In this world it is not at all uncommon to find "trial lawyers" who've never tried a case, to whom juries are alien entities. That's why real trial lawyers—criminal-defense counsel, personal-injury practitioners, prosecutors—have always viewed their Wall Street counterparts as wimps, poseurs, paper pushers. And even by the minimal standards of the elite bar, Edward J. Reilly seemed like an unlikely litigator.

True, he had the looks. At fifty-five he resembled one of those idealized, Ivy-ish older men seen only in Brooks Brothers sketches: tall and robust, with a full head of silky silver hair and not an extra ounce of fat, equally at home in courts of law or squash. While Forger was elegant, aristocratic, Reilly was dashing. When one met him, though, he came across as something else altogether: timid, fragile, maybe even wounded. He spoke in a gentle and quietly melodic voice, one barely audible across a desk, let alone a courtroom. With his chivalric manners, his sweet little puppy-dog smile, his politeness, he seemed more minister than lawyer, presumably from some Episcopal congregation in Fairfield County, Connecticut. Even his signature was diffident; it was not the bold, aggressive, calculatedly indecipherable script of so many self-important people, but the gentle, cursive Palmer-method lines of an earnest schoolboy. Beneath all this, however, roiled a driven, tortured, angry man. Whatever might account for this trait—childhood adversity, a perpetual struggle to succeed, a problematic personal life—few knew, for few knew Reilly very well. But it helped explain the uncompromising way that he approached everything he did, be it combing his hair, keeping his crease, sailing his boat, or trying a case. Whatever toll they took on him personally, Reilly's demons made him a potent advocate. He was someone opposing lawyers rarely understood and invariably underestimated.

Reilly, like Johnson & Johnson, was born in New Brunswick, New Jersey, and, like Forger, had grown up in Westchester. His father, a first-generation Irish-American, worked for a bank; Edward was the youngest of the six children and the only son. Almost from the beginning, things had not been easy for him. His mother died when he was four. He stuttered. His father had a series of debilitating strokes. College was unaffordable without the G.I. Bill, and at seventeen, Reilly enlisted in the marines. The atmosphere of the corps, alien in many ways to a youth of his intellect and sensitivity, nurtured his instincts for self-discipline and perseverance. Reilly, whose only encounters with rifles had been in amusement parks, learned not just how to put together an M1, but to shoot one better than southern farm boys who'd been playing with firearms since childhood. By taking as many as nine courses a semester, all while working at a bank twenty-four hours a week, Reilly got through the University of Pennsylvania in three years. But despairing of a life whose bottom line was the bottom line, he abandoned thoughts of a business career and headed for Yale Law School instead.

Yale Law School in the early 1950s was filled with brilliant and ambitious students—the kind of place where, as one of Reilly's classmates later recalled, he'd spent his first evening listening to some Jewish boys from New York debate whose Phi Beta Kappa key contained the highest grade of gold. It was also a place filled with cocky and confident WASPs, sons of the Jazz Age, who rarely studied, played poker for five hundred dollars a pot, and, on weekends, drove their Buick roadsters to Vassar or Smith. In his pressed khakis and J. Press buttoned-down Oxfords, Reilly looked the part. But neither as scintillating nor as wealthy nor as self-assured as most of his classmates, he fell into no group comfortably. His friends tended to be other Irish Catholics, but when they played touch football or went out drinking, he rarely went along. He spent much of his time alone and much of that on school-work—driven, as one classmate surmised, "by the nagging thought that he was going to stumble, that he didn't have the natural ability." Sundays, he sometimes went to church.

Whatever time remained was spent making ends meet. Reilly kept the books at a Yale eating club, waited tables in the law school's dining room, taught economics at a nearby college, spent summers in the oil fields of West Texas. Still, he didn't always earn enough, and just as he couldn't pay his college fraternity bills until some friends bailed him out, he almost could not afford to return for his second year at Yale. Reilly was only an average student. His greatest triumph came during his third year, when he won a moot-court competition. Characteris-tically, it was his sincerity and passion, rather than his brilliance or flashiness, that proved persuasive. While studying for the New York bar exam, he literally stopped talking to his friends, even when he was with them.

In the rigidly hierarchical, credentials-conscious world of 1950s Wall Street, Reilly's record wasn't good enough for the most selective firms, and he'd gone to Milbank instead. As at Yale, he was careful, consci-entious, controlled, colorless—"a gimlet-eyed, very hardworking, no-sense-of-humor type," one peer put it. He still seemed ever on guard, lest he slip and fall. And he remained something of a grind, the kind of person who'd eat his tickets to the Yale-Penn game to work at the office. Impeccably neat, no hair ever out of place, Reilly rarely cracked jokes; only after a drink or two did he loosen up enough to laugh. Even then, there was something unnatural, almost stage-managed, about it. It was a laugh lifted off an unsynchronized sound track, a fraction of a second late and a little louder than it should have been. When he went into Milbank's "bullpen," the large, rectangular room where the firm stuck new associates, he was assigned corporate pension work. To the surprise of his peers, he soon switched into litigation. He discussed the move with no one, and when word of it spread, the guessing was that Milbank brass considered him too bullheaded and tightly strung to get along with corporate clients.

Milbank's record for promoting anyone whose ancestors came through Ellis Island rather than the Massachusetts Bay Colony was poor. It had named only one Catholic partner in its history, and begrudgingly at that. Further clouding Reilly's prospects was the second-class status of his department. Litigation, after all, was not what gentle-

man lawyers did. Whenever the need arose, the firm generally turned
to outsiders, usually Jews who'd set up their own practices a convenient
distance away. In the twenty years before Reilly got there, Milbank
had named just two litigation partners: A. Donald MacKinnon and
William Jackson. They were the only two litigation partners when Reilly
came to Milbank, and it was unclear whether the firm would name
another until one of them either retired or died.

Reilly, a trial-lawyer-to-be in search of a mentor, worked only occasionally for Jackson, son of the famous Supreme Court justice and
chief prosecutor at Nuremburg. (The stuffy younger Jackson was not
subtle about lineage. In his office was a portrait of the High Court when
his father sat there, along with the leather chair in which he'd actually
sat, perpetually covered with books lest someone defile it with his fanny.
Jackson's own public service consisted of heading the attorney disciplinary committee in Manhattan, a job for which he was selected only
because the man doing the selecting had a daughter whose middle name
was Jackson.) Bill Jackson preferred the more dignified and decorous
world of appellate work, something that did not interest Reilly. Instead,
he turned to MacKinnon. Here was a litigator from the old school: fast
on his feet, uncompromising, irascible, persistent, exacting, capable of
functioning without either a script in front of him or a phalanx of
younger lawyers at his rear. A ruddy Scotsman known to generations
of terrified Milbank associates as "the Bear," MacKinnon, who'd been
at the firm since 1923, had a near-religious devotion to his clients and
a deep-seated contempt for his adversaries. Taking their decision to sue
his client almost as a personal affront, he ridiculed or humiliated them
in any way he could—for instance, by butchering the names of their
lawyers. And if he was rude to opponents, he was brutal with underlings.
He shouted at them, belittled them, tore up motions he didn't like,
scolded them for the slightest imperfection. "What's this 'Dear' doing
in here?" he'd bark at someone who'd drafted a letter for him. Young
lawyers were either broken in or broken down by the apprenticeship.
Those who lasted learned how to try cases. They also came to think
that the only thing worse than losing was settling. Always, the objective
was complete capitulation.

Far from sparing the gentlemanly Reilly, MacKinnon heaped particular abuse on him. One lawyer recalled how the Bear would arrive in
his office around nine, send for Reilly, and immediately chew him out.
While absorbing one tirade, Reilly grew so enraged that he actually
bent the mechanical pencil in his hand. But true to his stoical nature,
he stuck things out. Along the way he met and married a member of

a wealthy and illustrious Chicago family. The union instantly enhanced
his status at the status-conscious firm. "With the engagement the aura
around him changed completely," one of Reilly's contemporaries said.
"All of a sudden, he was thought of as a person with prospects." When
Milbank opted to name a third litigation partner in 1965, he finally
got the nod.

Marriage further isolated Reilly, a man whose few close friendships
already tended to wither for lack of cultivation. He left New York for
a large ranch-style home in Greenwich. Over the next eighteen years
he practiced law in quiet obscurity, doing work for the Stock Exchange,
the Chase, or some Rockefeller interest. Rarely was he assigned anything
meaty, and he didn't always impress. "He couldn't ask simple, direct
questions," a lawyer who'd heard him argue in federal court later recalled. "I was almost embarrassed for him. I thought he had probably
never tried a case before." Still, he tackled every case as if the fate of
Western civilization depended on its outcome. To an almost eerie
degree, he re-created MacKinnon. A surge of testosterone seemed to
run through him when he walked into a courtroom. Litigation was war;
cases, causes. MacKinnon taught that fancy legal theories meant nothing without facts, and Reilly mastered every record he examined. He
became fanatically devoted to whomever he was representing. He demonized the opposition, and blew up if he caught associates fraternizing
with them. With Reilly the usual lawyerly code of camaraderie—that
knack, as Shakespeare said, to "strive mightily, but eat and drink as
friends"—went conspicuously unobserved. Joseph Alioto, the former
mayor of San Francisco, referred to him once as "my friend on the
other side of the table." "Mr. Alioto, you can call me anything you
want," Reilly retorted, "but please don't call me your 'friend.' "

More than once, Reilly charged his adversaries with unethical conduct, which was dirty pool in the collegial confines of civil litigation.
Always, the question was whether he did so out of conviction or for
tactical advantage, or whether, for him, this was a meaningless distinction. "Most people want to be omnipotent, and it's in the courtroom
that Reilly finds this feeling," a friend said. "When he thinks people
are cheating, it's not so much that they're violating the ethical code;
they're changing the only rules he can win by." Inevitably, opposing
counsel hated him; but if they'd complained to Alex Forger, they'd
have gotten nowhere. Forger knew what Reilly was doing and savored
it, even as he kept his distance. Far more often than not, his take-no-
prisoners tactics worked.

Occasionally, an interesting matter came along. In 1973 Reilly headed a team of Milbank lawyers challenging conditions in the state penitentiary at Parchman, Mississippi. He'd helped David Young, the onetime Milbank associate who went on to become one of Richard Nixon's "Plumbers," escape Watergate with his law license. He had a piece of the litigation arising out of the Iranian hostage crisis and defended a Roosevelt in a palimony case brought by a former Playboy bunny. And while Forger held Jacqueline Onassis's hand, Ed Reilly did her heavy lifting. He successfully argued the Christian Dior look-alike case as well as the suit against Ron Galella, besting Marvin Mitchelson. (Mitchelson, self-promoting and bombastic, represented everything Reilly loathed, and he treated the Californian with MacKinnon-like contempt, referring to him once as "Mr. Michaelson.") Jackie was much indebted to, if not in awe of, him. Once, when Reilly had brought her a draft of a document to review, she said that "marking this up would be like changing the Gettysburg Address." Another time, as she watched him in court, she turned to a Milbank paralegal. "Mr. Reilly never loses a case, does he!" she asked. After he won her case, she presented him with an inscribed volume of Yeats. "To Ed, whose words also have the power to move," she wrote.

After so many years spent on scarcely watched, intramural commercial squabbles, Reilly basked in the high wattage Jackie generated. But such cases remained the exception. Moreover, they were, at least legally speaking, insignificant. Tactically, too, they offered only limited satisfaction. In each Onassis matter, he had argued the sympathetic cause of a sympathetic client before a sympathetic judge. On the eve of the Johnson case, anyone pulling Reilly's clippings from a newspaper morgue or punching his name into a computer came up with next to nothing. Shy and self-effacing, Reilly actually promoted his own obscurity. He left his name off briefs. In his most triumphant moments he let colleagues or underlings take the credit. When he represented Jackie, Simon Rifkind fetched her in a limousine and came by the front door of her apartment building, where he was sure to encounter a flock of reporters; Reilly picked her up at the service entrance in a Milbank station wagon, and secreted her into the courthouse through the basement.

This was not just a matter of Reilly's reticence or Jackie's privacy. Steeped in, wedded to, an ethic that those lawyers are best who are seen least, Reilly hated all of the attention suddenly being heaped on the legal profession, especially the self-generated kind. Even yellow legal pads or notepaper bearing the firm's name annoyed him. The same went for pencils: DIXON TICONDEROGA was okay; MILBANK, TWEED, HAD-

LEY & MCCLOY was not. He'd posed for the group portrait of partners that accompanied a story Milbank had planted about itself in *Manhattan, inc.* magazine, but he'd worn an indignant, almost pained expression; when the article appeared, he was furious. In a more decorous age, he grumbled, law firms had been disciplined for puffery far less flagrant.

Among his peers Reilly was considered rigid, uncompromising, volatile—a "handle with care" personality to one, "a controlled inferno," to another. "Reilly never talks to people; he argues cases," one of his partners said. When changes came to the firm—when Milbank stopped paying partners strictly by seniority and began factoring in the business they generated, for instance, or started firing partners, he was invariably, and vocally, opposed; it offended his sense of collegiality, loyalty, and tradition. While others deviated into striped and colored shirts, Reilly stuck with white. He wore his suits as he had his dress grays, forever tugging at the legs to maintain a perfect crease, sending them out for pressing as soon as he checked into a hotel. At work, he would never remove his suit coat or loosen his invariably conservative necktie, whose motif was sailboats or teddy bears or crests, depending on whether he was to be in court that day. Reilly was one of those people who looked almost silly in casual wear. By sheer act of will the child stutterer came to speak with the same crisp precision with which he dressed. His sentences came out as prose; only rarely would he fall back upon the usual linguistic rest notes everyone else used. Through similar acts of discipline, Reilly, who'd once smoked three packs of L&Ms a day, quit on the spot one New Year's, then, on successive Januarys, quit drinking and eating desserts as well. Though a closet chocoholic, he always kept trim. Overweight people offended him; anyone who couldn't control his appetite couldn't be trusted, he felt.

Reilly was, as one junior lawyer put it, "absolutely manic about imperfections." Once, a young Milbank lawyer asked him to sign a routine pleading in another partner's case. Reilly took the paper, held it up to the light, and disgustedly handed it back, unsigned. "You can't use that; there's an erasure on it," he declared. The associate had it retyped and brought it back. "This is still wrong," Reilly admonished. "You've written 'New York, New York.' You can't write out the state. It has to be abbreviated." The associate had the paper done again, but by this point he'd learned his lesson; he handed it to another partner, who signed without even looking at it. Anything typed for Reilly, including drafts, had to contain a precise number of lines per page and his own distinct margins, both different from the Milbank norm. He liked papers stapled diagonally (the better to flip pages) and would return documents that weren't. And were a staple removed, its replacement had to go in precisely the same holes. He hated misplaced commas, footnotes of any kind, and words like "clearly" and "obviously." When an associate transgressed, the dressings-down he got from Reilly were not explosive, as MacKinnon's had been. Reilly didn't erupt so much as smolder; his pinkish complexion would deepen, he would sit up even more erect than usual, purse his lips, stare at you with his unblinking, sharklike eyes, and land.

Reilly's compulsiveness grew as Milbank came to occupy an increasingly large part in his life. A particularly painful divorce and the departure to college of his son, an only child, left him more isolated than ever. Always drunk on work, Reilly functioned on an ever-emptier stomach. He never seemed to leave the office; weekends, he could be seen hunched over papers from cases months away from trial. When Milbank decided to redesign its offices, Reilly, with his devotion to the firm and his attention to detail, was the logical choice to supervise the project. He tackled it with zeal, spending hundreds of hours selecting and inspecting materials, working with architects, contacting contractors.

So it was that Reilly, a man far too prickly ever to lead Milbank, nonetheless cast it in his image: lean, uncluttered, understated, uncompromising. For Reilly, even the most mundane accoutrements made philosophical statements. Associates were given no filing cabinets; whatever they were working on should be on their desks, and the rest could go to central storage (as a result, associates' offices invariably had piles of paper on the floor). There was no clock in the Milbank library, lest lawyers grow too conscious of the time (Milbank associates without wristwatches brought travel clocks with them, or asked the reference librarian). He set aside inadequate space for administrators, hoping, perhaps, that this new breed of apparatchik would go away. Even after the project was complete, Reilly remained Milbank's conscience, or Comstock. He decreed that offices were to be painted only certain colors, have only certain kinds of venetian blinds, have the same sorts of plants in the same types of pots. He patrolled the corridors, making sure the doors, made of English brown oak, swung properly on their hinges, that the ledges by the secretarial pools weren't messy, that any coffee taken from the cafeteria be in lidded containers inside paper bags. The smallest deviations—coatracks or desk lamps—caused conniptions. "I don't want to take it too far, but he had some of the same

ardor for the task that Basia Johnson did," one of his partners remarked.
What he meant was that the Milbank renovation was Ed Reilly's Jasna
Polana.

When he finally left his office, Reilly took the train to Greenwich,
picking up his Mercedes 350SE at the station, perhaps stopping at the
Grand Union to buy some frozen food for a microwaved dinner. He
lived alone in the large ranch house he once shared with his family,
and though he had a decorator fix it up, it had a forlorn, static quality
to it, like a winter home on the Fourth of July. Even the inside of his
refrigerator was austere, a bare light bulb shining on the bottles of
imported beer and splits of champagne he served to guests and the
Perrier he kept for himself. In the basement he'd set up a shop for
woodworking, a hobby he liked because it required enough concentration to get his mind off law. Around the back was a pond, complete
with ducks and geese. It took only one visit to Reilly's office, where
there was a brass duck on the desk, a duck ashtray, copies of *Ducks
Unlimited* magazine on the coffee table, and, on the wall, a drawing by
some artist of the Wild Turkey School, to realize his devotion to these
creatures. He watched them for hours as they taught their young to fly;
he might tell you that Canadian geese are among the only species besides
man that marry for life, and there was a certain sadness, almost envy,
in him as he said so. He tended to his birds devotedly, straining his
back every spring and fall carrying sacks of cracked corn from the feed
store. Come winter, he showed the same concern Holden Caulfield felt
for the ducks on the Central Park lagoon. One year, as winter loomed,
he discovered a duck with broken wings, who, he feared, would be
unable to fly away before the water around it froze. He'd promptly gone
out and bought a water heater, much like the one he kept around his
boat all winter, and installed it near the helpless creature.

Reilly had few other diversions. His friends and colleagues were
forever trying to fix him up, and he dated often, usually women considerably younger than he, usually not for very long. He had had season
tickets to the New York Giants dating back to the days of Y. A. Tittle,
but made games only occasionally. Even when the firm had its annual
outing, Reilly would often stay behind; someone, he explained, should
be around in case a needy client called. A friend told of getting up to
urinate in the wee-wee hours one morning, wondering suddenly whether
Reilly could possibly be at his desk, placing a call to Milbank, and
hearing Reilly say "hello." This "life of Reilly" was one he neither
savored nor recommended. Even as he was working them to death,
Reilly would chide young colleagues for toiling nights or weekends,

when, he told them, they should have been home with their families.

Around Milbank Reilly had a reputation as a Johnny-one-note, a lawyer who could handle only a single case at a time. When his good friend Forger told him about the Johnsons, Reilly was about to leave for London on behalf of the International Tennis Federation. But taking on a second case didn't faze Reilly nearly as much as the kind of case it was. He knew that most will contests are "strike suits"—that is, attempts by disgruntled (and often remote) heirs to gain by coercion what they'd been denied by bequest. Reilly was skeptical. He needed to know much more, and he'd have to learn it by August 10, the deadline Judge Roth had set for filing objections. The children were informed of that deadline both by mail and, in some instances, in person; Jay Gunther, Nina's Shearman & Sterling colleague, visited the Richards residence on Gin Lane in Southhampton and served Mary Lea herself with the court papers. On the affidavit of service he listed her age as "over 50" and her weight as "over 150." Gunther had always been a gentleman.

XIX

In mid-July 1983 Reilly, along with Forger and Brinck, flew to Florida
to interview several key witnesses and get a feel for the case. First
on their list was Dr. Schilling. As expected, he told them that the
Seward he knew had been mentally competent until the end, and, as
he put it, no more susceptible to undue influence in April 1983 than
he had been in April 1933. But Schilling couldn't say whether Seward
had been able to read a magazine or understand a television program,
and seemed surprisingly blasé about the affidavit he'd signed; all that
he could recall was that some "female attorney" whose name he couldn't
remember had asked him to sign it sometime between the tenth and
the fifteenth of April. Schilling struck Reilly as blustery, irritable, inarticulate, and argumentative, taking any questions about his work as
personal affronts. Now was the time for charming the doctor, and Reilly
made a point of telling Schilling how handsome his children were and
how they'd clearly gotten their good looks from their dad. But he quickly
concluded that once on the stand, with the proper prodding, Schilling
could be undone.

If Schilling made the case more appetizing to Reilly, dinner with
Keith and Elaine Wold brought further nourishment. As Elaine remained characteristically mute, Keith offered the Milbank lawyers a
tasty description of the Johnsons' life together—a life, he neglected to
say, to which he'd only occasionally been privy. He spoke of how simply
Seward had lived before Basia came along, described Jasna Polana's
lavishness, recalled how Basia had very nearly bought out an entire
antique store next to Maine Chance, and owned so many outfits that
she had installed one of those moving dry cleaners' racks in her closet.
He depicted Nina Zagat as more Basia's puppy and puppet than Seward's
lawyer. He said Seward was well en route to senility by the Knights of
Malta dinner, and how a saner Seward had told him twenty-five years
earlier that he planned to leave everything to his descendants. Reilly
did not know Wold had scarcely seen Seward during the last ten years
of his life. Nor did he think it odd that Wold was so much more exercised

about things than Seward's own daughter. Intent upon making a case for his new clients, he was looking less for holes than for openings.

The next day the Milbank lawyers bought lunch in Vero Beach for Bonnie Weisser, the chief nurse at the Fort Pierce house. They detected in her some residual loyalty to Basia and sensed she would probably say Seward had been competent on April 14, when she happened to have been on duty. But here, too, her tenor changed when she was asked specifics. Though Seward could read a little, she said, it was only with great effort. He struggled manfully to maintain an appearance of normalcy, particularly when Schilling was around. Seward's greatest loves were Junior and Harbor Branch; it was "inconceivable" to her that he'd have omitted the foundation from his will. Basia had run the Fort Pierce house with an iron hand, with everyone, including Peach and her brother, doing exactly what she said.

Reilly was eliciting information. But he was also proselytizing. Gently, subtly, he was prodding Weisser to rethink her thoughts. Could Seward have divided fifty-six by eight? Did he do anything a four-year-old couldn't do? Ultimately, what Reilly was really doing was recruiting, and with the same soft-spoken, ultracourtly supersincerity he extended to most women. Reilly made women, even women far younger than he, want to mother him. Weisser discovered she not only liked Reilly, but found him positively intriguing. So solicitous had he been that afterward Fran Cioffi, Weisser's friend and the nurse on duty when Seward died, teased her about it. Damn it, girl, that ole Ed Reilly has a crush on you!

Reilly talked next to John Peach. Peach was still working at Harbor Branch, but his days there were numbered: Junior hadn't forgiven him for extracting a raise as Seward lay dying, particularly under what he believed to be the false pretense of another job. (There was some evidence to support this: Questioned by Milbank, the widow of the man who'd supposedly made the offer called Peach a "snake oil salesman.") Junior planned to can Peach, but only after the Milbank lawyers had pumped him for whatever he was worth. Predictably, Peach, too, vouched for Seward's competence. Reilly listened, sizing up how he'd look on the stand. There was something about Peach—the way he blurted out his answers, the fact he never made eye contact, his weak mouth and chin—that convinced Reilly a jury would find him untrustworthy. After about an hour the meeting came to an abrupt end. It was crawfish season, and Peach was anxious to go out and catch himself a few. A few days, and a few crawfish, later, Junior fired him.

Quickly, the war of nerves intensified. On August 5, John Stroc-

zynski, Jasna Polana's superintendent, asked Junior to return the flatbed
truck he'd borrowed. Around the same time, Basia and Nina paid an
unexpected visit to Harbor Branch to scoop up Seward's papers. Four
days later Junior barred Peach from Harbor Branch property except
when heading to Basia's house. Even then, he insisted, Peach had to
be escorted to and fro, and promise to indemnify the foundation for
any injuries he sustained along the way. ("He might conveniently break
his leg on the way or something else that would embroil us in something," Junior speculated.) Basia's property, Junior feared, could become
a staging ground for something sinister, Harbor Branch's own Guan-
tánamo Bay. A twenty-four-hour guard was suddenly installed at the
foundation's main entrance; all electronic gate openers held by Basia's
employees were confiscated. By September Basia had to sue Harbor
Branch to regain unrestricted access to her own property. And Peach
sued Harbor Branch for breach of contract.

As the fact-finding proceeded, Forger, as was his wont, receded into
the background—watching, calculating, reporting to the clients, holding their hands. His ultimate goal remained settlement; it was just a
question of when and for how much. But settlement went against
Reilly's grain, and with every additional interview, every disclosure, he
became more convinced he could win. He brought two young Milbank
litigators into the case: Charles Berry, a clean-cut, straight-arrow Yalie
who'd soon be up for partnership, and Paul Shoemaker, a dark and
dour sort from Harvard who was a year Berry's junior. The staffing was
lean—for Reilly, characteristically so. As a unit, the Milbank men were
strait-laced, determined, grim, as crusaders were supposed to be. They
were also all business, even among themselves. Three years into the
case and eight years into their association, Berry still wasn't sure how
many children Reilly had.

Over the next few months the trio interviewed those who'd known
Seward before Basia had come along: Philip Hofmann, the onetime
president of J&J; Seward's old lawyer, Robert Myers; two of his secretaries, Fran Perree and Joan Kelsey. The picture that emerged was of
a gentle, simple, suggestible, and maybe bullyable man. From Jasna
Polana alumni they collected a sampling of Basia's temper tantrums,
all of which, they hoped, could add up to an undue-influence case. But
their best sources remained the Johnsons, or, more accurately, the
Johnson spouses. In and of themselves, they provided evidence of Seward's susceptibility to undue influence, though hardly of a sort Reilly
could ever use; in the uncanny way that each of them utterly dominated
one of Seward's children, they suggested Seward had had that trait to

transmit. In one twist or turn of the family's DNA, it was ordained
that the Johnsons' dominant trait was recessiveness.

Jennifer and Jimmy contributed little, some of that counterproductive. They conceded Seward had never been terribly family-oriented,
rarely discussed finances with them, and had had a series of affairs before
Basia came along. In some ways, they added, Basia had been very nice
to their father. It was quickly apparent that Jimmy didn't want to be
in the case in the first place and was going along—why else?—in part
because his wife wanted him to. It was Gretchen, after all, who told
the Milbank lawyers that Basia was "incredibly ruthless" and "unattractive" and had "controlled things with a viselike grip."

When the lawyers sat down with the Richardses, Mary Lea occasionally burbled something, but it was Marty who did most of the
talking. In his breathless, rapid-fire, gossipy way, he ladled out generous
helpings of exaggerations and embellishments. Seward, he said, had
been a prisoner in his own home. Basia was forever foisting papers on
him and forcing him to sign them; "Seward would have signed the
Magna Carta if you'd given it to him," Richards declared. Marty actually
had been nowhere near Princeton when Seward had had his testicles
removed in 1981; in an amazing mneumonic feat he recalled Basia
railing in the hospital lobby that Seward had yet to sign his will (in
fact, he had signed it prior to his admission). Richards talked ominously
of a Swiss bank account the Johnsons kept; indeed they did, though it
never had more than fifty thousand dollars or so in it. Basia thought
herself a Medici, he said, and Nina was a glorified gofer, a lawyer who
occasionally did housework for Basia. Marty knew of Basia's altercation
with Nina over the chapel in the fall of 1982, but his understanding
of the episode was far more dramatic than anything about it heard up
until that point: Six weeks before the will was signed, he told the
Milbank lawyers, Basia actually had fired Nina. But Nina had been
reinstated immediately, Marty went on, because it had suddenly dawned
on Basia that she knew where all the bodies were buried. This was
powerful stuff, particularly since there was no one around to contradict
any of it or to consider it with the skepticism it deserved.

Before the Johnsons could prosecute their case, however, they had
to crush an insurrection in their own ranks—from Mary Lea's children.
The Ryans had caught wind of the impending will contest quickly,
even before the first rains had fallen atop their Pop-Pop's new crypt.
Shortly after his funeral, as their plane back north lifted off, Marty
Richards spilled the beans. "Whatever the will is, we're going to protest
it," he said. "There's no way it's going to be fair. I'm sure she's gotten

everything." Now the contest was taking shape, and the question had become who was going to get whatever the Johnson family could keep Basia from getting. Mary Lea assured her children that whatever spoils she collected would go to them. But the Ryans knew all about their mother and money, and they did not believe her.

Actually, the Ryan children had nothing against Basia, who'd always been decent enough to them and, as far as they could tell, to their grandfather, too. Conversely, they had little contact or respect for their mother's family. Most of them barely knew Uncle Junior, for instance, and the Ryan who knew him best, Eric, once described him as "incompetence and boobery personified." But neither the will's probable legitimacy nor gratitude to Basia nor distaste for their kith and kin was about to deter the Ryans, most of whom were broke, from a crack at Seward's fortune. Sure, all stood to become millionaires in 1997, when the trusts Seward had set up for them were due to dissolve. Some money could come their way sooner if their ever-sickly mother died. But increasingly, that money looked earmarked for Marty, who continued to kill Mary Lea with kindness and keep her off-limits to them. "Richards's friends continually sought to isolate Mom from the rest of us," Hillary Ryan later charged. "They were mostly homosexuals. When we did visit Mom, we were either put in a hotel or in the guesthouse, where two gay lovers were living."

The Ryans were thwarted at every turn. Mary Lea blocked her eldest son, Eric, from attending the meeting at the Metropolitan Club. Eric's call to Uncle Junior went unreturned. So the Ryans did what came most naturally whenever anything or anyone stood between the Johnsons and Johnson money: they got themselves some lawyers. In early June three of them—Seward and Quentin Ryan and their sister, Alice Ryan Marriott—hired William Roos of New York. Hillary Ryan turned to another New York lawyer named John Tommaney, who promptly brought in Millard Midonick, a former surrogate in Manhattan who had just joined the famous Manhattan firm of Willkie, Farr & Gallagher. Shortly thereafter, the six Ryans and their three lawyers held the small-fry version of the Metropolitan Club summit in a Willkie conference room, only a few flights above Nina's quarters at Shearman & Sterling.

The children, already factionalized, promptly splintered ever further. The hardest-liner was Hillary, who wanted to enter the contest aggressively. The wiliest—and, therefore, most skittish—was Eric, apparently reasoning, then as later, that the surest route to his mother's millions lay in feigning blind loyalty to her. The rest were somewhere in between. Midonick told them their case was weak; they were not named in any of Seward's wills, and unlike Seward's children, they had no automatic right to object. Entering the contest on their own was probably a mistake, he warned, since it could antagonize Mary Lea and drive her still more firmly into the nefarious Marty's clutches. Their best, and perhaps only, bet was to stick with their mother and press her to renounce, or pass along, whatever she collected. Midonick was given a retainer and told to keep his eye on things. It was only a few thousand dollars, but it would be large enough to preclude Willkie from representing Basia and Nina and collecting the millions in fees their case could generate.

Both Tommaney and Roos spoke with the Milbank lawyers about renouncement. But if Forger, Reilly, and Brinck were heartened by what they'd learned in Florida, they weren't sharing their good news with everyone. Whatever encouragement it was giving its clients, for the purposes of getting rid of the Ryans Milbank became the picture of pessimism. Brinck "feels they probably will not be able to make a strong case on incompetency," Roos, a nervous type and a compulsive composer of memoranda to file, wrote the next day. "Although some family members feel Mr. Johnson had lacked testamentary capacity for many years, from talking to his doctors and others it seems he was able to understand what was going on around him, although at the end he was a very tired man. As to undue influence, again Mr. Johnson seems to have been very weary at the end, and perhaps had passed beyond caring what would become of his $400,000,000, but of course more would be required to establish a case of undue influence. Brinck pointed out that at the end Barbara seems to have been frantically attempting to prolong Mr. Johnson's life, and seemed to have been truly devoted to him. Although she did seem to have disagreements with the nurses and the doctors, her major concern seemed to be that Mr. Johnson be made as comfortable as possible."

Marty Richards's degrading description of Nina's duties quickly took on a life of its own; with each retelling, her posture became more servile. Brinck, Roos related, "said there seemed to be an almost 'unnatural relationship' between Nina and the Johnsons. Nina was seen to do menial tasks around the house, mopping the floors when asked to do so by Barbara, and cleaning out the bathrooms. She seemed to act more as a social secretary than as legal counsel." But, Roos went on, "Brinck emphasized that based upon the present evidence, Milbank does not believe that there is a good case, even on the undue influence ground, except perhaps with respect to the most recent wills. Thus,

being completely realistic, Brinck presently feels there is really no
chance of successfully contesting all the wills prepared for Mr. Johnson
by Shearman & Sterling."

But all this was down the road. Brinck made it clear to Roos that
for the time being, Mary Lea was disinclined to renounce a dime, and
wanted her offspring to butt out of whatever eventuated. Mary Lea, it
seemed, wasn't the only Johnson leaning on her children to stay away
from the case; according to Brinck, so were the Firestones, Wolds, and
Junior—ostensibly to protect Seward's good name. "The Wolds especially were anxious not to see information about the decedent and his
lifestyle falling into the public domain, and the less attorneys involved
in the matter, the better," Roos wrote. "Brinck said the Wolds 'really
stepped on their kids' to see to it that they would take no independent
action. I have the distinct feeling that there has been some sort of
verbal pact or understanding entered into between the decedent's children that each will see to it that grandchildren do not get into the act.

"Mrs. Richards additionally complained at length about feeling uncomfortable—[Brinck] emphasized 'very uncomfortable'—in that she
knows her children presently will receive no economic benefits with
respect to their grandfather's assets until the time that she herself dies,"
Roos went on. "He said she spoke of feeling she constantly has 'six
pairs of eyes upon her.' Consequently, although she does not wish to
see her children take an independent active role in the contest, she is
hopeful that some funds will be forthcoming from the contest which
could then be passed on to the grandchildren presently. I asked Brinck
if Mrs. Richards understood that, this being her goal, there could be
real tax benefits to be derived from direct participation by her children.
Brinck said that he and Mr. Forger had gone to great pains to see to
it that Mrs. Richards understood the estate and gift tax aspects of the
situation; he said it didn't change her mind in the least.

"In short," continued Roos's recapitulation, "Mrs. Richards feels her
children are preoccupied with the topic of money, particularly her
money." Brinck warned that "drastic consequences" could ensue for
the Ryans if they proceeded. Roos tried to find a legal leg for his clients
to stand on, but without success. Thus, the Ryans ended up in the
worst possible situation: They collected nothing under the will, could
not join the will contest, and, since their improvident mother would
undoubtedly dip into her trust to pay the legal bills, would effectively
subsidize a court battle in which they would have no say and from which
they were unlikely to collect anything.

With threats and prophesies of doom the Milbank lawyers were able

to drive away Mary Lea's meddlesome children. But in August, when
Forger and his colleagues met with their paying Johnson clients in
Nantucket, they must have painted a far rosier picture, for Seward's
children told them to proceed. On August 5 Milbank asked that the
deadline for contesting the will be pushed back to September 30. Two
days later it requested a similar extension for Harbor Branch, which,
as a claimant under the penultimate will, actually had a stronger case.
On August 24 Shearman & Sterling asked Judge Roth to release some
money from the estate to pay Jasna Polana's bills; keeping the place in
shape, and protecting a $50 million art collection, cost $1,007,806 for
the first half of 1983 alone. Forger resisted the request, providing yet
another sign that a will contest loomed. Nina's colleagues in Shearman
& Sterling's probate department set up a pool over just who would
challenge the will and when.

As the deadline approached, only Basia remained convinced a will
contest would never happen. But on September 30, as she gave a
luncheon at Jasna Polana, a Milbank messenger arrived at Shearman
& Sterling with a three-page document and six pages of attachments.
In it the Johnson children announced they were objecting to the probate
of "that certain instrument dated the 14th of April, 1983 propounded
herein as the Last Will and Testament of J. Seward Johnson" on three
grounds: first, that their father lacked the capacity to make a will;
second, that the will had been procured "by fraud, duress and undue
influence" on the part of Seward Johnson's widow "and some other
person or persons who acted in concert with her or independently or
both"; and third, that the document had not been executed properly—
that is, that Seward had not actually signed it in the presence of the
Shearman & Sterling lawyers. The children demanded a jury trial on
the matter. All but Diana Firestone—who was in Europe at the time—
signed affidavits claiming they believed their charges to be true.

A few weeks earlier Brinck had told Roos that Harbor Branch might
contest the will even more aggressively than the Johnson children; in
fact, its filing deadline quietly came and went. Harbor Branch need
knock out only the final will to collect something, but that would have
netted nothing for the Johnson children and, since it would greatly
simplify the case, far less in fees for Milbank. Milbank had two horses
in this race; clearly, it was betting on the children, who would require
that much more in services precisely because their case was so much
weaker.

If Basia was bothered by all the legal maneuvering, she didn't let
on. Following her brief recuperation in the Bahamas, she went on a

European spending spree. It was, perhaps, her way of saying "don't fence me in!" to everyone, particularly Nina, who had urged against any major expenditures while Seward's estate remained in limbo and who, as an executor and trustee, had to ensure both that Basia not spend any money from the estate, nor deplete the war chest she had created for her. It was also a sign of a change some people began detecting in Basia. Seward had always kept her reasonably humble; with him gone, she began taking herself more seriously, to think of herself more as a grande dame. Her relationship with Nina also changed. "Nina was a very good friend to Basia, but she was also a nanny," a friend said. "And she might have thought, 'Now that Daddy is dead, I don't need a nanny.'"

At Christie's sale in Kent, England, on July 6, Basia spent $23,284 for a pair of petit-point George I cushions. Two days later, at Sotheby's, Basia, in the words of *Art & Auction,* "tenaciously outbid" the representative of the combined French museums and spent $1.535 million on a Louis XVI cabinet that once sat in Versailles—the highest price ever paid at auction for a piece of furniture. Basia started out with nineteenth-century paintings and "got taken," a dealer told *Art & Antiques* magazine—overlooking, perhaps, some of the Johnsons' early bargains. "So she got rid of those and made a collection of old masters that she bought in London, and she got taken again. So when she found out that they weren't what they were supposed to be, she sold them at auction and started all over again with French furniture. And this time she learned all about it before she bought, and got good advice, and developed an eye."

The English grew curious about this mysterious Polish-American woman with the deep pockets, and it wasn't long before *The London Times*'s antiques correspondent, Geraldine Norman, asked for an interview. Nina gave Basia her own version of a Miranda warning: Whatever she told the press could be used against her. But Harry Ward Bailey and Adrian Ward Jackson, two of the socialite art dealers with whom Basia had become particularly friendly, convinced her it was time to go public; a serious article about her, they said, could only help her case. Basia agreed, with one precondition: no photographs, please. "I don't want people to recognize me when I go around," she told Norman. "I have many enemies. I think they envy me."

In "The Fine Art of Marrying Well: A Treasure House Built On Johnson's Baby Powder," Norman described Basia as "unostentatious," despite her taste for nice clothes and fine things. "Her soft brown hair has been simply dressed by a top hairdresser," she wrote. "She appears much younger than her years, sensuous and vital, with a stocky Polish build. It is not difficult to understand why Mr. Johnson fell for her. Her eyes sparkle with pleasure and amusement as she tells the amazing story of her romance." Largely in Basia's own words, the writer recounted that story, beginning with the young Pole's entry into the Johnson household. " 'Mrs. Johnson liked me immediately,' she says, somehow managing to pronounce the name in just that way that a servant refers to her mistress," Norman wrote. "That was the reigning Mrs. Johnson, whose place she was to take.

"But a life of domestic drudgery was not what she had in mind for herself," Norman continued, noting Basia's decision to quit the Johnsons, followed by Seward's extraordinary summons. "I came not knowing what is going on," Basia told her. "He said 'I fall in love with you when you were in our house working.' " Basia shrugged her shoulders, smiled, and continued. "I never expect it because we could hardly talk to each other," she told Norman. But as Basia explained it, neither chemistry nor electricity knew any language barriers, and before long she was learning how to dive, buying Mondrians and Monets, and building a "pillared and porticoed Palladian villa" in New Jersey. All that, Basia lamented, was now on hold pending the outcome of the will contest. "I had made friends with all of them," Basia said of her stepchildren. "Now I can spend nothing until the legal actions have been settled." But " 'Nothing' on Mrs. Johnson's lips is a relative term," Norman wrote, noting how Basia had just commissioned an English foundry to cast a bell for Jasna Polana's new chapel.

"Basia Johnson looks on her inheritance as enormous fun, but also, she says, as a sacred trust to the memory of her husband," the article continued. " 'I know my husband's dreams,' she says. 'That is why he wanted to leave it all to me.' " There ended the published version of the Norman piece. Cut for reasons of space was Norman's last sentence, which was, in some ways, her most prescient. "It remains to be seen whether the children's challenge to the will makes any headway," she wrote. "But Basia does not look as if she is at all worried."

Indeed, Basia informed all and sundry, in America as well as England, that she was unconcerned—and uncompromising. "I'm fighting until the end," she told some guests at Jasna Polana in late October. "I'm not going to give them the dust off half a penny."

XX

The preliminary skirmishing was over, and the will contest was sort of under way. No one could predict how far it would go, or what the net result would be. But some were already convinced the children's cause was hopeless, as Mayor Lindsay discovered at the December 1983 meeting of Mary Lea's trustees. He came, as was customary, cup in hand—this time, though, carrying bills from Milbank Tweed rather than from some interior decorator. He got a frosty reception. "Mr. Lindsay was advised by the Trustees that they were not in a position to approve payment of the Milbank Tweed statements because they did not have sufficient information," the minutes state. "They [the trustees] questioned the open-end [sic] nature and advisibility of any commitment to agree to underwrite Mary Lea Johnson's expenses in connection with this litigation. They also raised the basic question of how Mary Lea Johnson stood to benefit from it. Mr. Lindsay was frank to concede he really did not have the answers to these questions. He agreed to look into the matter further."

In the meantime Basia and Nina needed legal representation. Shearman & Sterling was handling most of the estate-related matters, and Werner Polak, who was monitoring the will contest for the firm, thought it would hold off for a time on hiring outside counsel. Others felt the firm needed them immediately, particularly as the dimensions of its problem became clear. Finally, belatedly, the firm's brass had learned just how much Nina stood to make from the Johnson estate, and they were horrified. The realization quickly spread that the firm had a colossal legal, or at least a colossal public-relations, problem on its hands. Rather than admit he'd misled them in May, when he said that Nina stood to collect only $1 million as executor, Ford tried blaming her instead. "She blew one past me," he said. Now, though, was no time for pointing fingers. One way or another, Shearman & Sterling was in a fix, and needed some good lawyers to get out of it.

The firm began drawing up a list of candidates: Arthur Liman and Bernard Greene of Paul, Weiss, Rifkind, Wharton & Garrison; Theodore Kurz of Debevoise & Plimpton; Thomas McGrath of Simpson, Thacher & Bartlett; Ira Lustgarten of Willkie, Farr & Gallagher; Joseph Kartiganer, then of White & Case; William Zabel of Schulte, Roth & Zabel; Philip Hirsch of Proskauer, Rose, Goetz & Mendelsohn; and Donald Christ of Sullivan & Cromwell. Ford had another suggestion. "What's that guy's name who used to be a judge and tries a lot of negligence cases? Maybe that's what we need." he remarked one day, referring to Jacob Fuchsberg, the personal-injury lawyer who'd won New York's first million-dollar verdict. But Ford wasn't being serious; Shearman & Sterling would choose counsel the way John Peach picked priests: by the address. Aggressive street-smarts were not high on the list of attributes S&S was seeking. It wanted a firm that would take care of things quietly, some gentlemanly lawyers for some gentlemanly lawyer-clients. In short, it wanted one of its own.

Quickly, the list was whittled down. Kurz had just become managing partner at his firm and withdrew from consideration. Lustgarten couldn't have taken the case once his colleague, Judge Midonick, had been retained by the Ryan children. Besides, when it came right down to it, Ford felt there were only two great litigating firms in all of New York—Sullivan & Cromwell and Paul Weiss—and he preferred the first. S&C was perhaps the most famous and respected law firm in the country. Further, Shearman & Sterling had used it before and been pleased with the results. Moreover, S&C had Donald Christ. Unlike the others, Christ (it rhymes with "wrist") couldn't be pigeonholed as either a litigator or an estates lawyer; he had been both. He worked in the firm's estates group and had headed the City Bar Association's section on probate law for three years, but he'd been raised as a litigator and was said to know his way around a courtroom. A few years earlier Christ had greatly impressed Ford with his handling of the contested estate of Charles Lachman, the cofounder of Revlon. Christ, then, could play the role of either Alex Forger, hand-holder extraordinaire, or Ed Reilly, or both. To Ford, Christ had the perfect personality for the Johnson case—tough but low-key, unexcitable, ironic, and charming, particularly with women—all skills that could help him tame the savage Basia and, incidentally, get along with either of Manhattan's two women surrogates, Judge Roth or Judge Lambert.

In October Polak met with Christ. The two agreed that since both Basia and Nina sought to have the April 14 will admitted into probate, they did not need separate counsel. Apparently, the strong likelihood that the case would eventually be settled—whereupon the women's interests could very well diverge—did not give pause to either of them.

Nina and Ford joined Polak and Christ for lunch at the Four Seasons, during which where two important precedents were set: First, Christ won the job, at least provisionally; and second, the proponents made it clear that however the case went, they would always eat well.

There was one caveat: Basia would have to approve of their choice. Upon her return from a European shopping spree in November, Basia met Christ in a Shearman & Sterling conference room. As convinced as ever that character flowed from physiognomy and that she could read a body like a road map, she inspected Christ in much the way Seward might have examined a prized heifer. She liked what she saw. She was pleased by Christ's steady, penetrating eyes and what she called his "good square jaw." Her one concern, oddly enough, was his sexual orientation. Though many of her friends, particularly the art dealers she hung around with, were gay, she did not want her lawyer to be; she felt they were too indecisive. "I hope you're not a homosapien," she told the twice-married Christ, using a malapropism she thought quite charming. If Christ was thrown by such a question, he didn't show it. "You needn't worry, Mrs. Johnson," he replied calmly. "My credentials in that department are excellent."

The firm that would represent Basia and Nina, that would take on Forger's Milbank, had a storied past. But Sullivan & Cromwell was not one of those institutions, so common in the local bar, that had grown arteriosclerotic clinging to its history. For all its nineteenth-century trappings the firm remained prosperous, vigorous, confident. That much one could have seen at the Old Custom House in lower Manhattan a few years earlier, when Sullivan & Cromwell held its gala centennial celebration.

At first blush, so ostentatious and public an occasion seemed utterly out of character for Sullivan & Cromwell. Despite its enormous power and influence, only rarely was S&C even mentioned in the press. The light brown coats that messengers wore around the office carried no identifying embroidery; even S&C's listing in the phone book remained in small type. Self-aggrandizement was not only deemed unseemly and counterproductive, but quite unnecessary. Those lucky enough to be at the Custom House that night felt like members of an elite secret society, a legal Skull & Bones. Times had changed, pretenders had proliferated, but as Sullivan & Cromwell reached the century mark, few in the room would have doubted it was the finest law firm in the world. Its client list was a roster of American industrial and financial might. Top law graduates still clamored to work there. The men for whom the firm was named had been an incongruous pair, and had actually practiced law together only briefly. But in their own sphere, Sullivan and Cromwell were as inextricably linked as Johnson and Johnson, as if Nature meant them to be merged. As word of the centennial spread, eminences bowed and scraped before the firm, sending obsequious birthday telegrams. "I know of no law firm that has better served American society over the years than S&C," went one, from Harvard president Derek Bok. "It has always set the standard for professional excellence."

Algernon Sydney Sullivan, a Hoosier whose father had named Indianapolis, was a populist who loathed corporations and represented underdogs. William Nelson Cromwell, the son of a Union officer killed at Vicksburg and twenty-eight years Sullivan's junior, was an accountant in Sullivan's firm when the older man spotted him, paid his way through Columbia Law School, and, in April 1879, made him his partner. Eight years later Sullivan was dead, and Cromwell took the firm in a vastly different direction. He became the prototypical business lawyer, the man who, as someone once said, "taught the robber barons how to rob." Whether corporations were forming, expanding, consolidating, or collapsing, Cromwell was there to advise them. He played a key role in building the Panama Canal, on land owned by a French client. He eventually retired to Paris, where he died in 1948 at the age of ninety-four, but his firm thrived on. Indeed, the top post there, like left field in Fenway Park, seemed to breed greatness; after Sullivan and Cromwell came John Foster Dulles, later secretary of state, and Arthur Dean, another distinguished diplomat.

The party line around S&C had always been that only two other "shops," Davis, Polk & Wardwell and Cravath, Swaine & Moore, were conceivably on a par with it. Cravath lawyers, the thinking went, did fine work but were drones, while at Davis Polk, birth mattered more than brains. S&C, on the other hand, always fancied itself an enlightened meritocracy. It liked to think it nurtured the best people, regardless of their backgrounds (which for many years invariably meant the best white Protestant men regardless of their backgrounds; while some of the "Our Crowd" crowd were once powerful there, the firm went thirty years in midcentury without naming a Jewish partner, and by the time of the centennial still had no women partners. As for S&C's black population, it consisted of the man who came around shining shoes each afternoon and the slaves, tapping time to fiddle music, in the Currier & Ives prints on the wall). Partners, like popes, were not so much selected as revealed, and invariably stayed through their dotages; just about the only one ever to quit S&C did so for what was, at least arguably, a higher calling: He became a priest.

The alumni on hand for the gala represented a vast network of lawyers, extending into America's major corporations and a constellation of lesser law firms. And although many of them hadn't cut the mustard while there, they'd become S&C's truest believers; professionally at least, everything that had followed Sullivan & Cromwell had been anticlimactic. The skeptics, naysayers, and underachievers hadn't come to the Custom House, just as they boycotted most reunions. But years, even decades, later, they, too, could still recall the firm vividly, though it was a side left uncommemorated at the Custom House. They remembered the dreariness of S&C's old quarters at 48 Wall Street, where the most handsome thing was the receptionist on the nineteenth floor. They remembered the rigid hierarchy, where everything from desks to windows to offices to views was apportioned by seniority. The story is told of how Louis Auchincloss, who toiled at S&C from 1946 to 1951, was once asked whether he worked nights, and he replied that he was never sure. They remembered how senior partners upbraided young lawyers for forgetting to wear hats. They remembered the acculturation process—of creating an elitist esprit, the better to convince recruits that the long hours and stupefying work, the prospect of measuring out careers in shelf feet of registration statements, was worth the toll it took on their private lives. They remembered how the firm, in order to bind its lawyers more tightly to its bosom, found secretaries from Seven Sister schools, thus assuring a steady supply of wives who understood the rigorous demands the firm made on families, demands that prompted one dutiful S&C spouse to drag herself to a firm function only hours after undergoing a double mastectomy. (The younger women also formed a handy source for extramarital affairs, many of which were consummated in the lounges outside S&C's ladies' rooms.)

They remembered, notwithstanding all the meritocratic rhetoric, just how capricious the promotions process could be. Appearance and personality mattered. One associate was doomed after wearing a fez to the office one morning. A Duke Law School graduate named Richard Nixon came in for an interview but did not receive an offer. "This man will go far but he's not for us," his interrogator reported. They remembered how people reacted upon getting the ax. In one story, perhaps apocryphal, the disappointed reject promptly brought in his girlfriend and fornicated on the desk of William Ward Foshay, then S&C's managing partner. In another, this one true, the lawyer started to vomit the moment he heard the bad news. They remembered the conformity. The firm had its mavericks-in-residence, but never too many, and they usually were cordoned off in trusts and estates. Traditional nineteenth-century gentlemanly pastimes like wine tasting or stamp collecting were acceptable; anything more exotic was suspect. One brilliant associate was passed over at least in part because he played the recorder. "It was not a firm for mullers," a former associate recalled. "You didn't mull; you did."

They remembered its apoliticality. True, S&C was vaguely Republican. Democratic partners had problems filling tables at party functions; at least one applicant was turned down—in fact, his résumé was ripped up before his very eyes—when he told S&C's resident right-winger he admired William Brennan and loathed William Rehnquist. More characteristic, though, was the experience of the S&C lawyer who watched with amazement as news of Anwar Sadat's assassination failed to bring even a momentary halt to a drafting session. Actually, in its internal affairs, the internationalist firm of Cromwell, Dulles, and Dean was curiously xenophobic. As S&C grew more venerable, it also grew more snooty, more convinced that its unique ethos could be instilled only in minds still young, malleable, and pristine. To import people from other firms, or to let lawyers leave and then return, meant allowing in alien notions. Thus, when someone suggested former treasury secretary William Simon be brought in to lead S&C's Washington office, the idea was summarily shot down.

Most of all, they remembered the straitened atmosphere. To many, Sullivan & Cromwell was a place of excessive propriety, repressed emotions, muffled voices, self-conscious conversations, and, as one former associate put it, "cool handshakes." That spirit was captured best by John Foster Dulles, who presided over the firm before he presided over American foreign policy. "If you went up to his office and dropped dead, all he would say was 'Remove the body,'" one former S&C lawyer speculated. Another recalled introducing himself to the Great Man at a firm dinner. "He treated me like a cockroach that had just crawled up on his seat," he said. Even at the State Department, Dulles continued to receive care packages containing S&C legal pads, tablets he evidently deemed peculiarly well-suited for sketching out the future of the planet. Both he and his brother Allen, who'd also practiced at S&C and later headed the CIA, returned regularly for firm functions. Once the waiters had been banished and the doors closed portentously behind them, one Dulles or another would regale his S&C confreres with the latest diplomatic scuttlebutt. The lawyers' smugness wore off, however, once they went home and read the same tidbits in that week's *Look* or *Saturday Evening Post.*

In anticipation of the centennial, the firm commissioned a free-lance author to complete the firm history that Arthur Dean had long labored on but seemed unlikely ever to finish. The author had wrapped up his appointed task a year before the dinner, and it was, unsurprisingly, a largely flattering account ("If the firm has professed a single watchword from its inception, it has been excellence," went one representative passage). It soft-pedaled John Foster Dulles's links to Nazi Germany and even supplied a novel explanation for his legendary unpleasantness. "If he appeared to look through people without seeing them, it was partly because of poor eyesight," partly because he was "steeped in thought," it stated. Still, Dean found the new history irksome, particularly its depiction of the aged Cromwell as forgetful and lecherous. "The chapter upon Mr. Cromwell, about his lack of memory, and that he is old, superannuated and mossbacked, is not something that we should put in our own office history," he groused in a memo. As for Cromwell's alleged tendency to kiss every woman in sight, Dean turned to his own foreign experience. "In Europe, people do not shake hands, they kiss," he explained. "This is now the standard greeting of the chi-chi society of Jacqueline Onassis et al." Beset by such criticism and hampered by uncooperative partners, the firm history was never finished.

With two-hundred-odd lawyers, Sullivan & Cromwell had grown too large by its centennial for one of those old-fashioned group photographs, taken by a pivoting camera, of prosperous-looking men in formal wear sitting back and smoking cigars. After the S&C partners assembled for a more standard portrait, dinner began. The food was mediocre, the drink excellent and plenteous. The meal was followed by dessert, cordials, and cigars, which even nonsmokers lit con brio with the help of "Sullivan & Cromwell 1879–1979" matchbooks. The acoustics in the cavernous room were dreadful, and many could scarcely make out what the toastmaster, William Ward Foshay, was saying. They could probably have guessed; among other things, Foshay boasted of how, immersed in a deal, he'd missed the birth of one of his children. Philip Howard, a well-spoken and suave associate seemingly destined for partnership, toasted the firm's founders. Then Dean got up to say how delighted Sullivan and Cromwell would undoubtedly be with Sullivan & Cromwell. Before the firm, he boasted, "another splendid century stretches out."

Still, by the time of the celebration, many things about the S&C

of old were no more. Just as Dean had grown into an old man, a Milky Way of dandruff ever on his shoulders, the tradition of autocratic one-man rule had disappeared; indeed, as if in reaction to so many years of authoritarianism, S&C had grown a bit anarchic. Wall Street's premier law firm had outgrown Wall Street and moved into an antiseptic, uninviting structure at 125 Broad Street, on the very tip of lower Manhattan. The firm also maintained a small uptown office at 250 Park Avenue, just north of Grand Central Terminal, for retired partners and probate lawyers. That was where Christ practiced.

Historically, trusts and estates had been far less important at Sullivan & Cromwell than at Milbank. S&C's probate department was small and idiosyncratic, inhabited by the usual collection of oddballs, geniuses, and women. It was the only place at the firm where one could be an associate in perpetuity and eccentric with impunity. Auchincloss had worked there during his S&C days, and it was widely assumed that one of his fictional characters was patterned after Henry Ess III, Esq., a corpulent bachelor who collected antique books and could as easily tell you what Napoleon Lajoie batted in 1910 as he could explain the Rule against Perpetuities. Sullivan & Cromwell was counsel to the Mellons, who brought in the National Gallery in Washington; its lawyers drew up the will of Chester Dale, who bequeathed his Impressionist collection to the museum. It had handled several will contests, including battles over the estates of Henrietta Lenox, Mrs. Frank Leslie, Viscount Astor, Mark Rothko, and Cromwell himself. But most of its probate work was dreary, and what was tasty was invariably private. For Christ as for Reilly, *Johnson* v. *Johnson* promised to be a break from gilded obscurity. And yet if Christ hungered for recognition the way Reilly did, he didn't show it. In fact, he rarely showed much emotion of any kind—except, that is, a mordant, even a wicked, wit.

XXI

C hrist's father, Marcus, had been a much-respected judge, pre- siding over one branch of New York's second-highest court. But unlike so many other sons of accomplished fathers, young Don- ald didn't seem tormented by his lineage. He worked in a backwater at S&C and didn't aspire to lead even that. He could not have cared less that his name rarely made the papers. He enjoyed his work but was not consumed by it; to hear him talk, he cared far more for fly-fishing. Some sensed in him an ambivalence about law and lawyers; if he had his druthers, they thought, he'd be hanging around Long Island lob- stermen. While Reilly switched between his private and professional selves, Christ remained resolutely the same: low-key, unrattlable, de- tached, and, ultimately, opaque.

If Christ's calmness reflected an inner peace, it might have come from his unusual sense of place. For 120 years his family had lived in New Hyde Park, a small village on the border of Queens and Nassau counties. His great-grandfather had given the town its name and ran the local hotel and post office. His grandfather used his feed business as a springboard to town politics. His father was born in 1900 in the family house on Miller's Lane, and it was there that Marcus Christ grew up, brought his bride, raised his four children, grew old, and, nearly ninety years later, died. Donald was the youngest of the children. He was also the most intelligent, ambitious, and promising. His parents sent him to Choate, the elite Connecticut prep school where John F. Kennedy had gone.

Choate in the early 1950s was, like Sullivan & Cromwell, a self- contained and insular place. Boys barely older than Christ were falling in Korea, the Rosenbergs were about to die, the civil-rights movement was stirring, but little dissonance reached the campus. The topics there were sports, prom dates, and the headmaster's wife, who as the only attractive woman in a two-mile radius became the subject of a thousand adolescent fantasies. For all their intellectual pretensions Choate and its ilk were jockocracies, where status depended less on brains than on

226

good looks, particularly with the school uniform on. Christ was a respectable student but became better known as a determined, hardworking athlete. He began to wrestle, and after being pinned by a Kent boy in his first match, "Crotch-Hold Christ" rarely lost. With headlines like CHRIST TRIUMPHS, the student newspaper came to look like *The Watchtower*. Other wrestlers were flashier, maybe even more talented, but Christ, in the 147-pound class, won through coolness, deliberation, and intelligence—a "wrestling machine," a teammate called him. His only loss, to an undefeated wrestler from Loomis, was a split decision following a disputed call. In the off-season he played lacrosse, in which he also excelled, and football, in which he struggled but persisted.

After graduating, and after a year in Scotland on scholarship, in the fall of 1954 Christ took the fifteen-mile trip down the Wilbur Cross Parkway to Yale. He toyed with medicine, but after enjoying an undergraduate course in the common law, he decided to follow in his father's footsteps. His love life, too, was traditional; he married his high school sweetheart during his junior year. At Yale as at Choate, his greatest glories were athletic rather than academic. Before the lacrosse game against Syracuse, the coach told his players to steer clear of the opposition's star player, a young man named Jimmy Brown, thereby sparing themselves for more important Ivy League matches. Christ followed his instructions until spotting Brown chasing down a loose ball. "You get the ball, I'll get the man!" he yelled at a teammate. With that, Christ gave Brown a cross-body block and knocked him over. It was good preparation for the Marine Corps, which Christ joined after graduation. To hone his legal skills, he participated in some courtmartials, in one instance reducing the sentence of a drunken marine in the brig for telling an officer to go fuck himself. In 1961 Christ entered Yale Law School. He compiled a good record and earned a spot on the *Law Journal*. Sullivan & Cromwell liked that sort of thing. His job interview there turned out to be his last—that is, unless one counted Basia's inquiry into his sexual orientation.

Christ was initially assigned to S&C's litigation department, where, over the next few years, he worked on matters involving asbestos and light bulbs. When it came to partnership, he was neither bright enough to make it on raw intellect, scintillating enough to make it on personality, aggressive enough to make it on ambition, dronelike enough to make it on hard work, obsequious enough to make it through a mentor, well bred enough to make it on family ties, nor conforming enough to make it on loyalty. But the firm took the steady, solid, likable Christ on his terms. With too many litigators gunning for too few spots, it offered him a slot in trusts and estates, subject to a brief apprenticeship. Some said that even this partial rejection crushed Christ; it was, in some ways, the first time he'd ever "lost" at anything. But in some ways will work was better suited to someone who didn't much relish the role of lawyer-gladiator. Two years later, in 1972, he finally became a partner.

Christ made partner, but he did not make waves. Mostly, he worked behind the scenes for his wealthy clients, holding hands and, sometimes, other appendages. "I handle all the trouble people get into with their cocks," he once said. While his professional life was uneventful, there was tumult at home. To the shock of his friends, Christ left his wife, the mother of his three children, and took up with Iris Russell, a thrice-divorced Long Island socialite several years his senior whose ancestors included Cornelius Vanderbilt and whose father was Earl E. T. Smith, former mayor of Palm Beach and America's last ambassador to Cuba. From resolutely middle-class Port Washington he moved into Long Island society. The wedding, in Palm Beach in September 1976, was big news among the swells. "EARL E.T.'S IRIS IS MARRIED," Suzy declared in the *Daily News*. "Everyone is thrilled. And the Piping Rock set is ecstatic." Christ became squire of "Wuff Woods"—the name he'd given the handsome new estate, in honor of the couple's respective dogs, he and his bride purchased in Mill Neck. Gone were the days of commuter trains; Iris's chauffeur now drove him to Manhattan each morning. Christ had gone upscale, and some thought, a bit soft. Still, it was around this time that he had a rare moment in the sun. It came during the fight over the estate of Charles Lachman, the man who contributed the L, but little else, to the name "Revlon." This was the case, Christ later quipped, in which "I was accused of murdering Charlie Lachman and screwing his widow." It was also the case in which *The American Lawyer* accused Christ and S&C of being "awash" in a conflict of interest.

In the early 1930s Lachman had merged the small chemical company he'd inherited with a nail-polish company owned by the Revson brothers, receiving half the stock of the new entity in exchange. As Revlon prospered, Lachman sat back, amassed a fortune, and chased women. By 1973 he was on both his third wife and third pacemaker, and had had many more mistresses, whom he not only kept but overhauled. Dentists capped their teeth. Hairdressers redesigned their hair. Couturiers gave them new wardrobes. Dermatologists cleaned up their complexions. Plastic surgeons gave them new noses. Lachman took them to Tiffany or Van Cleef & Arpels for jewelry, then bought them the newly renovated apartments in which they could install their newly renovated selves. When he got bored, he'd move on to the next nymphette.

In the late 1960s Lachman met one Jaquine de Rochambeau, wife of Patrice Rémy Donatien La Croix de Vimeur, the Comte de Rochambeau. The unlikely matchmaker had been Rita Lachman, Charles's third wife and the mother of his only biological child, Charlene. For someone on a lifelong search for respectability, a half-Jewish half-Catholic boy who'd become a pillar of Manhattan's Brick Presbyterian Church, a title like Jaquine's was irresistible. He and Rita divorced in 1974, and Jaquine divorced Rochambeau. Soon the two were sharing Charles's duplex on Fifth Avenue. Lachman's friends later insisted that Jaquine's divorce was a sham, and that she planned to remarry the count once she'd inherited Lachman's fortune. In any case, fearful that the two would soon wed and Charlene Lachman would be disinherited, in May 1977 Rita Lachman asked a New York judge to declare Charles incompetent. As Lachman's paramour, Jaquine was technically not a party to the case. But sitting at counsel's table was her lawyer, Donald Christ. A few days after the court threw the case out, Lachman married Jaquine. She was thirty-six; he was eighty, and by now on his fourth pacemaker.

If Seward Johnson was a professional testator, Charles Lachman was a close second: twenty-three wills and seven codicils between December 1955 and October 1977. His longtime lawyer Leonard Bisco soon made out another will for him, in which he left half his $30 million estate to his new bride. But Bisco quickly went the way of Seward's Robert Myers; soon Sullivan & Cromwell was representing Charles as well as Jaquine. Predictably, the marriage foundered. Jaquine complained that Charles's clothes were covered with food and dandruff. And, alas, there were some things even the Brick Presbyterian Church couldn't change; Charles's face, she lamented, "looked all hollowed out, and all you could see was his big Jewish nose."

Lachman's secretary later testified that Jaquine told Christ she wanted out of the marriage, and that he'd counseled her to stick things out or she'd end up with nothing. So she took a different tack. His doctor said Charles should not go anywhere above five-thousand feet; she arranged for him to visit Mexico City. The doctor said "avoid hot weather"; the Lachmans journeyed to Egypt. The doctor ordered nothing strenuous; she took him dancing. The doctor told him to watch his diet; the chef she hired specialized in everything he was forbidden to eat. The doctor said cigarette smoke was dangerous; Jaquine gave a dinner party in their apartment, to which she invited plenty of smokers.

In June 1978 Lachman signed a new will, providing Jaquine with half the estate but only, he specified, were she "living with me as my wife at the date of my death." Privately, Charles called Jaquine a "greedy, avaricious bitch" who made him "puke." He began having her tailed during her frequent trips, and once, when she was due home, he ordered the doors to his room taped so she could not enter. Shortly before his death, he told Jaquine he wanted a divorce. He also moved to change his will. When Christ's boss in S&C's estates group failed to return his phone calls, Charles grew convinced the firm had cast its lot with Jaquine, and began shopping around for other counsel. He opted ultimately to return to Bisco, only to learn he was vacationing in Europe until September. On the night of August 10, claiming he had "to do something very urgently," he tried hauling Bisco back, without success. "All the world is out of town," Lachman lamented. "I have to correct some mistakes. I only hope I last." The next morning he died, his marriage intact, his will unaltered.

Since his mental state was not in doubt, Rita and Charlene Lachman's principal hope of challenging Charles's will lay in proving that the peripatetic Jaquine had not really been "living with" him when he died. They had a point: Nursing logs showed Jaquine had spent a grand total of nine and three-quarter hours with her husband in his final seven weeks. But in December 1979 Judge Midonick—later, once he'd left the bench, to represent Mary Lea's children in the will contest—upheld the unorthodox union. "A somewhat unhappy marriage is still a marriage," he ruled. (Christ brought in his S&C partner and mentor, William Piel, to help try the Lachman case. "I don't think trial work was his thing," a lawyer on the other side later said of Christ.)

Both at trial and in their appeal, Charlene's lawyers flirted with a more desperate ploy. Jaquine was not living with Charles as his wife, they would argue, because she was having an affair with Donald Christ. But the former butler in the Lachman household, brought up from Acapulco to so testify, got cold feet before he reached the stand. Later, in a sworn affidavit, a former maid stated that Christ had "practically lived" in the Lachman house following Charles's death, and that after the funeral she'd seen Christ and Jaquine, along with her father, celebrating over champagne. "I was extremely surprised to hear he was married, as he spent so much time in the apartment and with Jaquine Lachman," she stated. She went on to surmise from a variety of things she supposedly saw that the two of them had had sexual relations.

Christ had become involved with a client before; he'd met his second wife while representing the Animal Medical Center of New York, the hoity-toity charity of which she was a trustee. But Jaquine vehemently denied the charge, and the maid's salacious observations were never even offered into evidence, perhaps partly because of what Christ warned his adversaries would happen if the issue were ever broached. "My wife will be sitting with her knitting needles right behind you," he declared. "And I can't promise that you won't find yourself with them sticking between your shoulder blades."

Tom Ford, for one, was impressed with Christ's work in the Lachman case. But estates lawyers already flabbergasted by news of Nina Zagat's potential windfall found Christ an odd choice for the Johnson case. They knew and liked him, but didn't regard him as one of the very best, in or out of court. "Ed Reilly will eat Christ alive," one who knew them both predicted.

Christ now needed to get up to speed. With that in mind, Nina quickly prepared for him a primer on the Johnson family. She began with Junior, whom she described as a "sculptor and foundation manager." Reviewing his early financial and marital difficulties, she wrote, "Father and uncle hired private detectives to investigate background of his fiance [sic] and concluded (I am told) that she [Barbara] was a Nazi. However, I remember hearing from other sources that she is Jewish." Nina's history of Mary Lea was similar, including tales of her financial woes and checkered marriages. Under Marty Richards she wrote "gay film and theatrical producer" and added: "Intelligent, sensitive. Accustomed to a lot of publicity and won't embarrass easily." Basia and the Richardses had once been close, she recalled, but there'd been friction during their Italian travels "because Mary Lea and Marty drank a lot and slept all morning, and Basia doesn't drink [in the morning] and wanted to get around and do things." There was less to say about the others. Of Elaine Wold: "Quiet and restrained. Probably hates Basia. Not intelligent. Is skinny, but spends most of her time at Maine Chance—I assume to get away from her husband." Of Keith: "Crazy ophthalmologist, but looks distinguished. Has been after Elaine's money for years." Diana Firestone was "compulsive" while her husband "probably changed his name and is thought to be Jewish." Jennifer was an "attractive photographer" who was "shy, but friendly" and had "two weird-looking sons." She described Jimmy as "quiet, painfully shy, immature." "Does not want to be involved in this case," she added. "Told a friend he was forced to sign the objections by his brother. May hire independent counsel."

Christ's first priority, like Reilly's, was to gauge just how sick Seward had been. Here he had a distinct advantage over Milbank: John Peach remained in Florida, hated Junior, and, now that he'd been sacked at Harbor Branch, had ample time to help track down doctors and nurses. Of course, as someone who had known Seward for years and seen him until the very end, Peach himself could prove an important witness. But upon meeting him, Christ instantly decided he could never be called. To him Peach sounded sarcastic, caustic, embittered. He was the consummate cynic, a quality only heightened by what another S&C lawyer described as his "ratlike physiognomy." He would never play to a jury, particularly with Milbank certain to stress his bias. Besides, with a trial unlikely and plenty of others around to attest to Seward's competence, S&C probably wouldn't need him. In late October, after checking with Nina and Polak, S&C put Peach on the payroll. He'd asked for fifty dollars an hour, the going rate for "consultants." To Ford that was a bargain; only the other day, he told his colleagues, he'd paid some "grease monkey" forty-eight dollars an hour just to lubricate his car.

S&C put its stamp on the case in one more way. Against the better instincts of several Shearman & Sterling lawyers and some of his own colleagues, Christ began steering matters away from Renee Roth and toward Marie Lambert. Of course, choosing between the two was a complicated business, hinging on all manner of quirks and surmises. Just a few weeks earlier, for instance, Roth had called Jay Gunther "one sick guy" as they fought over a parking place near Lincoln Center; that might have loomed larger in the calculation had not Gunther been wearing his motorcycle helmet at the time and probably been unrecognizable. On the other hand, with her legendarily long memory Marie Lambert surely hadn't forgotten how her law assistant, Harvey Corn, was married to a former Shearman & Sterling associate who'd been treated shabbily by the firm. Moreover, Basia, who continued to believe she could divine a person's character from the way he or she looked, favored Roth. She cast her lot after Nina showed her the Surrogate's Court visitors' brochure, which contained photographs of the two: Roth was an attractive, intelligent-looking brunette with her own rough-hewn, middle-aged sexuality; one of Basia's bodyguards quickly developed a crush on her. Several years Roth's senior, Lambert had a sterner, harsher, far less pleasing look.

But Christ prevailed. Lambert, he was convinced, would sympathize with another widow, and have little patience with the children's suit; she was far more likely to force the objectants to settle far more quickly at some piddling price. And in the unlikely event the case went to trial, Lambert would move it along more briskly than the indecisive Roth. When Polak had petitioned Roth to free up enough money to run Jasna Polana, she'd sat up on the bench, nodded agreeably in all directions, decided nothing, and disappeared, leading Christ to dub her "the Chipmunk." Moreover, Judge Lambert was his friend; Christ's father had lent her a helping hand earlier in her career. "She owes me one," Christ boasted to his colleagues.

Christ's legal team gathered for the first time on Election Day 1983. On hand were Robert Osgood, the litigation partner he'd chosen to assist him; S&C associates Howard Burnett, Robert Delahunty, and Susan Ganz; and Elizabeth Gorski, a Polish-speaking paralegal who was sure to come in handy. Christ reviewed the facts as he knew them and the law of testamentary capacity and undue influence. "I don't want to be funny, but every marriage has an element of coercion in it," he said lightly. "I've seen it in my own marriage." The mood was confident and anticipatory, as if a great adventure was about to begin. This same spirit was evident later that month, when Nina, Polak, Ford, and Christ met in Florida. They dined with Peach at the Brazilian Court in Palm Beach, then spoke with assorted doctors, nurses, housekeepers, and others, all of whom seemed unshakably sure of Seward's mental capacity. For ghoulish verisimilitude, Christ spent a few nights in the bedroom where Seward died; lying there one evening, he read the nurses' notes from start to finish. They, too, supplied ample signs of Seward's competence. True, there were a few disconcerting references to hallucinations, including something about hearing trains. But having been awakened one night by the far-off sound of the Florida Railroad as it rumbled past Harbor Branch's front gate, Christ quickly learned that at least some of these could be explained.

The parties prepared for discovery—that is, to exchange information. Osgood suggested to Nina that she "clean out" her files, legal parlance for throwing away anything embarrassing or destructive before the other side asked for it, and such conduct would become officially unethical. Nina declined his invitation. Finally, in December, the two sides did some belated trick-or-treating. Milbank demanded everything pertaining to Seward's medical treatment, as well as anything related to his "physical, mental and emotional condition" from 1980 to 1983. S&C requested information on the 1944 trusts and anything else Seward had given his children, plus any letters Seward had written them between January 1980 and his death and anything at all suggesting incompetence, undue influence, or improper execution of the

will. The exchange would take months. In the meantime depositions—pretrial interrogations of key witnesses, taken under oath, with
both sets of lawyers and, sometimes, the opposing parties, present—
began.

Or, actually, intensified. In October 1983, with Polak alone filling
the chairs Christ and Osgood would soon occupy, Milbank questioned
Robert Myers, Seward's old lawyer. For anyone plumbing Seward's past,
it was a logical place to start; few outsiders knew more about Seward's
affairs or had had more of a ringside seat at the family's follies. It was
Myers's father, after all, who had seen the entranced Seward trying to
"think like a cow" and had investigated the tax-deductibility of Seward's
Ark; Myers the younger had witnessed the coming of Basia and the
going of Essie before he was banished himself. He'd watched it all with
detached amusement. "Mr. Myers, did you approve of Mr. Johnson
marrying Mrs. Johnson?" he was asked. "I didn't give a damn. Excuse
me. It was none of my business," he replied.

As Myers portrayed him, Seward had always been an easy mark. "He
was very interested in many things, and a lot of people were perfectly
willing to impose on him," he said. He also debunked any notion that
Seward had been a corporate chieftain. Seward was "a very lovable guy,
but I never saw him have any managerial responsibility," he said. In
the end, Myers's testimony cut both ways. On the one hand, he produced a memorandum he'd written in 1973, a decade before he died,
in which he'd informed Basia that Seward's testamentary goal was "to
get the maximum part of his estate to you without having it consumed
by taxes." On the other, he told Milbank of the pledge Seward had
made to Ruth upon their divorce in 1937 to leave half his estate to
their four children.

Both Seward and Ford had long believed that this obligation had
been discharged seven years later, when Seward set up the six trusts
for his children. So, too, apparently, did Myers, for the wills he subsequently drafted for Seward would not have worked were the claim
still valid. But technically, the moneys Seward placed in the 1944 trusts
collectively represented only 15 percent of what was, at the time, his
$12.3 million estate. Moreover, his promise to Ruth was supposedly
irrevocable, and neither a judge nor Seward's children nor anyone
representing them had ever absolved Seward of that obligation. For
Milbank, casting about wildly for any legal hook into Seward's estate,
any cloud on Basia's title, the discovery was a godsend. In December
1983 it filed a separate, second action in Manhattan Surrogate's Court,

claiming that before any will was probated, Seward's four eldest children were legally entitled to half his estate.

In some ways this second action—what became known as the "claims proceeding"—was the height of chutzpah. How could anyone think, or any court rule, that a father who'd given his children what had matured into $600 million had actually shortchanged them? "It's worth less than my necktie," Christ said of the claim. Even Ruth gave it short shrift. Sitting in her English-style cottage at Merriewold, just down the road from the baronial mansion she'd built and shared with "Johnny" fifty years earlier, her second husband grumbling in the background about how the Johnson children already had too goddamn much money for their own good, Ruth told Nina, Polak, and Christ that Seward had been very generous to their children. Later, talking to free-lance journalist Joyce Hoffman, Ruth appeared undisturbed that Basia stood to inherit almost everything. "She might as well have it," Ruth said. True, she added, Basia could be "a handful," and Jasna Polana was "too grand" and "puts on the dog too much" for her taste. But "I like her very much," Mrs. J. Seward Johnson I said of Mrs. J. Seward Johnson III. To her mind, the entire will contest was "very wrong." Her children, she said disgustedly, acted as if "the world owed them a living." "They have plenty, for God's sake, plenty of this world's goods," she said. "Stupid asses! I think that it's a mistake myself to fight this thing. I'd just let it go. It's crazy, nuts." As things stood, she predicted, only the lawyers would get rich off the case.

The new claim gave the four oldest Johnsons another bite at the apple and increased their leverage in any settlement talks. But it also added another layer to Milbank's conflict of interest. Already, the firm had failed to file objections on behalf of Harbor Branch, even though it was the foundation's general counsel; the foundation stood to collect something only in the unlikely event that the children's behavior matched their lofty rhetoric. Now, if the claim prevailed, Seward's estate would be halved even before it passed by will. That would entirely eliminate the Q-TIP trust and thereby wipe out whatever modest legacy Harbor Branch could claim under Seward's last three wills. Thus, while maintaining their altruistic aura, the children and their lawyers were really cutting off Harbor Branch's legal legs.

Its conflicting positions buried in legalisms, Milbank blithely continued to serve several masters simultaneously. Only three months later did Junior acknowledge one part of the problem, and direct Harbor Branch to find its own lawyers. A newly formed committee of ostensibly independent directors, comprised of Marilyn Link and the three other nonfamily board members, would select that counsel. Its real independence was dubious; two of the "independent" directors were Junior's cronies, who could be expected to keep him apprised of all developments.

XXII

The depositions of the Johnson children, to be held for the most part either in Milbank's or S&C's New York offices, were due to begin in mid-December. For the Sullivan & Cromwell lawyers, it would be the first chance to assay the family and assess the strength of their case. For the Johnsons, it would be another chance to tell their story, though this time, for the first time, under oath. For both sets of lawyers, it would be a chance to ferret out the information on which they'd build their cases and to size up opposing counsel. Christ was to interrogate the children; his calm, ingratiating manner seemed better-suited to lull them into saying something stupid or self-destructive. To the more combative Osgood fell the task of questioning the more menacing in-laws. Basia also decreed that Osgood should question all ugly and scary witnesses. These included Junior's wife, Joyce; so frightening did Basia find her that she wore a custom-tailored bulletproof vest, one that made her walk like a robot and look like a linebacker, to her deposition. It also included Jimmy's wife, Gretchen, a stern sort whom Basia likened to the matron of a concentration camp.

Beginning with Jimmy, the most reluctant of the objectants, over the next several months S&C questioned six Johnsons, five of their spouses, and two of their children. What the witnesses said revealed as much about their psyches and their candor as it did about their case.

At one point Christ asked Elaine Wold's husband, Keith, to characterize the Johnson clan. Wold, whose testimony was consistently more extreme and dubious than anyone else's in the case, answered true to form here. "They are a very close family, very close-knit family," he said. How "closely knit" were the Johnsons? The examinations revealed that of them all, only Junior had seen or spoken to Seward with any regularity. Jimmy didn't know whether he'd ever informed his father that he'd adopted Gretchen's four children. Diana didn't own a single photograph of herself with Seward and her siblings. Mary Lea wasn't sure how old Seward was when he died. (He might have been eighty-nine, she said, but then again, she had a silver dollar that was dated 1896, and that might help her figure things out more precisely, but then her mother once said that Seward was eleven years older than she, and Ruth had just turned eighty, so Seward must have been ninety. In fact, he was eighty-seven.) Neither Junior nor Jimmy knew the date of Seward's birth. Not that this much mattered, for the Johnson children rarely marked the occasion. Junior did not know whether Seward had ever graduated from college. Jennifer first learned of the removal of Seward's testicles three years after it had happened. Junior could not recall ever taking a picture of Seward. Neither could Jennifer, and she passed herself off as a photographer.

The Johnsons also knew little about one another, with Seward's first family particularly ignorant about his second. Junior did not know the name of Jennifer's new husband, or when she'd gotten married. Mary Lea did not know about Jimmy's four adopted children. Joyce and Junior, like Mary Lea and Marty, did not invite Seward to their wedding; Jimmy couldn't remember whether he had. Asked why Junior had resigned from her trust, Diana replied, "I think he was mentally disturbed at the time. I think my mother told me that was the reason." Despite the syrupy sentiments Nina had incorporated into his will, Seward wouldn't back any of Mary Lea's shows, hated *The Boys from Brazil* (he thought it was about carioca dancers, not Nazis), and was unimpressed when *Sweeney Todd* won a Tony. "His only response was that he didn't know what a Tony was," Marty Richards testified.

When one learned how the Johnsons communicated with one another, these gaps became less surprising. Here is how Joyce explained how she and Junior interacted during train trips to Florida: "He would take his four briefcases with him, and I would take my books, and he would go through his briefcases and I would read my books, and sometimes, at dinner, we might, you know, he might say something or he might not." She claimed that in the twenty years they'd been married, she had never discussed Junior's trust with him, even though it was their sole source of sustenance. "Most of what he says to me takes place when we might be walking in the woods or something and he might just say one or two sentences and I might say 'Look at that tree' and then we never go back to it," she explained. Joyce was unable even to recall the meeting at the Metropolitan Club, though it had happened but a few months earlier. "If something is of great interest to me, I have a wonderful memory; if it is not, I can be quite hazy," she explained. "This meeting was not, you know. I never expected to use it in any fiction, and I wasn't paying attention in the way that you think

I might have been." Her relationship to time was similar: "I usually have a very good memory for most things, except for years, and my whole relationship is sort of a timelessness, and the fifty years in one year, it doesn't make a difference in ultimate things, so when it comes to years, I am quite poor." Gretchen had equally unusual perspectives on time and talk. She did not place things, in "1968" or "1983," she said, but "back when she still sprinkled dry dill in her soups." She recalled that as they headed off for the Metropolitan Club summit, she hadn't pressed Jimmy for details on what was about to take place. "A lot of times I don't ask Jim questions," she said. "If he asks me to do something, there is no reason not to do it. I just go along with it."

Most claimed the idea of taking Basia and Nina to court just bubbled up once the will was read, though that was clearly not the case; Junior revealed in fact, that before boarding the QE2 in January, Keith Wold—whom Seward previously had pegged as the most likely ringleader of any challenge—had urged him to retain counsel just in case Seward's will proved "questionable." "You know very well she is writing the wills and that she is in complete control," Wold told his brother-in-law. At the time, Junior said, he was unreceptive. "I said I didn't know what the will was yet, and I thought it was a waste of time," he testified. For his part, Wold insisted no such discussion with Junior had ever taken place. Then again, Wold initially testified under oath that the family summit following Seward's death had taken place in the River Club (it was the Metropolitan Club) in July (it was June); that the Richardses and the Firestones were present (omitting Junior, Joyce, Jimmy, and Gretchen); and that the conversation began shortly before dinner (actually, it started much earlier in the day). Moreover, Wold could not recall how he'd first heard about the meeting, who spoke, whether he'd said anything himself, or whether Seward's will had even been discussed. "I don't recall specifically, to tell you the truth," he said. Later, Wold magically remembered the Metropolitan Club meeting. ("When did you develop a recollection of having been there, Dr. Wold?" a skeptical Christ asked.) But Wold still could not recall when the decision to contest the will had been made or, amazingly enough, whether Basia's name had ever surfaced in the discussions at the River Club, the Metropolitan Club, or in Nantucket that August. Reilly, who'd attended the last meeting, listened uncomfortably to Wold's evasions.

Once the depositions got under way, however, it surely did. Asked about Basia as Basia sat there listening, the Johnsons hemmed and hawed and hedged. It was, after all, much easier to attack someone in

absentia. At one point, for instance, Osgood asked Joyce whether Basia
had taken good care of her father-in-law.

"I think she was very . . . very aware, very . . . there wasn't much to
be done, but . . ."

"Did she do what she could?"

"Yes, I think she did. I don't know what she did particularly, but,
I mean, I think she . . . I would say yes, she did."

Was Seward fond of his wife?

"I think she was very important to him."

"Was he fond of her?"

"That isn't the word I would have chosen."

"What is the word you would have chosen?"

"I don't know."

"Let me ask you this: Did she give him a new lease on life when
they were married twelve years ago?"

"Yes. I think, in her own way, she did."

"And did she keep him younger longer?" Osgood asked, making Basia
sound like some brand of dishwashing detergent or hair coloring.

"Well, he had a rather childish ego, and I think he felt that to be
able to marry such a young woman was something that he felt that . . .
well, that type of relationship to a person was very important. His ego
played a very strong part."

"And did it make him happy?"

"I think as long as he felt his ego was being expressed, he was happy.
And when he felt it wasn't, he was unhappy."

Diana Firestone also waffled on the subject of the marriage. "Oh, I
think they had—had a lot of concern for each other, but there was
also, in the last eight months, there was a lot of tension, too," she
said. Gretchen was more expansive. "Her care for him was really two-
sided," she said. "She really gave very good custodial care of him, but
in a way she almost tortured him, and she withheld something I think
he really wanted, that he'd watch her, his eyes would follow her around
a room and he'd look like he really wanted her near him, that he wanted
to touch her. And she just, she couldn't let him, she just skittered
away, even if she got near, she just wouldn't settle down, almost like
a little kid that's sick, and they know you're in the room, but they
really want you to sit down and pat them, or hold their hand, they
don't want all that other care. And I felt that she couldn't give him
what he really wanted—that contactual, settled comfort that . . . Yes,
she could give him whole-wheat bread and all these other meals, but
she couldn't give him serenity or dignity or cuddling, and I think those

were the three things that the end of that long life needed." Was it nonetheless fair to say that Seward was fond of his wife? "I assume he was," she replied.

Elaine Wold admitted she'd seen some tenderness between Basia and Seward, though she felt unqualified to say whether that amounted to love. At one point Christ reminded Mary Lea that she'd once written "I love you both" in Jasna Polana's guest book. Did she still feel that way toward her stepmother? "Yes," she replied. "I would say that, as far as Basia is concerned, I am disappointed in a few things, but I would say, yes, that I am very fond of Basia."

The harshest judgments about Basia came, characteristically, from Keith Wold and Marty Richards. Wold described her treatment of Seward as "unconscionable," and said he'd never seen a single sign of affection between the two. Richards professed residual loyalty to Basia— "This is a very painful situation to all of us," he said—but trashed her nonetheless. Indeed, he now likened the woman he'd praised so lustily at the Knights of Malta ceremony to "the bitch of Buchenwald." (Richards liked Holocaust images, at another point comparing his flight from the QE2 to deportation to a death camp. "We were left one suitcase, like when you go to Auschwitz," he said.)

Richards went on to recount a conversation he'd had with Basia in Assisi, one that would have made Saint Francis (Basia's personal favorite) blush. As he and Basia walked toward the cathedral, he claimed, her thoughts weren't spiritual but sexual; Seward, she complained, was incredibly cruel and insensitive to her in bed. "You don't know how lucky you are to be in love, because Italy is a place of romance and how sad not to share music and art and flowers and be romantic," she'd allegedly told him. And, she whined, there was nothing she could do about her predicament; Seward had given Essie the heave-ho and could do the same to her. The ever-pragmatic Marty proposed a solution: "Why don't you go out and get yourself a lover?" he asked her. (Basia offered a different, equally implausible account of the stroll: True, sexual problems with one's spouse had been discussed, but it was Marty who'd complained—a few days earlier, it seemed, Mary Lea had passed gas during a romantic interlude with him on the isle of Capri.)

Like Wold, Marty insisted he'd known nothing about a will contest until after Seward died. With considerable outrage he denied that he and Junior had discussed the subject en route to the Amtrak station near Fort Pierce a week before Seward died, as their driver had said. "Never, ever, ever!" he declared. Marty should have stopped, but couldn't. "I never ever heard him say it, and I never heard a Johnson child discuss money in my life!" added the man who had lived through so many of Mary Lea's jousts with her trustees. He then spotted Nina slipping Basia a piece of paper. "You can pass as many notes as you want, and I will never say anything that is untrue!" he declared. "I never once thought of my father-in-law's will in regard to myself, nor have I ever discussed my father-in-law's will after his death." All he wanted of Seward's, he insisted, was a pair of his suspenders, and he expected even less from Mary Lea. "The longevity in my family is generally fifty-five to sixty," he explained. "The longevity in my wife's family is generally to ninety. So I have never thought of my wife's trust agreement." To Mary Lea's wary trustees he later offered a very different diagnosis. What with her kidney problems and cirrhosis of the liver, he told them in early 1986, Mary Lea was "a walking time bomb," who could die at any time. That, he explained, was why she needed his love. This, and not the money, was the bond between them; after nearly eight years of marriage, he told them, his worldly assets were a twenty-thousand-dollar certificate of deposit and eight hundred dollars in his checking account.

Not surprisingly, all of the Johnsons and their spouses agreed Seward had been incompetent on April 14, 1983. But they had never settled on how long he'd been that way. Jennifer placed the magic moment at Thanksgiving 1982. (She also maintained that the signature on his last will was fraudulent not because it was so shaky but because it was so firm, far firmer than other "spastic-looking" scrawls she'd seen Seward make around the same time.) Jimmy put the date way back in 1979. Seward, he said, had been "slightly" senile for two, three, even five, years. Here, too, Keith Wold was the most extreme.

Technically, Wold hadn't practiced medicine since 1965, though he'd dabbled in scientific research, including his quest for the elusive cure for diarrhea. (Once, when Christ complained of feeling ill, Elaine pulled a vial of the stuff out of her purse and offered him some. "Mrs. Wold, I'm not taking any of that unless Mr. Reilly takes some, too," Christ said.) Nor, presumably, had he cracked a neurology text for many years. But Wold confidently dated Seward's degeneration back to 1960, when, during a routine ophthalmological examination, he said he'd detected hardening of his father-in-law's arteries. From that point on, Wold testified, Seward tumbled, until, during his prime will-signing season in 1983, he had become what Wold called a "functional illiterate." Wold related how, aboard the *Ocean Pearl* in the 1960s, Seward periodically became disoriented, one night poking his head through the hatch and crying out, "Essie! Essie!" Though Seward couldn't find his

way back from morning walks, he thought he could handle anything—
the sort of delusion, Wold noted, "true of even early senility." Seward
withdrew whenever Basia yelled at him—behavior characteristic of
someone who, as Wold put it, "is already somewhat senile, or in the
stages of senility." Seward, who'd always navigated with a sextant,
suddenly stopped using one because it was too much trouble; even that,
said Wold, was "typical of the early stages of senility."

In a letter written in the late 1960s, Wold recalled, Seward spelled
boat "b-o-t." "I was amused by it," he joked. "I thought I would like
to play Scrabble with him, but that would be taking advantage." Seward's senility was also apparent in his nautical activities. Once he'd
forgotten to put a down haul on a spinnaker. Then he'd commissioned
the Mazurka, a boat Wold described as "an abortion." ("That was about
as good as the Poles could make a boat, I guess," he'd quipped.) To
Wold's way of thinking, Seward's marriage to Basia was itself evidence
of senility. "I think the largest—another serious judgmental error that
he made probably was in taking up with a girl that was forty years
younger than he was, the two of them with no particular mutual interest
and so on," he said. Wold last saw Seward in April, shortly after
disembarking from the QE2. He "didn't seem to be with it mentally,"
Wold recalled. "Mentally, he was in the later stages of senility. He was
not clear, he was clouded, he had all the classic signs of senility."

Of all the children and their spouses, only Marty Richards came
close to corroborating Wold. True, what Richards told the S&C lawyers
under oath was considerably tamer than what he'd told Milbank a few
months earlier. Gone was all talk of how Seward "would have signed
the Magna Carta" had it been handed to him. But there was a new
story: how, during the same April visit, he'd heard Seward hallucinating
about Nazi submarines. His account lent a certain historic grandeur to
Seward's delusions: What with his babblings about war with Russia and
accounts of his own navy days, within a week of signing his will Seward
appeared to be hallucinating about World Wars I, II, and III simultaneously.

Under questioning from the S&C lawyers, Richards now revealed
the dark side of the Knights of Malta investiture. First, he maintained
that the organization itself was no big deal, "just a group of people
involved in supposedly the supporting of hospitals and health, or giving
something back to the world," he said. (Mary Lea was even nastier,
calling it "a glorified Elks club" that was after Marty's money.) Marty
now disclosed that the man he extolled so heartily that night had
actually been losing his mind. Three times, he claimed, he'd introduced

Seward to Mervyn Nelson, Marty's longtime mentor, roommate, companion, and fellow mischief-maker; the two had even tied Seward's tie for him. And three times, he said, Seward mistook Nelson for Marty's valet. He'd also been rude and ungrateful. "During the time I was speaking, he said, 'Oh, just get on with it and let's get this thing over with and get the hell off the platform!' " Marty testified. "My father-in-law couldn't care less about the whole thing. He wanted to go upstairs and go to bed. He left much earlier than all of us. He left directly after dinner." It was powerful testimony. But it also bore no resemblance to anything anyone else remembered.

Sullivan & Cromwell was learning what Milbank already knew: If there were any case at all, it would come from the Johnson spouses, particularly the ones who'd sailed on the *QE2* together. None of the children had anything very damning to say; either because they were too addlebrained or too honest or both, much of their testimony actually undercut their case. This was particularly true for Junior, who had seen more of Seward in decline than all of the others combined. It was only one of the ways in which Junior's role in the case was by far the most complex of any of the children. For his siblings, the battle with Basia had an element of sport to it; its outcome would not fundamentally affect the way they lived, except to permit another horse, another vacation home, another opening of another show. But for Junior, the stakes, psychological and financial, were substantial and growing. This was particularly true once Basia opened up a second front against him.

Though both he and Basia sat on Harbor Branch's board, Junior was clearly in control. If there was any doubt, one had only to look at the twisting and turning foundation executives went through when the S&C lawyers questioned them. Robert Jones, who'd been so moved by Seward's courage at the arc-striking ceremony that he'd written about it afterward in Harbor Branch's newsletter, now revealed he wasn't so sure Seward had been *compos mentis* that day. Cook expressed similar doubts. "He's a liar!" Basia began shrieking upon hearing that. "It's all lies!" (Reilly knew this was the kind of explosion that might help him prove undue influence, and he wanted it preserved for posterity. "Get that down! Get all of that down!" he bellowed at the court reporter.)

Now, wanting to remove the last vestige of Basia's influence over the foundation, Junior proposed changing its bylaws to remove her from the board. Basia counterattacked. She'd recently learned that under Junior's management, the value of Harbor Branch's portfolio had plummeted. Christ joked that his dog, Beaver, could have traded stocks more intelligently; another Basia loyalist said that Junior had "a home computer for his investments, and he plays Atari games on it." On February 13, the day before the foundation's meeting, Basia asked a court in Trenton to remove Junior as Harbor Branch's investment manager and hold him responsible for its losses: $48,772,931, or more than twice Junior's net worth. The meeting the following day was predictably chaotic. Harbor Branch's new outside counsel, Milbank's Jeffrey Brinck, ordered its old counsel, Nina Zagat and Tom Ford, to leave the room. Basia ordered Brinck to apologize for his discourtesy, and he refused. "You're just like a Nazi!" she told Brinck, a Germanophile with a well-known taste for Wagner. As Basia departed, she gave Brinck a "*Sieg heil!*"

Basia's lawsuit against Junior, like the claims proceeding, would overlap and intertwine with the will contest, but not in quite the same way. It behooved the children to open up as many fronts as possible, simply to increase the nuisance value of their case. But however cathartic it might have been for Basia, her suit against Junior was a needless distraction, and looked like an attempt to embarrass and impoverish him for challenging the will. Moreover, by hitting Junior in his two sorest spots—his ego and his pocketbook—the suit only made him more resolute.

Still, on the question of when Seward lapsed into incompetency, Junior could be only so vehement. The documents he produced for S&C demonstrated how Seward continued to function in his last year of life: offering stock tips based on *Wall Street Week;* receiving and commenting upon foundation reports ("Photosynthesis is the most powerful force in nature," he'd written on one); complaining to J&J's chairman about a plan to spend Johnson money to spruce up New Brunswick (the best thing that could be done for New Brunswick, Seward wrote sourly, would be to improve the train to New York). Furthermore, to the New Jersey court hearing Diana's lawsuit against her trustees, Junior described his father in late February 1983—when they'd talked all night in the hospital—as eloquent, indignant, loquacious, intelligent, intense. Seward, he testified, had been "very incisive," filled with "challenging" questions, exhibiting a "terrific" memory. Had Seward made sense all evening? Junior's lawyer in the case asked. "Absolutely," he replied; verbally and mentally he had been "very acute," "very responsive, challenging, imaginative—all of the things that I would judge someone to be completely there."

Questioned by Christ, Junior placed Seward's fall into incompetence sometime after that session with his father, sometime late in March. But there were clearly exceptions after that; one had to be April 1, or at least that portion of April 1 when, under pressure from Junior, Seward resigned his Harbor Branch post. Meanwhile, in Basia's suit against him, where Junior's managerial competence was at issue, a third set of his lawyers would argue that Seward's faith in his eldest son "remained constant until his death on May 23, 1983." So, too, then, must have his competence.

There can be no doubt that in his final months, Seward Johnson clearly had periods of lucidity *and* confusion, pegged usually to electrolyte imbalances; the nurses' notes attest to this. But in their depositions, the children described another, very different pattern. Seward, they conceded, had his moments of lucidity, but they lasted only long enough for him to bestow some benefit on them—in January, when he forgave his $1 million loan to Junior's atelier; in February and March, when he purportedly pushed to have Junior named as one of Diana's trustees; in April, when he resigned from Harbor Branch. When he'd done anything detrimental, however—most notably, when he omitted them from his will of April 14, 1983—well, then he had clearly been incompetent.

As it emerged in the depositions, the objectants' case on undue influence was no stronger. It amounted to a pastiche of assumptions, misinformation, impressions, trivia, and other assorted bits of circumstantial or conclusory evidence—eleven authors in search of a conspiracy. At least three of the children (Jennifer, Mary Lea, and Junior) placed great reliance on a story furnished by Clinton Wold, the thirtysomething son of Keith and Elaine, who'd related how he'd once seen Basia force a reluctant Seward to sign some papers. All had inferred these papers to have been his will; in fact, it was a routine release of medical records having nothing to do with his estate. And this turned out to be among the more solid bits of evidence the children had.

Jennifer testified that Junior told her the Shearman & Sterling lawyers were not in the room when the will was signed (they were; Junior was not). She offered two smoking-gun experiences of her own: once, it seemed, Seward had complained to her of being a prisoner in his own house; another time, she heard Basia shriek at him for taking laxatives against the doctor's orders. Gretchen labored under the twin illusions that the "tone" of the last will was "very different" from those immediately before it, and that those prior wills contained bequests to his children. Elaine cited Basia's threat in the early days of her marriage to leave Seward unless he revoked the prenuptial agreement, and her tendency later to treat Seward like a child. Jimmy advanced the novel proposition that there had been fraud, duress, and undue influence simply because Seward had been in Basia's care. Gretchen told of hearing Seward decree that no more money was to be spent refurbishing Jasna Polana, and Basia pulling her aside to say she'd do so anyway and Seward would never know the difference.

To prevail on undue influence, the children had to paint Seward as a pathetic, unprepossessing pushover. This the children themselves didn't seem to realize, for their descriptions of him were actually too flattering for their own good. Only the in-laws ridiculed the old man with the requisite gusto. Keith Wold described him as "not very deep intellectually." Marty Richards, whose expansive praises of Seward at the Knights of Malta party had to be cut back to keep the ceremony on schedule, now said he couldn't recall a single conversation he'd had with the guy that lasted more than a few lines. "He spoke more to the dogs than to any people," Richards observed. (Anxious to denigrate his father-in-law as a father, Richards charged indignantly that following her parents' divorce, Mary Lea and her siblings were reduced to living in a rat-infested barn. Asked later whether this was true, Diana Firestone replied, "No, I am not aware of that.") Joyce, who'd once earned Seward's scorn by agonizing over a plate of meatballs, now complained that Seward "seemed to miss the gestalt of situations and could be very fussy about something that just didn't matter—like whether he was going to have a piece of cake or not, and whether the piece was large enough." She also disclosed that the novel she'd long been working on contained an unflattering portrait of a Seward surrogate, "a wealthy man who is sort of out of touch with reality." S&C demanded, without success, to peruse the manuscript.

Only Junior offered a more nuanced portrait of the testator. Over the years depositions had become standard operating procedure for him, and lawyers' offices his native habitat; following Seward's death, Junior was questioned in at least five separate proceedings. "It's a pleasure to meet the patron saint of lawyers," Christ declared when they'd first been introduced. When, on day eleven of Junior's examination, Basia asked that he kindly smoke only during breaks, Junior stood his ground defiantly; smoking was something he normally did, he said firmly, and depositions were "becoming the norm of my life." At various moments, this latest and lengthiest of Junior's depositions, stretching over nineteen days and 2,615 pages, seemed more like psychotherapy to him than interrogation. To Junior, answering questions could be pleasant, even cathartic. Sometimes it appeared that, at least subliminally, achieving posthumous peace with his father was more important to Junior than breaking his will; what good was coming to terms with an incompetent? Thus, Junior's Seward was far sharper and more durable than the pathetic creature Wold and Richards described. As she listened to Junior, Nina was struck by how much a fifty-five-year-old man could sound like a wounded, needy child. Junior's problems made more sense, too, once S&C obtained his amazing divorce papers, which Seward had never mentioned either to Basia or Nina. Nina read them aloud to Basia, with what evolved from amazement to amusement to pity.

At times Junior sounded as if he had precious few bones to pick with Basia. He conceded that Basia had probably saved Seward's life in January 1983, at a time when, from a strictly testamentary standpoint, she'd have been better off letting him die. He disabused one reporter of the idea that Seward's final marriage had been a deathbed affair. "Oh, no, they were married eleven years," he said. "She paid." ("There wasn't any anger, any venom," the reporter recalled. "He was almost sympathetic that she'd had to put up with the old goat all those years.") On occasion Junior sounded positively jolly about the case. Once, Sullivan & Cromwell's Osgood walked into a restaurant as Junior was walking out. "Poison his food!" Junior chirped to the maître d'. Another time he drew a caricature of Christ, leading the S&C lawyer to fear his likeness would soon be cast in bronze. Junior loved the verbal jousting and badinage of the interrogations; from time to time Reilly had to kick his rambling rose of a client under the table to stop his blabberings, just as S&C did later with Basia.

Though the ratio was different, Junior under examination, like Seward during his final illness, had his lucid, unlucid, and pellucid moments. When equivocal or evasive, his speech was impregnated with commas and dashes—a grammarian's horror show, a court reporter's nightmare. With time and practice he improved, honing a style that could be pungent, punchy, witty. "Please describe Mrs. Zagat as you see her," Christ once asked. "I don't believe you wish me to go into height and weight," Junior replied. At another point, he was asked how his father reacted whenever Nina kissed him. "Preoccupied," he said. Junior could be disingenuous—claiming, for instance, that he couldn't identify the handwriting on his own suicide note. But at other times, he waxed lyrical. His relationship with Mary Lea, he said, "had wintry and summer seasons"; when Mary Lea made the mistake of inviting both him and his former wife to an art opening, he said, "a few years of winter" ensued.

Of all the Johnsons, only Junior expressed concern to Seward about Basia's domination, and he'd said it through sculpture—to be precise, through the statue of King Lear he'd displayed for a time at Jasna Polana. Junior's message was muddled. "I told [Seward] he was the one that inspired it, and that King Lear had signed over his kingdom, and so that would be sort of an oblique way of getting at the . . . he always said things to me obliquely also," Junior explained, sort of. He was particularly pleased, he recalled, when Basia banished the piece to a spot far away from the house. "I smiled and said, 'Well, that's perfect, Basia. That's part of the story.' And I put him with his back to Jasna Polana as though he was thrown out of his own castle." Junior's Lear was a victim, too, though not of Regan or Goneril. The statue was eaten by the elements, and was carted away from the estate a few months later.

Of all the Johnson children only Junior, who spoke the most cogently, had seen his father the most frequently, had botched up his life the most grandly, and was challenging the will the most aggressively, was worth a prolonged interrogation. How, Christ asked, had Basia managed to change the last will? "I think that she, through, I guess, ranting and raving, and with the help of Nina Zagat, and whatever," Junior replied. How would he describe Nina's role in the saga? "I think Mrs. Zagat was influenceable and, in fact, influenced by Basia Johnson. I would say that someone who was influenceable, in the long run, obviously is not very honest." Who were the other coconspirators? Tom Ford and Jan Waligura, Junior speculated; Waligura, he explained, was financially beholden to Basia, seemed to have been around Fort Pierce at all the most crucial times, knew about the psychology of cancer patients, and had given Basia a "quite sophisticated" medicine kit in early 1983. Waligura had once explained his experiments to him, Junior recalled, and the methodology "made me shudder." Anyone so "extremely cold," Junior said, was surely "capable of stretching his ethics."

Christ put the question bluntly: On what basis was Junior objecting to the will? In response Junior cited what he called "a general pool of provocative incidents" and "questionable" experiences. There was the time that Basia had almost fired Nina—which showed, he thought, it was she who controlled Seward's lawyer. There was the decision to probate the will in New York, which struck Junior as odd given all the efforts to make Seward a Florida domiciliary. There was the way Basia had cleaned out all of Seward's old advisers. There'd been Seward's ever-expanding bequests to her, the incredible complexity of his wills, and the fact that they always seemed to have been signed when Junior hadn't been around. It was a hodgepodge of suspicions, most of them either irrelevant, self-evident, dubious, or easily explained. But in early 1984 this was as much as Milbank had. Small wonder, then, that as Reilly went stonily about his task, Christ & Company were brimming with confidence; the children's case, they were convinced, would collapse in a matter of months, once Milbank had milked its six cash cows dry, or, more likely, the cows themselves either smartened up or went broke. Even one of the court reporters picked up the prevailing mood: Sullivan & Cromwell "thought they had it sewn up," he said.

Basia and Nina whiled away the hours during depositions whispering, giggling, passing notes in a way that reminded an annoyed Reilly of two schoolgirls. Between themselves they'd ridicule the Johnsons, making fun of Jennifer's dresses or Mary Lea's chin or Joyce's haggardness, much as the S&C associates came to call the thin, bespectacled Jimmy Johnson "Gumby." They'd joke about how, instead of donating Seward's house in Fort Pierce to Harbor Branch, Basia should hand it over to Cuban exiles or sell it to Weyerhauser. Smiling brightly, suppressing giggles as her shoulders rolled up and down with mirth, drawing dachshunds to pass the time, Basia was the picture of insouciance. Basia and Nina also speculated about who would play whom in the inevitable movie version of the case. Basia envisioned Meryl Streep playing her, Robert Redford as Osgood, and Harrison Ford as Robert Delahunty, the S&C associate who was her most ardent defender. Christ joined in the fun, mimicking the Johnson women, cracking jokes, lining up Lifesavers and handing them out. Around S&C, he bragged that the Johnson case was "open and shut."

He, incidentally, would be played by Paul Newman.

XXIII

s the two teams of lawyers sparred in New York, a quieter war
was being waged thirteen hundred miles to the south: a war
for the cooperation of key witnesses, mostly the nurses who'd
cared for Seward during the height of his testamentary season. A year
had now passed since Seward signed his last will, and no trial date was
in sight; there was still too much information to collect. The two sides
worked separately, and stealthily. But hiding one's whereabouts wasn't
always possible, as the Sullivan & Cromwell lawyer heading the Florida
theater of operations soon learned to his chagrin. Driving wearily into
a lonely Holiday Inn late one day, he looked up at the hotelier's distinctive logo and saw Milbank's fingerprints. WELCOME BOB OSGOOD, it
declared in large plastic letters. It might just as well have said MILBANK
WAS ALREADY HERE.

When Donald Christ looked for a litigator, Robert Mansfield Osgood
seemed like a long shot. Christ and Osgood had never really worked
together and didn't know one another well. The quirky world of real
people and their wills, the world Christ inhabited, was alien to Osgood,
who specialized in complicated corporate litigation. Osgood's cases
rarely made it to court, and then were almost always tried before judges;
in fifteen years at the bar, he had never argued to a jury. And yet, as
he traipsed around Florida, Osgood was in one way on familiar ground.
The skills he was calling upon now—winning people's confidence,
listening to their woes, allaying their apprehensions, overcoming their
resentment, making them believe he cared—were talents he'd used in
an earlier and very different lifetime.

Osgood's father had been a Methodist minister, and Methodist min-
isters led transient lives. Their bishops moving them around like pawns,
they'd spend a few years somewhere, living in a parsonage they did not
own, only to be summarily uprooted and sent somewhere else. Young
Osgood was born in Elmira, New York, just across the state line from
his father's small parish in Pennsylvania. There followed stops throughout New York in places like Presho, Whitneyville, Rome, Ilion, East

251

Quogue, and Buffalo, as well as layovers in Ohio. The locales changed, but the life, one of all-pervasive, abstemious religiosity, did not. It was a message young Robert heard his father deliver every Sunday for eighteen years, and one he hoped someday to deliver, too. When the bishop offered him a scholarship to Syracuse University if he'd minister to three country parishes, he readily agreed.

Not surprisingly, his was not the typical college experience. In four years on a football-mad campus, he attended one game. While others were rushing fraternities, he was delivering sermons, performing marriages, and talking parishioners out of suicide. But Osgood had always harbored some doubts, and when an ecclesiastic superior reprimanded him for baptizing the child of a local prostitute, he broke with his church and turned to law, which had intrigued him since his days delivering the *Rome Sentinel* to local barristers. For the next three years he led his class at Syracuse Law School, the same class in which his buddy Joseph Biden, later United States senator from Delaware, finished seventy-ninth, and that only with Osgood's help. Syracuse law graduates generally didn't stray very far or aim very high. But Osgood aimed for Sullivan & Cromwell, largely because he had always identified with John Foster Dulles, another minister's son from rural upstate New York who had foregone the pulpit for a career in public affairs. By now, Dulles was dead, but how better to pay him homage than to follow in his footsteps?

This was easier said than done. S&C may have been filled with small-town types, but they were from small towns by way of Yale or Harvard; the firm had never hired anyone from Syracuse. But the man interviewing Osgood was yet another minister's son, a litigator named Robert MacCrate. The two hit it off, and in the summer of 1968 Osgood—his colleagues called him "Preacherman"—moved his young family to Staten Island and joined S&C's litigation department. Defending Armour from a hostile takeover by General Host had little to do with the social gospel, and after a year, Osgood came close to quitting. He stayed, however, a decision that required accommodations by both parties. The nature of his work did not change, but his ties to the firm did.

By no standards but S&C's was Osgood a nonconformist, particularly by the mores of the 1960s. But there, he stood out. He was, as one colleague put it, "less swept up in the 'S&C is everything' mentality" than his peers; amid the Brooks Brothers machismo, in which neglecting one's family was chic, Osgood was a devoted family man, someone who rejected the usual show of working hard and ordinarily made it home in time for dinner. And home wasn't on Park Avenue or in some ritzy suburb but the middle-class town of Glen Ridge, New Jersey. There was something almost corny about Osgood's life; one associate recalled how he once cut short a business trip to Fiji to get back and shovel the snow in front of his house.

There are three kinds of partnership candidates on Wall Street: shoo-ins, sure losers, and the indeterminate middle. It is from the last group, the largest class of all, that the dark horses and suicides emerge. Osgood was in the top of this middle tier, solid but by no means brilliant. But as flashier lawyers burned themselves out, he made his way. He became known as a methodical worker and effective questioner, someone who applied his common touch well. His routine rubbed some people the wrong way; to them, whenever Osgood joined his hands together in his contemplative, priestly way, he was at his most manipulative. Some-times, the play-acting was too much even for Osgood to stomach, and his body betrayed him. "Bob could never lie without turning beet red," one lawyer who worked with him later recalled. "It was to his detriment, because lawyers have to shade the truth."

In 1975 Osgood made partner. His forte was mammoth corporate lawsuits, many on behalf of Exxon. Before long he was elected to the American College of Trial Lawyers, the self-styled Mensa of the liti-gation bar. Still, he kept his institutional distance. He was a committed Democrat. At his insistence he became the first S&C partner to have a black secretary. He passed up firm outings and dinners in favor of weekends riding and rearing horses on the spectacular spread he had assembled in the Catskills, where he hoped to build his dream house and spend his retirement. He talked privately about life after the firm, perhaps in a Biden administration. When "the Senator," as Osgood always referred to his old classmate, addressed Osgood as "Mr. Attorney General," Osgood would laugh, but he would also dream.

Osgood's political prospects were only one of the things on his mind that Friday afternoon in late October 1983 when Don Christ asked him to work on the Johnson case. Normally, Osgood would have quickly agreed. But Christ's sketchy outline made him uneasy. The world of rich, eccentric, squabbling socialites was one he didn't know or care about. Dealing with corporate executives and their desiccated legal problems was one thing, dealing with a temperamental Polish immigrant with oodles of money quite another. But buoyed by what he took to be Christ's assurance that the case would be his to try, Osgood signed on. Within a few weeks he met Basia, Nina, and Werner Polak, the Shearman & Sterling lawyer overseeing the case. (For Nina, the experience was a bit disconcerting. Christ had touted Osgood as the perfect man for the job, but when she'd first laid eyes on him, he was wearing a cheesy polyester sports jacket, and looked more like a lawyer from Schenectady than Wall Street. When she expressed her concerns to Tom Ford, however, he brushed them aside. Sullivan & Cromwell, he assured her, presumably knew what it was doing.) They agreed that once he'd freed himself from some other commitments, he'd fly down to Florida and go to work.

In the first half of 1984 Osgood made five separate trips south. With John Peach squiring him around, they began visiting the nurses (it was a time-consuming process; for the generously salaried Osgood, it made no difference, but Peach was getting paid by the hour and faithfully recorded his every nanosecond on the job). Initially, it seemed that wherever they went, even remote Holiday Inns, Reilly or his sidekick, Charles Berry, already had been. This couldn't be helped, for Milbank had a five-month head start. But with the favorable testimony Osgood and Peach began amassing, the timing seemed inconsequential.

The most enthusiastic of the nurses was the one who'd worked the longest, Judy Smith. Already, she'd given Christ an earful about the idyllic life Basia and Seward shared; the old man, she told him, was "eighty-seven going on thirty-seven," not senile "by any means," and fiercely independent, while Basia was his "number one nurse." Smith spoke from a hospital bed to which she had been relegated since a serious car accident, one that killed her niece and crushed Smith's own legs. Osgood dutifully recorded everything, then drafted it into an affidavit that Smith signed the next day. Simple, straightforward, disarmingly honest, and now, seasoned with sympathy, Smith promised to be ideal on the stand—that is, until Basia insisted on paying for whatever hospital costs Smith's insurance didn't cover. Christ cautioned his client not to taint a pristine witness. But this was precisely the sort of impulsive, individualized act of charity Basia loved, and she ignored him. She had to do what was right, to live her own life, she said. The shortfall was $22,957.63, and that was the amount of Basia's check.

Osgood quickly secured favorable testimony from several other nurses. One described Seward as a "strong-willed" and "proud" man who had been "in command of everything" and "adored" Basia. The nurse who'd presumably heard Seward's mutterings about "war with Russia" on April 7 now said the old man had been "coherent and mentally competent" at least seven eighths of the time that day. Asked whether, as Wold had said, Seward then had been in "the advanced stages" of senility, she replied, "I don't think he was senile at all."

Another nurse said Seward had been "coherent and mentally alert" on April 8, one of his worst days. Still another, who'd worked the nights of April 7, 8, and 9, said Seward hadn't been "at all disoriented or confused" in that period, and that Basia "was always there" for him. Osgood took it all down. Fran Cioffi, the nurse on duty when Seward died, told Osgood that the old man had been generally alert and responsive until his last weekend, and even after that had had only fleeting periods of confusion. Often, she said, she saw Seward and Basia sitting together, holding hands. She recalled one night when, as Basia prepared to leave his bedroom, Seward declared, "Oh, Basia, I love you so much," whereupon Basia walked back to his bed and said she loved him, too. Osgood got that down as well.

Another nurse recalled how Seward talked to her about Jacques Cousteau and Tylenol, read his mail, placed his own phone calls, chose his own clothes, took Basia to task. "If Mrs. Johnson got excited about something, he would say, 'Now Basia, just quiet down. I'm not paying any attention to you,' " she recalled. Luella Johnson, who'd been on duty during the striking of the first arc, said Seward's mind had been "strong right up to the end," that Basia had been "extremely attentive," and that it was Seward who had really been in charge. "If Mrs. Johnson raised her voice and criticized something I had done, Mr. Johnson would say something like, 'Stop it, Basia. I've had enough. Leave her alone,' at which point Mrs. Johnson would quiet down," she recalled. Seward's cancer made him tired, she said, but "he was mentally competent and knew what was going on even if he did not talk a lot." Seward's podiatrist said that in March and April his client had been "mentally alert and lucid." Seward's masseur recalled the old man's "witty sense of humor." His housekeeper called him "a very intelligent man with an active mind." The engineer handling Seward's various solar-energy projects in Fort Pierce said, "I hope that when I get to the end, I am as mentally alert as Mr. Johnson was." And though he found Osgood too "buddy-buddy" for his taste, Seward's pilot, Daniel Malick, told him Seward remained forward-thinking, curious, and intelligent until the end.

Crisscrossing Florida, Osgood must have felt omnipotent. He would walk into a nurse's house or garden apartment or trailer, humble homes of the sort he'd visited as a minister, decorated with lace and pennants and knickknacks and religious objects. Once Peach had introduced him, he'd put on his pious, soulful, sincere face, listen earnestly, tell them how much Basia appreciated all they had done for Seward during that anxious time and regretted any unpleasantness she might have caused them, then coax the most wonderful testimony out of them. And yet he knew he mustn't get too complacent; the reservoir of resentment against Basia ran deep. Basia, he came to realize, was a Jekyll-and-Hyde character, capable of both great cruelty and extraordinary kindness. Sheril Bennett, the nurse whom Basia had fired for wearing too much perfume, didn't even invite Peach and Osgood inside. (Though it was a depressing experience, the two men left laughing: Sure enough, she still reeked of perfume.) "I may not be worth five hundred million dollars, but I didn't have to take that shit," another nurse spat out. Such people had to be won over, or at least neutralized. Osgood's mix of sugar and saccharine usually worked well, though circumstances sometimes required extraordinary measures. A nurse named Mary Banks greeted them by declaring that no one had the right to treat another human being the way Basia treated her. But Banks was the local sales-person for "Herbalife," a health-food concoction, laxative, purgative, and panacea; perhaps, Peach whispered, buying some of the crap could cure an embittered nurse. It was not cheap—$49.51, according to the receipt Peach attached to his expense account—but it seemed to work. "Tell Mrs. Johnson it's time to bury the hatchet," Banks declared as the two men departed.

In their reports back north, Osgood and Peach warned Christ and Nina about these pustules of resentment. If the children had any case at all, Osgood surmised, it would be on undue influence rather than incapacity, and be based on the testimony of ex-employees still seething over Basia's abusiveness. But they invariably ran into what Peach called "a stone wall of optimism" at S&C. Even when Nina came to Florida, Peach thought, she seemed more concerned about the dinner menu than the will contest. Worse, most of those Osgood interviewed were bit players. The most crucial witnesses were the nurses on duty April 14: Patricia Reid and Bonnie Weisser. The case could hinge on what they said, and Osgood had yet to recruit either of them.

Clearly, Basia had not chosen her targets with a will contest in mind. In her short tenure Reid repeatedly felt her wrath, and she had not forgotten the sensation. "She picked the first person she laid eyes on, and began to scream and holler at me," Reid said later of one episode. "And I'm no animal, and nobody's going to talk to me like that." So ugly had the ordeal been that Reid gave notice the next day, abandoned private nursing care for lab work (secretions and tissues weren't so nasty), and moved back to Kentucky. Now, Basia needed Pat Reid more than Seward ever had. Osgood tried reaching her through her sister, who had also worked briefly at the Fort Pierce house. "Tell him

I'm dead!" Reid told her. Osgood was not deterred, nor could he be. For the next several months there ensued one of the more bizarre spectacles of the Johnson case: a partner at one of Wall Street's ritziest law firms, a man who hobnobbed with Fortune 500 executives and was doted on by underlings, stalking and importuning a lowly part-time licensed practical nurse all the way to some hick Appalachian town.

In January 1984 Osgood sent Reid a handwritten note. "I need your help," he declared. "Please, please, please call me. Call collect." In a more conversational vein he added, "Your sister was great when I saw her last week in Lake Park," then signed the letter "Bob Osgood." It didn't work. In February Osgood wrote her again. "I really need to talk with you about Mr. Johnson," he pleaded. "Please do not worry about getting involved. We will keep you out of it." Once again he ended in folksy fashion. "If you and your husband cannot make it to Lexington, I'll be happy to drive to your place. I'd love to see a little of Kentucky." This more reader-friendly approach also failed, and Osgood's next note, sent in April, was of the more formal, typewritten variety. "I write again to request an opportunity to visit with you briefly in your home, in Lexington or in New York," he said. "Basically, I am only trying to do my job of talking to everyone who spent any significant amount of time with Mr. Johnson during his final illness. I have now talked with all the other nurses who helped to take care of him from late January 1983. Although many of them had problems with Mrs. Johnson, all of them had respect for Mr. Johnson and say he was a pretty sharp old man. I ask you to look beyond any ill feelings you may have toward Mrs. Johnson and to call me collect."

Should his plea for forgiveness fail, Osgood appealed to Reid's sense of filial loyalty and devotion to the truth. "It is not right for Mr. Johnson's children to say after his death, when he is no longer here to answer back, that their father was an imbecile and incapable of knowing who he was, or realizing that he had children, or realizing that he was a wealthy man," he continued. "It is my job to demonstrate that even if he was a sick man, he still was competent and I strongly believe he was. I want to talk to you to be sure I am on firm ground. I respectfully ask you to give me another phone call." This plea, too, was signed "Bob Osgood." And this one, too, fell on deaf ears. Reid remained unreachable. Actually, it was worse than that. She was falling into Reilly's clutches.

Sullivan & Cromwell knew that Milbank, too, was chasing Reid. In one packet of materials it sent to S&C, Milbank had mistakenly included an internal memorandum. "If either Jerry or Pat Reid calls, send a messenger immediately to the courthouse to notify Mr. Berry," it said. Berry, a wealthy Yalie, had even less in common with Reid than Osgood did. But either because his sell was softer or his clients more palatable to her, Reid agreed to meet with him. Over lunch at a greasy spoon in Harrodsburg, Kentucky, she told Berry she'd seen Seward confused on April 17 and 23 as well as on the fourteenth; that even when he was clearheaded, his attention span was short; that his rare remarks did not reflect "any great level of understanding"; and that he'd sometimes sign his name ad nauseum on a pad, just as a child might.

However unwelcome her message, Sullivan & Cromwell kept chasing the elusive Reid. In the saga's most preposterous chapter Wall Street met Tobacco Road. One afternoon in July 1985 Ted Rogers, the senior S&C associate on the case, flew to Lexington, Kentucky, picked up a rental car, then made the thirty-two-mile-long drive down U.S. 68 to Harrodsburg. He was going uninvited, and had only a rural route number for Reid. The local postal workers would not give him her address, but the resourceful Rogers found it in the local land registry. He then drove out to her place, which he subsequently described in an internal firm memorandum as "a rather poor farmhouse in scraggly farmland." Alas, he'd just missed Reid, who had left for her hospital job in Lexington. But he chatted with her husband and stepson, who told him she'd refused Milbank's offer to fly her to New York to testify at any trial. "In a rather oblique way [Mr. Reid] stated it would take more than just travel expenses to get her to come to New York," Rogers wrote. "At another point, Mr. Reid referred to the fact that the estate was worth $400 million." In any case he gave Rogers his wife's phone number for nothing.

Reluctantly, Patricia Reid agreed to meet Rogers the next morning at her house. But when he showed up, her stepson informed Rogers she'd once more changed her mind, and wasn't even home. "While [the stepson] and I were speaking, a pickup truck appeared on the Reids' long, meandering driveway," Rogers wrote. "[He] stated that Mr. and Mrs. Reid were in the truck. When the truck reached a distance of about 50 yards from us the truck turned around and drove back out of the driveway. It was apparent that the Reids had seen that I was there, and left in order to avoid me." It was an understatement. Reid later told the Milbank lawyers she considered calling the local sheriff to remove Rogers from her property. When Reid finally did talk to S&C, after she'd been subpoenaed, most of what she said would have been better left unuttered. She offered a truly bizarre tale of how once, as

Peach, Gregory, and Basia talked nonchalantly nearby, Seward pulled down his pajama bottoms, crouched, and defecated on the front lawn of the Fort Pierce house. She elaborated on Seward's bouts of irrationality, when he would "be talking to persons not there" and "be out in left field." Even Rogers's attempts to rehabilitate Basia backfired. Might not her abusiveness be due to the stress of her mother's death and Seward's illness? he asked. "I don't know what she was under," Reid replied. "She was just not nice."

Perhaps, from the proponents' point of view, Pat Reid had always been a lost cause. But Bonnie Weisser was still up for grabs. In January 1984 she told Christ and Nina what she'd already told Forger, Reilly, and Brinck: that she wanted to remain "evenhanded." Only after Osgood bought her a drink at the Steak 'n Shake near her apartment did she begin to take sides, and the side she took wasn't Osgood's.

Osgood subsequently described their encounter as a low-key, businesslike review of the case. But according to Weisser, Osgood came more to proselytize and strong-arm than to listen or learn. Osgood, she said, told her the Johnson children were depicting the declining Seward as "a lunatic"; stressed that Seward had amply provided both for his grandchildren and for Harbor Branch; and noted that Junior was mismanaging the foundation anyway. He leaned on her to sign an affidavit, as the other nurses had done; if she wished, he said, she could fly to Harbor Branch on Basia's plane, take a dip, and work on it there. Moreover, should she be interested in a job with Johnson & Johnson, he offered to "hand-carry" her résumé to Basia, who, he stressed, had far more clout at J&J than any of the children. She found his whole pitch distasteful, and likened Osgood to a high-pressure shoe salesman.

The draft affidavit Osgood prepared for her only made things worse. His recapitulation of their conversation wasn't exactly untrue, but was so much stronger than anything she'd said that she refused to sign it, as well as a more tempered version he subsequently prepared. How could someone who'd been so debilitated be called "demanding and intelligent"? How could anyone call her brief exchanges with Seward "conversations"? Or say that any eighty-seven-year-old terminal-cancer patient was "generally" alert and oriented? She told him she found his pressure tactics repellent; if he thought his hyperaggressiveness was serving Basia, she said, he was sadly mistaken. In every respect, Weisser thought, the contrast between the two sets of lawyers was striking. The Milbank men came dressed in button-down shirts and business suits, while Osgood self-consciously dressed with polyester, double-knit Floridian casualness. Reilly and Berry had been polite, even formal, while

Osgood seemed like a hustler. Reilly listened to her intensely; Osgood talked almost the entire time, and when he listened, he patronized her.

Of course, Milbank was no less partisan than Sullivan & Cromwell. But it had cloaked its partisanship much more effectively, and with a witness like Weisser, that mattered. And that, in turn, mattered to the case. Because the other nurses respected Weisser enormously, she gave the Milbank lawyers entrée to them; she was a far more welcome sight than John Peach, whom many didn't much like anyway. With Weisser opening doors, Milbank picked up valuable information and ideas. From Fran Cioffi, for instance, Milbank first learned of the "mental-status examination," the test for acuity that nurses give patients but that Schilling had failed to administer to Seward before attesting to his competence. Weisser also did spadework for Milbank: reviewing nursing notes, interpreting nursing terminology. Moreover, however neutral Weisser might think she was, she'd end up testifying for someone, and that someone now seemed to be Milbank.

Before long, reports of Osgood's frayed relations with the most important witness in the case reached Christ, but he was unconcerned. Just what, he asked a colleague, had Osgood done to antagonize her so? "Do you suppose," he joked, "he was pinching her patootie?"

XXIV

hile Sullivan & Cromwell had requested a wide range of materials from the children, all Milbank had asked for were Seward's medical records. But in March 1984, as Osgood's travels and travails continued, Milbank asked for just about everything else.

Ordinarily, probate courts enforce a "three-two rule"—that is, only those events that occurred within three years prior to the execution of the will or two years afterward are deemed relevant. But in the twenty-five-page shopping list it filed March 9, Milbank reached back to Seward's first separation in 1937 and up to the present day. The rule was inapplicable, Milbank argued, where the fraud and undue influence had lasted a far longer period of time—the fraud from the time Barbara Piasecka first met Seward in 1968, the undue influence from their wedding day. Reilly sought entry into every nook and cranny of the Johnsons' lives—anything pertaining to Seward's two divorces or to the twenty-nine wills and codicils he'd signed since January 1962; every communication either he or Basia had ever had with Shearman & Sterling; anything about anything Seward had ever given Basia; all tax returns from 1969 forward; all bank statements, passbooks, or canceled checks from January 1980 until Seward's death; anything pertaining to the Johnsons' corporations or properties.

To learn of their encounters with the Johnson children, Harbor Branch officials, lawyers, doctors, psychiatrists, and faith healers, Milbank asked for all of the appointment books Basia and Seward had kept. To trace their every move, it requested logs from their aircraft, boats, and helicopters. There were demands for everything—catalogs, receipts, correspondence—pertaining to any paintings, sculpture, furniture, silverware, or other objets d'art Basia had bought. Milbank wanted all materials related to the new chapel and the employment records of anyone who'd worked for the Johnsons anywhere in the world since January 1969. Then there were odds and ends: information on Basia's educational and employment history in Poland; details pertain-

ing to Seward's funeral and the disposition of his remains; the scrapbooks
or recipe books Seward kept; the guest lists for the Johnsons' wedding,
the opening party, the Knights of Malta investiture, and any other
event to which forty or more people had been invited; and, perhaps
most perplexing, any document that either Basia or Nina had ever
destroyed.

Sullivan & Cromwell promptly complained that Milbank was seeking
"a lifetime (indeed, several lifetimes) of records," much of it either
privileged or irrelevant. This marked the beginning of a long, tedious,
expensive war over document production, one that would endure for
many months and fully test the lawyers' bombastic skills. Soon Milbank
was complaining of S&C's "pattern of stonewalling and obstruction"
and its "cavalier" attitude toward the case. Maybe Seward couldn't have
taken on Basia or Nina, Milbank sneered, but it could and would. First,
though, it had to convince Marie Lambert, before whom it had filed
this particular motion, that it really needed everything it had requested.
To accomplish this, a yarn had to be spun, a spell cast. The task called
for someone with a literary touch and an almost operatic view of life.
Among the very earthbound team at Milbank, that could only have
been Jeffrey Brinck.

Brinck, who'd been at Milbank since 1969, came across as the prototypical trusts and estates lawyer, which is to say, atypical. A chemistry
buff in college, he was a strange compound himself. Though only forty-
two, he already had a certain fuddy-duddyish, schoolmarmish way about
him. Far from shunning the image of a young fogy, he cultivated it.
He kept his glasses suspended from a chain and hanging on his chest,
in the manner of a spinster librarian; he favored sports coats and loud
bow ties over suits, greens and browns over blues and grays. A bird-
watcher who'd festooned his office with Audubon prints, he also collected butterflies, and the walls of his apartment on West Eighty-first
Street resembled something out of the nearby Museum of Natural History. Brinck was an unabashed Germanophile (that was why Basia had
regaled him with a "*Sieg, heil!*" at the Harbor Branch meeting in February), and legend had it he worked weekends in lederhosen. He loved
German opera, especially Wagner. Unable to get tickets one year to
Bayreuth, he asked his partner John J. McCloy, once high commissioner
of occupied Germany, to intervene.

Brinck's version of the Basia and Seward story read less like a legal
document, more like the program notes from a Metropolitan Opera
playbill. Forger spiced it up still more, equating S&C's storybook tale
of Basia and Seward at Jasna Polana to Fonda and Hepburn on Golden

Pond. Reilly grew ruffled over Brinck's flourishes and Forger's embellishments, and removed some of them. Still, what emerged made for extraordinary reading. The fifty-page document was officially entitled "Affidavit in Opposition to Proponents' Motion for a Protective Order Striking Objectants' Second Document Request." That is, Milbank was telling Judge Lambert why she should ignore S&C's objections to its shopping list. It became better known, however, as the "Forger Affidavit," named for the man who signed it and, thereby, swore to its accuracy.

"Forger" began his grim fairy tale by acknowledging his limited competence; since he'd never met Seward, Basia, or Nina, what followed was necessarily based "on knowledge and belief." But that was his last concession to uncertainty. Forger forged forward confidently, breezily, with none of the equivocations, uncertainties, and contradictions his own clients betrayed. One heard echoes of *The Blue Angel* in his account, with Basia cast as the Marlene Dietrich–like temptress, and Seward as the pathetic, elderly professor whose respectable life fell to pieces once he fell for a modern Lola-Lola.

"Late in 1968, Barbara Z. Piasecka (who has been referred to in deposition testimony as 'Basia,') immigrated to the United States," Forger began. "She was then 31 years of age and arrived with but modest means. Almost immediately she found employment as a chambermaid in the household of J. Seward Johnson, Sr. Seward and Esther, his wife of more than 30 years, were then living a quiet life in comparatively modest surroundings, an unpretentious home in New Jersey, the home in which their children had been raised and which the grandchildren frequently visited. Basia's duties included caring for the living quarters, occasional oversight of Seward's grandchildren, serving tea to family and guests and the like." One could only imagine how much the Milbank lawyers—and their clients—had savored the chance to rub Basia's nose in her roots.

"Notwithstanding the language barrier, she did succeed in communicating with Seward, who was then well into his 70's," Forger continued. "Esther proved to be no match for the youthful and attractive Basia. Within a year, the domestic tranquility of the Johnson household had been shattered and the marriage of Seward and Esther destroyed"; in November 1971 "Basia replaced Esther as Mrs. J. Seward Johnson, Sr." But this marriage, Forger declared, could only be a short-term proposition, for at seventy-six years of age, Seward "had already achieved an actuarially-determined full life expectancy" (in other words, by the time Seward married Basia, he should have been dead already). The "wide disparity in their ages was paralleled by the vast differences in their educational and cultural backgrounds, in their financial resources and business interests and in their philanthropic, recreational and social interests," Forger observed. "What then was the attraction that caused Basia to embark upon matrimony? One is drawn unmistakenly to the conclusion that the real attraction was the money."

Forger described Basia's growing stake in Seward's estate. That progression, he wrote, was utterly illogical given Seward's deeply held charitable interests and the modest provisions he'd always made for Essie. Just about the only loot Basia didn't stand to inherit, he claimed, was what she'd already received, quite possibly fraudulently, while he was alive—gifts of cash and artworks and Jasna Polana itself. "Basia relied not only on her ability to enchant and captivate Seward, but also on her violent temper and fierce outbursts which Seward, by nature a reserved person, became too weak to resist as time wore on," Forger continued. "Basia would fly into rages at the slightest provocation and, when her rage was directed at others and Seward tried to calm her, she would turn her wrath on Seward, calling him 'ga-ga' and 'stupid.' Partly as a result of her forceful and embarrassing outbursts, Basia came to dominate Seward's life in every way; he stopped resisting her wishes, perhaps because he was too old and sick to do so." He recounted how Basia had threatened to leave Seward unless he tore up their prenuptial agreement, and how Clinton Wold had seen Basia pressure Seward to sign certain documents—documents that Forger quite understandably left unspecified. And, because she'd "purged" all of Seward's old loyalists, there was no one around to protect him. Enter Nina Zagat, whom Milbank described as Basia's "accomplice," "contemporary, traveling companion, and close personal friend." Her principal loyalties were to Basia, not Seward; her reward "the extraordinary compensation— indeed a small fortune in itself—that she is to receive."

From will to will to will, Seward's "long-held philosophy of balanced giving" disappeared, and Basia's marital trust grew, from $10 million to $50 million to $100 million. Seward bequeathed $20 million to Basia's relatives, "persons unknown to him and residing in foreign countries." As he was "undergoing surgery" in 1981, Seward signed a will leaving Basia virtually everything; Basia's principal concern "was not the state of Seward's health, but rather the state of his will." And as Basia's stake increased, so did Nina's.

How could these nefarious women have pulled off their dastardly plot, one lasting a dozen years, all under the testator's nose, without ever getting caught? Forger, like Junior, depicted Seward as a man of conveniently intermittent lucidity, capable of detecting—and resisting—rip-offs, but only for short intervals. Forger's Basia and Nina, on the other hand, were single-minded, demonic geniuses. At first they stole subtly, leaving Seward's wills outwardly intact but fine-tuning obscure back-of-the-book provisions in ways that had huge dollar consequences. One ploy—allowing Basia to withdraw trust principal freely—could just as easily have been a bequest, Forger contended, "except that then its effect might have been too plain to escape Seward's notice." From time to time, Forger suggested, Seward regained his wits, detected these ruses, and rebuffed such encroachments. But instead of throwing the rascals out, he only beat them into temporary retreat. As his condition deteriorated, so, too, did his capacity to fend off such thievery.

In early 1983, Forger wrote, Basia "removed" Seward from New Jersey to Florida. And while Basia had isolated Seward at Jasna Polana, in Fort Pierce she all but quarantined him. "A Fortress America atmosphere prevailed," Forger charged. Seward was "shut off from the outside world and, in large part, from his family," "kept at bay while Basia consolidated her control." Occasionally, relatives penetrated Seward's gilded gulag long enough to see that the man who signed all those "inordinately complicated" wills in his final months—containing changes designed either to further enrich Basia, simplify things for Shearman & Sterling, or "buy off" the children—was in the last, pathetic stages of senility. Then and only then, it seemed, did Seward's children experience their collective epiphany. "For the first time Seward Johnson, Jr., and perhaps other family members, began to suspect that neither family nor Harbor Branch Foundation had any significant interest under Seward's will," Forger declared. "They came to realize that Nina Zagat was not Seward's lawyer but Basia's."

"The end result—the shift of Seward's wealth to Basia, complete and total—and the rejection of charity—is wholly unnatural and contrary to the decedent's lifelong instincts," Forger wrote. "When in command of his faculties and free of improper influences, he would never have dreamed of defaulting in his perceived obligation of stewarding his wealth for the benefit of mankind. His resolve and dedication were unswerving until old age and poor health gave others the opportunity to take unfair advantage and cause him to do that which was totally foreign to his very being." Forger prepared his concluding pitch. "In your deponent's 34 years of practice, he has not encountered a more extraordinary set of circumstances than exists in this proceeding," he stated. And this, he promised, was only the beginning. There was no telling what Milbank would unearth if Judge Lambert forced Basia and Nina to cough up everything it had requested.

By any standard, the Forger Affidavit was what Truman Capote called "faction"—that is, lying somewhere between fact and fiction. In some ways it was accurate, but it was filled with omissions, oversimplifications, and exaggerations. It failed to mention that Seward might have stopped giving money to Harbor Branch because he'd lavished $150 million on it already. The notion that Basia had tempted Seward out of what had been an idyllic relationship with Essie and their grandchildren, most of whom he would never have recognized, was poppycock, as some of Seward's children readily admitted. Forger's own clients also rebutted the notion that Basia maintained a "Fortress America" in Fort Pierce; if four of them stayed away from there, it was because they'd been aboard the QE2 much of the time he was bedridden. Forger could hardly have thought Seward's eleventh-hour will-making so unusual, for the dying millionaires he represented often do such things. And his "I am shocked, *shocked*" reaction to the Johnsons' marriage was particularly hard to swallow coming from someone who'd spent his career tending to the quirky rich. Forger had undoubtedly helped any number of clients either arrange for or extricate themselves from unconventional, even utilitarian, unions. "The wide disparity in their ages was paralleled by the vast differences in their educational and cultural backgrounds, in their financial resources and business interests and in their philanthropic, recreational and social interests," Forger had stated. "What then was the attraction that caused [her] to embark upon matrimony? One is drawn unmistakenly to the conclusion that the real attraction was the money." He was describing Basia and Seward Johnson, but he could just as easily have been writing about Jacqueline and Aristotle Onassis.

Anyone requiring further proof that Forger's affidavit was cynicism masquerading as pious outrage need only have considered another case then on Milbank's docket: an effort in Long Island to overturn the last will of Charles Shipman Payson. There, as in the Johnson case, the objectants were the unhappy, disinherited children of an earlier marriage: the four children from Payson's union with Joan Whitney Payson, onetime owner of the New York Mets. There, too, the enemy was a much younger (by thirty-one years) stepmother, Virginia Payson. She, too, was depicted as a fortune hunter. She, too, was said to have spent her husband's money prodigiously on things he'd never previously cared about. His bequests to her, too, had gradually grown. Her husband, too, hated taxes, was forever changing his will, and never expected to die. The four Paysons, like the six Johnsons, said their first priority was salvaging family pride rather than collecting family cash. They, too, claimed that their stepmother (for whom they, too, had professed great admiration until the last will was read) controlled their father, and that her affection for him, like Basia's for Seward, was strictly for show. She, too, was said to have built a "Fortress America" around her husband, firing longtime associates, keeping him from his children, controlling his care. She, too, had allegedly coerced him into signing things (in this case, a letter to the New York Racing Authority guaranteeing her his prized boxes at Aqueduct, Belmont, and Saratoga after his death). She, too, muzzled her husband when he grew tiresome, only no one had ever accused Basia, as they accused Virginia, of literally taping over her husband's mouth to shut him up. Old man Payson, like old man Johnson, was said to have had memory lapses and bouts of irrationality; if Seward defecated publicly, Charles shot at a wild turkey from inside his Hobe Sound home. Seward was betrayed—and Basia, abetted—by Shearman & Sterling; Charles was betrayed—and Virginia, abetted—by another old and prominent Wall Street law firm, Carter, Ledyard & Milburn.

The defenses, too, were all the same. Lawyers for Virginia Payson insisted that she, like Basia, had revived a dispirited old man. As a woman who'd driven an arctic dog team two hundred miles, who hunted for big game, who "filled out a bathing suit just right," Virginia, too, was depicted as a sexy dynamo who enlivened a septuagenarian's twilight years. A revivified Seward became a Knight of Malta; a revivified Charles danced at Derby parties, collected trophies from Mario Cuomo and kisses from Phyllis George. The allegedly incompetent Seward could converse about solar energy and ships; the allegedly incompetent Charles could still explain the twelve-meter rule and the economics of the horse business. Here, too, the young wife charged that what disinherited children were calling undue influence was really love—a love for poets, not lawyers, to describe. This widow also argued it was hardly unusual for a father to leave nothing more to children he'd already made fabulously rich. Indeed, in his last will Charles had applied the same salve as Seward, about how his failure to give them any more didn't mean he didn't love them.

Who were those lawyers who stood up so gamely for this young, wronged widow, who denounced the "empty-headed greed" of stepchildren? They came from Milbank, Tweed, Hadley & McCloy. In

fact, Virginia Payson had originally retained Ed Reilly, who ceded the
case to a partner because he was too busy making diametrically opposed
arguments in *Johnson v. Johnson*.

Sure, Tolstoy wrote that every unhappy family is unhappy in its own
way. But when they went to court, the unhappy families of Seward
Johnson, Charles Payson, and Charles Lachman followed the same old
script. They demonstrate that colossal will contests share certain characteristics: canned outrage, allegedly evil interlopers, purportedly doddering testators. Such wills are invariably accepted anyway, which
explains why whatever noises Milbank was making, most leaders of
New York's probate bar considered the Johnson case yet another "strike
suit"—that is, a holdup staged by disgruntled heirs designed to induce
a settlement—one that Milbank, blessed with wealthy clients too gul-
lible to know any better, and aided by Shearman & Sterling's own
assortment of mistakes, was milking for all it was worth.

Privately, Milbank had already conceded that the Johnson children
and Harbor Branch had conflicting interests and needed separate counsel. Still, words like "charitable" and "philanthropic" kept popping up
in Forger's affidavit; charity was what had always driven Seward before
Basia came along, he insisted, and what was driving his children now.
But Forger spoke a bit disingenuously. Arguing incapacity was a bit like
using chemotherapy: that is, it was impossible to confine. By suggesting
Seward had been incompetent before April 14—including, presumably,
those times in March when he'd made his only bequests to the foundation for several years—he was undercutting Harbor Branch's only
chance at collecting anything. True, Forger was saying that Seward had
been Silly Putty in Basia's hands from the beginning of their marriage,
and maybe even before. But it was hard enough to prove undue influence
even for an instant; no court had ever found it over a twelve-year
period. Thus, the children were destroying something in order to save
it. Why? To paraphrase Forger once more, the real attraction was the
money. Invalidating only the last will would help Harbor Branch but
net the children nothing. They—the children and their hired guns—
had to attack them all.

Despite its literate, gentlemanly facade, the Forger Affidavit breached
the social fabric of the elite bar. In it one major law firm was charging
another with criminality—of participating, in the words of an accompanying memorandum, in "a prospective or ongoing crime or fraud."
Except for Nina, the other coconspirators were never identified by
name. There were, significantly, no references to the partner with

ultimate responsibility for the Johnson file, Tom Ford, nor to Henry
Ziegler, his second-in-command. Perhaps Milbank really believed Nina
had hoodwinked them, too. More likely, it was far easier for Forger to
aim his artillery at an associate rather than a partner, and a female
associate at that. The Code of Professional Responsibility contains no
strictures against ruthlessness. Forger's hyperbole, as one leading trusts
lawyer later put it, was "the kind of lie one has to tell in this sort of
game." Of Nina Zagat the lawyer added, "Alex painted her as much
worse than she was. But he did what he had to do."

The Forger Affidavit accomplished its immediate, narrow purpose.
Anyone reading it had to conclude that simply to ferret out so heinous
a plot, the objectants should be given whatever information they sought,
maybe more. This, in turn, guaranteed that discovery would be lengthy
and painful, enough to tie up the estate indefinitely and help coerce a
settlement. The affidavit also gave Milbank the chance to tell its side
of the story first, to frame the debate in its own way. Only a few
cognoscenti would spot all the distortions; to everyone else it had that
official, IBM Selectric look of truth. When the case inevitably hit the
press, the affidavit was destined to become the Baedeker on which
reporters relied. Perhaps most importantly, it threw the opposition
completely off stride. Neither the proponents nor their lawyers had
expected anything so hard-hitting. Like the spectators at the First Battle
of Bull Run, they had come to this fight carrying picnic baskets. "What
can they say about me?" Basia would ask. "I've never done anything
wrong." Now, all pretenses of gentility and fraternity had suddenly and
irrevocably been dropped.

Privately, the proponents were outraged. Ever-ready with an apt pun,
Christ came to refer to the Forger Affidavit as "the Forger-y," or simply
as the "steaming turd." Osgood suggested taking Forger's deposition, so
that he could be forced to back up some of his claims. What Basia
found most offensive was not that the children called her dishonest or
scheming, but uneducated. How dare those "monkeys," who'd never
even been to college, call *her* uneducated?

At Shearman & Sterling reactions were varied. First and foremost,
there was outrage. Milbank, some thought, was acting like a bunch of
high-class call girls, a ritzy firm prostituting itself for its clients. There
was also pity. Perhaps, some speculated, the firm was in dire financial
straits. There were I-told-you-so's from Henry Ziegler, who had tangled
with Forger during the Onassis case and considered the affidavit completely in character. There was also some patronizing admiration.

"Forger seems to be writing for New York Magazine and his clients, and has done a good job with what he has," one trusts partner, Arthur Norman Field, wrote in a memorandum.

Most significantly and surprisingly, there was fear. On the Saturday after it was filed, Shearman & Sterling's managing partner, Robert Knight, read over the copy of the affidavit that had been hand-delivered to his home in Greenwich. And, staggeringly enough, his first instinct was to believe Forger's view of reality rather than Ford's. Page by page Knight's face grew graver, his voice more indignant, though his indignation was directed at the accused instead of at the accuser. How could this have happened? What had his underlings done? What was to be done about it now? Genteel Shearman & Sterling was suddenly facing the most public of scandals, and Knight, a cautious securities lawyer by trade, reacted defensively rather than defiantly, just as the firm was to do throughout the case. Instead of returning fire, he sent for his senior and most respected litigator, Arnold Bauman, handed him a copy of the affidavit, and asked him to investigate Forger's charges.

Bauman, sixty-nine at the time, had taken a strange route to S&S. He'd worked for Thomas E. Dewey in his rackets-busting days, then bounced back and forth between private practice and public service in various prosecuting capacities. Bauman was serving on the Knapp Commission, investigating police corruption in New York, when Richard Nixon named him to the federal district court in 1972. He was there only a couple of years when the financial strains grew too serious, and he returned to private practice—this time at Shearman & Sterling. S&S generally didn't import outsiders, especially Jews, into its upper echelons. But the firm's litigation department was weak, and it thought Bauman could bring some experience and seasoning to the place. By the time Knight sent for him, Bauman was leading the contented life of an emeritus partner. He picked his cases as he pleased; rarely were things so hectic that he couldn't spend a leisurely lunchtime at the Broad Street Club or the Down Town Association, have a couple of kirs, mosey on back to One Wall, light up a Hoyo de Monterrey, place his feet squarely atop his desk, and ponder how good his life had become (Bauman was a tall man, and although he'd stayed trim, all those years spent sitting so contortedly had caused him to sag a bit around the middle—a feature highlighted by his habit of hunching over, reaching into his pockets, and jingling his change). If things were really slow, he'd leave early. Otherwise, he'd hop on the 5:32 to Rye.

Bauman was a lifelong Republican, and though he was a closet humanist, he had grown more publicly conservative over the years. He was also an unabashed elitist, someone who knew all the best vintages and kept a charge account at Le Cygne. Still, in his decade at Shearman & Sterling he'd never cracked the firm's inner circle. His partners may have viewed him as too independent, too intelligent, and well, maybe just a little *too Jewish*, to be one of them. But these same traits made his advice on sensitive matters particularly prized. His stock-in-trade these days wasn't billable hours so much as sage counsel. And that was what Shearman & Sterling needed now.

Bauman spent several weeks questioning Nina, Ford, Ziegler, Gunther, Hoch, Polak, and anyone else who'd worked on Johnson matters. By all accounts, no one had ever conducted a witch-hunt so civilly. He spoke with Christ as well, and reviewed all relevant documents. To him, the most important of them was the May 1983 memo to Nina from Shearman & Sterling's management committee, authorizing her to serve as executor and trustee and keep the fees she earned. "Case dismissed," he told her when she showed it to him. Nina, he subsequently told the committee, had not been a rogue elephant; she had followed firm procedures and kept Ford and other colleagues apprised of her work. Nor, he concluded, had she violated firm policy or had a conflict of interest by drafting a will in which she was named as a fiduciary or by representing both Basia and Seward simultaneously. For Forger, whose firm was counsel to innumerable Rockefellers, to make such a charge was outrageous and typical, Bauman said; so intensely did he dislike the Milbank lawyer, whom he considered self-righteous and unprincipled, that he'd quit the board of the Legal Aid Society rather than sit with him.

The firm accepted his findings. But with the case still heating up, Shearman & Sterling knew the worst was yet to come. It asked Bauman to stay on top of things, to befriend Basia, work with Sullivan & Cromwell, act as S&S's eyes and ears. He became counsel on matters large and small—for example, in the ongoing debate over the precise definition of "ga-ga." Did Basia's favorite epithet mean "senile," as Nina thought and Milbank was contending, or "crazy," as in head over heels in love, as Bauman insisted? The dispute led the proponents to add *The Dictionary of American Slang* to their arsenal. The entry defined "ga-ga" as "adj. lit. and fig., crazy; silly; irrational; having lost one's objectivity and perspective." It was not helpful. Indeed, months would pass and millions more dollars spent deciding whether Basia's use of the term was "lit." or "fig."

XXV

W hen it came to adverse publicity, the firm of John Foster Dulles instinctively pushed for containment. Already it had tried, unsuccessfully, to keep Seward's medical records sealed. Now, Sullivan & Cromwell attempted to bury Forger's affidavit. In May 1984, with depositions under way and a trial date still far off, the Johnson case remained a delicious secret; now, any reporter stumbling upon Forger's fusillade had himself an instant story. Intent upon avoiding that and protecting Basia's tender sensibilities, S&C formally moved in Lambert's chambers to keep the affidavit under seal. Reilly, Christ, and Forger (who rationed his appearances to underline their gravity) listened. Osgood talked. "We like a good, clean, hard-fought courtroom battle as much as anyone," he began. "We expect to articulate our positions forcefully, and would expect no less from the other side. But we also expect that the battle should be confined to the courtroom. In this age, when many of the old amenities have fast faded away, I think it is important to conduct this proceeding with as much decorum and dignity as we can. I say to the court with the utmost sincerity that if this case is not handled with sensitivity, it has the potential for being transformed into sensationalism. I believe such sensationalism would reflect poorly on the parties, their counsel, and perhaps the Court.

"Unfortunately," Osgood continued, "an affidavit has been filed that we believe feeds the fires of sensationalism. It is replete with argument, speculation, and invective. It does damage to the reputations of two women that the lawyer has never met. That affidavit, without the slightest justification, charges that a lawyer at Shearman & Sterling is incompetent. I refer to an exceptionally talented lawyer named Nina S. Zagat, whom Mr. Forger in his affidavit has—one hesitates to say it—defamed in her profession." By charging Seward was senile, Osgood said, the affidavit defamed his memory. And in portraying Basia as a fortune hunter, it was just as unfair to her. But what really seemed to exercise Osgood were Forger's hints about Basia's breeding. "Without

272

any basis in fact whatsoever, the affidavit charges that Mrs. Johnson is an uneducated, uncultured Polish immigrant who captivated Mr. Johnson, held him a virtual prisoner and forced him to execute no less than twenty testamentary instruments during the twelve-year marriage," Osgood fumed. "This, from a lawyer, under oath, who has never met either Mrs. Zagat or Mrs. Johnson!"

"Your Honor, we are not concerned about our ability to show there is absolutely no substance to these charges," Osgood continued. "The truth will come out. We are concerned, however, about our clients' right to litigate to the court and not in the press, to be free from damage to reputation from unsubstantiated, highly charged, provocative statements about their character and their competence. Our clients have a right to privacy, our clients have a right to trial by an unbiased jury, and they have a right to due process."

Reilly, who had listened silently, promptly objected to Osgood's request. There was nothing irresponsible about the affidavit, he insisted, though in truth he had some private qualms about it; what really worried the proponents was its accuracy. Besides, he added, Milbank wasn't about to alert anyone to it. "We couldn't dream of calling in the press and telling them about this. Our attitude with the press on all matters is 'no comment,' " he said.

"I don't think Mr. Osgood is saying you would call them in," interjected Harvey Corn, Lambert's law clerk. "I think he is saying that the fact that it is on file would lead to its discovery."

"One does have to wonder why the objectants would have a problem sealing a court paper," Osgood, evidently emboldened by Corn's comment, interjected. "It will not hinder them in communicating their positions with the court; it will not hinder them in communicating with their clients. The only thing it will do is assure that this will not be picked up by the *New York Post* or the *Daily News* and made into cheap, sensational gossip."

The colloquy then returned to the substance of the affidavit, as Reilly took issue with what he called several "egregious misstatements" Osgood had made. Nowhere, for instance, had Forger used words like "uneducated" or "uncultured" to describe Basia Johnson. "Let me read from the affidavit," Osgood replied. "Paragraph eleven, page six, refers to the marriage of Mr. and Mrs. Johnson in 1971. 'The vast disparity in their ages was paralleled by the vast differences in their educational and cultural backgrounds, in their financial resources and business interests and in their philanthropic, recreational and social interests. What then was the attraction that caused Basia'—who should be referred to as 'Mrs. Johnson,' " he interjected—" 'to embark upon matrimony? One is drawn unmistakenly to the conclusion that the real attraction for Basia was the money.' Now, the fact is that Mrs. Johnson was far more educated than Mr. Johnson, but Mr. Forger doesn't know that, so he implies that Mr. Johnson, who had one year of college, was far more educated and far more cultured than his wife, who in fact had a master's degree in art history. It is that kind of insinuation and innuendo that is absolutely unfair."

"You read that in!" Corn, suddenly less sympathetic, interjected.

"That's right, you read that in!" Lambert echoed. "I don't read it that way."

"He could have been referring to the fact that your client is *more* educated," Corn added.

Corn's interpretation was a stretch, but Forger seized upon it. "That's right," he chimed in. "There is a *'vast difference.'* "

In the end Lambert compromised. She would not formally seal the "steaming turd," but it would remain in her chambers, away from the press's grubby paws. Already, though, there were multiple copies in circulation; copies had been given to each of the Johnson children, their lawyers, Harbor Branch officials, and other Milbank lawyers, one of whom found it so moving—or deemed it such a fairy tale—that he brought it home and read it to his children. In addition, Milbank filed an unsealed copy of it with the New Jersey court hearing Basia's lawsuit against Junior. It was there, in fact, that an enterprising reporter eventually tracked it down, just as Milbank had probably hoped one would.

However distasteful she found it, Basia urged her lawyers not to respond in kind to the Forger Affidavit—"The eagles will fly high, not get down in the gutter," she said—and that seemed to suit her uncombative counsel just fine. Sullivan & Cromwell's answer was exceedingly mild; apart from charging that Forger had "passed the bounds of legitimate advocacy," it focused on the more narrow issue that was actually before the court: just how much information Milbank could demand. S&C called Milbank's motion a "kitchen sink," "blunderbuss," illogical request, one that strayed far afield from Seward Johnson's state of mind on April 14, 1983. The Forger Affidavit, S&C asserted, was "an abuse of the discovery process and a sign that civil litigation has become irrational."

Christ and Ford also fashioned personal responses to Forger, more detailed but, if possible, even more pallid. Apparently unperturbed that his department had been accused of conspiracy, Ford merely reiterated Seward's testamentary tenets: to leave nothing to his children; to give

Basia as much as he could without triggering taxes; and to let her decide how much of that money would wind up with which charity. How Forger missed this, Ford said, "is incomprehensible to me." He called Nina "a highly skilled, competent and respected lawyer," but added that Seward's wills "represent the work of my firm; they were not the product of Mrs. Zagat alone." The will was being probated in New York, he added, because that was where Seward's bankers, lawyers, and most of his assets were; besides, one of the co-executors, Junior, was afraid to fly. Regarding the charge that Seward hadn't comprehended the changes in his last few wills, Ford wrote that "one must wonder what Mr. Forger is talking about." And as for the ethical charges against Basia and Nina, Ford wished them away. Such an insinuendo "does not deserve comment," he said.

In his affidavit Christ juxtaposed Forger's claims against the sworn testimony of his clients. How could the children have known their father's testamentary plan when, by their own admission, they'd never discussed it with him? How could Forger blame Basia for destroying Seward's second marriage, when Junior had testified that the old man sailed the seas to escape from Essie? How could Forger liken the Fort Pierce house to "Fortress America" when the six children visited him thirty times in 1983, and Basia had welcomed them there? Indeed, in a classic display of S&C compulsiveness, some bleary-eyed underling had determined that between January 1, 1983, and May 23, 1983, Basia had kissed Diana at least four times, Elaine at least twice, and Mary Lea at least once (and had hugged her to boot).

Eventually, Lambert gave Milbank everything it wanted. Perhaps, like most trial court judges, she thought it better to be generous than to risk reversal. Just as plausibly, she hankered to hear more of the story herself.

Perhaps one reason the proponents fought Milbank's document request so halfheartedly is that they were attempting something far more ambitious. In early June they asked Lambert to throw out the children's case altogether. Under the law, they conceded, any offspring can contest a will. But the Johnson children, S&C claimed, were insisting they wanted nothing for themselves. As incredible as that claim appeared— as S&C put it, the children's handling of their "vast and unearned wealth" had always been "more conspicuous for frivolity than for public spiritedness"—it urged Lambert to take them at their word, and dismiss the case. If Harbor Branch sought a share of Seward's fortune, it should have challenged the will itself.

Milbank reacted to what it called "the Sullivan & Cromwell greed test" with what was, for lawyers, the most contemptuous of all retorts: a brief brief. Essentially, Milbank's defense was that however lovely the children's charitable utterances were, they had no significance legally and represented no waiver of their rights. Lambert agreed. She, too, hadn't bought the children's altruistic rhetoric. The Johnsons, she ruled, had acted "as if they do indeed hope to gain a financial benefit after these proceedings," and should be allowed to proceed.

Lambert's ruling, while unsurprising, did contain one disturbing passage: Perhaps, she suggested, only certain portions of the April 14 will had been procured by undue influence; if so, in order to collect something, the children would not have to knock out twenty wills at all, but just pieces of the last one. The possibility of such "partial intestacy"—an argument even Milbank hadn't hatched—sent shock waves through the proponents' camp. Something as novel and imaginative as this, they knew, was not the handiwork of Marie Lambert but of Corn. Robert Delahunty, one of the S&C associates working on the case, investigated the partial-intestacy doctrine and concluded it was inapplicable. "In view of the craziness of the theory, should we now call Harvey 'Mr. Korn-Flake'?" Delahunty wrote Nina.

While S&C was trying to knock the children out of the case, Harbor Branch was belatedly trying to get in.

Though everyone claimed to care about Harbor Branch, a year after Seward's death it effectively remained unrepresented in the will contest. Its general counsel, Milbank, was representing another party with hostile legal interests and had filed nothing on the foundation's behalf. Finally, in June 1984 Harbor Branch's Florida lawyer decided it needed independent New York counsel, and began looking for recommendations. Oddly, the person consulted was the same soul who'd cast Harbor Branch adrift: Alex Forger. He recommended Dewey, Ballantine, Bushby, Palmer & Wood. Indeed, it was Forger who called William Warren, head of Dewey Ballantine's trusts and estates department, and offered him the case.

Why, of all firms in New York, would Forger have suggested Dewey Ballantine, the firm to which Thomas E. Dewey retreated after he'd "won" the presidency in 1948? One could say it was convenience, for Dewey's offices, in the Marine Midland Bank building, were next door to Milbank's, but Dewey's probate department had separate offices near Grand Central. It could also have been that Forger and Warren were old and trusted colleagues, but in fact this was the first case in thirty years that Forger had referred to him. Moreover, Warren, who'd drafted Dewey's last will and inherited two of his armchairs, personified the kind of probate lawyer Forger loved to ridicule and was so quick to point out he wasn't: a blue blood from the Auchinclossian wing of the estates bar, a tad stuffy, maybe a bit soft. A graduate of Groton, Harvard, and Harvard Law School, Warren had the formal, slightly cramped demeanor and diction of a New England aristocrat. Long after his student days in Munich, he remained a bit of a Junker. He attended tastings of the German Wine Society and dabbled in German history, at least of those years before it all became so terribly unpleasant. No, a more likely answer is that Dewey promised the peculiar combination of attributes Forger sought. That is, it sounded good, but was doing badly. It had a distinguished lineage, with links to former secretary of war Elihu Root, Grenville Clark, and the younger John Marshall Harlan, but simply by walking into the place, one sensed it was heading into a decrepit middle age. Forger, like any other Wall Street insider, would surely have known that in the spring of 1984 Dewey Ballantine was hardly a firm in top fighting form. And that's what might have made it so appealing. Here was a firm that was unlikely to get too uppity, that would ride Milbank's coattails and follow its lead.

Shortly after Forger's call, Warren and Robert Hirth, a sixth-year Dewey litigation associate, reviewed Seward's wills. They quickly realized how weak Harbor Branch's legal position was: Its only shot was to knock out the April 14 will, then wait for Basia to die, when it would collect whatever she hadn't spent of the Q-TIP trust. Whatever Milbank was telling its clients, Warren knew that knocking out twelve years' worth of wills was a pipe dream. The Dewey lawyers quickly saw that by failing to file objections for the foundation, Milbank had either accidentally or deliberately abandoned its client. Undeterred, on August 13 Harbor Branch, claiming that its interests were "totally at odds" with those of the Johnson children, filed objections of its own.

Sullivan & Cromwell immediately opposed the request. Harbor Branch, it argued, had missed the boat; allowing it in now would bollix things up with "an extraordinary gallimaufry of contestants." Besides, S&C went on, how "independent" was the foundation and, implicitly, its lawyers? Junior controlled Harbor Branch "as completely as Colonel Qaddafi dominates Libya"; the foundation was clearly just a "stalking horse" for the children. Sure enough, despite being "totally at odds" with the foundation, the children supported its attempt to intervene. From their standpoint, the stickier things got, the better. Harbor Branch also got a vote of support from the New York State attorney general,

Robert Abrams, who was mandated by law to protect charities in will contests and, now, began going through the motions of doing so here. It probably wasn't necessary, for no judge was likely to disenfranchise a charity because of the behavior of its general counsel. In October Lambert allowed Harbor Branch to intervene.

If the foundation's position was legally weak, the predicament of its lawyers was downright degrading. To S&C, they were Milbank's puppets; to Milbank, they were clumsy nuisances. Still, Harbor Branch had one trump card: its name. Should it remain in the case, the children could continue to pose as altruists. Without it, S&C could lay bare their greed. As Warren saw things, his role would be like Bismarck's at the Congress of Berlin: He would play the "honest broker," flitting between the two sides, trying to strike the best deal for the foundation. The bidding would open with S&C. Warren set his asking price for dropping out of the case at $25 million. It was too steep for the proponents; there were negotiations, but they were brief and fruitless.

In the meantime Christ was having problems with his client. Throughout the early skirmishing Basia had held her acquisitiveness in check, either because she lacked the cash or had been listening to her lawyers, who had told her how bad any extravagances would now look, particularly since the money in Seward's estate was not yet hers to spend. "Don't give the other side any bullets, Mrs. Johnson," Polak cautioned. Then a temptation arose that proved too great for her to resist. Something Basia (or, as she characteristically put it, Seward) had always wanted—a work by Raphael—was coming on the market, at a Christie's sale in London. The piece, a drawing dating from 1520, depicted the head and hand of one of the Apostles in *The Transfiguration,* a painting in the Vatican. With his curly hair and scraggly beard, the figure resembled the freewheelin' Bob Dylan. Only five such drawings existed; the other four were in the British Museum. Even to contemplate such a purchase in the middle of a will contest was folly. Nina counseled strongly against it. But, undeterred, Basia flew to London with Harry Ward Bailey, her transatlantic art dealer and socialite friend. Arrayed against her were several of the world's leading collectors and the Getty Museum.

The crowd assembled in Christie's "Great Rooms" around seven. The day had been torrid, and with no air-conditioning on the premises, it was even more stifling inside. Still, Basia remained cool. Only a few years earlier, she had been too timid to raise her hand at an auction. Now, she was doing her own bidding. Two great oil fortunes, baby versus crude, did battle. In half a minute or less the figure had rocketed up to £3 million. Then the ghost of J. Paul Getty blinked. When the auctioneer asked for £3.3 million—$4.8 million—Basia's hand went up, and the hammer came down. To that hefty price was tacked on a 10 percent commission. It was, as *The New York Times* later reported, "by far the highest price ever paid for a drawing in any medium by any artist." Basia—and Seward—had their Raphael.

Basia exulted, but not everyone was impressed. *The Economist* called the purchase a symptom of "dollarhoea"—too much American money driving up the price of art. It was the July 4 weekend, and Nina, vacationing at a phone-free home off the coast of Maine, found a pile of anxious messages waiting for her on the mainland. Christ read the news aboard the *Concorde* to London, and briefly considered punching a hole in the window and bailing out. Before long, Milbank was accusing Basia of looting the estate. Anxious to cut their losses, Christ and Nina told Basia she would have to get rid of the Raphael, and arrangements were made to sell it, at a modest profit, to the Getty. But before that could be done, Judge Roth, who continued to oversee the estate's finances, demanded a list of the estate's assets, and shortly thereafter ordered the proponents to post a $100 million bond, as well as to set aside $100 million in Johnson & Johnson stock in a special account at Citibank. Basia ended up keeping the Raphael. She paid for it by selling what had been one of Seward's favorite paintings, Modigliani's *La Rêveuse*, for $4.6 million. Basia and Nina toasted the newly framed drawing during lunch at Le Cirque; afraid to leave it in the checkroom, they dined with it at their side.

In November 1984 Lambert laid out a pretrial schedule. The proponents were to produce all requested documents by December 31; all medical witnesses were to be deposed by February 28, 1985. The all-important depositions of Basia and Nina were to begin by March 1, and by the beginning of June discovery was to be complete. The trial could begin shortly after that. The proponents began disgorging eighty-five thousand pages of documents, among them lists of everyone who'd worked for the Johnsons during their marriage, and everyone— friend, employee, guest—who had seen or spoken to Seward between January 1980 and his death. At fifty-two pages, the latter sounded long, though when one considers how many encounters ordinary mortals have each week, it was really the logbook of a recluse. On it was the veterinarian who serviced Seward's animals; the welder who'd struck the first arc; Chief Justice Warren Burger and Cyrus

Vance (whom the Johnsons had met briefly at a Washington reception); Nicola Bulgari (the maker of Seward's famous medallion); tennis player Wojtek Fibak, Mr. and Mrs. I. M. Pei, Barbara Sinatra, and Edmund de Rothschild.

Of all the documents they had to produce, one particularly troubled the proponents and their lawyers: the "letter" Basia had "written" to Seward the day he signed his will, that weird hybrid of sentiment and legalese in which she'd promised to leave the Q-TIP trust to Harbor Branch. Nina remained convinced it had no legal significance whatever. But having been accorded all the honors due a binding document, it had, just as Nina had feared, taken on a legal life of its own. On the one hand, the proponents couldn't tear it up or laugh it off. On the other, treating it so solemnly and secretively legitimized it in a way. Somehow, they had to hand it over, but subtly, inconspicuously, in a fashion that would not highlight its potential importance.

S&C had been sending Milbank its documents piecemeal, going so far as to include juicy tidbits around each important holiday as a kind of bonus. One such present was the May 3 "anchor to windward" trust Nina had prepared to provide Basia with living expenses during a will contest (Christ called this document "the earmuff trust" because of the racket Reilly was certain to raise upon discovering it). Now, after endless agonizing, S&C decided to make the April 14 letter, document number 53090, the proponents' gift for Thanksgiving 1984. It was inserted into a package of 8,087 pages of documents. No matter how well hidden it might have been, a handwritten message on note-sized, cream-colored "Barbara P. Johnson" stationery leaped out from the reams of the larger, bleached-white Xeroxes. A Milbank paralegal named Lindsay Black spotted it and handed it to Charles Berry.

The Milbank lawyers did not know what to make of this peculiar document, this handwritten gobbledygook, witnessed by Nina Zagat and Jay Gunther and signed by Basia with love. Was it a codicil? A release? A contract? Was it enforceable? Had it also been procured through undue influence or incapacity? None of this really mattered, of course; what it was was irregular. Because it bore on the will, Reilly charged, failing to file it had been improper, even criminal. Citing both the letter and the May 3 trust—signed, Reilly charged, when Seward was in even worse shape than on April 14—he now opened yet another front, asking Lambert to remove Nina and Basia as preliminary executrices. In opposing the motion, S&C finally showed signs of annoyance. It charged that the children's claims stemmed more from "disappointed envy," "greed," and downright bigotry than conviction. "They simply cannot bear the thought that their father loved a woman whom they and their attorneys contemptuously describe as 'a Polish immigrant,' a 'chambermaid,' " it stated.

XXVI

The Milbank lawyers had begun deposing John Peach in August 1984. The first day, for which Peach had flown up from Florida, went innocuously enough. But on the second day Charles Berry's interrogation turned from Peach's background to the work he'd been performing for Sullivan & Cromwell. How had that association begun? What kind of tasks had he done? Had he taken any trips for S&C? Had he interviewed witnesses? Nurses? Doctors? How many hours per week was he working? How much was he making?

Osgood refused to let Peach answer these questions, claiming they were both immaterial and privileged. Later he defended S&C's use of Peach. Given the man's long association with the Johnsons, he told Lambert, Peach was the "obvious" choice to assist them; the only party who'd misused Peach was Junior, who'd fobbed off all his filial responsibilities on him in Seward's final days. But Milbank pressed for answers. Peach, it said, was likely to be a key witness at the trial, and it was crucial to know just how tainted this supposedly "disinterested" character had become. Sullivan & Cromwell had bought off Peach, it charged, and, for all it knew, other vital witnesses, too. Suddenly, Shearman & Sterling was not the only firm in the dock. Milbank demanded to question Christ and Osgood, under oath, about their arrangement with Peach.

Milbank and S&C went back a long ways together. When Milbank lawyers were assembling the land for what would become Rockefeller Center, for instance, they allowed William Nelson Cromwell to keep his apartment on the site as long as he wished. Any outsider would have viewed the firms as rivals in the same, sporting sense as the eating clubs of Fitzgerald's Princeton: that is, competitive in ways so trivial as to magnify how much they were alike. Their lawyers generally came from the same schools, ate the same food in the same restaurants and private clubs, belonged to the same professional associations, worshiped at the same churches, had outings at the same restricted country clubs, rode in on the same trains from the same wealthy suburbs, married and cheated on and divorced and married the same kinds of women, found themselves with the same kinds of clients in the same kinds of cases. Even as adversaries, a certain reciprocal respect and class courtesy had always obtained between them.

But within their tiny world inconsequential differences loomed large. Sullivan & Cromwell considered Milbank a second-rate operation, and Milbank knew it. S&C's top litigator, Marvin Schwartz, put it best: "No one in his right mind considers Milbank in the same breath as Sullivan & Cromwell," he once said. Rather than laugh off S&C's arrogance, Milbank, particularly some older Milbank lawyers, suffered from an institutional inferiority complex. As law students, both Forger and Reilly interviewed at S&C, and thirty-five years later, the experience still rankled Forger. "If we were to offer you a position, would you accept it?" the S&C partner, apparently worried that some snot-nosed kid might actually spurn him, had asked. Forger said such pretentiousness turned him off, and he went to the more modest Milbank instead. Reilly, too, had an interview at Sullivan & Cromwell, though nothing ever came of it. But, if anything, he loathed the place even more than Forger did. Forger breezily ridiculed S&C's haughtiness; it gnawed at Reilly. Overconfident, overbearing, imperious, coasting on its reputation: These were Reilly's impressions of S&C, and they only intensified as the Johnson case progressed. He thought S&C's briefs to be like S&C itself: overstated, cocky, careless. Reilly may never have said, as others claimed to have overheard, that he would "bury" Sullivan & Cromwell in the case. But he must have wanted to.

Reilly, of course, was hardly cordial to any of his adversaries. But S&C, and particularly Robert Osgood, prompted from him new levels of frigidity. Arriving for depositions or conferences, Reilly never offered his hand. Instead, he'd simply sit, stiff, purposeful, preoccupied. He never joked with Christ or Osgood, nor would he laugh at anything they said, at least not without a good, tactical reason for doing so. Nor was there ever any small talk. In one instance Reilly challenged a question he considered repetitious. "Mr. Reilly," an exasperated Christ replied, "I will give you a quarter if you can point to any reference in this record where this witness was asked that question or any like it." "Please continue, Mr. Christ," Reilly replied. "Fifty cents?" Christ asked. "We are deadly serious about this," Reilly declared, somewhat superfluously. "There is no point in joking about it."

The S&C lawyers began devising schemes to distract or at least tweak Reilly. Knowing of his nautical interests, they held all depositions in a particular corner conference room at S&C that overlooked New York

Harbor. Before long they discovered something that worked even better than boats. Women, they came to realize, were Reilly's kryptonite. Put a pretty one near him, and he began losing his superpowers, particularly his powers of concentration. The most potent weapon in S&C's arsenal was a paralegal named Tracy Hudson. Hudson was young and blond and Texan, the kind of woman one could imagine kicking up a halftime storm in her Davy Crockett coat and cowboy boots at the Texas-Baylor game. Whenever she'd enter the room, Reilly's eyes quickly migrated toward her. His permafrost personality would melt a bit; on his stern visage would appear that plaintive, boyish, vulnerable smile, that painfully shy, aw-shucks grin. Whenever possible, Hudson would be placed directly across the table from Reilly. After each session, S&C staffers would try to estimate just how long he'd stared at her that day, and whether or not he'd set some new world's indoor record.

Though it was scarcely detectable at times, Reilly actually liked Christ; with his sardonic, irreverent ways and utter lack of pretense, Christ didn't strike him as the prototypical S&C lawyer. Even with the other S&C lawyers, Reilly could muster an occasional awkward pleasantry. But none of the Milbank lawyers liked Osgood, and Reilly least of all. In chambers, say before Judge Lambert, they considered him a champion apple-polisher, laughing lustily at her unfunny and often off-color jokes. Away from court, he was a sneering smart-ass, ever quick with the cutting, condescending remark. At one point Berry asked a nurse about Seward's incontinence. "What is your theory, Mr. Berry: that if someone is incontinent, they are incompetent?" Osgood asked. Berry bristled. Such interruptions were "highly improper," he complained. "I think it is highly improper of you to spend so much time on the bowel movements of Mr. Johnson," Osgood retorted.

Repeatedly, strains surfaced between Osgood and Reilly. Consider what occurred at Joyce Johnson's deposition. True, Osgood's questions were often long-winded and poorly framed, but these were things a friendly adversary might have overlooked. Instead, Reilly's objections derailed the entire proceeding; a session in March 1984 lasted only a few minutes before both Osgood and Christ stalked out. It took nine months for that deposition to resume, but Reilly's rage had only intensified in the interim. Osgood began by asking the sickly Joyce if she felt up to testifying.

"Yes, I . . . yes," Joyce replied.

"I understand that you have a vertigo problem?" Osgood added.

"I object and instruct her not to answer," Reilly snapped.

"I just want to be sure, Mrs. Johnson, that you are able to testify competently this morning, and that if you have any physical disabilities that would keep you from testifying competently, I would like to know about it," Osgood continued.

"If there had been any, we would not have produced her," Reilly growled.

From there, the situation only degenerated. Osgood wanted to show that the Forger Affidavit was one giant exercise in projection—that all the cultural and financial differences he ascribed to Basia and Seward could just as easily be said of Junior and Joyce—and that Joyce, a woman of almost infinite passivity, was likely to construe even the most timid display of wifely assertiveness as "undue influence." But again and again—130 times, by S&C's count—Reilly blocked Osgood's questions, which he variously described as "irrelevant," "totally improper," "unprofessional," "off-the-wall," and "God-awful." Why, Osgood asked once, had young Johnny Johnson, Junior and Joyce's son, dropped out of Lawrenceville? "None of your business, Mr. Osgood! That's why!" Reilly thundered. Another time Osgood chided the Milbank lawyers for returning from lunch five minutes late. That, Reilly retorted, was "just too bad," and besides, Osgood's watch was fast.

No opportunity to ridicule Osgood's lawyerly manhood went unexploited. "I'm hopeful, Mr. Osgood, that you'd place your watch in front of you to see if you could shorten the time that elapses between answers and the following questions," Reilly said at one point. "This deposition has been dragged out frightfully long, and most of it is because of the time it takes you to formulate your questions." Another time, Reilly declared: "You don't have to snarl and get all upset, Mr. Osgood. If you don't care for the way I conduct the deposition, you can just take on some other matter." Invariably, neither Osgood nor Christ counterpunched. With Christ, it simply went against the grain. One had to wonder how he could defend his clients when he wouldn't defend his partner. Osgood, on the other hand, had the temperament to fight back, but not the skill. Instead, he was left to utter plaintive, almost pathetic, complaints. "Mr. Reilly, if you have something insulting to say to me, you can say it on the record and you need not use Mr. Berry as a mouthpiece and whisper in his ear," Osgood complained once.

Only in its court papers, when it had enough time to fine-tune its invective, did Sullivan & Cromwell get off any retorts. Seeking another crack at Joyce, it described her examination up to that point as "an object lesson" in how "an ill-tempered adversary can come near to sabotaging a deposition," and charged that Reilly had set himself up as judge and jury, disrupting things "by becoming over-excited," "by yelling," "by shouting," "by constantly threatening to bring the deposition to an immediate halt," "by giving vent to unprovoked sarcasm," etc., etc. Milbank calmly replied that most of the 130 questions to which it had objected were in fact objectionable. "By Mr. Osgood's reasoning, if he had asked 390 improper questions, his motion would be three times stronger," it charged. The Court found Milbank's less fiery approach more convincing, and Joyce was spared any further interrogation. Osgood construed Reilly's enmity as a backhanded compliment: Reilly, he assumed, had checked him out and resolved that he could handle him only by hating him. Still, Osgood was puzzled by the personal animus. After all, he'd worked on cases with various other Milbank lawyers, John McCloy among them, and relations had always been cordial.

Lambert denied Milbank's request to question Christ and Osgood about Peach, which offended her sense of lawyerly decorum. "If you want to attack the other side's clients, that's fine; but I don't think you ought to demean lawyers," she told them in chambers. The mudslinging, she continued, should stop. "We will make every effort to, Your Honor," Christ, who hadn't done any of it, politely promised. Reilly, customarily so deferential to the surrogate, wasn't so obliging. "Thank you," was all he said.

Did the Milbank lawyers seriously think Sullivan & Cromwell had bought Peach's testimony? There was no way they could have known that S&C had been so turned off by Peach's cynicism and looks—his "ratlike physiognomy"—and was so sure they could win without him that they'd no plans to call him. But Reilly knew Peach had been in Basia's camp long before S&C signed him up. Thus, Milbank's attempt to taint Peach was silly; Why pay for testimony you can already get free? It was also brutally effective. Marie Lambert saw conspiracies everywhere. Her suspicions of skulduggery aroused by Milbank's preposterous charge, she allowed the objectants to pursue the matter obsessively. And they did.

Milbank forced Peach to explain virtually every bill he'd ever submitted, every task he'd performed, everything he'd done to justify his tab at S&C, which by the end of 1984 stood at $106,650—a figure Milbank aptly called "astounding." Where had the roof leaked at Children's Bay Cay? How long had it taken him to get a permit allowing Basia to bring her dogs there? Had the health insurance Basia had given him covered the cost of his wife's pregnancy? How much had he earned from his grapefruit trees in 1984? Milbank's inquisition was made infinitely easier by Peach's compulsiveness. No dime he had expended went unrecorded. He'd charged $300 for the time he'd spent dining with Christ & Company at the Brazilian Court, and $2,400 for the forty-eight hours he'd devoted to preparing for, traveling to, and suffering through the first two days of his deposition. "Did you incur an expense related to 'Herb Life' or a diet supplement?" asked Berry, having spotted the $49.51 receipt for the "Herbalife" Peach bought from Mary Banks.

Besides dragging things out and torturing their adversaries, the inquiry gave Milbank unparalleled access into S&C's strategy, for wherever Peach had been, Osgood hadn't been far behind. Peach however, found the whole thing baffling—and infuriating. As far as he was concerned, the inquiry was based on a false and degrading premise. "I have never considered myself 'employed' by Sullivan & Cromwell," he explained. "From Day One I considered myself a consultant." Sometimes, the tedium grew too much for him. "I would like to say, I've put up with four days of this garbage and I've been allowed to talk about Mr. Johnson twice," he grumbled. If nothing else, the ordeal confirmed Peach's conviction that lawyers were nothing but high-class whores. At one point Berry asked whether, in the course of his interviews with nurses, Peach had ever posed as a lawyer. "Mr. Berry, I've never told anybody I was an attorney," Peach replied. "I wouldn't be proud to make that statement."

Perhaps it was accumulated frustration, perhaps a desire to regain the momentum or to vent its spleen. But in November 1984, more than a year after the children first objected to the will, Sullivan & Cromwell finally got off its high horse and counterattacked. Its salvo came, like Forger's, disguised in a document request. Suddenly, there was no more lofty talk about confining things to the events of April 14, 1983, or of "soaring like an eagle." Seward the proud father, the stick figure Nina had fabricated and inserted into his last few wills, was gone; the proponents' newly unveiled Seward had given his children just what they deserved. To prove this, Basia and Nina asked the Court for permission to enter the children's closet, and to take inventory of all the skeletons they found inside.

Sullivan & Cromwell asked four children—Mary Lea, Junior, Jimmy, and Jennifer—for their psychiatric records. The first three were also asked for anything pertaining to drug or alcohol abuse, while Junior and Jimmy were asked to produce information on any suicide attempts, though there was no indication Jimmy had ever tried such a thing. The four divorced Johnsons—Mary Lea, Diana, Junior, and Jennifer—were asked for all documents related to their marriages. From all six S&C sought academic and disciplinary records dating back to grade school; press reports about themselves, their spouses and ex-spouses, issue (legalese for children) and "alleged issue." Mary Lea was to provide anything she had on the Finos and a copy of Marty's Knights of Malta speech; Junior, material related to his first wife's alleged lovers, to his military service, and to his truncated career at Johnson & Johnson (the company claimed it couldn't find anything on the subject, proving that even antiseptic corporations don't always come clean); Jimmy, on his efforts to avoid the draft.

Milbank dismissed the request as an attempt to delay, divert, humiliate, and intimidate. S&C, it charged, was trying to put the children on trial, and it wouldn't wash, particularly after "Seward" himself had praised them so in his will. S&C now found itself in the position Milbank had just been in; to justify its extraordinarily broad request, it, too, had to spin a tale. It turned to the most junior lawyer working on the case, Robert Delahunty. Like Milbank's Brinck, Delahunty was the most literate lawyer on his team. But for him, this assignment was not some operatic lark. Delahunty was Basia's truest true believer.

Delahunty had joined Sullivan & Cromwell only a few months earlier, but he did not look like a rookie. He was clearly older than his classmates, though just how much older it was hard to say. Some things about him made him seem more mature than his years, like his chivalrous manners, his formal dress, his hint of an English accent. "Where'd you come up with Charles Laughton?" a referee in the case once asked another S&C lawyer. At the same time Delahunty seemed frozen in an earnest, ungainly adolescence, accentuated by his boyish haircut and heavyset physique. No matter what his age, he retained the look of a boy bound for First Communion.

Delahunty was a passionate and romantic man. He loved Proust and listened to Brahms by the hour. Like Reilly, he was a zealot, and poured himself into whatever he believed. But while Reilly demonized Basia, Delahunty canonized her. In his chiaroscuro universe Basia embodied the noble but wronged woman. He admired her dynamism and vitality, her passion for art, her loyalty to Seward. He also loved her Polishness and her ties to that gallant, long-suffering people. Mostly, he loved what he saw as her bluntness, her unambiguous sense of right and wrong, her sense of justice. As the case progressed and what he considered the calumnies against her accumulated, his attitude toward her grew from respect to almost fanatical devotion. After depositions Delahunty would collect Basia's doodles and pin them to his office wall. He told one incredulous colleague he was willing to die for her. Conversely, to Delahunty the children were barbarians. He took their unproductive, dissipated lives almost as a personal affront, and he viewed their protector, Ed Reilly, as the personification of evil.

For all his Anglophilia, Delahunty's Irish-American roots actually lay in East New York, a Brooklyn neighborhood of ethnics before becoming one of the city's worst ghettos. He was a good student, and won a scholarship to Regis High School, an intensely rigorous Jesuit establishment on Manhattan's Upper East Side. There, he took four years of Latin and three years of Greek; after school he'd translate Cicero or Homer for the fun and love of it. Stephan Dedalus would have recognized the regime: Every class began with a Hail Mary, every Friday with Mass; every year every student attended a retreat upstate, in which he'd reflect on the life of Christ, on heaven and hell, on death and judgment. Delahunty contemplated the priesthood until experiencing a sudden, jolting loss of faith one day. It happened while walking under a flowering cherry tree, when he suddenly realized that no matter how earnestly one believes, even those beautiful blossoms would soon turn to dust. He steered away from the seminary and toward Columbia University.

Insulated by the classics and his own conservatism, the man classmates called "the British Marquis from Brooklyn" was largely oblivious to the Vietnam-era convulsions on Morningside Heights. He was admitted to Yale Law School, but put that on hold to study philosophy at Oxford. He remained there for seven years, studying, teaching, immersing himself in Aristotle and Spinoza. For three years after that he taught "at university," as the British say. By 1980 Delahunty had spent nearly a third of his life abroad. He knew it was time to return home when he heard Dvořák's *American Quartet* on the BBC one night and it moved him to tears. Yale's patience with him having run out, he enrolled in Harvard Law School instead.

After so many years spent in search of truth, Delahunty found Harvard grubby, dreary, humiliating. His straitened finances, which forced him to live in an unheated attic in Somerville, made things worse. But he struck up some friendships, including one with a professor who urged him to try a summer on Wall Street. Delahunty chose Sullivan & Cromwell, in part because one of his interviewers there was also a Regis alumnus. He spent the summer of 1982 at S&C and, after graduating and completing his magnum opus on Spinoza ("We are still, to an extent which we have only recently begun to realize, the children of the seventeenth century," he wrote in its introduction), he returned to the firm. The Johnson case arrived around the same time he did, and Osgood brought him into it.

Delahunty attacked the assignment with the same gusto and intensity he'd just devoted to the Dutch philosopher. Late into many, many nights he could be found in his office, the Chinese lamps on his desk burning bright, a lock of graying hair falling over his eyes, his hyperactive tongue dancing over his lips as he read cases or wrote, and wrote, and wrote, deliberately overstating things so that S&C's censors could do their duty and still leave something spicy behind. "None [of the children] has been gainfully employed for any meaningful period; one of them could not even hold down a middle-rank job at Johnson & Johnson," he wrote in one early, never-filed motion. "The vast wealth their father lavished on them has been spent both stupidly (e.g. on horse-farms which came near to bankruptcy, or on an expensive divorce settlement) and selfishly (none of the children has made a significant contribution to charity from his or her own resources)." He charged that Mary Lea's "uncanny gifts for publicity seem to stem from lack of more genuine theatrical talents," and that Junior's past conduct had been "if anything, even more spectacularly decadent" than Mary Lea's.

Everything he wrote out longhand, cutting and pasting, cutting and pasting, before heading back to his mother's apartment in Queens. Like many misfits in the law, he'd gravitated toward or stumbled onto or been banished into the right niche: in his case, an antiquarian one. For the law is precedent, and what is precedent but history? When Delahunty wasn't in his office, he was in S&C's leathery library, hunched over piles of dusty, disintegrating volumes of *New York Reports*, reliving the poignant dramas of long-forgotten people, retrieving the neglected erudition of long-forgotten judges. "You gotta give Delahunty credit; when he researches something, he researches the shit out of it," a colleague once noted. And whatever he learned, he could convey. Delahunty had read Orwell's essay on the English language at Regis, and he'd taken it to heart—particularly its emphasis on conciseness. If, as Orwell wrote, "the great enemy of clear language is insincerity," then among its greatest allies was conviction, and in that Delahunty abounded.

Now, the time had come to tap his passion. In mid-December 1984, S&C filed Delahunty's first broadside. Accompanying it was a "*This Is Your Life*" collection of titillating morsels from the Johnsons' pasts, including Junior's divorce petition; tabloid articles (e.g. DRUG CO. HEIR WINS DIVORCE AND WIFE WINS A BIG WAD; or HEIRESS SAYS SPOUSE WAS

HOMOSEXUAL); Seward's 1965 "troublemaker beyond my imagination" letter to Mary Lea; papers detailing the decline in the value of Harbor Branch's portfolio under Junior; and Seward Ryan's "too bad about the goddam money" letter to his grandfather. Its signatory was Osgood, but the rhetoric was Delahunty's.

What was the relevance of this sordid history? Anything related to the children's prodigality and ineffectuality, Delahunty argued, was crucial to understanding why Seward wanted to leave them nothing more. Data on lifestyles, suicide attempts, and artistic endeavors would help highlight Seward's awareness of what wastrels they were ("Three of the children are self-described 'artists,'" Delahunty sneered in a footnote. "None holds down a regular job. The requests directed at their 'accomplishments' in the arts are directed to the only meaningful 'careers' they have had"). Travel records would help establish how, far from shooing away the children, Basia had reached out for them. Psychological records could help explain the children's twisted perceptions of their father's final marriage.

Delahunty took shots at all the children, but he zeroed in on Junior. In the 1960s and 1970s, he wrote gleefully, Junior gave his father "copious" evidence of psychological and emotional instability: indeed, he wrote, "more erratic conduct is hard to imagine." "Whether or not J. Seward Johnson, Jr. is mentally ill, there is in fact abundant evidence that he needed psychiatric attention: he did, after all, attempt to commit suicide once or twice," Delahunty added in another brief. "Moreover, there is a firm evidentiary basis for thinking that his psychological troubles stem in part from his relationship with his father, and that they may therefore color his testimony about the decedent—one has only to read his divorce complaint to be struck by its eerie similarity to his allegations in this proceeding about his father's marriage."

Delahunty then recounted the story of Junior's first marriage, larding his story with quotations from Junior's own divorce papers. The whole ghastly spectacle, he wrote, gave Junior great notoriety, "a notoriety which his need for self-dramatization apparently still drives him to seek." "The similarity between Mr. Johnson Jr.'s account of his first marriage, and his theory of the 'undue influence' which his father's wife supposedly practiced on the decedent, is so palpable that it suggests that Mr. Johnson, Jr. is engaged in projecting from his own unhappy experiences," Delahunty wrote. "The jury will surely be entitled to test Mr. Johnson, Jr.'s ugly portrait of his father and his father's marriage against the evidence that his own first marriage was a nightmare, that no sense of shame constrains him in what he will say, and that his psychological problems concerning his father have been traumatic." In those years and beyond, what Delahunty called Junior's "unique combination of misjudgment and misconduct" drained his own trust, which would have been worth $110 million if left alone, of all but $23 million and, more recently, caused the value of Harbor Branch's portfolio to plummet by at least $35 million.

Sullivan & Cromwell now offered an additional explanation for Seward's disinheritance of Harbor Branch, apart from the riches he'd already bestowed upon it: Junior. "His dilettantism, his sensational divorce, his bitter quarrels with his father's brother, his role in lawsuits which have fractured his family, his disastrous career at Johnson & Johnson, the depletion through his own mistakes of the assets in the great trust which his father had created for him, and his record of unsuccessful investment all bear directly on his father's estimate of his competence, and thus on his father's decision not to leave substantial sums either to this son, or to commit further funds to a Foundation managed by him," Delahunty wrote. That decision was further spurred on by the "monumental insensitivity" Junior showed in strong-arming Seward into relinquishing his post. "A mind as acute as the decedent's could well have wondered what Harbor Branch's fate would be with his elder son in unfettered control of its affairs," Delahunty stated.

Delahunty ridiculed Milbank's claim that the document request was needlessly intrusive, particularly given what the children had already asked for. "It comes ill from people whose private lives have been so sordid—and so much flaunted before the public—to object that the proponents' requests transgress the 'limits of decency' or to lament that their 'privacy' is being invaded," he wrote. And with Basia and Nina having produced materials whose volume was "more on the scale of a large antitrust case than of a probate proceeding," the children could not very well claim S&C's demands were unduly burdensome. The children, Delahunty wrote, "have demanded documents by the tens of thousands; they have pried into the most intimate details of a marriage; they have made liberal use of insult and innuendo; and now they complain of 'irrelevance,' 'burden,' 'overbreadth,' and 'embarrassment.' It will not do."

In its reply Milbank dismissed what it called S&C's "cracker barrel psychoanalysis" of the Johnsons, and Lambert agreed. True, she wrote, she'd provided for broad discovery in the case. But there were limits, particularly where much of what S&C sought was "palpably improper" and inadmissible. "This Court is hard-pressed to see how school disciplinary records, records of divorces and information concerning military service would be or lead to admissible evidence," she wrote. And so, whatever else the Johnson case would become, it would not turn into a trial of the

children, at least not in court. It was hard to quantify the Johnsons' capacity for embarrassment. But whatever leverage such embarrassment
might have provided was lost.

The ruling was ominous for another reason. It provided further evidence that a crucial element in Christ's strategy—his decision to steer
the case toward Marie Lambert—was backfiring. Donald Christ had
played Russian roulette, and there were now numerous indications that
he'd picked the wrong chamber—or chambers.

XXVII

More than six years earlier, on New Year's morning 1978, Marie Macri Lambert stood triumphantly at the front of the ornate courtroom on the fifth floor of New York County Surrogate's Court, preparing to speak. Her ample frame swelled with pride, as it hadn't in all her fifty-seven years. The assembled throng filled the main floor, wound up the staircases to the balcony, and spilled over into the corridor. And every single one of these folks was there for her.

On hand was a splendid assortment of people: judges, including judges who'd served on the court she was about to join; lawyers, many of whom would be appearing before her over the next twelve years, and others who would not, like her new good friend Roy Cohn; a priest and a rabbi; family members and cronies. In the very front were her campaign workers, the people who hadn't listened when everyone had insisted Marie Lambert would never reach this point. Today, though, nothing seemed impossible. "Will she end her legal career as New York County Surrogate?" a reporter for the *New York Law Journal* had asked. "She admits, with a slight touch of embarrassment, that she would like to wind up as a Justice of the Supreme Court of the United States."

The air was thick with praise. Judge Edward Re recalled how, when he was a fourth grader fresh off the boat from Italy, the young Marie had translated for him. Geraldine Ferraro recounted how the Queens Women's Bar Association had supported Marie Lambert, even though its members couldn't vote in Manhattan. Standing on a chair in the back of the room, Allard Lowenstein called the occasion "a love-feast for Marie Lambert." Former Mayor John V. Lindsay also offered some kind words. A lawyer representing her old comrades in the personal-injury bar joined in. "At last, we have a shirtsleeves judge," he said.

Few of her many detractors, the bar Brahmins who were still not reconciled to her victory and, to her mind, were still trying to undo her, were here today. But their animus wouldn't, couldn't last. She'd show them she was the best surrogate Manhattan ever had. Moreover, even if they never did like her, they'd better get used to her, and if they didn't, she'd crush them. "Marie, isn't it a pleasure to see these hypocritical fucks kissing your Italian ass?" a friend asked her before the ceremony began, pointing to the few patricians who'd swallowed their pride and shown up. "You can say that again," she'd replied.

The judge-to-be beamed. Change her wardrobe, take her out of this solemn setting, and she was a figure from Frans Hals, dumpy and frumpy, coarse and crude. She was a washerwoman of a woman, a Katzenjammer character. Heavy, bespectacled, her pageboy hair a shade of red more customarily found in a box of Crayolas or on a Sherwin Williams paint-chip chart, she bore little physical resemblance to the sleek, striking Mediterranean-looking woman who'd led her class at New York University Law School thirty-five years earlier. (As is the case with anyone tampering with hair color, the top of her head was out of synch with the rest of her face.) But psychically, she hadn't changed all that much. Her personality had never been buried beneath layers of culture and hypocrisy and pretense; everything she was—tough, profane, street-smart, loyal, unforgiving, peremptory—was there for all to see.

Though she was about to become one of New York's most powerful judges, presiding over estates large and small, dispensing vast amounts of patronage, inside Marie Lambert was still the Italian immigrant girl, craving approval and acceptance. The sentiments swirling around her now were to her parched ego what a downpour is to a desert; only a little of it would ever sink in. It would take praise far more sustained than today's to make up for all the years of neglect and disparagement. Much of what she'd now hear would be prompted less by conviction than by the self-serving obsequiousness lawyers always lavish on judges. But in her court praise of any provenance was always admissible. "Marie always wanted to be respected," a lawyer once said. "But she wants to be loved even more than respected, and feared even more than loved."

The ghosts—and, in some instances, the portraits—of her predecessors peered down at her. In one form or another the Surrogate's Court has been around since New York's Dutch days. It has jurisdiction over all those who live in Manhattan or own property there. When anyone, millionaire or pensioner, dies, it is to the Surrogate's Court that his chosen representative comes to file his will. And, should no interested party object, a surrogate will issue the decree admitting the will into probate. The court also handles adoptions, guardianships, and the estates of those who die without wills, and intervenes on behalf of those who haven't lawyers themselves. Each year a surrogate names hundreds of lawyers to handle such tasks, giving him or her colossal powers of patronage.

The courthouse had stood in its current incarnation, on the corner of Centre and Chambers streets in lower Manhattan, since the turn of the century. Built when New York's self-image was at its apex, the eclectic, Beaux Arts structure stood out even in the cluster of monumental government buildings surrounding it, all designed to exude solemnity, stability, nobility of purpose. Its classical Greek motif, including the Corinthian columns over its main entrance, connoted the usual justice and rectitude; but that severity was tempered by French touches, which gave the building elegance and refinement. It was further eased by the rococo statuary around the facade. Standing sentry were Revolutionary War soldiers, Pilgrims and Indians; Peter Stuyvesant (complete with wooden leg), DeWitt Clinton, and other early political leaders; allegorical characters representing Childhood, Philosophy, Poetry, and Maternity. Like many public buildings of its era, there was something wonderfully and wackily pretentious about the Surrogate's Court. Its lobby was modeled after the Paris Opera, its walls lined with warm yellow Siena marble, its ceilings studded with Ravenna-like mosaics on classical and astrological themes. Such buildings can never be reproduced; what was particularly pathetic was that its current custodians couldn't even keep it clean. Still, the place was a favorite of filmmakers, commercial makers, soap-opera makers—anyone seeking an elegant, antiquarian environment.

The Surrogate's Court, like many structures with noble facades, sat on tawdry foundations. It had taken a dozen years and three mayoralties to complete; it cost more than three times original estimates, and even at that, some of its "marble" turned out to be plaster. This same gap between aspirations and reality also characterized those who presided there. The court had had its share of Solomons, but there'd been plenty of hacks as well. Periodically, attempts were made to clean up what Fiorello La Guardia once called "the most expensive undertaking establishment in the world," the most serious spearheaded by Senator Robert F. Kennedy. "Don't die in New York if you want to leave anything to your wife and children," he once said. Reformist rhetoric was plentiful; Lambert had been only the latest to use it freely. But cronyism and corruption seemed woven into the place. Real reform was rare.

Now, in one of those startling, only-in-America tableaux, frail, elderly Nicola Macri stood on the dais and, with the help of his grandson, placed the judicial robes on his daughter. Nearly sixty years earlier, he'd left Calabria for Brooklyn, then sent for his wife and baby girl, the girl he stood by now. "This is the only country in the world in which the daughter of a poor barber could come so far," he told *Il Progresso*, New York's Italian newspaper. Marie was convinced her father had lived to see this day only through a supreme act of will, and in fact he died but a few weeks later. She was convinced her late mother, wherever she might be, was watching, too.

From her earliest days in Brooklyn Lambert had imagined herself a lawyer, a daring notion for a woman of her generation and background. She hadn't spoken any English until kindergarten, hadn't become an American citizen until her third year at NYU Law School, which she entered in 1941. One of only a handful of women there, she'd encountered all the usual sexist skepticism of that era; a dean told her tartly that were she searching for a husband, there were better places to look. She paid her own way, selling dresses and tutoring. These were the war years, a time when classes were unstable and rankings unreliable. But when she graduated in 1944, Marie Macri collected a fifty-dollar check for maintaining the highest average over the previous three years. Even so, she'd had trouble finding work. Firms simply were not hiring women; as Malcolm Wilson, once governor of New York, later put it, "When I first met Marie Lambert, seeing a woman lawyer was not unlike seeing an eclipse of the sun." The firm that eventually hired her wanted a legal Rosie the Riveter, someone to fill in until the real lawyers came back from overseas. When she married one of those returning G.I.'s, a southerner named Grady Lambert, and got pregnant, she was let go.

After the birth of her son, Greg, who was to be her only child, she joined another, smaller firm; then, in 1949, she opened a twenty-five-dollar-a-month office of her own in midtown Manhattan, sharing a phone and secretary with some other lawyers. Later, she moved down to 160 Broadway, amid the ant farm of personal-injury lawyers near City Hall. Most of the time she was in court; only after it shut down for the day did she reach her office. Her desk, like the backseat of her battered Chevrolet, was strewn with file folders and office detritus.

Always, Lambert had her doubters and detractors. "She's such a nice girl and she wants to be a trial lawyer so badly; it's such a pity she'll never make it," Moe Levine, a titan of the negligence bar, once said. Others were less charitable. "You never saw her when there wasn't four inches of slip hanging under her dress," another lawyer recalled. She was "an obese, sloppy, slovenly, slatternly whale of a woman," said a third. Professionally, her plate was filled with scraps: the nickel-and-dime cases that other, fancier lawyers wouldn't touch. "Lambert tried the worst junk that you had in the business," one lawyer said. "If you had a piece of shit where there was an injury, you got Marie to take it because no one else would."

But whatever she lacked in grooming or erudition she made up for in hard work, theatricality, and outrageousness. She learned all of the classic cheap tricks of trial lawyers: letting a witness relax throughout cross-examination, only to hit him with a "by the way" at the very end, for instance, or knocking over her open purse when the opposing testimony got good. The stained Lane Bryant dresses, the shopping bags she used in lieu of a briefcase, gave her the look and feel of a hausfrau. If it helped to seem wifely, she'd mention her home; if it helped to sound motherly or even if it didn't, she'd talk about her son. She won some large judgments. But these were the exception, and there were big gaps between them, when bills would mount, rent money was hard to scrape together, the telephone service came precariously close to being cut. Mostly, she made her money on volume, getting and settling cases as quickly as she could. She was a good nudge, hanging on people's lapels until they finally paid up. So primitive, so obnoxious, could she be that it was easy to underestimate her. In fact, though the field was admittedly small, Marie Lambert was really the premier woman trial lawyer in New York. In a sense, though, her professed feminism was skin-deep. She'd always preferred the company of men, and could swear with and at the best of them. A group portrait taken at a trial lawyers' convention in 1962 showed all the giants of the New York personal-injury bar, Jewish guys like Jack Fuchsberg, Al Julien, Aaron Broder, Jerry Edelman, and Charlie Kramer, horsing around for the photographer. And in the middle of them all, entirely at ease, was good old Marie.

In the New York State Trial Lawyers Association, the fancy-sounding name for the negligence lawyers' trade group, you rose through the ranks as you proceeded in a bakery: by taking a number, then waiting to be called. But in 1974, when Lambert's turn at the presidency came up, the men balked. For lawyers forever fighting their image as shysters and ambulance chasers, it was one thing to allow Marie on the letterhead, quite another to have her speaking on their behalf. While her opponents scurried around for an eleventh-hour alternative, Lambert campaigned, ultimately crushing her opponent. She was the first woman ever to head the group, and, equally noteworthy, the first Gentile in memory, though with all of her Yiddishkeit, it wasn't always so easy to tell. "Where'd you learn to speak Italian?" a Jewish lawyer once asked her. As president, Lambert took on all the usual comers: insurance companies, defense lawyers, doctors. In a letter to the *Times*, for instance, she complained of doctors trying to curb malpractice suits so that, as she put it, "they can kill anybody and it won't make any difference."

Lambert had always been a joiner. At Brooklyn College classmates knew that if they ever needed anyone to mimeograph something overnight, Marie Macri was happy—indeed, would almost beg—to do it. By the time of her swearing-in her life had become a perpetual round of bar dinners, award ceremonies, committee meetings, conventions. Events most people dreaded, Lambert loved, for they filled two voids. One was for recognition. The groups gave her a slew of awards, which mattered to someone who, more than fifty years later, still talked bitterly about the WASP classmate who'd received a prize that had rightfully been hers and who still boasted of going to City Hall and complaining to Mayor La Guardia about it, who had never fully overcome the humiliation of hearing her parents ridiculed for speaking no English, who had been laughed at for wearing handmade clothes. No matter how comprehensive her résumé—the 1986 edition still noted that she'd been valedictorian at P.S. 176 in 1934—she'd felt she'd never gotten the respect she deserved.

The other void was more personal. Marie Lambert had friends, but like Basia's, they were forever falling in and out of her favor. Her husband, a salesman for Abercrombie & Fitch who was as inconspicuous as she was loud, appeared to play a minor role in her life; he was away so often that even she wondered whether he was actually a CIA agent. Eventually, he fell sick and entered a nursing home in Queens, from which, one day, he disappeared. Two months later his decomposing body was found in a stairwell there. (Convinced that his death had been in reprisal for her anti–Vietnam War activities, she brought in the FBI to investigate.) Her family life was built around her son. She worked tirelessly to advance his legal career, eventually, through Roy Cohn, landing him a job with Representative Mario Biaggi. Lawyers practicing before her came to learn that all business, no matter how momentous, would stop whenever Greg Lambert called.

The rat race of solo practice grew too much for Lambert, and in 1972 she joined Manny Katz, one of the city's better-known (if not more highly regarded) negligence lawyers. With characteristic bravado, she insisted that her name appear first on the new letterhead, and when she couldn't get that, she compromised. The result was one of the stranger-sounding firm names in New York: Katz, Shandell, Katz, Erasmous & Marie M. Lambert. What she really craved, though, was a judgeship. She'd maneuvered for an appointment, but never got past the screening panel. What she needed was an elective post, where she could circumvent the bosses and go directly to the people—*her* people. So, in 1976, she ran for surrogate.

As improbable as Lambert's career had been up to then, what followed was even unlikelier. Lambert's candidacy struck nearly everyone as a colossal lapse of judgment, an act of supreme chutzpah, a bad joke. Quite apart from her poor prospects, she was the consummate advocate, with no aptitude whatever for judging. Furthermore, she was a complete stranger to probate work, someone who knew more about whiplash than wills. Undeterred, she stood on the steps of the Surrogate's Court, called the institution "a citadel of patronage" and a "billionaire boondoggle," and promised to do better. "Maybe it's time we had a woman here who can say she is not connected to clubhouse politics," she said. "I owe no favors or obligations to anybody." Unfortunately, the reverse was also true: She had no real backing, and finished third in a five-person race.

Unexpectedly, she got another crack at the job the following year, when the man who'd beaten her, Samuel Spiegel, suddenly died. Under Jewish law a body must be buried by sundown of the day following death. Poor Spiegel was still above ground when Lambert revived her campaign, imploring his supporters to back her for an interim appointment until the next election. Sam would have wanted it that way, she assured them. Instead, a panel picked Arthur Blyn, the runner-up in the previous election. He took office only eight weeks before the previously scheduled Democratic primary in September.

Even without the aid of incumbency, Blyn would have been the odds-on favorite in the race, which in Democratic New York was in fact the main event. He was endorsed by both the regular and insurgent wings of the party, by six of seven mayoral candidates, by two former mayors, by *The New York Times,* and by a host of powerful lawyers, including Alex Forger. Many thought Lambert was actually angling for a deal: withdrawal in exchange for a seat on some other, lesser court. Still, she had some points in her favor. First, it was a good year for women candidates; Elizabeth Holtzman, Carol Bellamy, and Bella Abzug were in various races. Some conservative lawyers feared Blyn was a closet socialist, and wondered whether anyone opposed to private property could be trusted with their clients' money. The machine opposing Lambert was only a rusty relic of its former self. And precisely because Blyn was such a shoo-in, his supporters grew complacent.

Up to now, races for surrogate had been low-key affairs. That would change, quickly. Lambert's first attack was not on Blyn's character or fitness, but on his very being. Claiming that "Arthur Blyn" didn't exist—as a young man, Blyn, born "Elitzik," had taken the name of his stepfather, but never changed it officially—she sued to have the name removed from the ballot. She dredged up other charges: for instance, that Blyn had not been admitted to the bar for six years after completing law school, a delay attributable to McCarthyite scrutiny of his left-wing past. "She said everything but that he sodomized little children," one observer recalled. Blyn's lawyer called Lambert's suit "obscene and disgraceful," part of "a shabby effort to obtain publicity for her floundering campaign." A referee agreed, and threw out the case. But the stench lingered.

Blyn conducted a traditional, which is to say an almost invisible, campaign. Having spent twenty thousand dollars of his own money the previous year, he resolved this time to campaign on the cheap, and accepted no contributions larger than one hundred dollars. Lambert suffered from no such constraints. Hitting on her fellow trial lawyers, digging deeply into her own pockets, she spent lavishly. Her name appeared everywhere. There were Marie Lambert T-shirts and buttons, Marie Lambert shopping bags and bumper stickers. MARIE LAMBERT FOR SURROGATE posters sprang up on buses and in subway stations. Marie Lambert flyers found their way, like Chinese restaurant menus, under apartment doors. Marie Lambert campaign workers stood on street corners (the choicest spots were by newsstands that sold the Sunday *Times* on Saturday night) handing out Marie Lambert literature. Always, it was short on specifics, long on tone—populist, shrill, accusatory. Blyn, she charged, was the candidate of Samuel DiFalco, the incumbent surrogate, who had been indicted for various irregularities. (In fact, Lambert herself had gotten several cases from DiFalco, while Blyn had not.) She assailed both those who doled out patronage and those who took it. "Politicians and political lawyers profit from death," declared one advertisement, which charged that more than half of those on Blyn's campaign committee had accepted patronage from him. The ad listed some of these malefactors and their ill-gotten gains: Simon Rifkind and his partners ($45,000); William Shea of Shea Stadium fame ($157,000); former Mayor Robert Wagner ($120,000); and even Alex Forger ($10,500). All, she said, had taken money "out of the pockets of widows and orphans." "MARIE LAMBERT isn't willing to let politicians and well-connected lawyers profit from misery and grief," the advertisement stated. "MARIE LAMBERT ISN'T A POLITICIAN. MARIE LAMBERT is independent of the political clubhouse. MARIE LAMBERT has spent over thirty years fighting for the people. NOW

MARIE LAMBERT is running for Surrogate to clean up the mess."

All told, MARIE LAMBERT sent out some 300,000 pieces of campaign literature. Some was "women-oriented," stressing her status as mother, widow, head of "the male dominated" state trial lawyers association and enemy of the macho political establishment. One Lambert flier charged that Blyn belonged to a bar group that discriminated against women: the B'nai B'rith Lawyers Lodge. To Harlem residents, she promised to deposit court money in black-owned banks and boycott institutions redlining minority neighborhoods. To Italian-Americans, she became Marie *Macri* Lambert and soft-pedalled the anti-DiFalco rhetoric. Many of her campaign workers were gay, and to them she promised equal rights regardless of "sexual or affectional preferences." But she saved her strongest pitch for the key bloc in any Democratic primary in Manhattan: Jews.

This ploy came naturally. Lambert had, after all, spent much of her life among Jews. She'd been the only Catholic in the Brooklyn College chapter of Hillel; she'd refused to join a sorority at NYU that wouldn't admit Jews. She regularly attended Jewish functions, even those sponsored by the Lubavitchers, a Hasidic sect. Many of her friends were Jewish, and she'd picked up their mannerisms, their language, their customs. She could talk about matzo and hamentaschen without a hint of self-consciousness; when in Europe she'd gone to the death camps, when in Israel to Yad Vashem. Some even saw in her a resemblance to Golda Meir, others to Bella Abzug. She seemed like the perfect *bubbe*. (No one ponders the etymology of surnames with quite the fervor of Jews, but "Lambert" was ambiguous enough to stump students of such things.) Some even swore she'd told them her husband was a Jew, though Grady Lambert in fact had been a Protestant from Georgia.

Among her Gentile friends, Lambert grumbled that Jews had impeded her advance. But campaigning for Jewish votes, she stifled any such feelings. She placed ethnically androgynous advertisements in Jewish newspapers, whether in English, German, or Yiddish, filled with the sights and sounds and flavors of Hester Street. These ads stressed how she'd canceled a trial lawyers' trip to Mexico after that country endorsed the United Nations' "Zionism is racism" resolution, how she'd once locked horns with a PLO official on a local radio program, how she'd won "the coveted 'Citizen of the Year Award' " from a previously unknown group called the "Westside Zionist Coalition for Israel." And there were Holocaust allusions aplenty. Stressing that judges shouldn't shrink from controversy, she asked, "What do you think would have happened if the lawyers and judges in Nazi Germany had spoken up?"

She also claimed that shortly after World War II, she'd helped spare a visiting group of Eastern European rabbis from being sent back to the slaughterhouse from which they'd just escaped. One flyer stated:

> A young lawyer was engaged to see if there were any possibility to remedy this seemingly impossible situation. Her name—MARIE LAMBERT. The atrocious stories these holocaust survivors told caused her to become emotionally involved in each and every case. She vowed that she would do more than humanly possible in order that this remnant should not have to go back to the blood-soaked land from whence they came. Marie Lambert put aside her then blooming law practice and worked day and night for this newly adopted cause she cherished. Her entreaties and pleadings with the Department of Immigration were successful. Not one of these 248 people were returned to Europe. Marie Lambert did not take one penny for this brilliant Hatzalah [rescue] and much was offered. She did this because it was the humane thing to do and G-d was with her.

There was, in fact, such a rescue mission. But years later, no one connected with it could corroborate her account, or, indeed, even recognized her name.

The campaign for votes, particularly Jewish votes, saturated the airwaves as well. Lambert ran numerous radio spots, primarily on all-news or classical stations favored by elderly Jewish listeners. In one, against the backdrop of martial music and bombs bursting in air, she pledged that no court funds would ever be deposited in banks participating in the Arab boycott of Israel. "I will not support the genocide of the State of Israel, to satisfy those banks whose greed aligns them with ARAB murderers," she stated in one of her flyers. "I will not finance the HITLERS of this generation with the monies of widows, widowers and orphans." The advertisements drew immediate criticism; the state Code of Judicial Conduct barred candidates from making any such "pledges or promises." And since court funds went by law into banks barred from overseas investment, the entire issue was irrelevant anyway.

Then, only a few days before the vote, a new circular appeared. It charged that Blyn, along with Bella Abzug and another candidate, were "ENEMIES OF THE JEWISH PEOPLE," who had remained mum while Stalin and Hitler slaughtered their coreligionists; had opposed the creation of the State of Israel; had supported the Arabs during various Middle Eastern wars; and had said nothing when the PLO murdered Israelis. "THEY ARE GUILTY," it shrieked. "Please go to the POLLS and take with you the memories of the SIX MILLION murdered by

HITLER and STALIN." Nowhere on the flier did Marie Lambert's name actually appear. But Blyn and his staff were convinced that Lambert's campaign was responsible. On the day of the primary Blyn's wife spotted an old Jew handing out Lambert literature on the Lower East Side. She asked him why, in Yiddish. "She's Jewish and he's a goy," the man replied. In this campaign, at least, Blyn should have stuck with "Elitzik."

In the end the indefatigable Lambert won by nearly twenty thousand votes, prompting comparisons to another Italian underdog: Sylvester Stallone, aka "Rocky." So unprepared were her troops for victory that they'd made no plans to celebrate. Lambert promptly sent some flunky to a delicatessen for sandwiches and coffee. One worker later recalled everyone singing a chorus of "We're in the Money." And, indeed, barring some debacle in the November general election, the judgeship was hers. But leaving nothing to chance, Lambert immediately began mending fences. She met with lawyers from several large firms, including some of the "profiteers from death" she had just condemned. Some of her erstwhile targets even contributed to her campaign, and she gladly accepted their funds. Thus, Bill Shea, whom she'd accused of pocketing $157,000 in patronage, now gave 1/157 of his loot to her. Other contributors included Bernard Greene and Buck Finkelstein of Paul Weiss; Tom Ford of Shearman & Sterling; and Bill Warren of Dewey Ballantine. Even Louis Auchincloss chipped in. Staggered by the prospect of Marie Lambert on the bench, some reform Democrats, Liberals, and Republicans sought frantically for a fusion candidate. But due partly to the intervention of Roy Cohn, who convinced Republican leader Vincent Albano not to enter a major candidate in the race, the already token opposition splintered into two.

Lambert's sole remaining hurdle was more a matter of ego than electoral prospects: the Association of the Bar of the City of New York. As the organization's dignified "Meeting House" on West Forty-fourth Street attested, this was the most patrician of all bar groups, dominated by the very Wall Street types she loathed; it was one of the few legal fraternities within a ten-mile radius in which she'd never been active. Because so much of its brass had been vacationing during the primary, at retreats in which a Marie Lambert never would or could have tread, the prestigious group hadn't assessed the candidates when such an evaluation might have mattered. But undaunted by its irrelevancy, it now proceeded to do so.

Normally, such inquiries were perfunctory. But the two association lawyers assigned to scrutinize Lambert thought they sensed something fishy about her. She always seemed to be cutting corners, like failing to file a list of contributors, then offering Beaver Cleaver–like excuses—that someone had burglarized her office, for instance, or broken into her car. They probed whether she'd really led her class at NYU and really served on the *Law Review*; in each case, they couldn't prove she hadn't. In the end it was her style to which they objected, the style of someone who promised to protect widows and orphans, then went out and exhumed her rival's adoption records. They found Lambert "not qualified" on the grounds that she lacked judicial temperament. To Lambert, the decision smacked of snobbery and sexism, and she was furious. "If I were a man, and if I did all the things they said I did, they would say that I'm a fine fighting lawyer for my client," she told one reporter. Privately, she dismissed the decision as the work of the "blue-blooded bastards," and savored the retribution she would wreak when they appeared before her. She promptly called Milton Gould of Shea, Gould, Climenko & Casey—another of the predatory firms she'd attacked in her late campaign—to represent her in an appeal to the bar group's executive committee. She also solicited support from more than one hundred state judges and lawyers and lined up several character witnesses. But in the end the finding stood. "So be it. Let the voters decide," she told the *Times*. Besides, most of the association's members didn't even live in Manhattan.

The general election was anticlimactic. The *Times* railed against her—"Having been criticized often before for lack of judicial deportment, she managed to demonstrate in the campaign that her critics understood her all too well"—but it didn't matter. Marie Lambert had the air of a winner. Shea's law firm threw a party for her atop the Pan Am Building, to which she arrived in a limousine supplied by the suddenly ubiquitous Roy Cohn. On Election Day she piled up nearly two thirds of the vote. "All my heartfelt congratulations on your well deserved victory. What a happy ending it was!" Auchincloss gushed in one of the many congratulatory messages she received. "I am sorry about the unpleasantness at the Bar Association, but at least it brought you and me together so I shall consider that a silver lining." Two weeks later, when her campaign staff threw her a surprise fifty-seventh birthday party, the lettering atop the cake was even sweeter than usual. "Happy Birthday, Your Eminence," it said.

The swearing-in was still two months away, and in the meantime there were bills to pay. Though funds trickled in from belatedly brown-nosing lawyers, Lambert was shackled with a deficit of $175,000, half of which had come out of her own pocket. She and her staff mapped out a series of fund-raisers. One of them, at Studio 54, promised to be particularly profitable; Steve Rubell and Ian Shrager, clients of Cohn, were supplying the place free. But the grandest shindig was to be a $250-a-plate reception and birthday party at the Top of the Beekman Tower in early December. Immediately, the judge-elect came under fire, for many of those invited were lawyers who would soon be appearing before her. The president of the City Bar Association called the gala "manifestly improper." Others were equally blunt. "During this year's campaign for Surrogate, the successful candidate characterized herself as a widow, who, if elected would look after the interests of widows and orphans," Judge James J. Leff of State Supreme Court wrote the *Daily News*. "She has begun to live up to her campaign promise even before taking office by looking after the FIRST WIDOW: herself." And at $250 a pop, he continued, "we may assume that subscribers become honorary orphans who will be taken care of after January 1st. Simply stated, it stinks!" So controversial did the event become that most would-be guests, including the birthday girl herself, stayed away. Marie Lambert's party turned into a wake. The brouhaha triggered the interest of New York's Commission on Judicial Conduct, which monitors the state's judges and, in rare instances, judges-elect. But before it could get down to anything serious, Inauguration Day arrived.

Never one to underdo anything, Lambert arranged to be sworn in with not just one Bible but three: a Catholic version her son had given her; a King James edition furnished by Judge Theodore Roosevelt Kupferman, who would administer the oath; and a Hebrew version that Harvey Corn, the Cornell-educated lawyer who was to become her law secretary, had received for his bar mitzvah and now, sixteen years later, had inscribed to her. "As our futures are intertwined, I rest safe and secure in the knowledge that mine is in the most capable hands," he'd written. Private citizen Marie Lambert pledged to faithfully follow the United States Constitution and the laws of the state of New York. Then, amid sustained and lusty applause, *Judge* Marie Lambert, *Surrogate* Marie Lambert—the terms could be used interchangeably, and either sounded just fine—took out her prepared remarks and began to speak.

Now, it could be admitted: In a sense, her detractors had been right. She knew nothing at all about this court. Her uncertainty came across in the unnatural way in which she read her text. Normally, her voice was sharp, even piercing, better suited to waitressing than judging. Like many trial lawyers, she was more comfortable speaking extemporaneously than from a text, and she delivered her address in a kind of constrained, singsongy monotone. Mostly, it was a rehash of her campaign rhetoric. Her peroration was a characteristic blend of pride, defensiveness, defiance, confidence, and conceit.

"I am deeply conscious of my special obligation to the voters of this county who have given me such a clear mandate," she said. "I enter this office with no animosity but with the courage to do what is right. I will not be intimidated. I will not be forced to abandon my commitments to the people of this borough. I will prove to my detractors that they were wrong, and I will justify the faith of my supporters. It is with great humility that I leave private life to assume this burden and responsibility. I hope and pray that I, as Surrogate, will always be compassionate and understanding and that I will dispense justice equally to all."

Rabbi David Seligson said the benediction from, appropriately enough, the Book of Numbers. And with that, the ceremony ended. There was a brief party in the rotunda, and then lunch at Luchow's. Later, Lambert and twelve of her apostles headed off to dinner at a downtown club, where she broke out a hundred-year-old bottle of cognac. The headline in the next day's *Progresso* was straightforward in Italian, prophetic in English. UN'ITALIANA LA PRIMA DONNA DELLA SURROGATE'S COURT, it declared.

XXVIII

Marie Lambert went about her new business, but for her first five years on the bench there was a sword hanging over it. The Judicial Conduct Commission subpoenaed her campaign manager, an unsavory genius named Gary Nicholson, along with five of her campaign workers (the workers either refused to answer any questions, or, in the case of a man named Vincent Catalfo, claimed to have forgotten everything as a result of a mugging). Nicholson, along with Lambert, challenged the entire investigation, claiming that scrutiny of her electoral activities violated her free-speech rights.

To Lambert, the probe was a witch-hunt: Unable to kill her openly, her enemies had moved behind closed doors. Those enemies, she was convinced, were everywhere. Just as she had thought her campaign headquarters were bugged—that was why she always discussed sensitive matters at the nearby Wolf's Deli—she now believed the walls of her chambers had ears. When touchy subjects were to be discussed, she and her comrade might go to the courthouse basement. If her interlocutor were somewhere else, she would wander outside, taking care not to use the same pay phone too frequently. Periodically, she had the locks in her chambers changed. One Lambert employee recalled placing a personal phone call from her chambers, only to have a court officer order him to hang up. "Don't talk about the judge!" he said. "The phones are bugged!"

Her election having been deemed, as one reporter put it, "an unnatural act by the city's political parties and an obscenity bordering on bestiality by its legal establishment," some hostility remained. Three liberal Democrats walked out of a ceremony where she presided, for instance, and Alex Forger, among others, declined her offers of guardianships. Still, she established her turf. In a lightning raid she seized some chairs from her courthouse colleague, Surrogate Millard Midonick. And jurisprudentially, she quickly earned a reputation for knocking heads and disposing of cases. "A poor settlement is better than a trial," she'd say. Many lawyers steered their cases to Midonick, a known quantity. But enough Manhattanites died to keep her busy; the estates of Lotte Lenya, Yul Brynner, Leon Klinghoffer, Lillian Hellman, Béla Bartók, Joan Crawford, and Lee Strasberg passed through her hands. In the latter case a star-studded cast, including Paul Newman, Al Pacino, Eli Wallach, and Ellen Burstyn, came to her courtroom; a star-struck Marie Lambert did everything she could to accommodate her famous guests. "Relax," she told Pacino as he took the stand. "Nobody is going to bite you—not if I can help it." She even gave him some coffee while he testified.

Lambert approached her job with one fundamental conviction: She was smarter than most people. Not necessarily book-smarter, mind you, but street-smarter. She felt she *felt* more than others, that she was closer to the ground, that her instincts were purer, sounder, more common-sensical. Where the brittle old law didn't work, she ignored it or bent it into something new. For a couple who'd raised a foundling but never formally adopted him, so that when he died without a will, they were barred from inheriting his estate, she devised what she called "the de facto adoption." She fashioned new rights for gays as the wills of persons dying of AIDS came into her court. And she kept at least one of her campaign promises when, following the 1981 death of a journalist named Fred Sparks, she injected herself into the Arab-Israeli conflict.

Sparks, né Siegelstein and a Jew, left most of his $300,000 estate to charity. But he earmarked 10 percent of it to the Palestine Liberation Organization. Whether that bequest represented a political statement or self-hatred or the last laugh of a onetime humorist was impossible to say. The law was considerably simpler: A person was generally free to do with his money as he wished. Lambert nonetheless blocked the bequest pending what she promised would be a full-blown investigation of the structure, aims, and activities of the PLO, one that would de-termine just how "charitable" it really was. Thus, issues that had divided diplomats, scholars, and politicians for years would finally be resolved in Marie Lambert's Manhattan courtroom. The American Jewish Con-gress and the Anti-Defamation League solmnly thrust themselves for-ward as "friends of the court." Zehdi Labib Terzi, the PLO's representative at the United Nations, also agreed to testify, and why not? The group usually couldn't buy a platform in the United States, let alone get one free. "I talked to the State Department, but was promptly told, 'It's your baby. Do with it as you want,' " Lambert later recalled.

Marie Lambert was one of those people who love to be paranoid; after all, that someone cared enough to hurt you was a sure sign you really mattered. Now, she became convinced the Palestinians were out to murder her, a fear reinforced one day when she found the hood on her Cadillac Seville slightly ajar. She promptly installed a device enabling her to start the car from a block away. She also insisted that all elevators in the Surrogate's Court be cleared before she boarded.

By the time the Sparks hearing got under way in May 1982, the proceeding had escalated, or degenerated, into farce. The Jewish groups sent over not just one but two heavy hitters: Morris Abram, onetime president of Brandeis University, and Louis Craco, incoming president of the City Bar Association, each accompanied by legions of acolytes. Also on hand were representatives of the American Civil Liberties Union, the National Lawyers Guild, a lawyer for the PLO, a lawyer for Sparks's executor, and three lawyers from the office of New York's attorney general. At one point Lambert ordered Terzi to produce a copy of the Palestinian political program, only to learn it was in Arabic. At another she proposed to review the group's charter *in camera.* When some questions remained unresolved, Lambert offered a simple solution: "Is Mr. Arafat within the United States?" she asked.

The *Times* called Lambert's performance "cheap grandstanding" and assailed her for "making good on her campaign pledge to spice her work with ethnic politics." The *Daily News's* Ken Auletta knocked her "do-it-yourself foreign policy, New York style" and called the hearing "a cross between a Marx brothers movie and a Joseph McCarthy inquiry." In the end Sparks's money ended up with the International Red Cross, to be spent "for the betterment of the living conditions of the Palestinian people." Everyone could claim a victory, but it was the PLO representative who was most grateful. Thanks to her, he wrote the judge, America, or at least the American judicial system, had finally recognized the PLO. Marie Lambert had become a certified hero of Fatah.

The Sparks case to one side, Lambert kept a low profile. Still, the stench from the election lingered. In February 1979 she found herself the subject of a cover story in the *Village Voice,* headlined WHERE THERE'S A WILL, THERE'S A WAY: MARIE LAMBERT BRINGS PATRONAGE BACK TO SURROGATE'S COURT. The article, written by Joe Conason, examined the appointments Lambert made in her first year on the bench. But it also offered a devastating account of her campaign, furnished in large part by a former Lambert worker named Roy Hollander. He charged that Lambert, ignoring the rules for judicial candidates, had been intimately involved in raising funds for herself—writing solicitation letters, planning events, drawing up guest lists, even determining the most favorable furniture arrangements. "How are we going to make any money if we don't charge to get in the door?" he said she'd once complained. "They will just show up to have free drinks, cheese and crackers, and then they will leave." And she reviewed who'd donated how much. "This is an insult!" she allegedly declared in disgust after reviewing one pledge card. "I know how much he makes a year, and he could afford a lot more!" Aware her conduct was improper, Hollander said, Lambert suggested various subterfuges, including what he called a "golly-gee-whiz-innocent-girl-routine" as the hat was passed. The judicial-conduct commissioners, she chortled at one point, "would have shit" in their pants had they known the degree of her involvement.

Over the next few months the *Voice* repeatedly revisited the Lambert story. "If this is 'reform,' " Conason wrote at one point, "we were better off with Boss Tweed." One story was headlined MARIE LAMBERT MAY RUN, BUT SHE CAN'T HIDE. The accompanying picture, which the *Voice* photographer Fred McDarrah managed to take after the man accompanying the surrogate hit him over the head with his briefcase, showed Lambert, in dark sunglasses, in apparent flight from her own courthouse. The pictures, a *News* reporter later wrote, "would have embarrassed Frank Costello," suggesting as they did "that orphans got a better deal in the days of Dickens." Lambert dismissed the *Voice* stories as yet another prong in the plot to destroy her. As for the sunglasses, she said she'd been wearing them on doctor's orders after dust from the repair work in her apartment had irritated her eyes.

Prompted by the *Voice* articles, the Judicial Conduct Commission broadened its probe. Repeatedly, it sought her testimony; just as repeatedly, she stalled. Always, there was a different excuse: Her lawyer had suffered a heart attack; the First Amendment question had to be resolved; Midonick had been hospitalized, and she was too busy running the court. Only in September 1980 did she finally appear, to vehemently deny all charges. She insisted she'd known nothing about her fundraisers, including that funds were actually being raised at them, or that she'd ever monitored who gave how much to her campaign. "I never looked at contributors—never, ever, ever, ever, ever," she declared.

The commission found Lambert's testimony unpersuasive, and in December 1981 formally charged her with engaging in prohibited political activity both during and after the race. It started taking testimony in September 1982, five years after Lambert's primary victory. The commission's principal witness was Hollander, who came without counsel (a friend had recommended John Dickey of Sullivan & Cromwell, who declined to take the assignment. "I ran it past my partners; they tell me we do a fair amount of business in Surrogate's Court," he explained). Lambert's counsel, the noted criminal-defense lawyer James LaRossa, subjected Hollander to a wilting cross-examination, in which he suggested Hollander was a former drug dealer whose mind had been corroded by Quaaludes and LSD. He also trotted out Lambert's usual covey of character witnesses. Lambert failed to take the stand in her own defense.

In October, commission administrator Gerald Stern urged the panel to censure Lambert. "Far from shielding herself from the fund-raising aspects of her campaign," he concluded, Lambert had been "an active, visible participant," and "was determined to make a 'pitch' to attorneys that it was in their interest to contribute." He continued, "In throwing the weight of her potential judicial office behind her request for funds— however subtly or indirectly—[she] was in fact asking for funds that would go into her own pocket." Whatever misconduct Lambert had committed, Stern said, had been compounded by perjury. "Only a candidate who had become too greatly involved in fund-raising—and who knew that such conduct raised serious ethical questions—would fabricate a position of total non-involvement," he wrote. "There is no alternative but to conclude that she has testified falsely." In the end it didn't matter. With both Roy Cohn and two of his powerful law partners, Stanley Friedman and Tom Bolan, pulling strings for her, the commission decided not to punish Lambert in any way. At long last, she was in the clear.

Once their initial jitters wear off, many new judges come to believe in their own omniscience. And why not? All around them they see obsequiousness, from court officers, litigants, and most of all from lawyers. Indeed, no one has yet invented a protractor finely calibrated enough to measure the angle to which even the most respectable of them bow and scrape before the bench. Behind their backs lawyers curse judges as tyrants, lambaste them as lightweights. What do you call a lawyer with an IQ of less than 80? the old joke goes. "Your Honor." But standing before them, they compliment them on their appearance, lavish them with honorifics, praise their decisions, double over with laughter at their lamest jokes. Only the strongest judge can resist the feeling that all this is entirely deserved, and realize that what these lawyers are groveling before are the robes rather than what's beneath them. For Lambert, the metamorphosis promised to be especially extreme. The same lawyers appeared before her frequently; their livelihoods depended upon her goodwill. Moreover, as she was the court's first woman, the usual fawning would be compounded by phony chivalry; lawyers could be expected to treat her with all the unctuousness of prep-school boys pouring the headmaster's wife some tea. Most important, Lambert would feel all the deference was not just due, but overdue.

From the beginning of her tenure Lambert became known as impulsive, arbitrary, and partisan. Harkening back to her trial-lawyering days, when she'd eyeball cases for their dollar value, she'd take a dispute, view it viscerally, and decide the merits, often without the luxury of testimony. "From the day I met Marie Lambert, there was a sign hanging over her head that said, 'My mind is already made up. Don't confuse me with the facts,' " a clerk in her chambers once said. Everything—her demeanor, her rulings, her attitude toward counsel—flowed from this initial determination. Quickly, she became known for manhandling lawyers, or at least those lawyers representing what she'd deemed to be the greedy bastards or ungrateful children or gold-digging next-of-kin appearing before her. She would shriek at them, snap at them, threaten them, cut them off, put them down. Her bias was all-pervasive—"If they needed time they got it; if I wanted to take a leak, I couldn't," one lawyer recalled—and unrelenting: It could manifest itself in her chambers or in court, with or without a jury. Conversely, those lawyers and witnesses whom she liked could do no wrong. She would joke with them, coach them, set them at ease, wink at their mistakes, grant them their every wish, make them look omnipotent.

Initially, both the ongoing judicial-conduct probe and her junior status at the court held Lambert's ego somewhat in check, just as Seward's very presence curbed Basia. But once Midonick retired and the investigation fizzled out, all bets were off. The Brahmins started currying favor. Among the chief sycophants were Paul Weiss's Bernard Greene, Willkie's Ira Lustgarten (her frequent dinner escort), and Alex Forger, the same Forger who'd once eyed her so suspiciously. ("I hope your life is easing a bit with a new colleague in place at the court," he'd written her in April 1983, shortly after Renee Roth had replaced Will Midonick. "You certainly had a long period when you had to juggle more responsibility than you should have had to cope with. From all accounts you did so superbly!") Finally, she had the Forgers of the world where she wanted them, doing what she wanted them to do: on their knees, groveling, or, as she put it, "kissing my ass." Pillars of the probate bar, more anxious to protect their pocketbooks than publicize her shortcomings, could now be counted on to overlook whatever mischief she made. "Those fellows were on all fours, licking not only her feet but the floor in front of her," one lawyer recalled. Lambert concurred. "I don't have any trouble with the big firms," she said. "All they want is for me to give them their fees." Even the judges of the Appellate Division, her ostensible superiors, went easy on her; once they left the bench, they wanted appointments. Marie Lambert could at long last be herself. Through courage, doggedness, and ruthlessness, she had attained what Basia had attained through marriage and widowhood: the right to shed all inhibitions, to give vent to her impulses, to be irresponsible with impunity.

Her ego ran rampant. She fashioned all kinds of superlatives for herself—"the highest elected Catholic official in New York City," the "most important woman lawyer in the state," "the most powerful woman judge in New York," "the second most important Catholic in the state" (next to the cardinal, and ahead of the governor). She pushed for even more. She lobbied to become grand marshal of the annual Columbus Day parade, for example, as well as for the "SURROGATE 1" license plate. She grew livid at the slightest slight; at the Catholic Diocese's annual Al Smith Dinner, she raged when she wasn't within the purview of the television cameras and, when a Jewish judge was placed closer to the center of the dais than she, she complained to John Cardinal O'Connor. Her uncouthness, however, was ecumenical. At a Lubavitcher dinner, she grew furious when she was relegated to one side of the dais, away from all the male judges, and threatened to investigate the rebbe's tax exemption. Nor was she mollified upon being told that men and women had sat separately at such events for at least the past 5,700 years.

She lobbied tirelessly for still more awards and titles, and laminated plaques soon filled her chambers. From some Jewish lawyers came the "Golda Meir Award." The Columbus Alliance in the Bronx gave her its "Jurisprudence Award." There was the "Harlan Fiske Stone Award" from the trial lawyers; the "Rapallo Award" from the Columbia lawyers; the "Helen M. Wolfsohn Memorial Award" from the Brooklyn Women's Bar Association. When the National Ethnic Coalition of Organizations prepared to award its Ellis Island medals for distinguished immigrants, her whole office was enlisted to tout her. So indignant did she become over the eventual recipient of one of the Italian-American slots—"Who the hell is Joe DiMaggio? He's just some stupid ballplayer!" she complained—that she quit the group in a huff. Though, like many judges, she didn't write her own decisions—that task invariably fell to Harvey Corn; in their nine years together, he was to write all but one sentence of the entire body of Lambert opinions—she'd rail over how infrequently hers made the front page of the *New York Law Journal*. During trips to Italy and China she grew miffed when local officials did not turn out to greet her.

Officially, Lambert's term ran for twelve years. That would see her through until 1990, when she would reach the mandatory retirement age of seventy. But even before Judge Kupferman administered the oath, she had her eye on higher office. She spoke of an appointment to the Federal Court of Appeals in New York, where Learned Hand once sat. Twice, she applied for vacancies on the New York Court of Appeals, the state's highest, where Benjamin Cardozo once sat. But her real goal was the United States Supreme Court, where John Marshall, Oliver Wendell Holmes, and Louis Brandeis once sat. Everyone knew Ronald Reagan was looking for a woman to appoint, and Lambert was convinced she had the inside track; Roy Cohn had seen to that. She was crushed when Sandra Day O'Connor got the nod, and crushed anew a few years later when Antonin Scalia became the first Italian-American justice. Things would have been very different, she lamented, if Cohn, recently deceased, were still around.

One has to wonder how hard Cohn, the quintessential pragmatist, ever pushed Marie Lambert for anything, or how close the two really were. But the relationship was useful to each; it made Lambert feel like an insider and offered other assorted perks, like her son's job with Congressman Biaggi. Conversely it gave Cohn access to yet another court and judge. In any case Lambert became a member of Cohn's crowd. He added her to the roster of judges he invited to his famous functions—the birthday parties every February at Studio 54, the barbecue every July in Greenwich—and arranged for her to attend Reagan's inauguration in 1981. Conversely, Lambert called Cohn as often as three or four times a week. She joined the select few   S. I. Newhouse, Jerry Finkelstein, Donald Trump, Ron Perelman, George Steinbrenner, Estée Lauder—whose calls Cohn always took. What they discussed wasn't clear; frequently, though, she appeared almost frantic to reach him. Sometimes Lambert would show up at Cohn's town-house-law-office on East Sixty-eighth Street in the wee hours of the morning, and the two would have breakfast together, either on the second floor or at the Polo Bar of the nearby Westbury Hotel. Cohn was smart enough not to show up very often at the Surrogate's Court; when his firm had business there, an underling always handled it. He made no contribution to her campaign and accepted no patronage from her. But as it became known that his tentacles reached into Lambert's chambers, others with cases before her turned to him for help. "I'll talk to Marie" or "I'm going to see Marie tomorrow" or "I'll see what I can do with Marie" were phrases frequently overheard in Cohn's office at Saxe, Bacon & Bolan.

Sometimes, when Saxe Bacon was involved in an estates case, the opposition tried to move the matter to Roth. That was what Milbank did upon learning that Cohn might be representing Cosima von Bulow in the fight over her grandmother's will. Or they tried removing Lambert from the case, as New York lawyer Stanley Arkin did in April 1983, in a case pitting Cohn client Ronald Perelman against his estranged wife, Faith Golding Perelman, whom Arkin was representing. Given the "close and abiding friendly relationship" between Lambert and Cohn, argued Arkin, it was "inappropriate" for her to hear any case involving his firm. The motion enraged Lambert. "Let's have some facts, Mr. Arkin!" she barked when it reached court. "You stated that I have a 'close and abiding' relationship with Mr. Cohn. I don't know what that means."

"Very friendly," Arkin replied.

"I know many lawyers in this state," she said. "I probably have a friendly relationship with approximately fifty percent of the lawyers in this state, including every member of the New York State Trial Lawyers, including many members of the Association of the Bar, including many members of the New York County Lawyers' Association, including ninety percent of the women lawyers who belong to the Metropolitan Women's Bar, the New York Women's Bar, the New York State Women's Bar, and the National Women Lawyers Bar Association. I have many, many friends. For your information, Mr. Cohn has never visited at my home. Mr. Cohn is not a close personal friend of mine. He is a friend as many members of the bar are."

"You have not visited his home?" Arkin asked incredulously.

"I have not visited in his home *alone*," Lambert replied, conveniently ignoring all those early-morning visits. "He has had parties at his home to which dozens of judges were invited, dozens of lawyers were invited, and I have been one of the individuals invited to those parties. If you know anything about the parties that Mr. Cohn gives, you know that they consist of three or four hundred people, and I am one of the guests who have been invited. Sometimes I've gone, and sometimes I've not gone. So now we've taken care of my alleged close personal friendship."

Lambert did not recuse herself in the case. Two years later, when Perelman and gossip columnist Claudia Cohen married, Marie Lambert officiated. And a few years after that, when Cohn died, Marie Lambert mourned the man she described as "my closest friend in the whole world."

Lambert had opposed the candidacy of Renee Roth for Midonick's seat, at least partly because she didn't want another woman sharing the spotlight, particularly one more experienced in probate work, one who'd been endorsed by the *Times*, one who was twenty years younger and several dress sizes smaller. Lambert—and Cohn—backed another candidate, but for naught. From January 1, 1983, forward, Manhattan would have two women surrogates. Tensions are almost inevitable when two judges with identical authority and jurisdiction serve together. Still, no one was quite prepared for the tong war that developed between these two. Privately, Lambert called Roth "that bitch" and wasted no opportunity to ridicule her. She bristled whenever Roth was accorded the barest preference, real or imaginary, in any publication, on any platform. When an official prepared a brochure on the Surrogate's Court (the one Basia had consulted to access the two women's respective physiognomies), he took great pains to devote an identical number of lines to each. So mortified by the feud were their fellow surrogates in the metropolitan area that they arranged a summit between the two. In fact, things only worsened as Lambert lobbied mightily—and, ultimately, successfully—for the largely ceremonial post of the court's "supervising judge."

Lambert actually presided over very few trials; she transacted most of her business in chambers, which came to resemble a bizarre bazaar. Here, she'd hear arguments, take telephone calls from her son, conduct settlement talks. Years later, one lawyer recalled how, without interrupting her harangue against one set of lawyers, Lambert went behind a screen and readied herself for a dinner engagement, donning a lamé dress and one of the many fancy coats she bought at a discount from Harvey Corn's furrier father. She would also transact her own business. A second lawyer told of how, while Lambert was conducting talks in another case, a character came into her chambers, reached into his pocket, and handed her a wad of cash, which she proceeded to count (it was, she later explained, her nephew bringing his rent money).

Everyone knew Marie Lambert took sides; the only question in a given case was which. A science of Lambertology gradually developed, one that, like all sciences, had to be constantly tested, refined, reevaluated in the light of additional data. Truths appeared, then new truths, and sometimes they clashed, and newer truths emerged. Lambert's biases, like Lambert, were basic, and could be traced to her own experiences as lawyer, woman, widow, daughter, mother. She loved first wives, as long as they hadn't cheated on their husbands. She loathed second, third, or fourth wives, particularly when they were strong-willed, determined types who'd enticed away much older, wealthier men from their devoted, long-suffering spouses. And she almost always favored children, at least when they weren't fighting their mothers. The law did not prohibit disinheriting a child, but to her it was almost inconceivable. She preferred families over charities. She favored settlements, and struck back harshly at anyone she deemed to be resisting one unreasonably. If one's legal position was sound, one went with Roth, even though she was slow. Conversely, if one was weak on the law but strong on sentimentality, or sought a wild card, or wanted to settle, or had ties to her, Lambert was preferable. But even this was dangerous: There was no telling what kind of settlement she'd arrange, or how much she'd beat on a party to nail it down. Moreover, one had better be sure that settlement was plausible; otherwise, she'd preside over a trial, and all bets about her behavior would be off.

Just about the only moderating influence on her was Harvey Corn. An unusually savvy and mature young lawyer, Corn counseled her on the bench, steered her clear of pitfalls, protected her from herself. By and large, Lambert surrounded herself with flunkies, sycophants, and schnorrers. Many had played roles in her election campaign, and for their dogged devotion and subservience she liberally doled out patronage bones, awarding them massive fees for work for which they showed no particular industry or aptitude. A frequent recipient and companion, Vincent Catalfo, had been suspended from law practice for three years once after forging a client's name on a check. In any crowd, but in this crowd in particular, Corn was a class act. He was also ambitious; he wanted to be surrogate someday and saw this as the most direct route, as long as he played his cards right and kept Marie Lambert under control.

Sullivan & Cromwell was not Lambert's favorite law firm; three S&C partners had been complicit when the City Bar Association found her unfit for office. But with his characteristic cool confidence, particularly when it came to women, Donald Christ thought he knew Lambert, and believed he could harness her to his ends. After all, he had two things working for him: his charm and his genes. Apart from her affection for Christ's father, Christ himself had been among the few lawyers who'd ignored the blue bloods' blockade around her during her early days on the court. Christ felt that Lambert's abrasive, impatient, partisan style was just what the Johnson case called for. As a fiery, strong-willed immigrant woman herself, she would understand Basia. She'd have little use for a strike suit, and would let Milbank and the children know it. Christ thought she disliked Forger, the embodiment of her patrician detractors. Even on the law, she seemed well disposed toward his case. In one of her several highly praised rulings involving the estates of AIDS victims, one whose issues applied equally to the will contest, Lambert had construed undue influence narrowly and "lucid intervals" broadly; that the testator had been incoherent both before and after he'd signed his will, she ruled, by no means invalidated something he'd signed while "cheerful and ambulatory" in between. Sure, Christ might have reasoned, Marie Lambert took sides. But in this case she would surely take his. The Milbank lawyers thought so, too. Every time Lambert turned to Christ in chambers and said, "Don, how's your dad?" Forger and Reilly winced, though at no point were they tempted to take Marty Richards's advice and add Cohn to their legal team. But as Lambert ruled their way on several successive issues, they stopped worrying. Christ, meanwhile, remained convinced he'd made the right choice. Besides, what difference did the judge make when, as he had told Basia, there was a "zero percent chance" she'd lose the case!

In early 1985 an old friend of Christ's, a New York lawyer named J. Robert Lunney, appeared in Lambert's courtroom on behalf of Mrs. A. Chauncey Newlin, widow of a partner at the New York law firm of White & Case. It was a variation on a familiar theme: Newlin's three sons by a prior marriage were trying to set aside a $2 million "charitable unitrust" their father had set up, one whose income went to their stepmother. They charged that, due to a degenerative brain disease, their father was obsessed with unitrusts, having touted them monomaniacally to law partners, doctors, doormen, and even Mayor Koch, whom he threatened to sue for $400 billion for failing to place New York City's assets in one. ("You would lose your job as Mayor and also the possibility of your ever becoming president," Newlin warned him. "I shall hate to do this because you are such a nice guy. I would rather sue Governor Carey, but he is in Albany and I do not have the time to run back and forth".) One lawyer testified that Newlin was in "never-never land." A neurologist put it more bluntly, calling him "a little meshugah." His lawyer-landlords recounted how he'd ordered five hundred neckties at once from a local haberdasher. Newlin sent *The Odd Couple*'s Felix and Oscar a rambling seven-page proposed plot. He sent some 154 people, including the board members of the Metropolitan Opera and Lincoln Center, copies of a letter he'd mailed to Ms. Lillian Carter, in which he recounted how he'd dreamed she'd been buried alongside fifty thousand gallons of scotch, enough "from time to time to reach over and take a few nips."

Lunney's formidable task was to show that while Newlin was "inimitable," he was not demented. But Lambert didn't seem interested.

She had apparently decided that the second Mrs. Newlin, a former editor of the *Ladies' Home Journal,* was a fortune hunter, and that any trial was superfluous. She refused to give Lunney adequate preparation time, denigrated his evidence, and cut off his examination, all the while coddling opposing counsel. "Donald, the woman is crazy!" Lunney told Christ. "Depending on which side she decides to come down on, you either luck in or luck out. You may want to rethink where you're going." But Christ was unperturbed. "You must have pissed her off," he replied. "Don't tell her you know me."

Christ appeared equally unconcerned by Lambert's conduct a few months later in a lawsuit over the estate of a New York businessman named Milton Kimmelman. Kimmelman left the bulk of his estate to his wife; their son, Peter Kimmelman, was challenging the will on the grounds of incapacity. The Kimmelman trial began in October 1985, and with the Johnson case on deck, scouts from S&C, Milbank, Shearman & Sterling, and Dewey Ballantine filled the gallery. (So frequently did Christ come to court that Lambert called him to the stand one day to read some testimony into the record.) Quickly, Lambert's biases surfaced. This time the winners were Mrs. Kimmelman, her lawyers, and her witnesses. To Mrs. Kimmelman's lawyer, Steven Kaufman, and his star witness, Paul Weiss partner Bernard Greene, she was unfailingly deferential. For one of young Kimmelman's lawyers, Seth Rubenstein of Brooklyn, getting even the most minor exhibit into evidence was Sisyphean. Lambert brutalized his principal lawyer, Ira Turret, even worse.

A losing party doesn't often have good things to say about the presiding judge. But he generally keeps his feelings to himself, particularly while the case is still under way. Twice during the trial, however, Peter Kimmelman complained to the Commission on Judicial Conduct about what he called Lambert's "almost complete abandonment of judicial restraint." "From 11 A.M. to 5 P.M. each day the Judge, with brief intermittent breaks, castigates and screams, scowls and scolds," he wrote the panel. While Lambert insulated his mother's witnesses, Kimmelman wrote, she subjected his to withering cross-examination. Now, he suggested, was the time to reign in this rogue judge. "Our trial, which is preceding immediately in time the probate contest in the Johnson estate, is being followed with interest by numerous major Wall Street law firms involved in that controversy," he wrote. "I believe that your commission is in a position to ascertain rather quickly whether the judicial misconduct of which I complain has occurred." There was no response. Three weeks later, as summations were about to begin, Kimmelman again urged the commissioners to see for themselves Lambert's "egregious and shocking bias." Again there was no response. Incidentally the jury found for Mrs. Kimmelman.

Kimmelman was a harbinger, but of what? To Michael Levin and Paul Shoemaker, the two Milbank associates sent to observe the proceedings, the message was sobering. They, like Rubenstein, were representing objectants. If this was how Lambert viewed anyone trying to overturn a will, the children were in deep trouble. Nina, too, was struck by Lambert's bias, but took comfort for the very reason Milbank was so apprehensive. Christ remained unconcerned. Frequently, he'd amble into Lambert's chambers during breaks for some amiable schmoozing. "They looked like they were good friends," a Lambert employee recalled. Christ's cohorts at Sullivan & Cromwell noticed this as well, and took solace from it. "It must be terribly hard to go through what you're going through," one S&C lawyer told Rubenstein. "But she won't do that to Donald."

XXIX

One day early in 1985, while perusing her new *Fannie Farmer Baking Book*, Nina Zagat came across a recipe for "Osgood Pie." As Ms. Farmer described it, it was an old-fashioned confection, "a snappy mixture of raisins, walnuts, spice, and vinegar, with under-pinnings of a little butter and sugar." Osgood Pie, unlike Osgood the lawyer, was of southern origin, its name a contraction of "oh so good." But why be fussy? Nina photocopied the recipe and gave it to Basia. Not long afterward, when Basia invited Osgood and his family to Jasna Polana, she had her cook bake one. Alas, it was better on the page than the palate; its crust was hard, its innards leaden. But no one saw anything ominous in this. Nina and Basia even took to calling the S&C litigator "Oh So Good."

Life in the proponents' camp still bordered on frolicsome. Christ regaled Basia with his mordant wit; realizing that the way to Basia's heart was through her animals, he told her tales of his wife's llamas and his own beloved dog, Beaver. Basia decreed that he need no longer call her "Mrs. Johnson"; "Basia" would do just fine. But as warmly disposed as she was toward Christ, Basia positively had a crush on Osgood. She became girlishly playful whenever she was near him. She graded his neckties and grew giddy with him over drinks and dinner at Petrossian. When he entered a room, she might gush something like, "Doesn't Mr. Osgood look handsome today!" Christ she called "Perry Mason," the smart but rather asexual attorney; she likened Osgood to the far more dashing Paul Drake. Osgood joined in the merrymaking. During one of his periodic trips to Chautauqua, where he'd been de-veloping a new hotel, he discovered a winery named "Johnson Estate." He bought himself a case of "Johnson Estate" Seyval Blanc 1983, and, one afternoon at Jasna Polana, presented everyone with a bottle, along with one of his periodic poems. Basia's included allusions to the various men she thought were in love with her, like Gregory Peck. Later, Nina got her own custom-made doggerel.

Dear Nina:
The label on this bottle of wine
Brought you fondly to mind.
Save it not for victory celebrations
When our inevitable victory occurs,
There shall be extensive libations.
Bob 9-7-84.

Osgood became Basia's great champion, her Prince Valiant. During one deposition, after Reilly called her "Basia," Osgood sprang into action. "Mr. Reilly, my client's name is 'Mrs. Barbara P. Johnson,' and I would appreciate it if you would show enough respect to refer to her as 'Mrs. Johnson,'" he huffed. (Reilly complied, though he still took care always to mangle "Piasecka.") The proponents had recently launched a campaign to burnish Basia's image—an element of which included an English translation of her thesis, "Jan Stanisławski: Master of Polish Landscape Painting"—and Osgood did his part. By now, Basia had largely shed her former lumpenproletarianism, the humble origins that had come in so handy in the Krasinski case, and Osgood accelerated the revisionism. It was misleading to characterize her as a "former upstairs maid," he lectured one reporter; she'd come from a "brave and aristocratic family" of landowners and been born of "wealthy parents." Nor was she a mere fortune hunter. "Mrs. Johnson loved Mr. Johnson, who was a dashing man," Osgood explained. "And he was madly in love with his wife. Here was a man who could have any woman, who had an 'active social life,' but he wanted to marry her. She was one of the few people Mr. Johnson met who had the attributes of attractiveness, intelligence, and strong character."

The tie between Jasna Polana's queen and Sullivan & Cromwell's poet laureate only intensified during his many visits to the estate, where he was preparing her to testify in the Harbor Branch case. So cozy did the two of them become that when Basia got some new dachshunds, she joked that she had named one of them, "Eros," after him; she likened "Bumble Bee," whose squarer belly hung closer to the ground, to Christ. Even Osgood's own colleagues began making veiled jokes about just what he was doing during all those hours at Jasna Polana, with Christ joining in the merriment. "He's down there screwing the client," he quipped. Whether or not that was true, or whether Christ actually believed it, at one point Basia complained to Nina that Osgood had kissed her too enthusiastically for her taste. Nina considered the matter serious enough to report it to Christ and Bauman, and even to

suggest that Osgood be taken off the case. Later Osgood heatedly denied
any romantic involvement with Basia, and in one way his denial rang
true: He was at least thirty years too young for her.

But with the Forger Affidavit, Lambert's adverse rulings, and the
difficulties with the key nurses, a vague sense of disquiet began building
in the proponents' camp. Osgood, forced to live out of Holiday Inns
in godforsaken Florida, resented Christ, whom he felt was back in New
York doing nothing. Peach resented Nina, thinking that she, too, was
unduly complacent. And Basia seemed to resent everyone, especially
her lawyers. As a species, she did not like lawyers much; they were too
cautious, indecisive, evasive for her taste, forever clouding issues, getting in the way, slowing her down. "Speed is half of victory," she liked
to say, and now, the only speed she saw from S&C was of the "all
deliberate" kind. The preliminary wrangling droned on and on, no trial
date was yet in sight, and her lawyers seemed powerless to pick up the
pace.

By June of 1985 most of the doctors and nurses had been questioned.
So, too, with the sole exception of Junior, had the children and their
spouses. Still, more than two years after Seward's death, Reilly requested
and received yet more time for depositions: an additional ten days each
for Peach, Ford, and Jay Gunther; two weeks for Basia, three weeks for
Nina. Now, the earliest the trial could possibly begin was November
1. Danny Katz, an art dealer in London who'd sold Basia a collection
of Renaissance bronzes, told her to ditch her "society lawyers" and get
herself some smart, aggressive Jews: "Cohen & Cohen" was his generic
name for them. For Basia as for many of her countrymen, the very
thing that made Jews so distasteful—their purportedly superior intelligence—at times made them more desirable; even anti-Semites, after
all, want Jewish doctors for the children. Basia remembered Katz's
suggestion, as well as Peach's credo: that "all attorneys are whores."

Basia's unhappiness grew as Milbank besmirched her and S&C appeared too paralyzed and ineffectual to respond. With a naturally laconic
style that could easily be taken for passivity, Christ fell from grace first.
Basia suspected him of being a closet compromiser, willing to sell out
her honor and settle if the right offer came along. She grew exasperated
with what she deemed his lethargy. He mumbled, and worse, put his
feet up on the nearest table or desk as he did. Things she'd initially
found so endearing about him became annoyances, like his frequent
references to his pets. "That lazy slob! All he cares about is Beaver!"
she'd complain. Soon, she bestowed on him one of her favorite epithets,
one she'd already applied to characters as diverse as Count Krasinski,

Cyrus Vance, and Junior Johnson: Donald Christ, she concluded, was a "soft-boiled egg."

Basia's growing disenchantment with Christ led to an even more crippling confrontation with Osgood. At Jasna Polana in the late spring of 1985, without Christ or Nina around to inhibit him, Osgood confessed to Basia that he, too, felt frustrated. Reilly had seized the initiative; the proponents seemed listless. He went on to suggest how much better things would be if, as he believed Christ had promised him, he were in charge. That that much was said seems beyond dispute. But in Basia's version of events, things got more dramatic. Christ, she recalled Osgood telling her, was like a brother to him. But he was lazy, indifferent, and ultimately unconcerned for her; his real loyalties lay with Nina. Rather than roll up their sleeves and get this case over with, Osgood complained, the two of them did little more than sit around and gossip. But he, Osgood, was different: He was a fighter, like Basia herself. Put him in charge, he told her, and he would *really* defend her. He would tell her inspiring life story. He would win her case and rout the children.

Or so Basia said he said. As much as she sympathized with Osgood's message, however, she recoiled as he said it. Bad-mouthing his own partner like this, she thought, was betrayal of the worst sort. By her standards of loyalty and honor, anyone—even the plodding, dim-witted Christ—was preferable to someone so treacherous. Suddenly, "Oh So Good" became "Oh So Bad"; Basia began treating Osgood the way Fannie Farmer told her readers to treat Osgood Pie—that is, to "beat until stiff," "prick all over with a fork," then test "by inserting a knife in the center." Basia took to calling Osgood "the Peacock," a reference to what she considered his vanity. She subjected him to petty humiliations, at one point instructing him not to speak to her without obtaining Christ's permission first. Her tongue-lashings grew more caustic, more frequent, more public. The coup de grace came during Nina's examination, as several colleagues looked on. "When I defend you at your deposition . . . " Osgood began, turning to Basia, only to be cut short. "What makes you think *you're* going to defend me?" Basia shrieked. "You're not going to defend me! Mr. Christ is going to defend me!" Osgood turned his usual shade of scarlet and said nothing. Afterward, Osgood put his arm around Christ. "Congratulations, Donald," he said bitterly. "You have won the grand prize."

To compound matters for the proponents, Milbank renewed and broadened its attack on Sullivan & Cromwell. Now, it accused S&C of having had improper contacts with several witnesses—among them

Bonnie Weisser (whom Osgood had supposedly harassed), John Peach, and Judy Smith, the nurse whose hospitalization Basia had underwritten. Once more the objectants demanded to question Christ and Osgood under oath. S&C called the complaint an attempt by the children to spy and pry and try to delay the start of trial. "It is unfortunate when litigation descends to such an uncivilized state," it stated. "Scurrying from the merits, they fabricate delays, dirt and diversion." In the same motion S&C called the children "six avaricious multimillionaires" and "six nabobs who have lived off trust funds for forty years, and whose greed for still more millions has led to this litigation." And Delahunty, S&C's designated scrivener of screeds, was only getting warmed up.

"The six unhappy children have squandered tens of millions of dollars, with nothing to show for it but broken lives," his motion continued. "They still have plenty left: none of them is in any danger of going on welfare. But they seem to want more, more, MORE. Not content with their father's gifts of great wealth, the children have laid siege to his estate." Now, "with fourteen weeks to go before trial and the key facts lining up against them, the children have thrown a little tantrum. Their motion strikes out at the lawyers and witnesses who seem to be standing between them and their father's money. They call the lawyers rude names; pound on the table; demand to take lawyers' depositions; and suggest that if they lose this contest their defeat will result from the undue influence of lawyers on witnesses—not because their father saw no need to heap more millions upon them."

"To maintain that their father was 'very acute' when he assisted THEM, but 'incompetent' when he left his estate to others, is self-evident bad faith," the S&C motion concluded. "Rather than coddle the children's fantasies, discovery should be brought to a swift conclusion, so that their objections to the will may receive the judgment they deserve."

As the lawyers bickered, the press enjoyed a Roman holiday. Articles on the case appeared everywhere from the *Dallas Times Herald* ("It's not unlike *Dallas*," Alex Forger remarked, referring to the television program rather than the city), to *Star Magazine* (where Junior called the will contest the worst scandal ever to hit his family and boasted that the Johnsons had always liked "to keep our skirts clean") to Suzy's column in the *Daily News*. "Suzy" was friendly with Iris Christ, and her item was certainly the most sympathetic to Basia; it described how Seward had forsaken Essie for this "much younger, vivacious, bright woman" and how from that moment on "in every will it was Basia all the way." The first full-length feature was written by John Taylor of *Manhattan, inc.* magazine. In it he described Basia as "a stocky woman with a sensual face, dark blond hair sometimes worn in Marie Antoinette ringlets, and an engagingly imperfect command of English."

While, on the standard but counterproductive instruction of counsel, Basia and Nina remained mum, Junior Johnson was accessible and voluble. On the front page of the *Trenton Times* he described how the Johnson blood had been polluted, leached, and, now, aroused by an alien antigen. Seward, he said, "always thought in sort of dynastic terms," and it was incredible for him to have left his fortune outside his bloodline. "When did he last have a will?" he asked. "I think it was before he married Basia." He continued, "I think that a family that would have allowed what appears to me to be an invasion, socially and financially, is weak and undeserving and does not represent the strengths that made the fortune. Frankly, I think the Johnson blood is up, and we're not about to back down." So frequent were his blabberings that Sullivan & Cromwell accused Milbank of researching and scripting his periodic "press releases" as well as providing him legal counsel. In *Us* magazine, Junior called Basia "the merry widow." In *New Jersey Monthly*, he predicted that the will contest would "blow high, wide and handsome" and was "going to be a lulu." And in a lengthy interview with *The New York Times*, he described Basia as "a combination of Marie Antoinette and Hetty Green," adding, "She knows how to furnish a yacht. What she doesn't know is social responsibility." At another point he joked, "When she was asked to come and clean house, she took it idiomatically instead of literally."

Reilly chuckled at his client's bon mots, and one sensed that for once his laughter wasn't just strategic. He genuinely enjoyed Junior, perhaps because Junior was his polar opposite: irresponsible, irrepressible, insouciant, filthily rich enough to buy his way out of whatever messes he made, however horrible or irreparable they were for others. For Junior, life was a kind of sport; Reilly, for whom nothing had ever come easily, seemed to view him with wonder and to delight vicariously in his naughtiness. Even with his commanding presence, Reilly could not always keep Junior under control. He repeatedly undermined his own case, as if he preferred hearing himself talk to winning. In his *Times* interview, for instance, Junior made it sound as if Basia and Seward were strangely compatible. "All they did was talk about spending money," he said. "He saw himself as wealthy enough that he didn't have to worry, that he could spoil her, spoil her, spoil her, spoil her."

Though Basia appeared dominant, Junior said, he'd always felt his father remained quietly but firmly in control. "He was placating her, but he had his own ideas of what he was doing," Junior opined. Nor, he suggested, was Seward's silence on his wills particularly surprising. "There was no going up to him and saying 'Hey, Dad, what the hell is going on with your will?' He didn't like to talk about gifts, wills, money, anything like that. He would sidestep it right away."

And in some ways, he went on, the will's contents weren't all that shocking; asked how much he had expected the children to collect under it, he hesitated, then replied, "Just a few million dollars each." Because of the 1944 trusts, he confessed, any additional bequests would have been "generous." (Mary Lea said the same thing. "We had a very good trust fund which was certainly adequate to take care of us," she said.) And, if Milbank hoped to portray Basia as a homewrecker, Junior couldn't help much. Asked about Seward's prior philandering, he sputtered, "Ah . . . well, no, it . . . I wouldn't say it was . . . there maybe had . . . yes there had been a couple of instances. I wasn't too involved with them, you know . . . it's hearsay."

For the same *Times* article the scene shifted a few days later to the Sixth Avenue offices of the Producer Circle, where Reilly produced Mary Lea and Marty Richards. All around, one could see the trappings of Mary Lea's glamorous new life: autographed pictures of Harold Prince, Stephen Sondheim, and Angela Lansbury, along with a Hirschfeld caricature of Marty and Mary Lea which, like the children's case against Basia, had a "NINA" in the middle of it. Not knowing any better, the reporter naively directed his initial questions to Mary Lea. More candid than her brother, she confirmed that her father was priapic, and that before Basia came along he would periodically "disappear for a day or two" with one woman or another, sometimes one of Mary Lea's friends. She recalled that she hadn't met Basia until shortly before Seward married her ("They'd been traveling, and our paths just didn't cross") and that the union "really did not concern me one way or the other." "There seemed to be a great deal of physical attraction between the two," she said. "When she'd get up he'd pat her on the bottom, little things like that. They seemed very much in love," she added, what with all their "handholding and baby talk and stuff." That, though, was about all Mary Lea was inclined to say—or, more accurately, could get in edgewise. For two hours Marty Richards cut her off at every pass, completely dominating the conversation.

By now Marty had already discussed the case twice with the Milbank lawyers and been questioned by S&C, so his account was polished.

Once again, he talked of how close he'd been to Basia and how much it pained him to knock her now. Once again, he anesthetized himself quickly. Once again, he compared her to the "bitch of Buchenwald." ("When you find out how she treated help, for someone who was help herself, I mean, it was outrageous! I have never seen anyone more horrible. When she had her hook in, she tortured them to death.") Once again, he claimed Basia's favorite English words were "stupid" and "idiot." Once again, he offered his apocryphal account of how, during Seward's hospitalization in 1981, Basia had gone around yelling, "My God, he didn't sign the will yet! He didn't sign the will yet!" Once again, he compared Basia to a Medici, claiming that her art dwarfed Getty's (by his count, source unknown, she had nineteen Monets, fifteen Picassos, and several Rembrandts), that she'd once spent forty thousand dollars on tablecloths, and had sunk $5.5 million in a chapel when, as Richards put it, "there's a starving world out there and she comes from a country that's been starving." And for all that "she buried him in Florida for tax reasons and he's laying there God knows where in between a bunch of people he never heard of, behind a little slab in the wall."

Once again, he depicted Nina as a glorified maid. Until Seward's death, he said, her workload had been "ninety percent domestic and ten percent legal," while afterward it was the other way around. Seward had little use for her, he said, usually referring to her as "that Zagat woman." ("Now if you call someone 'that Zagat woman' I don't think you leave them anything.") And once again, he described how Basia had turned Seward into pulp. Sure, Seward wore a Bulgari necklace, but "he would have put garbage on his neck if she told him to do it." Away from Basia, Seward had spoken in "a radio voice," articulate and mellifluous; near her, he was simpering, babylike, and pliable. "I'd seen him sign papers and things that she just threw in front of him and he'd say, 'Can't we just do it tomorrow?' " he recalled.

But old Seward wasn't always helpless. Once, Marty said, his father-in-law told him his third marriage was his best because "I don't understand a word she's saying and I can turn her off at any time I want." On another occasion, Marty related, Seward cut short one of Basia's tirades. "Don't teach me anything!" he snapped. "What I have forgotten you will never learn!" In fact, according to Marty, a specter haunted Basia: that Seward might unload her. That was why, he explained, she'd surrounded him with elderly, obese, mustached, Polish-speaking nurses. "She made sure that there would be no competition," he said. Her fear, he went on, was warranted. He recalled how, in Italy, he'd seen the elderly Seward survey a nude beach through some binoculars, then grumble, "There isn't a decent pair on the bunch!" "This is what my father-in-law said, and he was no baby at the time," Marty recalled impishly. "Something I must say: Basia had a 'decent pair,' I guess."

As Richards prattled and tattled, Mary Lea sat largely mute. "The only reason I'm speaking a great deal and my wife isn't is that they're a very low-key, lovely family, very quiet, they donate many things to this country and never talk about it; you don't read about it like the Rockefellers and the Fords," Marty gushed. In their own quiet way, he went on, the children had loved their father "very, very much." (This time, at least, there were no references to any rat-infested barns.) When the reporter asked Mary Lea whether she was pained by the court case, Richards, naturally, answered for her. "It bereaves her a great deal, it really, really does," he said. "She cries a great deal about it, she's embarrassed by it, and she also misses her father terribly, which is the truth."

"We were great friends," Mary Lea finally chimed in.

Over the next few months, however, Marty began circulating a story he failed to mention to Milbank, S&C, the *Times* or Seward's assembled admirers at the Knights of Malta ceremony. Among those to hear the story was one of Mary Lea's trustees. Over lunch at Windows on the World in January 1986, the trustee later told his colleagues, Marty "launched into a long tale of what a cruel early youth Mary Lea had experienced, how badly she had been treated by her father, including some rather revolting details that I will not put down on paper." What Marty had told him, along with several other people around the same time, was that as a child, Mary Lea had been the victim of incest— and that the villain had been Seward. It was a claim Mary Lea had bandied about intermittently, but that, for obvious reasons, she had stopped peddling during the will contest. Moreover, it was one that various members of her own family either did not believe or knew nothing about, and that her friends invariably discounted, chalking it up to her vivid imagination and lifelong craving for attention and affection. For whatever reason, Marty Richards now seemed determined to give it a wider audience.

Sticking to its press quarantine, Sullivan & Cromwell would not allow the *Times* to speak with either Basia or Nina. Instead, it dispatched the elaborate press kit it furnished anyone writing on the case. It was organized with characteristic S&C meticulousness into six convenient categories:

It was not necessary to read through all the chaff; for handy reference, the wheat had been pre-underlined in green ink.

Under "I" were some of the notes Seward had written to Basia over the years. Seward had never been the epistolary type, and the selection was pretty skimpy—for instance, a receipt from Judy's Flower Shop in Princeton, showing that Seward had once ordered a $72.45 bouquet of roses with an accompanying card to read "To Basia: Welcome Home. Love, Seward." Under "II" was a letter written by a Polish nobleman during the Biblioteka Polska flap, describing Basia as "very intelligent, feminine, and full of character." Under "III" were deposition excerpts attesting to Seward's competence and Basia's ministrations. Category "IV," by far the thickest file, was a sampler of the children's peccadillos, inadmissible in court but not in the press. There were Junior's divorce papers, Seward's "troublemaker beyond my imagination" letter to Mary Lea, and clippings from the D'Arc case, all designed to counter suggestions that the unhappy Johnsons were the Happy Hollisters. For "VI" S&C culled the children's every backhanded compliment and begrudging admission regarding Basia. There was, for instance, the following illuminating exchange from Elaine Wold's deposition:

CHRIST: "Did you believe that your stepmother took good care of your father during his last illness?"
WOLD: "Yes, I do."
CHRIST: "Did you ever tell her so?
WOLD: "No."

What with all of their childhood traumas, one thing the Johnsons had learned to do well was write thank-you notes, and S&C supplied several sent to Basia, or, as the children also addressed her at various times, "Bisha," "Basha," and "Bashia." "We know you worked hard durring [sic] the past weeks to plan every detail—you even cut and arranged the beautiful flowers," Diana Wold Marszalek wrote after her wedding reception at Jasna Polana. Elaine wrote of her thrill at owning the "lovely Pisarro [sic] painting" Basia had sold her. There were condolences on the death of Basia's mother, including one from "Jim, Gretchen, Tucker, GoGo, Christy, Scarlet, Jazz & Jamie," another from Jennifer ("You have my affection, love, and support"), a third from Elaine, complete with a check for "the needy and hungry of Poland" in memory of Basia's mother. There were the notes Ruth and Evangeline had sent Basia after Seward's death, as well as Junior's letter saluting her "delicious spaghetti" and "very nice effort to pull the family together."

In the *Times* article on the case, which appeared on June 18, Christ remarked that the first collective gesture taken by the fragmented family Basia had helped unite was to turn around and maul her. It was not that charge, though, but a description of his early marital problems, as depicted in his 1962 divorce petition, that angered Junior most. "By his own admission," the story stated, "Seward Jr. was reduced to the role of babysitter, chauffeur, cook and cuckold," subjected to such humiliations "as serving breakfast in bed to his wife's lover and pouring tea at a women-only bridal shower."

That statement, Junior correctly noted, was wrong. True, Junior had charged that his first wife allowed one of her lovers to move into her home, send her love poems, and "embrace and fondle her amorously while she was scantily clad, and to kiss her lips, legs, thighs, and other parts of her body," while Junior was reduced, among other things, to serving her breakfast in bed and acting "as babysitter, chauffeur, and errand boy." Nor did Junior dispute that Barbara had allowed a second man to sleep with her, dress and undress her, watch her take baths, showers, and bowel movements. But never, *ever* had Junior actually served breakfast in bed to any of her paramours, and he fumed at the suggestion. "Such an act would be sexually and socially perverted," he huffed. Junior spoke with one of his lawyers about suing for libel. Later, he demanded a correction, only to back off; unfortunately, the same mistake reappeared in the newspaper eight months later, as the trial was about to begin. This time, Junior insisted on, and got, a correction—one of the more unusual ones in the annals of the *Times*. "The petition said the younger Mr. Johnson's first wife forced him to serve her breakfast in bed after she had become involved with another man, not that she forced him to serve her lover breakfast in bed," it stated.

Oddly, Junior played his own role in perpetuating the mistake. Not

long afterward he "sculpted" a piece he called "Between Appointments," depicting a man snoozing on a park bench. The man had
covered his face with *The New York Times* of June 18, 1985, opened
to the offending story. Long after versions of it in newsprint or microfilm
had disintegrated, then, the calumny would be preserved in bronze.

XXX

Osgood may have been denied the honor of handling Basia's deposition, but he won second prize: handling Nina's, which finally got under way on June 3. Take Nina's long association with the Johnsons, add her encyclopedic knowledge of their affairs, sprinkle in her lawyerly caution and penchant for agonizing over every syllable, sauté that with Milbank's meticulousness, and you have a recipe for interminability. Even with Lambert crony Harry W. Davis serving as referee—he would pocket $160,000 from the estate for his labors— the proceeding dragged on for twenty-eight days and 3,689 pages.

Reilly's demonization of the opposition was on schedule. Already, he had little use for Nina. He was, to be sure, convinced of her cupidity, but her offensiveness to him was as much a matter of aesthetics as ethics. Every morning of her examination he'd watch her scarf down the banana she brought (Osgood thought the potassium was good for her) and nibble on the coffee cake Milbank provided; afternoons, he'd look on as she pumped herself up with Coca-Cola. As a man of con-summate self-control—this, after all, was the fellow who'd sworn off candy, cookies, and cake on successive New Years—he couldn't abide such noshing; he loved making wisecracks to his colleagues about Nina, calling her things like "Piano Legs" and "Fat Pig." But he did not let his prejudices interfere with his task. The fireworks would come later. Now was the time to learn.

For one thing, he could learn more about the testator. "What would you say were the most distinctive traits or characteristics of Mr. Johnson?" he asked Nina at one point. "Extremely imaginative, intel-ligent, kind, very broad interests in a lot of areas, and not superficial interests," Nina soliloquized, a bit hesitantly at first, though more out of surprise than uncertainty. "He was wise. He had a very good sense of humor. He could be impatient. Very precise and demanding of precision in others. He liked people who were direct and honest and didn't like people who were superficial. He was very involved with words and the meaning of words and would be very impatient with people who were sloppy about it. He respected hard work. Although he had enormously broad experiences in his life, he wasn't the kind of person who would sit back and just talk about the past, except in those special occasions where there was something very relevant about it. He was always planning for the future in a way that was very rare for a person his age. I always felt that was part of what kept him so young. He was loving. He took extremely good care of himself. He was quite an authoritarian in a very quiet way. He knew what he wanted and he would see that what he wanted was done. He would tease people sometimes. He loved animals. He loved being a farmer. He was proud of himself as a sailor. He loved the sea. And he was a great teacher. He would be exacting with others. He was generous. He was very proud of Johnson & Johnson and the part he had played in the development of the company, in participating in the selection of the young men who eventually were to rise to be the management of the company. And he was deeply in love with Mrs. Johnson. He had enormous respect for her and pride in the things she did and in her helping him to develop interests that he had more deeply. He was a great gentleman, and enjoyed dressing in his own special, individual style, and extremely distinguished in his appearance, his manner, his speech, in every way."

She had called Mr. Johnson "loving," Reilly noted. Did that apply to loving his children? "It's hard to answer that because Mr. Johnson was different in that way from most people of his age," Nina replied. "Many people talk more about their children and grandchildren than Mr. Johnson did. He just wasn't the kind of person who would say, 'My grandchild took his first two steps last week.' It just wasn't his nature." Reilly pressed. Had Nina any doubts that he loved his children? Nina squirmed. "Love is just such a hard word . . . I mean it has so many different levels to it," she replied. "I have no reason to think that he *didn't* love his children."

Nina realized instantly that she would soon be asked the same thing about Basia, and that she'd better be better prepared. Then, there would be an additional complication: Basia would be sitting next to her. The following day—the twenty-second day of Nina's deposition—it came. "Mrs. Zagat, what would you say are the most distinctive traits of Mrs. Johnson?" Osgood objected; the question, he said, was irrelevant. He was overruled. Nina asked that Reilly's query be repeated, as she often did with even the most straightforward questions, to collect her thoughts and guard against curveballs. Her S&S colleague Werner Polak advised her to do so; taking such pauses was, in fact, one of what he called his "Fourteen Commandments" for surviving cross-examinations. The hypercautious Nina reviewed Polak's injunctions before every session; with certain questions, she seemed to run through all fourteen of them sequentially before answering.

"I'd say Mrs. Johnson is a very loving person, with very strong beliefs in the importance of family and family relationships, and who devoted herself, during the course of her marriage, to Mr. Johnson, to building relationships between Mr. Johnson and his children, and among the children themselves, that had not existed in any meaningful way prior to that time," she began. "Mrs. Johnson is a perfectionist, always striving to increase her knowledge and to perform every responsibility that she undertakes with great enthusiasm and in the best possible way. Mrs. Johnson is extremely generous, understanding, kind, and has a great intuitive sense that enables her to understand people and communicate with them in a very meaningful way. I have to say . . . " she began. The word "naive" had suddenly popped into her head. She wanted to say that Basia sometimes saw things as she wanted them to be, that she misjudged relations, that she thought people liked her when they really didn't. But it was too risky. She stumbled through a few additional observations—Basia's devotion to Harbor Branch and *her* love of animals—before she decided how she could say it. "I think sometimes Mrs. Johnson assumes that other people have the same motivations as she does, and sometimes that leads to disappointment," she said. "And, likewise, she assumes that other people have the same drive to do things perfectly in the way she always tries to do them. And sometimes that leads to disappointment."

"You used the phrase 'leads to disappointment,' " Reilly said. "You used that expression twice. My question is: 'Leads to disappointment' of whom? Disappointment of Mrs. Johnson?"

Nina tried to duck. "I thought my answer was clear on that point," she replied. "Don't you think?" she asked, turning to Osgood. "It is not clear to me," Reilly declared. "That's why I asked the question."

"What I meant was that she would be disappointed," Nina said.

"How did she express her disappointment?" Reilly asked.

Nina was tempted to acknowledge the tirades, but Osgood objected before she could, and this time he was sustained, just as he had been when Reilly asked for some examples of Basia's sense of humor. And a good thing, too; the only examples Nina could think of were Basia's nicknames for the opposing lawyers; Reilly was "Ratley"; Shoemaker, "Screwmaker," etc., etc.

Reilly, undeterred, pressed on. "Did she become angry?" he asked. Again the referee sustained the objection.

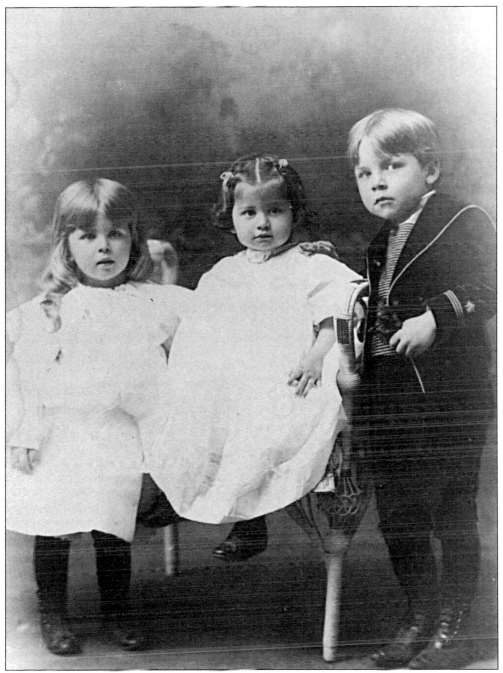

Seward Johnson *(left)* with his siblings, Evangeline and Robert Wood Johnson, circa 1900

Seward at various stages during his gilded childhood

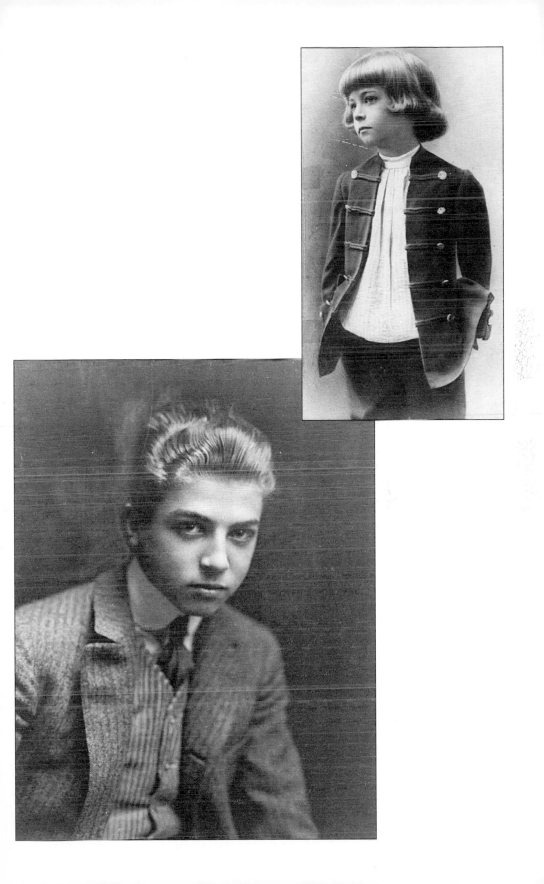

Seward as a naval officer during World War I. It was his sexual exploits, and not his maritime ones, that earned him the nickname "Speedy."

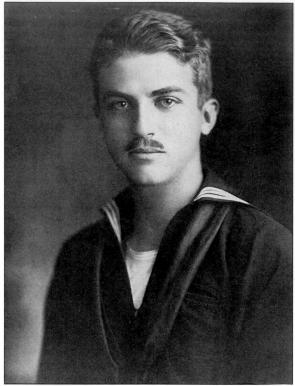

Seward ties his first knot, with Ruth Crockett, London, 1924.

Seward, Ruth, and their brood in the early 1930s. Seward is holding Diana; beneath him (*left to right*) are Seward, Jr., Elaine, and Mary Lea. *NYT PICTURES*

With Mary Lea (*right*) and Elaine, as they boarded a ship bound for Sweden, 1932 *NYT PICTURES*

Seward as a middle-aged roué

Seward as a Johnson & Johnson executive, 1969. It was in this incarnation that he first laid eyes on Basia. *NYT Pictures*

Evangeline Johnson (*above*), age twenty-four, in 1921; (*left*) with her first husband, Leopold Stokowski, circa 1929; (*below*) with her third husband, Charles Merrill ("Big Paw"), 1988

Basia's Polish tourism
group card, 1956.
At age nineteen, her
life abounded with
friends and "fiancés."

Basia (*left*), newly arrived in America, comes to the Johnsons' Oldwick, New Jersey, farm for
her fateful job interview, 1968.

Some thought it a subterfuge,
but Basia's position as curator of
Seward's fledgling art collection
came complete with business
cards. The address was the East
Side love nest they shared prior
to their marriage.

Barbara Z. Piasecka, A.M.
Curator

Fine Arts Mutual, Inc.
Apartment 4-L
45 Sutton Place South
New York, N.Y. 10022

(212) 755-4037

Seward and Basia frolicking at Children's Bay Cay, the Bahamas, mid-1970s. Legend had it that Basia, similarly clad on Cape Cod a few years earlier, had very nearly made Seward run his boat aground.

The Johnsons in Fort Pierce, 1979 COURTESY HALINA RODZINSKI

As a Shearman & Sterling tenderfoot, Nina Zagat found herself in a man's world. Though at her side during a 1968 firm dinner in Paris, her forgetful boss, Tom Ford (*fourth from right*), left her hanging eighteen years later in New York.

Basia and Nina in the Bahamas, mid-1970s. Nina was Basia's best friend, although that friendship came with a quarterly statement for tens of thousands of dollars attached.

In 1975 Basia and Seward sponsored the Chopin piano competition in Warsaw and presented first prize to Krystian Zimerman.
LASKI/SIPA PRESS

Jasna Polana. What Seward envisioned as a "simple country house" eventually rivaled Hearst's San Simeon as America's most expensive residence. MICHAEL MELFORD/THE IMAGE BANK

Jasna Polana's air-conditioned doghouse. Here, one of its pampered occupants strolls alfresco. TOM HERDE/THE TIMES OF TRENTON, NEW JERSEY

Menu for Jasna Polana's opening party, May 1978

Jasna Polana

M13

Chassagne – Montrachet 1976
"La Romanée"
Fernand Chauvet

Château Haut – Brion 1964

Chambertin 1966
Grivas Père et Fils

Krug 1964

Oeuf de poule au caviar

Soupe de truffes V.G.E.

Homard en terrine
Sauce cressonnette

Sorbet pamplemousse au Noilly

Suprême de volaille en vessie
"Baria"

Foie gras frais du Périgord
Salade gourmande

Fromages de France
Pain Poilâne

Farandole de desserts

aux fourneaux: Paul Bocuse

Marty and Mary Lea Richards. Each craved the only thing the other had to give.

The Richardses and Basia, shown here in 1980, quickly became fast friends, in part because, as flamboyant, dynamic ethnics who married in the same wary, WASPy family, Marty and Basia had so much in common. *RICHARD CORKERY/NEW YORK DAILY NEWS*

Mary Lea (*back row, fourth from left*), Marty (*back row, second from right*), and some of Mary Lea's children and grandchildren shortly after the settlement in *Johnson* v. *Johnson*. Within a few years everyone (minus the smallest fry) would be embroiled in another will contest, complete with everything but a corpse.

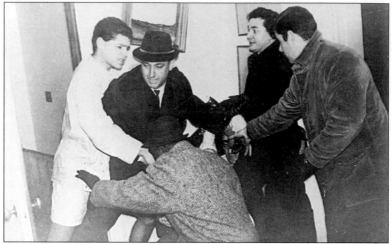

As Junior Johnson waited outside, the detectives he hired raided his own home, February 1963. One man lost an eye, another his detective's license, but Junior emerged unscathed.

Junior contemplating his bust of Seward, 1976. The creation, one of Junior's hyperrealistic works, was part art, part kitsch, part a son's attempt to win a father's respect.
RICHARD HAITCH/ NYT PICTURES

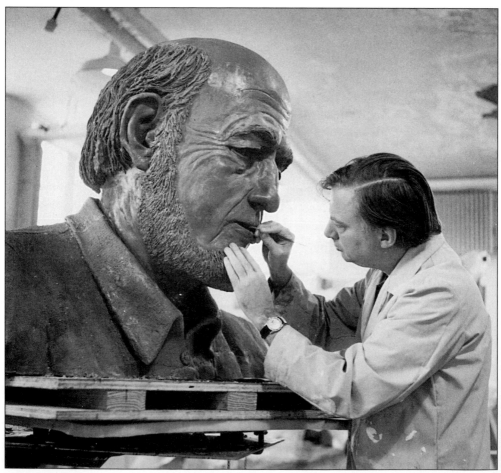

After Marty Richards extols his virtues *(top)*, Seward becomes a Knight of Malta *(center)*, then receives a congratulatory kiss from his son-in-law *(bottom)*. Once Seward died and the will contest raged, Marty denigrated the organization, the occasion, and the father-in-law he had so lustily praised.

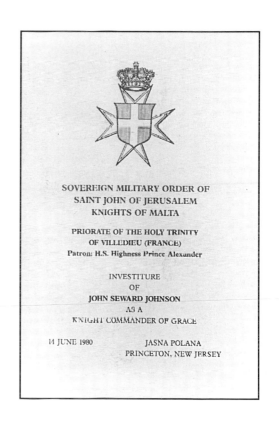

SOVEREIGN MILITARY ORDER OF
SAINT JOHN OF JERUSALEM
KNIGHTS OF MALTA

PRIORATE OF THE HOLY TRINITY
OF VILLEDIEU (FRANCE)
Patron: H.S. Highness Prince Alexander

INVESTITURE
OF
JOHN SEWARD JOHNSON
AS A
KNIGHT COMMANDER OF GRACE

14 JUNE 1980   JASNA POLANA
PRINCETON, NEW JERSEY

Even at an advanced age, Seward remained interested in the sea. He continued his undersea exploration *(left)*, tinkered with Ed Link *(bottom, at left)* at Harbor Branch, and, as a sailor *(center)*, came to resemble the *Old Man and the Sea.*

ELECT
Marie
LAMBERT
An Independent Democrat
for
SURROGATE

IF SOMETHING HAPPENS TO YOU TODAY——WHAT WILL YOUR FAMILY DO TOMORROW??

The SURROGATE COURT is really a FAMILY COURT, responsible for insuring that families receive their rightful inheritance when a loved one passes away. This should be done quickly and compassionately.

HISTORY OF THE SURROGATE COURT

The SURROGATE COURT HAS BEEN THE POLITICAL BOSSES' PRIVATE CLUB. ITS FIRST PRIORITY WAS FILLING THE POCKETS OF MACHINE POLITICIANS. Only after the politically connected "Club House" lawyers raked off their share did families get their rightful inheritance.

WHY DOES LAMBERT SCARE THE BOSSES??

 • LAMBERT IS INDEPENDENT—She has never been part of the "Club House" and has spent the better part of her career fighting them.

 • LAMBERT IS A WIDOW AND A MOTHER—She knows and understands what it is like to face the uncertain future alone.

 • LAMBERT HAS A RECORD OF INTEGRITY—She has been fighting for the oppressed and disadvantaged since the beginning of her legal career when she secured asylum for over 200 Jewish concentration camp victims. Her efforts were recognized when she was awarded the coveted "CITIZEN OF THE YEAR AWARD" by the WESTSIDE ZIONIST COALITION FOR ISRAEL. As Surrogate she will not deposit inheritance monies in any bank that participates in the Arab boycott against Israel.

 • LAMBERT IS A WOMAN WITH DETERMINATION—Her father was a barber who lost his job during the depression. LAMBERT sold dresses to put herself through Brooklyn College and NYU's Law School. For over 30 years she has been a practicing attorney and is highly regarded as one of the best in the State of New York. Her excellence was recognized when she was elected President of the male dominated New York State Trial Lawyers Association.

The SURROGATE COURT NEEDS A COMPETENT WOMAN
On Thursday Sept. 8, Elect Marie Lambert Surrogate

Lambert campaigned tirelessly for her job, papering all Manhattan with her incendiary flyers.

Marie Lambert, lioness of the New York personal injury bar, fraternizes with some of the lions. *From left to right:* Charles Kramer, Jacob Fuchsberg, Lambert, Alfred Julien, unidentified, Aaron Broder, Gerald Edelman. COURTESY OF MARIE LAMBERT

While becoming surrogate, she found a new crony: Roy Cohn. BILL MARK

The street-smart, tyrannical, uncontrollable surrogate of Manhattan

Harvey Corn. For eight years—until she went too far even for him—he wrote Marie Lambert's opinions, gave her wise counsel, protected her from herself.

Alex Forger *(left)* stands grimly by the side of his most famous client, Jacqueline Kennedy Onassis, 1983.

Edward J. Reilly of Milbank, Tweed, Hadley & McCloy. The Johnson children profited handsomely from the near-religious zeal he brought to their case, only to abandon him at the end.

The will contest prompted the six Johnson children to make an almost unprecedented joint appearance, united less by physical resemblance or philosophy than by their desire for more of their father's riches. *From left to right:* Junior Johnson, Elaine Wold, Jennifer Duke, Mary Lea Richards, Jimmy Johnson, and Diana Firestone. *HEMSEY/GAMMA LIAISON, INC.*

Bubbling over with optimism, a fur-clad Basia arrives for the beginning of the trial, while a fur-clad Nina greets her lawyer, Donald Christ of Sullivan & Cromwell, and his fur-clad wife, Iris.
MEL FINKELSTEIN/
NEW YORK DAILY NEWS

Basia in another uncharacteristically amicable moment with Donald and Iris Christ. Basia later dismissed him as "a sack of potatoes" and her as "the Peacock." *HEMSEY/GAMMA LIAISON, INC.*

Robert Osgood (*right*) escorts Seward's cantankerous doctor, Fred Schilling, into Surrogate's Court. In their own ways, each eventually stalked out of the case. *HEMSEY/GAMMA LIAISON, INC.*

The Inquiring Photographer

By John Stapleton

Today's Question: What do you think of a multimillionaire who left his wife and former chambermaid $500 million and left nothing to his six grown children?

Jocelyn Lim
Banking
"He should have left something to everyone, maybe half to his wife and splitting the rest among his children, or giving it to charity."

Joseph Plecka
Salesman
"It must be awesome to have so much money. I feel for the children, but his will is a legal document and this is the way he wanted to disburse the money."

Darlene Rigney
Banking
"He must have known his children would contest the will; his wife's attorneys say they had frittered away millions when he was alive. But $500 million to the wife doesn't seem right."

David Bowers
Utilities foreman
"It was his money, to do with as he chose. I'm surprised that he didn't leave any to an undersea project he had funded. This was his 20th will, so he seemed to have trouble making up his mind."

Cheyenne Johnson
Securities clerk
"His children have a right to contest the will. It's possible his wife used undue influence to get him to leave everything to her. It's up to a judge to decide."

The *Daily News* Inquiring Photographer polled passers-by about the case. The result? A hung jury.

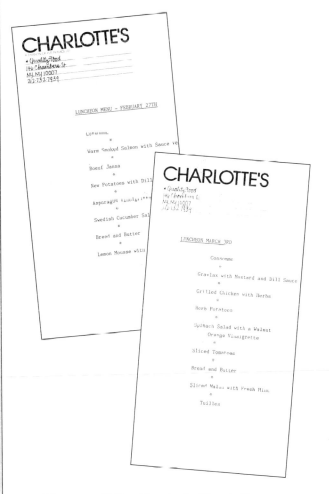

Two typical bills of fare in the Titanic Room. Neither a hostile judge nor an implacable adversary nor their own floundering could stay the proponents and their lawyers from their elegant catered lunches.

THE AMERICAN LAWYER

MAY 1986

MARKETING AND MEDIA 1986
PULL-OUT MANAGEMENT REPORT

THE EIGHT MILLION DOLLAR ASSOCIATE

Shearman & Sterling associate Nina Zagat
fights for her cut of the Johnson estate.

by Ellen Joan Pollock

Nina Zagat was tried not only in court but in the press, most notably in *The American Lawyer*.

Ed Reilly (*left*) and Charles Berry (*right*) escort a triumphant Izabella Poterewicz out of court. Armed with a mini-cassette, one former maid proved another's undoing.
ROBERT EBERLE/THE STAR-LEDGER

A manacled John Stroczynski (*center*) is hauled off to jail after fifteen Jasna Polana employees disrupt the trial. Later, in open court, he apologized abjectly to Basia for the episode, though it turned out he had been only following her orders. *PIM VAN HEMMEN/THE STAR-LEDGER*

As the trial wore on, the faces in the proponents' legal team grew longer and longer. *Left to right:* Basil Zirinis, Donald Christ, Arnold Bauman, Ted Rogers.

Robert Delahunty of Sullivan & Cromwell. He once said he was willing to die for Basia.

Sister Mary Louise Flowers (*left*), with colleague, comes to court for Basia. "Mr. Schwartz," Reilly told his opposing counsel caustically, "the only thing she can do for your case is pray for it."

Junior Johnson

Joyce Johnson

Alex Forger

Marty Richards

Keith Wold

Diana Firestone

Jennifer Johnson

Jimmy Johnson

Surrounded by relatives and lawyers, Junior Johnson tells the press that his family had performed a "service" in the case, though precisely what that was or who was served—besides, that is, themselves— he does not say. SARA KRULWICH/NYT PICTURES

Basia *(left)*, Marvin Schwartz, and Nina Zagat present a united front following the settlement, shortly before heading their very separate ways. AP/WIDE WORLD PHOTOS

"Basia," the cow Donald Christ bought following the trial, then had ground into "Basia burgers." The patties, he reported, were tough and stringy.

NEW YORK POST

Tuesday June 3 1986

35 CENTS

METRO | SPORTS FINAL

TODAY: Sunny, 65-70.
TONIGHT: Clear, mid
50s. TOMORROW:
Sunny, mid 70s.
Details: Page 2.

TV listings: P. 87

THE $340M WOMAN

Johnson widow settles in bitter battle over drug mogul's estate

SEE PAGE 5

Barbara Piasecka Johnson, 49, widow of drug company tycoon J. Seward Johnson Sr., gives victory sign as she leaves Manhattan court yesterday after settlement in battle over the $500 million estate her husband left her. She gets to keep $340 million.

New York Post: Neil Schneider

TOT FALLS 17 FLOORS — AND LIVES!
PAGE THREE

Despite the battering she had just taken, with a strategic "V for victory" Basia emerged the winner. *NEIL SCHNEIDER/NEW YORK POST*

The jubilant chatelaine during a belated press tour of Jasna Polana *Keith Meyers/NYT Pictures*

In her new, regal state

Basia and Lech Wałesa in the Lenin Shipyard, Gdańsk, Poland,
September 1989, and on the cover of *The New York Times
Magazine*, October 1989. "What's a delicate woman like you
doing in a shipyard with cranes and rusting metal?" he asked her.
"You belong in a garden of flowers, or in a coffee shop, with me."
The honeymoon, however, was brief.
ANTONIN KRATOCHVIL/DOT PICTURES. COPYRIGHT © 1989 BY THE NEW YORK TIMES

Poland's two most powerful expatriates meet, 1989. LASKI/SIPA PRESS

"Have you ever observed Mrs. Johnson being critical of others?"

"Objection. Irrelevant," Osgood interjected. It was more wishful thinking than legal logic, and this time he was overruled. Osgood told Nina to disregard the question, a luxury he would not have in the courtroom.

"Would you characterize Mrs. Johnson as being impatient?" Reilly asked. Osgood's objection was sustained. "Would you say that Mrs. Johnson is intolerant of the shortcomings of others?" Nina said she wouldn't characterize Basia that way. "Are you aware of any occasion when Mrs. Johnson appeared to have lost her temper?" Once again Osgood told her not to answer. "Are you aware of any occasion when Mrs. Johnson appeared to have lost her temper with persons other than Mr. Johnson?"

"That has to be, on its face, one of the most irrelevant questions asked in the last twenty-two days," Osgood charged. "Objection." Here, too, he was sustained, at least for now.

Reilly returned to how Seward felt about his children. Here, he knew, Nina was bound by the treacly language she'd inserted into the last two wills. It had to be with a certain sadism that Reilly asked her to elaborate on her understanding of just what Seward had meant when he alluded to the pride he took in his children. Nina ran down the list, trying to find something good to say about all six of them. It was not easy, but eventually she made it, then asked to take a break, presumably for something stronger than a Coke.

The deposition dragged on. To lighten things up, S&C's resident bard, Bob Osgood, began writing poems on the paper bags he brought to each session, containing Nina's minimum daily requirement of sucrose and fructose. The verse for June 21, 1985, went like this:

For our great witness
        to keep going
When the pace
        today is slowing
And the unvarnished
        truth to tell
Here is a little help
        from Sullivan & Cromwell.

Two months later, Nina—and Osgood—were still at it.

Congratulations to our star
For coming this far

It is day 24
There should be no more!

Like the previous effort, it was signed "Your devoted lawyers." This time, though, there was a small postscript.

You say it's day 25
And you still
            got out alive.

Brushing aside S&C's complaint that Nina's examination had lasted longer than those of all of the children combined and that Milbank was simply running up its fees, Lambert allowed the objectants to ask just about anything they wanted. Reilly—and, later on, Paul Shoemaker—asked Nina thousands of questions, including whether she'd ever tapped anyone's telephone or had anyone tailed; whether she had charged the Johnsons for attending the Jasna Polana opening and Knights of Malta parties; and how much time she spent working on the *Zagat Restaurant Survey*. ("Who paid for your expenses in attending this place called 'Maine Chance'?" Reilly asked with obvious revulsion. "I did," Nina replied. "There goes their case!" Osgood joked.) Though he was being paid by the hour, even the referee became frustrated when Shoemaker asked Nina whether, at the time of Jasna Polana's opening, anyone had accompanied Seward and Paul Bocuse to the wine cellar. "What is the need for all this?" the referee asked. "Did you ever see the movie *Notorious*? They went down to the basement to look at the wine cellar, and they found something else in the bottles. You are not looking for that, are you?" He was no more sympathetic when Shoemaker asked Nina to list the mourners at Princey's funeral.

"Is this relevant, Mr. Shoemaker?" Christ interjected.

"Yes, I think it is," Shoemaker replied.

"To the will contest?"

"How could it possibly be?" the referee chimed in. "The death of a dog and its funeral?"

"That particular fact may not be, but I think the events that happened on that occasion may be relevant," Shoemaker said.

"You mean you want to know if the dog's relatives came?" the referee asked acidly.

"No," replied Shoemaker. "I am only asking about human beings."

Nina told Milbank she discussed Seward's wills with Basia only in Seward's presence; that she never mentioned any rumblings of a will contest to her; that Basia had never told her of her days as a maid; and that in all their years together, the only gifts Basia had ever given her were a few trinkets and a kitten. All this cast doubt on whether Reilly could prove the two women were partners in crime. Still, the deposition gave Reilly a chance to dissect a crucial character, and what he saw was more encouraging than what he heard.

It is conventional wisdom that most lawyers make lousy witnesses. They tend to be argumentative, calculating, cautious, condescending, cute. But Nina was particularly problematical. Her innately hypertechnical approach to law, compounded by her discomfort under questioning and her compulsive desire to omit nothing, left her utterly unable to answer questions crisply, forthrightly. She could be unduly literal—Q: "Are you licensed in any other profession?" A: "Yes, driving."—or lawyerly: Q: "Was that a gift from Mrs. Johnson?" A: "No, it was 'a gratuitous transfer of funds.' " She avoided unpleasant subjects altogether: In hundreds of hours of testimony about Seward's final years, his cancer came up but once. No matter how trivial the issue, she would bob and weave and dart and duck, then furnish either more or less information than was called for. Reilly fired on her king, and Nina moved an extraneous pawn. Alarmed at her style, Arnold Bauman, the former federal judge watching over the case for Shearman & Sterling, pleaded with her to be more straightforward. Though she was telling the truth, it sounded as if she were not.

Nina's credibility was all the more crucial because Tom Ford, the only man who could back up what she said, was proving to be singularly useless. Ford, whose own deposition began in September 1985, was a man most everyone liked, and why not? So hale a fellow was he that even after Forger had all but called him a crook, he'd have greeted good old Alex heartily at their next encounter had Nina not reined him in. An Irishman with a ruddy complexion, robust laugh, and shock of white hair, he'd come to Shearman & Sterling in 1947, without, as he usually put it, "a pot to piss in." He'd eventually attained the second-highest post in the firm, along with places in Palm Beach and the Social Register. Just as one never had to ask whether his partner Henry Ziegler was around (one could always hear the high-pitched sound he made when clearing the frog lodged in his throat), with Ford you need only take a whiff. A cigar, perhaps one of the Havanas Nina bought him whenever she got beyond the American embargo, was forever stuck in his mouth. They were more than smokes; they were props. He'd punctuate his stories with puffs, chew on them for emphasis.

Ford had always been your big-picture kind of guy—someone who prized practicality, cut corners, hated long explanations, rarely beat around the bush. "Fuck it, let's do it!" he might say when someone brought him a new idea. And of all the wills he had handled, only one had ever been challenged. But the estate of Arnold Schwartz was not the estate of J. Seward Johnson, Sr. Nina would need someone of authority to back her up, and Ford couldn't help her. One cannot remember what one never knew, or had been too lackadaisical to learn correctly, or had conveniently chosen to forget.

Though no one at Shearman & Sterling expected Ford's understanding of the Johnson file to be encyclopedic, one could hardly have anticipated how rasa his tabula would be. Ford outdid even Keith Wold in I-don't-recalls: 189 of them in his first day of testimony alone. He did not recall why he had assigned Nina to the Johnson account; whether he had told Nina she had been passed over for partnership or the reasons he'd given her; what precautions he had advised her to take against a possible will contest; whether he had reviewed any drafts of the April 14 will or even been told why Seward wanted to make the last change. As for Seward's state of health, the only ailment Ford had heard about was a case of tennis elbow. He was not even sure he could recognize Seward's signature. "I don't really think I saw enough of his handwriting to recognize it one way or the other," he said.

Ford could not recall talking with Seward about his estate at any time after 1976. Nor could he recall ever going to Fort Pierce for any social occasions. ("I assume the funeral is not a 'social' occasion,' " he said.) On the matter of Nina's fees, there was no more talk, as there had been with the Shearman & Sterling brass, of how Nina had "blown one" past him. To Milbank, Ford said he had left it all to her. "I told her to work it out with Mr. Johnson—whatever he wanted to do is all right," he testified. He had never discussed the size of Nina's fees with Seward. "Did you remark to [Nina] at any time prior to Mr. Johnson's death that the amount of commissions she stood to receive was quite substantial?" Shoemaker asked. "Not that I can recall," he said. This from someone who had in fact teased Nina about them whenever Basia or Seward was being difficult. "That's why you're getting those big commissions!" he would joke.

Even the Milbank lawyers, who had Ford pegged as an affable light-weight—"a cheerful, avuncular fellow," Shoemaker called him in a memo—were shocked by his ignorance. There was no there there. Someone on the proponents' legal team theorized that Ford was depressed. An exasperated Christ had another hyothesis: Ford must have been lobotomized. In any case, he was clearly unfit to testify. This would not hurt Ford, who would soon retire to Palm Beach. But it meant that Nina, notwithstanding all her imperfections as a witness, would be on her own.

Already, two of the proponents' key witnesses, Peach and Ford, were disabled. Now, Milbank went to work on two more: Jan Waligura, the Polish-born doctor with whom both Seward and Basia had been so friendly, and Gregory Piasecki, Basia's brother. Under the best of circumstances, Waligura would not have been a perfect witness; from 1977 to 1982 more than half of his hospital salary had come from the Johnsons' charitable trusts. Still, in the Johnsons' transient circle he passed as a lifelong friend; the old man had shared many intimate thoughts with him, on his marriage, his family, his illness, his legacy. It was to Waligura that Seward had said, six weeks after his orchiectomy, that he planned to leave Basia everything. Moreover, Waligura specialized in the psychology of terminal-cancer patients; unlike the experts Milbank would produce, he could base his opinions on more than records. He had visited Fort Pierce eight times during Seward's last season, and could attest to Seward's continued clarity until very nearly the end. He also knew some of the children, and had been particularly close to the Richardses. Mary Lea told him lurid stories about her love life; when she and Marty went off on the *QE2*, it was with Waligura that they left their itinerary. But loyalties mattered little in this universe; now, Waligura was fair game. Reilly pounced on Waligura's legal problems at Sloan-Kettering, stemming from his supervision of student research, for which Seward had offered him Nina's services. He interrogated Waligura about them, demanded all related documents, moved to question hospital officials. Sullivan & Cromwell charged that the inquiry revealed the "gutter tactics" to which the children would descend; if their "squalid life histories" were inadmissible, surely Waligura's work problems should be as well. Lambert agreed, which was not to say that Reilly would not attempt to raise them again should Waligura ever take the stand.

The Milbank lawyers questioned Basia's brother, Gregory Piasecki, with equal minuteness, on everything from Seward's courtship to the cows he sent to Poland. As they did, Christ grew rambunctious. When Shoemaker asked whether the old man had read newspapers every day of his illness, Christ reminded him that on May 23 he'd died before the morning papers had arrived. When Shoemaker asked whether Seward ever talked about Junior's work at Harbor Branch, Christ interjected, "Has it been established that Mr. Johnson, Jr., *did* any work at Harbor Branch?" When Shoemaker asked Gregory if he'd ever heard

Basia ask Seward for something, Christ queried whether that included "Will you please pass the butter?" One particular question—whether Gregory had ever seen Basia operating any farm equipment in Poland— prompted a particularly heated reaction. "This question seems designed to be fed to the press, in which the children's interviews appear so frequently," S&C later charged. "It would doubtless amuse them to be able to portray their stepmother behind the wheel of a tractor."

Even Lambert had to agree with that. "I am asking you: How is it relevant if she drove a tractor?" she asked Shoemaker.

"I interpreted that to be a tractor," Christ interjected. "Perhaps it could include a combine or a washing machine or a reaper."

Gregory Piasecki's testimony was neither as intelligent, threatening, vivid, nor convincing as Waligura's. The amorous exchanges he recalled sounded flat; he testified to hearing Seward say "I love you very much" to Basia, and Basia replying "I love you, too, very much." He described the two as an "ideal" couple, who would "jump into the fire for one another." One typically unilluminating exchange concerned their courtship.

> SHOEMAKER: "Did your sister ever tell you that Mr. Johnson asked her to marry him?"
> PIASECKI: "Yes, she told me."
> SHOEMAKER: "Did she tell you what she said on that occasion?"
> PIASECKI: "She said 'yes.' "

The Milbank lawyers were barred from asking Gregory whether Seward had spoken at Princey's funeral. But even without such information, they realized there was little either to learn or fear from Basia's brother. True, even in his last few months, the Seward he described swam like Johnny Weismuller and sailed like Ernest Hemingway. But this came from someone who also said he had never heard Basia and Seward argue and had hardly ever heard Basia raise her voice. Despite his lofty title—"deputy of the general director of Jasna Polana," for which he received the munificent sum of $17,000 annually (plus room and board)—Gregory Piasecki was clearly terrified of his sister. Whether Basia had stripped Seward of his free will was debatable; with Gregory it was not. "He is not just her brother," Shoemaker said during one conference. "He is in effect her servant." Indeed, though nothing Gregory said should have displeased Basia, she castigated him horrendously when his examination was over.

Repeatedly, Milbank asked Lambert for more time with each witness.

Just as repeatedly S&C countered that "six insatiable multimillionaires" and their lawyers were dragging out what was quickly becoming "the twentieth-century equivalent of *Bleak House*" Dickens's novel about an interminable lawsuit and its consequences. But for all its alleged eagerness to get under way, S&C itself was in no shape to start. Morale slipped lower with Basia's every tantrum. The highest on her Richter scale occurred one afternoon at Shearman & Sterling; at the epicenter was Christ. Her seismic shrieking penetrated even the linen-lined walls; from all over the firm people scurried to learn what was happening. Nina's paralegal, Carolina Sanchez, immediately placed calls to both Werner Polak and Arnold Bauman. "Mrs. Johnson is screaming like I've never heard her scream before!" she told Bauman excitedly when he called in from Grand Central Terminal, ten blocks downrange from Basia's tirade, where it apparently could not be heard. Once, when a Milbanker asked Waligura whether Basia ever lost her temper, Christ objected. What did "losing one's temper" mean, after all? he asked. "It's different strokes for different folks." This time, there was nothing ambiguous about it.

Basia's iciness toward Osgood continued. Nor did she like Sheryl Michaelson, a young S&C associate who was arguably the most industrious of the lawyers on the case. For some reason Basia grew convinced Michaelson was actually a Milbank mole, funneling information to Reilly, and pressed to have her taken off the case. Meantime, Michaelson and other underlings on the case felt adrift. While mastering the facts in the case, Christ vacillated over decisions, sat on briefs, assigned tasks randomly, failed to define themes or articulate strategy. September came; scarcely two months now remained before the scheduled start of the trial, and who would actually lead S&C in court still hadn't been determined. Osgood pressed Christ to be placed in charge, as Christ, he felt, had promised to do. Even here, it took Christ two weeks to reply, and his response was brief. "The client wants me to handle the case," he replied.

Just about the only solace the proponents received was over something for which they could claim no credit. In late September a New Jersey judge, concluding that neither Diana nor Junior was believable, dismissed Diana Firestone's lawsuit against her trustees. ("The court has no confidence in the accuracy of Seward, Jr.'s testimony" on his conversations with his father, the judge said at one point.) With characteristic speed—two weeks later—Sullivan & Cromwell forwarded a copy of the ruling to Lambert. "The opinion demonstrates that Mr. Johnson, Jr. and Mrs. Firestone have put little value on truth and consistency in their sworn testimony, whether here or in New Jersey," S&C declared.

Up to now, Junior's inquisitor in the will contest had been Christ, and the witness could just as easily have been on a couch or in a confessional. Christ, the onetime wrestler and former marine, proved once again he was almost pathologically nonconfrontational. Now that Robert Dela-hunty was doing the questioning, however, this promised to change; for of all the villains Delahunty saw in this morality play, Junior was the most nefarious. Delahunty asked him questions designed simply to sting—like whether or not Junior felt his own first marriage had been tainted by fraud or undue influence—or to censure, like about the frequency with which Junior had emptied his father's bedpan ("Only once or twice," Junior admitted). Had he ever called Seward "stupid?" "Weak?" "A stupid jerk?" Had Junior ever committed a crime? (When Junior said no, Delahunty reminded him that under New Jersey Statute A:170–25.6, in effect in January 1958, attempted suicide was a criminal act.)

Delahunty pressed Junior to explain his view of Seward's conveni-ently intermittent competency. Had Seward been functioning on March 31, when Junior forced his resignation from Harbor Branch, or was Junior, too, exploiting a defenseless man? "I wouldn't want to make a judgment on that," Junior replied. Would he have approached his father had he thought he was incompetent? "I think if that had occurred to me, that I wouldn't have, but I was preoccupied with what I felt was happening. The thought of his competency, quite frankly, didn't occur to me." Had Seward been competent in April 1982, when he'd sup-posedly encouraged Junior to become one of Diana's trustees? "Well, I don't know what day we are talking about. I don't know . . . and it was over the telephone. I don't think there is . . . as a layman, I would feel that I could answer that question responsibly. I assume it is supposed to be a responsible answer from a layman, and being a party, I don't want to be estopped if the facts that come up that I don't know that would have shown that he was competent to write a will sometime in April. . . . " he rambled.

Delahunty demanded a more direct reply. "Your Honor, I suggest that a witness who understands a term like 'estoppel' is certainly able to understand a word like 'competent,' " he said. Eventually, he got Junior to say that Seward had been of sound mind at least as late as December 1982, when the will then in effect would also have left the children nothing. As of the following March, Junior said, his father had been "up and down and in and out of what I would normally think of having testamentary capacity."

The ardent associate also attempted to flesh out the children's true objectives, and just how committed they really were to Harbor Branch. When Reilly objected that such talk was "speculative," Delahunty, unlike Christ, pressed his point. "Your Honor, it has been extremely hard for us in the course of two years to find out what this case is about and what Mr. Johnson, Jr., and his siblings want," he complained. "And every time we have tried to have them lay their cards on the table and to tell us what they think their father really intended, we have been blocked." Later he asked Junior whether Seward had often expressed his testamentary wishes to his family, friends, and associates, as the Forger Affidavit claimed. "I don't know," Junior replied.

Basia had given the objectants plenty of bullets, like buying Raphaels and paying a potential witness's hospital bills. Now, it turned out, Junior had given the proponents at least a few pellets. One of the few people who'd seen Basia and Seward from the beginning was Junior's aunt Evie, the General's widow. Junior had had little to do with the old lady over the years, partly because he'd feuded so with her husband. But upon learning that S&C would soon be questioning her, he sent her a passionate appeal for family solidarity. True, he said, Basia had helped his father "loosen up." But over time she'd turned him into "moral mashed potatoes," and Evie mustn't side with her. "Evie," he continued, "you are a most important member of the Johnson family and I guess there comes a time when we are all going to have to make a decision on which side of the knife we are going to fall. Otherwise, we find ourselves cleft in two."

The elderly Evie had always liked Basia, as she had shown in the effusive condolence note she sent following the death of Basia's mother, in January 1983. Basia, she wrote, had always been "the kindest and most loving of daughters," and, she added, "will surely be given a ringside seat in Heaven for the beautiful arrangements you made for your mother." Now, in answering S&C's written questions, Evie made clear that Junior's blood-is-thicker-than-water appeal had failed dismally. Asked to describe Seward's third marriage, she replied, "Well, it seemed to me to be a very happy one." That her brother-in-law left Basia everything hadn't surprised her; "I knew he had settled sizable sums on each of his children before he married Basia." But S&C was not about to let the matter drop. Calling Junior's epistle "a demented threat to an important witness" and "a transparent attempt to bully her into silence," it pressed Junior to explain himself. "I spoke my mind," Junior told Delahunty. "I don't know whether that would be . . . I don't think that she could be influenced on her testimony. I was attempting to have her maybe see a little bit rounder picture of the situation."

By late September the scheduled start of jury selection was scarcely five weeks away, and Reilly was once more running out of time. Several depositions remained incomplete, and Basia's hadn't even begun. Once again he implored Lambert to postpone the trial, this time until December. Osgood resisted the idea; there was "no reason on God's green earth," he argued, why it couldn't get under way on time. Lambert stuck to her schedule. But when November 1 arrived and several depositions remained open, she had no choice. Once more she postponed things, though not without a broadside. The frustration was hers; the rhetoric, characteristically, Corn's. "The parties have done everything short of throwing sand into the legal machinery to grind these proceedings, and each other, to a halt," she stated. "Employing the maxim 'do unto others before they do unto you,' they have raised every objection and utilized every strategem to frustrate each other into submission. While this Court has allowed the parties wide swath in conducting their discovery, that liberality has been viewed as an occasion for legal sniping worthy of a swat team."

But if the pace picked up, it was barely perceptible. Christmas, New Year's, even Groundhog Day would come and go before the Day of Reckoning arrived.

XXXI

For months now, the Milbank lawyers had been preparing themselves to question Basia. It would be a gargantuan undertaking: More than demystify Basia's past, they wanted to divine her character. Apart from their foreign origins, their tempers, and their egocentricity, Basia Johnson and Marie Lambert shared one trait: Some aspects of their life stories seemed embroidered. Learning the truth was more complicated in Basia's case, however, because her background was shrouded in the fog of wartime and postwar Communist Poland. Milbank grilled Gregory Piasecki about his sister's past—had she ever been engaged or married to anyone else? Had she ever had a prior marriage annulled? Had anyone else ever proposed to her? Had she borne any children?—but learned little. Reilly doubted there was anything useful to find. But Forger and Junior were curious and resolved to go to the source, or at least to send someone there.

A Harvard Law School chum of Shoemaker's at the Boston firm of Choate, Hall & Stewart, who was Polish-born and spoke the language, volunteered to review Basia's autobiography, as culled from her past statements on her origins. In July 1985 the lawyer offered what he pompously called his own "somewhat paleontological" finding: that there was definitely "something false" about Basia's version of events. From his report it was clear that he had quickly absorbed the objectants' skeptical, patronizing view of the enemy. Basia, he surmised, had twice failed to gain admission to the University of Wrocław; her thesis topic was "noncontroversial and uninspiring"; and, judging from the grade she got—the equivalent of a "B"—the thesis itself "must have been mediocre." Moreover, something was awry in Basia's account of her postgraduate years and employment history. He urged that she be subjected to "detailed questioning" on these subjects, and invited Milbank to launch a more ambitious probe, one that he would presumably lead. "Such investigation could uncover such facts as marriage or a relationship with a man who supported her or a history of employment which, for some reason, she is unwilling to disclose," he wrote.

347

Milbank was buying. With the firm's approval, Shoemaker's friend hired a Polish investigator, code-named "Jan," to retrace Basia's perambulations. Masquerading at times as a journalist, he interviewed people in Wrocław, Cracow, and Warsaw, then sent his findings to Boston. His research, which was forwarded to Milbank in December, documented several minor discrepancies. Basia's background wasn't as lofty as she now claimed. Her parents were of "humble origins" and spoke a "peasant dialect"; eyewitnesses recalled seeing Basia plowing fields (hence, Shoemaker's question to Gregory Piasecki about his sister riding tractors) and taking vegetables to market by cart. "It seems obvious to me that Mrs. Johnson is ashamed of her humble origins and is trying to embellish her past," the lawyer wrote. No one "Jan" spoke with could remember any of the articles on art Basia said she had written. Jan confirmed that Basia had never married, but found at least one "fiancé"—with whom, he said some believed, she remained intimate even during her marriage—and caught wind of her rumored affair with the pianist Malcuzynski. But learning anything about Basia in Poland was becoming harder, Jan complained, because "somebody has been actively working on covering her tracks." Indeed, even the intrepid Jan was becoming skittish. "He fears that someone may connect him with our case and thus expose him to Mrs. Johnson's vengeance," the Boston lawyer reported.

For a time the Boston lawyer played "Jan" domestically, calling up at least one former maid at Jasna Polana to ask her about Basia. But the woman panicked as soon as he announced his purpose, and it took him nearly half an hour to convince her not to hang up. When he called back a week later, he reported to Milbank, it sounded as if S&C had reached her in the meantime. The woman's husband "spoke as if he read from a brief," and together "they sounded as if they were coached by an attorney who was trying to prove the case against us." He urged that Milbank authorize a "concerted all-out effort" to pin down Basia's past and to import anyone in a position to discredit her to the United States or at least to Sweden, where they could give depositions. At this point Reilly pulled the plug. Even if something was to turn up, how could one get it into evidence? Subpoena some Polish peasant? The decision displeased Junior, who remained convinced that something sensational would turn up if only the snoops looked hard enough.

Domestically, Milbank interviewed Seward loyalists like Andy Potvin, his old chauffeur, and Fran Perree, from 1962 to 1972 his secretary at Johnson & Johnson. For a time, Perree recounted, she'd gotten along with Basia; she attended the wedding and, later, processed her citizenship papers. Before long, though, Basia was threatening to reduce Perree to "cooking for us in Italy," then demanding she be canned, just as Basia canned anyone who had ever seen her as a maid. Seward let her do so just to keep her quiet; indeed, it was Myers, not Seward, who'd told Perree she was let go. Over the last ten years of his life, she said, she'd seen Seward twice.

Milbank lawyers tracked down Zofia Koverdan, who'd worked with Basia at Oldwick. Motivated at least in part by guilt—having brought Basia to the Johnsons, she blamed herself for Essie's exit—she spoke freely to them. "She has information about Barbara's past that can be helpful (at least to unnerve her by creating the impression that we know all about her)," Berry later wrote. They spoke, too, to Dan Malick, Seward's longtime pilot, and, in Poland, Tadeusz Leski, Wallace Harrison's assistant at Jasna Polana. They also found Steve Brack, the Johnsons' first site manager during the construction of Jasna Polana. He declined their invitation to talk about the experience, except to call Basia a "bitch" and add, "It's too bad you can't talk to some of the people who died" during the project. They interviewed J&J executives Philip Hofmann, James Burke, and Richard Sellars; Hester Diamond, Basia's interior designer, and Lyuba Rhodes, Evangeline's daughter by Leopold Stokowski (she had little to contribute except an odd recollection of Uncle Seward and Aunt Essie playing tennis in the nude on Cape Cod). A former Jasna Polana worker told Reilly she'd seen Seward ward off one of Basia's tirades by pretending to read a newspaper he was actually holding upside down. She'd be a good witness; not so Kenneth Rooney of the Knights of Malta. Irked at Marty Richards for failing to honor his knightly obligations—indeed, convinced Richards had betrayed a fellow knight by fomenting the will contest—Rooney refused Reilly's pleas for help.

Basia's deposition, for which Lambert had budgeted two weeks, was scheduled to begin October 7. Never one to underestimate herself, Basia predicted she'd be "cool as ten thousand cucumbers" for it. In her scheme of things the deposition, like the case itself, was merely a distraction from more glamorous and grandiose projects.

Alas, there'd had to be some retrenchments. Around this time, *American Funeral Director* magazine reported that the will contest had delayed Basia Johnson's $5 million chapel project. But in other ways life went resolutely on. In May Basia unveiled her Raphael drawing at a gala in Princeton. Putting aside a speech written for her by Jack Raymond, the former *New York Times* reporter she'd recently hired as her publicist, she ad-libbed awkwardly, her voice cracking when the topic turned to Seward. "When Basia testifies like that, she'll win her case," an impressed Iris Love, the archeologist and socialite, said.

That done, Basia embarked upon her most grandiose project to date: converting Jasna Polana into a center for Central and Eastern European studies. The idea had come from Czeslaw Milosz, the Polish-American poet and Nobel laureate, who'd proposed that such a facility be built either in New Haven, Cambridge, or Ann Arbor, and had written to Basia for funds. Basia fell in love with the idea partly because it was pro-Polish, partly because it was anti-Soviet, partly because she fell in love with Milosz, yet another brilliant and charismatic older man. "Doesn't he look like Witold?" she asked. She pledged $15 million, a figure chosen deliberately to outstrip the endowment of Columbia's Harriman Center on Soviet Studies; later she talked of devoting half her fortune to it. As she envisioned it, the institute—"the J. Seward Johnson, Sr., Center for Central European Studies," it might be called, or "the Barbara Piasecka Johnson Center"—would be based on the estate, with branches in Paris and Florence. Even as the will contest proceeded, Basia journeyed to Italy to scout out villas in the Tuscan hills, with Nina tagging along to ensure that she make no more foolish puchases en route. To chart out the center's future, Basia invoked extraterrestrial assistance, holding aloft a magical plumb bob given to her by a Polish bishop, monitoring the telltale direction in which it swung.

That fall, as her lawyers recruited witnesses, Basia recruited faculty. One weekend she invited Alex Schenker of Yale, Wiktor Weintraub and Stanislaw Baranczak of Harvard, and Milosz to the estate. All spent several days there, with Milosz getting the Malcuzynski memorial room. The scholars left liking and respecting Basia more than they had anticipated. They'd expected a scheming, primitive character; what they found was a charming, enthusiastic woman, naive almost to the point of defenselessness. Nina cautioned that nothing could be done until the case was resolved, something that Basia still insisted would happen in a matter of weeks. "You wait and see: the children will be suing their own lawyers before this is over," she predicted. With the mansion now earmarked for scholarly uses, she began planning new, more modest quarters for herself elsewhere on the estate.

The plumb bob was but one of the supernatural aids Basia invoked for her emotional and physical well-being. She grew infatuated with another Polish faith healer named Stanislaw Nardelli, speaking of him so rapturously that when she hosted him on the estate people began speculating about their having an affair. Jasna Polana came to resemble

Lourdes, as thirty employees lined up to receive Nardelli's ministrations. Iris Christ's astrologer gave Basia a celestial checkup—recording her pars fortunae, vertex/anti-vertex angle axis, current transits, eclipse cycles, lunar highs and lows, one-year progressions, and Mercury retrograde positions—from which she ascertained that Basia had a lot of money in her future (she did charts for Donald Christ and Nina, too). Basia also heard reassuring things from Norman Mitchell, the psychic and clairvoyant she retained. She escorted him to Seward's old bedroom, where Mitchell claimed to see Seward, sitting on the bed. The old man—can spirits be old?—told Mitchell, and Mitchell told Basia, how he'd really wanted Basia to have his fortune, how unhappy he was to see her subjected to a will contest, how Junior was mentally unstable, and how his other children were spoiled brats.

Basia's English was respectable, but she'd stopped working at it well short of total fluency; what incentive was there when it already sufficed to get whatever she could conceivably want? Seward hadn't helped much, discouraging her from taking lessons because he found her foreignisms so charming. While she easily made herself understood, her accent remained heavy and her vocabulary, though occasionally colorful, still limited. In her everyday speech, in her expressions, in her expletives, her larder of idioms was sparsely stocked. What she wanted to say sometimes yielded to what she could say. Mrs. Malaprop visited regularly; when her memory failed her, Basia might say she was very "forgettable," one thing she most certainly was not.

In short, Basia's English was treacherous: not quite good enough to forgo an interpreter in a case of this magnitude, more than good enough for her to think she could. The unpolished, Polished English Seward had found so frisky in bed could prove risky on the stand. "Please state your full name to the court," the clerk in the Harbor Branch case told her. "Nine-two-one . . ." Basia replied, offering her telephone number. "Do you think your husband was ignorant of the true facts as to what happened in 1982?" Junior's lawyer, Richard Altman of Princeton, asked at one point. "I already told you that my husband was never 'ignorant'!" replied Basia. "Don't use this word!" Language problems were at least partly responsible for the bad taste Basia ultimately left with the Court. "It couldn't have been worse," one of Basia's lawyers said after Basia stepped down. "The judge hated her, and she looked dishonest."

Not surprisingly, Milbank wanted Basia deposed in English. As they saw it, a translator might be present to help Basia out, but only if the referee thought it necessary; Milbank feared that having everything translated, as S&C had proposed, would give Basia more time to consider her answers and her lawyers more time to object. Milbank proposed a strict schedule: five days a week, with an hour off for lunch and two ten-minute recesses. Christ called the regime "clearly punitive and harassing," designed "to cause Mrs. Johnson the maximum possible strain and exhaustion." He had one more factor to consider: what some delicately called Basia's "recurring condition." It was no clearer now just what caused Basia's rages; the menstrual, the astrological-lunar, and the screwy-chromosome schools all had their adherents. In any case, each month Basia pinpointed for her lawyers the ten-day stretch when she would be out of sorts. Basia's menstruation also figured into S&C's defense. Sheryl Michaelson was asked to investigate premenstrual syndrome, should it become necessary to argue that Basia's rages were really beyond her control. (Basia never knew such a defense was under consideration.) Meantime Milbank fashioned its own elaborate chronology of her tantrums, designed to show they fit no discernible pattern.

When Basia tapped Christ to handle her examination, she treated it as a kind of prize. But at Milbank, it was the other way around; Reilly passed on the assignment to Shoemaker. One might have thought Reilly would relish the task, not so much to size Basia up—this he'd already done, concluding she was selfish, self-centered, and cruel, someone who grew to hate her husband because he lived far longer than he was supposed to, someone without a single redeeming quality or anything that justified her existence as a human being—but to bloody her up. Instead, he carefully kept his distance. Some people could be schmoozers and killers simultaneously—Forger, for one. Smearing someone on paper was no reason to snub her in person; thus when Basia came to Milbank for her deposition, Forger greeted her cheerily. ("Hello, Arnold," he'd said to Bauman, who accompanied her. "This must be your client. How do you do?" Basia ignored his outstretched hand, just as she had once refused to shake Wernher von Braun's because of his Nazi ties.) But for Reilly, there was a time for pleasantries and a time for war. He could hate only by keeping his distance; proximity bred familiarity, and familiarity, sympathy. Thus, he sealed himself off from Basia. He studiously avoided all eye contact with her, or even the faintest acknowledgment of her presence. To coexist with Basia, even for a few weeks, might de-demonize her.

On October 7, Basia's deposition finally began. On hand in the

Milbank conference room, besides Shoemaker and Christ, were Bauman, Nina, and Tracy Hudson, the paralegal who so rattled Reilly. Shoemaker, a soft-spoken fellow and a plodding questioner, began by walking through Basia's curriculum vitae. She retold the story of her beginnings with the Johnsons, taking care to understate her problems in the kitchen. She began crying as she recalled her first visit to Seward's J&J offices. How had she felt when he made his extraordinary proposal? "I was pleasantly surprised," she answered. She told of her wedding, her first meeting with Nina, and of her early, and largely friendly, encounters with her stepchildren. She depicted a happy marriage, with Seward very much in control. True, she occasionally called him things, but they'd been pet names like "Sewardo" and "Romeo," not epithets like "stupid American." Yes, she had called him "ga-ga" on occasion, but only to throw back jokingly an expression she'd picked up from him. If she dressed him down, it was to dress him up, to keep her impractical husband from catching a cold. He yelled at her over equally mundane matters, like failing to squeeze toothpaste from the bottom of the tube. She said she'd never struck him, though on occasion she had spanked him.

Basia insisted her marriage had been built on love, not lucre. "I knew he was a wealthy man but I was not interested in how much money he owns," she said. She said she'd paid little attention to their prenuptial agreement; it was untrue, as various Johnson children had testified, that she threatened to leave Seward unless he tore it up (or unless he fired Perree and Myers). She said she had never known much about Seward's testamentary planning, including the size of Nina's stake. Of one thing, though, Basia was sure: Seward wanted her to have everything, so that, as she put it, "our dreams will be executed." "Remember, everything is for you," she recalled him saying. Basia's Seward was not only healthy until the bitter end—she said she'd not witnessed a single instance of irrationality—but literate (he read William F. Buckley's Atlantic High) and religious (he kept a Bible in his bedroom and called it the "wisest book of all").

By this time "Basia the peacemaker," as Junior once described her, was long gone. Even Seward, she now testified, considered his children and their mates to be birdbrains, boors, and leeches. Asked whether, in caring for Seward, she'd brought in nurses from a Polish convent who spoke no English, Basia said the first part was true, but not the second. "Each of them spoke an excellent English—sometimes they speak better English than Mr. Johnson's children," she said. She described how, as Seward lay sick and Basia's mother lay dying, Elaine

Wold proposed a champagne celebration at Jasna Polana and demanded a chauffeur for a New York shopping spree. She said Seward considered Keith Wold a parasite, and wrote him off altogether after he'd called Elaine a "bitch." "My husband was stupefied by the fact that the man who is running after women is using this kind of words in connection with Elaine," she said. She claimed the Firestones spoke to Seward about two topics only—their horses and their trust—and that Mary Lea actually seemed upset to find Seward so well after her hasty evacuation from the QE2; it meant they'd interrupted their trip unnecessarily.

But Basia saved most of her venom for Junior, and packaged it in the way it hurt him most: by attributing it all to Seward. Basia's Seward believed Junior could do nothing right at Harbor Branch, found Junior's loudness grating, and considered his sculptures trash. "Why did you come?" the senior Seward supposedly asked Junior one of the last times they met. "Do you want more money?" She recalled another occasion, in mid-May, when, as the three of them sat in Seward's bedroom, Seward declared his love for her, said their years together had been the happiest of his life, then turned to Junior and told him that he felt sorry for him. Why? Junior asked. "You know perfectly well why I feel sorry for you," he'd supposedly replied.

Shoemaker asked Basia the total cost of Jasna Polana (she didn't know); whether she'd ever been arrested (twice, at the ages of two and five, by German soldiers); whether she'd ever been previously married, spied on anyone connected to the case, told Keith Wold that Nina was "stupid," held up one of her dachshunds to lick Seward's face, or signed a contract for a book about herself (all "No"). She was asked whether she ever lied to Seward ("No"), whether he ever lied to her ("That I don't know"), whether he'd ever expressed any belief in the supernatural. He asked a whole series of questions related to Basia's comments to The Times (London), including her tale of a mesmerized Seward ogling her on a Cape Cod beach. Several times Christ grew exasperated. "If Mrs. Johnson, as a cook, burned the eggs one day, I don't see how that could possibly be relevant to the preparation or execution of Mr. Johnson's will in 1983," he complained once. Later, when Shoemaker asked Basia to review, name by name, everyone who'd ever worked at Jasna Polana, Christ finally boiled over. "Mr. Shoemaker, this is pointless, it is absolutely pointless!" he snapped. "This is not discovery; this isn't even a fishing expedition. This is a snipe hunt!" At another juncture he lamented, "Mr. Shoemaker, if it weren't for some slight bit of discipline being exerted on you, this would go on to the next century." But far from ending things, Milbank asked Lambert for an additional ten to fifteen days of questioning.

Christ objected. Describing Milbank's interrogation as "irrelevance and triviality run riot," "a legally-sanctioned means for working out personal grudges," and "a relentless quest for the minute and the immaterial, the collateral and the remote," S&C declared, "This is not an examination conducted in good faith. It is a game of Trivial Pursuit, designed to annoy, hector, and embarrass." "Why are the children so obsessed with Mr. Johnson's tea drinking in 1968?" it continued. "Since it has no bearing on the issues in controversy, it must be because the answers could provide colorful material for another of Mr. Johnson, Jr.'s press releases." Questions like whether Basia had ever flunked a course at the University of Wrocław were "surely objectionable," it argued, "in view of the court's ruling that the children's (dismal) academic records were not discoverable." It went on, "The real reason for these idle questions is evident: sheer rancor. The children's antagonism toward their stepmother flared into existence on the day their father's will was read, and has raged on since then. At every stage of this contest, through the legal process and in the press, they have sought to humiliate and to harass her. The court should stop the flow of the children's bile. Just as the children misapplied the fortunes which their father gave them, so they have chronically wasted and abused the liberal opportunities for discovery which have been provided to them by the court. And just as they demand more and more unearned wealth from their father's estate, so they incessantly demand more and more discovery. For the Johnson children, enough will never be enough."

Even Lambert called Milbank's request "ridiculous." "While it might be interesting to know that the witness took scuba-diving lessons at the decedent's insistence, this information is not designed to ascertain whether the propounded will should be admitted to probate," she wrote. She had not given the objectants "a license to hunt and peck at every minute detail" of Basia's life. But S&C did not get off unscathed. Lambert chastised Basia for failing to put in an honest day's work and her lawyers for their "carping" objections. The lawyers, she said, "should be ashamed to have this transcript cluttered by colloquy such as the following," citing what ensued after Shoemaker asked Basia whether she'd bought out virtually an entire antique store near Maine Chance.

> CHRIST: "Is this relevant, Mr. Shoemaker, to the case?"
> SHOEMAKER: "If it wasn't, I wouldn't be asking the question."

CHRIST: "Will you give me some small indication as to why this might be relevant?"

SHOEMAKER: "No."

CHRIST: "Do you have any? You don't have any. There is no reason whatsoever for you to ask this question today, is there?"

SHOEMAKER: "I told you before, I don't see the point in getting into these kinds of discussions. Of course I could answer you, but I won't."

CHRIST: "It is clear from the redness in your face that you cannot answer these questions."

SHOEMAKER: "It is clear from the way that you are shouting that you are losing control of yourself."

CHRIST: "Oh, Mr. Shoemaker, now, now, now. Is there any reason . . . "

SHOEMAKER: "Please sit down, Mr. Christ, and don't wave your arms."

CHRIST: "Mr. Shoemaker, is there any reason whatever for you to ask these questions?"

SHOEMAKER: "Mr. Christ, I told you I am not answering your questions. Apparently, Mrs. Johnson isn't going to answer that one, either, because you are not permitting her to, so I will ask another one."

BAUMAN: "I would like the record to indicate that Mr. Shoemaker has used the expression that Mr. Christ has 'shouted,' that he has 'waved his arms,' and the third factor, which eludes me at the moment, and I would like the record to indicate . . . "

CHRIST: "And that he was standing."

BAUMAN: " . . . and that he was standing. And I would like the record to indicate that none of those things, in fact, has happened."

SHOEMAKER: "I would like to proceed with the examination without your remarks or Mr. Christ's."

"It is time both sides in this matter stop playing games," Lambert-Corn concluded. "While a definitive trial date has not as yet been set, the parties are on notice that the day of Armageddon, in the judicial sense, is fast arriving. Those who fail to conclude their discovery expeditiously are in danger of failing to 'Beat the Clock.' " Basia's deposition nonetheless dragged on for ten more days stretched over the next several weeks, and didn't conclude until the following February.

Time was money. Mary Lea asked her trustees to cover what was by now the more than $400,000 in legal fees she had racked up, and for her children to approve such a payment. Her lawyers, she told them, were now predicting a good settlement; she was referring, presumably, to Forger, since Reilly was still counting on a full-blown trial. But "just like there is no free lunch, nothing comes cheap," she went on. "The legal struggle is lengthy and expensive—very." The trustees refused to fork over the money. But the Richardses had found something even more precious than pliable trustees, and right beneath their noses: a smoking gun.

It came from Anthony Maffatone, their trusty and handsomely paid ($55,000 in 1985 alone) bodyguard, who in a meeting with Reilly and Berry in late January 1986 made a few startling disclosures about Basia. To say Maffatone disliked Basia was a bit of an understatement. He described her to the priggish Milbank lawyers as "the biggest cunt I have ever seen"—someone who, he added, "deserves to be put in quick lime." One of his stories, which Berry called an "incident of great significance," concerned Basia's behavior with someone Maffatone described as a "dude from Italy" at the *Night of 100 Stars*. "[Maffatone] said that Basia was holding her escort's hand in both of hers and then put her hand on his lap and was rubbing against his thigh," Berry wrote. "He said that he was amazed that Basia was 'flaunting it' with this 'Don Juan.' If properly presented, this incident could be very helpful."

But another revelation promised to be more helpful still: During a visit to Jasna Polana nearly six years earlier, Maffatone told the Milbank lawyers, he'd seen Basia "smack the shit out her husband." Maffatone claimed he had been sitting and chatting with Seward and Basia on the rear patio when, he said, Seward suddenly and inexplicably asked him who he was and what he was doing there. With that, Maffatone said, Basia "physically grabbed" the old man and "smacked him over the face." "Stupid man! Stupid man!" she'd shrieked. As for Seward, he "didn't say shit." (That, plus an incident the following morning when Basia forced Seward to eat his cereal, convinced Maffatone that Seward was "spineless." "He said that if anybody had spoken to him as she did to Mr. Johnson," Berry wrote, "he would have pulled the James Cagney routine of pushing a grapefruit into her face.")

Milbank had combed the earth for such a horrifying tale, suggesting as it did both incompetence and undue influence, and come up with zilch. Now, on the eve of trial, one of their clients' most trusted confidants conveniently dropped it in their lap. The tale was inherently implausible, and not just because no one had ever seen anything remotely similar. Why would Basia "smack the shit" out of Seward in front of one of her wary stepchildren's most slavishly loyal lackies—a man who, one would have supposed, was all but certain to report what he had just seen to his employers? And why did Maffatone then fail to do so for the next five and a half years? More particularly, why had he remained mum since the fall of 1983, when, as he surely knew, the children began amassing evidence against Basia, and such a disclosure would have earned him brownie points? Why had he said nothing when the Milbank lawyers questioned the Richardses, especially since, as their faithful bodyguard, he was undoubtedly hovering somewhere nearby? What finally prompted him to let Marty and Mary Lea in on his secret only when the trial loomed? But if any of these questions—or this sudden serendipity—seemed at all suspicious to Berry, he didn't show it. All that the Milbank lawyer noted afterward was that with his "good appearance" and "direct" manner, Maffatone would make a great witness.

Sophie Zdziechowska, Basia's erstwhile friend at the Biblioteka Polska, gave Milbank more ammunition. Meeting with Shoemaker's Polish-speaking friend from Boston a week before Maffatone's session with Reilly and Berry, she described Basia as a "madwoman," prone to frequent, horrible temper tantrums. At various times, she said, she'd seen her throw things at Seward, scream at him, call him an "idiot," blame him for rough seas, torture him by speaking Polish to him. "Mrs. Zdziechowska said that Basia told her that Seward had not wanted to marry her and that, by screaming at him and throwing fits, she forced him to do so," Shoemaker wrote in a memorandum.

Basia was uncouth, the Polish noblewoman sneered. She recounted how Basia had learned etiquette from a book, and how she'd once seen her, tipsy, dancing and screaming in Venice's Piazza San Marco. But that wasn't surprising; she told the Milbank lawyers a psychiatrist friend of hers once diagnosed Basia as mentally ill, given to paranoia, drunkenness, and wild, uncontrolled behavior. The Krasinskis called Basia a "mad dog." Seward's old secretary Joann Farinella, recalled how, in late 1982, Basia had exploded when Seward, anxious for some hot oatmeal, had sent out a bodyguard in the middle of the night to buy him a Crockpot.

Though Basia's infidelity was not grounds for overturning the will, the Milbank lawyers searched assiduously for any evidence of it. A former security man told them that on occasion Jasna Polana's elaborate electronic alarm system showed Waligura intering her bedroom late at night. Mme. Zdziechowska wasn't so equivocal: Malcuzynski, she declared, had been Basia's lover, though, disappointingly from Milbank's perspective, it had been with Seward's approval. "Mrs. Zdziechowska said that Seward himself knew about it, but that he was a very 'gentle spirit' and 'well-mannered' and did not oppose the affair," Shoemaker wrote. "Seward told Mrs. Zdziechowska that he preferred Basia have a lover like Malcuzynski, someone who was honest and older, instead of

a younger man who would have exploited her." At one time, he continued, there was even some talk about Malcuzynski marrying Basia.
But try as it might, Milbank never could prove that Basia had been
unfaithful to Seward, with Malcuzynski or anyone else. If the children
were to make the charge, it would have to be through innuendo.

Indeed, they had more success proving the converse. Joann Farinella
recalled one of the eighty-five-year-old Seward's antics from the fall of
1980, when Basia was off in Europe and the old man had Jasna Polana—
and, he apparently hoped, Farinella—all to himself. "Johnson called
Farinella to his rooms at 2:00 p.m.," the Milbank interviewer, Paul
Shoemaker, later recorded. "When she arrived, there was a fire in the
fireplace and music was playing. Seward said to her that he was very
unhappy with Basia, that Basia was not satisfying him sexually, and
that he hoped that Farinella could. Farinella rejected his advances."

Sullivan & Cromwell also collected information, albeit less vigorously. Its task was simpler; it needed to show only that Seward had
been competent and independent, not to raise dust wherever and however it could. Christ's most thought-provoking conversation was with
Charles Merrill, aka "Big Paw," husband of Seward's sister, Evangeline.

It hadn't been easy for Christ to find a member of the Johnson family
to speak with him; the pursuit of Seward's fortune had united them as
genes and love never had. But Big Paw was different. Like Basia, like
Marty Richards, he was the third and much younger spouse of a Johnson,
sneeringly regarded by the stepchildren as an interloper and fortune
hunter. Like them, too, he had an eclectic background, with stints as
a laundry worker, furniture refinisher, soda jerk, tractor operator, horse
groomer, cook, photographer, and Tarot card reader. He'd first met
Evangeline in 1967, in the Palm Beach beauty parlor where he worked
to subsidized his painting. Evangeline, who'd purchased Kandinskis and
Jackson Pollocks long before they became fashionable, liked Merrill's
oeuvre and invited him to see her own collection. Shortly thereafter,
Merrill moved in with her. The two lived for a time in Dublin, where
Merrill launched an arts magazine, and in September 1977 they'd married, with Captain J. Seward Johnson, Sr., of the *Mazurka* officiating.
"Until the death of love!" Evangeline declared in a champagne toast.
Shortly after that, the eighty-year-old bride and the groom, forty-three,
moved to "World's Edge Farm," an aptly named spread outside Hen-
dersonville, North Carolina. Having named his home, Merrill renamed
himself: "Merrill" hadn't worked very well; Palm Beachers, thinking
he was connected to "Merrill Lynch," had attached themselves to him,
only to dump him in disgust upon discovering he wasn't. "Big Paw"

became his legal name, and his license plate, in 1983.

Though Seward hadn't trusted Evangeline and even feared she might contest his will, Basia thought of her as an ally. In fact, Evangeline never much liked Basia. But Big Paw identified with her. He had seen how she had invigorated Seward; moreover, he considered Seward's offspring a sorry lot. While Mary Lea could not hold an intelligent conversation, Marty, her "blue-rinsed husband," was a nonstop talker. Elaine Wold was a nitwit, Keith a philistine. When the Merrills had stopped by the Firestone estate in Ireland, Diana and Bert spent the whole time necking—acting "like morons," Evangeline said afterward. Big Paw had met Junior only once, but likened his artwork to bronzed baby shoes, the kind of kitsch a Nixon or Eisenhower would collect.

Inevitably, tremors from the will contest reached even World's Edge Farm. Both Junior and Mary Lea called to enlist the Merrills, with Mary Lea suggesting there might be something in it for Evangeline if she came on board. Later Keith Wold's sister Betty, widow of the General's son, began sending her five thousand dollars every three months—intended, she said, to make Evangeline's life a bit easier. Big Paw found the children's sudden interest disgusting. But something Junior said intrigued him. Junior related how, in an effort to prove Basia had been abusing Seward, the children had bugged Jasna Polana, and had somehow gotten Basia ranting and raving on tape. It was an amazing disclosure; while Basia had always worried about surveillance, it was the KGB, not her husband's family, she feared. Big Paw, who surmised that the children had co-opted a Jasna Polana employee into doing the dirty deed, hadn't mentioned this to anyone until Christ called. Better than any lawyer in the case, Christ knew the sound of Basia screaming, and how piercing that sound would be should it ever reverberate around a cavernous courtroom. S&C had previously asked Milbank to produce tapes "of any meeting of two or more persons" in which either Seward or Basia had been present, and the objectants had furnished nothing; this meant either that Milbank had withheld such tapes, had not been told of them, or had told whoever had them to hold on to them for the time being. In his sworn deposition Junior said he knew nothing of any tape recordings.

Who could have done the taping? S&C assigned Basil Zirinis, a darkly dashing recent Columbia Law School graduate who'd joined the firm a few months earlier, to interview Jasna Polana employees, past and present, and round up some suspects. Zirinis learned little from most of those he interviewed, but paused over the case of a former handyman named Edmund Sulikowski. He couldn't figure out why Sulikowski left Jasna Polana, since by all accounts he'd been happy there. Moreover, Sulikowski was raising nine children by himself; anyone with so large a brood, he surmised, could be bought. Zirinis called Sulikowski and arranged to meet with him at his home in Fairless Hills, Pennsylvania, a few miles outside Trenton.

At first Sulikowski seemed confused about whom Zirinis represented, and upon learning it was Basia, he equivocated; perhaps, he said, he should talk to Junior Johnson first. The comment seemed doubly odd to Zirinis—first, that Sulikowski even knew Junior; second, that he would seek his permission to talk with anyone. But the night was bitterly cold, and Sulikowski, a hospitable sort, invited Zirinis in. For the next three hours, over coffee and cake, the young S&C lawyer listened to his loquacious host. Sulikowski talked about himself, his wartime experiences, his busted marriage, his financial woes, the Johnsons' fabulous wealth. He said he needed money to send his kids to school; how nice it would be, he added, if an angel came along and dropped $100,000 in his lap. Repeatedly, Zirinis steered him back to Jasna Polana, and whenever he did, Sulikowski bad-mouthed the Johnsons' marriage. His comments tracked the Forger Affidavit, making Zirinis wonder whether Milbank had already gotten to him. On a couple of occasions, Sulikowski hinted obliquely he had made some tape recordings, but then either changed the subject or said he wasn't sure he had them anymore. Sulikowski obviously had something to say, but he wasn't saying much of it to Zirinis.

Zirinis paid a return call a few weeks later. He learned nothing more about any recordings, but Sulikowski suggested he contact Mariusz and Izabella Poterewicz, a husband-and-wife butler-and-maid team Basia had hired, then fired, in Seward's final months. Basia had never mentioned them to S&C; unable to acknowledge her own fallibility, she was hardly in a position to identify for her lawyers anyone she'd alienated. But another employee informed S&C that within days of being fired, Izabella Poterewicz had miscarried; that she had been unable to conceive ever since; and that she and her husband blamed Basia for their tragedy. "She's going to pay for this," Mariusz told this co-worker. "We'll find some lawyer, and we'll make her pay for this." When the co-worker asked what he meant, Poterewicz pointed to a small rectangular object in his pocket and said, "I have it here. I always have it here." What he was pointing to was a small tape recorder.

Sulikowski's co-worker warned Christ and Nina that he could probably be persuaded to testify for the children. She also urged the S&C lawyers to contact Izabella Poterewicz, if only to neutralize her. But

Christ, she later recalled, seemed uninterested in what she had to say, and, as she put it, "talked more about his wife's llamas than about the case." In fact, the S&C lawyers split on the point. Osgood recommended tracking down Izabella, taking her deposition, finding out what she knew, even if it meant alerting Milbank to her existence. Christ felt it preferable to let things lie. Besides, what the Poterewiczes and Sulikowski had said—or recorded—was plainly inadmissible, on the grounds of irrelevance and prejudice. Ultimately, Basia had the last word. "That stupid girl, she doesn't know anything!" she declared. She urged her lawyers to ignore her.

They did.

XXXII

B y December 1985 the preliminary bouts were just about over, and the main event loomed. Nina had already had a new phone line installed in her apartment, to which only Basia and Christ had the unlisted number. She had also asked a Saks shopper to stock her with clothes for the trial, having no way of knowing that Elaine Wold had retained the same woman. Shearman & Sterling had just billed the estate another $600,000, bringing its tab since Seward's death to $2.9 million. (By now, Ziegler wrote in one of Nina's evaluations, she was really more of an S&S client than S&S lawyer; once the Johnson matter ended, he added ominously, this "special relationship" would have to be reviewed.)

The two sides had questioned 54 witnesses for 170 days, producing 20,000 pages of verbiage, and still S&C had little idea what Milbank's case would look like. Seeking to find out—or, as S&C put it more altruistically, to assure that the trial would be "managed professionally, thoughtfully, and efficiently" rather than degenerate into an "unruly circus" or game of "Blind Man's Bluff"—the proponents asked that Milbank be made to disclose the names of the witnesses it planned to call, a routine procedure in many trials. Milbank resisted, raising the novel claim that naming names might actually endanger the people on the list. To buttress that argument, Milbank offered three more instances in which, it alleged, Osgood had manipulated potential witnesses. One was Patricia Reid, the nurse to whom he had sent his series of entreaties. Milbank had obtained copies of those letters, and charged they were improper in several ways. First, it charged, it was "a gross distortion" for Osgood to have told Reid that the Johnson children considered Seward to have been "an imbecile" in his final weeks. Imbecile, according to Milbank's *Webster's*, "connotes retarded intellectual or mental development that has been suffered since birth or early youth," and that was plainly inapplicable to Seward. Equally untrue was Osgood's claim that the other nurses considered Seward "a pretty sharp old man." Moreover, by assuring Reid she could speak to him in

363

confidence ("Please do not worry about getting involved. We will keep you out of it."), Osgood had tried to hide a crucial witness. But his deviousness didn't stop there. So calculating, so Machiavellian, so shamelessly manipulative was Robert Osgood, Milbank maintained, that he'd enlisted the United States Postal Service in his diabolical plot. What Reilly described as Osgood's "unbecoming and desperate effort to ingratiate" himself with Reid extended—or descended—"even down to the subliminal messages conveyed by the postage stamps" he used. The stamp on one envelope, a copy of which Milbank submitted to the court, showed two hands poised to touch, in the fashion of Michelangelo's God and Adam in the Sistine Chapel, and exhorted the reader to "Volunteer: Lend a Hand." The stamp on the other envelope was more pernicious: "L♡ve L♡ve L♡ve L♡ve L♡ve," it said. "One cannot help but conclude that the stamps were purposefully chosen," Reilly said.

Osgood stood accused of manipulating two other potential witnesses. One was Seward's former pilot, Dan Malick, who said Osgood had misled him, belittled what he'd said, flattered him, jerked him around. "Mr. Osgood made a big effort to engage in friendly conversation with me not relevant to the lawsuit," Malick stated in an affidavit. "He even mentioned that he used to be a Methodist minister." The other was Sheril Bennett, the overly perfumed nurse. "It really made me mad," she said of his treatment. "I felt he was harassing me in an unprofessional and improper manner. I thought that kind of thing only happened on television or in soap operas."

Sullivan & Cromwell used terms like "desperate," "diversionary," and "wildly inaccurate" to describe the latest assault. Milbank had clearly spoon-fed Bennett and Malick their statements, it maintained; as for its use of "L♡ve" stamps, S&C noted that another envelope sent to Reid had been stamped by a postal meter. "What 'subliminal message' is conveyed by such a mark?" it queried. Were Pitney and Bowes in on the conspiracy, too? As it turned out, Milbank's animadversions weren't even necessary. To an old trial lawyer like Marie Lambert, trial by ambush was a great American tradition. She was not about to steal the children's thunder by making them disgorge the names of those they planned to produce. That would rob the proceedings of much of their suspense and entertainment value.

The children *were* ordered to file a bill of particulars, laying out what they proposed to prove in their forthcoming case. But S&C promptly complained that what Milbank supplied was little more than a glorified press release, a "bill of generalities." From S&C's standpoint, it included only one new element, but it was a disconcerting one at that. "The acts of fraud, duress and undue influence," Milbank stated, "were accompanied by acts of physical violence." Sullivan & Cromwell now demanded to ask each of the children to state the time, date, and location of each episode of violence. Once more Milbank successfully resisted. Along with everyone else, Sullivan & Cromwell would just have to wait to hear Maffatone's tale.

The few clues Milbank did provide about its upcoming case came voluntarily, in a motion urging Lambert to allow it great latitude to prove undue influence. Undue influence, Milbank argued, could rarely be seen or touched; it had to be shown inferentially, through threads and patches of evidence. All of Basia's temper tantrums, and not only those aimed at Seward, were relevant, because they demonstrated her "tyrannical disposition" and the "coercive and oppressive atmosphere" in which he had spent his final years. Unless the court objected, then, a procession of Basia's targets would likely be paraded into court. S&C countered that courts rarely upheld undue-influence claims, particularly against spouses. "No matter that children or family are disinherited," the S&C brief stated. "No matter that the spouses quarrelled frequently or even violently. No matter that the testator was aged, diseased, or dependent. No matter that the spouses differed in age or in financial resources." Representing the widow in the Payson case, Milbank concurred. "It is almost inconceivable that a will by one spouse leaving property to the other spouse in a relationship of love and understanding could be looked upon as the product of undue influence, and no reported New York decision in the last seventy-five years has so held," it argued.

While Milbank was making much of Sullivan & Cromwell's conduct, it may have been involved in some skulduggery of its own. It concerned the Richardses and John Fino, the frustrated actor who blew the whistle on Victor D'Arc's purported murder plot. By the eve of trial Fino had emerged from prison, his hatred for Marty Richards greater than ever. At one point he filed a $2 million lawsuit against Richards over property rights to Fort Apache, The Bronx; three years later he made a series of threatening phone calls to Richards's home, prompting John Lindsay to call the police for his clients. Concerned for their safety, Mary Lea and Marty paid Tony Maffatone an additional three thousand dollars a week for extra security, services that Mary Lea once more petitioned her trustees to bankroll (the Richardses ultimately sued Fino for harassment, seeking $1 million in damages from their impoverished tormentor). By himself, Fino posed little threat to Marty and Mary Lea. But in early 1985 Victor D'Arc also reappeared, claiming Mary Lea had shortchanged him in their divorce settlement. D'Arc and the Finos promptly teamed up. Fino's father resurfaced to say D'Arc had never discussed murdering Mary Lea with him, and that the famous tape had been doctored by Marty Richards. Then, mysteriously, the elder Fino recanted his recantation. And, besides dropping their harassment case against Fino the younger, Marty and Mary Lea began paying his legal fees in another matter arising out of a fight Fino had had in a bar with an off-duty policeman.

What caused this sudden rapprochement? The minutes of the January 28, 1986, meeting of Mary Lea's trustees, held two weeks before the will contest was to go to trial, provide a clue.

> John Swink [one of the trustees] asked Mary Lea if she cared to comment on the Fino matter since she was asking the trustees to pay some legal fees for him. Mary Lea stated that there were certain tapes which Fino had relating to the renewal of the D'Arc divorce case. She said that the attorneys for the will contest did not want these to be made public at this time. She then said by promising to pay some legal fees that they would secure an affidavit from Fino stating that these tapes were untrue. She said they had bought Fino. She remarked that she did not want the tapes brought up at this time in view of the Estate trial. She told us she is committed for the balance of Fino's legal expense.

It was but another chapter in the twisted Fino saga, one that both Mary Lea and her trustee had garbled still further. But no matter what the Finos, Victor D'Arc, and the Richardses were trying to do to one another, at least one thing was clear: Mary Lea and her lawyers wanted Fino to disappear for the duration of the will contest, lest he surface and embarrass her, and they were willing to pay him to butt out. In fact, Mary Lea gave a lawyer named Douglas Eaton nearly twelve thousand dollars to defend Fino. Documents suggest that Mary Lea's personal lawyer, Phillip Broughton of Thacher, Proffitt & Wood, handled the paperwork, but Mary Lea's remark to her trustees indicated that Milbank, too, was involved. Forger denied the charge, but could not offer any explanation for Mary Lea's comment about "the attorneys for the will content." If what she said was true, Milbank's misconduct was far more serious than Osgood's clumsiness with a few witnesses in Florida.

By Christmas all depositions except Junior's and Basia's were complete. Now that Basia had decreed that Christ would try the case, Osgood had no alternative but to prop him up, and for that, he had to find out how bad things actually were. The best way to take stock was to hold a simulated minitrial before a mock jury, a process that would force Christ to get on his feet, state his case, and see how he fared. Thus, one evening in late December, S&C's Johnson team, along with some support staff, assembled in the lawyers' lunchroom. For some, it was their first foray onto the premises: The S&C cafeteria was normally off-limits to anyone without a law degree. Twelve firm employees, working overtime, were to serve as jurors. Ted Rogers, the senior associate on the case, would play Ed Reilly, while Sheryl Michaelson would be the as-yet unspecified Dewey Ballantine lawyer arguing for Harbor Branch. Basil Zirinis was cast as Marie Lambert. Christ had a leg up on them all; he had only to play himself. Moderating the proceedings, which were to be videotaped, was Osgood.

Zirinis laid out for the "jury" the ground rules of the case: the elements of testamentary capacity, a testator's right to change his will willy-nilly, and, if he chose, to disinherit his children. What the jury had to decide, he said, was whether Seward Johnson had acted freely, not whether he'd acted wisely or well. Then, as he would soon do in Surrogate's Court, Christ ambled up to the lectern and began to speak. Or, more accurately, to read. Worse still, he read listlessly, haltingly, almost mournfully, as if he had so little confidence in his case or himself that he had to sound solemn to compensate. There was neither passion nor punctuation in what he said. His gestures appeared wooden, and he clung to the lectern as tenaciously as to his script, as if he were afraid of tipping over. His remarks were not only poorly delivered, but poorly conceived. They contained more about the law than the facts. There was little about Basia and Seward, their marriage, their personalities, their interest in one another's affairs, his generosity to Harbor Branch, her longtime stake in his wills. Nor was there anything about Seward's frayed relations with his children or their real reason for challenging the will. Thorny issues Milbank was certain to raise—Seward's health, Basia's temper, Nina's fees—were glossed over. Christ's performance was disastrous. A palpable discomfort filled the room when he sat down.

Rogers, who was next to argue, was one of those bright but cautious young men who advance at Sullivan & Cromwell and places like it by performing well but never too conspicuously. Though only thirty-two at the time, Rogers, sober, serious, wearing wire-rimmed glasses, had the look and air of an older man; one needed no computer enhancement to imagine what he'd be at fifty. Or where, for he would almost surely make partner and spend the rest of his days at S&C. By temperament and experience, Rogers was no Reilly. Moreover, he'd dashed off his opening statement on a plane. But he made a compelling case for the children. It was hard enough for a healthy man to comprehend forty-eight pages of legalese, he declared; how could it have ever been understood by an old and cancer-ridden man, unable to read a newspaper, receiving round-the-clock nursing care, given to hallucinating and talking to people who weren't even there, who, the nursing notes confirmed, had been confused only a few hours before? Rogers held up the will before the jury, much as a dog owner holds a loaded Poop-R-Scoop. This will, he said, had been "manufactured" by Basia and Nina, the people who'd controlled Seward Johnson; the older and sicker he got, the tighter their net around him grew. This will, he said, simply *had* to be a hoax.

Rogers sat down, and Michaelson rose to speak. A solid, heavyset woman with short hair and a flat, no-nonsense manner, she had been at S&C barely a year, but had a calm worldliness that suggested prior seasoning. While Rogers was a lifer, Michaelson was just as surely a bird of passage, someone who saw her time at S&C as training for something more politically congenial. Even as she worked on the Johnson case, she'd represented some gay G.I.'s seeking to march in New York's Veterans' Day parade. Michaelson now argued that Harbor Branch was Seward Johnson's dear child, embodying two of the keys to his character: his love of the sea and his dedication to charity. Was it believable that a man who wanted to die on the premises of his proudest creation, contemplating his beloved boats, wouldn't leave it a penny? Besides, if Seward distrusted Junior enough to strip Harbor Branch of its legacy, why had he kept him on as an executor? And what possible explanation was there for Basia's April 14 letter, except to deceive Seward into thinking Harbor Branch still stood to collect something? Michaelson, too, had had little time to prepare. But her presentation was another tour de force—if anything, even stronger than Rogers's.

The formal presentations were over, and an ominous silence fell over the room. Here it was the eve of trial, and two associates, one scarcely a year out of law school, had whipped the partner running the case—or, as one of the "jurors" later put it, had "blown Christ out of the water." The jurors were riddled with doubts about the home team's case; all they could talk about in the question-and-answer period that followed was how decrepit Seward was. How could he ever have rebounded from his confusion in time to sign his will? one asked. Wow! another said. This man was in real bad shape! Even the exhibits were a disaster. One was a photograph of Nina and Seward talking, designed

to show their closeness; in fact, one juror said, it made Nina look shifty
and untrustworthy. "I wouldn't be a bit surprised if there's a case between
Mrs. Johnson and S&C when this whole thing is over," one paralegal
said to another.

Christ quickly reverted to his old droll self once "court" had adjourned. When one juror expressed concern over Seward's hallucinations, Christ quipped that hallucinating wasn't all that bad; some people
do it all the time. Osgood, too, took refuge in humor. Did Nina really
stand to make so much money? he was asked. Yes, Osgood replied;
would the questioner like to meet her? The crowd, sworn to secrecy,
began to disperse. First, though, a sadist in their midst polled the jurors.
Eleven of them said they would have given the money to Harbor Branch;
the twelfth favored the children. Even the juror who told Rogers beforehand that she had a crush on Donald Christ had voted against him.
Christ was not told the results. Nor was anyone at Shearman & Sterling.
Nor were Nina or Basia, who in fact never knew the simulation had
even occurred. By November 1985 Seward's estate had already paid
Sullivan & Cromwell nearly $3 million in legal fees, and it was getting
precious little bang for so many bucks.

Behind their Maginot Line of confidence, some S&C generals still
thought victory was inevitable. When Christ asked whether anyone
could imagine losing the case, only Michaelson raised her hand. Some
tinkering was in order; Rogers was told to revise Christ's opening statement. The more hawkish S&C lawyers urged him to juice up his message, to confront Basia's "tempestuousness" head-on, to elevate what
could otherwise be perceived as abusiveness into panache and passion.
Heathcliff was "tempestuous"; so was Anna Karenina. But Christ nixed
the idea; the entire issue of Basia's fits, at least those not directed at
Seward, was irrelevant, he said.

Privately, Basia kept complaining about her counsel. Christ had bad
eating habits, spoke too quietly, and, depending on the day, was either
dragging out the case needlessly or attempting to sell her out through
settlement. As for Osgood, he was a typical Bolshevik—or was it a
Nazi? As her dissatisfaction filtered down, threatening to demoralize
even further an already troubled camp, Arnold Bauman made a modest
proposal. "Mrs. Johnson," he said one night in early January 1986,
over dinner at the Quilted Giraffe, "I've lived a long time, and I know
there are two kinds of people in the world: those who feel you get more
out of people by applying the lash to the back . . ."

"Like me!" Basia blurted out, apparently proud of that distinction.

" . . . and others like myself who believe you do better by patting

them on the back," he continued. "These people at Sullivan and Cromwell have worked day and night, weekend and holiday, bringing a
measure of devotion beyond any requirement, and I think it would be
very nice if you were to take them all to dinner and tell them, 'Look,
ladies and gentlemen, I know I've been a difficult client, but I also
know how hard you've been working for me, and I appreciate it
deeply.' "

Minus a husband, with few friends, her pleasure trips and shopping
expeditions curbed by the case, the usual toadies less toadying while
her purchasing power was limited, Basia had little social life. So isolated
was she that she'd had to beg Nina and her family to spend that
Christmas Eve with her at Jasna Polana. Basia's lawyers had become
her most dependable companions, and she readily agreed to Bauman's
suggestion. The dinner, set for the following week, would be solely for
the S&C team; apart from Nina, no one from Shearman & Sterling,
including Bauman, would attend.

Now more than ever, picking restaurants was Nina's department.
Almost overnight, the *Zagat Restaurant Survey* had moved from the
realm of samizdat to a brash, much-discussed, and increasingly important part of the New York scene. Nina selected Primavera, an Upper
East Side establishment ("surely among best Northern Italians and considered 'the best' by many; patrons come from NYC's power elite of
fashion and finance") Basia loved. She called Nicola, the owner, and
booked the tavernalike private room downstairs.

The troops gathered around seven, sipping cocktails and noshing
fried zucchini. Nina and Basia sat at opposite ends of a long, rectangular
table, with Christ and Osgood across from each other in the middle.
Flanking them were the other lawyers—Delahunty, Zirinis, Rogers,
and Michaelson—along with four paralegals and Christ's secretary.
Nina had already arranged for the menu (pasta and roast rack of veal)
and a steady supply of a Brunello. Gradually, the melancholy yielded
to alcoholically assisted good cheer, though how much *veritas* there
would be in this *vino* was hard to predict.

Before dessert, a radiant Basia gave a pep talk to her troops. "Sometimes I don't show my appreciation, but I want you to know you're
terrific," she said, parroting Bauman. Seward would have liked all of
them, she speculated, because he enjoyed young people and thought
like them, too. "Sometimes I get excited, but one must show one's
emotions," she went on. She closed by urging them once more to "fly
like an eagle," to soar above the dirt and debris the enemy would hurl
their way. Christ gamely offered a toast, in which he saluted Basia for

being a good client, so active and interested in her own case. Osgood followed, then Nina, then Delahunty. "You are our case," he declared solemnly, looking directly at Nina. He and Rogers then stood up, walked over to Basia, put their arms around each other in the best Whiffenpoof fashion, and boozily led everyone in a lusty chorus of "For She's a Jolly Good Fellow," the kind of revel Delahunty had so often seen during his student days in England. Barely had the words " . . . that nobody can deny!" faded into the stone walls when Basia rose and gave each of the men a hug and a kiss. The two choristers then ambled over to the other end of the table and serenaded Nina with a salute of her own. The dinner was a smashing success. But all evening long, the younger lawyers had noticed Osgood was eerily subdued, then left early. Afterward, Zirinis, Delahunty, and Elizabeth Gorski, the Polish-speaking paralegal, went out for more drinks. "What's going on with Osgood?" someone asked. No one had an answer.

Christ remained convinced the children would fold short of trial. Sooner or later, he felt, they had to realize that a court battle was irrational, costly, and futile, even if their own lawyers wouldn't tell them. In fact, Forger refused to talk settlement, at least, he said, until the depositions were complete. Instead, Christ renewed his courtship of Harbor Branch.

Everyone at S&C well knew how much stronger its case would be with the foundation out of the picture, with the children no longer able to masquerade as Seward's stewards. Privately, at least some Milbank lawyers felt the same way. Harbor Branch "provided the children with their entrée, their respectability," one of them said later with remarkable candor and cynicism. "I could see saying Seward had a ball in the early years of his marriage, that it was a Walter Mitty–like blowout," he continued. "I could see, too, that he had little use for the children—he'd left them nothing since the 1960s. And there's nothing so peculiar about giving the widow everything: Charity was not an abiding interest of his, but his hobby. So Basia didn't have a cookout, so she didn't want him to have a hot tamale on a sore stomach, so she sent him to bed and screamed at the help—a lot of this could be explained off. She was influencing him since 1968, but when did it become 'undue'? I'm not sure it ever did. Maybe he wasn't incapable of saying no, but just didn't want to." He concluded, "The children and Harbor Branch together are an awesome combination. If Harbor Branch had been eliminated, we would have had our legs cut off. Without them, all we had was a screaming woman."

Both in late 1984 and early 1985 Christ met with William Warren, the Dewey lawyer heading Harbor Branch's team. The parties were far apart: Christ offered Harbor Branch the present value of the $75 million Q-TIP trust—around $8.7 million, by his reckoning—while Warren insisted on that plus a substantial premium, totaling around $20 million. But before things could proceed any further, word of the talks reached Junior, and through him, Milbank, presumably from one of the "independent" directors. Basia, who had maintained that she'd never settle with anyone, felt she had been made to look like a liar, and ordered that all discussions cease. "Close the door from the other side!" she told Christ. Now, with the trial nearing, S&C would presumably pay still more to remove the foundation from the case. Dewey might then extract a promise from the children to match or top the offer. The foundation could effectively coerce the children to be charitable.

But in his role of "honest broker," Warren got very different receptions from the two sides. He got along famously with Don Christ and liked Nina, too. (In January, for instance, he sent her a "Dear Nina" note at Shearman & Sterling, asking if she'd be good enough to mail the Harbor Branch legal team four copies of the 1986 *Zagat Restaurant Survey.* "Many thanks and best wishes for the New Year," he cheerily closed.) And though he really didn't know her, the thrice-married Warren even had a certain respect for Basia. For all her faults, Basia struck him as a pretty damn good wife. That was why he considered the children's undue-influence claim absurd. But Milbank refused to extend the Dewey lawyers even the most basic courtesies, like providing them with documents, let alone keep them apprised of developments or encourage their clients to pledge funds to the foundation. That happened only when Basia put some of her own cash on the barrelhead.

As the trial neared, Basia agreed to put $30 million—she called it "pocket money"—on the table, to be picked over like carrion by the children, Harbor Branch, and Uncle Sam together. Bauman suggested something higher, around $75 million, which Basia rejected. But even that wouldn't have worked. On February 13, with jury selection about to begin, Forger finally forwarded Milbank's figure: $200 million. The number was deliberately outrageous, a clear indication that a trial was imminent. The two sides began digging trenches. Sullivan & Cromwell rented quarters from a court reporter on Duane Street, around the corner from the Surrogate's Court, for use as a lunch-and-war room; workmen arrived from Jasna Polana to make the place combat-ready. Milbank arranged for less swank quarters a few blocks away.

Meanwhile the Harbor Branch lawyers tried to negotiate a separate peace with S&C. "You gotta be nuts wanting to litigate this case with a white knight here," Bob Hirth, the Dewey associate on the case, told Christ. For $25 to $30 million, he said, the foundation's board would have to settle, no matter how stacked with Junior's cronies it might be. Christ offered $15 million, but subject to three conditions: The money would be in trust; it could be used only for research vessels like the *R/V Seward Johnson*; and the deal would be off should the children win either the will contest or the claims proceeding. That meant Harbor Branch would have to drop its neutrality, and take on Seward's children.

The new offer, while posing a dilemma for Dewey, was not really a close call; no additional money was needed to run the ships. But it reflected S&C's flexibility, and Dewey thought it could do better. Lambert suspended jury selection, which had just begun, so that the two firms could continue talking. Soon Christ's offer had risen to $20 million. Rather than grab it, the Dewey lawyers asked Milbank to match it. On the morning of February 17, as the *Johnson Sea Link 2* probed the Caribbean floor for chunks of the space shuttle *Challenger*, lawyers from Dewey and Milbank, along with foundation officials, met at Junior's Princeton house. Meanwhile Reilly, salivating for a trial and anxious to keep Harbor Branch on board, paced around the courthouse—acting "like a fruitcake," an eyewitness recalled.

The Dewey lawyers gave Milbank their terms: Harbor Branch would continue to challenge the will, but only if the children guaranteed it the present value of the Q-TIP trust plus one sixth of whatever they recovered in court. Forger refused. As the meeting ended, Warren prepared to advise Harbor Branch's independent directors to accept Basia's offer. Then Junior Johnson played his trump card. If Harbor Branch settled, he warned, he would cut off all funding from the Atlantic Foundation, which he also controlled. He was holding Harbor Branch, the institution his father had entrusted him to lead, hostage, and Harbor Branch's own general counsel was helping him. The Dewey lawyers reacted with disbelief. Convinced they could not represent their client properly, they pondered withdrawing from the case. Instead, they returned to Christ, begging for an offer that even the "independent" directors couldn't refuse. The next morning Christ upped the ante once more: $20 million, but outright rather than in trust, and earmarked for ocean engineering. Now, Milbank interposed another obstacle: the independent directors, it told Lambert, had no authority to settle. To the Dewey lawyers, it was another eleventh-hour effort at sabotage, done in typically amiable Forger fashion. "He would walk up to us and say 'friends' when he was doing everything in his power to screw us," one later recalled. Forger, another Dewey lawyer said, was "ruthlessly protecting his own interests. You knew where Christ was coming from," he added. "Forger was more Machiavelli and less Jefferson than I might have expected."

Of course, it was improper for someone to manipulate a charity for his own ends. That was why the New York attorney general was designated to look out for charities in cases of this kind. But throughout the talks, the office of Attorney General Robert Abrams was invisible, and despite its frustrations, Dewey never approached it. Dewey offered Milbank a new ultimatum: Unless the children matched the offer— that is, guaranteed Harbor Branch the first $20 million of whatever they collected—the foundation would support Basia and Nina. The children wouldn't do it, but agreed to give Harbor Branch one sixth of whatever they collected in the claim. By any standard it was a poor deal, since the claim would probably net nothing. But it was the best Dewey could do with Milbank. (Even then, Milbank dragged its feet, refusing to sign the pledge for another six weeks.) When the dust settled, the charity remained in the case, allied with the children, and was none the richer for it.

For all they revealed about Forger, the settlement talks also showed something about Marie Lambert. Christ had steered the case toward her partly because he thought her more likely to force a settlement. But her efforts in that direction were strangely perfunctory. Rather than lean on the foundation to strike a deal with the proponents, Lambert undermined the talks by setting arbitrarily short deadlines. She chastised Christ's settlement proposals, including one that would have given the children $1 million each. "A million dollars isn't an offer; it's an insult!" she declared. Indeed, to some of the S&C lawyers, she seemed at least as vigorous a defender of the children's cause as Forger was. The only person she pressured to settle was Nina, to whom she spoke alone once in chambers. She had a great love of lawyers, Lambert told her, and she hated to see one of them, particularly another woman, forced to take the stand to defend herself. Unless Nina could convince Basia to settle the case, the judge seemed to be saying, things could turn nasty for Nina. Shaken up, convinced Lambert was urging her to betray Basia to save her own neck, Nina promptly reported the conversation to Bauman.

Like Reilly, Lambert seemed more anxious to begin the trial than to simplify the case. Her impatience confirmed what people who knew her suspected all along: She didn't want any settlement in this, the biggest and most highly publicized case of her judicial career. With jury selection in *Johnson* v. *Johnson* now at hand, her moment in the sun was at hand, and she would not be a party to any eclipse.

XXXIII

There was a slight air of unreality in Marie Lambert's courtroom at two o'clock on the afternoon of Tuesday, February 18, 1986, when Robert Osgood rose to introduce himself and the other lawyers to the jury pool. Nearly three years had now passed since Seward Johnson's death, and the contest over his last will was finally going to trial.

The prospective jurors could not be blamed for feeling a bit skeptical. Many had already languished in the courtroom a few days, unaware of the frenzied settlement talks taking place around them. The smart ones had brought books, mostly the kind with embossed covers found at airport newsstands. One had spent the previous Friday, Valentine's Day, reading something called *Deadly Medicine;* he'd entered the room at page 100 and left at page 390. It was apt reading, for the newspapers were filled with the latest tales of tainted Tylenol, which had sent J&J stock—and therefore, the value of Seward's fortune—into a temporary tailspin.

On hand, though they had yet to be introduced, were some of the principals. Three future witnesses—Jennifer, Mary Lea, and Mary Lea's bodyguard, Tony Maffatone—were in the front row of the seats to the right of where Lambert would soon sit. Basia, Nina, Bauman, and Delahunty were two rows behind them. People who'd never seen each other before, thrown together by the vagaries of jury duty, conversed animatedly, while two factions of the same family, people who'd known each other for years, sat only a few feet apart, studiously ignoring one another. Some of the S&C lawyers chatted casually in the corridor, while Reilly and his Milbank cohorts sat erect at counsel's table.

Lambert appeared but twice: first, to excuse everyone for lunch, and later, around four, to order the first six candidates into the jury box and direct Osgood to begin his questioning. Twelve people had to be picked: six to hear the case, the others as alternates. The ever-ingratiating Osgood introduced the lawyers and litigants to the audience and prepared for his interrogation, only to run aground on his very first

376

question. "How many people would have a problem sitting for a trial that lasted three or four months?" he asked, citing the commonly accepted estimated length of the trial to come. There was a forest of hands. "May we ask in the alternative: who would *not* have a problem?" Three people raised their hands. "I think at this point we should ask the judge for some guidance," he said helplessly. Jury selection was promptly suspended after a few seconds. The courtroom emptied, almost. A few moments later a court officer who'd checked to make sure the room had been cleared reported what he'd seen. "You won't believe this, but Mrs. Johnson is in there, swinging around in the witness chair," he said. Despite everything, for Basia the case remained a carnival, the witness stand a merry-go-round.

Few in the jury pool appeared to relish the chance to participate in one of the most sensational will contests ever; their energies went instead toward devising novel excuses. "I just had an operation on my rectum. It would kill me to sit three or four months," one explained. But Lambert showed little mercy to malingerers. To a recalcitrant schoolteacher, she snapped, "If tomorrow morning you had a burst appendix, you'd be out for two or three months. This case is just as important as anybody's education." She told a reluctant bureaucrat she would call Mario Cuomo to ascertain whether New York State could survive without the fellow for a few months. Soon people knew better than to argue. Asked if she could serve, an asthmatic woman told the judge, "Provided I don't turn blue, you don't have a problem."

"Are you going to turn blue on me?" the judge asked playfully. "We don't allow that."

"No, Your Honor, I wouldn't," the woman replied. "I wouldn't dare."

The process of picking jurors, known as "voir dire," is more an art than a science, and more a pseudoscience than either. Fancy sociological studies, demographics, ethnic stereotyping, and professional mythology aside, a lawyer must proceed largely on instinct. Still, the process helps ferret out those with conspicuous biases and affords lawyers a chance to put themselves and their cases on display while jurors' minds are still malleable.

The American ideal has always been a jury of one's peers. Everyone connected with the Johnson case knew, though, that these litigants would have little in common, culturally, economically, or psychologically, with those judging them. Actually, there was something quite absurd about the whole arrangement. Basia and five of the six Johnson children lived outside New York. Only Nina Zagat and Mary Lea Richards were city residents, and they lived on Central Park West and at

River House, respectively—precincts few of the civil servants, retirees, and yuppies making up the pool frequented. At issue were amounts of money unimaginable to everyone in the room. No one had ever heard of Harbor Branch or of J. Seward Johnson, Sr., and few could afford to patronize many of the establishments listed in the *Zagat Restaurant Survey*. As the parties cruised away each evening in their limousines, the jurors descended into the Lexington or Seventh Avenue IRT. Reilly, Christ, Osgood, Forger—none of them lived in New York, either. In their funereal pinstripes and wing tips, neither they nor the other lawyers in the case had much feel for the potential jurors, and they looked incongruous and ill at ease among them. Only Marie Lambert seemed at home with them, even though, in her exalted judicial state, her address had changed from the Lower East Side to Park Avenue.

In selecting jurors, Reilly was content to rely on his instincts. He had a few preferences: intelligent, middle-class, middle-aged men with traditional values, steady marriages, and employment, or people who would be most dismayed by Basia's opportunism, extravagance, and abusiveness, would be best. Sullivan & Cromwell, on the other hand, retained Jay Schulman, a pioneer in the science of jury selection. Schulman, fifty-nine at the time, had the look and sound of an aged eccentric, a lifelong lefty who, having never fit into the mainstream, had gone off and created a niche of his own. He had assisted in scores of cases, working for litigants like General William Westmoreland (in his libel suit against CBS), Kathy Boudin, Claus von Bülow, and the estate of Karen Silkwood. He was a big bear of a man, a Greenwich Village Santa Claus, with huge hands, a deep voice, a mane of unkempt white hair, a long beard, and a prominent gut, one accentuated by the tight red turtlenecks, invariably stained, he liked to wear. Here was a case of no political or social significance whatever, but still, Schulman signed on. Acting out some old redistributive urge from his days with Saul Alinsky—or, like so many others connected to the Johnson case, simply viewing it as a gravy train—he jacked up his usual fee an extra twenty-five dollars an hour.

Schulman met first with Osgood, who supplied him with press accounts and pleadings in the case, then with the entire S&C team. What most impressed him, apart from the views from S&C's office windows—God, you could get hypnotized just watching the beautiful boats go by—was how passive both Christ and Osgood seemed. They sat there like doyens, delegating tasks to the younger lawyers. These two were what he'd come to call "gentlemen litigators," lacking jugular

instincts to begin with, then grown softer still in their plush surroundings. The younger lawyers were more eager, but naive. Schulman recognized that the case would turn on people's perceptions of Basia.
Women jurors, he knew, could be vicious toward other women, particularly women who are wealthy and attractive; for this case, he preferred men, preferably older ones who'd like Basia's youthful good looks
and could imagine how she'd served Seward emotionally and physically.
He wanted educated jurors, less likely to buy into Milbank's primitive
fairy tale of the wicked stepmother. But the combination of education
and youth could be lethal: They tended to be anti-authoritarian, anti-
establishment, and might look askance at Basia's anticommunism. No
way did he want blacks or Hispanics deciding Basia's fate. Here was a
woman who'd forgotten her origins, something sure to turn them off.
Basia must be portrayed simultaneously as wife and mother—resolute,
courageous, loving—but should not be sanitized; it wouldn't work. The
jury would inevitably see Basia as capricious, unpredictable, tempestuous, and it was better to deal with that directly.

But Schulman quickly found his working conditions impossible.
Clearly, he had to interview Basia, but afraid he would spook her, the
S&C lawyers kept him away. What he saw when he finally did lay eyes
on her horrified him: She was surrounded by bodyguards, who for all
the physical protection they furnished would leave her defenseless before
resentful jurors. From what Schulman could see, Christ and Osgood
were reluctant to lean on Basia, afraid of her even, unwilling to push
her to do what was in her own best interests. They also seemed intimidated by Lambert and the Milbank lawyers. By the end of the first day
of jury selection, Schulman could sense that he and his new employers
were operating on entirely different frequencies. Sure enough, Ted
Rogers called him at home that night and fired him, ostensibly for
talking to prospective jurors. Schulman collected his nine-thousand-
dollar fee and moved on to the next case.

Osgood, whose overly colloquial, patronizing touch had already offended so many potential witnesses, stuck to his shtick during voir dire.
As he began to speak, he sounded a bit like Art Linkletter talking to
schoolchildren. He introduced himself as "Bob" Osgood, described Sullivan & Cromwell as "a law firm downtown here in the city," then
proceeded to introduce the rest of the "cast of characters," including
"Mr." Keith Wold. When he got to Nina, he asked, "Has anybody
read Mrs. Zagat's restaurant guide?" Did the names of any of the former
Johnson spouses "ring bells" for them? Did they use any Johnson &
Johnson products? He assumed everyone did, and, alluding to the day's

headlines, he bet there was one product they weren't going to use anymore!

Much of Osgood's work consisted of collecting biographical data from the jury candidates. Both sides were interested in whether the potential jurors had relatives who'd died of cancer or had even watched anyone go senile. Both sides looked for persons connected with—and, therefore, partial to—doctors or nurses. Osgood asked about hobbies and favorite television programs. Did they have any problems with a marriage that had its "ups and downs"? How about the difficulties that ensue "where people grow old and aren't quite as sharp as they used to be"? How did they feel about divorce and remarriage, or marriages between people of drastically different ages? Or about inheritance, and whether one who had already made his children millionaires should be required to leave them more ("I don't know," one candidate replied. "I've never really been in that situation.")? Any bias toward Polish people? Osgood asked for a show of hands. There were none. Anyone particularly admire Polish people? Again no one raised his hand. As Osgood probed, Rogers kept score, tabulating totals for each candidate. Over lunches at Ecco, an Italian restaurant nearby, they compared intuitions with Basia. She made her feelings known, not always quietly. One of those present described a particular harangue as an "E. F. Hutton kind of scene," with everyone in the restaurant nearly choking on their antipasto as she shrieked.

Reilly, by contrast, made no attempt to endear himself to anyone— except, perhaps, the pretty dark-haired woman in the jury pool to whom he smiled periodically (Reilly did not select her for the jury, but did select her for a couple of dates). When he introduced himself, it was always as "Edward," not "Ed." When he read his questions—through a pair of thick lenses that made him temporarily look his age and that, therefore, he removed as quickly as he could—he seemed formal and humorless, but genuine. And, more effectively than Osgood, he used the exercise to lay the groundwork for his case. Could the panel members recognize that a signature on the bottom of a document didn't always prove its validity? Could they believe what a nurse said, even if she contradicted a doctor? Could they credit the testimony of experts who hadn't actually seen Seward but had reviewed his medical records? Could they accept that, on occasion, a husband *could* be unduly influenced by his own wife?

When Osgood finally began propagandizing—during the selection of alternates, when Lambert was out of the room—he was far less subtle. "We contend that Harbor Branch is here attacking the will because

Mr. Johnson, Jr., lost more than twenty million dollars . . . " he began.

The point was clearly improper, since Lambert had ruled that nothing happening after Seward's death would be admissible. Immediately, Reilly was on his feet. "Counsel, I object!" he declared.

" . . . in the stock market following his father's death."

"Counsel, I am going to ask for the judge to come in!" Reilly shouted.

"We contend that Harbor Branch is here . . . "

Reilly dispatched one of the court officers to fetch Lambert. "Counsel, I asked for the judge to come in. I ask you to desist!"

" . . . trying to recover . . . "

"I asked you to desist until the judge comes in! You have no right to proceed over my objection!"

" . . . money in a will contest . . . "

"I am not going to get in a shouting match with you!"

" . . . that was lost in the stock market."

"You have no right to continue, Mr. Osgood!"

There were four raps on the door, and Lambert strode regally into the room. "You know you're not supposed to do that!" she scolded Osgood after she'd taken her seat. "I hope I don't have to be a monitor and sit here while you pick a jury. Do you think you can continue without me?"

"Yes, Your Honor," Reilly said. But Osgood, the naughty boy, was more begrudging. "I think so," he said reluctantly. After all, Lambert had entered just as he was nearing his punch line: "We contend," he was about to say, "that the children have come to this court with their pockets stuffed with their father's millions, and their hands outstretched and open for more." He never did get it off. Nor, for that matter, did he or anyone else at S&C over the next fifteen weeks.

" . . . because if you can't, I'll end up picking this jury, in about three minutes," the judge continued. "You may not like it."

But in the end that wasn't necessary. By the afternoon of February 26 there had emerged twelve people acceptable to everyone—except, perhaps, to Schulman. He'd advised against women of any age, minorities, and younger educated people; of the six who would actually hear the case, four were women under thirty-five years old, several of them with college degrees, one of them Dominican. The most intriguing was Debra Califia, thirty-three, an admissions officer at Columbia. Like Basia, she was young, attractive, and widowed; five years earlier, she'd nursed her husband as he died from Hodgkin's disease (like Basia, she, too, still wore her wedding band). Neither of the two men fit Schulman's profile, either. One of them, a thirty-nine-year-old sanitation worker named José Santana, had been born in Puerto Rico. The other, a gregarious yuppie named Jeffrey Schwab, was a computer specialist at his father's textile company. Thirty-three, single, and flirtatious, he clearly relished his role at center stage.

"The jury is satisfactory to the proponents," Osgood declared.

"The panel is satisfactory to Harbor Branch," added Hirth.

It was Reilly's turn. "We have a jury," he said triumphantly. Clearly, he was the happiest of them all.

Lambert swore in the jurors, then promptly placed them in intellectual quarantine: They were, she told them, to steer clear of all reporters, lawyers, and litigants, and not to read or listen to any accounts of the proceedings. A great believer in the grand but hollow gesture, Lambert directed that no one could ever stir until the jurors left the courtroom and reached the elevators. (Earlier, she barred the court officers even from bidding "good morning" to the jury pool. "I know it may not seem polite, but it's the best way to assure that the parties get justice in this case," she said.) She directed the jurors to report the following morning, February 27, for her preliminary charge and opening arguments.

The next day the parties assembled around ten. Basia had driven in from Princeton with her bodyguards, but by the time she reached the fifth floor of the courthouse, she had shed them, entering instead on Arnold Bauman's arm. A couple of the jurors wondered whether he was her boyfriend, an impression that did not bother Bauman in the least. (Bauman clipped a newspaper photograph of the two of them walking together and sent it to his son. "As Mayor Koch is wont to say, 'how'm I doin'?' " he wrote.) Basia was clad in her best courtroom attire, elegant but understated. She took her place on the west side of the room, near the press section and directly in Lambert's line of sight. Nina, who had arrived separately, sat two seats away. Bauman planted himself between them, as if to keep the two alleged coconspirators from looking still more conspiratorial. Also on hand was Tom Ford. Just because he was unfit to testify didn't mean he couldn't come watch, particularly since he would bill the estate seven hours for his presence.

With the press amply on hand, the world got its first extended look at the dramatis personae. What it learned was that ordinary English seemed inapplicable to them. "Widow" sounded inapt for someone as youthful as Basia, so fresh-looking that Junior urged one of the many courtroom artists already sketching her likeness to sprinkle in some wrinkles. "Children" seemed no more appropriate to describe the Johnsons and their spouses. Individually, they were an ungainly menagerie, something out of a box of Barnum's animal crackers. Perhaps the first picture ever taken of them all together, appearing in *Time* magazine, showed six people appearing to be of different parentage, on different planets, looking off in six different directions. All they had in common was that as a group, they were unattractive, unappealing, shopworn, a bowl of bruised fruit. In the front row, befitting his role as ringleader, was Junior Johnson, a man of pale skin, yellowed, stubby smoker's teeth, the jowls of a walrus, and the drooping eyelids of a *Doonesbury* character. Alongside him was his wife, Joyce, who looked like one of those haggard, haunted characters from the paintings of Edvard Munch. Behind them were the Richardses. Mary Lea was a large, disassociated, androgynous woman who looked eerily like the character ZaZa in *La Cage aux Folles*, the Broadway musical she and her husband had produced. At her side, looking more like an escort than a spouse, was Marty, boyish, diminutive, immaculately coiffed. The thin, birdlike Elaine Wold, her hair done up like a 1950s doll, was nearby. Occasionally, she exchanged words with her husband, Keith, a red-skinned, beady-eyed man with thin lips, aviator glasses, and slicked-back silver hair. Jimmy Johnson looked owlish and perpetually befuddled. Diana Firestone had undergone the peculiar metamorphosis of animal lovers, and had come to resemble one of her own beloved horses. ("Doesn't she look like her mother! Doesn't he look like his father!" a juror had overheard Diana remarking one day as she surveyed some photographs. The pictures, the juror discovered with a start, turned out to be of horses.) Only Jennifer Johnson and her new husband, Joseph Duke, could be called attractive.

Even some members of the extended Johnson family appeared. On hand, for instance, was Keith Wold's sister Betty, who'd once been married to the General's son and had inherited his vast fortune. She was accompanied by her husband, Douglas Bushnell, who after squiring around a succession of prominent Princeton women (in an incident much talked about at the time, Stalin's daughter, Svetlana Alliluyeva, had tried to run him over after he jilted her) had finally bagged himself one. By contrast, Basia had come without any relatives at all. True, hers was a much smaller family, but in some ways it was even more dysfunctional. None of her brothers could afford her any comfort, either because she'd terrorized them into servitude, like Gregory, or antagonized them into unavailability, like Piotr (who lived in Canada) and Roch, who kept an even greater distance from Basia, remaining in Poland.

The lawyers took their places at counsel's table, a long mahogany

rectangle in front of the bench. Christ, Osgood, and Rogers sat to the
right, directly in front of Basia and Nina, with Delahunty, Michaelson,
and Zirinis seated in the gallery. To Osgood's left were four lawyers
from Milbank: Reilly, Berry, Shoemaker, and Michael Levin, a litigation associate who had helped with jury selection. To their left were
the Harbor Branch lawyers: Jack Kaufmann, a litigator; Bob Hirth, the
senior associate on the case, and a second associate named Deborah
Neff. As they awaited the opening gavel, reporters attached themselves
to anyone offering a bit of insight. One began chatting with Forger,
who sat in the gallery. His mind was on what had happened in Seward's
bedroom shortly before the will was signed, or at least his version of
it. "Can you imagine, she read him the whole will, *the whole fucking
will,* all forty-seven pages of it?" he sneered. "And she did it alone,
with no one else in there!" He fixed his gaze on Basia, and said he was
looking forward to seeing his lawyers strip away her "demure" image—
to, as he put it, "pull her chain and get her screaming before the jury."

The jury filed in, largely unobserved. A few minutes later a dissolute-
looking court officer rapped his knuckles three times on the door leading
from the judge's chambers to the courtroom. "The Honorable Marie
M. Lambert, surrogate of Manhattan!" he declared. And in she strode,
removing her huge tinted glasses as the lawyers rose and said "Good
morning" to her in unison, then remained standing like schoolchildren.
"Oh, be seated, I'm sorry," she said. Corn tapped the microphone on
the bench, a superfluous contraption if ever there was one. Lambert
took a deep draught of water. "That's to save my voice!" she joked,
with a voice that sounded like the least endangered of species.

Reading off handwritten notes on a yellow pad, she explained to the
jury some of the legal issues they would be considering: who can write
a will, when someone can be said to have "testamentary capacity," the
meaning of "undue influence." The newly installed jurors, like most
people suddenly thrust into that peculiar position of responsibility, hung
on her every word. As she went on, the illustrators, wearing minibi-
noculars that made them look like diamond cutters, honed in on the
largely impassive Basia. The judge pointed to the contestants. All but
one of them, she noted, had been "virtually disinherited"; the exception, she editorialized, received "what might seem to you a large bequest
but in the context of this estate is a small bequest." Harbor Branch,
too, she noted, had had "a much greater interest" under some prior
wills.

She then laid out the order in which testimony would be presented.
First the proponents would offer the will for probate. Then came the

children, then Harbor Branch, then the proponents' rebuttal case, followed by closing statements. "You are the sole, exclusive judges of the facts," she declared. "Neither I nor anyone else may invade your province. I shall make every effort and endeavor to preside impartially and not to express any opinion concerning the facts. And views of mine on the facts would, in any event, be totally irrelevant to your determination of the issues of fact." She read listlessly from her prepared text, as if she barely cared about—and maybe didn't even entirely believe—what she mouthed.

Lambert asked if the lawyers had any objections to her instructions, and Christ asked to approach the bench. Soon, in a scene that would be replayed repeatedly, nine lawyers and Nathaniel Weiss, the court reporter, were huddled around her desk, where Christ complained that she had failed to stress that when a husband and wife were involved, all sorts of influence was not necessarily undue. The judge promised to consider that when giving her charge, and the herd headed back to their seats. Lambert urged those in the overflow crowd standing by the doors to find seats. Meanwhile, Christ wrote out a short message and handed it to Osgood. "I'm leaving," it said. "Good luck." Osgood knew it was in jest, but also knew the ambivalence and anxiety that lay beneath the joke. "Leave me your notes," he wrote back. It was five past eleven.

"We will now hear the opening statement by the attorney for Mrs. Zagat and Mrs. Johnson," Lambert declared. "I believe that's Mr. Christ."

"That's correct, Your Honor," Christ replied.

Donald Christ walked up slowly to the lectern and fiddled with it, then opened up a manila folder. He had rehearsed repeatedly in front of a video camera in recent days, determined to appear looser and more at ease than in the S&C cafeteria a month earlier. "Good morning, ladies and gentlemen of the jury, Your Honor. My name is Donald Christ," he began in a cool monotone. "I'm from Sullivan and Cromwell. Together with my colleagues Bob Osgood and Ted Rogers, we have the privilege of representing Mrs. Johnson—Mr. Johnson's widow—and Mrs. Zagat—Mr. Johnson's lawyer—in this proceeding." As he spoke, Christ looked directly at the jury and moved his fist finely, as if hammering in some half-inch nails. He peeked occasionally at his notes and strayed periodically from his lectern, but only a bit, as if on a chain. His casualness seemed scripted.

"The question here is whether Mr. Johnson's will of April 14, 1983, is Mr. Johnson's last will, and the issue that you will be asked to consider is whether Mr. Johnson knew what he was doing when he signed that document," he continued. "During the course of this trial you will get to know Mr. Johnson quite well. He was a very private man. Mr. Johnson was a very intelligent man. He was a very wealthy man. He had the good fortune to be the son of the founders of the Johnson and Johnson Company. For fifty years Mr. Johnson was a member of its board of directors."

Christ told the jury of Seward's love for farming, for sailing, for Harbor Branch. Then he spoke of Basia: how she'd come from Poland with her art degree, gone to work for the Johnsons, been courted by Seward, and spent twelve years married to him. "The life they led was virtually a dream," Christ said. "They owned homes in Europe, in the Bahamas, in Florida, and in New Jersey. They traveled by private plane. They amassed a collection of beautiful art and antiques. They had ninety people working for them. The Johnsons, as I say, lived a dream. And it was one, I believe, that you will come to see gave Mr. Johnson great pleasure in the later years of his life."

Basia watched as Christ spoke, her hands clasped on her pocketbook, a slight smile frozen on her face. She heard him refer—twice—to their "dream" marriage, a choice of words he would soon enough and predictably enough regret. But Basia, for one, was touched. Her eyes began to water, and a tear began to trickle down her right cheek. Normally, we wipe away our tears, for they itch and irritate and embarrass. But there are certain times we don't, either because we're too saddened to bother or too intent to put our sadness on display. Basia let the tear run and run and run. Only when it passed her nostrils did she remove a purple handkerchief from her pocketbook and brush the remnants away. By that time Christ had reviewed Nina's life history as well.

Christ told the jurors they would hear a good deal about the Johnson children, particularly Junior, and of Seward's $400 million estate, which included more than 7 million shares of J&J stock. But despite the figures involved, he said, Seward's last will was really "rather simple." Christ laid out its provisions, identified the executors, and described how Nina and the witnesses, Jay Gunther and James Hoch, would testify "in no uncertain terms" that Seward had known what he was doing when he signed it. So, too, would Seward's doctor, Fred Schilling, who would say that the cancer that was killing Seward had not affected his mind. "You are going to hear how, when Mr. Johnson was terminally ill, his wife cared for her husband with devotion, day after day, virtually twenty-four hours a day," he continued. "You'll hear how Mrs. Johnson, in a story that is really very touching, took good care of him, as she tried to ward off the inevitable. You'll also learn something about the Johnsons' marriage. You'll find that they shared this life together, shared this dream which I told you about, and they did it in the way that we all promise to do when we take our wedding vows. It's a life they shared in sickness and in health, in joy and sorrow; and it was, you'll find, a good marriage. You'll find that Mrs. Johnson is a vital, vibrant, exciting, and intelligent person. You'll see why Mr. Johnson was attracted to her, and you'll find that he loved her and that she loved him."

Christ told the jury it would have to consider the April 14 will in context, particularly in light of what Seward had already given his children and Harbor Branch. Christ described the six 1944 trusts, and how, had they been left intact, they would collectively have been worth $660 million when Seward died. All told, he said, Seward gave his children stock worth over $700 million, and set up additional trusts worth $70 million for his grandchildren. But as far back as 1966, Christ went on, long before he'd even met Basia or Nina, Seward said "Enough, no more," and he'd reaffirmed that decision in the thirty wills and codicils that followed. As for Harbor Branch, Seward had endowed it with $150 million—more than enough, Christ claimed, to cover its operating budget. And contrary to what they would soon hear, Christ said before Reilly objected and Lambert sustained him, Basia had always seconded Seward's support of the place.

Christ then launched into a hypertechnical discussion of Harbor Branch's leadership structure, all of which led him to describe how Junior had forced Seward's resignation on March 31. "Mr. Johnson was not happy with that, he was upset by it," Christ said with such understatement that it seemed only tangentially related to the topic that followed: Seward's last testamentary change, the one removing Harbor Branch as remainderman. "You'll see that by virtue of that change, Mr. Johnson did not benefit Mrs. Johnson in any significant way," Christ said. "She does not receive a nickel as a result of that change." He then mentioned the "letter" Basia gave Seward after the will-signing, describing how it began "Dearest Seward" and ended "Love, Basia" but omitting all the gibberish in between. In that letter, Christ said, Basia promised to look after Harbor Branch, and no matter how the children tried to twist and turn the thing around, Basia's commitment still stood.

"I told you that you will get to know Nina Zagat," Christ went on. "You are going to see her testify. You are going to get to be able to measure her yourselves. And I think that you will see she is a competent lawyer, a good person. I think that she will demonstrate to you the reasons Mr. Johnson selected her to carry out the responsibility he gave to her." He mentioned how Seward had named Nina an executor in 1976, literally writing her into his will. Then he tackled the sticky point of her fees. Sure, he confessed, they were large: $6 million as executor, plus $750,000 annually as trustee. "But as you consider that," he continued, "bear in mind that Mr. Johnson appointed his wife and his son, Seward Johnson, Jr., to receive those fees also.

"I think that when you've heard this testimony, you'll conclude that Mr. Johnson's will was properly executed on April 14, 1983, and that Mr. Johnson possessed testamentary capacity when he signed that will," Christ said. The children might produce doctors and nurses to say otherwise, he noted, but they either hadn't seen Seward around the time he signed his will, or, in the case of the children's experts, seen Seward at all.

"I'd like you to bear in mind that this is, as the judge said, a will contest," he went on. "It's not a divorce case. We're not here to try Mrs. Johnson or Mrs. Zagat. And you'll find, I think, that since Mr. Johnson is a private man, it's perilous for us to try to put ourselves into his shoes. We're not going to be able to see his children through the eyes of their father, to see his wife through the eyes of her husband, to see his foundation through the eyes of its founder. And I think that after this testimony has been heard, you will conclude that he did what he wanted and he knew what he was doing when he did it."

Seward Johnson, he reiterated, had really been disposing of his estate for forty years. Over that time he'd given half of his J&J stock to his family, a quarter to charity, and now, the final quarter to his wife. Viewed in that way, Christ said, Seward hadn't "disinherited" his children: "To suggest otherwise is to pervert the word. I think you'll find that the real question that the children are asking of their father in this case is, 'What have you done for me lately, Pop?' " That, it turned out, was as indignant as he got. Christ thanked the jury, gathered his papers, and returned to his seat. This time there would be no "jury" offering instant feedback. The only immediate reaction came from Reilly, who looked up at him briefly. "Very well done," he said quietly.

And so it was, for anyone who knew nothing about the case. But as Reilly must have realized with relish, Christ had sidestepped or glossed over almost every issue Milbank was likely to raise. If Osgood was the peacock in the S&C aviary, Christ had become the ostrich.

There was, for instance, the issue of Basia the homewrecker. Christ knew all about Seward's philandering; in chambers once, he'd joked that the "R/V" in "R/V Seward Johnson" stood not for "research vessel" but "recreational vehicle." But instead of reviewing Seward's sexual history candidly, Christ sidestepped it altogether, leaving Milbank free to depict Basia as a temptress rather than merely his latest and most serious extramarital adventure. Three times he'd called the Johnsons' marriage a "dream." It was an image begging to be contradicted; one could almost see Reilly write in "nightmare" in his own typed statement as Christ spoke. There was nearly nothing about Seward's precarious health and bouts of confusion. There was nothing about Basia's explosiveness or extravagance. And if Christ ignored the weakness in his case, he also underplayed his strengths. He said next to nothing about the children's motives, their prodigality, their indebtedness, their estrangement from their father, their absence during his last illness, their double-talk on Harbor Branch. Compare Christ's style to that of Richard Nolan, the Davis, Polk lawyer helping the widow Payson fight off her stepchildren in Nassau County. Each of "the quote, 'children,' was worth more than everyone else in the courtroom combined," he declared. "Why do I call them, quote, 'children'? Because they've never done a thing in their lives to earn money. Every dime they've gotten has come from their mother or their father." These "children," Nolan continued, "should get down on their knees and thank God that Charles Payson had Virginia during the last part of his life, but they don't. Instead, they are here saying that their father was a doddering old man, demented, an old drunk. Perhaps that's gratitude and love in the world of the smart set, but I don't think it's love and gratitude in the real world." Christ decried such martial airs, and played the jury some Muzak instead. "We're going to be nice," he told a reporter afterwards. "We're going to let them be strident."

It had worked, for now. But one person who hadn't been fooled was Lambert. From all of her years in court she knew the Cinderella bit wouldn't sell. The only way to present an unsympathetic client was directly. Christ, she quickly concluded, was an amateur. "Need a break?" she asked the jurors. When one of them nodded, she declared a five-minute recess to let everyone use what she called "the facilities." The jurors filed out, taking care as jurors do to look as inscrutable as possible as they did. As everyone stretched, the recess did, too. But within a few minutes the courtroom had reassembled expectantly and everyone was looking up toward the bench.

"Mr. Reilly?" Lambert said.

XXXIV

S lowly and stiffly, Ed Reilly walked to the lectern. He put on those
thick glasses of his, and began speaking in his deep voice, a voice
with a hint of sadness in it. The words were Charles Berry's; the
passions Reilly's own. "Ladies and gentlemen, may it please the Court,"
he began. "You will hear a great deal of testimony in this trial and have
an opportunity to examine many documents, but your ultimate responsibility is to decide one primary issue. Is this document, dated April
14, 1983, truly the will of J. Seward Johnson?

"There are two principal reasons why the six children of Seward
Johnson believe that this document is not his will," he continued.
"First, they believe, and the evidence will show that on April 14, 1983,
Seward Johnson lacked the mental capacity to execute a valid will. He
did not understand who all of his family were, all of those who were
near and dear to him. Nor was he capable of comprehending the very
significance and consequence of signing this document. The other reason is because, as the evidence will show, it was obtained through the
undue influence of two people: Barbara or 'Basia' Johnson and her
lawyer, Nina Zagat. In other words, this document is not a true expression of the intention of Seward Johnson, but rather the intention of
others.

"As you will see, its contents were dictated by someone who hopes
to become one of the richest women in the world. As you will also see,
that woman, Barbara Johnson, was assisted by Nina Zagat who, herself,
will become an instant multimillionaire if this document is admitted
to probate." How the two women twisted Seward Johnson's wishes into
the document before them, he said, "is one of the most extraordinary
stories ever to be heard in this court." Join me in reliving this adventure,
Reilly was telling the jury, but let *me* be your guide.

While Christ hadn't mentioned the childrens' greed, Reilly led off
with their altruism. What persuaded his clients of the will's illegitimacy,
Reilly said, was that it left nothing to Seward's "very life blood": Harbor
Branch. As if that weren't enough, Reilly quickly gave the children a

second charitable purpose, one that they might not really buy but that
he surely did. The case was important not just because it involved a
lot of money, he said, but because of the questions it raised about the
way in which doctors and lawyers deal with the old, the ill, the mentally
impaired. This was not just a tiff in which some rich people were fighting
to become richer; it was something in which everyone had a stake, at
least everyone who would ever grow old or knew someone who would
or had. "Bear these issues in mind when you hear how Nina Zagat
prepared documents for Seward Johnson's signature without even conferring with him before they were prepared," like the April 14 will, he
told them. In drafting it, Reilly charged, Nina "took her instructions
solely from her real client, her real boss: Barbara Johnson."

Reilly briefly described Seward's marriages, and, crediting "none
other than Nina Zagat" as his source, described the "great pride and
pleasure" he had taken in his six children. (In fact, Nina had done
Reilly a great favor; as loyal as he was to them, even for Reilly finding
something praiseworthy to say about each of the Johnsons was a bit of
a strain.) "You will hear of all the ties of affection and pride that bound
Seward to his six children and their families and, in turn, their quiet
love and respect for their father," he continued. "You will hear that it
is those mutual feelings that have brought the children here today.
Some of the children were surprised that their own children—Seward's
grandchildren—did not receive something under his will; some of them
were hurt that they did not receive some token, some memento, of
their father; but the overwhelming motivation of the children is to see
that justice is done to their father's memory, that his dedication to
charity and particularly his dream for Harbor Branch is not violated."

Reilly's Seward, like Christ's, was generally a sympathetic character,
even though Reilly himself had little respect for someone who'd made
so little of his life and wealth. Reilly described the simple life Seward
led before Barbara Piasecka—as usual, Reilly abjured "Basia" and mis-
pronounced "Piasecka"—came along and, "although she spoke virtually
no English, caught Seward's fancy." He related how, nine months before
marrying her, Seward bequeathed Basia nine thousand shares of J&J
stock—a change effectuated, he noted, by "none other than Nina
Zagat." For better or worse, the name lent itself nicely to denunciation,
and Reilly was to utter it repeatedly: *"Nina Zagat." "Nina Zagat." "Nina
Zagat." "Nina Zagat." "Nina Zagat."* With every reference Nina, listening intently, twiddling her thubs, gazing forward stonily, sucking
on one of the candies Arnold Bauman had given her, appeared to
swallow harder and age almost before one's eyes. "That was the first

appearance of Nina Zagat, but she soon became the attorney that Barbara relied upon and, as you will see, the means by which Barbara rewrote Seward's will. As you will also see, Nina Zagat expects to be handsomely rewarded for her services."

If Seward's will of November 12, 1971, had been his last, Reilly said, Basia would still have ended up a wealthy woman. Harbor Branch would have had much of the rest, and, he said, "none of us would be here today." Instead, he went on, Basia solidified her hold over Seward. "Barbara did not physically force Seward to do any specific thing, but you will hear that she accomplished the same result by exerting a psychological influence over him," he said. "She threatened him with abandonment. She threatened him with public humiliation. She threatened him with the most common fears of all elderly and infirm people regardless of their wealth: isolation, loneliness, and embarrassment in front of others.

"When Barbara married Seward, she became Mrs. J. Seward Johnson, and with that dramatic change in status came a dramatic change in her personality or at least in her behavior . . . " Reilly continued, only to be interrupted as Christ rose. Basia's personality, he protested, was not an issue in the case. It was wishful thinking, and both Lambert and Reilly quickly swatted Christ away.

" . . . and if I may continue," Reilly pressed on, as if nothing could now stop him, "this change in Mrs. Johnson's behavior was evidenced by her giving vent to outbursts of temper that became such a regular feature of the way she behaved with virtually everyone, including, most significantly, her husband—whether she was frustrated because Seward lived longer than she had planned, or whether she simply could not control herself, or for whatever reason."

Christ got back on his feet. "I object to that, Your Honor," he mumbled. "I don't think that's proper. This is a summation. This is not what . . . " But Christ's words were like lighter fluid on smoldering charcoal. Up to now, Reilly had been reading undeviatingly off neatly typed white pages. Suddenly, he departed from his printed text and began reading off some deeper, more visceral script. "Your Honor, I am telling the jury the proof that we plan to present," he boomed, in a manner both ferocious and controlled. "It is going to be a bitter pill for some people in this courtroom. I don't feel I should have to sugarcoat it for Mr. Christ or his clients. It is going to be very graphic, explicit, and the jury is entitled to know what it is I now plan to prove, and that's exactly what I am doing. If I may continue . . . "

Lambert issued a mild rebuke and then Reilly resumed, giving no sign of heeding anything he'd just heard. The spectators, whom Christ had lulled into a comfortable, fireside frame of mind, now sat upright, spellbound. Reilly, who'd seemed so mild during depositions, who'd struck the proponents and their lawyers as a mediocrity, had caught fire. He had been transformed.

"It will become apparent to you that the marriage of Seward Johnson and Barbara Piasecka was highly unusual," he went on. "It was not extraordinary simply because he had wealth in an amount that is difficult for most of us even to comprehend, while she was penniless. It was not exceptional simply because he came from a family of social and economic prominence while she had an austere upbringing behind the Iron Curtain. It was not remarkable simply because he was old enough to be her grandfather or because she barely spoke English or because he met her when she was serving as a maid in the house he had lived in with his wife of thirty-two years. What really set their marriage apart, I am sorry to say, is the way in which Barbara Johnson bullied and terrorized her husband.

"You will hear testimony that time and time again Barbara Johnson insulted and demeaned Seward Johnson in public. On countless occasions she called him 'ga-ga,' 'stupid,' 'stupid man,' 'stupid old man,' 'stupid American,' 'senile old fool.' And those were not occasional epithets that happened to slip out in the heat of a marital spat. Those were insults which she hurled at him consistently, frequently, deliberately.

"It is hard to imagine without having witnessed it the verbal abuse that Barbara Johnson leveled at her husband, but you will hear testimony from many who did witness it, including those who were themselves the object of her fury. Her tantrums were sudden and devastating. Sometimes they lasted literally for hours, and she often shrieked in anger for so long that she became hoarse and could barely even talk. When Seward was dying of cancer, she would launch into tirades that were terrifying both to him and to the people who witnessed them. You will hear that when she learned he had ordered a Crockpot so that he could cook oatmeal in his bedroom, she exploded in a rage, seized his cane, and threatened to hit him with it. She screamed insults at him and told him never to do anything like that again without her permission. Seward was pale with fear. He was also eighty-seven years old, and his body was riddled with cancer.

"You will hear that she became completely enraged when Seward was not wearing an overcoat on a cool evening in Manhattan. She screamed at him and her own personal bodyguard and humiliated Seward in such a cruel manner that her bodyguard decided to quit. This, too, happened when Seward was eighty-seven years old, only months before he succumbed to the cancer that even then had metastasized to his bones.

"You will hear that when Seward's children were visiting at the villa in Italy or on an island that he owned in the Bahamas, Barbara would scream at him in front of them. When he expressed an interest in having a barbecue with his family, she came down on him like a ton of bricks. She actually sent him to his room like a mother might do to a boy who has been bad, and he went. At restaurants she would shout at him, calling him 'stupid' and 'ga-ga' so that everyone would look around in embarrassed disbelief. You will also hear that Barbara did not stop short of physically striking Seward even in the last years of his life. On one occasion she and Seward had been talking with a visitor for about half an hour. Out of the blue, Seward turned to the visitor and said, 'Who are you?' With that, Barbara sprung to her feet, struck Seward across the face, and repeatedly called him 'stupid American!' 'Stupid old man!' Abuse of that sort was frequent and flagrant.

"Of course, not every waking hour that Barbara and Seward spent together was punctuated by such outbursts. There may indeed be photographs of Barbara and Seward taken when she was not screaming at him, threatening him, or hitting him. Her public abuse of this frail and gentle old man, however, cannot be erased by a few smiling snapshots. You will see that her most characteristic pose was when she was inflicting terror. And how did Seward Johnson react to this barrage? Seward Johnson tolerated his wife's insults and threats just as a small child would accept the scolding of a mother. He would be embarrassed and humiliated by her abuse, but he would not stick up for himself or fight back. Quite simply, he would withdraw. If Barbara Johnson told Seward Johnson to go to his room, he would go. If Barbara Johnson told Seward Johnson to finish eating his oatmeal, he would finish eating his oatmeal. Barbara's behavior continued throughout the eleven long years she was married to Seward. She did not give him a new lease on life; she taught him a new servitude. If she opened new vistas for him, they were vistas that would have been better left closed. It was not 'a dream,' as characterized by Mr. Christ. It was at times a nightmare."

Reilly ticked off other ways in which, he said, Basia terrorized and isolated her husband: by firing his old associates; by speaking only Polish around him; by threatening to leave him or actually doing so, by ranting and raving. And she abused the old man in another way: by running through his money. "The testimony will also show that Barbara indulged in phenomenal spending binges at Seward's expense," Reilly said. "She amassed a collection of art and antiques, and her tastes became increasingly extravagant. She set world-record prices with many of her purchases and came to be a favorite of the auction houses and art dealers to whom she had given so much business. Some of the items she bought are a desk from Versailles for one and a half million dollars, the highest price ever paid for a single piece of furniture. Also a small chalk drawing by Raphael . . ."

"Objection, Your Honor," Christ said. His reason was unstated but clear: Because the drawing had been purchased after Seward's death, anything about it was inadmissible. But Reilly ignored Christ and continued.

" . . . for almost five million dollars—far and away the highest price ever paid for a drawing by any artist."

"Is this during his lifetime?" Lambert asked.

"Yes, Your Honor," Reilly responded. Christ said nothing, and Reilly resumed (Reilly later said he had "misunderstood" the judge's question). "Barbara acquired artworks on a grander and grander scale, and even when Seward was in the final weeks of his terminal cancer she was busy pouring through auction catalogs. The most significant aspect of Barbara's accumulation of art is that it was virtually all purchased under the name of a company which Seward was required to leave to her under the prenuptial agreement.

"Dwarfing any of Barbara's art purchases, however, was the palatial residence she built to house her collection. This huge mansion, called 'Jasna Polana,' cost more than $20 million to construct, and it is probably the most expensive private residence in the country. Barbara hired and fired scores of workers and craftsmen, many brought over from Europe, to fabricate and install the marble staircases and the wrought-iron gates. She ordered entire exterior stone walls torn down, because she didn't like the color of a few of the stones. The finished product is a vast, cold museum which costs more to run in six months than most families earn in a lifetime. It requires a full-time staff of more than fifty, and utilities alone run more than four hundred thousand dollars a year. All this was very foreign to Seward. He felt lonely and neglected in this huge new mansion. He vastly preferred Florida, where he built a house next to Harbor Branch." But Basia, Reilly said, went South only occasionally and briefly; she preferred going on art-buying binges with Nina Zagat or traveling with Jan Waligura, "a psychiatrist who, like herself, had emigrated from Poland, and with whom she had a very warm relationship." At that a titter spread across the room. So

Reilly's yarn had sex in it, too! The gallery began savoring what sounded like the tasty revelations still to come.

Reilly traced the gradual accretion of Basia's stake, and described how Nina's numbers grew in tandem. Once the cap on executor's fees was removed, Reilly said, Nina stood to become "enormously wealthy. Clearly, it was the reward for all the good work she had done for Barbara," he said. "We shall all listen with interest when Nina Zagat tries to justify this extraordinary arrangement." He reviewed the flurry of last-minute wills, signed amid repeated hospitalizations, blood transfusions, frantic phone calls to priests. He described the confusion the nurses had noted—the non sequiturs, the hallucinations, the illusions of war with Russia, the public defecation—as well as his growing weakness, fatigue, and helplessness. When two of his children and their spouses arrived in April, Reilly related, Seward hadn't even recognized Keith Wold, whom he had known for thirty-seven years; another son-in-law, Marty Richards, heard him hallucinating about Nazi submarines. Yet shortly thereafter, on a day when one nurse described him as "continually confused," he signed his last will, the one Nina Zagat had drawn up in New York at Basia's behest. True, the two Shearman & Sterling lawyers who witnessed the will-signing would say Seward had been competent at the time. So, too, Reilly conceded, would Dr. Fred Schilling. But the lawyers had engaged in mere "social chitchat" with Seward, while the doctor had only examined him briefly and failed to test his mental acuity properly.

Reilly mentioned the payments to Judy Smith and John Peach, both of whom, he noted, were likely to testify for the proponents. He described Basia's bizarre April 14 letter to Seward—a letter, he noted, that Basia "feels free to tear up any time she chooses." He brought up the May 3 trust, the war chest Nina had created to fund a defense of the will—from which, he mistakenly noted, Nina stood to enrich herself still more. Then he touted the nurses who would be his most crucial witnesses. Although they'd come and gone like everyone else in Basia's employ, they had had "a unique opportunity" to witness Seward's physical and mental decline.

Precisely an hour after he'd begun, Reilly wrapped things up. He thanked the jury for listening to him and returned to his seat. Lambert promptly declared a recess. It was one o'clock; Harbor Branch, appropriately enough, would make its own largely anticlimactic statement after lunch.

In the meantime the jury, along with everyone else, could ponder how much Reilly had accomplished. In strong, forceful rhetoric imbued with his own clear conviction, he had laid out his case. Like Forger before him, he had defined the issues—for the jury, for the judge, for the public. Not surprisingly, it was Reilly's more compelling, better-articulated version of reality that led the newspaper stories the next day. "TALE OF RAGES TO RICHES: JOHNSON JURY TOLD WIDOW WAS SHREW," the *Daily News* reported. "WIFE BULLIED DYING JOHNSON OUT OF FORTUNE," declared the *New York Post*. Both *The Wall Street Journal* and *The New York Times* (which described Reilly's Basia as "a vicious, screaming harpy") also gave the man from Milbank top billing.

Out of oatmeal and overcoats and aborted barbecues, Reilly had concocted a grand conspiracy. He had turned Basia's temper tantrums and profligacy and Nina's casualness and naïveté into indictable offenses. He had also elevated his case into a cause. All along, Reilly had urged the associates writing briefs in the case to make it sound like more than "a pissing contest"; now, a selfish grab for money had been transmuted into a class-action suit on behalf of old people everywhere, a crusade to clean up two sullied professions. There was no sense that Reilly, like Forger, was doing all of this cynically. Reilly actually believed what he was saying. Paradoxically, it was his very gullibility that made him so credible.

In some instances—his suggestion that Basia hadn't offered her step-children any mementos of their father, for instance, or that her physical abuse of Seward was "frequent" and "flagrant"—Reilly had skirted the truth. This was, perhaps, simply good advocacy. But in one instance he crossed the line: his clear suggestion that Basia and Waligura had been lovers. Reilly knew Waligura was gay. But he was a closeted gay, which meant he could rebut the charge only at devastating cost to himself. But for Reilly in battle the distinction between belief and strategem blurred: To need was to believe. Sure, Waligura was gay, but maybe he was bisexual; if not, Reilly reasoned, he was so beholden to Basia—the research money and all—that he'd surely have serviced her sexually if she so desired. Others on his team, less overwrought, were more objective. "Of course we knew they weren't involved; he was a fag," another Milbank lawyer said laughingly in the corridor shortly after Reilly's opening.

As if laying out his case weren't enough, Reilly had accomplished one more feat: He had made his clients feel good about themselves. Sitting in the courtroom, the Johnson children were, in a sense, like their father lying on his hospital bed near the end of his life, an intravenous line hooked into his gnarled octogenarian arm. As Reilly uttered his kind words about Junior and Mary Lea and the rest, it was as though vital psychological nutrients were coursing into their anemic egos. When it was over, Junior stood up and greeted Reilly heartily. "It was beautiful!" he exclaimed to Forger. "He just kept hitting and hitting." Reilly strode triumphantly out into the corridor. His clients were paying him handsomely for his services, but two things he knew: One, he was giving them good value for their money; and two, the best was yet to come.

PART THREE

THE TRIAL

XXXV

N ina Zagat was outwardly placid on the afternoon of February 27, when she placed her left hand atop Harvey Corn's bar mitzvah Bible and was sworn in as the first witness in the Johnson case. It was the calm, however, of someone benumbed. Her head was saturated not only with key facts, figures, and dates from the Seward Johnson era, but tips from Christ, Osgood, Bauman, Polak, Rogers, and Zirinis about how to be a better witness than she really was. Now, there were even refinements to Werner Polak's Fourteen Commandments; when asked a question, one of them went, look straight at your interrogator, then swivel your chair around and address the jury, preferably smiling as you do. Nina had not wanted to be the keynote witness in her own case. Even without Reilly certain to try to dismember her and Lambert glowering at her before she'd said a syl- lable—perhaps, Nina sensed, the judge had not forgiven her for ignoring her admonition about settling the case—she knew her shortcomings as a public speaker. Ford should have been the one to get things under way, but he had failed her. Basia, too, could have been called; that was what Reilly had been expecting, not knowing that S&C was ag- onizing over whether to risk calling her at all. It was just as Delahunty had said: Nina *was* their case. By default, she was batting leadoff and cleanup at the same time. "The Eight Million Dollar Associate," as the *American Lawyer* christened her, now had to earn her keep.

Nina sounded programmed even as she recalled her high school days on Long Island, smiling nervously, twiddling her thumbs, fighting off a dry mouth with frequent gulps of water. Her voice was thin and barely audible, prompting Reilly, whose hearing had never quite recovered from the Marine Corps rifle range, to lean forward and cup his ear. Repeatedly, Lambert asked her to speak up. "Just pretend you're yelling at your children," she suggested. Christ managed to elicit a few more biographical details, but Reilly successfully objected when he asked Nina to explain the vocabulary of the trial: terms like "will" and "trust" and "codicil." It was a role Lambert had let her friend Bernie Greene play

401

only a few weeks earlier, in the Kimmelman case, but that role she now decreed, lay within "the province of the Court." Then, when Christ tried to introduce the April 14 will into evidence, Reilly derailed things altogether, convincing Lambert that the attesting witnesses first had to do their attesting. It was now five o'clock, and court adjourned. Christ had gotten off to a peculiar, disconcerting start.

Jack D. "Jay" Gunther, Jr., Phillips Exeter '59, Princeton '63, Columbia Law School '67, had spent his entire legal career in Shearman & Sterling's trusts and estates department, and would probably spend the rest of it there, too, marking at least one anniversary of his arrival there by hanging a black crepe bow from his office door. Gunther was a precise man in his mid-forties, whose preppy surface accentuated his outrageousness. He was the type to file his fingernails during departmental meetings, to ride Kitty Carlisle Hart around town on his motorcycle, to wear LaCoste shirts with suspenders to work on hot summer days. His office, a few doors down from Nina's, was as meticulously tidy as hers was chaotic: Among the few gewgaws was a can of genuine Bon Vivant vichyssoise. On the wall was a poster-sized picture of himself playing tennis, taken before he'd stopped dyeing his prematurely gray hair. Nearby was a photograph of his close friend Ellen McCloy, wife of the famous Milbank partner, whom he visited regularly in a nursing home. Knowing of that tie, some of Gunther's colleagues urged him to complain to her husband about Forger's shabby affidavit. But the gentlemanly Gunther thought it might upset the old man, and he refused. There were some things even more important than victory, and decency was one of them.

Gunther spent his off-hours either exercising or hanging around his Park Avenue bachelor's pad, cooking meals for friends, baking pound cake, doing needlepoint. When he wasn't home, he was most likely swimming, jogging, playing tennis, ballroom dancing, or hobnobbing at one of his clubs—the Racquet or the Links or the Brook in the city, the Lawrence Beach or the Rockaway Hunt Club on the Island. Gunther loved to gossip—he and Nina were forever whispering to one another— and for a while had moonlighted as "man about town" for a New York television station. Years afterward he continued to pay his annual dues to the Screen Actors Guild.

The same compulsive orderliness that marked Gunther's personal life had earned for him the reputation as Shearman & Sterling's premier testamentary draftsman, the lawyer of choice to make the complicated comprehensible. He'd written hundreds of wills and codicils, usually while standing at the lecternlike desk he used to compensate for a childhood case of polio. But Gunther's world was not only the genteel world of the wealthy's wills, but the sedate world in which those wills worked. Never before had he had to soil himself in a will contest. Before he took the stand on February 28, he'd rarely set foot in a courtroom, and never, ever, to testify, let alone on such short notice; he'd been told he would not be called for several days, but Nina's cameo appearance changed all that. Sitting in the witness box in his blue suit, red tie, and buttoned-down Oxford, he seemed particularly vulnerable.

Questioned by Christ, Gunther traced his relationship with Seward Johnson from their first encounter in the early 1970s until his last visit in April 1983. He recalled how the group gathered that last afternoon, and how Seward, after substituting "April" for "March," signed the document, smiling as he did. The court officer reached into a dark brown folding envelope and pulled out a sheaf of papers, labeled "Proponents' #1 for Identification," and handed it to the witness. Whole trees had been turned into photocopies of this exhibit; sometimes, in the Xerox age, it is easy to forget that original documents, with signatures that actually smudge when moistened, do exist. Christ asked Gunther if he could identify the document. "Yes," Gunther replied. "This document is the last will and testament which Mr. Johnson signed on April 14, 1983." Printed on heavy, ivory-colored bond, festooned with red satin ribbons, a blob of sealing wax on the back page, Seward's will looked unassailable, at least physically. Twice more, Christ tried to introduce it into evidence, only to have Reilly object twice more: First because Christ had forgotten to ask Gunther whether Seward had been of sound mind when he signed it, second because the other attesting witness had yet to be heard. Christ then yielded the floor to Reilly. One had to wonder how anyone having such trouble getting a will admitted into evidence could ever get it admitted into probate.

Reilly walked to the lectern. "Good morning, Mr. Gunther," he said. "My name is Edward Reilly. I'd like to ask you a few questions." In fact, he had dozens of them, more than a day's worth in all. His mission was to show that Gunther was either too irresponsible or dishonest or blind to be believed. And if that didn't work, he could at least bloody him up. For one couldn't help but sense that along with the contempt Reilly felt for Gunther as an adversary, he also considered him less of a real man than he. It was hard to imagine more of a mismatch, physically, temperamentally, and verbally. To compound matters, S&C had not prepared Gunther well, and apart from dispatching the court officer to fetch him more water, Christ's witness-protection program was minimal. A false fire alarm that briefly halted the proceedings was more helpful to Gunther than anything Christ did for him.

Gunther fended off Reilly's suggestions that the old man had actually thought it was April 4 rather than the 14 and that someone else had inserted the *1*, or that Seward hadn't known what month it was. But he was tripped up when Reilly asked him about the extra loop in "Aprul." Seward's hand had the predictable tics and tremors of old age; the misspelling would have been harmless had Gunther not insisted it wasn't there. "I think it's just—it's a question of how you read it," he said meekly.

"How do *you* read it?" Reilly snapped.

"A-P-R-I-L."

"Is that the way you make an *i*, with two little marks, like a *u*? Is that the way you make an *i*, Mr. Gunther?"

Reilly suggested Gunther was second-rate for failing to make partner or write any scholarly articles. Then he depicted him as a high-priced hack by noting that though Gunther had drafted the clause removing the cap on Nina's fees, he'd never asked Seward about it. "Did you feel it would be in the best interest of your client, or in the best interest of Nina Zagat, to remove that limitation?" Reilly snarled. "It was in the best interests of my client because that's what he wanted to do," Gunther replied quietly. "You think it was in the best interests of your client to raise executors' commissions from two million to twenty-four million?" Reilly asked in mock disbelief.

Next, Reilly asked Gunther whether he'd done anything, apart from chitchatting with the man, to ascertain Seward's mental condition on April 14. Had he talked to the nurses or to Schilling? Had he asked him how many quarters there are in a dollar or to name the United States senators from New York? Of course, neither Gunther nor any attesting witness was obliged to do any such thing, just as Seward need not have identified Alfonse D'Amato to have had testamentary capacity when Shoemaker had asked Gunther the same question during his deposition, the referee rebuked him. "In Mr. Johnson's case, I had known him for twelve years and he acted as normal on April 14 as he always had and as normal as anyone in this courtroom," Gunther replied.

Reilly established that Gunther had taken no notes of the will-signing ceremony. This might not have mattered had Gunther's memory or powers of observation been keen. Instead, his barren, lifeless recollections made Seward sound like a robot, an impression Reilly hammered in by asking Gunther what he had already asked various nurses: whether he'd seen Seward do anything that day that a six-year-old child could not have done. "Isn't it a fact that you didn't take any notes because there simply was nothing to record . . . " he asked.

"Absolutely not!" Gunther blurted out.

" . . . and that Mr. Johnson simply nodded . . . and nodded . . . and nodded?" he continued, sounding as if he was offering his own, very different recollections of the afternoon.

"Absolutely not!" Gunther repeated.

"Can you tell us why you didn't take notes of this conversation?"

"I didn't think it was necessary," Gunther said pathetically. He had conceded nothing of importance, but seemed vanquished anyway.

Many years earlier, perhaps during his happier "man about town" phase, Gunther had been invited to Jennifer Johnson's debut. But when a bloodied Gunther limped off the stand, it was Jennifer who crowed the loudest. "You made dogmeat out of him!" she gushed to Reilly. Gunther, too, knew that something had gone desperately wrong. "It's the only time in my life I've told the truth and nobody believed me," he lamented.

The second attesting witness, James Hoch (pronounced HOKE), performed more admirably. He seemed more bemused than bullied by Reilly, dispatching his questions with contemptuous courtesy, cockily appending a "Mr. Reilly" to thirty-five of his answers. He had the good judgment, rare for a lawyer, to admit to what he didn't know, like the legal significance of Basia's increasingly famous April 14 letter. ("Mr. Reilly, I have no idea what this document does," he said. "That's my legal opinion, or lack thereof.") Standing his ground, maintaining his insouciance, he made the fire-breathing Reilly look overwrought and a bit silly. Wouldn't he have been surer of Seward's mental capacity had he discussed something like American foreign policy with him? "No, Mr. Reilly," Hoch replied, "I don't feel that having an opinion on foreign policy is necessarily a requirement to being able to sign a will." What if he'd just seen him play a game of chess, or watched him do a *New York Times* crossword puzzle? "Mr. Reilly, I don't think that watching someone do a *New York Times* crossword puzzle would add much more to the degree of certainty that I had." Hoch, too, hadn't taken notes, but was candid enough to admit he should have. "Mr. Reilly, if I had known that I was going to be sitting in this courtroom three years hence, I might have taken copious notes to help withstand this," he said. On the questions of capacity and undue influence, Hoch was unequivocal. "He was under no constraint," he testified. "He certainly had the requisite capacity to sign a will. His conduct was quite rational." With that, the April 14 will was at last admitted into evidence, and on the following Monday, March 3, Nina tried once more to tell her story.

But as presented, it was a tale without any discernible plot. Christ did not have Nina articulate any grand testamentary themes, themes jurors could remember when their minds grew numb with dates and numbers and details. Instead, he immediately escorted her back to her first days with the Johnsons, thrusting the court into a quagmire of trivia, like where the will of August 3, 1973, had been signed (the office of one Mr. Drake). Nina eventually drew the main outlines of the proponents' case: the growing bequests to Basia; the large transfers to Harbor Branch, which ceased once Seward considered it self-sustaining; the consistent disinheritance of the children. But only the late, lamented Princey could have sniffed out these themes in the fog of esoterica and legalese that descended over the court. Even Nina occasionally lost track of precisely where Christ was headed, a problem that might have been averted if, as she had requested beforehand, Christ had given her an outline of his examination.

And things only got worse. It was hard to say which was duller, Christ's questions or Nina's answers. The first were methodically read off a prepared script in a lifeless monotone; the second sounded rehearsed and defensive even under friendly fire. Christ led Nina through twelve years of testamentary history, and his examination seemed to last nearly that long. Reading his questions through half-moon glasses, checking them off one by one, Christ was taking inventory, not testimony. As for Nina, her answers sounded compulsively lawyerlike, spoken with all the spontaneity of a schoolgirl in a spelling bee. Things were slowed down still further by Reilly's repeated objections. Many were meritorious; others, however, stemmed from Lambert's unusually restrictive reading of the hearsay rule. Because of it, Nina's testimony on several key topics—the background of Basia's April 14 letter; Junior's pleas to Seward for preferential testamentary treatment; Junior's report to her of "noises in the underbrush" about a will contest—was either omitted, eviscerated, or shredded to the point of unintelligibility. Weeks later, when one of Harbor Branch's witnesses sought to describe an argument between Basia and Seward and she evidently wanted to listen in, Lambert reversed herself. Immediately, S&C demanded to introduce everything that had previously been excluded, or, if that was ineffective, to have her declare a mistrial. "Stop having pipe dreams!"

Lambert, who maintained any harm was minimal, scolded them in chambers. "Nobody is going to have any mistrials in this case." Reilly, predictably enough, agreed. "The whole thing is a blown-up, exaggerated attempt to create an image of prejudice which I think is very unfair," he said. That was untrue. Whether one believed Nina Zagat or not, she never got to tell her story.

At least as seriously, Lambert blocked all references to the amount of money Seward had already given his children. When Christ tried to tell the jury that the six trusts Seward had set up for them were collectively worth $430 million—the firm had prepared elaborate charts illustrating the point—Reilly made the extraordinary claim that such information was irrelevant. More extraordinarily, Lambert sustained him, and with a healthy helping of sarcasm. These trusts, for heaven's sake, dated back to 1944. "We will start with 1928!" she cackled, referring to the date of Seward's first will. "Let me tell the jury that they're going to be here for two years, because we are going back to 1929!" The colloquy moved to Lambert's chambers, where Reilly argued that because the children wanted nothing for themselves, how much they already had was immaterial. Christ countered that the children were hiding "behind Harbor Branch's skirts," and that keeping out the present value of the trusts would leave the jury with "a very lopsided view" of Seward's estate plan. Lambert ultimately decided to split the baby, but with S&C getting the toes and Milbank everything else. She would let the 1944 trusts themselves into evidence, but permit no discussion about what they'd ballooned into. The jury, then, could learn that forty years earlier, Seward had given each of his children $476,000 in Johnson & Johnson stock, but not that each of those chunks, if left intact, would have been worth $110 million now.

On March 6, 1986, Christ and Nina finally reached April 14, 1983. To a hushed courtroom, with only the sound of traffic on the Brooklyn Bridge in the background, Nina recalled the moment she'd entered Seward's bedroom to discuss his will. There was a ripple of knowing laughter when she recalled Seward's reaction to her suggestion that he write Basia a letter urging her to consider Harbor Branch in her own will: "No. We will just end up with a lot of lawyers." But Lambert left little time to savor the irony. All afternoon, she had been smoldering. Her beef was ostensibly over the testimony's torpid pace—part of a deliberate effort, she believed, to wear down jury and judge alike. More generally, though, she seemed offended by Nina Zagat. Not just by what she said, mind you, or by how she said it, but by Nina's very essence. Those who knew Lambert well would have recognized what was happening, and just about on schedule: She had already sized things up and, as was her wont, was taking sides. In the privacy of her chambers she began calling Basia and Nina "the dolls." It was her way of saying that these two women might think they were hot stuff, but she knew better. Lambert had not seen all that much of Basia yet, but she was on to Nina. Nina was always fidgeting with her hands, a sure sign of untrustworthiness. Privately, she told one Milbank lawyer that Nina would be lucky to keep her law license once the case was over. Lambert suspected something else, too: that Nina hadn't only been Seward's lawyer, but lover. "Nina Zagat came and took over this guy like Grant took Richmond," she later said. Now, just as Nina closed in on the most crucial portion of her story, Lambert cut her off as Grant choked Vicksburg. "I am going to take a ten-minute recess, and I would suggest that the jurors call their homes and tell them that we are going to be late tonight!" she suddenly announced. "We are going to work tonight until we finish at least the direct with this witness."

"Fine, Your Honor," Christ said wanly.

" . . . because I think that we have had this witness on the stand long enough, and if it takes until midnight, we will work until midnight. So the lawyers please call your homes, jurors please call your homes, and tell them not to expect you until you get there." She then ostentatiously instructed a court officer to arrange rides home for the jurors.

Christ objected tepidly. "Your Honor, if I might, we will go as long as the Court directs, but I do except to the possibility of pushing the witness beyond a point where she may not be able to continue, Your Honor," he said.

"Mr. Christ, don't let me make speeches in front of the jury!" said the judge, flaunting for all the world to see what she considered her great restraint. "Wait until the jury leaves, and then I will tell you why I'm doing this!"

The tirade then shifted into her chambers. "Tonight, we are working until you finish your direct!" she told Christ. "I don't care how long it takes. It may be four in the morning. I am a very hearty soul. I need very little sleep."

"Your Honor, we have approached the critical day with respect to the will offered for probate," Osgood pleaded.

" . . . and we are going to do it tonight," the judge reiterated. "You had all day to know you were getting to this. Let me tell you something. All day it has been very slow. The words come out of Mrs. Zagat's mouth as if she didn't go past elementary school. She . . . speaks . . . at . . . this . . . rate. And then there are pauses and there are pauses between the questions and it really has gotten to the point at which it begins to give an appearance of stretching this out."

As the Milbank lawyers watched, silently and delightedly, the S&C lawyers begged for mercy. To force the jurors to miss dinner and get home late and then blame it on the witness would be highly prejudicial, Osgood argued. Christ voiced some concern about Nina's stamina. "I thought it was *Mrs. Johnson* who didn't have the stamina!" Lambert acidly replied. "Now, we have *a lawyer* who doesn't have stamina?"

"Your Honor, all I can . . . " Christ began.

"How old is she? Forty-six?"

"I don't remember."

"A lot younger than I am!"

"She might not have your strength, Your Honor," Christ said.

Court resumed and adjourned at six, as it invariably did whenever Lambert made such threats. Christ concluded his questioning shortly after court resumed the following day.

But Nina's real ordeal had yet to start. Throughout her direct examination, as six or seven other lawyers listened inertly, Reilly was hunched over his legal pad, furiously scribbling questions for his cross-examination.

XXXVI

E ven before Reilly asked Nina his first question, March 7 was a
red-letter day for his clients. The judge hearing Basia's case
against Junior in New Jersey cleared him of any liability for the
foundation's stock losses, and excoriated Basia for filing the lawsuit in
bad faith. Lambert denied Milbank's motion to allow the opinion into
evidence. But even if the jury couldn't consider it, Lambert could, and
did. It further confirmed her suspicion that Basia and Nina could not
be believed.

Reilly looked up toward the bench. "May I proceed, Your Honor?"
he asked decorously. "You may inquire," she responded in kind. He
took a final sip of water, walked up to the lectern, slowly opened up a
black binder and yellow legal pad, and looked warily at Zagat. Then
he pounced.

"Mrs. Zagat, could you tell us who the man is who is seated next to
Barbara Johnson?"

Like everyone else, Nina was startled by the question, and she fumbled around for the name of Basia's publicist, who had come to watch
the first few days of testimony. "His name is Jack Raymond," she finally
replied.

"What is his business?" Reilly boomed.

The jury never got an answer to the question, but that didn't much
matter; merely by posing the question, Reilly had impressed upon them
that something ominous was afoot. At the bench, he made the same
point more explicitly. Raymond was "a public-relations representative,"
he told the judge, as if he were describing a Communist spy or child
molester. In fact, Raymond symbolized Basia's largely futile attempt to
shape public attitudes toward her and her cause.

Press coverage was predictably intense in a case replete with the
embarrassments of riches—a case that, as one anchorperson put it,
"makes *Dallas* look like *Romper Room.*" Throughout it all, though, Basia
remained muzzled. Raymond urged that she be allowed to give a press
conference, so that the world could warm up to her, but the reflexively

410

press-averse S&C lawyers nixed the idea. Instead, Raymond unhappily schooled Basia and Nina in the fine art of stonewalling: to remain expressionless and keep on walking when reporters approached them, for example, or leave the courthouse only when there was a waiting limousine into which they could duck. He struggled mightily to erase Basia's humble history from the reportage, but the phrase "former chambermaid" crept into most accounts—usually condescendingly, though in the case of Newsday's Murray Kempton, describing her demotion from cook to domestic at Oldwick, admiringly. ("No new arrival's initial failure was ever more fortunate," he wrote, "for she fascinated Johnson's 76-year-old but still unclouded gaze with her feather duster as she never could have with her saucepan.") Eventually, Raymond drafted a statement for Basia to parrot the next time her background arose. "Since when is it a bad thing to be a maid and work hard?" she was to say.

By contrast, Junior seemed to open his mouth like a goldfish whenever a microphone or notebook was thrust beneath it. He lamented to Alex Michelini of the Daily News, for instance, that large legal fees had forced him to sell the family boat and lay off thirty-five employees at his atelier. At one point Junior charged Michelini with bias, an accusation that so irked Michelini that he complained to Reilly. "I know the fucker never graduated from college, but can't he read?" Michelini asked.

Lambert did not seem perturbed by the gossipy tone of the evening news broadcasts. What really agitated her was a column by Jimmy Breslin, which appeared during Nina's direct examination. Breslin had little use for the trial—which, he wrote, showed "more about the contemptuous attitudes of the nation's rich than perhaps anything the public has seen since the 1920's"—or the players, as he made clear when a reporter uttered to him that Fitzgeraldian cliché about how different the wealthy really were. "Yeah," Breslin spat back, one-upping Hemingway. "They're all scum!" The real story of the case, he quickly determined, wasn't in Nina's turgid testimony but on First Avenue and Tenth Street, where Juror Number 4, José Santana, swept curbs and cleaned catch basins when he wasn't divvying up $400 million fortunes.

Breslin informed Santana's fellow sanitation men that their buddy was a juror in the Johnson trial, then gave them his take on the case: There were these six "children," who were actually much older than children but who had made so little of their lives that everyone called them that. One had had a husband who wanted her to have sex with other men as he watched, and some sons who once upon a time injected the family dog with heroin. There were the lawyers, who were as greedy and corrupt and parasitic as their clients. There was old man Seward, the Band-Aid heir, and his wife of eleven and a half years, the former maid with "a thin mouth and high cheekbones," who smiled a lot and pretended she lived in Cracow whenever you asked her something. "She put up eleven years with this old bum, she should get the money," one street cleaner said. "LET THE MAID CLEAN UP, SAY THE SANITMEN," Breslin's subsequent article declared.

The day that it appeared, an irate Lambert called the column "a disgrace" and "an absolute attempt to influence the jury." Somehow, she had come to see Breslin as S&C's stooge, manipulated into touting Basia's cause. Reilly stoked her suspicions by claiming Osgood had fomented such stories by sending reporters his "despicable" care packages of clippings, whose "seamier parts" were already "marked with yellow crayon or yellow pen." Now, back in court, as he prepared to question Nina, Reilly offered up Jack Raymond as another culprit. "I believe he's responsible for a lot of things that are of concern to the Court and the parties," he told Lambert at the bench. He neglected to mention that the children themselves had just retained John Scanlon, a prominent New York publicist. Scanlon, a cumulus cloud of a character with his white beard, curly white hair, and ample belly, was a conspicuous presence in court, until delegating the account to an underling.

"All honorable lawyers understand that the one who is called upon to draw a will is the agent and advisor of the testator and of him only," a judge once wrote. "And if one so called intentionally mislead[s] the feeble or pervert[s] the intention of his client, no terms are too severe for his baseness." That neatly summarized Reilly's take on Nina Zagat. He now had to make the jury think similarly.

He began his inquisition not with April 14 but May 3, the date Seward had approved the "anchor to windward" trust Nina set up to tide Basia over in the event of a will contest. Why hadn't she called Seward before setting it up and carting it to Florida? Was it because she knew he could no longer even hold a telephone up to his ear? Didn't she have any ethical qualms about naming herself trustee? Wasn't she familiar with the Code of Professional Responsibility? How long had she been a lawyer, anyway? Nina scraped together answers, but her meek responses, however meritorious, were invariably far less memorable than the questions.

Continuing his oblique attack on Nina's credibility, Reilly introduced the minutes of various shareholders' and directors' "meetings" Nina had conducted on May 3 for the Johnsons' holding corporations. Between 9:30 and 11:50 that morning there'd supposedly been ten of them, concerning art, real estate, and charities. The minutes faithfully followed Robert's Rules of Order, down to phrases like "the chairman stated that the first order of business was the election of directors", each had been dutifully signed by Nina Zagat. Unfortunately, none had really taken place, at least with all the formalities described. Perhaps, as Nina's defenders said afterward, this is the way meetings of closely held corporations are always reported, but once again, this was something jurors wouldn't know; to them, the image of the pajama-clad and cancer-ridden Seward gaveling a series of sessions to order from his sickbed was too ludicrous to be believed, and anyone attesting to them was a liar.

Much of what Nina had done—drafting instruments in advance, taking calls and, at times, instructions, from a testator's spouse, flying to distant places at a moment's notice—was standard lawyerly operating procedure. But the combination of Reilly's questions, laced with outrage and incredulity, Lambert's own hostility, and Nina's awkward and overly literal answers made whatever she had done seem conspiratorial, culpable. (At one point Reilly asked whether she had drawn a check on Seward's account, payable to her own firm. "Payable to *Shearman and Sterling,*" she corrected him. Why, he asked exasperatedly, couldn't she have just said "yes" or "no"? "Because 'your own firm' can mean a lot of different things, and if 'your own firm' means that I own the firm, no, I don't," she replied.)

Reilly turned next to Basia's April 14 "letter" to Seward. Three years after it had been written, no one yet knew how to describe it—whether it was just good, clean lawyerly fun, like those certificates printed on foolscap and loaded with legalisms handed out at testimonials; or a binding contract; or a codicil. Asked for her explanation, Nina hadn't the nerve to call it what it was: her friend's misguided, grandiloquent, clumsy attempt to express herself. Instead, she took the heat, describing it as Basia's way of "expressing an enormous amount of love to her husband and to Harbor Branch."

"You are saying *this* is an expression of 'an enormous amount of love'?" Reilly asked ridiculingly.

"That is correct," Nina replied.

"When she refers in fairly technical language to provisions of the will and then says, 'I hearby agree not to exercise a limited testamentary power of appointment,' you consider this an *expression of love?*"

"It certainly was. I was there."

"Signed by her and acknowledged by him?"

"That's right."

"And witnessed by two lawyers in your firm, and you are calling this a love note?"

As Nina's back rose, Reilly, clasping his glasses behind him and peering at her directly, pressed forward.

"If this was an expression of Mrs. Johnson's 'enormous love,' or however you phrased it, for Harbor Branch, why did she need two lawyers to draft it for her?" he asked sarcastically.

"She didn't need two lawyers to draft it for her, I guess," Nina replied.

"Then why did two lawyers do it?"

"That's just the way it happened."

"Why did you sign this document as a witness?" he asked.

"Because Mrs. Johnson asked me to," Nina replied. What Nina said was correct, but her choice of words wasn't wise.

"And-if-Mrs.-Johnson-asked-you-to-do-it, then-Nina-Zagat-does-it, is that right?" Reilly asked, his voice becoming louder and more mechanical as he went along.

"No," Nina replied.

When Reilly finally reached the subject of Seward's will, it was once more Nina's credibility rather than Seward's capacity he probed. He focused on her habit of dealing with Basia rather than Seward, of flying wills down to Florida in finished form, complete with ribbon and seal. "Your testimony, Mrs. Zagat, is that if Mr. Johnson for any reason had decided, 'No, I am not going to sign this,' then you and Mr. Gunther and Mr. Hoch would have just turned around and gone back to New York?" Reilly asked her. Nina insisted that she would.

"Isn't it really the fact, Mrs. Zagat, that you knew, because Mrs. Johnson had dictated the terms of this will to you, that Mr. Johnson was definitely going to sign it and there was no way that he would decline to sign it?"

"No."

"It is a fact, isn't it, that he did sign it as presented to him without making a single change in this so-called draft?" Yes, Nina said. "Did the thought ever enter your mind, Mrs. Zagat, that perhaps Mr. Johnson would want to make some change other than what was communicated to you by Mrs. Johnson?"

"Yes."

"Or that he might not want to make any change at all?"

"No."

"You were satisfied that if you got it from Mrs. Johnson, then it must be Mr. Johnson's intention, is that your testimony?"

"No."

"Then why didn't you call Mr. Johnson to be sure of it?"

"Because I felt it was something that I should discuss with him in person."

Reilly was not done yet with this line of questioning. Why, he asked, hadn't Nina just written Seward a letter with a proposed draft, and solicited his comments? Nina replied that he'd already said what he wanted, and that he wanted her down pronto. "Isn't it also true, Mrs. Zagat, that the message you got from Mrs. Johnson on the eleventh was that Mr. Johnson's death was imminent and that Mrs. Johnson wanted the new will signed before he died?" Again, Reilly sounded as if he, too, had been in Fort Pierce that day and was refreshing Nina's faulty recollection.

"Ab-so-*lute*-ly not," she snapped back.

With a sadistic flourish Reilly forced Nina to elaborate upon the candy-coated disinheritance clause she had inserted into the last couple of wills. Once more she had to go through the humiliation of describing just how proud Seward had been of his children. Then Reilly turned to the shaky state of Seward's health, a topic Christ had failed to address either in his opening statement or his direct examination of Nina.

"Weren't you aware on April 14, 1983, that Mr. Johnson was a terminal-cancer patient?" Reilly asked. Christ, attempting to throw Nina a lifeline, objected that the question was imprecise. "We are all terminal," he said lamely.

"Let me put it this way, Mrs. Zagat," Reilly went on. "Didn't you know that on April 14, 1983, Mr. Johnson was dying of cancer, and it was only a question of how soon he would actually die?"

Nina, who always seemed ill at ease discussing Seward's illness, once more equivocated. "I wouldn't say it that way," she replied. "If you can let me just . . . "

"No, I am asking it this way," he said. "Is your answer to that 'No'?"

"I can't answer it that way," Nina said forlornly.

Nina admitted that prior to April 14 she had never asked Schilling or any of the nurses about Seward's medical condition. She wasn't even sure she had known that Basia had once summoned a priest. If Seward were really so "wonderful"—that was the word she used in her deposition—why was she preparing his obituary on February 7? Reilly then pilloried Nina for the nearly $12 million in loans she'd arranged in Seward's final months, most of which went for Basia's art purchases.

Wasn't this an extraordinary amount to spend in so short a time? Nina's response was characteristic: "What do you mean by 'extraordinary'?" she asked. Riffling through receipts, Reilly showed the jury where the money had gone: $2,203,185.19 to Sotheby's; $935,000 for a Louis XIV bureau; $550,000 for a Zurbarán Saint Sebastian; $440,000 for some candelabras and rafraîchissoirs; $24,200 for a George III five-piece silver tea service; nearly £10,000 for some ivory buttons and a seventeenth-century gold chain from Christie's. The purchases had little legal significance, but they sure were alienating. Reilly seemed especially curious about this last item. "This was jewelry purchased by Mrs. Johnson?" he asked. "Jewelry purchased by R.E.I. Company," Nina, ever the hypertechnocrat replied, listing the name of one of the Johnsons' holding companies.

"To be worn by whom?" he asked.

"I don't know."

"You didn't wear them as vice president of R.E.I. Company, did you?" he asked sarcastically. Nina said that she had not.

Reilly plowed through the proponents' paper trail, which was liberally strewn with examples of bad judgment or self-dealing—for instance, bills prepared by Nina Zagat and paid by Nina Zagat for services rendered by Nina Zagat. Having elicited from her that Seward's shaky signature on one document hadn't given Nina any pause, he showed that the same scrawl raised doubts among Citibank officials. He also showed how, though Seward had supposedly authorized her to transfer $3.76 million to Basia's account on May 3, Nina hadn't done so until May 20, a point at which even Seward's own doctors were no longer sure of his competence. He introduced Exhibit 78, documenting a seemingly innocuous transfer from Citibank to Seward of a mere $180,000 on May 23, 1983. Perhaps, as Christ insisted, it was routine paper shuffling. But as Reilly quickly reminded the jury, the timing was anything but routine. "Mrs. Zagat," he asked, "if Mr. Johnson died at four-forty A.M., how could Citibank have loaned him one hundred and eighty thousand dollars later in the day?"

Next, in a long and tortuous series of questions, an increasingly exasperated Reilly pressed Nina to explain why she'd bowed out in Hoch's favor as one of the attesting witnesses for Seward's last two wills. With Seward having expressed concerns about a will contest, Nina replied, she and her colleagues thought it better, for a couple of reasons, to have someone else serve in that capacity. One was that since anyone weighing a will contest could only question the witnesses to that will, Nina would be off-limits to the children unless they filed formal objections. What was the other reason? Reilly asked. Wasn't it because someone at Shearman & Sterling had decided it was improper for a person with so large a financial interest in a will to witness it? No, Nina said. While it was entirely lawful for an executor to serve as a witness, it was thought more prudent here that she not. But why, if the law didn't require it, was it more prudent? Reilly asked. Why? Why? Why?

For three days now, Reilly had assaulted Nina's honesty, intelligence, independence, and competence. Nina had kept her composure, but even that hadn't helped, since her peculiar brand of stoicism made it look as though even she believed she'd done something wrong. When Reilly wasn't tormenting her, Lambert was. Or Basia was. Or Bauman was. Or her husband, horrified by the direction the case had taken but banned from court since he might yet be called as a witness, was. Finally, when Reilly pressed her to explain the substitution, she could contain herself no longer. "Because," she suddenly exclaimed, "there are people like you, who will turn anything around!"

In most settings it would have been a perfectly normal response for anyone under siege. But a courtroom is not a normal setting. Amid all its artificiality, in language and decorum and dress, such outbursts are almost eerie. Courtroom etiquette allows lawyers to hector and harass, but not for witnesses to hector back, particularly witnesses under attack from counsel's table and the bench simultaneously. The courtroom momentarily lost its collective breath as everyone awaited Reilly's, and Lambert's, response. Reilly wisely decided to leave well enough alone for a few seconds; Nina had transformed him from a zealot to a martyr and, besides, he could count on the judge to defend him. With him, at least, she fully earned the title of "surrogate."

"Your Honor, I was going to ask that the answer be stricken, but I think it is better to leave it on the record," he finally said, almost mournfully. "But I do think the witness ought to be admonished that it is not a properly responsive answer."

Christ tried dousing the flames, only to be cut off. "Don't make me make speeches in front of the jury!" Lambert speechified in front of the jury. She declared a recess and herded the lawyers into her chambers, where Christ again tried to defend his client. Reilly's prolonged attack on Nina, he said, did not place her "in a position of calm silence." That brought forth from Reilly all of the anger he had suppressed in court. It was his right to tell the jury how "obscene" and "disgusting" Nina's fees were, about how she had effectively written into Seward's will a $900,000-a-year "pension plan" for herself, without being insulted by such a lowlife. As for Nina's tattered reputation, well, she should have thought of that earlier. "Chickens come home to roost," Reilly said. "Now, they're here."

"I would suggest that you talk to your client," Lambert told Christ. "She really owes Mr. Reilly an apology. For her to make the statement 'Because of people like you! . . . '" She paused for a second. "Let me tell you something: If I had been the attorney, I would have said, 'At least I'm not a crook and a thief!' That's what my answer would have been. He restrained himself from saying that."

It was a startling statement for a judge to make, even away from a jury. In a flash all of Lambert's bias gushed to the surface. Oddly, this woman who was so incapable of curbing her tongue was smart enough to want to clean up after herself almost instantaneously. For Marie Lambert talk was cheap, but she sensed here that she'd better buy it back. "I mean, for her to make these kind of comments—that is what he thinks she is," she said, trying to fob off her sentiments on Reilly. She turned to him. "Am I right?"

"I become more convinced about it every day," Reilly obligingly replied. None of Nina's lawyers objected to the judge's comments, or asked that they be stricken from the record. Nor did they bother telling Nina about them. Only several weeks later, when she read them in a motion, did she even learn they had been made.

When court reconvened, Reilly focused explicitly on Nina's fees. He contrasted the $225,000 she would have made under the May 1976 will with what she stood to collect now: by her own reckoning, $6.2 million. "You expect to receive six million how much?" Reilly asked with his well-practiced air of surprise.

"Six million two hundred thousand dollars is the amount for each executor," Nina replied, determined to make her own treatment seem less singular.

"I'm only asking the amount *you* expect to receive," he countered. "Six million two hundred what?"

"Thousand dollars."

"That's only for being an executor?"

"I've said that is the amount of the executors' commissions, yes," Nina replied.

"And how much do you expect to receive as trustee of the trusts for which you have been nominated in this will?"

Once again, Nina hedged, seeking refuge in the passive voice. "The amount is calculated as two hundred fifty thousand as of the date of death."

"I'm not asking for the formula," Reilly said angrily. "I'm asking for the amount."

"I can't give you an amount," Nina replied. "There are no trusts yet."

"I'm asking you for an estimate of the amount you expect to receive."

Lambert offered a figure, culled from Nina's earlier testimony: $750,000 a year.

"You expect to get seven hundred fifty thousand dollars a year for how many years?"

"I can't tell you what it would be, because it would depend on what's in the trusts and the value of the trusts each year," she said.

"But your estimate is that it would be seven hundred fifty thousand dollars to start?" Yes, Nina acknowledged elliptically, that was the figure she used with Seward in 1979, based on the rates then in effect.

"And the rates of commissions have increased since then, haven't they?"

"The Legislature of the State of New York has changed the commission rates, yes," she replied.

"The answer is, 'Yes, they've been increased'?"

"That's correct."

"And under the increased rates, it would go from seven hundred fifty thousand dollars to what? About nine hundred thousand dollars?"

Nina threw in a number, raised several technicalities, caveats, and conditions, then agreed.

"Nine hundred thousand dollars per year?" Reilly asked again.

"That's correct," Nina replied.

"That you, Nina Zagat, would receive?"

"Correct."

"As testamentary trustee?"

"Yes."

"And while that amount may vary in the future, it should last as long as Barbara Johnson lives. Is that right?"

"The trusts will continue during Mrs. Johnson's lifetime."

"Excuse me," Reilly snapped back. "Is that right?"

"That's correct."

At this point it was Reilly who could contain himself no longer. "Couldn't you just say 'yes'?" he sighed.

In his opening statement Donald Christ told the jurors they would soon see Nina Zagat and could "measure her yourselves." It had not been a fair test. Lambert had not let Nina tell her story, allowed Reilly to run over her, and made her own feelings manifest with her every grimace. But Nina had not helped her cause. She came across as wooden, awkward, evasive. All of her preparation backfired, even the happy pirouette toward the jury box that the Diaghilevs of S&C had choreographed for her. "Her smiles made me sick," one juror later said. Whatever Seward's mental state had been on April 14, another said, the will should be thrown out, just so Nina couldn't collect a nickel. "Zagat should be disbarred," one juror whispered to another as she testified. To the menagerie of romantic liaisons, real and imagined, that had already sprouted up in the case, some jurors added a pairing neither Milbank nor Lambert had considered: Basia and Nina, they speculated, were lovers. Appearing as she did to be getting her just desserts, Nina was hard to pity. Oddly enough, only on the day when her eldest son, a sweet-looking eleven-year-old, came to court was one suddenly jolted into realizing that she, too, had feelings, and recognizing the trauma she and her family were undergoing.

The trial was young, but observers sensed the case had already taken a fundamental turn. "After Reilly's attacks on her credibility, motives and legal work," Ellen Pollock wrote in the *American Lawyer,* "the jury has to be wondering whether Zagat's judgment hasn't been clouded by too much fun, too much travel, and too close a relationship with her good friend Basia Johnson. For the first time, it seemed, Basia stopped smiling. And for the first time, too, there were smiles in the children's corner." Some reporters, either fearing the premature end to a delicious story or feeling sorry for the man, tried bucking up S&C's general. "Hey, Christ!" Alex Michelini of the *Daily News* barked one day in front of the courthouse. "When you're in a street fight, you have to fight like a street fighter!" Christ kept walking, but his wife, Iris, turned around and smiled. "Donald's not used to street fighting," she said. "He's too nice."

In the public at large, though, attitudes remained unsettled. New York *Newsday* surveyed the buffs who attended the trial each day. "It's all so nauseating," one said. "They're all such creepy people, but you have to be on someone's side, so I'm on the kids'." The *Daily News*'s "Inquiring Photographer" posed the following question to a handful of pedestrians: "What do you think of a multimillionaire who left his wife and former chambermaid $500 million and left nothing to his six grown children?" The response was a hung jury. The *Nowy Dziennik,* the Polish-American newspaper Basia had helped keep financially afloat, remained oddly silent about the case. But a publication called the *Friends of Poland News* claimed to have surveyed eleven hundred Polish-Americans around the country on the subject. The results of the "Pole

Poll" were disseminated in court by its editor, a burly gentleman named Raymond Paluch, who strutted around in a loud sports coat, straw hat, and bright red socks. Nearly three quarters of the respondents wanted Basia to share her loot with her stepchildren, while 16 percent said she should keep it all. The rest said they didn't really care.

XXXVII

T he will now admitted into evidence, it was time to consider Seward's state when he signed it. On March 10 Osgood, who was to handle all medical testimony, called Fred J. Schilling, M.D., to the stand.

As one of his own medical histories might have put it, Schilling was a heavyset but muscular man of sixty-eight, with a full head of wavy white hair. He had an unmistakable air of authority about him, and well he might, for he'd come of age at a time when patients still revered their doctors. His time treating Seward had done little to humble him; for nearly four months he'd been ferried to Fort Pierce and back by helicopter, arriving and departing like some banana-republic potentate. In forty-four years of practice, Schilling had never set foot in a court of law, as a defendant or even as a witness, and that suited him just fine. Like many doctors, he viewed courtrooms as alien, unfriendly places and lawyers as, well, he wasn't a proctologist, but they were a pain in the ass. "You know, one attorney is just like another to me," he'd huffed during his deposition. "You say 'Sullivan and Cromwell.' I wouldn't know if it was 'Cromwell and Sullivan.' " Doctors saved lives; lawyers complicated them.

By now, lawyers had been hounding Schilling for nearly three years. His deposition had been stormy; he called one question "below my dignity to answer" and a follow-up "an absolute insult." Now that he'd been dragged back north to this dreary place in the dead of winter, things had really bottomed out. To Schilling, Seward had been functional on the fourteenth of April and for some time after that, and that was that. Now, he had to go through this charade. After an endless recitation of his credentials—for what it was worth, the world now knew he'd once given rectal examinations to executives of the Continental Insurance Company—Schilling reviewed the course of Seward's care. Seward, he said, had been "alert, clear, and of good humor" when they'd first met. He'd remained so after that, even when Basia summoned the priest in what was a clear overreaction to a temporary

422

electrolyte imbalance. On April 14 he was your perfectly normal ter-
minally ill cancer patient, and there was no evidence that his disease
had in any way affected his brain. He went on to recount how Nina—
he repeatedly called her "Mrs. Zagrat," and even that was an improvement; in some interviews he'd referred to her simply as a "female attorney"—asked him to sign a form attesting to Seward's mental
competence.

But as had become clear during Nina's testimony, there was something about April 14, 1983, that made Lambert want to butt in. Here,
it was as if Schilling's doctorly demeanor had sparked a flashback in
her, the kind of "disassociative state" produced among Vietnam veterans
by the smell of rice or the sound of helicopters. Suddenly, unceremoniously casting Osgood aside, the old lioness of the negligence bar was
once more trying to trip up some loathsome physician. "Who was in
the room when you signed the document?" she asked accusingly.

"Mrs. Zagrat . . . "

"Just a minute!" the judge snapped. "Was anybody else in the room
when you signed the document?"

"I believe there were two other gentlemen, but I didn't know who
they were," he replied, apparently referring to Gunther and Hoch.

"What did you do with the document from the moment it was handed
to you *already typed?*" she added, broadcasting to all her belief that
because the document had been prepared beforehand it had to be a
sham.

"I am at a table," Schilling droned wearily, apparently having concluded that in the strange world of lawyers simple stream-of-
consciousness, uncluttered by tenses, was the least safest way to speak.
"I am unaware that anything is going to transpire other than my visit.
I read the document."

"And everything was typed in except what?" the judge asked.

"My name, the date, and the notary public's signature."

"Now, when the document was given to you, you said you read it,"
the grand inquisitor continued.

"I consumed its significance of what I was being requested to concur
in," replied Schilling, whose sentences, if ever diagrammed, would have
resembled double helixes, and were often ladened with Greco-Roman
gobbledygook (asked about the medical arrangements in Fort Pierce,
he replied, "You never had the epitome of a Utopia").

Initially, one might have thought Lambert was simply playing Annie
Oakley, showing the S&C lawyers that anything they could ask, she
could ask better. Instead, what she was saying was that she didn't trust

424

DAVID MARGOLICK

the Milbank lawyers to be sufficiently aggressive when their turn came, so she would soften up the blackguard for them beforehand.

"Now, Doctor," she continued, "did you think it important to tell Mrs. Zagat about an entry in your notes on April 7, 1983, at eleven-thirty A.M., which read, 'Some confusion noted. Illusions of war with Russia, etc.' Did you think it was important to mention that to Mrs. Zagat before you signed that document?"

Schilling said he hadn't, primarily because his daughter, who had written that entry, had simply recorded what another nurse had said.

"Oh, you don't think she observed it?" the judge said sarcastically.

"I don't believe so," he replied.

Osgood, reduced to the role of spectator, asked the date of the note.

"April seventh!" the judge replied triumphantly, as if she'd ferreted out something that might otherwise have gone overlooked. "That's the date you skipped in these notes!"

When Osgood attempted to introduce the affidavit into evidence, Reilly objected. Lambert overruled him, but in a way that let everyone know how low she considered its probative value to be. "Don't want it in evidence?" she asked the Milbank lawyer incredulously. "I would allow it. It is a statement made by this witness. The jury has the whole picture. It was not prepared by the witness, it was signed by him and filled in. I am going to allow it." And she did. Within a few moments, then, she had cut off Osgood's questioning, accused him of misleading the jury, ridiculed one of his key witnesses, and disparaged a vital document. As the jurors filed out for lunch, Osgood left the lectern, a sardonic smile on his face. "In my nineteen years as a lawyer, I've never had a judge like this, who wouldn't let me conduct my own examination," he bitterly told a reporter.

After lunch Osgood asked Schilling to describe Basia's role in her husband's care. The doctor was not allowed to say Basia had been "concerned" or "interested"; those, Lambert said, were things one couldn't actually see. But quietly and unemotionally, he recounted some of what he had witnessed. "I saw her occasionally bathe the patient," he began. "I saw her assist him with his ambulation. I saw her take orders from me regarding his nutrition. I saw her assist him to the bedside commode, to the cleansing of his anus. I saw her provide him with [a] beverage if he required it." As he spoke to a hushed courtroom, Basia's eyes began to water. Quickly, she lifted her head, as if to reassert her will.

Having rehabilitated Basia a bit, Osgood, whose style was far crisper than Christ's, moved to rehabilitate Seward. What, he asked the doctor, had he observed about his patient? It was a simple question, but one Schilling had great difficulty answering. As Reilly's objections mounted—the witness, he complained, was offering opinions rather than observations—the doctor grew increasingly testy, making his already leaden locution heavier still. "I observed a kindly, elderly gentleman, who was, for a sick person, impeccably attired, who was warm in his mood, who attempted to give me a few bodily complaints, who was interested in, from my observation, current events," he said slowly. "*The New York Times* was there. I did not actually see him read *The New York Times*; it was on his bed. It would have shown that it would have been opened. If I was there in the morning or the late afternoon, there would be one of the TV programs usually pertaining to news. He had an apparent interest in the first Tylenol situation's effect upon his investment in Johnson & Johnson, because he discussed it with me. We had many short discussions about the production of the new vessel by Harbor Branch. We touched upon his interest in sailing. In his backyard was a sailboat . . . "

Reilly objected again. All these references to "we" made it impossible to tell who was saying what.

"It seems pretty obvious to me 'we' is Mr. Johnson and myself," Schilling pouted.

"No!" Lambert interjected. "You have to tell us what you said and what Mr. Johnson said separately."

Schilling seethed. These lawyers had tied him in knots. First, they told him he couldn't give his feelings. Then, he couldn't say what someone else said to him. Now, they were telling him he couldn't use normal pronouns. "For example, there is a sailboat, I don't know how many feet, maybe fifty feet, maybe sixty feet, just within a stone's throw from here to the other side of the building," he continued agonizingly. "On one occasion he's sitting there with a blanket over him. I arrive. I sit down next to him. We just don't shove him into his room and examine him. We have some rapport. He starts describing the boat. There's no paint on it, I believe it was teak, and no specific details, but several apparently sizable voyages that he had. I am not a chic sailor, but I, too, have interest in marine things."

How was it clear to him, Osgood asked, that Seward Johnson understood what was being said to him? "Practicing medicine for forty-four years—that is the basis," Schilling replied. "I believe that that permits me a certain ability to ascertain whether, in the course of a conversation one of the individuals is able to stay with the subject, drift from the subject, go asleep, be aware of. This is a medical conclusion. He had that faculty."

Given the minimal requirements of the law and Schilling's background, this seemed to be all Osgood needed. As he rose to cross-examine the doctor, Reilly had a more difficult task: Essentially, he had to prove that both Seward and Schilling were incompetent. Reilly, unlike his new friend behind the bench, was not one of those lawyers whose office decor included vertabrae charts and plastic torsos alongside the diplomas. Nor, like Christ, had he the luxury of delegating medical testimony to a partner, for he had no partner assisting him at all. And yet he didn't appear fazed by the assignment.

Reilly began by bringing up something he'd touched on with Gunther and Hoch: the "mental-status examination," the test administered by psychiatrists, neurologists, and clinical practitioners to test a person's cognitive functions, in which they ask patients to name the president or the number of dimes in a dollar or something similar. The test was not only more formal than anything Schilling had performed on Seward, but far more formal than anything the law required. Like most doctors, Schilling believed you could test a man's mental state just as effectively by asking him what he'd had for breakfast or whether his bowels were regular, and the law agreed with him. But through his own inventiveness, Reilly hoped to make Schilling look slipshod to the jury.

"Dr. Schilling, did you, on April fourteenth, ask Mr. Johnson any questions designed to evaluate his reasoning ability?" he asked.

"No specific questions, no, sir," he replied.

"Did you ask Mr. Johnson on April fourteenth any questions designed to evaluate his judgment?"

"No, sir," Schilling confessed.

"I understand from your testimony that you are a cardiologist with many, many years experience, forty-four years, I believe?" Reilly asked matter-of-factly. Schilling, lulled momentarily, boasted that he was an internist as well.

"Are you from time to time called upon to express an opinion as to the condition of someone's heart?"

"Quite frequently."

"Would you express an opinion to someone about the condition of my heart today, right now, on the stand?" Reilly asked. Schilling admitted that he would not, but that he would not necessarily need to test him to offer one.

"Well, even if you saw me complete three sets of tennis, would you express an opinion on the condition of my heart?"

"If I had an opportunity to watch you play, I might," Schilling replied.

"Would you express an opinion of the condition of the heart of Jim Fixx if you watched him complete a marathon?" he asked, referring to the famous runner who'd recently dropped dead during a jog.

Schilling attempted to stand his ground. "If I knew something about his personality and how he conducted himself in a daily manner in his other work environment and observed him, I might be able to express that opinion, yes."

Reilly leaned over the lectern and stared at Schilling, and addressed him indignantly. "And if you expressed an opinion that his heart was in good condition because he completed a marathon or completed three sets of tennis, but you did not conduct a physical examination of him and he died the next day, wouldn't that be an act of malpractice?" Osgood's objection was sustained. The comparison was ridiculous. But it was also a bit disconcerting.

Reilly turned next to the *Physicians' Desk Reference* manual, which gave him an excuse to list every conceivable side effect of every medication Seward was taking when he signed his will: psychotic reactions, irrationality, dizziness, hallucinations, apathy, visual disturbances, psychosis, drowsiness, confusion. Had Schilling taken all this into account when he'd signed Nina's affidavit? Reilly reminded everyone that Schilling had never written any scholarly articles about senility, mental illness, or confusion, raising doubts about his qualifications to evaluate them. And if Seward had been so sharp, why had Schilling not discussed the use of heroic measures with him, too, instead of only with Basia and Junior? Schilling rose to defend himself, only to fall promptly into a ditch. "I profess to have feelings for a patient," he began solemnly. "Never in forty-four years have I seen the individual who is ready to die. We are now talking about whether or not, in a terminal situation, there's no hope, whether we are going to do heroic measures on that patient, knowing full well that we are taking a whip to a tired animal, a horse, a human, and whipping him on."

"Is that how you characterized Mr. Johnson in April of 1983? A 'tired animal'?" Reilly retorted indignantly. As Schilling tried to respond, Lambert again entered the ring. "Just a moment!" she declared. "Doctor, you are not here to defend yourself. Mr. Reilly is asking you whether you think that the patient had the right to decide, 'I want to live another five or ten days,' or did you decide that the patient didn't have that right, that Mrs. Johnson had that right? That is basically his

question." Even the children conceded that heroic measures of the kind
Reilly mentioned were irrelevant in Seward's state. But Reilly was
determined to discredit the doctor however he could, and the judge
was happy to help.

For two days now, Schilling had been on a treadmill far more grueling
than the one he kept in his office. Inevitably, a combination of ingredients—being second-guessed about prescribing drugs that the lawyer
interrogating him couldn't even pronounce, fighting nonsensical rules
of evidence, having his answers trampled upon—soon proved too much
for him to bear. Rather than crack, as Nina had, he began openly
defying Reilly and Lambert. That gave Lambert the chance to drag him
into her chambers and dress him down. Thirty years of hatred for
doctors, a hatred honed in hundreds of courtrooms, now rained down
on him.

"Doctor, so we understand each other: I make the rulings in this
court," she said. "In the hospital, you're God; in this court, I make
the rulings. Now just hear me out. The lawyer asks you a question, and
you sit there and you demean the lawyer in front of the jury. I do not
allow that in my courtroom. These lawyers, as far as I'm concerned,
are as important as any doctor in the entire country. In my courtroom
I consider the lawyers the most important people in the world. I am
maybe one of the few judges who remembers that I was once a lawyer,
and that lawyers perform a very important function in the world. Without lawyers, we would have Fascism, Communism, and anarchy. That's
what we have behind the Iron Curtain. We don't have it here in the
United States. And we are not going to have a lawyer demeaned in
my court by anyone." They were lofty sentiments, which the lawyers
at S&C would have many occasions to ponder over the next few
months, and minutes.

Schilling hadn't helped himself with his imperiousness. Nor had S&C
prepared him sufficiently; amazingly enough, he did not seem to know
that Patricia Reid had thought Seward confused on the morning of
April 14. But if he had been neutralized, the credit belonged largely
to the man at the lectern. Peering icily at a hostile witness, tapping
time with his wing tips, swinging his glasses in small semicircular motions, Reilly was not given to histrionics. He worked with the peculiar
calm of suppressed passion, of someone in a kind of trance. No one
ever said "Good morning" or "Excuse me" so menacingly. Like many
trial lawyers, he had a convenient case of tunnel vision, one that
permitted him to see only 50 percent of reality, but he did not appear

partisan. He could be merciless or cynical or contemptuous or resigned or humorless or sometimes so stiff that he'd bray like a horse, but always, he seemed genuine.

Reilly's fervor made the S&C lawyers look like dilettantes. It also made them extremely uneasy. Reilly and Christ rarely spoke, and when they did, it was invariably Christ who initiated things. Basia forbade such contacts; how dare her lawyers be civil to the enemy? But courtesy, Christ realized, was the best way to combat Reilly; anyone needing to loathe his opponents could be killed with kindness. When Reilly entered a stall one day during a joint trip to the men's room, Christ stood by the sink, enduring Reilly's every peristalsis; this way, he could accompany him collegially back to court.

At first Lambert had Reilly pegged as a cold fish. But within the first few days of the trial he had become the teacher's pet, while Christ had been relegated to the corner, a dunce cap on his head. Lambert sustained virtually all of Reilly's objections, and overruled nearly all of Christ's. She allowed Reilly to object at length, while labeling even the tersest of Christ's comments "speeches" and shutting him up. While she cut off Christ's flawed questions angrily, she gently amended Reilly's. While allowing Reilly to ask his witnesses leading questions, she straitjacketed Christ through overly literal readings of the rules. She and Reilly were members of the same tag team. The irony was that Reilly didn't need her help, while Christ dearly did. Marie Lambert, who campaigned as the champion of the underdog, was now going with the winner—and helping him to win.

Concerned about her one-sidedness, Christ invited a lawyer friend to come to court and offer his appraisal. After witnessing a typical display of Lambert partisanship, the lawyer offered two hypotheses: Either Lambert was bending over backward to help Milbank, so as to protect herself when the children appealed an adverse verdict; or she had chosen sides and was simply out of control. If the latter were true, he said, Christ either had to confront her privately or attempt to have her taken off the case; no one could win with such bias and bile flowing from the bench, particularly since the jury clearly liked Marie Lambert. To them she seemed authentic; they listened, and deferred to, what she said and did. If juries go through stages of maturity, this one was still in adolescence, and it had a kind of crush on her. On Saint Patrick's Day, for instance, one juror brought her a green carnation. S&C was not ready to take the steps Christ's friend recommended, opting instead for less frontal approaches. At one point Osgood tried befriending the judge's son, a fellow graduate of Syracuse Law School. Unfortunately, Greg Lambert worked in Washington; his visits to New York were too rare to do S&C much good.

Still, Christ remained one of the two lawyers in the courtroom who refused to recognize Lambert's bias. "This judge is killing us!" Osgood cried. "Just wait," Christ replied. "She's going to be equally rough on them." The other believer was Reilly. Every day, in the biggest case in his career, he was dazzling an entire courtroom. Few in his heady position could have conceded the painful truth: Sure, he was throwing hard and well, but to an artificially enlarged strike zone. Far from seeing Lambert's shortcomings, he praised her at every opportunity for the "magnificent" job she was doing. The one thing she *was* doing magnificently was making Reilly look even more magnificent than he already was.

On Saint Patrick's Day—in addition to the judge's carnation, Basia was dressed in evergreen, Nina wore a green jacket, Junior a dark green coat, and Reilly a green variant of his usual club tie—the witness was Jonathan Wideroff, one of the round-the-clock doctors brought in to tend to Seward toward the end. The move did not surprise Reilly. Figuring that unimaginative old S&C would do things strictly by the book, he surmised it would house its out-of-towners at the Vista Hotel, the only ritzy establishment close to the courthouse. Thus, Berry would call the place periodically, asking for whomever Milbank expected S&C to call next, and when the front desk put him through, he knew he'd surmised correctly. S&C eventually caught on, and took to registering its people in the name of a secretary unknown to Milbank.

Wideroff, a dark-haired young man of the Elliot Gould–Gabe Kaplan school, was, like his mentor Schilling, a Northeasterner who had fled to Florida. But unlike him, he had not traveled to New York under protest. S&C had turned his trip into a junket, paying not only his way but his wife's, his children's, and some of their friends'. Not that he'd needed all those enticements. From the time he'd first drawn blood from Seward—by coincidence, only hours before the old man had signed his will—he'd found the case intriguing. Now, he could take part in the final act.

That first day in Fort Pierce, Wideroff testified, Seward had greeted him with a "Good morning," shaken his hand firmly, and discussed the appropriate place to insert the needle. It was, Wideroff said, a fairly difficult procedure, and Seward impressed him with his ability to help. Unlike the nurse on duty that morning, he'd seen no signs of confusion. "He seemed like a normal individual to me," he told Osgood. Only much later, during the week of May 12, had Wideroff noticed a change, and by May 20, he said, "I don't think he was competent. I mean, no way." Wideroff had his problems with Basia—several times he'd almost quit—but he said she'd tended to Seward faithfully. He recalled once hearing Seward say he loved her, and another time when they'd kissed (like coins, kisses in the case could be evaluated by their date and mint mark; 1983 kisses from Florida, the kind Wideroff was talking about, were clearly the most valuable).

Wideroff was on notice that however S&C wined and dined him, the trip to New York would be no free lunch. When Schilling returned to Florida, his face grew purple and contorted as he described his court-room humiliations. Osgood, too, warned Wideroff that the judge, whom he described as a hack former personal-injury lawyer, would try to trip him up. But Reilly got to him first. Young, flippant, a bit of a wise guy, Wideroff was easier prey than Schilling. Reilly honed in on Wideroff's lazy days in Fort Pierce, spent sleeping, reading, or chatting with his good buddy Ray Gore, skipper of the *Ocean Pearl*, who, for all his friendliness, had turned around and told Milbank Wideroff's quip that tending to Seward was like "baby-sitting for a dead man." Reilly asked an embarrassed Wideroff about that. And he focused on the unusual manner in which Wideroff and his young partner had been paid: in cash, thirty thousand dollars of it in all.

"You find that a pretty cumbersome thing to deal with, checks?" Reilly asked snidely, as Berry suppressed a snicker.

"I find it— yes," Wideroff replied.

"You find it easier to haul around a big bag of cash?"

"Occasionally, yes."

"Eight thousand dollars, nine thousand dollars, you just get on a helicopter and go back with it and say, 'Ten for you and ten for me'?" Reilly sneered.

"I never did it like that," said Wideroff.

"What denominations were these bills, thousand-dollar bills? Hundred-dollar bills?" Wideroff couldn't remember. "Twenties?" He still couldn't remember. "You mean you got five thousand dollars or six thousand dollars in twenty-dollar bills?"

"I honestly can't remember," Wideroff said forlornly. "I think it was hundreds, but I can't remember." (On at least one payday, he conceded, he requested a check. "We had more cash than we needed. It was building up pretty quickly.")

Reilly then brought the questioning back to Basia, asking Wideroff about the frequency and duration and decibel level of her tantrums. It was the first time he had touched on them since his opening. Wideroff denied ever seeing her throw any "missiles" at nurses, but confessed that he had found Basia a "thorn in my side."

"You observed that she had a lot of power and was running the show, didn't you?" Reilly continued.

"Right," Wideroff replied. "In general, she was the household."

"Would you say she is the type of person who was used to getting what she wants?"

"She seemed to be, yes," Wideroff said.

Wideroff acknowledged that he, too, had never administered a mental-status exam to Seward. And as the day drew to a close, Reilly asked him, too, whether he'd seen Seward do anything a child of six could not have done. The question didn't work as well with Wideroff. "There is no way a six-year-old child would cooperate with me in starting intravenous lines, drawing blood samples, moving his arms around, sitting still for a complex cardiovascular physical examination, discussing things with me about complex research vessels that were made by the marine institute," Wideroff declared.

Wideroff held his glibness in check until Osgood's redirect examination, when he was asked what he had observed when Basia had lost her temper. "The common behavior pattern that women act like when they are about to become a widow, I guess," he said blandly. He'd used the same line during his deposition, and nobody made a fuss; it might even have drawn a laugh. This time, though, Reilly was promptly on his feet, defending all of womankind. "I object!" he boomed. "I think this is entirely improper and offensive to a lot of people in this room!" Lambert concurred. "It is very offensive about the common conduct of women," she said schoolmarmishly. Wideroff abjectly begged her pardon. "No," Lambert said sourly. "You have said it. Forget it."

A wholesome midwestern nurse named Catherine Williams, testifying in the sugar-and-pectin tone nurses use when injecting terrified children, said that in her five weeks in Fort Pierce, Seward had always been "well orientated." Sam Watkins, a Florida doctor who'd seen Seward in January and February, said he'd never detected any "confusion or delusional ideations" in him. Their testimony, along with a brief appearance by Seward's former masseur, completed the proponents' functional but unmemorable case on capacity. Unfortunately, those who could have painted a more vivid portrait of a more vital Seward were either in the children's camp (Bonnie Weisser) or too tainted

(John Peach, Jan Waligura), or too risky to call, at least at this point in the case (Basia).

While Reilly projected his unmistakable air of authority, a sense of chaos emanated from the other side of counsel's table. The trial was still young, yet four S&C lawyers—Christ, Osgood, Rogers, and Michaelson, none of whom had much courtroom experience—had already questioned witnesses. With Lambert's repeated reprimands, at times the proceedings resembled a law-school moot-court competition. "Ask Mr. Christ, discuss it with Mr. Osgood, and frame the question properly!" she scolded Michaelson during one bench conference. "This is Sullivan and Cromwell, not some two-by-four outfit that I have to ask the questions for." A few minutes later she was less maternal. "The Court is not going to be subjected to Amateur Day, unless you want me to tell the jury that this case is so unimportant to your office that the lawyer has no knowledge of how to ask a question!" she complained at the bench. "Do you want me to tell this jury that a first-year law student wouldn't have asked such a question?" Lambert's shrill voice reached into every corner of the courtroom, including the press gallery and, presumably, the jury box.

In early March, three weeks into the trial, Milbank once more raised the issue of Sullivan & Cromwell's conduct with witnesses. In a stinging fifty-page memorandum, Milbank now argued that the jury had a right to hear how, by "bribing, intimidating, and otherwise improperly influencing" seven key witnesses—five nurses, plus Seward's pilot and Peach—S&C had tried to scuttle the children's case. Nothing less than the continued integrity of Lambert's beloved court — "historically and currently the preeminent court in the country"— was at stake.

From S&C's standpoint, it was one thing to sling mud in court papers, quite another to do so publicly, when reputations could be ruined and institutions embarrassed. In chambers Christ assailed what he called Milbank's attempt "to place Sullivan and Cromwell in the dock" and asked that the motion itself be kept under seal. Osgood called the charges a "smear"—filed, he said, to discredit him with the judge as well as the jury. S&C's written response reflected just how seriously it took the matter; signing the brief were not just the Johnson lawyers but two of the firm's senior litigators: Marvin Schwartz and Robert MacCrate, president-elect of the American Bar Association and the man who'd interviewed Osgood for his job two decades earlier. Sullivan & Cromwell's brief, like Milbank's flattering description of the Surrogate's Court, was custom-made for Lambert, appealing to her sense of lawyerly etiquette and camaraderie. Milbank, it noted, had thrown around variations of the term "corrupt" seventeen times and "bribe" eight times, an unheard-of breach of professional decorum. Should she credit Milbank's "flimsy and tendentious" charges, S&C warned, it would "end any semblance of civility among counsel," produce ad hominem attacks on Osgood in open court, and lead to a mistrial. There were also some bows to Lambert's ego, including citations to some of her own decisions.

Schwartz and MacCrate joined Christ, Delahunty, and Osgood when the motion was argued in Lambert's chambers on March 20. Accompanying Reilly and Berry was Forger, who visited the courthouse much as Bob Hope visited Johnny Carson: occasionally, briefly, and with a great sense of self-importance. A few months earlier, when MacCrate entered the race for the bar presidency, it was Forger who'd nominated him; now, the two bar brothers merely glowered across the room at each other. Schwartz, a small man with curly whitish hair and owlish glasses, had difficulty containing his disgust for Milbank's charges, which he called "junk" and "filth." Reilly, by contrast, was in his finest "friend of the court" form, feigning pain over having to raise such charges against a colleague. "My initial contact in this case was with Mr. Christ, of whom I became quite fond and certainly respectful," he said. "You know, you can be a zealous advocate, as I'm sure many litigators at Sullivan and Cromwell properly are. But you should stay within certain limits. And we believe that representatives of the Sullivan and Cromwell firm have gone beyond those limits."

Schwartz rose in Osgood's defense. "We're here, may it please the Court, because Mr. Reilly wants to demean Mr. Osgood," he said. "Mr. Reilly is not attacking the justice of Mrs. Johnson's cause; he wants to attack Osgood the man and Osgood the lawyer." Osgood, Schwartz said, had done nothing but try to find facts and hire people to help him. He called Peach "a God-given litigation assistant" and added: "There cannot be anything wrong in hiring him for the munificent sum of fifty dollars an hour." And paying Judy Smith's hospital bills, Schwartz said, had been "a Christian and decent thing to do." "No single piece of evidence amounts to a witness saying, 'Mr. Osgood offered me money to testify.' 'He told me that if I came into the jurisdiction, I would have my legs broken or my nose broken,' nothing in the nature of unequivocal misconduct," Schwartz said. "All we have is people suggesting that they were offended by the questions which

Mr. Osgood asked, and perhaps offended that he seemed to believe in the justness of his clients' cause."

Schwartz then returned to the theme of collegiality. Litigation, like war, was supposed to be played by certain rules, and Reilly, he seemed to suggest, had introduced mustard gas into the proceedings. "I do not accuse a fellow lawyer of misconduct in the course of litigation," Schwartz said. "If my adversary has acted unethically or improperly, I'll tell him so to his face, but I'll wait till it's over, and then I'll go to the Grievance Committee. I personally, by my code of conduct, do not seek to take advantage, on the merits of the case, of what I perceive to be inappropriate conduct by my adversary. So I would not, in this case, even if I believed it, accuse the Milbank firm of impropriety."

Schwartz's presentation left Robert Delahunty in tears. But Reilly greeted Schwartz's suggestion about the Grievance Committee—it hadn't been called that for many years—contemptuously. "It's not sufficient to say to the six children of Mr. Johnson, 'We lost the case, and Barbara Johnson is going to walk off with at least half a billion dollars, but I'll tell you what: There's a disciplinary committee up on Madison Avenue and Twenty-fifth Street, or wherever they are located now, and I'll be sure that whoever is responsible for this devastating disaster is censured or disciplined or whatever,' " he said. Nor was he impressed by Schwartz's sense of ethics. "I think it would be a really sorry day if the test on intimidation of witnesses was whether you threatened to break their legs or break their nose," he added.

Privately, Alex Forger made the same point afterward to the judge, and in terms she was sure to appreciate. S&C's argument left him feeling "distraught for the profession," he said, adding, "I have a higher opinion of the Court Street lawyers now." (The pejorative term is one New York's fancy lawyers use to describe their ostensibly less ethical brethren of the personal-injury bar, lawyers of the sort Marie Lambert had once been herself.) The judge nonetheless ruled in S&C's favor, concluding that while Milbank could cross-examine any of the seven people about Osgood's activities, it could not raise the subject on its own. But whatever Lambert had formally ruled, she seemed more convinced than ever that S&C was untrustworthy. Meanwhile Osgood breathed yet another sigh of relief. For the fourth and, probably, final time, Milbank had tried, and failed, to besmirch him publicly. Still, he knew the charges, fair or unfair, could hurt him if they ever even surfaced. He approached Reilly in the courtroom.

"Out of a sense of decency, I would appreciate it if you would with-draw your papers," he pleaded. "This could really hurt someone's reputation."

"I'll consider it!" Reilly barked back.

Instead, once the case was concluded, he managed to find the "griev-ance committee"—it *was* on Twenty-fifth Street and Madison Avenue, just as he had said—and supplied it with a complete set of Milbank's Osgood file.

XXXVIII

No matter how badly things went in court, the proponents always had one consolation: lunch.

If anyone wanted to see just how differently the two legal teams were approaching the Johnson case, he need look no further than their respective lunchrooms. In Milbank's makeshift office on Broadway, a few blocks from the courthouse, the fare was simple, comparatively inexpensive, and lean—"aggression food," in the words of Donald Saxe, the SoHo caterer who prepared it. Reilly and his associates ate protein-laden sandwiches suitable for carnivorous litigators, generally Black Forest ham and Emmentaler cheese or roast beef on French bread; for dessert there was fruit and, for the chocoholic Reilly, an ample supply of Toll House cookies, perfect for quick afternoon ergs. Everyone served himself and ate off paper plates; drinks—soda or mineral water—were kept in a makeshift refrigerator and taken in plastic cups. The tab: around $10.50 a person.

At Basia's Duane Street hideaway, though, it was a very different story. Things might have begun rockily for the proponents in court, but neither snow nor sleet nor a hostile judge nor an implacable adversary nor their own ineffectuality could stay them or their lawyers from their elegant midday repast. For them, eating well was the only revenge.

In Poland—and, therefore, at Jasna Polana—the midday meal was traditionally the day's biggest, and the mere fact that there would be a trial sandwiched around it was no reason to change Basia's traditional routine. So, before the court proceedings had begun, Nina had scouted out caterers in the vicinity of the courthouse, and selected Charlotte's ("highly professional," "innovative," "try their Scandinavian-style specialties," the Zagats' new *Food Sources Survey* said about it). "Here is THE group that tailor-makes your party," Charlotte's promotional literature boasted. "Lighting to linens, ambience to aperitifs, soups to service, flowers to entertainment and food, food, ambrosial food!!"

Charlotte and her helpers began their task by creating a setting

437

worthy of their cuisine, removing years of accumulated grime from the schlocky offices of Larry Urban's Court Reporters, the unlikely oasis the proponents had found for themselves a few steps from the court-house. A SoHo florist delivered three bouquets there every Monday morning: winter flowers like amaryllis, tulips, and narcissi when the trial began, daffodils and hyacinths by the time it concluded. To brighten things still further, the colors of the table linens were changed weekly. Once the trial began, one of two young men, each resembling an earnest young S&C associate, walked over from Charlotte's every morning around eleven o'clock, donned some black trousers, a white dinner jacket, and dress shirt with black bow tie, and set ten places at a long, rectangular table. Shortly thereafter, a van filled with the day's fare would arrive. Basia and her entourage came around 1:10 or so. The lawyers would walk the two short blocks; Basia would be driven over in her limousine.

What was for lunch? Lest there be any uncertainty, the bill of fare appeared daily on a printed menu. The cuisine seemed better suited for a country club than a war room, or, as it was coming to be, a funeral parlor. After Reilly's devastating opening statement, for instance, the proponents dined on "warm smoked salmon with *sauce verte*," "*boeuf janna*," "new potatoes with dill," "asparagus vinaigrette" and "Swedish cucumber salad," with "lemon mousse with almond *tuiles*" for dessert. On March 3, after Nina had eaten crow on the stand, she and her group enjoyed "grilled chicken with herbs," "spinach salad with a walnut orange vinaigrette," and "sliced melon with fresh mint" next door. On other occasions, after other disasters, there was lobster tail or pheasant mousse. The cuisine got four-star ratings (or, in the numerology of the Zagat surveys, high twenties) from almost everyone. Indeed, weeks after his own testimony had ended, Jay Gunther often found some excuse to tool downtown on his motorcycle and stop by for a free lunch. Sometimes he'd bring his Tupperware and take some leftovers home for dinner. On one occasion, so did Nina.

Before stepping outside (so that the players could discuss official matters privately), the waiter poured what could be called the "*vin du jour*." All were selected by Roberta Morrell, president of Morrell & Company, specialists in "wine catering." Though the weekly order was, by her standards, piddling—a dozen bottles, six white and six red—Mrs. Morrell decided to make the selections personally; after all, these were folks who knew their vintages. She decided to start with good French wines in the twenty-dollar range: reds like Château Talbot St. Julien 1981 or Château Grand-Puy-LaCoste Pauillac 1979, Chambertin

Grand Cru "Clos de Beze" 1980, whites like Mersault Premier Cru Louis Latour 1983 and Puligny-Montrachet, Domaine Girard Chavey 1983. Bauman, an oenophile, especially appreciated the assortment, and each day made a beeline for the table in the corner, where he would stand inspecting labels and savoring bouquets. Even if only a single glass had been poured, a bottle was never recorked: After all, it might have been poisoned in the interim. With fine wines as with Tylenol, the safety seal had to be in place; opened bottles were returned to and consumed by the happy staff at Charlotte's.

Doctored wines were not the only security concern. Around noon Basia's bodyguards, armed with the latest electronic gadgetry, swept the lunchroom for bugs (the only ones they ever found were cockroaches). One bodyguard stood sentry outside the room during meals, while another was stationed at the entrance to the building and a third remained with the car, lest someone, perhaps the same fiend who once stalked Marie Lambert, plant a bomb in it. It was all part of the elaborate daily routine Basia's bodyguards followed throughout the trial. Every morning her car was started an hour before it left Jasna Polana; armed with mirrors, her security men inspected its tail pipe and underbelly for explosives. Basia would step outside the house only after a Jeep had circumnavigated Jasna Polana, while other agents checked beneath the estate's bridges for more bombs. Basia's Mercedes had bulletproof glass and steel plates so heavy that the car's shock absorbers had to be replaced constantly. To foil would-be kidnappers, Basia's route from the estate to the New Jersey Turnpike changed each day; minutes before leaving, her drivers would open a locked drawer in the control center and pick one of ten index cards, each containing a different itinerary, at random. All of the bodyguards were trained in evasive driving, in case anyone tried anything foolish en route to New York.

The security fetish did not interfere with the proponents' repasts, in which Nina played impresario. It was she who seemed most interested in what was being served; who, mindful of that moment in Eastern Lambert Time—usually fifteen or twenty minutes after it was supposed to—when court was due to resume, would usually finish first; who would summon the waiter when it was time for coffee and tea to be poured; who most enjoyed the "finger-food sweets"—chocolate cups filled with lemon mousse or strawberry tartlets—that accompanied the coffee. The tab: thirty dollars a head, and that didn't include the fancy wine. For all that, Basia sipped some beef consommé but ate little else. She seemed to prefer the ham sandwiches with lettuce on salt-free Jasna Polana bread she brought from home each day in the large basket from "21" that Mary Lea had given her during happier times. Sometimes Basia brought too many sandwiches, and when she couldn't pawn off them on her bodyguards, she had them handed out to homeless people on the street. (Occasionally, she supplemented the spread with other items; once, having opened a bottle of soda and found that the cap entitled her to fifty cents off on a dozen Dunkin' Donuts, she instructed a bodyguard to fetch her some.)

But before long, what was most striking about these lunches was less food than mood. From the first few days of jocularity, the atmosphere degenerated into depression. The lawyers sat glumly picking at their fine cuisine. Bauman, who'd initially regaled his fellow diners with war stories about court battles he had seen, began talking about how Lambert had to have been fixed; Basia speculated over whether Ed Reilly beat his women before or after he made love with them.

Though they, too, sat at the counsel's table, Harbor Branch's lawyers were largely inert. Milbank still kept them almost entirely in the dark on all strategic matters. Whenever Reilly rose to object, one of the Dewey lawyers—Bob Hirth or Jack Kaufmann—would invariably rise an instant later, and following Reilly's cross-examinations would chip in a question or two of his own. Even this was too much for Reilly, who seemed annoyed at their very presence: The slightest involvement of the Dewey partners, whom he considered boobs, threatened to throw off his own carefully laid plans. Still, the children's public devotion to Harbor Branch remained crucial. That was why Reilly wanted Marilyn Link, the foundation's former managing director, to be his keynote witness. Dewey agreed, but at a price. First, it finally extracted a guarantee from the children that the foundation would collect at least one sixth of whatever they won in the will contest—still far more speculative than what Basia had promised weeks earlier, but something. Second, Dewey would present Harbor Branch's own makeshift case first. Harbor Branch was ostensibly what this court battle was all about. In fact, its case lasted but three days. Reilly held his breath for all of them.

Marilyn Link had followed her half-brother Ed into aviation and, later, into marine research at Fort Pierce. Now in her sixties, she projected the aura of an aged tomboy, someone who had lived a lonely, unmarried life in a man's world. Despite a dry, creaky voice that betrayed her age, she remained athletic, an attribute that could help her walk the testamentary tightrope she now faced: to make Seward incompetent in April, when he left nothing to Harbor Branch, but competent when he'd made his token bequest to the foundation a few weeks earlier. She sidestepped the topic altogether for a time by giving a simulated tour of the foundation's facility, aided by a pointer and a giant aeriel photograph. When she finally did talk about Seward, it was only to note his gradual decline into sickness, forgetfulness, and eccentricity. She also talked disparagingly about Basia—or, as she pointedly and distastefully called her, "Barbara"—just as she had done during her deposition. (Q: "Ever see Seward kiss Basia?" A: "Once—on the cheek." Q: "Ever see him pat her?" A: "Only to calm her down.") She had little to contribute to the proceedings except two conversations with Seward: one in 1975, in which he told her of plans to remember Harbor Branch in his will; and another in January 1983, when she'd greeted him and he'd replied, "I shaved myself this morning."

Link was followed on the stand, as she had been at Harbor Branch's helm, by a hulking Texan named Robert Jones. He testified that Seward's memory began fading in the late 1970s and only got worse; on Election Day 1982, he recalled, Seward summoned him to his office, only to forget what he'd wanted him for by the time he'd arrived. On a prior occasion, Jones testified, Seward had been thinking about nuclear war. "He was telling me about some things he had been reading," Jones recalled, "and they involved early civilization in the Mediterranean, when some city had been sacked, and the only thing that had remained was the library, which had been imprinted on clay tiles. And he said, 'That's probably a good idea. Why don't we do that with our Harbor Branch papers?'

"I thought he was joking," Jones continued, "and I said, 'Mr. Johnson, we would have to strengthen the footings of the library in order to hold the clay tiles.' He said—and this is what surprised me most; he wasn't joking—he said, 'Well, if we have to, we'll do it.' I tried to make the point that if we were close to ground zero, the clay tiles would probably be pulverized anyway. And I said, 'There is also the possibility, Mr. Johnson, there wouldn't be anybody left to read our library entries.' He said, 'Well, we may be recolonized by someone from outer space someday. And they would be interested in what we were doing.' "

Harbor Branch's final witness was Roger Cook, the foundation's director of marine operations. Seward had once complained that Cook, a cherubic man with bristling gray hair who held the world's record for the deepest lockout dive, spoke like a machine gun, and as Cook explained how a Harbor Branch submersible operated, his Uzi-like diction was readily apparent. His testimony, like much of Link's and Jones's, seemed lifted from an old Lloyd Bridges *Sea Hunt* show, and was enough to give anyone the bends. Eventually, though, he returned to the surface, and the will contest. In 1983, he told Dewey's Kaufmann, he was never quite sure whether Seward recognized him, and their conversations were basically one-sided. But Cook, a navy demolition expert in Vietnam, quickly proved adept at self-destruction, too. Unable to recall many seemingly simple points, he admitted that ever since he'd been in a serious car accident two years earlier, his memory hadn't been so good. When, Christ asked him on cross-examination, had the mishap occurred? "I think in May or June of 1984," he replied.

The Harbor Branch witnesses gave Christ his first crack at cross-examination, which came to him no more naturally than other phases of trial work. He did little to highlight how the children were really undermining the foundation; or how, by energizing and encouraging Seward, Basia had been an integral part of Harbor Branch's development; or how Harbor Branch was arguing that Seward had been competent far longer than the children said he had been; or how Cook and Jones had dealt with Seward as a normal, functioning fellow until almost the end. Instead, his examination was just what S&C had called Milbank's examination of Basia four months earlier: "a relentless quest for the minute and the immaterial, the collateral and the remote." Standing at the lectern, half-moon glasses perched on his nose and hands on his hips like a little teapot, Christ darted from one topic to another; key issues got lost amid queries about Seward's interest in sediment on the ocean floor or more ethereal questions like "Was Mr. Johnson a gentleman?" or "Would you say Mr. Johnson was competitive?" or "Would you say Mr. Johnson liked to win?" All were designed to show Seward's enduring intellectual powers, but Christ's message was too subtle for just about everyone. "Your questions don't relate to the lawsuit," Corn told him once. "They could refer to football games."

Christ gathered points as squirrels gather acorns, husbanding them for use months later, presumably during his closing statement. His larger purpose could not be gleaned by the naked eye, in part because that eye was usually half-shut. "The jury is falling asleep," Lambert complained during one bench conference. "The judge is about to fall asleep." Her impatience sometimes spilled over into open court—for instance, when Christ tried to ask Link about the letter on national defense policy that Seward (assisted by Tim Zagat) had written to President Reagan in June 1982. "I think we ought to subpoena the president!" she jeered. Reilly joined in the merriment. "We will take his deposition!" Reilly chirped.

If nothing else, Christ was persevering. At one point he sought to establish that Basia had barred Marilyn Link from the Fort Pierce house not to immure Seward in "Fortress America," as the objectants were saying, but because he found her tennis games disturbing. Dewey's Robert Hirth did not see the relevance of the entire inquiry.

CHRIST: "Are you familiar with the tennis court at the Johnson property at Fort Pierce?"

HIRTH: "Objection, Your Honor."

THE COURT: "Sustained."

CHRIST: "Do you know whether the Johnsons have a tennis court?"

HIRTH: "Same objection."

THE COURT: "Sustained."

CHRIST: "Did you ever play tennis at the Johnsons' house at Fort Pierce?"

HIRTH: "Same objection, Your Honor."

THE COURT: "Sustained."

CHRIST: "Did you play tennis in January of 1983?"

HIRTH: "Same objection."

THE COURT: "Sustained."

CHRIST: "Did you play tennis there in February of 1983?"

HIRTH: "Same objection."

THE COURT: "Sustained."

CHRIST: "May I ask the basis, Your Honor, of the objection?"

HIRTH: "The basis is relevance."

CHRIST: "Miss Link, do you know, when someone plays tennis at Mr. Johnson's tennis court in Fort Pierce, if it's possible to hear the play from the house?"

HIRTH: "Same objection, Your Honor."

THE COURT: "Sustained."

CHRIST: "Do you know whether it would disturb people in the house if people used the tennis court?"

HIRTH: "Same objection."

THE COURT: "Sustained."

CHRIST: "Did there come a time, in February of 1983, when you were asked not to play tennis at the Johnsons' court?"

HIRTH: "Same objection."

THE COURT: "Sustained."

CHRIST: "Were you told that it was . . . "

HIRTH: "Your Honor, I don't believe this is proper, to continue to ask questions about Miss Link's tennis."

THE COURT: "The Court has ruled that this question is inadmissible. We can ask it a hundred ways; that's the Court's ruling."

CHRIST: "Miss Link, were you told that it was disturbing to Mr.

Johnson to have people use the tennis court in February of 1983?"
    HIRTH: "Same objection."
    THE COURT: "Sustained."

But Christ still hadn't reached match point. Only a few minutes
later, while questioning Link about Junior's visits to Fort Pierce, Christ
returned for yet another set, serving up the following question:

    CHRIST: "Didn't he tell you that it would be better for you not to
    go back and play tennis at the house?"
    HIRTH: "Objection."
    THE COURT: "Sustained. I don't want to hear the word 'tennis'
    again."

In a way Christ didn't have to discredit the Harbor Branch witnesses;
much of what they told their own lawyers harmed the children's case.
They portrayed a man who was firmly at Harbor Branch's helm, who
had remained vital well into his ninth decade; Jones told Kaufmann
that when he'd first met Seward in 1975, the eighty-year-old man was
in a wet suit, under sixty-five feet of water in a Bahamian "habitat."
And had Seward's oxygen supply been cut off that day, the children
still would not have collected a dime.
    It was Jones who had composed that emotional account of the arc-
striking ceremony four days before Seward's death for the Harbor Branch
newsletter. "The strength and resolve of this man has never ceased to
amaze us," he'd written. "He is wide-eyed, and his pleasure and anticipation are evident." Though Christ asked Jones to read it aloud, he
predictably had not forced the witness to dwell on this powerful testament to Seward's endurance for more than a moment, to dissect it
phrase by phrase. In this comedy of errors it was Harbor Branch's own
lawyer who did that. Kaufmann put the question to Jones: On May 19,
1983—that is, more than a month after he had signed his last will—
had Seward Johnson been rational or irrational?
    Jones, whom Junior had once compared to Jell-O, fidgeted, then
hesitated, then hesitated some more. True, his account might have
been a bit exaggerated, an attempt to butter up the family and inspire
the troops. Still, he'd seen Seward sitting there smiling that day, and
even though he couldn't tell what the old man had been thinking, or
whether he was thinking at all. . . . Jones began an answer or two, then
tried to slither out of the question sideways. "I am pausing because I'm
not sure I know what you mean by 'rational' and 'irrational,' " he said.

"Was he raving or throwing the pillows or what? I'm not sure I understand. Was he . . . "

"I think the question was, from what you observed of Mr. Johnson's acts, was he rational or irrational?" Kaufmann asked again.

"All right," Jones finally said. "I have to say he was rational."

It was a stunning admission. A Harbor Branch poobah was now saying Seward was still with it four days before he died. Reilly was livid. If he'd had a bazooka, he told one of his colleagues, he'd have blown away Dewey Ballantine's entire litigation department; they were hurting him far more than S&C ever did. Strangely enough, Lambert seemed just as indignant, complaining afterward to another Dewey lawyer that the foundation's case had been "a disaster." Apparently, things were not going as she wanted them to, either.

The judge chose this unpropitious moment, on the eve of the children's case, to take one more stab at settlement. Basia herself remained adamantly opposed to any deals, as she disclosed one day to one of her few sympathizers in the courtroom, a horse trainer who smelled of his craft and planned to christen one of his trotters "Basia." Why, he asked, couldn't they all just split the pie and go home? She shook her head piteously. "What is life without principles?" she asked. The children, too, were disinclined. The case was going swimmingly, and they'd yet to fire a single of their own salvos. But by late March the disparity between the Johnsons' rhetoric and their conduct was apparently bothering even Marie Lambert, and one afternoon after court, she invited them all into her chambers.

Basia, she told them, was offering something around $50 million—more than enough for Harbor Branch, she said, if the children were willing to forgo something themselves. How much of their settlement share, she asked, would each of the Johnson children be willing to give to the foundation? Suddenly, the Johnsons and their spouses grew vague, talking about family solidarity and "principles" and, in the case of Junior's wife, Joyce, children. ("All you have to do is put your kids through school," the judge reminded her. "I realize that you're the poorest, but $30 million is enough.") Gretchen Johnson, in her customary role as Jimmy's ventriloquist, was the only one willing to cede a share. Forger categorically rejected the offer: There wasn't enough for Harbor Branch, he said, and maybe, well, not quite what the children wanted, either. "We all knew that what Forger said was bullshit," one Dewey lawyer later recalled. "But what this did was put on the record, for the first time, what the children and Milbank were in it for."

Once again, Reilly had been granted a reprieve, and this one was likely to last. For he was about to begin his case, and the ensuing stench would take some time to clear. This was particularly so given his sensational first witness—someone who, oddly enough, thoroughly meticulous Milbank had managed to overlook, but who had miraculously materialized at the eleventh hour, carrying what was to become the most crucial exhibit in the Johnson case.

XXXIX

Anyone attending the Johnson trial on March 27 could not be blamed for mistaking the Surrogate's Court for some provincial airport. Officers stationed in the corridor frisked everyone entering the courtroom, lawyers, parties, and visitors alike. The haywire, crackling sound of primitive handheld metal detectors could be heard in the halls.

The day before, Marie Lambert had learned that two of Basia's bodyguards, both moonlighting New York City detectives, were carrying guns to court. The news sent the judge into orbit. "No one carries guns in our hallways! No way!" she declared. "JOHNSON WIDOW'S BODY-GUARDS ORDERED TO DISARM BY IRATE JUDGE," the *Newark Star-Ledger* reported the next day. Lambert promptly procured additional security men, and they had their hands full. This, after all, was the day the children were to begin their case, and a large crowd had come to court expecting fireworks. Leaving nothing to chance, a Harbor Branch publicist had been working the phones, urging various reporters not to miss the "bombshell" testimony that morning. Even the press-shy Reilly called a *New York Times* reporter at home to urge him to cover the day's events.

"Mr. Reilly, do you have a witness?" Lambert asked solemnly. Up until very recently, Reilly could not really have said he did, at least one he was entirely happy with, one who could sound the two grand themes of his case: Seward's decrepitude and Basia's abusiveness. Then, at least as the story was later told, serendipity had struck.

"Yes, Your Honor," Reilly replied. "We call Izabella Poterewicz."

Unlike "Piasecka," this bit of unpronounceable Polish tripped perfectly off Reilly's tongue. A small, pretty woman of Slavic countenance, her brown hair tied in a bun, made her way to the stand. She appeared to be in her twenties, but her deep-set, sad eyes made her seem older. She was wearing a simple blue dress and a heart-shaped pendant. She had never been in a courtroom, at least an American one, before. Even so, her look was not of nervousness but of determination and righteousness.

So, Christ and Osgood quickly realized, Milbank had found the Poterewiczes, the embittered husband-and-wife, butler-and-maid team who blamed Basia for the loss of their baby, after all. Actually, the Poterewiczes had found Milbank. As Izabella later explained it, she and her husband had been in their small basement apartment in Brooklyn, watching televised accounts of the trial, listening with mounting disbelief and indignation as Basia's lawyers depicted their client as a good woman and loyal wife. It was neither just nor fair to the Johnson children to let such claims go unrebutted, Izabella thought. One day, as she sat in her doctor's office on the East Side of Manhattan, she resolved to help stop this travesty. She looked up "Surrogate's Court" in the phone book, boarded the Lexington Avenue IRT, exited at the Brooklyn Bridge stop, and made her way to the courthouse. Luncheon recess had just been declared when she reached the fifth floor and approached Jennifer Johnson, whom she recognized from television. For a moment all Jennifer could see was the umbrella under the woman's arm, and she thought it was a gun. But quickly, she learned the woman was carrying a different kind of ammunition. "I used to work for Mrs. Johnson," Izabella told her. "Maybe I can help you." Before she could explain how, Basia and her entourage approached. "Give me your phone number, and I'll have one of my lawyers call you," Jennifer said quickly. Izabella complied. "I want to give her back some of what she gave me," she said. Then she returned to Brooklyn and told her husband what she had done.

Within a few days Charles Berry arranged for the Poterewiczes to come to Milbank. So elated was he by their horror stories about life with Basia that after he escorted them out, he walked into Reilly's office and exclaimed, "There's just no way we're going to lose this case!" Berry's next rendezvous with the couple was in their Brooklyn flat, and Reilly was with him. It was during this visit, an enterprise every bit as incongruous as Ted Rogers's trek to Pat Reid's old Kentucky home, that the couple suggested the Milbank lawyers speak to Edmund Sulikowski, the same disgruntled Jasna Polana alumnus who'd hinted to S&C's Zirinis a few months earlier that he had tape recordings for sale. Berry, too, then journeyed to Fairless Hills, Pennsylvania, where, over hamburgers at a local greasy spoon, Sulikowski revealed he'd taped Basia screaming, and suggested the Poterewiczes had as well.

In fact, Izabella had made three recordings. The first, from Jasna Polana, was unusable; unfamiliar with her new machine, she had set the volume too low. Besides, Basia had held her temper. The third had been made in Florida, where recording someone surreptitiously was arguably illegal. But in a Milbank conference room only a few days before the children's case was to begin, Izabella played the second tape for Reilly. The interchange was in Polish, but substance was secondary. What mattered was the sound, which was so horrifying, so piercing, that it penetrated Paul Shoemaker's office wall a few doors down. Suddenly, Basia's bloodcurdling rages need no longer be left to the jury's imagination. Reilly decided then and there to begin his case with her, before she could possibly get cold feet. Berry promptly purchased a cassette player powerful enough to project over a huge room (actually, the first contraption he bought jammed, almost as if the sound of Basia's screaming was too much for it to take), and on the morning of March 27, the clean-cut, preppyish Yalie carried the machine to court, drawing covetous glances all along Nassau Street and an incredulous one from Nina, who spotted him crossing Chambers Street. (The cost-conscious S&C paralegal who subsequently bought the proponents' considerably more modest model was promptly chastised by Ted Rogers, who thought it disgraceful that Sullivan & Cromwell had been so thoroughly outclassed by Milbank in anything.)

"Your Honor, I request that the witness not be required to disclose her address," Reilly said forebodingly. Of course, she would not have been hard to track down, but Reilly's request lent a nice chill to the proceedings and played well to a judge already filled with visions of gunfights in her courthouse. Lambert had the witness write the information on a piece of paper. "I am giving the address to my law secretary, and that will be safeguarded in our safe," she assured the Milbank lawyers as she played right into their hands.

Under Reilly's gently questioning, Izabella began recounting her life story, one that initially echoed, then overlapped, that of the other onetime Polish maid sitting nearby. Happily, Izabella's vision grew cloudy when she was tense, so she could not see Basia well enough to feel intimidated. Just in case, the ever-attentive Reilly positioned himself between the two. She told of coming to the United States with her husband in 1981 and of writing the rich Polish woman in Princeton she'd heard about, requesting work; she sent the letter care of Johnson & Johnson, at the address she lifted off the back of a baby-oil bottle. In the fall of 1982 Basia invited the couple to Jasna Polana and hired them on the spot: Izabella to work around the house, Mariusz for maintenance. Speaking calmly in accented but clear English, seeking only occasional assistance from the Milbank translator for terms like "dust-

ing" and "drawing the curtains," she described her domestic routine—
serving the Johnsons breakfast; cleaning their bedrooms, bathrooms,
and the rest of the house; feeding the dogs, turning down the Johnsons'
beds before going home each night.

Like their innumerable predecessors, the Poterewiczes had been
fired—and, in their case, rehired, then fired, then hired, then fired
again, this time for good, in late March 1983. Izabella described how Seward had declined noticeably during her tenure, particularly in Florida.
Never, she said, had she seen Basia address him with affection. Instead,
she yelled at him for eating the wrong food, wetting his bed, refusing to
relinquish the remote-control device so she could watch what she wanted
on television. "She yell at him, 'Give me that machine! Give me that
machine! I want another channel!' and she grabbed the remote control
from his hands," she said. Reilly asked whether she'd ever heard Basia
call Seward names. "She was yelling at him and calling him names like
'stupid Englishman,' 'idiot,' and even I heard . . . "—here she hesitated
demurely for an instant—" 'you son of a bitch.' I don't want to say
that," she added shyly as the courtroom broke out into sympathetic
laughter. In fact, she continued, she'd called him that twice.

The "stupid Englishman" part didn't ring true, and Reilly pressed
her to correct it. "She called him 'stupid—'what?" he asked. Osgood
objected; the question was leading. Lambert, obviously enjoying herself,
not only overruled him but hammered in the damaging testimony.
"She's already testified that she said 'stupid Englishman,' 'idiot,'—I
don't want to say that word," the judge chortled, as laughter broke out
anew. "It's an insult to his mother. You can call me names, but not
my mother." The objectants and their lawyers laughed heartily. The
S&C team sat unamused.

The proponents had anticipated that Milbank would dredge up evidence of marital discord and offer it to prove undue influence. In papers
it submitted to Lambert, S&C argued that frequent arguments didn't
equal undue influence, that courts recognized discord to be as much a
part of marriage as bliss. Nor was it enough to show that Basia leaned
on Seward into leaving her everything; they cited one case in which a
wife had hectored her husband so vigorously he'd poisoned himself, and
still, no undue influence was found. To permit the jury to hear such
"idle and malicious chatter," S&C claimed, would be reversible error.
"It would offend the dignity of the court and set a menacing precedent
if the children were allowed to put the Johnsons' harmonious, twelve-
year marriage on trial in what is supposed to be a probate proceeding,"
it argued. Osgood had attempted to make these points in chambers

shortly before Milbank began its case, only to run into a judicial buzz saw.

"Your Honor, because we are now in the area where briefs were submitted on the question of undue influence," he began, "I would like to review some of the ground rules briefly, Your Honor, so that . . . "

"No! No!" Reilly cut him off.

"Wait a minute!" Lambert said sharply. "You don't 'review ground rules' for the judge!"

"I put that poorly," said Osgood sheepishly. "I don't . . . "

"You better believe you put it poorly!" she said angrily.

"I want Your Honor to . . . "

"You'd better believe you put it poorly!" she reiterated. "Let me tell you what I am going to do. I have read the briefs. Enough said. I will rule on a question-by-question basis, and in the presence of the jury. Now, we've settled that problem."

Milbank, then, had its mandate, and it was a great victory not just for the children but for journalists, court buffs, busybodies, and voyeurs everywhere. The trial was now certain to turn into an ad hominem soap opera, albeit a one-sided one since Lambert had ruled long ago that the children's own past peccadillos were inadmissible. Moreover, Lambert was posed to go one step further. The discord to be testified to need not even be between husband and wife, but between wife and anyone else. And as if that weren't enough, she routinely overruled Osgood's objections and offered Reilly assistance.

"Your Honor, may I ask that *counsel* ask questions of the witness, rather than the Court?" Osgood said on one such occasion.

"Your Honor, I think that's insulting!" Reilly replied huffily. Lambert, unsurprisingly, thought so, too.

Izabella's Jasna Polana (and, briefly, her Fort Pierce) was a place where brutality reigned. Maids and butlers, gardeners and nurses, appeared briefly, then vanished. Presiding over it all was a woman who didn't so much lose her temper as seem incapable ever of finding it.

"Did you observe Mrs. Johnson yelling at people in the house other than Mr. Johnson?" Reilly asked.

"Oh, yes," Izabella replied.

"Who else did she yell at?"

"Everybody."

"Was Mr. Johnson in the house at the time the yelling was going on?" Lambert interjected, supplying Reilly with one of his two missing evidentiary links.

"Yes."

"This yelling, can it be heard throughout the house?" the Judge continued, furnishing the other.

"Objection, Your Honor," Osgood declared. "May I ask . . . " Once more, he was going to request that Reilly, and not the court, be the children's lawyer in the case. This time, the court cut him off.

"Whenever you heard yelling, where were you?" the judge continued.

"May I ask that counsel ask the questions to the witness?" Osgood repeated.

"Well, you objected, so I'm trying to lay a foundation," the judge replied. "You have said you wanted those answers. I'm trying to get them for you."

"That is counsel's job," Osgood said pathetically.

Reilly took the tag. "In what rooms in the house did you hear or see Mrs. Johnson yelling?" he asked.

"In every room. When she was yelling very loud, you could hear her in every corner of the house."

How many ways can one describe a scream? How accurately can one ever reconstruct the sound? Was it really enough to drive a nurse to tears, make the help tremble or an aged millionaire cower in abject terror? There was really only one way to know.

"You mentioned that Mrs. Johnson fired you on January sixteenth?" Reilly asked.

"Yes."

"Where were you at the time?"

"I was upstairs in that big bathroom."

"Where was Mr. Johnson?"

"In his bedroom."

"And Mrs. Johnson started speaking to you?"

"Yes."

"What did she say?"

"She stopped me, and she start to yell at me," Izabella replied. "She said I am not good worker, I don't do a good job, I am lazy, I am not responsible, and I don't know how to do even minor things, and she said it is not her problem if I plan family—because I was pregnant at the time—and she said it is not her problem, and this is not a shelter, she will not help stupid people."

"Was this near Mr. Johnson's bedroom?"

"Yes."

"Where did this take place?" Lambert asked. The question had already been asked and answered twice. Now, with the judge's prompting, the maid had another chance to elaborate.

"In that big bathroom, and you could go straight from that big bathroom to Mr. Johnson's bedroom, and the door was always open," she said.

"Did you make any tape recording of Mrs. Johnson's voice at that time?"

"Yes," Izabella replied.

A murmur filled the courtroom: The maid had captured her mistress's voice. Nina suddenly realized why Berry had been carrying that mammoth cassette player this morning. The only remaining question was whether Lambert would admit the tape into evidence. Actually, it wasn't much of a question at all. She dismissed the jury, led the lawyers into her chambers, and began going through the motions.

Sitting to the judge's left, Reilly argued that the tape was not only relevant, but "about the most relevant evidence we have." Since the decibel level and tenor of the tirade were similar to what Seward had absorbed, he argued, listening to it would help one understand how Basia had browbeaten her husband all those years. " 'Yelling' just doesn't do justice to the manner in which this woman expressed herself," Reilly said. " 'Screaming' is a much more appropriate word." The only alternative to playing it, he went on, was to have the witness stand up "and shout and scream and wave her arms."

Osgood's retorts flew like buckshot: The tape had been doctored. It was redundant. It might have been made illegally. It had nothing to do with undue influence. Seward wasn't in the room, and didn't understand Polish. But even if he had been and even if he did, berating a maid in January did not prove undue influence over a husband in April.

Before she decided anything, the undoubtedly curious judge wanted to hear the tape for herself. Izabella handed the cassette to Berry, who inserted it into Milbank's shiny new twenty-two-inch Sony CFD5 stereo cassette recorder and pushed "play." By now Berry, who had already heard the tape seven times, knew the script: A scratchy hum gave way to an apparently normal conversation between two women. But quickly, one of the voices rose into a shriek—not a sustained shriek, but a series of cries that even Dolby was powerless to reduce. As the S&C lawyers sat like statuary, Elizabeth Gorski, their Polish-speaking paralegal, whispered translations into Christ's ear. "You are the ones who asked for work, and not I who looked for you!" went one scream. "You are doing lousy work! You are taking it easy! Lazy, you are lazy!" went another. Izabella told her meekly that her pregnancy had not been planned. "Oh, you never planned? Then where is it from?" Basia shrieked. "Love and responsibility. Do you have anything in your head? I have no intention of helping stupid people! Everyone is responsible for his own life!" Suddenly, there was the sound of a slamming door, and it was over. Gorski wrote out a note and handed it to Christ. "This sounds like a set-up to me," it said.

Ostensibly, Lambert had to balance the tape's probative value against its prejudicial effect. The first was speculative, since Seward hadn't been the target of the tirade, might not have heard it, would not have understood it, and might never have been spoken to such a way. The second was not; it was a devastating document. After calling two other judges for advice—the law of evidence, or the law of anything else for that matter never having been her strong suit—Lambert issued another of her pseudo-Solomonic rulings: The tape would be admitted into evidence, but for its tone, not its content. Thus, the jury could hear Basia screaming, but would not be given the slightest idea of what she was screaming about.

Osgood made one last eloquent attempt to block the tape. "This is out-and-out hearsay, and it is totally irrelevant to the question of undue influence, because I again say it is a spat between a widow and a member of her staff," he pleaded. "To permit the jury to hear this, and to suggest that they draw an inference that because Mrs. Johnson had an argument with somebody on her staff that she didn't think was doing a good job, that she therefore unduly influenced, coerced, and practiced duress upon her husband on April fourteenth is patently erroneous."

"You have been very patient listening to Mr. Osgood, incredibly patient, and I don't think I could be so patient, and I really admire your ability to tolerate it, but I ask that the Court instruct Mr. Osgood to desist," Reilly replied. "We just can't sit here for the rest of the day."

"I'm not going to sit here for the rest of the day," the judge parroted. That was that.

By three everyone was back in the courtroom, where, before the tape was played, Osgood would have the chance to question Izabella about it. There was panic in his voice and on his face, which had reddened in its predictable fashion. It was an odd spectacle: a suave Wall Street lawyer, a veteran of a hundred courtrooms, ill at ease and flustered, while the woman he faced, an immigrant clerk in a Brooklyn five-and-dime, sat strangely, icily calm. As Osgood questioned her about her activities on January 16, 1983, the day she'd made her fateful recording, she clutched her trusty silver Sony in her hand. Osgood asked about the size of the room where the recording was made, about who'd held the tape since then, about whether it had ever been altered. Since making the tape, Izabella told him, the only persons to learn of it were her husband and her psychologist, conveniently omitting Sulikowski and perhaps others. She said she had informed the lawyers at Milbank about it only three days earlier, and played it for them for the first time only the day before yesterday. Osgood was eliciting information, but he was also fomenting suspense. In fact, by filibustering until late into the afternoon, he assured that the recording would cap the day's events. The next day was Good Friday, and on Monday Lambert claimed to have "a meeting in Albany"—shorthand for one of her periodic, perfunctory stabs at settlement. The jury was certain to have a good, long time to ponder what it would soon hear.

Once more, Osgood objected to its admission. And once more, he was overruled. Then, Lambert read the cautionary instructions Corn had drafted for her, as much to protect her on the appeal that would certainly follow as to enlighten the jury. The tape, she told them, "is not being offered to prove the truth of its contents, but to show the tone of voice which this witness alleges Mrs. Johnson addressed to the decedent on certain occasions. In weighing this piece of evidence, you shall give to it only such weight as you deem reasonable, keeping in mind that this is not a conversation with the decedent and that the tone of voice may depend upon the reason why a conversation occurred." The jurors could be expected to pay about as much attention to her warning as a chain-smoker does to the surgeon general's. Lambert directed that the windows in the courtroom be closed, perhaps to protect passersby below from the shock. Once more, Berry, who had now heard the tape eight times, pushed "play."

After Osgood had emerged from Lambert's chambers to say how awful the upcoming tape would be, Nina had tried preparing Basia for it. "We are going to hear something that's going to be extremely upsetting," she explained maternally. "We're not going to let it bother us. We'll take a deep breath, we'll look straight ahead, and we won't get upset." Basia followed her instructions well. As she sat impassively, a congealed smile on her face, the staccato sound of her own high-pitched hysteria filled the courtroom. The nightmarish cries went on and on, sounding even more horrific because, with only a few exceptions— notably, the two former domestics now facing one another—no one had any idea what they were hearing. All told, the tape lasted only four minutes. But, as is often the case with traumas, listeners lost their sense of time; some insisted it went on for at least fifteen. Both Osgood and Jack Raymond had been urging Christ to let Basia be Basia, to take off her muzzle and let her talk. Now, the jurors had finally heard Basia speak. Heretofore, it had been nearly impossible to reconcile the demon Milbank had been portraying with the silent woman they saw, but no longer. "She'll never recover from this," John Scanlon, the children's publicist, predicted afterward. Just about the only people who weren't shocked by what they heard were Christ and Osgood. The rest of the world was merely catching up with what they'd already been subjected to, live rather than on Memorex. When recess was declared, they sat back and smiled sardonically at one another. "I didn't think that was so bad," Christ mumbled. "We've heard a lot worse," Osgood replied. Later Christ predicted sullenly to a reporter that the television news shows surely would "go apeshit" over the recording.

Court stood in recess. The crowd milled in the hallway while Milbank's interpreter, Theresa Romer, speaking in the crisp, antiseptic English of Radio Moscow's North American service, supplied curious reporters with instant translations. The interchange ended only when Basil Zirinis of S&C stumbled upon the scene and called it "a fucking outrage." In the meantime, to a smaller audience, Basia insisted the tape contained only "mild swears" like "Go to hell," once one of her father's favorite expressions. She also speculated on the tape's origins. "Why do you think she made this tape?" she asked, smiling the peculiar, self-satisfied smile of the persecuted. "She was ordered to." It was, she suggested, the handiwork of the KGB.

The next day the press was filled with Romer's minitranslations, including claims that Basia had called Izabella "a dumb broad," a "whore," and a "monkey," none of which was true. "JOHNSON'S WIDOW'S A SCREAM ON TAPE," the *Post* declared. *People* magazine compared the tape to "a Wild Kingdom sound track." After two television stations brought in lawyers to get permission, millions of viewers heard the tirade for themselves. Only the *Nowy Dziennik*, the Polish-American daily, was subdued. True, the episode prompted the pro-Basia paper to run its first article on the trial, but the gist of the story was that in light of the dastardly deed of one Pole, jobs at Jasna Polana might now be harder to come by.

Had they been inclined to feel the slightest sympathy for Basia, the jurors might have been offended by the episode. They might have resented a maid for striking back at someone who had taken pity on her and given her a job. They might also have been enraged by an employee furtively recording her employer, and felt like eavesdroppers for overhearing it. They might have wondered how Reilly, who claimed to be fighting for the integrity of the legal profession, could kick off his case with such ill-gotten evidence. They might have been puzzled, too, about why the tape had been made in the first place. At least one juror was convinced Junior had put Izabella up to it, but the others seemed disinclined to probe Izabella's motives too deeply; they were already convinced of Basia's villainy. Bad enough that she abused the help; worse still, she had forgotten her own past. Henceforth, whenever anyone described Basia flying off the handle—or, as it became known in the proponents' camp, "doing a Poterewicz"—the jury would mentally replay the tape. One juror was so upset by the recording that he begged off an invitation to ride home with an alternate; he needed to be alone.

Osgood nonetheless thought he saw a way to salvage something out of the debacle. Playing the recording on a large machine in open court exaggerated the harshness of Basia's voice, he argued: Why not bring the jury to Jasna Polana, where they could hear it in the more intimate setting in which it was made? At first blush his idea seemed insane. Why take a jury already alienated from Basia to her gilded palace and play that awful tape all over again? Milbank, amazed at S&C's poor judgment, quickly embraced the proposal, as did Lambert; she was as anxious to see "JAZZ-na Pa-LOW-na," as she called it, as anyone. But Osgood had an ulterior motive. He knew that on her own turf Basia could be a charming hostess; a field trip there might actually humanize his client. The trek was set for the following Tuesday, April Fool's Day. Now, at least, the jurors had something other than Basia's shrieking to ponder over the long weekend.

Basia, too, had things to consider besides playing hostess for twelve working stiffs. As the trial progressed, she continued to feel increasingly isolated. Nina and Christ, she thought, were in cahoots. Osgood's stock fell to a new low when, as she dictated some off-the-wall questions she wanted him to ask Izabella on cross-examination, he'd looked away momentarily. "Mr. Osgood, pay attention!" she shrieked. "You're not listening to me!" Old acquaintances were boycotting her, either because Basia had no business to throw them or because Christ wanted them uncontaminated in the event they were called as witnesses. So starved was she for companionship, so desperate was she for a sounding board, that one night she invited one of the reporters covering the trial to spend a night at Jasna Polana. This he did, with Basia's blue Mercedes picking him up on the corner of Chambers and Church streets, a few blocks west of the courthouse. More swayed than he suspected by Reilly's advocacy, the reporter—who rated only the room next to the one in which Malcuzynski had always stayed—slept fitfully, afraid that Basia would either shoot him or seduce him, but surely never leave him alone. Over bottles from Seward's private stock, the reporter and Basia spoke until the wee hours of the morning; but how much consolation could Basia get from someone taking down everything she said on a laptop computer?

In other words, Basia had plenty of yes-men and yes-women around, but no real confidant, and at a time when she needed one most. Into this vacuum entered John D. Fox. A twenty-seven-year-old man she'd met the previous fall through a friend in Poland's Solidarity underground, Fox was an enigmatic fellow. As a Princeton undergraduate, he'd had strong and conspicuously conservative leanings, which he shared periodically in the school newspaper. But his résumé stopped there. The last several years of his life were a blank. Fox had the cocky confidence and worldliness of the journalist he claimed to be, but his clippings were strangely sparse. His few extant articles, which had appeared in publications like the *Reader's Digest*, were often on anti-Communist themes; so impressed had Basia been by one of them, on Jerzy Popieluszko, the priest murdered by the Polish authorities, that she'd had copies of it distributed in court—presumably so that the press could read about another Polish martyr. Fox now appeared to have nothing better to do with his time than tend to Basia Johnson; his business card listed no occupation and gave as his address 15 West Forty-third Street in New York: the Princeton Club. As her case progressed, he and his Polish-born wife visited her lonely estate with increasing frequency. He laughed at her jokes and lent her counsel—for instance, upbraiding her for drinking too much one night in the sole company of that reporter she'd just invited to Princeton.

Basia's friends were perplexed and a bit threatened by this strange interloper. "This guy is going to be trouble," Harry Bailey warned Nina. Members of Basia's circle hatched theories about Fox, most notably that he was with the CIA; Bailey, who had himself worked briefly for the Company, deputized a Princeton friend to look up Fox in the university's alumni records, only to find that his history had been erased—standard Agency operating procedure, he thought. So, too, was landing a sinecure at *Reader's Digest* and annexing oneself onto someone like Basia, who had lots of money to give away with no strings or congressional oversight attached. Discussing Fox's background one day as they drove together to Jasna Polana, Bailey declared, "Oh, John, you'd be perfect for the CIA!" There followed, Bailey later recalled, "a deathly pause"; looking into his rearview mirror, he could see that Fox had turned scarlet.

To Basia, convinced the KGB was either at Jasna Polana's wrought-iron gates or had already penetrated them, such exotic rumors only made Fox more appealing. Even before the trial started, she tapped him to head her new center on Central European culture, and once testimony in the case began, their conversations grew even more frequent. After Izabella's appearance, Basia sent Fox an S.O.S. in Berne, where he was conducting one of his periodic, vaguely defined "research" missions. "You've got to come back immediately!" she told him. "I really need you! It's a disaster! Everything is going against me! These lawyers are not working for me! It's an impossible situation!" Fearing her line was tapped, she said nothing more.

Fox dutifully, and hastily, returned, and the two spent Easter Sunday pacing the presumably bug-free grounds of Jasna Polana together. Basia briefed Fox on the sorry state of her case and the nastiness of a court system that could be used—unlike Poland's, she maintained—to assassinate someone's character. She complained about awakening at six each morning, making the long trip to New York, sitting bound and gagged in the courtroom as the lies rained down upon her. And she chastised her lawyers. Christ was "lazy," "a wet noodle," "a dishrag," "a knucklehead," "a sack of potatoes," "a soft-boiled egg." She again fantasized that Christ and Nina were lovers, and lamented that she hadn't fired him long ago. She directed Fox, a man with a million contacts, to check Christ out. Fox reported the mixed reviews he'd received to her, along with a recommendation: She needed her own counsel, someone beholden only to her. "The plane you are riding in is a two-seater, it's been hit, it's out of control, and it's going down," he told her. "You're in one seat, Nina's in the other." Moreover, that lawyer shouldn't be some namby-pamby type but a "junkyard dog," someone unafraid of mixing things up.

Basia already had her own candidate, the same man Lambert lionized and Marty Richards had nominated to Milbank months earlier: the ubiquitous Roy Cohn. Apparently unaware that he was a "homosapien," Basia thought Cohn ideal; here, she reasoned, was someone who knew both the Red Menace facing the Free World and the redheaded menace perverting the trial. If Lambert were looking for a payoff—as Basia came to suspect after the judge, chatting with her and Nina after court one evening, lamented how expensive it was to send one of her relatives to college—Cohn could presumably take care of that as well. "I'm so excited! I've got an idea that will save the case!" she told Fox. Fox promptly called Cohn's office, only to be told he was vacationing in the Caribbean. In fact, Cohn had just learned he had AIDS. ("Should I commit suicide now or later?" he'd asked his doctor upon hearing his diagnosis.) Unbeknown to Basia, he was in no condition to help her, or himself.

XL

On March 31, on the eve of the scheduled Jasna Polana tour, the proponents and their lawyers huddled in a private dining room at the Broad Street Club. From the moment she walked in, Basia was incensed. The first thing to offend her was the fancy food: Given everything else on their plates, she complained, they should be eating the same simple sandwiches as she. When Osgood broached the subject of Lambert's upcoming settlement talks, she branded him a defeatist, a fifth columnist like all the others. He was helping the KGB, she charged; he didn't believe in her cause. "Now, Basia, that's not fair," Nina said. Osgood, who said nothing, pushed back his chair as if to leave. He may well have, had not Christ calmed things down by assuring Basia that her case was strong and there would be no need to settle anything.

The next morning two white vans, usually used to ferry sequestered jurors to and from their hotel, pulled up in front of the Surrogate's Court, ready for the trip to Princeton. "JOHNSON JURY GOES TO THE JOHN," the *Post* declared. But there were some hitches. First, two television stations had convinced Lambert to let them tag along. Moreover, the judge decreed that the jury could see the bathroom where the tape was made but nothing else, thereby dashing Osgood's hopes for an ingratiating tour. Upset over the changes in the rules, Basia abruptly canceled the visit. The jurors went away bitterly disappointed, as did the twenty press people who'd already gathered at Jasna Polana's gates. Just about the only winners were Basia's security men, who got to eat all of the victuals the kitchen had cooked up for the entourage.

Actually, S&C did not abandon the idea of a house tour. It subsequently proposed a no-frills excursion, with no questions asked, little commentary, no meals, and little press. But only a few days before the proponents revived the idea, Lambert claimed to have received some threatening phone calls both at home and in her chambers. One of the callers, she said, warned that she would soon "die! die! die!" while theother said she'd be killed, killed, killed, unless she declared a mistrial. "Just tell Lambert she better be good to Johnson or else," another caller said. Such a message would have been ambiguous, to say the least, were it not delivered in what the judge's law assistant identified as an Eastern European accent. Lambert promptly called in the FBI. Henceforth, court officers escorted her to and from work, and policemen buzzed by the courthouse hourly. She cut back on her quota of awards banquets, and announced she would go to Jasna Polana only if accompanied by an armed posse of court officers, FBI agents, and New Jersey State policemen. "If anything were to happen to me there, rest assured it isn't going to make any difference," she declared. "This case is going to continue if I have to continue it from a hospital bed and if I have to bring the jurors to the hospital." The Sullivan & Cromwell team quickly realized that a trip taken under such conditions would do more harm than good, and dropped the idea forever.

John Fox rarely showed up in court, and apart from Nina, no one on the proponents' team even knew what he looked like. But gradually, Basia's entourage began sensing his influence. She talked about him, made them talk to him, parroted his lines. When she walked triumphantly into the Duane Street lunchroom one day reciting with obvious gusto Shakespeare's line about killing all the lawyers, it was evident Fox had been teaching her the classics. His fingerprints were also apparent on April 1, when John Merow, S&C's managing-partner-to-be, received a phone call from one of Fox's Princeton classmates, who had himself practiced briefly at the firm. He told Merow how unhappy Basia was with her lawyers, then forwarded two demands: First, she insisted that Osgood, whom she deemed a détente-nik naive about Russian perfidy, not be allowed to cross-examine Izabella. Second, she wanted to meet personally with the S&C brass to discuss how unhappy she was with her legal team, and her desire to add Marvin Schwartz, whose heroic defense of Osgood before Lambert had so dazzled everyone, to it.

Merow immediately summoned Osgood and recounted the conversation. Osgood had no objections to the meeting Basia had proposed. But snatching away Izabella's cross-examination, particularly on such ludicrous grounds, was a personal affront, only the latest he'd had to endure in this star-crossed case from his client, his partner, his adversaries, the judge. Osgood walked back slowly to his office, sat down at his desk, and stared out his window toward New York Harbor and the

Verrazano Bridge. Normally, it was unheard of, unethical, to abandon a client in mid-trial, but not, Osgood rationalized, if that client fired you first. He had areached the stage Wallace Harrison had reached with Basia at Jasna Polana a decade earlier: "*I'm not going to take this bullshit anymore.*" He resolved to quit the case, and informed Christ and Bauman of his shocking decision over lunch at the Down Town Association. Bauman simply didn't believe him. Basia's abusiveness was nothing new; why walk away now? "You're like two guys who've been through the wars together!" he said to Osgood. "You can't leave Donald." "Arnold, it's not going to work," Christ interjected. "This time he's *really* pissed."

After lunch, Osgood walked back to S&C with Christ, and handed him the questions he'd prepared for Izabella. Then, around five, he headed home. In the lobby he encountered Nina, who'd come for the meeting Basia had demanded and that, Nina had presumed, Osgood, too, would attend. "I'm leaving. I'm going home," he said cryptically. When he arrived in Glen Ridge, New Jersey, he promptly went out for a two-hour jog. If anyone from S&C called, he told his wife, she was to say he was not in.

Merow had asked MacCrate, one of the firm's most distinguished senior litigators, the bar-president-to-be who had accompanied Schwartz to Lambert's chambers when Osgood was under attack, to meet with Basia and Nina. Soft-spoken, genial, wholesome to the point of corniness, MacCrate was the ideal diplomat, a man at ease among movers and shakers. He flaunted those ties, dropping so many names into so many conversations that associates called him "Thud." Tall, thin, bespectacled, square, MacCrate looked like the father in "American Gothic." But Basia never liked Grant Wood, and soon she didn't much like MacCrate, either. She didn't like how he stood up for Osgood. She didn't like how he resisted her call for Schwartz, offering an experienced but less renowned litigator named Philip Graham instead. And she didn't like what she considered his condescension. At one point in their meeting MacCrate stood up, looked out of his office window, and pointed toward Brooklyn, where his forebears had settled. It was in yon place that his grandfather, a poor Scotsman, had first settled, he explained; nearby, he said, pointing out another spot, his father had practiced law, in an office he shared with the local blacksmith. And over there, well, that was where MacCrate himself had grown up. Perhaps, MacCrate said, he hadn't come all that far; Wall Street was just a stone's throw away. He had regaled countless visitors and S&C associates with this Algerist routine, some of them more than once. In this instance it was perhaps his way of saying he, too, was an immigrant, and could understand Basia's problems. But she felt he was patronizing her, and dismissed him afterward as a "stupid blockhead" and "nothing but a Methodist preacher."

Word that Osgood had walked off the case sent shock waves through the proponents' camp. At Shearman & Sterling, where the development was discussed at a management committee meeting, there was speculation that Osgood had suffered a nervous breakdown. Between themselves Nina and Christ theorized that Osgood's exit reflected not only humiliation but the petulance of a suitor scorned. Over the next few days there were repeated pleas to Osgood to return, from Nina, Christ, Polak, and several partners at Sullivan & Cromwell. All were unavailing. Bauman called MacCrate, demanding he compel his junior partner to come back; MacCrate threw up his hands and said he could do nothing. Some of the associates on the case made more personal appeals. While Rogers and Zirinis had aligned themselves with Christ, the loyalties of Delahunty and Michaelson lay with Osgood. As Delahunty once put it, "We have a minister who fights like a marine and a marine who fights like a minister." Fearing that the case was salvageable only if he stayed on, they implored Osgood to return; if Basia had fired him, they said, they were prepared to quit the case in protest. Osgood would not budge. Only one person might have changed his mind. She never called.

When court resumed on Tuesday, with Izabella once more taking the stand, Osgood's chair was conspicuously empty. Henceforth, the only trace of him in the courtroom was the gold chain he had given Basia, which she continued to wear around her neck. Christ told anyone seeking Osgood's whereabouts that he was in some unspecified place, "working on the case." Initially, the Milbank lawyers feared he was attempting to have Izabella either deported or indicted for taping conversations illegally. (Apparently fearing that, Izabella consulted Peter James Johnson, Mario Cuomo's personal lawyer. How she found him, much less could afford him, wasn't clear.) When his absence became permanent, Reilly came to assume Basia had fired him. While Osgood thought the Milbank lawyers would exult over his departure, they were actually quite dejected. Osgood, they felt, had turned several witnesses and the judge in their favor. "Hey, maybe now we're in trouble," Reilly told one of his partners. In the meantime, despite Nina's warnings that he could never manage alone, Christ carried on uncomplainingly. A man who had both coveted responsibility and feared it was finally on his own. "You've done me a real favor," he told Osgood after his first day solo in court. "You've helped me to grow up."

Back on the stand, Izabella had by now shed her Hester Street look and appeared almost glamorous. She made the tape, she told Reilly, as a matter of self-defense. "I did that after I was fired for the first time and because I want to secure myself," she explained. "I mean, I didn't know exactly maybe if I will go to an unemployment office or something." ("We weren't sure why we wanted to do it," she said after the trial. "It was something like instinct.") Every day, she said, Basia yelled at someone—a housekeeper, a maid, or Seward himself, once for wetting his bed, another time for walking instead of using his wheelchair. Sometimes, she said after some prompting from Lambert, Basia yelled at Seward even louder than she had in the recorded tirade. What triggered her final departure, she continued, was a dirty bathtub. "I said, 'Mrs. Johnson, I am pregnant. I am doing my best,' but she wasn't listening," she testified. "She said, 'If I can do it, you can do it,' and when she was going upstairs, she was near the door, I heard her call me a 'whore.' "

"What is the Polish word that she used?" Reilly asked.

"I don't want to say it," Izabella said coyly. "It is very bad word in Polish. It is . . . I have to say it?"

"*Kurwa?*" asked Reilly.

"Yes, exactly."

"Objection," Christ said. "I'm not sure that Mr. Reilly is a qualified Polish translator, and I don't think there's any reason for him to prompt the witness or dazzle us with his knowledge of Polish."

"I am really not dazzled of his great knowledge of Polish, since he knows one word," the judge said, joking as she often did when the only alternative was to sustain an S&C lawyer's objection.

"I am learning, Your Honor," Reilly added.

Christ faced a choice when he rose to question Izabella. He could either grill her or leave bad enough alone. In fact, he struck his usual unhappy compromise, questioning her laboriously but inflicting little real pain. As always, he appeared ill at ease when confrontational, speaking so quickly it seemed he could hardly wait for his own unpleasant questions to end. Several times he allowed her to revisit or embellish what she'd already said—for instance, to inform the jury that Basia had forced her to use, and, therefore, to inhale, ammonia during her pregnancy. Though Christ hinted she had provoked Basia into exploding and been paid for making the recording, Izabella was generally spared any discomfort, either because Lambert blocked the most difficult questions or Christ didn't think to ask them. At times Izabella appeared to mock Christ, a point that did not elude Basia. "She was smarter than he was," Basia bitterly told a friend afterward.

Once Izabella stepped down, dark rumors began emanating from Basia's camp. By now, the pattern was becoming familiar: Incapable of discrediting witnesses on the stand, the proponents and their lawyers opted for ex post facto innuendo instead. Milbank, one rumor went, had really known about Izabella all along, but kept mum so it would not have to disgorge any tapes during discovery. Another was that Izabella's recorder was a state-of-the-art machine costing three hundred dollars, a budget-busting item for someone so poorly paid and, therefore, clearly supplied by others. Still another was that Izabella had been put up to the job, either by the Polish government (a theory favored by Basia) or by the Johnson children. In fact, the machine was routinely available for under a hundred dollars. Apparently, the cost was inconsequential to the Poterewiczes; months after the trial concluded, their tape recorder sat unclaimed, presumably alongside the scrap of paper containing their secret address, in Lambert's office safe.

But the objectants' story had inconsistencies of its own. According to one Lambert confidant, long before Izabella had allegedly stumbled into the courthouse with her recordings, Forger, seeking to impress the judge with the strength of his upcoming case and to justify his unwillingness to settle, had hinted privately to her that the children had such tapes (Forger later denied this was so). Then there was Charles Big Paw's assertion that months earlier Junior had told him he had a hysterical Basia on tape. (Junior later denied that claim, too). One way or another, Izabella Poterewicz seemed peculiarly, incongruously, cozy with the Johnson children. She regularly referred to them by their first names and, shortly before her testimony was complete, went out with them for a quick snack at Ellen's, a bakery-restaurant across the street from City Hall. It was a strange sight: a collection of multimillionaires sitting at the counter, breaking pecan butter strip and bran muffins with yet another Polish maid. (Junior liked to recount the story of how, before some of Basia's relatives arrived for a visit, his father had allegedly asked him whether he should have them fumigated first. The comment sounded more characteristic of the son than the father; in any case, neither Junior nor his siblings felt constrained to check Izabella for lice.) Elaine Wold, who had the 1950s look of the various Miss Subways posters lining the restaurant's walls, picked up the tab—for $12.70. It was the best investment one of Seward's children ever made.

During a break in court one day, as the two men stood urinating side by side in the fourth-floor bathroom, Jack Raymond reminded Junior Johnson that it was in just such a setting that Gromyko and Dulles had settled the Korean War. But with Izabella's tape, the children had crossed the Yalu. As Basia dug in, if only to clear her blackened reputation, the children savored all of what Junior called the "good stuff" still to come. Indeed, for the next five weeks a steady procession of the disgruntled, displaced, disenchanted, and disinherited marched into court, swore to tell the truth, the whole truth, and nothing but the truth, and offered their own sordid versions of life with Seward and Basia.

For everyone who testified, several others had been considered. Seward's former secretary, Joann Farinella, was rejected because she was too attractive; the jury might wonder why, if Basia were as protective of her prized bird as Milbank claimed, she'd have kept this pretty woman around. A former cook begged off. "I cater parties where there are bowls of cocaine on the table," he told a Milbank lawyer. "How would my employers feel if they knew I go around talking about them afterwards?" Despite Reilly's impassioned plea—he flew to Paris on the Concorde and offered her comparable travel arrangements to New York—Mme. Zdziechowska, the matron of the Biblioteka Polska who'd feuded so bitterly with Basia, declined to testify. So did a Jasna Polana alumna who worried that Basia could block her daughter's admission to Princeton. Indeed, despite the wide net that Milbank cast, when court resumed on April 4, Reilly's witness was a familiar face. He'd been sitting in the courtroom from the beginning, and always in the same place: alongside Mary Lea and Marty Richards, the people he was paid to protect. "Your Honor," Reilly intoned solemnly, "contestants call Anthony Maffatone." With a tough act to follow, Milbank had decided to unveil its next star witness, the only man who claimed ever to have seen Basia strike Seward.

Robert Carswell, the man who had succeeded Robert Knight as

head of Shearman & Sterling (and someone who wanted to learn first-hand whether things in Lambert's courtroom were as bleak as he'd been led to believe), was among those on hand when Maffatone, a small man with thinning hair and a closely cropped salt-and-pepper beard, made his way toward the witness stand. With his intense, dark eyes and world-weary mien, Maffatone had an ascetic, almost priestly air about him. But here was someone in a perpetual state of combat readiness, who loved to boast, as he had to Berry and Reilly and many others, of being in the "death and mayhem" business. He'd been a navy SEAL in Vietnam, and had gone on to become not only Sylvester Stallone's bodyguard and buddy, but also, some said, the inspiration for *Rambo*. Maffatone hailed from Paterson, New Jersey, but traced his spiritual roots back to Japan and Japanese military mythology. Now, Maffatone was about to go over the hill for his samurai.

Maffatone told Reilly of first meeting the Johnsons, at what he called Seward's "indoctrination" into the Knights of Malta, then of returning to Jasna Polana to inspect its security system. It was during that visit, after thirty or forty minutes of chitchat, that Seward suddenly leaned across the table, looked at him, and asked, "Who are you, and what are you doing here?" Reilly asked him what happened next. Maffatone looked down at his feet and began to speak. "With that, Mrs. Johnson spun around and she screamed at him, 'You stupid, stupid man! This is Tony!' " he said. "And she smacked him in the face, and she went into a tirade, screaming at him, that he was a 'stupid,' 'ga-ga' man. When she smacked him in the face, he grabbed his mouth, and there was like a look of shock on his face."

"Can you describe any more specifically how hard she hit him?" Reilly asked. "Did she hit him with her hand?"

"The back of her hand," Maffatone said. "She stood up when she did it. It was all like in one motion. And she just smacked him, and she stood over him, and she was screaming, 'You stupid, stupid man! This is Tony! You know who Tony is! He was invited here!' "

As Maffatone now recalled the scene, Basia's outburst shook him up far more than any Vietcong mortar barrage. "I just started fumbling around with my papers," he said. "It was just like very, very confusing to me. I just couldn't wait to get out of there. I was, like, mortified."

"Can you describe Mrs. Johnson's tone of voice on that occasion?" Reilly asked.

"She was screaming at the top of her voice, and her voice was hysterical."

Maffatone told the court, as he told Milbank, of how Basia ladled out another helping of humiliation when Seward balked at eating the breakfast mush placed before him. "She screamed at him and told him he was a 'stupid old man' and a 'stupid American' and 'That's very good for you!' and 'You eat it!'" he testified. Another time, Basia chewed him out for requesting a birthday barbecue. "She just started to scream at him and told him again he was a 'stupid old man' and a 'stupid American' and that he was irresponsible and he would burn the house down and 'How could you think of such a stupid thing?' and 'The food is bad at the cookout and it's no good for you,'" he said. "And she said that he was 'ga-ga,' and she told him to get into his room because he was bad." What, Reilly asked, had been Seward's response? "He did an about-face and went into his room," Maffatone replied.

But it was Maffatone's description of Basia's battery that stuck. In its own way Maffatone's stroke was far more powerful than Basia's could possibly have been, suggesting Seward's incompetence and Basia's dominance all at once. "A SLAP AT MRS. JOHNSON," the *Daily News* reported. Or, as the *Times* put it, "WITNESS IN SUIT SAYS MRS. JOHNSON STRUCK HER HUSBAND'S FACE." The Sullivan & Cromwell lawyers thought Maffatone had invented the entire incident and that they could prove it: The security men watching the Johnsons' every move on closed-circuit television would surely have seen it. They resolved to find the men on duty at the time and bring them into court. In the meantime Christ cross-examined. Lacking Reilly's killer instinct, he failed to ask Maffatone the question Milbank would pose so effectively to several of Basia's witnesses: whether he was so beholden to his employers that he would say or do anything for them. Nor did he ask Maffatone why he'd never mentioned anything about the episode to anyone for six years, particularly to the daughter of the man being abused. Maffatone's sworn testimony—that he was "like, mortified" by what he'd witnessed, suggested he'd been too shaken up to tell anyone about it. Later, though, he claimed the experience had actually been too inconsequential to bother bringing up. Grizzled veteran of the "death and mayhem business" that he was, he explained, "seeing an old man get slapped in the face is not earth-shattering to me." Maffatone couldn't keep his own story straight. He could not decide whether what he'd seen at Jasna Polana was too traumatic or too trivial to tell anyone about, and Christ did not force him to choose.

When Christ finally embarked upon a commando mission of his own, seeking to show Maffatone's hatred for Basia, he stepped on a land mine. "Isn't it a fact that you don't like her?" he asked the bodyguard. "No, I don't," Maffatone answered glumly. It was a simple and unilluminating exchange. But under the rules of evidence Reilly could not ask Maffatone for opinions—unless, that is, Christ opened the door for him. "I bet you a nickel Reilly gets up and asks, 'Why?' " the judge whispered to Corn. "No further questions, Your Honor," Christ declared.

"I have just one," Reilly said, as he strode toward the lectern. "Mr. Maffatone, is there any particular reason *why* you do not like Barbara Johnson?"

"Yes, there is," he replied.

"Will you tell us what it is?"

Almost from the beginning, there'd been bad blood between Basia Johnson and Tony Maffatone. Basia told the Richardses he was incompetent and courted trouble rather than avoided it. She'd also said he'd made advances toward her. Now, his reciprocal hatred enabled Maffatone, a man who usually spoke in police jargon and Pentagonese, to summon the same primitive eloquence he'd already shown with Reilly and Berry. However stage-managed the rest of his testimony had been, this part came from the heart. "I feel that she enjoys berating people," he said. "My mother and father were working-class people, and when I witnessed the way she treated her employees and everyone that she felt was beneath her, it brought out an anger in me that . . . I put myself in empathy with the people that she would scream and yell at and berate and hold their jobs in the palm of her hand, and it was like if they didn't become subservient to her, they would lose their jobs. And it disgusted me."

"Did that include also the way she treated Mr. Johnson?" Reilly asked.

"When I see a man humiliated . . . " he began.

Christ objected, and was promptly overruled. "You opened the door!" the judge exclaimed gleefully.

" . . . in front of someone else . . . "

Christ objected again, and was again overruled.

" . . . it repulses me, and I just kept wanting him to react or do something, to defend himself. And it just . . . it turned me off like a switch. I just wanted to be away from her and the whole thing."

"I have no further questions, Your Honor," Reilly said.

Court stood adjourned. It was Seward who'd allegedly been slapped, but it was Basia who'd been bloodied, and badly. A journalist approached Reilly with his verdict: After Maffatone's peroration, Milbank would have to work overtime to lose.

XLI

When testimony resumed the following Monday, the jury got its first look at a Johnson, albeit a Johnson by marriage. The law of wills assured de jure what had already happened de facto: that the in-laws would take the leading role in the case. Under New York's "Dead Man's Statute," witnesses standing to gain financially cannot testify about their alleged conversations with the testator. To allow such testimony, a judge once explained, would "imperil the estates of the dead by subjecting them to the uncontradicted perjuries of the mendacious." But while the children couldn't testify about very much, their spouses could, even though Marty Richards, Keith Wold, and Bert Firestone were at least as self-interested as their mates, and would, if the past were any guide, end up spending far more of whatever a will contest would produce.

Reilly began with Wold, the onetime ophthalmologist whom Seward had tagged years earlier as the likeliest ringleader of any will contest. By now, Wold was a familiar figure in the courtroom; no one, including any of the Johnson children, attended the proceedings so faithfully. He wore a gray pinstripe suit and wire-rimmed aviator glasses. His silvery hair was slicked back, and his complexion, befitting a country squire from Boca Raton, was red. He had slitty eyes and thin lips, which he pursed frequently as he talked. He spoke in a folksy, phlegmy voice, one that sounded a bit like Nelson Rockefeller's. And if Rockefeller was now a distant memory, so, too, was much of what Wold had to say. Had a movie been made from his testimony, it would have been in the bleached tones of early Technicolor.

Wold began with an Andy Hardy–like account of his introduction to the Johnsons. He'd first met Seward in 1946, he said, through the General's son, Bobby, who'd married his sister Betty. Betty offered to fix up Keith with one of the Johnson girls, apparently Mary Lea. But young Wold wasn't fussy about his heiresses: When Mary Lea came down with a cold, he'd gone out with Elaine instead, and married her. Here was a real fairy tale, not the bogus one Christ had offered in his opening statement. The Wold-Johnson saga was so storybook, in fact, that no one in it ever died. "Bob Johnson, is he General Robert Wood Johnson's son?" Reilly asked, referring to a man who'd died sixteen years earlier. "Bob Johnson is General Johnson's son," Wold replied. "And he's married to your sister?" "He's married to my sister, yes," Wold said, neglecting to say she'd been married twice since.

The Seward that Wold described was a simple man, who loved boats and cows, drove Chevys and Dodges, drank cheap Bordeaux (Wold neglected to mention Seward's private wine cellar, which pre-dated Basia), wore canvas and corduroy from the local army-navy store; his idea of "art" was the Bull Durham bull on the side of a barn. All of this changed, Wold maintained, when "Barbara" entered the picture. He depicted a metamorphosis like Kafka's, though here the hero turned into a mouse rather than a cockroach, and a profligate mouse at that. The Dodges became Rolls-Royces; the cheap wine, Lafite-Rothschild; the rented single-engine plane, a jet. The farming and sailing supposedly ceased, the clothes became tailored, the art turned to Pissarros and Picassos and Monets. ("I'm sure some of them had cows in them," he quipped.) Gone, too, were a half-dozen of his old friends, though Wold neglected to note that two of them died before Basia left Poland and a third succumbed shortly thereafter. The Shaker-like furnishings at Oldwick yielded to the gaudiness of Jasna Polana, where, he said, "you played a game called 'How Many Monets Are There in This Room?' "

Wold, who'd seen little of Seward and Basia in their first decade together, conveniently fast-forwarded to 1980, when he and Elaine paid them a visit at Children's Bay Cay. The topic of conversation that day turned to the pavilion, of her design, that Basia had hoped to build in honor of Wallace Harrison at the Metropolitan Opera. "I asked her what her qualifications were—where, you know, did she go to architecture school," he recalled. "She said 'no,' she had just learned it in life, through experience, looking at buildings and that sort of thing. And she said, 'Besides, all architects are stupid. I could do a much better job than that anyway.' Seward said, 'Well, now, Basia, we have some pretty good architects for this.' She said, 'No, they're all stupid, and they aren't any good at all. Seward, if you don't think that they're stupid, then you're stupid, too.' "

That declaration, Wold related, was followed by a tirade at the cook and, when he came to the hapless employee's defense, at Seward, too. Wold said he witnessed something similar at Ansedonia, when Seward, unable to explain the word "oatmeal" to the Italian waiter, went into the kitchen himself to get some, thereby detonating Basia.

"She was again calling him 'stupid' and 'crazy' and 'cruel,' and also she used an expression, 'ga-ga,' which I don't know what that is, but she called him 'ga-ga,' " he testified. When Seward slunk away, Wold went on, Basia turned to Elaine and said, "You'll never know how difficult it is to live with someone as stupid and cruel and crazy as your father."

Wold could recall no instances where Basia had hit his father-in-law, but that was only because he'd never seen her touch him at all.

REILLY: "Did you ever see Barbara Johnson kiss Mr. Johnson?"
WOLD: "No, never."
REILLY: "Did you ever see Barbara Johnson pat Mr. Johnson on the shoulder or on his head?"
WOLD: "No."
REILLY: "Did you ever see Barbara Johnson hug Mr. Johnson?"
WOLD: "No, I don't think so."
REILLY: "Did you ever see her express any affection toward him?"
WOLD: "Not that I recall."

Perhaps because even he found it unbelievable, Reilly did not have Wold retrace what he'd described in his deposition as Seward's twenty-five-year-long descent into senility. Instead, he had Wold recount the condition in which he'd found his father-in-law in April 1983, just after the great escape from the QE2. "Moon-faced, pale, almost yellowish," Wold said. "He appeared to be tranquilized. He was not active at all." Had Seward known who he was? "I don't think he recognized me," Wold replied. "Elaine reached over to him and said, 'Dad, this is Keith. You remember him, don't you?' And he looked at me and said, 'Fine.' " When he questioned his father-in-law about the new ship, Wold said, Seward stared at him uncomprehendingly. The next day, Wold said, Seward lay inert in bed, staring straight ahead "as though he were in a catatonic state or something."

"Dr. Wold, did you form an opinion as to whether Mr. Johnson was of sound mind and memory?" Reilly asked. By Reilly's own standards, the question could not be answered satisfactorily without administering a "mental-status examination." But that did not deter Reilly, or Wold, here. "My opinion was that he was not of sound mind and memory," Wold said. "He didn't recognize me. He was unable to answer my questions."

Christ tried, agonizingly and maladroitly, to chip away at Wold. The doctor's credibility did not suffer grievously, for instance, when Christ demonstrated that Jasna Polana, like Oldwick, had a herd of cows.

Asked whether Seward had been senile in 1983, Wold grew curiously cautious. "I don't know what you mean by 'senile,'" he replied. On those few occasions when he had Wold on the ropes, Christ invariably let him off. Aside from proving that Wold was either a liar, a cretin, or a tad senile himself—Wold claimed not to know that the painting he and Elaine bought from Basia and Seward for $160,000 was a Pissarro—Christ hadn't laid a glove on the man.

Word of Christ's agonies was spreading. A senior S&C associate not involved in the Johnson case stopped by the Surrogate's Court one day to see if what he'd been hearing was exaggerated. "Don couldn't try his way out of a paper bag," he reported to his colleagues when he returned. As Forger told someone that same morning, it was as if Christ were dribbling with a half-inflated basketball. No one could argue with the message on the T-shirt Elaine Wold goofily unveiled in court that day: MY LAWYER CAN BEAT UP YOUR LAWYER, it said. Indeed, with a single question to him in the corridor after he'd completed his testimony, Mary Civiello, the reporter covering the case for the local NBC affiliate, challenged Wold far more than Christ had. "If you considered Seward Johnson your best friend, why didn't you see him for three years until April of 1983?" she asked him. "Ab . . . ip . . . " he burbled. "That's a very good question. We had a lot of . . . ah . . . we spent a lot of time trying to figure this out . . . it . . . I didn't want to cause any further problems with his wife."

Next came Elaine. Speaking in a thin, breathless voice with a slight lisp, holding on to the witness's chair for dear life, she proved anew that far from hampering his case, the Dead Man's Statute was Reilly's secret weapon, allowing him to get the Johnsons on and off the stand before they could do too much damage to their case. Elaine, for instance, recalled a conversation she'd had with Basia, Marty, and Mary Lea at Jasna Polana in the summer of 1971, in which Basia had boasted of forcing Seward to tear up their prenuptial agreement. Unfortunately, Jasna Polana had not yet been built, and Mary Lea and Marty had not yet met. ("She's not a bad sort," Christ said afterward. "Just dumb as hell.") Hoping to slip one by her, Christ raised the still-verboten topic of the children's wealth. "Isn't it true that your net worth is approximately $75 million?" he asked. Instantly, Reilly objected. "Sus-*tained!*" the judge angrily declared. "Her net worth doesn't make one particle of difference in this case! Not one particle of difference does it make! If she had twenty-five cents in her pocket and that's all she had, she would have the same rights in this court as if she were a multimionaire!"

Civiello buttonholed Elaine, too, in the corridor afterward. How, she asked Elaine, would she describe her father's condition during the period under discussion? "Gravely ill," she replied. But had he been senile? "I did not say that. I did not say that." Well, then had he been of sound mind? "I did not say that." Well, then had he been unduly influenced? "I do not know." Eventually, the Wolds' two children, "Dindy" and Clinton, also took the stand. Dindy, who had thanked Basia so effusively for the wedding reception her stepgrandmother had thrown for her at Jasna Polana a few years earlier, now recalled only that a few days prior to the event, she'd heard Basia called Seward "stupid." For her part, Elaine, who'd previously thanked Basia for making "everything so perfect" at the shindig, now disclosed that this was not quite so; she remained miffed that Basia had stuck her with the liquor bill.

Reilly turned next to Seward's skipper, Captain Raymond Gore. With his erect carriage and close-cropped graying hair, Gore had the look of a military man. Though fiercely proud of his aristocratic lineage, he had spent his life in gilded subservience, the kind of life in which he could never call an employer by his or her first name. First there was a certain Mrs. Palmer, owner of the *Guinevere*, then a Mr. Taylor, aboard the *Barunita*. In 1959 he joined Seward, to whom he referred, even in death, as "Mr. Johnson." But Basia had come along and ruined everything, and even before Nina axed him in 1985—in other words, while he was still on Basia's payroll—Gore volunteered his services in the will contest to Keith Wold.

Gore had survived so long in part by keeping Seward's secrets. Like the gondoliers of old Venice, who maintained cabins with curtains for such purposes, Gore kept his patron's assignations private; now, pressed by a judge intensely curious about Seward's sex life, he scrupulously observed the chauffeur's code. Only when forced to, for instance, did he disclose that the "friend" who accompanied Seward and Carter Nicholas on their seven-week-long cruise to Central America in 1969 was a young lady, whose name he had somehow forgotten. He had standing orders not to list such people in the ship's log, and even after Seward's death, his secrets were still safe. Like Wold, Gore was a lifestyle witness, someone who could describe how much Seward had changed over the years, how dreadful that change was, and how much of it was attributable to big, bad Basia. But his account of Seward's evolution was far less dramatic than Wold's, and far less critical of Basia, who had struck him as "very pleasant" and a "nice person to have around" when they'd first met in 1970. Just about the most negative thing he could say about her was that Seward found Jasna Polana too "drafty" for his taste.

The physical decline Gore retraced was the familiar trajectory of a septuagenarian turned octogenarian. By age eighty-two, Seward wasn't as alert or responsive as he'd been at seventy-two; at eighty-seven, when Gore left him at the helm for an instant, Seward ran the boat aground. But piloting a boat and signing a will were entirely different skills, and Christ objected. "I think we have really run aground in this examination," he complained.

"You may think it is irrelevant," Lambert retorted, "but they may want to use this as to questions of judgment and things of that nature."

"Sailing a boat?" Christ asked unbelievingly.

In Seward's last year, Gore continued, he and the old man took five daylong trips together, and Seward hadn't said a word to him on any of them. But Gore recalled that in their last trip of any consequence, a May 1982 journey to the Florida Keys, Seward turned comparatively loquacious, making three significant statements—all, strangely enough, germane to the case. It was neat: One reflected on his competence, another on his testamentary wishes, while a third touched on the children's undue-influence claim. First, he expressed an odd desire to be buried on the *Ocean Pearl*, lashed to a table in the main cabin and sunk somewhere east of the Bahamas. Second, he said he planned to leave Harbor Branch a large sum of money, though his will at the time said no such thing. Then he gave Gore a warning. "By the way, Ray, watch out for Mrs. Zagat," he supposedly said. "I don't trust her."

"Were those his exact words?" asked Charles Berry, who was conducting the examination.

"Exact words," Gore replied.

In a case with no real victims, in which it was difficult to feel especially sorry for anyone, Reilly had to entertain as much as enlighten. He had to keep the jury interested. That meant producing people who were colorful, lively, true to life. Already there had been a maid, a bodyguard, and a ship captain, and people began wondering: Just *whom* would Reilly come up with next? It was a closely held secret; even Junior wasn't told, lest he blab to the press. Shortly after Gore departed, Reilly escorted into the courtroom a gentle-looking, elderly man with a white goatee. If Izabella Poterewicz was too vulnerable to be impugned, here was someone who was too lovable. "Your Honor, contestants call Mr. Mervyn Nelson," Reilly said.

Nelson, wearing a blue blazer over a white cardigan, looked like a cross between Zorba the Greek and Orson Welles, and spoke like a cross between Welles and Vincent Price. Né Rosen, he described himself as "a teacher of film and theater technique," but in fact had led a far more varied life. Hovering around stardom and genius, he wrote and directed scripts and plays and revues and dinner theaters and nightclub acts and even a few films. He'd taught hundreds of aspiring actors; worked with Harold Prince, Leonard Bernstein, Cy Coleman, Betty Comden, and Adolph Green; discovered Rue McClanahan and Harry Belafonte; and, until Mary Lea and her millions came along, lived with Marty Richards.

For thirty years the two had not just lived together, but worked together, scraped by together, schemed together, made mischief together, and now, were waging a will contest together. They were, Nelson said, "as close as I guess any two friends could be." In fact, strains had developed between them; Nelson thought Mary Lea's money had made his old friend more arrogant and less appreciative, and he resented it deeply. But for Nelson the courtroom was but another stage; he made that clear during a break in his testimony, when he asked a bystander when court went back into session. Told this was one show that truly could not go on without him, he smiled approvingly, then he peeked through the courtroom door. "I don't want to make my entrance until everyone is seated," he snickered.

Nelson, who'd spent a lifetime memorizing lines, claimed to have no memory for names or dates or places; at one point he called Diana Firestone "Mrs. Livingston," and he stumbled over the name of the Johnson estate as well. "I can't pronounce the name . . . Lola Polana? . . . Am I saying it right?" he asked amid laughter in the court. "Mr. Nelson, join the club!" Lambert chortled. "I have trouble pronouncing it, too." "Good," Nelson retorted. "I feel better." But on matters of greater moment his memory, either of the facts or the script, was considerably sharper. He recounted how, as he tied Seward's bow tie before the Knights of Malta ceremony, the old man had repeatedly mistaken him for a butler, dresser, or valet, even though the tie-tying had actually been done by someone else. He told of how Basia had introduced Nina to him as "my lawyer," and how Nina in turn praised Basia's ability to "do anything she sets her mind to." He recalled his 1982 visit with Basia and the Richardses to Florence, where, he said as he gestured skyward, Basia boasted to him of hearing "heavenly voices that told her that she should go out and make her way in the world."

Another time, he testified, "she said she was lying down—I think it was on the grass when she was a girl when she heard these things happen inside, this inspiration—this heavenly inspiration."

Nelson went on to describe the far less sublime way Basia treated Seward, using judgment-laden language Lambert hadn't tolerated from the other side. "He was like a child," Nelson said. "I felt . . . I felt no happiness." He paused for a second, then resorted to a language with which he was more familiar. "I must tell you also that I'm answering these things in terms of my work as a director," he continued. "So, therefore, I am very conscious of character things, and I found that there was . . . it seemed to me that . . . no, no, not it seemed to me: It was, the thing I saw was this lady had tremendous control in a very strong, adamant attitude toward this man who would like . . . not who like: who was resigned, almost like resigned to the position he was in. It was not healthy at all, at all."

With the Johnsons, breakfast was clearly the cruelest meal; Nelson recalled one when Seward would not eat whatever Basia was offering. "You will eat that and no one else will give you anything but that!" he recalled her saying. "I remember him clenching his fists and sitting like a . . . not like: sitting like a kid who . . . "—he clenched his fists and moved them up and down, as if throwing a tantrum—"inside there was a fury that he wasn't going to let out, like a little boy, like a child, like a four-year-old."

For a change Christ began his cross-examination with a bang.

"Mr. Nelson," he asked, "have you ever won an Oscar for your acting?"

Instantaneously, Reilly was on his feet. "I object!" he thundered. "I think that is offensive, grossly offensive!" The objection, not surprisingly, was sustained, and the questioning all went downhill from there.

With Maffatone having already appeared and Nelson onstage, the Johnson case was coming to resemble a Producer Circle production, and one of the longer-running and quite possibly more profitable ones at that. Once Nelson finished, in fact, his understudy took his place. Marty Richards, a short, immaculately groomed man, whose hair had the texture and swirl and, one suspected, the feel, of cotton candy, smiled wanly and rose from his seat as his name was called. He had played some strange gigs in his day, but none as improbable as this: the gay Broadway producer, son of a Jewish bookmaker in the Bronx, cast as the defender of one of America's WASPier clans. He'd been practicing the part, kibitzing with reporters, annotating testimony, bad-mouthing Basia from the beginning of the trial. But those were only previews; this was Opening Night. A couple of his in-laws gave him fraternal pats as he walked to the stand.

"My name is Martin Richards, and I live on Gin Lane in Southampton," he began. Richards's voice, like Richards himself, was part man, part boy. It had a certain mature, smoky raspiness to it; he'd just given up Pall Malls, and one could still hear all the years of accumulated tar and nicotine. But it also had a childish lilt and fragility to it, making him sound like a tattletale no matter what he said. This veteran of a thousand theaters added to his boyish charm by affecting an endearing stage fright. "I'm a little nervous," he giggled meekly, bringing forth from Lambert the same motherly reassurance she'd extended to Al Pacino in the Strasberg case.

Richards ticked off the plays and movies he had produced and the functions he'd attended with Basia and Seward—the Richardses' wedding reception at the Stork Club; the White House dinner for Pope John Paul II; the Black and White Ball, where Seward, hating all the noise, had departed just as Frank Sinatra was about to sing. Marty described Seward, whom he'd thought worthy of knighthood only a few years earlier, as something of a bore, able to talk only about his boats and his dogs. With Basia, he related, the subjects were loftier but just as predictable: travel, art, clothing, money. Once, he said, she told him that if the U.S. government went belly-up, she was ready. "She said that she and my father-in-law had put around fourteen or sixteen million dollars into banks in Switzerland, because they had no intention of living any worse than they did if the country should go under," he said. Another time, he said, Basia had boasted of outspending the queen of England. Where did all of this money go? Clearly not to Seward, according to Marty. Once, his father-in-law complained bitterly to him that Basia wouldn't even buy him a couch for his bedroom.

Six years earlier, resplendent in his Knights of Malta regalia, Chevalier Richards had praised Basia extravagantly. Now, he crooned a different tune. "Basia was very much a disciplinarian and acted like a very stern mother, and my father-in-law spoke like a baby—in baby talk," he said. "He would say, 'Basia, can I please have a roll?' 'Basia, can I please go and take that?' 'Basia, can I please go on the boat?' " Richards recalled, scrunching up his face and speaking in a cloying, childlike, whine. "It was sort of embarrassing because he didn't speak the same to us." He then listed the explosions he'd witnessed, several of which were by now no more than summer reruns. There was the

incident at Children's Bay Cay witnessed by the Wolds. "It was hor-
rendous!" Marty said excitedly. "It was . . . there was an explosion of
hysteria toward the young man that was serving and cooking, the steward. He apparently had been an alternate chef (the chef, I believe, was
fired). He was serving us and he was cooking at the same time and I
believe he put a plate down in the wrong place, and all hell broke
loose. There was such screaming and hysteria, and then it just got
louder and louder, and then my father-in-law . . . "

"Screaming by whom?" Reilly inquired.

"By Basia!" Richards tattled. "And then my father-in-law said,
'Basia, please!' and as soon as he said, 'Basia, please!' she started screaming at him and call[ing] him every kind of 'ga-ga,' 'fool,' 'stupid,' and
it went on and on and on; and then she threw her hands up, and she
just looked hysterical. She followed the steward into the kitchen area,
and then my father-in-law turned to us and said, 'No one say anything,
because if you say anything, it gets louder and it gets worse. Just keep
quiet.' "

Then there was that cookout in Ansedonia. "No sooner did he finish
the word 'barbecue,' Basia started screaming and calling him every name
in the world and saying that he was a 'fool' and a 'horrible, stupid old
man' and he was going to burn the house down, and it got louder and
louder until we all choked," he said, holding up his hands limply to
his throat. "There wasn't a moment that there wasn't screaming at the
help and where help didn't walk around shaking with dishes right above
our heads in terrible fear," he said. It was, he added, "like they were
working at a penal colony." After again recounting Basia's lamentation
in Assisi about Seward's sexual cruelty, Richards described how, shortly
after arriving in Florida from the QE2, he'd heard Seward hallucinate
about Nazi submarines. Pay him no mind, he said Basia told everyone;
he was dying and deluded.

Convinced Richards was stage-managing the will contest, S&C had
prepared assiduously to cross-examine him, going so far as to hire a
private investigator to check him out. But Christ's questioning had all
the fire of a television editorial. Far from discrediting Richards—for
instance, by having him recite his Knights of Malta speech, so full of
praise for both Basia and Seward, to the jury—Christ permitted him
to elaborate upon hurtful testimony. On Basia's treatment of others:
"Basia called everyone stupid and incompetent—anyone, of any position, whether it was a person that built her home or a gardener." On
Seward's speaking habits: "They've made him this great conversation-
alist. I've never heard him talk very, very much about anything but

the sea, and they were never lengthy conversations. He spoke to the dogs more than he spoke to human beings." On the hysteria-filled meal at Children's Bay Cay: "I don't know whether you'd call it 'eating' or 'choking' lunch that day." On the bow-tie incident prior to the Knights of Malta party: "My father-in-law said, 'You have a wonderful valet.' I said, 'He isn't my valet. It's my friend.' And he said, 'That's wonderful. Give my best regards to your valet.' Again I said, 'No, he's my friend.' And later, when we left, in the evening, he said, 'Please say good-bye to your valet.' "

The story was a distinct improvement over Nelson's version of the same nonevent, and the gallery laughed appreciatively, with Reilly laughing loudest of all. It even one-upped the version Marty told in his deposition, which had Seward retiring shortly after dinner and, therefore, unable to have bid good-bye to the departing Richardses. Once again, Marty maintained Seward was a reluctant and ill-tempered Knight, a Knight—dare one think it?—only by dint of Basia's undue influence. "My father-in-law wanted it to be over before he started," he testified, ignoring, as Christ did in cross-examining him, his own role in paving Seward's way into the order. "He just kept pulling my jacket and saying 'Can we please get this over with?' Apparently, Basia wanted him to be a Knight more than he wanted to be a Knight."

With his gallant defense of his brothers- and sisters-in-law, his self-deprecating and gossipy asides, his cultivated vulnerability, Marty Richards had been an endearing witness. In fact, he was a smash hit. When he was finished, an exuberant Reilly walked over to Mary Lea. "Marty captivated the jury!" he gushed. There was one more thing that Richards did, though no one, apart perhaps from the Milbank lawyers, picked up on it. He took an odd and unconvincing position on the subject of Maffatone's sensational disclosure.

Maffatone might have remained inexplicably silent for nearly six years after purportedly seeing Basia slap Seward, but he acknowledged mentioning the matter to Marty and Mary Lea before taking the stand. Yet in response to one of Christ's final questions, Marty, seemingly discomfited by the entire subject, insisted Maffatone's story caught him completely by surprise. Milbank had announced months earlier that the children would claim Basia had abused Seward; even the S&C lawyers knew it was coming. But Marty? Though he had taken such a keen interest in the case, though he and his bodyguard were so close, well, it was all news to him. "No, I never heard that story before," he testified. "It was quite shocking. He didn't want to upset my wife prior to this case, I guess." (Richards professed not only ignorance but indignation: So thunderstruck had he been by the story, he later maintained, that he'd reprimanded Maffatone in the corridor immediately afterward. *How could you never have told us about this before, Tony?* But Marty and Maffatone could not reconcile their recollections. The bodyguard not only failed to remember such a reprimand, but dismissed out of hand the notion it ever happened. How could it have, after all, if Marty had known all along what Maffatone was going to testify?)

Once as Marty Richards answered his question, Christ, characteristically, did not follow up. But his apparent acquiescence did not lay the matter to rest, particularly after the will contest had concluded and the children's façade of solidarity crumbled. It was then that Quentin Ryan, who'd been in touch with Mary Lea and Marty during the trial, offered a bombshell of his own, one that could explain his stepfather's odd response to Christ's question: Marty and Mary Lea, Ryan declared unequivocally in court papers, had paid Maffatone to lie on the stand.

XLII

In the next few days Reilly called the three remaining Johnson daughters. Diana Firestone took the stand briefly, murmured something about her children and her horses, then sat down. Next came Jennifer Johnson, the only one of Seward's daughters who did not seem stuck in an era when Betty Furness still sold refrigerators. She described how Seward's departure "devastated" Essie, and how years later Basia, upset over Seward's insistence on taking laxatives against doctors' orders, threatened to leave him. Then came a slightly befuddled Mary Lea, who, after listing her six children, described herself, appropriately enough, as "a producer."

Understandably, Reilly did not delve into Mary Lea's past. Instead, he put her to other, more ingenious uses. The jury, he knew, still felt shortchanged over its aborted trip to Jasna Polana, so he had Mary Lea provide a simulated tour of her own, courtesy of a huge aeriel photograph of the estate. A few years earlier Mary Lea left Jasna Polana all agog, writing Basia and Seward afterward that "your home is the most beautiful I have ever seen." Now, pointer in hand like some Palladian scholar, she was considerably more subdued.

"This is where the help lives and, also, Basia's family lives up here, and . . . " she began. Basia watched the proceedings with obvious revulsion, as if a plague of locusts had descended upon her domain. " . . . Now, these little black ball things here are cameras for security reasons. . . . " These people are so primitive, Basia thought to herself. " . . . One, two, three, four, I can see four, because there are some back here in the garden. I have never counted them, but when you come up here, the gates mysteriously open . . . " I think she's too stupid to know what her lawyers are up to, that they're using her to try to humiliate me, Basia thought. " . . . and this wrought-iron fence along here and gates were made in Poland . . . " I actually feel sorry for her. " . . . This is the front door and you enter into here into a great hall and in here there are a couple of Rembrandts. . . . " There is not a grain of culture in any of them. "Upstairs here was Dad's bedroom. A good portion of this center in the back is the marble bathroom that belonged to Dad. Over this side there is Basia's bedroom here. Then behind that, there is a little tiny bedroom which is done like a railroad car, one of those old Pullman cars. It is a just very small, little cozy place."

In some respects her tour was dated. There had never been a Michelangelo, for instance, and by now the Monets and Modiglianis had gone the way of Princey and Clara. But the jurors got the message: Here was a house in which the mistress had been master. The jury was seeing a huge, opulent monument to a woman's ego, an ego surely strong enough to overwhelm anything that got in its way.

Christ's cross-examinations of the Johnson daughters were unproductive, in part because it was difficult to confront people who seemed so insignificant and inoffensive. Unlike their spouses, there was nothing conspicuously venal about them. Christ attempted to undot Reilly's every i, uncross his every t. He posed his questions mechanically, as if, unsure just what he was looking for, he decided to cover everything. During breaks, he even asked reporters whether there was anything he'd neglected to ask. He chose his targets poorly—for instance, asking Marty Richards his real name. "Very proudly, Klein," Richards told the jurors, four of whom were Jews. "But, you see, Eddie Fisher was not yet a star. Fishers and Schwartzes didn't make it as singers at that time, and my grandmother used to call me Martin Richard, so I figured, it worked for her, it worked for me." That impressed Lambert, who still sported all of the stigmata of her Brooklyn Italian childhood. "You mean prejudice used to rear its ugly head?" she asked in mock surprise.

Shortly after Mary Lea concluded her testimony, Mary Civiello of WNBC caught up with her in the corridor. She asked what Mary Lea hoped to gain from the contest, and Mary Lea quickly spouted the Johnson family line. "I'd like to see Harbor Branch get its fair share because I know that that's what he would have wanted," she said earnestly. "He *loved* the sea."

Civiello wasn't satisfied. "And the money has nothing, means nothing to you?" she asked.

Her script having run out, Mary Lea momentarily looked terrorized. Her eyes widened suddenly, and she looked off frantically, first to her left, then to her right, for help. It was as if her personal computer had just crashed. A second or two later power was restored, but only partially, for the family's altruistic software had not yet been reactivated. Her defenses still down, she began nodding her head, as if savoring something very tasty, then resumed speaking. "Anyone could use it," she finally stated cheerfully.

It was more of an admission than anything Christ had obtained. Or, for that matter, anything that S&C had procured for all its millions in fees. But in fairness to Christ, his impotence stemmed, in large part, to the second, far more public orchiectomy of the Johnson saga: the castration Lambert was performing on him. She would not let him ask a host of crucial questions: whether the children had ever given anything to Harbor Branch, for instance, or felt Basia had taken good care of their father. Frequently, she ridiculed him. "The jury is getting impatient," she declared during one of Christ's examinations. "They want some estimate of when this case is going to be finished. Do you want my best estimate? Before Christmas!" Or, "He said he didn't know four times already. Let's ask the fifth time!" Whenever Christ honed in on something crucial, she would call recesses. "Does anybody here need to make a phone call?" she blurted out during a key moment in his interrogation of Diana Firestone.

Lambert forced Christ's witnesses to answer the most complicated questions "yes" or "no," but let anyone testifying for the children roam far and wide over the historical and psychological map. While torturing Christ's witnesses, she coddled, coached, and comforted Reilly's. While she'd let Reilly pummel Nina ("Everyone has their own way of asking questions," she told Christ after he'd complained) she cautioned the soft-spoken Christ not to use "an attacking voice" while cross-examining Reilly's witnesses. While Reilly objected expansively and without interruption, she cut off the laconic Christ after only a few words, warning him not to "make speeches." One had to wonder how any lawyer, even one more combative and faster on his feet than Christ, would have fared. "I really don't think that if Jesus H. Christ were the lawyer for Mrs. Johnson it would have made any difference," Arnold Bauman later said. Publicly, Christ remained stoic. But privately, he compared entering Lambert's courtroom each morning either to battling at Iwo Jima or getting caught in a trash compactor.

Meanwhile Reilly continued to play Lambert like a virtuoso, appealing to her sense of decorum, her professional pride, her vanity. "I'm not teaching anybody how to try a case—and that includes you, Mr. Reilly," she said once. "We have all learned a lot from you, Your Honor," Reilly oozed. Another time S&C announced plans to bring in an Italian interpreter for one of its witnesses. That wasn't necessary, Reilly purred; "We have the best one on the bench." "You have the best Italian interpreter sitting right here," the beaming judge reiterated.

As April wound down, Reilly unveiled a series of other witnesses. There were Louise Eberle and Judy Abramovitz, two nurses who'd tended to Seward in late 1982 and early 1983. Olindo "Zip" Carnevale had been chief of security and, briefly, estate manager at Jasna Polana (his job description: "I hired people as necessary and fired them at Mrs. Johnson's request"). Reid Edles, John Pellegrini, and Mary Howard also worked on security. Joan Kelsey had succeeded Fran Perrec as Seward's personal secretary. Vincent Stalski had been a butler, and Michael and Andrea Emery another husband-and-wife, cook-and-butler team. Reilly questioned them all crisply, concisely, and—with the exception of one overstuffed former bodyguard whose pants split along the crotch just as she was about to testify, exposing her bikini underwear—without mishap.

One could question the integrity and independence of Izabella Poterewicz, Marty Richards, Mervyn Nelson, Keith Wold, and Tony Maffatone. But the second wave of witnesses consisted of solid citizens— pithy and persuasive, well prepared and eager. Several of them, still smarting over Basia's harsh treatment and anxious to settle scores, had come forward on their own. Though they spanned a decade and observed the Johnsons from a variety of vantage points, their stories were strikingly consistent.

Collectively, Reilly's witnesses covered many topics. A principal one was Basia's tantrums. They occurred around the globe: in Poland (according to Gore); Italy (the Richardses, the Wolds, Maffatone, Nelson); the Bahamas (Marty Richards, the Woldo); Jasna Polana (Carnevale, the Emerys, Kelsey, Abramovitz); the Princeton hospital (Eberle, Abramovitz); and Florida (Poterewicz, the Emerys). They'd been precipitated by Seward's secret purchase of a Crockpot (Abramovitz); a waiter putting out too many wineglasses (Stalski) or putting a dish in the wrong place (Marty Richards); inclement weather and Seward's inability to stick to his Scarsdale diet (Andrea Emery); the loss of a pair of Seward's underwear (Eberle); reserving a single room instead of a suite for Basia in a Paris hotel (Kelsey). Descriptions of Basia's treatment of Seward ranged from "intolerant" to "demeaning" to "debasing" to "denigrating" to "abrasive" to "abrupt." Her epithets ran from "stupid!" (Gore) to "stupid old man!" (Carnevale) to "stupid American!" (Carnevale, Andrea Emery) to "stupid Englishman!" (Poterewicz) to simply "stupid, stupid, stupid!" (Michael Emery). Milbank's witnesses dissected her rages with precision. Her muscles would tense up, she would clench her fists or point menacingly at her target, and her face would redden (Andrea Emery); her face would grow contorted with anger (Michael Emery) or become unusually flushed, with veins sticking out of her neck (Carnevale). Her movements would become "flighty and jerky" (Louise

Eberle). If she was calling someone stupid or crazy, she would gesture with her hands and point to her temple (Howard).

So searing were these rages that even the most inarticulate witness could summon the requisite images to describe them. "If she yell on the people," said Stalski, a seventy-six-year-old Pole who said he had quit a cushy job with David Rockefeller to work for her, "she was very red, red face, mad you can see big eye, red, red face." Finally, when Basia berated him over a tarnished piece of silverware, Stalski had had enough. He testified that he finished serving the dinner, washed the pantry floor, went back to his room, and packed his things. "After she scream at me and I know it wasn't true, I come to the pantry and my hands start to shake, so I realize it is very bad with my heart," he explained. "I couldn't take it any more, the scream, so I left. Next morning, I call Mr. Johnson. I said, 'Sir, I leave. I will not come down because Mrs. Johnson scream at me and that is not true. I did nothing wrong, and I will not come down for work anymore, and I just want to say, 'Thank you very, very much for everything, because I have enough. I can't take it any more.' "

However halting his English, Stalski at times demonstrated a better command of the language than Lambert.

"Can you recall anything else she said when she was yelling at people?" Reilly asked him.

"Yes," he said. "Outside I hear one time she demand—the man was outside and they talk something together, Mrs. Johnson went out and start to scream at them. Then she call him, 'Why you stand here like a pederast?' "

"Do you recall anything . . ." Reilly continued.

"Like a *what*?" the judge blurted out. "I'm sorry. We didn't get the last word. The stenographer had trouble with the last word of his answer."

"*Pederast*," Stalski repeated.

"Is that a Polish word?" the judge asked.

"Polish word," the witness said obligingly.

"Do you know the American word?"

"It is man like a gay," Stalski replied.

Still the judge seemed baffled. "Do you know the English word for 'pederast'?" she asked.

"It is like a gay would be," Stalski answered.

"A what?" asked the judge.

"Gay, the gays, yes," Stalski told her.

"It is the word for 'gay,' " the judge affirmed.

"I object and move to strike, Your Honor," interjected Ted Rogers, the S&C lawyer cross-examining Stalski.

"Overruled," Lambert said firmly. "He used a Polish word, and the judge asked for a translation, and he translated it into English, and he said that pederast is 'gay.' "

Estimates of the periodicity of Basia's rages varied wildly. Carnevale said he'd seen "a good half-dozen" of them in his three years on the estate, or an average of one every six months. Gore, who appeared to chart Basia's tantrums with the same precision he recorded ocean currents, estimated that between 1974 and 1981 they occurred two or three times a week, but by 1982 that number had risen to three or four times weekly. Whatever their frequency, Seward's reaction was the same. He would grow "frustated and submissive" (Eberle); "stand there and lower his head and not say a word and just stare at the floor" (Carnevale); bend over the table and look "verbally or physically whipped" or hang his head and walk away (Michael Emery); or become quiet and look "very sad" (Howard). Later, though, she told another story that cut against the image of Seward's defenselessness. Once, it seemed, Basia told Seward he was crazy. "Hah!" he replied. "Look who's talking about being crazy!"

While Sullivan & Cromwell suggested that particular fits were provoked, it made no attempt to explain Basia's propensity for them. In all likelihood Christ did not know of the history of mental illness in Basia's family; certainly he never raised it as a defense. Instead, it was a Milbank witness, Joan Kelsey, who hinted that these tirades were really beyond Basia's control. "I left the room to go out and tell Mrs. Johnson I was sorry she was so upset," she said, after describing one tantrum. "She turned around and told me she didn't remember a thing she said to me."

Of all of Milbank's witnesses, it was Abramovitz, a registered nurse who'd cared for Seward at Jasna Polana in December 1982, who provided the most graphic account of what working for Basia Johnson was like. Wearing a dress that was the color of a Creamsicle, she described what had ensued when, unbeknown to Basia, Seward sent out late one night for that star-crossed Crockpot. Basia, she said, "started to scream and yell and shout 'How dare he? How could he? He had no business doing that!' " She paused. "Mr. Johnson used a cane to walk with," she continued, "and she picked up the cane and stood up, not completely straight, but somewhat towered over him and did attempt to come down on him with the cane but never connected, and she was screaming the entire while. Some of the things she said were he was 'senile,' 'stupid old man.' I was just trying to keep one eye on Mr. Johnson to see if he would be abused and another eye on the back door for a quick escape." The next evening, she continued, Seward was still thinking about the episode. "Why, Basia, I'm afraid of you," she recalled him saying. "Yes, I am very afraid of you."

But the Crockpot contretemps paled by comparison to the "papaya-juice episode." (Like many of Basia's explosions, this concerned food, usually food she felt Seward shouldn't have been fed. "If Mr. Johnson didn't eat, they wouldn't have a case," an S&C lawyer later remarked.) One night in early January 1983, Seward had complained of indigestion—a common enough gripe at Jasna Polana, Abramowitz noted, where carbohydrates were king. At Seward's insistence, the nurse poured him some juice, even though Basia had specifically said it was too old—two days old—for him to drink. The next morning Basia learned she'd been countermanded. "The screaming started, louder and more furious than I had ever heard, and I never thought it was possible that she could get louder, but she did," the nurse recalled. "You would have to be there to appreciate it. If anybody has ever done any work in institutions, psychiatric, they would know what I was talking about. She raved like a lunatic. She had a cup and saucer in her hand, and one cup came flying across the room toward me, and I immediately decided I should leave but was in fear again, for Mr. Johnson and tried to—I thought I could last until three P.M., and I tried desperately to stay, but I could not. She raged for an hour and a half, and it seemed to simmer down, and the minute she would come back into the area, they would start again. By twelve o'clock I gave up the ghost. I had to leave the premises for my own mental health. I couldn't stand another minute."

Each of the witnesses had stories to tell, some horrible, some just bizarre. Carnevale, one of those no-nonsense working men who look uncomfortable in a coat and tie, recalled what Seward told him one day as they returned from the Jasna Polana construction site to Skillman. "Look, Zip, look at this quaint, nice farmhouse," he said as they pulled into the driveway. "I love it here, and I have to put up with that monstrosity over there." Another time, he said, Seward sent him to fetch the gun he kept by his bed, but only when Basia wasn't there. "I'm afraid she's going to use it on me," he said. Pellegrini told of a time Seward asked him to buy a gun. "He just said he was afraid of his wife Basia and her brother Gregory," Pellegrini recalled. "He said that Gregory was crazy." Pellegrini purchased a Luger .357 magnum revolver and a box of ammunition for the old man, only to be summoned a week later by a livid Basia. "She said that I had no right to give a handgun to her husband, that he's like a baby, and he doesn't know what he wants, and that he doesn't know what he's doing," Pellegrini said.

Seward's fears were a bit hard to fathom, and to Basia, who by now had loosened up a bit and was conversing more freely with the press, they were positively laughable. "He lived with me happily for twelve years," she told a group of reporters after Pellegrini stepped down. "Besides," she added smilingly, "he died of natural causes." She did not dispute, however, that Seward knew from firearms. "My husband was a very good marksman even into his eighties," she said on another occasion. Were he to know what his children were up to in court, she continued, "he would bring in his pistol and shoot them all like rabid dogs."

Pellegrini told of a time Basia returned from New York at three in the morning, ranting, raving, and abusively drunk, and summoned him to open a door that wasn't locked. Louise Eberle described how, when Seward returned to Jasna Polana briefly from the hospital in December 1982 to visit his dogs, Basia complained that he'd disrupted her day. And, with some coaxing from Reilly, various witnesses sprinkled around more hints about Basia's extramarital liaisons. Michael Emery talked of seeing her and Jan Waligura "walking arm in arm and talking with their heads together" in Florida. Both Edles and Pellegrini recalled how Basia, unaccompanied and unencumbered by bodyguards, paid nocturnal visits to New York—where Waligura lived. Edles, a security man who'd been fired because, he was told, Basia "didn't like his face," described how, around nine-thirty on the night of Jasna Polana's opening party, Basia banished a reluctant Seward to bed, then flirted with one of the musicians. "They had a couple of drinks in their hand and they were conversing, obviously it was in Polish because I couldn't understand it, and Mrs. Johnson had her hand around him and he had his hand around her and he touched her breasts and then he moved his hand around and touched her buttocks and they kept walking down the hall," he said. What had Mrs. Johnson done then? Reilly asked. "I think she took another sip of her drink," Edles replied. Thus, after two years of investigations and eight weeks of testimony, the children had uncovered evidence that Barbara Piasecka Johnson had allowed someone to touch her breasts. "As histories of twelve-year-long marriages go, that is a record for trespass rather more impressive than Dwight Gooden's earned run average," Murray Kempton later wrote.

Pellegrini, who'd witnessed the same scene, supplied further details.

Basia's boyfriend, he said, was somewhat shorter than she, balding, and "a little on the chubby side." The cad he described was more octopus than musician, capable of drinking and walking and fondling and pinching simultaneously. "He had his arm around her waist, and he was caressing her behind," said Pellegrini, a Florentine by birth. "And then he would squeeze more and reach the front and grab one of the . . . breasts, I guess you call it."

In its typically reactive mode S&C immediately launched an all-points search for Basia's mystery lover, the fellow they dubbed the "Tits-and-Ass Man," hoping he could be brought in to refute these scurrilous charges. The search narrowed to one Piotr Janowski, a violinist. Nina tried tracking down the allegedly fondling fiddler, but without success.

Reilly was on a roll, confident enough for occasional bursts of bonhomie. "We're calling Basia's first husband," he told Christ once between witnesses. Still, the people he produced didn't speak with a single voice. Judy Abramovitz's Basia was a shrew, but her Seward was a curious, cantankerous, intellectually active man, capable of conversing about horses, artwork, the Republican party, J&J's Purpose soap, and CAT scanners. Pellegrini and Carnevale said Seward loathed Jasna Polana; Abramovitz said he loved it. Gore described how Basia berated her eighty-five-year-old husband once for attempting to drag the *Ocean Pearl* ashore, then boasted when he desisted. "See! See!" she said. "He does exactly what I tell him to do!" Sure, the story documented Basia's dominance, but it also showed Seward's nimbleness.

The children were delighted with Reilly—"He loves to win," Joyce Johnson said wondrously one day as she left the court. "He's got blood on his teeth," Junior added—and impressed with Lambert-style American justice. One reporter approached Junior in the corridor and dredged up the recurrent image of *Jarndyce* v. *Jarndyce*. "I think the system has improved since then," Junior remarked. Basia was thinking of another author. "It's a pity Kafka isn't here to see this," she told a reporter. "He would understand the reality of it all." In fact, after all of the attacks on her character and stability, her principal reaction wasn't embarrassment or remorse or regret, but the self-righteousness of the persecuted perfectionist. Like the Zurbarán Saint Sebastian she'd hung at Jasna Polana, she felt pierced by dozens of arrows, but arrows fired by dishonest, corrupt, jealous, and greedy people. Though observers thought she looked increasingly haggard, she said she'd never slept better. "I was like a strong oak facing a storm," she later recalled.

XLIII

Even the most outrageous tales can quickly become routine. How many times can one describe a woman's screams? In how many ways can one detail an old man's decline? By mid-April the children's case, for all its outrageousness, actually threatened to become routine. Reilly needed another rabbit.

He did not seem to have him in Edmund Sulikowski, a tall, thin man of fifty-four who'd worked maintenance at Jasna Polana from 1980 to 1984. Sulikowski, who took the stand on April 15, offered more unhappy snapshots of life on the estate, in the broken English he continued to speak thirty-five years after coming to the United States. Basia was always abusing the help, though for what was not always clear. "Sometimes when Mrs. Johnson talks with her high voice, I can't make out because the tone of voice kills the words of what was said," he testified. Once, Basia said to Seward, "This is my house, and if you don't like it, you can leave!" (When? Reilly asked. "Oh, I don't know," Sulikowski replied. "It was different times.") So withering was one of Basia's fits that it sent a cook named Ewa Grudzien to the hospital. All this finally drove Sulikowski to leave Jasna Polana and return to his roofing business.

Five months earlier Sulikowski had all but told S&C's Basil Zirinis he had Basia on tape, and now he, like Izabella, had come to court, minicassettes in hand. Sulikowski said he wasn't sure just how many tapes he made. At one point he said "a half dozen or more"; the one he brought to court was marked "#13." "I didn't pay attention to it, how many," he said. "I just made them and put them away." Why had this man, whom Basia had apparently treated reasonably well, who hadn't lost any baby, made his recordings, and with the same kind of machine—a Sony M-9—that Izabella had? "Well, because I felt that, when Mrs. Johnson increase her screaming, you know, I felt that if something is going to happen to somebody and I don't know whether it was me or somebody else, and I want to leave the tapes in case something will happen to me or whoever." Had he ever taped a phone call? "Well, I'd rather not to answer." Had anyone paid him off? "What money? I came on my own! I didn't ask for anybody money, and I don't want anybody money." To whom, Lambert asked him in chambers, had he first disclosed the existence of the tapes? "To Mr.—Marty . . . What is his last name?" he replied. The only "Marty" around was Richards. But before he could elaborate, Reilly cut him off, and he never finished his answer.

In the Polish crowd around Jasna Polana, there were suspicions that the children had paid both Izabella and Sulikowski to make their tapes. This Sulikowski later denied (though his stories contained certain discrepancies; for one thing, he said that Mariusz Poterewicz had called him "many months" before the trial to say he'd heard from the Milbank lawyers). But in a brief conversation with a reporter outside the Sulikowski homestead, one of his daughters confirmed that some money had changed hands. "All he got out of it was fifteen hundred dollars," she said. "He thought he'd get more. He's friendly with the son at the atelier—what's his name?—Seward. That's the guy who wrote out the check." But Milbank later paid Sulikowski $1,650 for the time he devoted to the case; might his daughter have been thinking of that?

In this courtroom, however, motivation didn't appear to matter. The gallery roared with laughter as Sulikowski recalled his yearlong effort to record Basia—how, chasing after one tirade or another, he'd sometimes forget to bring his machine; how, threatened with discovery once, he locked himself in a linen closet for twenty minutes. Lambert joined in the raillery. "Are you *nosy?*" she asked the witness playfully. A year after Seward's death, Basia upbraided Sulikowski for failing to clean up after her dogs, and Sulikowski got down every immortal moment on tape. Apparently unable to stop, Reilly now asked that this tape, too, be admitted into evidence. Whether to play Izabella's tape, made while Seward was in the next room, had arguably been a close call. Sulikowski's tape, however, was not only prejudicial, but irrelevant, having been made after Seward's death, and redundant. But in Lambert's court, whatever Reilly wanted, Reilly got. In obliging one of her favorite lawyers, though, Lambert crossed another. From the beginning of her judicial career, her trusty law secretary, Harvey Corn, had been at her side. And from the beginning of the trial, he'd sat alongside her on the bench, dispensing wise counsel, protecting her from herself. "Thank God he's up there; otherwise she'd go completely out of her gourd," Christ told a friend. But as loyal as Corn was, he had his standards. Marie Lambert's performance in the Johnson case was turning into an embarrassment, in part because she was no longer listening to Corn.

It was one thing for her to lean on the proponents to force a settlement; it was quite another for her to join in a gang rape, and Corn wanted no part of it. Within a few days he, like Osgood, disappeared from the courtroom, ostensibly to catch up on work in chambers. One might have expected Lambert to resist. But she knew people considered her overly dependent on Corn, and seemed to feel liberated without him.

April 16, 1986, the second day of Sulikowski's testimony, began early for most of the players in the Johnson drama. Sulikowski had to drive into court from his home, two hours away. Reilly, who, to the chagrin of his ducks, had been spending nights in a Manhattan hotel rather than commuting from Greenwich, arose early to prepare for his next witness; after all, Sulikowski's tape would take only a few minutes to play and discuss. Christ's mornings were all early; his driver would swing by Woof Woods around seven to fetch him and Iris for the trek to New York. Similarly, the sun had barely risen over Jasna Polana when Basia called her bodyguards, twice. "Get Mr. Stroczynski for me, immediately!" she demanded. "Where is he? Where is he?" When he showed up, he was promptly escorted to her room. "We have a surprise. You'll see. We can fight back," Basia had just told John Fox. Fox had assumed she was speaking of a surprise witness. He was wrong.

When Stroczynski returned, he came carrying orders. Round up some of the estate workers, he told a security man. Tell them only that they'll be going to court in New York, and that they needn't worry about missing work, they'd be paid anyway. Within minutes, fifteen workers had been assembled. Stroczynski divided them into groups and loaded them into the four-car caravan that soon snaked out of the estate and onto Route 206. Meanwhile Basia and her bodyguards hopped into her blue Mercedes. Accompanying them was Norman Mitchell, the psychic who had spoken to the spectral Seward the previous fall. Mitchell told her she'd soon see something white, which would augur well for her in court. And sure enough, on the way out of Jasna Polana that morning, they saw a white squirrel. Soon a new, bilingual sign appeared along the road leading into the estate: BEWARE OF WHITE SQUIRREL, it warned in both English and Polish. Basia did not want her newest talisman to be run over.

Things began slowly that day in court. But a few minutes before noon, as Sulikowski sat on the stand, the suddenly routine sound of angry Basia filled the room. As the tape played, the workers from Jasna Polana filed into the lobby of the Surrogate's Court and made their way to the fifth floor. John Pellegrini, the short-lived director of security at Jasna Polana who was to testify next for the children, saw them walk out of the elevator and instantly recognized Stroczynski, looking oddly agitated. It was a chilling sight, for he believed that Stroczynski would stop at nothing for Basia, even murder. "Something's happening here!" he told Paul Shoemaker, who promptly walked into the courtroom and told Reilly. The phalanx of workers, by now split in two, entered behind him through the near and far doors.

The new arrivals were hard to miss. The trial had thus far attracted a wide variety of types, but had been a largely middle-class affair. The workers, by contrast, wore cheap polyester flannels, blue jeans, and nylon windbreakers; their faces were Slavic and weather-beaten, their hair slicked back. They were figures from the steel mills of Nowa Huta or the shipyards of Gdańsk. They looked ill at ease, even lost. Only Stroczynski, dressed in a herringbone-tweed sports jacket, and another older man in a blue blazer were wearing normal courtroom attire.

Sitting in the second row, Nina looked up and saw Stroczynski. *He's not supposed to be here,* she thought; anyone who might be called as a witness was supposed to stay away. She told Bauman, who told Christ, who told Rogers, who told Zirinis to get him out of there. Zirinis ambled over to the superintendent, taking pains to look casual as he did. "John, you'll have to leave," he whispered. But Stroczynski didn't budge. Nina glanced at Lindy Anderson, one of Basia's bodyguards, who shrugged her shoulders as if to say, "I'm just as baffled as you are." Then Nina looked at Basia, who seemed absolutely serene. It was two minutes to one. The court would break for lunch in a few moments, Nina thought, and everything could be straightened out. She looked at Basia again, and again and again. Each time Basia was utterly, disconcertingly expressionless.

Sulikowski remained on the stand, answering Christ's last few questions. The judge then instructed him to leave the witness box. "Next witness," she declared. "We're going to work until one-thirty today." At that instant the man in the blue blazer suddenly spoke up. "He's spying on our property!" he shouted at Sulikowski.

"He's a Communist spy!" Stroczynski chimed in.

Then, like a Greek chorus, the workers on the other side of the courtroom also stood up. "Liar! Liar!" they yelled in Polish. Others shouted Slavic catcalls. "Swine!" one shrieked.

In the official transcript the court reporter noted simply, "There was a disturbance in the courtroom." But it was far more than that. The carefully cultivated, controlled calm of the place had suddenly been pierced. Pandemonium broke out. All along, Milbank had tried to depict Basia as a sinister, unscrupulous, ruthless megalomaniac who'd surrounded Seward with aliens, and all of a sudden that picture, like Basia's voice before it, had come to life.

"Just a minute!" shouted Lambert, who snapped instantaneously, seemingly instinctively, into military mode. "These two gentlemen will be brought up here! The jury will be taken out!"

Reilly, too, switched modes immediately, as if he had been expecting the ruckus all along. Within milliseconds, judge and lawyer were functioning like two parts of a single well-lubricated machine.

"Your Honor, I ask that the doors be closed and the names and addresses of all these people taken!" Reilly boomed.

"These people are not to leave this room!" declared the judge, who had the doors locked. "The jury will step out! Please! Get the court attendants in here! Just get the court attendants in here! Just be quiet! The jury is to disregard anything that's being said in this room! Get the court officers and the sheriff!" The officers hustled the jurors upstairs, then remained posted outside their door. Rather than let them venture outside, a guard took their lunch orders. Another accompanied anyone wanting to use the bathroom.

"Your Honor, I also understand that one of the people here is the estate manager for Jasna Polana!" Reilly said. "I want to get them all up here, and I want them under oath!"

"Let's find out who they are!" the judge, by now standing up behind the bench, said sharply. "There is somebody over there that opened her mouth, in the red dress, the red blouse. Up here! Come on! Up here!"

"Which one is Stroczynski?" Reilly continued. "I want Stroczynski on the stand, Your Honor!"

Lambert needed no coaxing. "We are going to get everybody up here!" she said. "Nobody will leave this room until we get names and addresses! Get me the sheriff down here! Who else spoke back there? Come on! Everybody who spoke back there! Up here! You were the first to speak," she added, addressing the man in the blazer. Give your name and address to the stenographer!"

"Heliodor Bartosinski," the man said quietly in accented English.

"Mr. Reilly, are you able to identify any of the people who stood up and disrupted this courtroom and attempted to create a riot in the courtroom in the presence of the jury?" the judge asked the Milbank lawyer, even though the S&C team was actually far more likely to know such things. "The Court is going to do something very serious about this, and I mean serious!"

Reilly called again for Stroczynski, and this time he found him. "May

I have him take the stand?" he asked. "I want to ask him some questions!"

"Relax, Mr. Reilly, trust me!" Lambert replied. "First, let's get all the names, then he'll take the stand. Nobody is leaving this room, if we have to stay here until midnight tonight. No one is leaving this room until every one of these people is questioned. I am not going to allow this kind of thing to go on in my courtroom!"

One by one, she summoned the workers, took down their names, then sentenced them to the jury box, where they sat, motionless, frightened, bewildered. At one point Basia was spotted flashing a "V for Victory" sign at one of them. "Be quiet!" Lambert exclaimed as a low murmur filled the courtroom. "I will not hear one more word! This Court will not be intimidated, no matter how many people come in here! This judge does not intimidate, and this judge does not get frightened. Is that clear?"

Amid the chaos, the Harbor Branch flunkie who regularly accompanied Junior to court angrily approached one of the children's publicists, Chris Policano, with an urgent demand. "Why aren't you on the phone?" he exclaimed. "We have to get the press here!" (Half a dozen local television stations were promptly called.) Basia and Nina began making their way to the Duane Street lunchroom. The *plat du jour* was cold lobster in the shell, but no one had much of an appetite. Meantime, accompanied by a small armada of observers—lawyers, reporters, stenographers, artists—Lambert moved the proceedings into her chambers. Lambert took her accustomed place at her long, rectangular table. Nearby was a plastic plaque declaring A CLUTTERED DESK IS A SIGN OF GENIUS and a package of red cocktail napkins with WHERE THERE'S A WILL THERE'S A RELATIVE printed on them.

"Did you see the size of some of those guys?" Lambert asked. "I'm going to find out how *this* was orchestrated!" She then spotted Jack Raymond, Basia's publicist. "You're not a lawyer, you are not a party, you are not a member of the press! Get out!" she snapped. "Get me Bellacosa!" she barked at her secretary, referring to the state's chief administrative judge. "Tell him it's an emergency!" For the judge, things were coming into focus. "I'm beginning to understand the phone calls that come in here at night, when the people hear my voice and hang up," she said. "I absolutely don't believe this! In thirty years of practicing law . . . " Then she turned to Reilly, who remained standing nearby. "Do you want to question them or do you want me to?" she asked.

"You're doing so well, I hate to interfere, but I have a few suggestions," he replied. One was that the chief perpetrator was not among those cowering in the jury box. "I have no doubt that Barbara Piasecka fully understands what was done, and the timing of it, the orchestration of it, and her involvement in it is of greater concern to me than some lower-ranked employee of hers," he said.

Almost as an afterthought Lambert asked Christ if he wanted to say anything. "I'm as interested as the Court to find out what happened," he quietly replied.

Then, in turn, the court officers ushered in each of the "Jasna Polana Fifteen." Never had there been an unlikelier group of rabble-rousers. Most spoke too little English to heckle intelligibly for very long, let alone understand the modified Miranda warning the judge now gave them. Acting simultaneously as schoolmistress, settlement-house worker, policeman, prosecutor, judge, and jury, Lambert questioned each about the episode. To all, she offered several alternatives: remain silent and be punished; confess and be fined; apologize abjectly and walk away with a slap on the wrist. Bartosinski, for instance, was initially given a day behind bars, but had his sentence commuted to a $250 fine after saying he was sorry. But how was he to pay? "I don't have no money with me," he pleaded.

"Well, then you can make other arrangements," Lambert retorted.

"I have a credit card," he chimed in.

"The Court doesn't take credit cards!" she replied, unamused.

Stroczynski did not fare nearly so well. "Who decided that all of you people could come down here today?" Lambert asked him angrily. "Who gave the eighteen people the day off to come down to court today?"

"Nobody give us day off," he replied meekly. "I just told them I want to go, all people with me to court."

"And did you tell them that you wanted them to speak up in the courtroom?"

"Well, I didn't tell them to speak up, but I would like to hear what the man testified."

"And you organized this?"

"Yes."

"Fifteen days in jail!" she announced. "Okay. That's my decision!" The sentence was to begin that night.

Moments later, when an uncomprehending maid was given a night in jail and unceremoniously ushered out of the room, Christ protested. It was a humane gesture by a caring man, but one that eluded Reilly. "Do you represent her, Mr. Christ?" he snapped nastily.

"No, Mr. Reilly, you know I don't represent her," Christ responded.

"No, I don't know that at all," Reilly retorted. "In fact, I thought quite the contrary." Eventually, the woman was freed.

A gardener named Marian Fryc, who had known Sulikowski for twenty years and was godfather to one of his children, attempted valiantly to explain why he'd come to court. "Every time morning I go greenhouse," he said. "Everybody talk come on New York court, newspaper is no good read. Everything no good Lady Johnson. This is no, no true." Lambert asked him if he'd shouted out in court. "Yes . . . no, I go inside, go, you talk go front, I go front," he replied.

"No, no, but when the people were standing up shouting in the courtroom, were you shouting?" she asked.

"Yes," he replied.

"What did you say?"

"I said . . . was I talk my friend?"

"No, no, were you talking in the courtroom? After I said, 'Everybody be quiet,' did you say, 'He's lying!'?"

"No, I know nothing," he said. "Nothing talk."

"You didn't say that?"

"No."

"Did you make any statement out loud in the courtroom?"

"No perfect understand, no translate. Maybe I need to translate."

But Lambert would not give up. "When everyone else stood up in the courtroom and they were shouting, did you say anything out loud in the courtroom?" she asked.

"Well, first time the court in the United States," Fryc replied.

"I didn't ask you that!" she snapped. "I asked you if you said anything out loud in the courtroom."

"I don't understand."

"Do we have someone here who speaks Polish?" the judge pleaded, only to meet with silence. "Okay," she declared. "We will get a Polish interpreter."

"Sorry my English," Fryc said sorrowfully as he was escorted back into the courtroom.

An interpreter was soon procured. But try as Lambert might, she could not get to the bottom of things. Even in their Pidgin English, the workers clearly felt genuinely angry at Sulikowski. They'd known and liked the man in his days on the estate, and even helped him financially; now, several of them suspected, he'd been paid to betray their boss. But had Basia put them up to the protest? No one would say. Frustrated as prosecutor, Lambert instead began lecturing them on American democracy and proper courtroom etiquette.

"What happens to people in Poland who stand up and disrupt the court who have no business being there?" she asked Jaroslaw Slabinski, a hearty man with a flowing dark beard and a plaid work shirt.

"Maybe they will have problem," he replied.

"They will have problems?"

"Yes, but this is a free country," he replied.

"Yes, I know it's a free country," Lambert repeated, momentarily speechless.

"That's why I came here," Slabinski added.

He was fined $250.

Moments later Slabinski's wife offered a different response. During the heyday of Solidarity, she said, such courtroom disturbances were commonplace—and honorable. "Even though it is a free country, I feel that sometimes we felt more free there than here," she said through an interpreter. She, too, was fined $250.

Fryc, too, said he'd thought what he'd done was proper because "America is a free country."

"Do you know why it is a free country?" Lambert responded. "It is a free country because people do things the way they are supposed to do." Having listened politely to her homily, Fryc was fined only one hundred dollars. The questioning complete, the press departed, and only the lawyers remained in Lambert's chambers.

"Your Honor, I wanted to say at the outset that we deplore this disturbance, and we are as distressed as the Court that it happened," Christ began. "I don't believe from my observation of what happened this morning that it was in any way directed at the jury." But the outburst, he went on, "may have fatally affected the ability of this trial to go forward." On that basis, he said, he was reluctantly asking for a mistrial.

The request was desperate—and doomed. Convinced Basia was behind it all and that her lawyers had been accessories, Lambert was not about to reward them for their treachery. But before she could deny the motion, Reilly pounced. What Christ's plea proved, he declared, was that the uprising had been a deliberate attempt to taint the proceedings, plotted by people who knew they could not win legitimately. "Even if [Basia] did not dream up the idea—I think she is probably a little bit dumb and maybe unimaginative to have thought it up—she surely knew of it and I believe expressly countenanced it," he told the judge. There was not going to be any mistrial, he declared; the day of reckoning was coming, and the final judgment would be made by a jury, not a mob. At that moment, one need not have been a Polish immigrant to have thought that it was Reilly, and not Lambert, who was presiding over the case. Moments later, when Lambert officially denied Christ's motion, it was as if she were affirming a lower court.

Lambert decreed that henceforth court officers would drive the jurors to and from the trial. Mindful that so incendiary a step could itself trigger a mistrial, Robert Hirth of Dewey Ballantine tried to discourage the idea. "Are *you* going to protect the jury?" she snapped at him. She dropped the idea but announced that were any juror harmed, Basia's lawyers would bear the blame. "I hold Shearman and Sterling responsible, since Mrs. Zagat is in close association with this lady day after day, and Judge Bauman talks to her," she declared.

Bauman, a stickler for propriety from his own judging days, had come to loathe Lambert, but as a backbencher, he'd had no real outlet for his rage—until now. "I want to say with all due respect, Your Honor, that I reject that responsibility, that that statement is baseless, that there is not any suggestion in this record to suggest the involvement of Shearman and Sterling in any aspect of this," he declared. "I respectfully decline responsibility and respectfully suggest to you, madam, that it is beyond the power of this court to assign that responsibility in the absence of the slightest evidence."

It was the sort of challenge Lambert had never heard from Christ, and she promptly backed down. But seemingly unable to stop, Reilly pressed the collusion charge. "The fact that Mr. Christ moved for a mistrial removed any doubt in my mind as to the real purpose in getting them here," he declared.

"I totally reject that, Mr. Reilly," Christ responded. "It is unprofessional of you and outrageous, and you ought to know better."

"You can reject it like you rejected everything else," Reilly said. "I have seen enough of what has happened in this case to know well enough. It is comforting to know that there will be no mistrial."

Court finally resumed at five-thirty, more than four hours after the uprising. "All the jurors are present, safe, and seated," the court officer declared.

"I'm sorry for what occurred in the courtroom this morning," Lambert told them. "This is a court of law. This is the United States. We do not have prospective witnesses standing up and shouting in a courtroom. That is not the way we do things here." She asked whether any of the jurors would be unable to overlook the outburst, and when there was no reply, she sent them all home, where, that night and the following morning, they could hear and read accounts of the uprising. "It reminded me, sort of, of what happened in the beginnings in Germany, when the Nazi party would move in and take over things," Junior told one reporter. "That's what money and fear can buy," Marty Richards said to another. "UPROAR AT JOHNSON HEIR WARS' TESTIMONY," the *New York Post* proclaimed. "JOHNSON TRIAL MELEE: WIDOW'S RETAINER JAILED FOR DISRUPTION," declared the *Newark Star-Ledger*.

In the wake of the disturbance a series of macabre jokes began circulating. (Q: "What's another name for Jasna Polana?" A: "Serf City." Q: "What do you say when a Jasna Polana worker is on the second floor?" A: "Serf's Up.") Basia herself went through the motions of perturbation. "I'm very upset, and it's unfortunate that it happened," she told one reporter. "And I'm upset especially for the judge," she added enigmatically. "I am sorry for her that she had to work so hard." Later that day Raymond issued a canned statement from Basia, who in the interim had gone from "very" to "terribly" upset by the outburst. "The persons involved apparently sought to help, but it was wrong for them to do this," the statement went on. "I can only say that I regret it deeply."

It sounded like double-talk, and it was. That night, as bedlam reigned at Shearman & Sterling, a radiant Basia, back in Jasna Polana's bosom, exulted about the day's events. "Look how they love me!" she said. "Look how devoted they are to me! They're willing to go to prison for me!" These people, and not the slackers and malcontents the children had dredged up, were her real employees. "Today was our biggest victory!" she told a friend that night, shaking her fist in the air. "We showed them what the Poles could do." She was rejuvenated.

Around S&C the feeling grew that the case was now irretrievably lost. Only one man connected to the case was even unhappier than the S&C lawyers: Stroczynski. As the jurors went home, the hapless estate manager was manacled around his wrists and ankles, escorted to a paddy wagon, and driven to the Bronx House of Detention. There, he was photographed, fingerprinted, and thrown into a cell with eight other inmates, one of them bleeding and several others either drunk or strung out. Trying to lay low, he slowly started unraveling his necktie. "Hey, Pop! What are you in for?" one of his new roommates suddenly asked. Stroczynski swallowed hard. "I choked a man with my bare hands," he replied, trying to sound as menacing as possible.

Stroczynski wound up in a spartan cell, which, he assured his anxious wife by phone, was more like a hotel than a jail. He was served three pieces of fried chicken—much to his surprise, it was tastier than what he got at home—then spent his first night ever in incarceration. Meanwhile an indignant Fryc telephoned Sulikowski. "Son of a bitch!" he said to him in Polish. "How much money did they give you for the tapes?" Sulikowski promptly brought the call to Reilly's attention, and the next morning, with Alex Forger's first appearance at counsel's table bringing a new degree of gravity to the proceeding, Reilly solemnly asked Lambert to dismiss the jury. Then he apprised her of the latest developments.

"Your Honor, I want to inform the Court of an incident that is as disturbing to us as the intrusions into the court yesterday by fifteen employees of Barbara Piasecka Johnson," Reilly declared. He described Fryc's phone call, one filled with the kind of profanity, he said distastefully, "we are more accustomed to hearing from Barbara Piasecka Johnson." Basia and her lawyers, he charged, were continuing their efforts to intimidate the children's witnesses, and the jury should know about it. He asked that he be allowed to take the depositions of Basia, Stroczynski, Fryc, and any others connected with the courtroom uprising. That included S&C's Basil Zirinis, who, Reilly noted, had been seen speaking with the estate manager moments before the outburst. "The least he could have done, as a matter of professional responsibility, was to escort Mr. Stroczynski out of the court," Reilly charged.

It was a stinging remark for a senior partner to level at a junior associate from another firm, one at the very beginning of his legal career, and Christ complained to Reilly about it. That was not enough to satisfy Zirinis, however, and as the court broke for lunch, he walked over to his accuser and prepared to defend himself. "Mr. Reilly?" Zirinis said, only to get no response. "Mr. Reilly?" Reilly continued to ignore him, looking down toward the floor. "Mr. Reilly," Zirinis continued, "you'd better look me in the eye, because I have something to say to you, and it will be very brief." This time Reilly muttered something that Zirinis couldn't quite make out. "What did you say?" Zirinis asked. Finally, Reilly looked up at him. "Oh, fuck off!" Reilly said. Then he walked away.

In the wake of the disturbance Christ sent out a notice to all Jasna Polana employees, in English and Polish, warning them not to try influencing or intimidating anyone testifying against Basia. "If anyone does that, it is Mrs. Johnson who may be damaged," he wrote. Mary Lea, too, moved into action, writing her trustees to say that the episode proved she needed increased security (and, incidentally, the money to pay for it). "There have been several scary instances in and around the court lately and each time they have left me very anxious, nervous and fearful," she wrote to her financial keepers two days after the uprising. "This past week there was an incident in the courtroom which could have turned into a nasty riot. I am besieged by crowds, not only the press, and it is frightening!" The trustees stood firm. By May, Mary Lea's security tab for the trial stood at forty thousand dollars.

With the approval of the court, the Milbank lawyers eventually questioned twenty-three people—the fifteen who'd come to court, plus Gregory Piasecki and his wife, two secretaries, and all of the bodyguards on duty the day of the uprising. Besides the usual lawyerly colloquies (Lawyer 1: "Did you see Mrs. Johnson do anything with her hands [during the courtroom disturbance]?"; Lawyer 2: "Could you make it more precise, please? You could wipe your nose with your hands."), two distinctly different versions of the events emerged. In the official "Stroczynski" version, backed up by most of the Poles in the entourage, the expedition was like a field trip, in which various workers, having read of Sulikowski's testimony, resolved, simultaneously but independently, to go to New York to hear him; their cries of protest in court were entirely spontaneous and uncoordinated. The non-Poles offered a somewhat different account: that Stroczynski had ordered them to assemble, then dispatched them to New York. But in each account, Basia remained blameless. Stroczynski swore he had not spoken to her at all over the previous ten days.

The Milbank lawyers charged Stroczynski with covering up and, briefly, Lambert threatened to ask Manhattan District Attorney Robert Morgenthau to consider bringing perjury charges against the estate manager. (At one point the superintendent's family took his legal problems seriously enough to ask William J. Brennan, III, a Princeton lawyer and son of the Supreme Court justice, to consider taking his case; instead, the superintendent was represented by Edward Gorski, a Polish-speaking New York lawyer.) It was maddening: Both Reilly and Lambert were sure Stroczynski had been following Basia's orders—"Nobody will ever convince me that tomato wasn't behind the whole thing," Lambert told Christ—but yet they couldn't prove it. The judge telegraphed her skepticism to one and all when John Pellegrini finally took the stand. "Incidentally, let me ask you a question," she interjected. "Would the employees at Jasna Polana do something on their own without consulting either Mr. Stroczynski or Mrs. Johnson?"

"Your Honor," replied Pellegrini, "all of the employees of Jasna Polana were so terrorized and intimidated by Mrs. Johnson, they wouldn't even dream of doing anything without her permission and without her knowledge."

No one at the estate was ever fired, docked, or even reprimanded for the fiasco; in fact, Basia discreetly arranged to pay their legal fees. As for the faithful Stroczynski, he returned to court the day after the debacle, still manacled, still wearing the same shirt and herringbone-tweed sports jacket, but with a day's stubble on his face. His son brought him a bottle of Zantac for his ulcer. Late that afternoon, after publicly acknowledging Lambert's power to punish him as she did, apologizing for his dastardly behavior, and promising never, ever, to do it again, Stroczynski had his sentence commuted to time served. His mea culpa complete, he then turned to Basia. "I would like to apologize also to Mrs. Johnson what I done and I am very sorry, Mrs. Johnson, because without your permission, I done on my own," he said. He then bent down, and, in the fashion of a Polish gentleman, gently kissed her hand. Some said there were tears in Basia's eyes as he did.

XLIV

F ew of the children's witnesses had actually seen that much of Basia and Seward Johnson. From these cameo characters and their sordid snapshots, Reilly had had to cobble together a case. But Milbank's witness on April 24 was different. She, too, had horror stories to tell, but for reasons she could not explain even to herself, she felt treacherous and disloyal telling them. Despite everything, she still thought of Basia as her own daughter. She'd not wanted to testify at all, but when Charles Berry threatened to try to subpoena her, she'd reluctantly headed north.

Berry escorted a heavyset woman with white, boyishly cut hair and a warm face to the witness stand. Zofia Koverdan was one of those people whose lives mirror their tumultuous times: She was born in Russia, educated in Poland, interned in a German concentration camp, picked clean by Polish Communists, washed ashore in the United States. She'd emigrated in 1967, and found her first job in the home of J. Seward and Essie Johnson. It was Koverdan who'd gotten Basia a spot in Oldwick's kitchen, then protected her through all those incinerated or undercooked meals. More than anyone else, it was she who had set the whole fairy tale in motion. The sadness Koverdan felt over testifying against her old friend only intensified as she set eyes upon her, for the first time in six years. Entirely gone was the "fresh Polish beauty" she'd known. The only thing radiating from Basia now, she thought, was a deep and profound unhappiness.

Koverdan recounted Basia's beginnings in America: her halting English, her cooking misadventures, her personality. "She was a very nice girl," she said. "She was charming. I liked her very much. We were very close then." She described how their paths diverged when Basia left the Johnsons in August of 1969, and how they crossed once more in the spring of 1971, as she leafed through the Manhattan telephone book and came across a "Piasecka, Barbara" at 45 Sutton Place. When Koverdan called, she'd learned Basia and Seward would soon wed and move into a house they'd bought in Skillman. "Well, in that case you will need a cook," Koverdan said. And they did. She began working for them in September 1971. For the most part relations between the two women picked up where they left off: amicable, even intimate. Once, during a visit to the bank, Basia removed Seward's latest will, one leaving her $50 million, from a safety-deposit box and showed it to her. Koverdan left Skillman in 1972. But eight years later, at Basia's initiative, she came to Jasna Polana, where she replaced Countess Krasinski as head housekeeper. Koverdan soon learned you cannot go home again, even if the home was never yours.

By 1980, she testified, Seward and Basia were no longer the lovebirds they'd once been, and Basia was utterly unable to control her temper. One tirade, over an errant box of fruit, lasted an hour and a half. Another, over—well, she couldn't even remember what it was over— set some sort of record: two hours. "Finally, finally, it was finished," she recounted. "I went upstairs, and I was so disgusted that . . . and I was so hurt and upset that I thought, Well, this night I am not going to sleep. I tried to take a sleeping pill, and being in such a state, I didn't notice what I'm doing. I put the whole handful of pills and put them in my mouth. And when I took the water to swallow it, then I noticed, 'My God, what's going on?' And then I spit it out. But I was awful upset." The story, like much of the evidence in the case, was technically irrelevant; Seward had been in Fort Pierce at the time. But by now, the trial had degenerated even beyond the divorce case Christ had feared. Basia was now on trial for crimes against humanity. Seward had been around, and tried to comfort Koverdan, in January 1981, when she was reeling from another tongue-lashing. "I said, 'Mr. Johnson, why? Why don't you say something? Why don't you say that it isn't right to do this way?' " she testified. "He said, 'Well, you cannot cross Basia. And I am tired, and I'm sick. I'm a sick man.' "

While Koverdan was testifying, her eyes occasionally met Basia's. Whatever each woman was thinking, both remained expressionless. When she finished, the older woman felt a strange mixture of disloyalty and pity, love and fear. Anxious to avoid any contact with her erstwhile friend, she had the Milbank lawyers escort her out of court and lock her in the sheriff's office upstairs until she left for the airport. When she returned to Palm Beach, she refused to tell her daughter what had happened. Basia wasn't so troubled. Koverdan, she declared, was an "ingrate."

Next up was Robert Myers, Seward's lawyer until 1973. Myers, a pleasingly plump man with a pumpkin-shaped head, testified for several stupefying days in late April. He traced Basia's swelling stake in Seward's estate, recounted the gradual disappearance of Seward's old cronies, and told of how, at least back then, Harbor Branch had been an "integral part" of Seward's estate planning. He explained why he'd thought Basia and Seward needed separate legal counsel. And he chipped away still more at the myth of Seward the corporate magnate when Christ asked him what Seward's job as "chairman of the finance committee" entailed. "I don't know," Myers replied. "The chairman of the board told me it never met."

Myers had attended the Basia-Seward nuptials, which had been marked, he testified, by "a very warm feeling of friendliness and happiness." And he depicted Essie's reaction to Seward's philandering very differently than had Jennifer a few weeks earlier. "Esther Johnson said to me she was fully aware of Mr. Johnson's relationship with Barbara Johnson and why didn't I do something about it," he testified. Myers knew better than anyone how Seward wanted to leave his children nothing and Basia everything, points Christ touched upon but failed sufficiently to stress in his cross-examination.

As the parties battled publicly in court, the paper war raged on behind the scenes. As issues arose, Lambert would bark, "Find me some cases!" and the lawyers would oblige. Among the judge's staff—the ones who had to read all the stuff—the blizzard of motions became a big joke. "Here is the memo de jour," one of them wrote. "These guys must be getting paid by the word," another scrawled. Press interest, too, remained high. Liz Smith of the Daily News described how, after court each day, the children compared notes via the cellular phones in their respective limousines. When Marty Richards, whom Smith called "my pal," complained about the item, she advised him to relax. "Looks to me as if their side is far ahead in the fight against their stepmama," she wrote.

It was hard to argue with that, though no one knew what the jurors were thinking. They were much scrutinized, of course; several times daily, they were ushered in and out for all to inspect. Some, including José Santana, the sanitation man Jimmy Breslin made famous, remained completely impassive. The other man on the jury, Jeffrey Schwab, a tall wiseacre who was obviously drinking in the drama as much as the evidence, appeared enthralled by Reilly. By far the most intriguing—and inscrutable—was Debra Califia, the young widow. Lambert ostentatiously insulated them from any contamination, admonishing them repeatedly to avoid all press reports of the case. But even her protectiveness proved partisan. At one point in April Basia turned to Arnold Bauman and smilingly wished him a happy Passover. Lambert, suspecting they were savoring some courtroom success in front of the jury, angrily decreed that henceforth, the proponents were to move back a row, farther away from the jury's view and earshot. For the rest of the trial the ringside seats remained vacant.

Until well into the trial the judge remained a hit with most of the jurors. True, one of the alternates thought her biased, but she was an unpleasant woman, disliked by her fellows. The others continued to laugh at Lambert's jokes, listen deferentially when she spoke, and lap up her exaggerated solicitude, uttered in the same gooey, babyish tone of voice Marty Richards attributed to Seward begging Basia for a boat ride or a roll. To them, Marie Lambert remained a New York original, a hot pastrami on rye with Cel-Ray tonic, a yellow Checker taxi. But their feelings slowly but surely changed as they saw her pampering Reilly and his witnesses, then barking at Christ like a chihuahua, her mouth crinkling with contempt, her bottom teeth exposed. The detested alternate was right. The reservoir of respect that any jury initially holds for almost any judge was evaporating.

Even the most jaded reporters watched Lambert's display of partisanship with amazement. "In fifteen years of covering the courts I'd never seen a judge who tilted so outrageously, who was so out of control, so absolutely incapable of impartiality," said Tim O'Brien of the *Newark Star-Ledger*. "She made you cringe." Had such sentiments made their way into print—or had Lambert, like the next generation of judges, had her every indiscretion televised—she would surely have shaped up. As it was, only S&C could make an issue of Lambert's conduct, and thus far it had been too scared to try.

The only question now was not whether Lambert was biased, but why. One theory, favored by the Milbank lawyers, was that their case was just so overwhelming—and, incidentally, so well presented. Others thought she'd become enraged over Sullivan & Cromwell's ineptness or indignant over its purportedly underhanded tactics, and was taking it out on its clients. Conversely, some believed she was turned off by Basia, and was taking it out on S&C. And it was true that she'd grown skeptical of Basia; how genuine could her marriage have been, she once asked, when Seward had been castrated shortly into it? Basia made things worse for herself when, during a private conversation with the judge, she claimed that the Polish Communists deemed her their second-most-dangerous expatriate, exceeded only by the pope. Come to think of it, Basia quickly added, perhaps they considered her even more dangerous. Lambert was always arrogating such distinctions to herself but apparently disliked it in someone else.

Some, noting Lambert's well-known hatred of her judicial colleague Renee Roth and other accomplished women, speculated that she felt threatened by and resented Nina Zagat. Some felt her one-sidedness was her way of coercing Basia to settle. Some felt that as the fanatically devoted mother of an only son, Lambert was again demonstrating her preference for children, even prodigal or profligate ones, over a childless stepmother. Some felt that given her own husband's gruesome death, she instinctively hated anyone who had been by her husband's bedside when he expired. Some felt a self-made woman from Bensonhurst, who had clawed her way to the top against all odds and looked it, could never forgive another immigrant girl for her good looks and fortune. One thing was certain: For all of her oft-expressed faith in the adversary system, Lambert would not let it run its course here. Her hand was always on the scale.

Finding and assembling ammunition for a mistrial motion—a real motion, not the halfhearted attempt Christ made after the courtroom uprising—would not be a problem. From the first day of the trial, Osgood had maintained a black looseleaf entitled "Lambert's Erroneous Rulings," to which he'd added several pages each week. Of course, such a motion was clearly doomed. While mistrials have been granted where jurors or lawyers have misbehaved, few judges have ever said, in effect, "You're right. I've done a terrible job. Let's start all over again." But both Osgood and Bauman pushed for one anyway, if only to sober up the judge and to preserve their complaints for an eventual appeal. Only Christ opposed it, fearing it might rile up Lambert even more. Also, alone among the S&C lawyers, his business was primarily in Surrogate's Court; long after Basia was just a bad memory, he would still be appearing before Marie Lambert. The idea was shelved.

The abuses continued. Lambert made the proponents' every task Sisyphean. If they wanted to introduce photographs into evidence, she insisted on the originals. If they wanted to read something to the jurors, she insisted it be shown to them instead. If they wanted it shown, she insisted they hold it up rather than hand it over. If they asked to show it to the jurors now, she insisted they wait until a break. When they asked to take a break, she refused. If they wanted to break for lunch until two, she insisted they return twenty minutes earlier. When they approached a key point, she took over the questioning, interjecting her own hypertechnicalities and irrelevancies. When they introduced deposition excerpts into the record, she blocked them or ostentatiously tacked on a few additional lines, just to let the jury know she felt the portion selected had been ripped dishonestly out of context. She cut off relevant lines of inquiry, blocked key points. In Lambert on Evidence, charts depicting the children's wealth were inadmissible; charts showing how many days Harbor Branch vessels had spent at sea were let in.

So blatant were Lambert's biases that one of the Harbor Branch lawyers, Bob Hirth, asked Reilly to approach the judge quietly and urge her to settle down. That he never did, though he eventually did speak to Corn. But the abuses mounted. On the afternoon of April 22, as Christ's examination of Robert Myers inched agonizingly along, Lambert seethed—in this case, not entirely without reason. José Santana, the juror-sanitation man, consumed his last few No-Doz, but they didn't help. "I will let him ask anything he wants!" Lambert finally remarked at one point. "Let's see how many weeks we can go on with this!" Once, Myers said he did not understand Christ's question. "Neither do I," Lambert added. She ridiculed Christ for eliciting "all this great information." Later she proposed that the court meet part time, so that the jurors could tend to everything they had neglected over the past two months. Of course, she explained, this would mean either an additional twenty weeks of trial or starting at six each morning.

Finally, as Christ tried to pinpoint some inconsequential meeting Myers had attended thirteen years earlier, Lambert lost whatever self-restraint remained. "Let's find out!" she cackled. "Was it May ninth? Was it May tenth? Was it May twelfth? Was it May thirteenth or May fourteenth of 1973? It's very crucial to find out if it was any one of these days! Would you tell us, please? We will do them one at a time. Did you meet with them on May ninth?"

"I don't know, Your Honor," Myers said.

"Did you meet with them on May tenth?"

"I don't know, Your Honor."

"Did you meet with them on May eleventh?"

"I don't know, Your Honor."

"Did you meet with them on May twelfth?"

"I don't know, Your Honor."

"Did you meet with them on May thirteenth?"

"I do not know, Your Honor."

"Let's go!" she snapped. "Go ahead, Mr. Christ! Keep asking!"

Finally, even Christ crossed the Rubicon; there was nothing left to lose. Late in the afternoon of April 22, in Lambert's chambers, Sheryl Michaelson of S&C handed Corn a seventy-nine-page document in which the proponents officially asked for a mistrial. Corn, who had been expecting it, shrugged his shoulders and said nothing. Lambert's intemperate and unjudicious conduct, a topic people had been whispering about for weeks, was finally on the table. Accompanying the motion was an application to keep it under seal, undoubtedly to spare the judge any undue embarrassment. Of course, a copy in the hands of the right reporter could have worked wonders, just as the Forger Affidavit had done. But Sullivan & Cromwell, schooled in discretion, afraid of censure, devoid of imagination or street smarts, couldn't think that way. When news of the motion emerged, as it inevitably would, it would dribble out, thereby having minimal impact on the public and, therefore, on the judge.

The first hint that something was afoot came the following morning, when Ellen Joan Pollock of the *American Lawyer* overheard Lambert say something to Christ about his "three-hundred-pound motion." Two days later, Tim O'Brien of the *Newark Star-Ledger* heard about it firsthand from Osgood. O'Brien had discovered, and written about, the ethical charges Milbank had leveled against Osgood, and the S&C litigator had called pleading for him to stop. "Please don't print that garbage!" he begged. "Regardless of what I say, just printing that will ruin me! I'll never be able to practice again in this town!" People were asking his young daughter whether her daddy bribed witnesses, Osgood complained, and looking censoriously at him each morning in the Glen Ridge train station. O'Brien, who had no plans to write anything further anyway, instead offered Osgood some free advice. "You people have to fight back," he said. "If you haven't filed for a mistrial already, you should do it." Osgood informed him they just had, and O'Brien reported the news that Sunday.

In court Monday morning Lambert complained to the lawyers that even this tad of adverse publicity was unfair to her. "I certainly concur in that," Reilly obligingly chimed in. Osgood's partners, who never knew he'd spilled the story, also expressed indignation. But with the word already out, Lambert had little choice but to order the motion unsealed. Soon the fecund photocopiers of S&C began churning them out. The motion made the expected bows to propriety, stating that the proponents sought a mistrial "with great reluctance" and with no desire to "criticize the Court." But, it went on, the trial had become "so infected with irreparable error" that any verdict for the children would surely be overturned. "The question has become not whether a new trial will be ordered, but when and by whom," it stated. For seventy pages the proponents listed their grievances against the entity to which they referred euphemistically as "the Court." They spoke of a "pervasive pattern of prejudice," demonstrable in wisecracks, questions, and evidentiary rulings; by what reckoning could the fact that a Polish musician allegedly fondled Basia's breasts and buttocks six years earlier be admissible, while Seward's lifetime bequests to his children not be? Many of the worst offenses could not really be described at all. "A smile, a sneer, an exclamation, an inflection of the voice in giving a ruling, may be far more prejudicial than the average erroneous ruling," S&C argued.

Both Milbank and Dewey now found themselves in a delicate position: They had to defend Lambert without sounding silly. Dewey did so straightforwardly and tersely, in twenty-nine pages. Milbank took twice as long, with hardly half as much wisdom. It labeled the motion "a cynical attempt to intimidate the Court," one that "distorts the record beyond recognition, is without legal basis, disregards the responsibilities of the Court and, when all is said and done, seeks to gain advantage from counsel's tactical and legal errors." If Lambert treated the lawyers differently, it was only because of S&C's "inept advocacy"; a mighty institution, "reputed to be one of the nation's premier law firms," had been humbled, and didn't much like it. During one stretch, Milbank noted gleefully, Christ had objected seventy-eight times and been sustained on only thirteen of them. "In baseball terms, Mr. Christ was batting an embarrassing .167," the brief sniped.

"Unable to cope with the evidence, the proponents chose instead to torpedo the judicial process by challenging the integrity of the Court," Milbank charged. It dismissed the complaints against Lambert as "a grabbag of worthless nit-picks"; that this was all S&C could come up with was "a compliment to the Court and its sound, practical management of this complicated case," which it had handled "fairly, smoothly and efficiently." Milbank urged Lambert to stand firm. "Others may have been pushed aside by Barbara Johnson and Nina Zagat in their relentless pursuit of Mr. Johnson's fortune, but surely neither the objectants nor this Court nor the jury will be intimidated by the monumental arrogance of these proponents and their counsel."

Short of getting a mistrial, S&C considered asking Lambert to throw out the children's undue-influence claim, which, it argued, they had by now failed to prove. Robert Delahunty's brief on the subject included his usual antiquarian cases, his usual ringing defense of Basia, his usual idealized portrait of the Johnsons' marriage (so fervent that it led a husband to name a yacht after his bride and buy her a Mercedes "in a particular shade of gray, obviously as a gesture of love"), his usual assault on the children ("Their themes are the banalities of many unsuccessful will contests," their evidence "trash"). The rights of the elderly were indeed at stake, just as Reilly had said: Specifically, their right to bequeath things as they see fit. "This Court must choose whether it wishes to render every will in this state insecure," he urged. "If Mr. Johnson's will can be invalidated, then *any* will in New York can be invalidated." The only problem was that the motion was never filed, due largely to Christ's opposition. It was Delahunty's last oration in Estate of Johnson. In fact, it was to be his last at Sullivan & Cromwell.

Most assumed Lambert would be affected by the mistrial motion; whether she would be chastened or antagonized was not so clear. For the next few days, she seemed more subdued, and, on occasion, actually overruled Reilly and sustained Christ. It turned out she had a cold, and sure enough, when her temperature returned to normal so, too, did her behavior. In the meantime, as the parties exchanged their venomous motions, Law Day arrived. The holiday, the American Bar Association's answer to May Day, had never really caught on, but one place where it was observed with all due solemnity was Marie Lambert's courtroom, whose doors she ostentatiously locked once everyone had assembled so that no rash intruder could detract from the proceedings. A hush descended upon the premises as Lambert began her holiday sermonette.

"I cannot, as a lawyer, as a judge, allow the day to go unnoticed in this, my court," she said. "I must tell you something that I think is very important. We are one of the few countries left in the entire world where we have a free and independent judiciary, a judiciary that does not allow itself to be intimidated by the president, the governor, or the mayor. It doesn't allow itself to be intimidated by the executive branch of government, by the legislative branch of government, or by any of the powerful law firms that appear before it or by any of the power brokers that bring their cases to this court." She turned to the jury. "I want to thank you for sharing with me today, Law Day," she said—a day, she went on, "that I think is at the very foundation of our democracy. There, but for the grace of God, go you or I in a lawsuit, and we would want the kind of justice that we get in the United States." One side of the gallery nodded in agreement.

As the festivities drew to a close, Sullivan & Cromwell's mistrial papers remained on Lambert's desk. But she had told one of the lawyers she would decide the matter "in about three seconds flat," and she may have overestimated by a second or two. "There is no basis for the motion," she declared the following morning. "I therefore deny it."

In a less judicious moment with Christ, Lambert had called S&C's brief "a bunch of garbage." Even so, it evidently made her a bit uneasy, as she revealed in an exchange with Alex Michelini of the *Daily News*.

"What do you think of the mistrial motion?" she asked him as she headed into her chambers during one recess.

The diplomatic Michelini tried to beg off. "Judge, I'm just a reporter," he pleaded.

"No, really. What do you think?" she insisted.

"Do you really want to know?"

"Yeah."

He paused for a moment. "I think they're right."

XLV

B y early May, with the children's case gradually drawing to a close, Charles Berry placed a most peculiar exhibit on the easel behind the witness box. It was a tick-tack-toe board of twelve fuzzy black-and-white oval-shaped images, four rows of three apiece. The more literal-minded in the room might have thought they'd come from NASA. Or they might have been a Rorschach-like test, for if one looked at them long enough, the faces of certain cartoon characters— Tony the Tiger, Olive Oyl, Felix the Cat—seemed to emerge. In fact, each square depicted a different slice of Seward Johnson's brain, as it appeared on October 29, 1981. What gave the pictures their lunar look were the brain's constituent parts: The white spots were bone, the dark areas spinal fluid, and the gray matter, well, gray matter. Though they'd shown little interest in Seward's mind while it actually functioned, Mary Lea Richards and Elaine Wold craned their necks to study it now.

The focus of the trial was shifting. Now, the object was to depict Seward as a victim of a different process, one even Basia couldn't control: old age. Up to now, the vocabulary of the case had been simple, even primitive: "Stupid!" "Ga-ga!" Now, the air would be heavy with a tongue-twisting array of diseases, drugs, and psychobabble. In his opening Christ had said Seward was someone "you probably will know more about at the end of this trial than you could have learned if he were still alive." On this he proved prophetic. Seward Johnson, who'd spent eight decades and millions of dollars protecting his privacy, was now about to be undressed—dissected, really—in public.

To catalog Seward's mental and physical decrepitude, Milbank was calling three experts: a specialist in geriatric medicine, a neurologist, and a geriatric psychiatrist, all vying for the distinction of having the lengthiest résumé. Dr. Richard Besdine weighed in with a comparatively modest eleven pages' worth of appointments, awards, assignments, and publications. He was quickly topped by Dr. Martin Samuels, whose curriculum vitae measured fourteen pages. Together, they were dwarfed by Dr. Barry Reisberg, whose accolades took an astonishing twenty-seven pages to list. It is not easy to boast self-deprecatingly, and as the Milbank lawyers asked them about their accomplishments, the doctors spoke with the kind of false humility generally found in locker-room interviews. For instance, Samuels, a handsome and intense Harvard specialist in the neurological complications of medical illnesses, spiced his story with comments like, "Well, it is a rather immodest display," but . . . " and "I have been fortunate enough to have . . . " and "I can't believe it myself, that I do all this. . . . "

But in rounding up his experts, Reilly had sought more than eminence. It was something he remembered from his law-school moot-court competition, when his opponent had foolishly selected a highly credentialed windbag: You needed people who were not just erudite, but persuasive and likable. You also needed people who were fresh enough to testify with conviction, and hungry enough, whether for recognition or intellectual excitement or kicks, to work at it rather than wing it.

The forty-six-year-old Besdine, another Harvard man, had spent the previous fifteen years studying and treating confusion and delirium among the elderly. He had never testified before, but liked Charles Berry when the Milbank associate came calling to Boston. Moreover, the records he was showed left him stunned, enraged. Here was the kid brother of Robert Wood Johnson, whose foundation pumped more money into geriatric research than any other, and he'd been cared for absymally. Obviously, Besdine had no fixed fee for courtroom work. He figured, however, that he was worth at least what his divorce lawyer had just charged him: $200 an hour. It was a price worthy of another local landmark: Louis Filene's Basement.

On April 30, when Reilly asked him to describe the state of Seward's health the day he'd signed his will, Besdine was raring to go. "Mr. Johnson was a very frail, dependent, chronically ill man with a long list of serious medical problems—quite a number, an extraordinary, really, array of medical problems," he replied. Lest there be any doubt, at his back was a giant poster, mounted on Styrofoam, containing an inventory of Seward Johnson's sicknesses. On display only a week after Passover, the poster looked like a list of the plagues God had visited upon the Egyptians. The Pharaoh had to endure only ten calamities. For Seward there had been twenty-three, the twentieth of which was depression. "With this array of diseases, this is not very surprising," Besdine said.

Besdine gave a macabre tour of Seward's cancer-ridden system, describing the catastrophic chain reaction that had occurred as his disease metastasized. By charting changes in his hematocrit, or cell count, Besdine showed statistically what the nurses had noted empirically: how Seward had wilted between blood transfusions. What the disease didn't trigger, the treatment did. Chemotherapy brought nausea, bloody diarrhea, and cramping. His drugs could cause confusion, dizziness, somnolence, psychosis, hallucinations, disorientation, visual disturbances, alteration of color vision, drowsiness, and lethargy. Seward's liver was too crippled to detoxify these medications; in effect, then, the old man had been poisoning himself with his beloved Tylenol! But most deleterious of all was Prednisone, an anti-inflammatory agent. It impaired the adrenal gland, thereby reducing the level of electrolytes in his blood. More than anything else, Besdine said, it was Seward's electrolyte imbalance, measured by his low serum-sodium count, that explained his weakness, lethargy, and confusion. On April 14, that count was lower than it had been on March 18, when Peach combed the Yellow Pages for a priest.

Samuels noted how the 1981 CAT scan revealed that at some point Seward had sustained "encephalomalacia" or a "loss of brain," in those areas responsible for understanding language and recognizing objects (including, presumably, the natural objects of his bounty). As of April 1983, Samuels said, "this man did not have a normal brain." Rather than stabilizing Seward's condition, the doctors testified, Schilling and his associates made things worse by feeding him too many drugs and too much fluid. The Seward who signed his will, Besdine testified, was a shell of a man. "In the aggregate, I am impressed by the fact that Mr. Johnson was even awake," he said.

As he questioned his experts, Reilly continued to perform his own brand of surgery. His operation was a kind of graft, in which he was still attempting to stitch a notion from medicine—the mental-status examination—onto the law. It would not take easily. Ever pragmatic, the law recognized that most people don't want or didn't need or wouldn't think of or couldn't afford to have a doctor around when they signed their wills. So, while mental-status exams were nothing new, no court or legislature had ever required one to prove testamentary capacity. Milbank's cocounsel in the Payson case acknowledged as much, calling such a requirement "sheer baloney." But through repetition of the idea, Reilly gave it legitimacy.

The variant Besdine and Samuels favored was rigorous. Because even a demented octogenarian could identify the president during World War II, you might ask him to name the president's dog. And even someone who remembered Fala should be tested further—say, by in-

terpreting an aphorism. Besdine's example was well suited to the case
at hand: "People in glass houses shouldn't throw stones." Casual talk—
what Samuels called "cocktail conversation"—simply didn't suffice.
Amazingly enough, Besdine admitted to Philip Graham, the S&C litigator who had taken Osgood's place as the proponents' medical maven,
that even were the two of them to have a long lunch together, he could
not vouch for Graham's mental competence. Seward's meager shards
of conversation in his last few months proved nothing, the doctors said;
indeed, his obsession with topics like the new ship suggested "over-
learning" or "perseveration," itself a form of dementia. "So a doctor of
forty years' experience treating patients, including elderly patients, did
not, in your opinion, have a basis for forming a judgment about Mr.
Johnson's competence because he did not get a mental-status examination?" an understandably incredulous Graham asked Besdine. "Precisely correct," Besdine replied.

Together, the Harvard professors took an almost sadistic pleasure in
skewering Schilling. They depicted him as an obsolescent hayseed, a
relic of an older and more ignorant age of the sort still found occasionally
in the provinces. In attesting to Seward's capacity on so little evidence,
Besdine explained, Schilling made the kind of rudimentary mistake
today's medical students were routinely taught to avoid. "Are you saying
that Dr. Schilling's testimony was neutral, or are you saying that it
actually was evidence of noncompetence?" Graham asked. "Whose
competence? Mr. Johnson's or Dr. Schilling's?" Besdine replied.

Having stated there was no way Schilling, who had seen Seward
repeatedly, could have assessed his acuity without a mental-status examination, Milbank's witnesses, who had never seen Seward at all, let
alone asked him about Fala, now insisted Schilling's assessment had
been wrong. The nurses thought Seward only intermittently confused;
they, too, were way off base. "My opinion is that he was continuously
confused and that he was only intermittently noted to be confused,"
Samuels said. Besdine put it a bit differently. "In the docile or quiet
intervals between his confusion, he had seriously blunted intellectual
function," he said. Asked whether he'd felt Seward had been "of sound
mind and memory on the afternoon of April fourteenth," Besdine replied: "It is my opinion that he was not." (Samuels concurred.) Assume,
Reilly then directed Besdine, that Seward had been subjected to eleven
years of his wife's rantings and ravings. What effect, if any, would that
have had upon him on April 14? "I would expect it to have a devastating, demoralizing, demeaning, unmanning effect on Mr. Johnson,"
he replied. "It would powerfully inhibit him from exercising his judg-

ment if he felt that his judgment were in conflict with Mrs. Johnson's wishes."

Reisberg, a psychiatrist at New York University School of Medicine and an authority on Alzheimer's disease and the psychological problems of old people, elaborated on that point. In choppy, cut-and-pasted prose, the doctor, a short, scruffy man of thirty-eight who looked like Mel Brooks, testified that on April 14 Seward had been in the middle phase of dementia—that is, unable to function on his own—and subject to intermittent delusions and hallucinations. Had anyone bothered to ask him, Reisberg said, Seward probably could not have named the schools he attended or the president of the United States; perhaps he could have counted from one to ten, but not from ten to one. To the extent Seward *seemed* competent, it was all just a brave act; that was why he held up newspapers without reading them, watched television without understanding it, put up a front whenever Schilling came. Only certain "emotional memories" remained intact, encoded on some deeper level of consciousness and thereby protected from the disease raging all around. That was how he could have remembered how scary Basia really was. "I think he would have been intimidated, very likely enormously intimidated, by such tirades," he said.

Berry, who'd been doing the questioning, now moved to tie Milbank's entire case together. "Dr. Reisberg," he began, "I would like you to assume the following facts: Mrs. Johnson frequently screamed both at Mr. Johnson and at others in his presence. Her voice was often shrill and piercing, and her verbal tirades varied in frequency and duration. Sometimes they were daily or even more than once a day. Sometimes they lasted for a minute or two and sometimes for an hour and a half. Mr. Johnson's characteristic reaction was to say little or nothing and to leave the room. Mrs. Johnson frequently called Mr. Johnson such things as 'senile old man,' 'ga-ga,' 'stupid American.' Sometimes she spoke to him in that fashion in public places or in front of his relatives. On occasions when he was addressed by her in that fashion, Mr. Johnson customarily failed to respond verbally. He sat quietly, lowered his head, or left the room.

"Mrs. Johnson yelled at Mr. Johnson often during the course of their marriage, including during the final two years of his life, when he was dying of cancer. She yelled at him when he soiled his bed. She yelled at nurses in his presence. Mrs. Johnson sometimes refused to give him certain foods that he asked for. When he wanted a barbecue for his birthday, she told him that he could not have it and sent him to his room. When he wanted to drive his car, she refused to permit him to do so and ordered him to get out of his car immediately. In December 1982 or January 1983 Mr. Johnson told Mrs. Johnson that he was afraid of her. In January 1981 he explained to a housekeeper that he did not say anything when Mrs. Johnson was screaming at him or others because he was tired and sick and 'You cannot cross Basia.' He asked one chief of the security personnel at his home to remove a gun from a table in his bedroom because he was afraid that Mrs. Johnson would use it on him. He told another security chief that he wanted to have a gun to protect himself against her. On one occasion, Mrs. Johnson struck Mr. Johnson on the face and called him a 'stupid old man.'

"About four or five months before his death, Mr. Johnson, without consulting Mrs. Johnson, instructed one of the security guards to buy a Crockpot in which he could cook oatmeal. When she found out what he had done, she started screaming at him. She took his cane and threatened to hit him with it and called him a 'senile, stupid old man.' Mr. Johnson sunk down in his chair to protect himself. When he was hospitalized at the Princeton Medical Center in December 1982, he came home one day to have lunch and to be with his dogs. Mrs. Johnson became angry with him and complained that he had disrupted her whole day. She often told him to go to his bed or to his room, and he followed her command. At times after Mrs. Johnson's verbal tirades he would have tears in his eyes."

Finally, Berry's cadenza was complete. "Assuming these facts to be true," he said, "and taking into consideration the various medical records and testimony and trial witnesses that you have reviewed, do you have an opinion with a reasonable degree of medical certainty as to what effect, if any, all of Mrs. Johnson's behavior had on Mr. Johnson on the afternoon of April 14, 1983?"

Even in his debilitated state, Reisberg replied, the one thing Seward Johnson was capable of realizing was how helpless he was without Basia. "Under these circumstances," he said, "Mr. Johnson must have been enormously intimidated by Mrs. Johnson."

"Do you have an opinion as to what Mr. Johnson would have done if, on April 14, 1983, his wife had made any request of him?"

"I believe that the effect of the intimidation and of Mr. Johnson's insight into his degree of incapacity, combined, was such that Mr. Johnson would have felt obligated, in the interests of his own survival, to acquiesce, to concur, with his wife's wishes."

"I have no further questions," Berry said.

*   *   *

Milbank's medical case provided the first long look at Philip Graham, the litigator Sullivan & Cromwell had hastily substituted for Osgood. The new arrival, whose only technical knowledge of human anatomy came from some asbestos litigation he'd once handled, faced the daunting task not only of digesting Seward's massive medical history almost overnight, but of understanding it well enough to challenge Milbank's doctors. It was a job for which Graham, a soft-spoken, almost sweet man, seemed ill-suited. But he more than held his own.

When lawyers, particularly Wall Street lawyers more familiar with corporations than anatomy, confront doctors in a courtroom, anything short of outright embarrassment must be considered a win. Part of their problem is the tortuous subject matter; even the best questioner cannot hold a juror's attention for long with it. "I have to prepare for the doctor's testimony this afternoon," Santana, the sanitation-man-juror, once remarked to a reporter, reaching into his pocket and pulling out his second box of No-Doz. Graham kept things moving and reasonably interesting, but this was not his only accomplishment. His low-key competence helped hide the turmoil in his own camp. And, proceeding quietly, politely, and deferentially, he was the perfect person to dispel any lingering notion that Lambert's biases stemmed solely from his colleagues' clumsiness. Indeed, Graham was baptized on his first day before her.

"Your Honor, move to strike. This is just . . . " he said at one point.

"I'll take no speeches!" Lambert retorted. "You haven't been here, so you don't know our rules. The rules are no speeches!"

It was not his only lesson that day. At one point Graham challenged Besdine's account of how feeble Seward had been at the end of March 1983. "Would it surprise you to learn that Mr. Johnson rode his Exercycle for ten minutes without shortness of breath on the twenty-eighth of March?" Graham had asked. "He was a very tough man, wasn't he?" Besdine said nothing. "Wasn't he?"

"Sounds it," the doctor finally admitted.

So spoiled had she become by this point in the trial that Lambert took even the objectants' smallest rhetorical setback as an affront. "Do you *know*, Doctor, that he was a very tough man?" she interjected. "What does that mean? What does 'a very tough man' mean, medically? Does it mean anything?"

"No, it does not," Besdine, sprung from his trap, replied.

It was during his cross-examination of Reisberg, however, that Graham caught his purest glimpse of life in Lambertland. He'd asked the doctor whether Seward, even in his enfeebled state, could still have

understood whether Basia had been yelling at him or at a nurse, and
Berry had objected, claiming that the question had already been asked
and answered twice.

"He has already answered that," the judge parroted. "He has answered it twice."

"May I ask what the answer was?" Graham asked politely.

"I don't remember what the answer was," Lambert replied. "But he
did answer it."

Graham accomplished one more thing. While he could not discredit
Milbank's experts, he made them sound dogmatic, partisan, and extreme. In a sense, it was not so difficult. For despite their vaunted
antipathy toward each other, in many instances doctors and lawyers
are not all that different. Some lawyers, particularly litigators, are persons for hire. Once retained, they undergo a striking transformation,
one that can conveniently blind them to any moral, legal, or factual
ambiguity in the case before them. For doctors, the impetus isn't so
much economics as ego; having made their diagnoses, they became
wedded to them, sometimes going to ridiculous lengths to defend them.
That stubbornness can be even more pronounced in the courtroom,
where there are no living, breathing patients involved. When Reilly
examined his doctors, he was speaking not only to brilliant clinicians
but to kindred souls—people who were, by discipline and training,
every bit as partisan as he, who, having taken a position, would defend
it to the death no matter how untenable it might be.

Wherever, however, he could, Graham highlighted the doctors' dog-
matism. He got Besdine to advance the extraordinary proposition that
whether Seward loved Basia for the decade prior to his illness was
irrelevant to the perniciousness of her hold over him at the end. And,
not content to let Reilly finesse his way around so sensitive a subject,
he pinned down the doctors on the onset of Seward's incompetence.
Besdine placed the date at March 31 and appeared ready to say it arrived
even sooner until the judge cautioned him not to. With no such warning, Samuels was far more sweeping. Seward, he said, had been incompetent from the moment he arrived in Florida that January, maybe even
earlier. What Samuels was saying, then, was that Seward was incompetent before his nightlong chat with Junior at the Boca Raton hospital,
before making his two bequests to Harbor Branch, before meeting with
the president of Johnson & Johnson, before yielding the foundation
presidency to Junior, maybe even before approving the construction of
the *R/V Seward Johnson* and forgiving Junior's $1 million debt. No matter
how irrefutable the medical logic, empirically this just hadn't been so.

Anyone listening carefully really had to question everything the doctors said. And of course, regardless of where they placed the start of Seward's incompetence, it was years after he'd last left anything to his children.

When it came right down to it, the most reliable judges of Seward's competence were not the Harvard doctors or the children or Schilling or Basia, but the nurses who treated him around April 14. In order of their shifts, they were Mary Banks, Judy Smith, Patricia Reid, Bonnie Weisser, and Fran Cioffi. By all accounts, the most reliable and crucial of them all was Weisser, who had been on duty when Seward actually took pen in hand. Three years and two weeks afterward she took the stand, for the children.

Even before she stated her name, the jurors knew quite a bit about this cheerful woman of forty, with her boyish haircut and powder-blue dress. In a case where just about every issue was contested, all agreed she'd been the most competent and conscientious of all Seward's nurses. Bonnie Weisser. Even the name conjured up something sweet, sunny, reassuring. One could instantly see why she became Seward's favorite nurse, and would probably become the jury's, too. Enlisting Weisser, perhaps the pivotal witness in the case, had been one of Milbank's most impressive coups, just as losing her had been one of Osgood's most calamitous bungles.

And yet. Though she was testifying for the children, though she'd so helped Milbank prepare for trial, there always seemed to be an "and yet" tacked on to Weisser's version of events. Everyone else—Reilly and Christ, Schilling and Samuels, Junior and Basia, Peach and Lambert—had their easy answers to every question about Seward's competence and Basia's character. Of all of them, only Weisser was close enough to know what had really happened in Fort Pierce, dispassionate enough to assess it fairly, intelligent enough to know there was nothing simple about it, and honest enough to say so.

Weisser had lasted long enough to see Basia's many shortcomings. "There was often shouting and screaming, and her favorite word to holler at people was 'stupid,' " she said. At the same time, she noted that Basia had a more pleasing side. Both Reid and Banks had described the Johnsons' marriage as an arid, loveless union. (Reid had been no more flattering to the children, saying she couldn't recall Seward ever talking about them. "I didn't know he had any for a long time," she said.) But in a case where every kiss or caress was crucial, Weisser disagreed. Had Basia been interested in the quality of Seward's care?

Graham asked. "Very much so," she replied. Had Basia been attentive to his needs? "Yes." Was she involved virtually every day in his activities? "Very much so." Had she kissed Seward on the cheek? "Yes, she kissed him good night." She'd do that every night, wouldn't she? "Usually." And say she loved him? "Yes." And he'd say it back? "Yes."

Weisser graphically described Seward's declining physical and mental powers. Sometimes, she said, he would look at the same newspaper article for half an hour. There even came a time when he no longer asked her to read him the stock quotations; clearly, when Seward stopped caring about the price of J&J, the end was near. If anything, she told Reilly, the nurses, fearing for their jobs if they got too gloomy, deliberately understated Seward's mental problems. Weisser herself had described Seward as "alert" more than a dozen times in her notes, but "alert" to her meant only that Seward had not been dozing or hallucinating, just as "attentive" referred more to posture and attention span than retention. Sure, she'd given the nurses innumerable instructions designed to keep Seward happy, but that by no means meant she'd considered him competent. "Even though his reaction to things was not appropriate, I still maintained that we needed to treat him as if he were oriented at all times," she explained. "We did not take it for granted that he won't know the difference."

But as Weisser drew it, Seward's chart did not contain the unremitting, precipitous tumble Milbank's experts had traced. "He didn't just get very sick. He was sick, very sick, intermittently," she said, struggling to describe precisely what she meant. "He would be very ill and get just a little bit better and then very ill again. So there were transient periods. It wasn't an exact progression." Similarly, at times Seward became confused, but he was not confused continuously. "When someone is confused in this minute or five-minute span does not necessarily mean they are the next," she said. "Conversely, if they are very well oriented at this time doesn't mean that they are not confused within the next five minutes." Seward Johnson, she seemed to say, had his lucid intervals. That was all the law required. The only question was whether one of them occurred at the right time on April 14.

That morning, nurse Patricia Reid had made her two notations of confusion, at 8:25 and 8:40. "He was quite tired that day," Reid had said later in her deposition, which a pretty Milbank paralegal had read into the record before Weisser took the stand. "He had been having several bouts of confusion that kind of ran along through the entire morning." Reid had then been asked whether the confusion had ended earlier that morning, as her notes suggested. "No," she'd replied. "It had lasted almost the entire shift, but it would . . . it kind of came, you know, would come and go. This particular morning he would not always be aware of the day or where he was at. And he had times when he thought there were other people in the room that were not there. I don't know . . . it just kind of came and went in waves." Anything read into the record was soporific, and even though Reid's testimony was crucial, the exercise made little impression on anyone. Indeed, what people were likely to remember most wasn't anything Reid had said but the way in which the Milbank paralegal read what she said—specifically, when she began to describe rubbing ointment on Seward's coccyx, only to get stuck on the first syllable of the word. The two men on the jury started to snicker, then ripples of ribald male mirth spread across the courtroom.

Weisser had taken over from Reid at three o'clock. In her notes, she had recorded how Seward had taken some broth, watched some television, and, sometime between four and five, had gone to the dining room "to sign some papers." Around eleven that night, shortly after Seward told her he felt "much stronger," she'd prepared to leave. "No confusion noted this shift," she wrote before departing.

As Reilly completed his direct examination of Weisser, he did his best to help her explain that potentially damning statement away.

"Why did you make that entry?" he asked.

"Because he had no obvious manifestations of confusion or hallucinations," she replied.

"Does that entry indicate that Mr. Johnson was not, in your opinion, confused?"

"It only states that I noted no evidence of confusion," she replied.

Finally, Reilly asked his most crucial witness his most crucial question at the most crucial moment in his case, just as it was about to conclude. "Miss Weisser," he began, "do you have any opinion as to whether or not Mr. Johnson was rational or irrational on April 14, 1983?"

Weisser had seen Seward Johnson as much as or more than anyone—more even, arguably, than Basia—during the most critical phase of his long testamentary career, and with a keener eye. She'd seen his confusion firsthand, and, after speaking with Reid, had been looking for it on the fourteenth. More than anyone else's, her answer to Reilly's question was definitive, and everyone, Reilly among them, awaited it eagerly. It was as if she wasn't a witness so much as foreman of the jury.

All morning long, she had been pausing for long periods of time before giving her answers. One Milbank sympathizer in the gallery said she'd sounded "constipated." It was all a function of her compulsive carefulness, her ambivalence about what she was doing, and the illness that had overcome her since arriving in New York: a compound of the change in climate, cabin fever, and fear for her own safety, stemming from what she'd heard about the recent courtroom uprising. The pauses were a bit exasperating. This time, though, the wait seemed particularly interminable.

Actually, her thinking on the question of Seward's competence had never really changed, though she was not beyond persuasion. Perhaps if Osgood had not been so heavy-handed with her, she might have landed one way. If her initial chemistry with Reilly, which led her friend Fran Cioffi to think he had a crush on her, had persisted, she might have landed the other way. But on the subway to court that morning, she'd seen Reilly become unglued over something, chewing out Berry so crudely that everyone on the train could hear him. The S&C lawyers had repeatedly seen Reilly treat subordinates that way, and would not have been shocked. Nor would some folks at Milbank, who had pondered the paradox of a man who went through secretaries the way Basia went through butlers criticize someone else for abusing inferiors. But it surprised, and disturbed, Weisser. She'd become uneasier still at lunch, when Reilly's iciness suggested he was displeased with her testimony thus far. It dawned on her that Reilly's high-mindedness, his talk about principles, his commitment to seeing justice done, was all a facade. Perhaps, when it came right down to it, Reilly and Osgood weren't so different after all: Perhaps truth was something Reilly, no more than Osgood, really wanted to hear.

There were other forces working on Weisser. First, she'd learned from press accounts that Seward's last will really wasn't all that different from the ones before it, as Junior Johnson had led her to believe. Second, she'd now laid eyes on Basia for the first time since Seward's funeral, and when she did, she felt a strange surge of sympathy. Whatever else Basia was, Weisser knew she was not the one-dimensional demon Milbank was making her out to be. Seeing Basia again reminded her of what they shared. Both women were perfectionists. Both had endured hardships alone: If Basia had watched her husband die, Weisser had raised three children by herself. Both shared an intense and terrible time: Those two months in Fort Pierce during which each stood by helplessly as a man they loved, however differently, slowly faded away. "I don't care about any of this," Basia told Weisser, clutching her by her wrists, during one break. "All I care about is that you took very good care of my husband, and I still really like you." Feverish and confused, in a dizzy, dreamlike state, Weisser barely heard Reilly say, "Miss Weisser, do you have any opinion as to whether or not Mr. Johnson was rational or irrational on April 14, 1983?" She answered it anyway, as best she could.

"No," she said. "I don't."

Reilly, and everyone else in the courtroom for that matter, was dumbfounded. Hers was the last syllable in Milbank's case; Sullivan & Cromwell's rebuttal was now at hand. And if Bonnie Weisser couldn't hazard a guess about the state of Seward Johnson's mind when he'd signed his will, how in heaven's name could anyone else?

XLVI

Sister Mary Louise Flowers sat politely in the witness box on the morning of May 8. She was wearing the same outfit she'd worn every day for the past thirty years: a crisp, bleached white habit, one that stood out in the sea of gray flannel all around her and seemed miraculously immune to the city's grit and grime. Sullivan & Cromwell had interviewed dozens of potential witnesses for this, the leadoff spot in its rebuttal case. But of all those it could have called, the demure, benevolent nun was the most fitting. For even after Bonnie Weisser's key admission, it seemed that only divine intervention could spare Basia Johnson, Nina Zagat, and S&C from going down to defeat.

Actually, the task facing the proponents was more like a rehabilitation than a rebuttal. Before they could build anything of their own, they had to clean up eight weeks' worth of debris, and it was difficult to know what to pick up first. Seward's mental state on April 14 remained paramount, and witnesses would be called to recount his every utterance. More than that, Seward had to be transformed from the docile, doddering Milquetoast his children had portrayed into a vital, strong-willed soul, capable of thinking for, asserting, defending himself. His third marriage had to be recast into something he'd entered into lovingly and remained in freely. Basia, like Seward, desperately needed refurbishment. Nina's battered credibility also needed tending to. Then there were dozens of brushfires to extinguish, concerning everything from guns to dirty bathtubs to Crockpots to fondled breasts.

It was a tall order, and good witnesses were few. For when it came right down to it, the Johnsons had everything but friends. To make matters worse, whoever Sullivan & Cromwell called would testify with the clock running out. The judge, who'd let the objectants luxuriate, was hectoring S&C to wrap things up quickly, and for a reason; as the days grew longer and warmer, the jury was growing more restless. Even the juror who was perpetually chewing gum seemed to be masticating more slowly. During one lunch break one of Basia's bodyguards thought he saw two of the jurors sharing a joint in City Hall Park.

Morale in the proponents' camp continued to ebb. By now, Sullivan & Cromwell had stopped bringing potential recruits to court to see the kind of sexy cases awaiting them. One night at S&C Basia screamed so hysterically that one of the firm's security guards poked his head into the conference room. "Everything all right, Mr. Christ?" he asked. On another occasion she'd berated Christ quasi-publicly in the corridor outside the courtroom. "You're no litigator!" she told him. "Society lawyer" joined "soft-boiled egg" and "sack of potatoes" in Basia's arsenal of epithets for him.

Basia's relations with the other Christ—Iris—had also grown frosty. Christ's loyal wife liked coming to court, to buck up her husband and follow his exploits. Before the trial had begun, Christ had asked Nina whether such visits would pose any problems, and Nina assured him they would not, even though she came to believe Iris's presence, and occasional sickliness, proved a distraction to her husband. Almost from the beginning, though, there had been tensions between Christ's wife and Christ's client. For one thing, Basia objected to Iris's wardrobe—the Adolfo suits, the furs, the makeup, the jewelry, including one bauble that, as Marty Richards felicitously put it, was more rink than ring. Such lavishness, Basia felt, completely undermined her own aggressive underdressing. Privately, she bestowed upon Iris a name she had already given Osgood: "the Peacock."

Things nosedived still further when, in an attempt to be helpful, Iris tried furnishing an alibi for Basia's initial silence with the press: Her English wasn't good enough. Conversely, Iris grew fed up with Basia's treatment of her husband. "He's not used to dealing with cruds like this," she remarked at one point. Soon Basia chafed at Iris's every move. "The next thing you know, the llamas will be coming to the courtroom, too," she once complained. Finally, she decreed that Iris be barred altogether, and gave Nina the unenviable task of informing Iris's husband. Donald Christ was forced to choose between his client and his wife, and, like the prince of Wales, he opted for the woman he loved. There was no way he could or would keep Iris from coming to court, he said. That brought Bauman into the picture. A compromise was struck: Iris could still attend court, but would sit in the demilitarized spectators' zone, far away from Basia, but not so far away from her husband that he couldn't throw her an occasional kiss. There she remained, facing a jury that must have been perplexed by her sudden exile.

And there matters stood, or sat, until April 29, when an item appeared in William Norwich's society column in the *Daily News*. "VAN-

DERBILT TRIBE GAINS ONE MORE," it announced rather innocuously, and, indeed, most of the column was devoted to the birth in London of **Serena McCallum,** daughter of **Serena Vanderbilt Van Ingen McCallum,** an actress and model, and **Rick McCallum,** executive producer of *Pennies from Heaven* and other films. The proud grandmother was identified as "the very beautiful **Iris Smith Van Ingen Paine Russell Christ** of Locust Valley and Oregon." The aforementioned Iris, Norwich went on, "recently jolted society when she appeared (unidentified) on the front page of this newspaper, escorting **Basha Johnson** to court." Since Iris loathed press coverage, Norwich reported, everyone wondered what she was doing there. Then he supplied the answer: Iris's husband, **Donald Christ,** was "Basha's" lawyer, and Iris had dutifully befriended the widow.

"Now, however, I am told that Basha is complaining loudly to attorney Christ about the progress of the trial," Norwich went on. "Needless to say, Iris isn't exactly singing Basha's tune these days. You see, when oil and water try to mix, the water would do well not to push the oil around." Basia was aware that Iris had known Norwich for years, and held her responsible for the item. It was enough to make Basia take her "Ban Iris" campaign even higher, to Robert Carswell and John Stephenson, the heads of Shearman & Sterling and Sullivan & Cromwell.

Come what may in court, the van from Charlotte's arrived daily at 52 Duane Street, carrying its latest lavish repasts. Fearful that her discriminating customers might be growing bored with her twenty-dollar selections, Roberta Morrell, the wine caterer, tried livening things up by inaugurating what she called "a mini wine course": a sampling designed to replicate the average millionaire's wine cellar. She stretched for some thirty-dollar varieties like a 1984 Corton Charlemagne, Domaine Delarche. From the standard French repertoire, she branched out into California, Spain, Italy, and Australia. To make things really festive, she'd occasionally send down something even better, like a thirty-five dollar-a-bottle 1981 Château Decru Beaucaillou. Once, she included a bottle of vintage port. But while Morrell knew nothing about the case, she did notice one curious thing: Never were there any requests for champagne.

As matters deteriorated in court, the tensions inevitably spilled over into the dining area. No longer were Marie Lambert's integrity or Ed Reilly's lovemaking techniques the principal topics under discussion; now, the fighting turned fratricidal. Basia's tongue-lashings at her lawyers became as much a staple of the lunchtime menu as her beef consommé. One Sullivan & Cromwell lawyer succinctly described the transition from courtroom to lunchroom: "You went from one woman screaming to another woman screaming."

There were other signs of stress. As his star fell with Basia, Arnold Bauman, who had initially cruised over to the lunchroom in her limousine, was forced to walk. Bauman's once-cordial relationship with Iris Christ, another lunchtime regular, also soured. Not so far back, she'd given him a photograph of one of her pet llamas, who happened to be named "Arnold." But as time passed, and Bauman repeatedly entered the premises wailing "Reilly owns the courtroom!" or something similar, she came to regard Bauman as a Cassandra—or, as she put it, "a crepe-hanging creep." Eventually, the two stopped speaking, and Iris vowed to rechristen "Arnold" once the whole confounded mess was over. Relations between Iris and both Basia and Nina sank to new lows. Once, when Iris wore purple to court, Basia complained that she was allergic to the color. As for Iris, she began calling Basia "the witch" and Nina "the stupidest lawyer I've ever seen."

Morale was especially low among the S&C underlings. Associates and paralegals despaired as they prepared blistering cross-examinations for Christ, only to see their best questions be frittered away or go unasked. Privately, they started improvising sardonic scripts. One depicted Christ's idea of interrogation.

CHRIST: "Mr. Smith, just where *do* you live?"
SMITH: "Boston, Mass."
CHRIST: "No further questions."

Another skit featured Lech Wałęsa and His Holiness Pope John Paul II appearing as character witnesses for Basia. "I tell you, that Basia, she's a scream!" the pope told the court.

As their spirits plummeted, some junior members of the proponents' legal team gave the lunchtime retreat a new name: "the Titanic Room." Robert Delahunty—who had taken to burying himself in Plato's *Republic* and listening to Mendelssohn psalms for solace; for all his labors, the only reaction he got from the firm fathers was a reprimand from Bob MacCrate for letting his hair grow beyond S&C's regulation length— kept his colleagues posted as S&C headed toward the fateful iceberg, then struck it and began to sink. Though Nina and Bauman remained on deck, some erstwhile lunchtime regulars, like Christ, stopped showing up, opting to eat more plebian fare on shore. On any given day in the Titanic Room, there might be as few as four people sitting around a table set for ten. Since no one informed Charlotte's, piles of food were left untouched, conjuring up images of Paul Bocuse's fare at the Jasna Polana opening, until the normally brown-bagging court reporters working next door began pillaging the daily remains.

Isolated by her lack of friends, unable to lean on the already-beleaguered Nina, spurned by those few remaining loyalists who found her either too frazzled to be with or too hamstrung to buy anything from them, Basia became increasingly dependent on John Fox. The ever-accommodating Foxes spent hours, days, at Jasna Polana, largely listening to Basia's lamentations. Sitting around the estate, Basia would talk about her trial, and trials. She would explain how a confluence of forces—WASPs, Wall Street, the Kremlin, the American legal system, the American character, America itself—were torturing her, all because they couldn't stand to see a Pole collect so much money. Or God, or Jesus, was subjecting her to all this for His own purposes. Only occasionally were there moments of levity. She'd ridicule her stepchildren, calling them "wimps" and "cretins" and "half-wits." Or she'd describe the karate lessons she was getting from her bodyguard, how she could now poke out eyes Three Stooges–style, and how she was tempted to use her new skills on Christ.

As Milbank's case concluded, Basia again resolved to replace Christ, or at least shove him to one side. Around seven on the morning of April 23, she called Nina and, in an agitated tone, declared she would go ahead and hire Roy Cohn by day's end if her legal team wasn't beefed up. Nina hastily arranged a meeting at Shearman & Sterling's downtown offices, attended by, among others, the heads of both S&S and S&C, Carswell and Stevenson. If nothing else, Basia was at last getting the attention she felt she deserved. "Mrs. Johnson, I just want you to know that if there's anything you need, if you have any problems at all, just yell," Carswell said to her as the meeting concluded. Basia didn't blink. "Do you have your tape recorder on?" she asked.

Short of Cohn, the smart Jewish lawyer Basia said she wanted was Marvin Schwartz, the S&C litigator who'd so impressed everyone with his impassioned defense of Osgood a month earlier. When they met, Schwartz listened politely to Basia rant and rave, assailing Bauman for failing to warn her how long the case would last, deriding the absent Christ as a "soft-boiled egg" and a "stubborn blockhead." Privately, Schwartz had to admit she had a point. Much as he loved Christ, the firm should never have let him try the Johnson case; Schwartz himself had always assumed Osgood would handle it. Schwartz quickly agreed to join the proponents' legal team and help present its rebuttal. But on one point he was adamant: He should not, and would not, take over for Christ. Even if he could bring himself up to speed, he said, it would be seen as an act of desperation. Christ would remain in charge, at least nominally. Christ had qualms about the move, and not because he felt threatened or rebuked. Lambert would hate the guy, he warned Nina, and the jury wouldn't like him, either. "Look, Don," Nina responded, "would you rather have Roy Cohn?" MacCrate, the senior litigator Basia had met with earlier, was also skeptical. "You think Osgood's egotistical and you want *Schwartz*?" he'd once asked Basia incredulously.

For Schwartz, fixing sticky situations was nothing new. He'd been at the firm since 1951, and had come to be known as Sullivan & Cromwell's smartest and scrappiest litigator. He'd had to be. Anti-Semitism, rife on Wall Street in the first half of the century, was one charge that could not be routinely thrown at S&C; by the Woodrow Wilson administration the firm had already had several Jewish partners. But for decades afterward it named none, at least not any who'd own up to their Jewishness. The logjam was finally broken in 1953, when a Jewish protegé of Arthur Dean was elevated; those who carried Dean's bags invariably got bag carriers for themselves. But S&C circa 1920–1950 had little room for Marvins *or* Schwartzes. It didn't help that Schwartz was short and, with thick eyeglasses encased in black fifties frames, bookwormy—hardly a figure from the genteel Dulles school. Schwartz was brighter than his peers (he'd led his class at the University of Pennsylvania Law School and clerked for Supreme Court justice Harold Burton), and more industrious, too. But he'd initially been passed over for partnership, and was out looking for another job when S&C relented and let him in.

Even then, he hadn't stopped scratching. His work was invariably brilliant; he earned a reputation as a quick study, someone who could spot issues instantaneously, who had an encyclopedic knowledge of federal securities laws, who could dictate arcane memoranda and capture a courtroom with equal ease. "Swaying back and forth as he speaks," the *New Yorker*'s Lillian Ross wrote in 1966, Schwartz projected "a deep, resonant voice, which immediately makes him sound authoritative." When the occasion called for it, Schwartz could be tough, even brutal. In a story as well known around S&C as MacCrate's tales of his Brooklyn forebears, Schwartz once found himself up against Abe Fortas, who had just left the U.S. Supreme Court in disgrace. "Mr. Schwartz, I really must intervene, you are badgering the witness. That's improper," Fortas said at one point. "Mr. Justice Fortas," Schwartz shot back, "when I want to take lessons in ethics, the last person in the world I'd go to is you."

A few years later, when it came time for Schwartz to submit an autobiographical statement for Sullivan & Cromwell's centennial volume, some smugness had crept into his account. "Mr. Schwartz is well-known at the bar as a securities lawyer," it declared. But "while he has certainly handled many securities cases his career contradicts any notion of specialization." And there were those who felt that by the 1980s Schwartz was coasting and boasting a bit too much. Both personally and professionally, Schwartz grew somewhat self-indulgent and careless. He was living the good life; he sported a solid-gold Rolex, shared a tailor with Henry Kissinger—"The guy says he knows me, but I don't remember meeting him," he once said of the former secretary of state—and sent back food or wine a bit more often than he should. Indeed, he was a charter participant in the increasingly popular *Zagat Restaurant Survey*.

Schwartz came to court less prepared than before. When he couldn't find the right citation, he would say things like "reason and common sense dictate that . . ." He tended to wing things, to paper things over with pomposity. "It didn't occur to him that he wouldn't be brilliant," recalled one former associate. Another remarked, "Marvin believes that the jury is privileged to be there listening to him." Said a third, "He's sometimes wrong, but never in doubt." Two months before Basia demanded Schwartz's services, Kidder, Peabody & Company, enmeshed in the insider-trading scandal, had unceremoniously dumped him and S&C as counsel; Schwartz, it felt, had needlessly antagonized government prosecutors, at one point hectoring one of them with the same wisecrack about legal ethics he'd used with Fortas. Schwartz had come to consider himself a celebrity; in fact, he fully expected his entry into *Johnson* v. *Johnson* would make the eleven o'clock news.

Despite his concerns for Christ, Schwartz quickly became, to all appearances, the man in charge of the proponents' case. He handled most of the rebuttal witnesses, with Graham continuing to work with doctors and nurses; Christ was left with only a few family members and bit players. Day in and day out, witness after witness, Christ sat silently at counsel's table, head down, pen in hand, writing, writing, writing. Just what he was writing was difficult to determine. Perhaps he was taking notes, but that was pointless; transcripts were available almost instantaneously. Perhaps he was writing out questions for various witnesses, but if so, why did he never hand those questions to the folks doing the questioning? More likely, what Christ was doing was preserving his own dignity; if he kept his head down, he wouldn't have to hold it high. Whatever suffering Christ was experiencing, however, he suffered in silence (to cite just one example, he was grinding his teeth so much that he developed abscesses and needed extensive root-canal work when the trial was over). He never grew testy, never complained, never pouted, never played the martyr, never placed any blame. His very detachment from things, which made him so poor an advocate, was now his best defense.

Time and mortality had shrunk the circumference of Seward's already-limited circle of friends. Most of those who'd lived through his arid second marriage or his final courtship were either gone, had fuzzy memories, or, in the case of various J&J panjandrums, were sworn to neutrality. Johnson & Johnson stuck together on *Johnson v. Johnson* as resolutely as it did on Tylenol, though it was not always easy. The company's chairman, James Burke, liked spouting platitudes about what he called the "long-standing and greatly admired tradition in the Johnson family that family is family and business is business." That, of course, had always been nonsense, as the sagas of Robert Wood Johnson, Seward Johnson, Junior Johnson, and Bobby Johnson proved, and it remained nonsense in the will contest. Johnson & Johnson talked neutrality, but its decision to lie low was, in and of itself, highly partisan. For one thing, Burke himself had often seen Seward and Basia together and could have contradicted the children's portrait of the marriage. Moreover, he'd had firsthand evidence of Seward's competence, having spoken to him in February 1983 about the Tylenol crisis. ("I can't tell you how pleased I am that you are doing so well," Burke subsequently wrote the old man. "Your voice sounded strong.") For another, David Clare, J&J's president, had met with Seward only a month before the will-signing and heard the old man describe Harbor Branch as his "life's work." Clare's older brother, Robert, had once headed Shearman & Sterling; indeed, it was he who had recruited Bauman to the firm. But when Bauman asked him to speak to his younger brother about that encounter, Robert Clare came back empty-handed: his brother, he told Bauman, remembered nothing. Bauman found Clare's report not just unconvincing but deeply disturbing; his oldest friend at the firm, he lamented to a friend, was not telling him the truth.

Basia, too, had few potential allies to enlist. In court proceedings as at her Jasna Polana galas, there were not enough people to invite. After all, she had spent most of her time in the United States securely nestled in Seward's cocoon. Furthermore, given her perfectionist nature, mercurial temperament, and fleeting loyalties, she had forged few enduring bonds. Most of her "friends" weren't friends at all, but sycophants, parasites, and purveyors, who barely knew her or were too beholden to her to be of any use. Her lawyers contacted plenty of big names—Millicent Fenwick and I. M. Pei, Cyrus Vance and the Smithsonian's Dillon Ripley, among them—all of whom said they'd have had little to contribute. They considered calling Gregory Peck, but feared his loyalties lay with the Richardses. Clive Harris, the faith healer, was too dicey to call, and besides, Basia had stiffed him. Others, like Dr. Jacqueline Mislow, who'd treated Seward in late 1982, declined to testify, and it was a pity for Basia. "Only through your insistent and determined efforts was Mr. Johnson able to enjoy an extended period of his life," the doctor had written her shortly after Seward's death. "You demonstrated with great courage what a truly devoted and loving wife would do for her husband."

Still others could not be called either because they had been among the Jasna Polana Fifteen or were so slavishly loyal to Basia as to be utterly incredible. And there were those whom S&C overlooked, like Krystian Zimerman, the Polish-born pianist who had won the Chopin Competition the Johnsons had sponsored in 1975. He'd spoken to Seward from England in mid-April 1983, within days of the will-signing, and could have said that even by transatlantic cable Seward had conversed intelligently. He also could have described how Basia had rejuventated Seward in much the way a younger woman had rejuvenated Artur Rubinstein. Zimerman's agent called Sullivan & Cromwell to offer the musician's services. And S&C did return the call—once the case was over. S&C had long since deemed John Peach too embittered, unattractive, and tainted to testify. Basia's brother Gregory, would surely have crumpled on the stand, for fear of Basia at least as much as of Reilly. Waligura had taken money from the Johnsons and, besides, had been painted as Basia's lover, a charge he could not refute without disclosing his own homosexuality.

With all of the emphasis on Basia, it was easy to forget that Nina, too, needed a makeover. Shearman & Sterling made one last-ditch effort to prepare Tom Ford to testify, but the S&C lawyers remained unimpressed. "A bumbling horse's ass" was how one of them described him. Christ considered calling several other Shearman & Sterling lawyers—Werner Polak, Arthur Field, Edward Reilly—but opted against it. (For better or for worse, then, the jury would never get to hear Edward Reilly cross-examine Edward Reilly.) Christ also considered and rejected George Gillespie of Cravath, Swaine & Moore, whom he'd paid twenty-five thousand dollars to review Seward's wills, to attest to

Nina's good work and Seward's testamentary consistency. He also opted not to call any of the character witnesses Nina suggested, including Orville Schell, past president of the Association of the Bar of the City of New York; Peter Zimroth, a Yale classmate and later New York City's corporation counsel; and Scott Greathead, right-hand man of New York attorney general Robert Abrams. Indeed, for all of Basia's talk that Christ and Nina were in league together, Sullivan & Cromwell was curiously nonchalant about rehabilitating Nina.

Calling Basia to the stand appeared to offer the last, best hope of salvaging the case. Completing it without her, as the ever-erudite Arthur Field once put it, would be "like producing *Hamlet* without the Prince." But as her disastrous appearance in the Harbor Branch case had proved, such a move was dangerous. As Basia's lawyers debated the idea, a parade of less risky, less revealing witnesses took the stand.

Like Milbank's first witness, Sister Mary Louise Flowers, vicar of the Order of the Little Servant Sisters of the Immaculate Conception of the Blessed Virgin Mary and administrator of St. Joseph's Seniors Residence of Woodbridge, New Jersey, was a volunteer. She, too, had been following the trial in the paper and felt outraged by what she read. So she picked up the phone and dialed (609) 921–1200—Jasna Polana—to offer her services.

It was, well, a godsend. The good sister was not just a nun but a nurse who had specialized in geriatric care for forty years. She had seen the loving Johnsons together in the fall of 1982, when she visited Seward both in the Princeton hospital and at Jasna Polana. The jurors would surely find her appealing; at least one of them, Santana the sanitation worker, came to court for her second day of testimony in his Sunday best. And she could handcuff Lambert, whose own conspicuous Catholicism would presumably overcome her prejudices. Schwartz put it more simply: the nun (who, like most nuns, seemed both elderly and ageless and, in any event, saintly) would drive Marie Lambert crazy. On May 8, after a day spent cloistered on the sixth floor praying to God and eating Mrs. Field's cookies, she took the stand and swore to tell the truth. "That's kind of silly," one observer noted as she took the oath.

Because Sister Mary Louise hadn't seen Seward after he'd made his final migration to Florida, her testimony was directed not so much to competency as to character. With her, the usually laconic old man had been comparatively chatty. Many of their exchanges were of the *Heaven*

Knows, Mr. Allison, variety, in which the nun gushed goodness and Seward tended toward impish irreverence. She described Seward the loyal son-in-law, who brought flowers, spring water, and homemade bread to his hospitalized mother-in-law in September 1982 and lamented that he could no longer take walks with her. "I looked at him skeptically and said, 'But you have a language barrier, don't you?' " she recalled. "And he turned to me, and he said—it was really beautiful— he said, 'I love her. We love each other. Basia knows that I love them both.' " Sister Mary Louise paused to ponder just how lovely it had all been, then turned to share her pleasure with Lambert. "I thought that was so beautiful, Your Honor," she said. The judge looked slightly annoyed.

Schwartz pumped her for more examples of Seward's sense of humor, and the nun happily obliged. Once, the old man compared nuns to penguins. Another time, he expressed amazement that some nuns were actually good-looking. A third time, he asked what a nun did for fun. When informed that a feast day was coming, he asked whether any "Blue Nun" would be served. "I said 'Oh, yes. All of our teachers wear blue habits in the wintertime,' " Sister Mary Louise recalled. "At that time I didn't know what 'Blue Nun' was, truthfully," she added sheepishly as the gallery burst into laughter, quite possibly the first sympathetic laughter S&C had heard. "And so he said, 'Sister, I'm talking about wine. I'll see that I ask Basia to order something for you for that jubilee.' " And, sure enough, he did. Shortly before he left for Fort Pierce, Seward told the sister he was sorry he couldn't bring all of the nuns along with him. "I'm sorry I can't go there, too," Sister Mary Louise had replied, "because I have a doctor nephew there, and my other nephew is a lawyer, aspiring to be a judge." That didn't impress Seward. "I abhor both," he'd said. "I looked at him kind of hurt," she went on. "And he said, 'No aspersions on your nephews.' And then we both laughed. And then he said, 'But we'd all be better off without them, wouldn't we? Without doctors and judges and lawyers, it would be a better world.' And we laughed at that. It's the truth." At that moment, three years into a will contest his millions were financing, Seward seemed not just competent but clairvoyant.

Once, the nun related, Seward asked her what she thought of Jasna Polana. "Plush," Sister Mary Louise replied. "Yes, Barbara has expensive taste," he'd said, but so, too, did he—at Harbor Branch. He expressed regrets to her that until Basia had come along, he'd not been "a giver." In a single afternoon the nun saw Basia and Seward exchange more kisses than Keith Wold and Marilyn Link combined said they'd seen in a dozen years. She insisted that in her time with him, Seward had always been alert. "He was always cognizant of the time, place, that he was in," she said. "He was rational."

Reilly realized that the best cross-examinations weren't the bloated, interminable inquiries Christ had conducted, but short and to the point. He needn't even highlight the nun's beholdenness to Basia—some $350,000 from Seward's charitable trusts had gone into the order's nursing home—since she'd already done that herself. "With thanks to the Almighty God and to the Johnsons, we were able to begin with our building," she'd said beamingly in her direct examination. Thus, Reilly's cross lasted all of one minute and consisted of one real question. "Am I correct that you did not see Mr. Johnson after January 24, 1983?" The nun conceded that he was.

Reilly realized, too, that cross-examination is superfluous if one could derail direct testimony. Rarely could Schwartz get in more than a few questions before Reilly was on his feet, objecting. His most ingenious cavil was that the nun's conversations with Seward were akin to confessions and, therefore, privileged. That Seward, a non-Catholic man of little faith, viewed himself as a penitent and the nun as his confessor was silly. Moreover, the cases uniformly held what the church taught: that nuns were not clergy and, therefore, could not hear the confessions of Catholics, let alone those of lapsed Protestants. But Reilly had an uncanny ability to *sound* correct, at least partly because, in the judge's eyes, he always was. Once again Reilly was performing sorcery on Marie Lambert, and Marie Lambert was the Sorcerer's Apprentice.

Even before the confessional issue arose, Lambert had repeatedly cut off Schwartz to conduct mini-inquisitions of her own. At times, she all but called the nun a liar. Now, interrupted only by the occasional kibitzing of the Jew from Sullivan & Cromwell, Lambert and another lay Catholic, this one from Milbank Tweed, presumed to tell a nun just who can administer the sacraments and when. Seemingly determined to reverse two millennia of church teaching, the judge decreed that Seward's conversations with Sister Mary Louise were legally off-limits. She proposed interviewing her outside the presence of the jury, then reenacting for it whatever portions she deemed appropriate—much as some animals chew their food before giving it to their young. Of course, such reconstituted testimony had no impact at all, and Schwartz objected with a ferocity heretofore unseen from his side of the table. "What Your Honor is doing is cutting the guts out of this woman's testimony!" he complained at the sidebar. "And it's highly unfair and prejudicial." Finally, a Sullivan & Cromwell lawyer found a case that stated, unambiguously, that a nun is not a priest. Sister Mary Louise was finally allowed to testify.

Around this time Forger made one of his periodic, portentous trips to court, where he watched contentedly as Reilly scored point after point. "You can't be happy with how Lambert is conducting herself," a reporter sitting alongside him commented. The implication was clear: The more the judge ran amok, the more certain was reversal. Forger maintained a judicious silence. But as the rebuttal continued, Reilly's objections dropped dramatically, and not because S&C's questions were any better framed or because the judge, whenever she looked skyward after Reilly rose, was any less certain to find the word "sustained" carved into the ornate entablature. Even the Milbank lawyers had determined her partisanship was becoming too apparent, and decided to stop goading her into further indiscretions.

Despite his advance billing, Schwartz did not answer the proponents' prayers. Far from being the facile questioner he was cracked up to be, he seemed stilted and uncomfortable on his feet. He croaked more than talked and had only a smoker's wind, which hurt him with two quick-witted adversaries like Reilly and Lambert. The jury didn't like him. "He reminded me of Ed Begley and the sleazy roles he used to play," one of them later said. And, just as Christ had feared, Schwartz patronized Lambert, and she quickly detected the condescension. "He thinks he's a really brilliant trial lawyer, and he isn't," she later said. "He's a pompous ass." If Schwartz annoyed Lambert, he enraged Reilly. To the Milbank litigator, Schwartz exemplified S&C's signature arrogance. From the moment during his defense of Osgood when Schwartz promulgated his peculiar test of legal ethics—that intimidating a witness meant threatening to break his bones—Reilly wasted no chance to display his contempt for him. Things boiled over during one sidebar conference on an evidentiary issue.

"If you wanted to learn something about your case, maybe it would do you some good," Reilly said acidly.

"I don't appreciate remarks like that," Schwartz replied. "Why don't we try to be professionals, civil to each other?"

"I don't need any lectures from you on any case," Reilly snapped back, cribbing a line from Schwartz's own libretto and speaking so loudly that Lambert moved the colloquy into her chambers. As they headed in, Reilly got in his last licks. "Other than broken noses and broken legs, I don't need any lectures from you on anything!"

"Let's get some ground rules set right away," the judge said once the group had moved out of public earshot. "We don't shout at the sidebar so that newspaper reporters who are sitting there can hear, and the jury. We try to keep our voices down. That's why I dragged you in here. Okay?"

"May I add, Your Honor, that after Your Honor left, Mr. Reilly threatened to break my legs and my nose," Schwartz declared.

"That is false, Your Honor, totally false!" Reilly retorted. "Mr. Schwartz was giving me what I believe was some sort of a lecture on behavior, and I said I don't need to get a lecture from anyone in view of your comments on broken noses and broken legs." When things calmed down, the lawyers headed back to the courtroom. As they did, Reilly turned to Schwartz yet again, then nodded toward the nun in the witness box, who had spent the recess showing to the jurors picture postcards (never placed in evidence) of the nursing home Basia's money had built. "Mr. Schwartz," he said caustically, "the only thing she can do for your case is pray for it."

Henceforth, Reilly wasted few chances to tweak and belittle Schwartz. Once, the S&C lawyer accidently bumped into him as he rose to make an objection. "Excuse me! You can rise without contact with me!" the recoiling Reilly shouted. "I want the record to show that Mr. Schwartz was unable to stand and make an objection without bumping into me!" ("If I'd wanted to touch him, I would have kicked him in the balls," Schwartz said later.) When the *American Lawyer* criticized Christ (SULLIVAN & CROMWELL GETS ITS WHITE SHOES SCUFFED), using words like "vapid," "long-winded" and "aimless" to describe his questioning, Reilly offered him some soothing words. If Sullivan & Cromwell knew what it was doing, he told Christ, it would send Schwartz back to the office. As the case had grown more bitter, Reilly had gone from calling Christ "Donald" to "Mr. Christ" to nothing at all. But by now he was so far out in front—it was, he later said, "ten to nothing in the bottom of the eighth"—that he could afford to be magnanimous.

Sister Mary Louise Flowers went back to New Jersey. It had, in some ways, been an upsetting experience for her, and not just because the toilets in the Vista Hotel, like so much of the proponents' machinery, didn't work. The brand of justice she'd seen in Marie Lambert's courtroom was nothing like what she'd taught her fifth and sixth graders. Lambert herself, she was convinced, was "one-sided," and Reilly was "a wicked man." But there had been compensations. One night the dashing Zirinis had taken her and two other sisters to Windows on the World, where the waiters brought them matches with which to light candles for them when they got back to the convent. Even more important, she'd had a chance to testify for Seward Johnson, who had apparently worked the same magic on her he had on many other women in his life. "I'm sorry that he's gone. I miss him very much," she told a reporter shortly after concluding her testimony. She began to walk away, then sighed. "And such beautiful blue eyes . . . "

XLVII

aria Pia Fanfani barely knew Basia Johnson. Their relationship
flowed largely from the three days she and her husband Amintore, president of the Italian Senate and one of postwar Italy's
most famous politicians, had spent with the Johnsons in Ansedonia
during the summer of 1982. Short on familiarity but long on prestige,
the elegant white-haired Italian woman now found herself testifying on
behalf of Basia, who'd once underwritten (to the tune of sixty thousand
dollars) the cost of publishing a book on her charitable activities in the
Third World. The courtroom she entered was presided over by one of
her nation's many expatriates, and that expatriate thought she smelled
a rat.

So suspicious of the proponents had Marie Lambert become by now
that when Mrs. Fanfani was introduced, the judge immediately asked
one of her flunkies to make sure this woman was really who she claimed
to be. Even after verifying Fanfani's bona fides, Lambert wouldn't let
down her guard. She'd seen the Fanfanis at some Italian-American
functions, and had concluded the Mrs. was always pushing the Mr.
around. She wasn't about to let that happen to her. Even Mrs. Fanfani's
interpreter was suspect. "Keep your voice up, because the judge understands Italian and probably speaks Italian more fluently than you
do," Lambert warned her. In fact, the only problem with the interpreter
was that Schwartz did not use her enough.

"Mrs. Fanfani, in your visit to the Johnsons in Italy, did you observe
them together?" Schwartz asked.

"Yes, they was very . . . " she began, only to have the S&C lawyer
cut her off. Schwartz could tell she was about to volunteer an opinion,
for which the judge was certain to pounce on her.

"What did you *see?*" he asked.

"Very nice together, in love, affection."

"Objection, Your Honor!" Reilly bellowed.

"Sustained!"

"Your Honor, that is a matter as to which lay opinion is acceptable," Schwartz pleaded.

" 'Very nice together'?" the judge repeated mockingly.

"Yes," Schwartz insisted. "That's what a lay person can observe, seeing a married couple together."

Lambert, who had allowed Mervyn Nelson to opine so freely on the happiness and healthiness of the Johnsons' marriage, was not convinced. So Schwartz had to start all over again. "What did you *see,* when you saw them together, of how they dealt with one another?" he asked. This time, Fanfani had the interpreter sitting next to her translate the question. But Fanfani, apparently fancying herself a citizen of the world, insisted on responding in English.

"Normally, as always people . . . "

Quickly, Reilly was up again. Generalities were no more acceptable than opinions. "I object!" he said.

"Sustained," the judge repeated, then turned to the interpreter. "Explain to the witness: What is normal to you may not be what is normal to other people," she said. Fanfani nodded, as if she understood.

"Very affection, with a kind . . . "

"Same objection, Your Honor," said Reilly.

"Sustained!" an exasperated Lambert declared. "What did you see with your eyes?" Then she turned to the interpreter. "Explain that to her!"

"Kindness between both," Fanfani said. "She was kind, very nice. She . . . "

"Same objection," Reilly said. "It is all conclusory."

"I don't know how to say," a flummoxed Fanfani lamented as Reilly moved to strike whatever she had just said, and Lambert complied.

"Did you hear Mrs. Johnson . . . " Schwartz began when the judge interrupted him. "What did you hear Mrs. Johnson say, and what did you hear Mr. Johnson say, and what did you see? Not what you concluded from what you saw."

"I saw to offer coffee, for instance, kindness, no, so," Fanfani replied, gesturing. "Kindness."

"Objection!" Reilly repeated.

"And he was thank, thank, nice."

"Sustained," the judge declared. "Mrs. Fanfani, kindness is not something that you can see with the eyes."

"Smiling."

"Well, that you can see with your eyes, so tell us that," Lambert said. "Kindness is not something you can see with your eyes."

"But if I give coffee, kindness, so, and I give . . . ?"

"No, that's not kindness," the judge barked. "What did you see her do when she gave coffee?"

"Coffee smiling, with . . . nicely, I don't know. I don't . . . "

"I will strike the word 'nice,' " the judge declared.

"Smiling, giving coffee, smiling, just with the arm around the shoulder, so . . . coffee."

Maria Pia Fanfani, the wife of the president of the Italian Senate, chatelaine of Palazzo Giustiniani, was blabbering. To Lambert, however, Fanfani's performance wasn't the bumbling of a poorly prepared foreign neophyte but one more element of the proponents' plot. This fancy Italian lady was no hayseed; she could not possibly be as discombobulated as she appeared. "This is an American court, and she's well aware of what goes on," Lambert scolded Schwartz at the sidebar. Fanfani, she claimed, was trying to "volunteer information all over the place," and she was not going to permit it. The judge continued to ridicule and hector Fanfani throughout her testimony, so much so that when it was all over the Italian woman considered complaining to President Reagan about her. Instead, she sent a letter to the Judicial Conduct Commission, whose Lambert file was already thick with complaints that never got anywhere.

Schwartz doggedly pressed ahead. "Did you see any other displays?" he asked.

"Yes," Fanfani replied. "During the lunch Mrs. Johnson offer the plates who Mr. Johnson ask, 'I like this,' and Mrs. Johnson she prepare, she give him smiling."

"Did you see any displays of physical affection?"

"Objection!" stated Reilly, who had asked a virtually identical question of Keith Wold a few weeks earlier. "Leading."

"Sustained!" the judge replied.

"Did you see any displays of affection?"

"Objection!"

"Sustained. It's leading."

"Your Honor . . . " Schwartz began.

"Mr. Schwartz, you are giving the answer to the witness," Lambert snapped. "And if we are going to have a speech to make, let's make it at the sidebar, Mr. Schwartz!"

Once out of the jury's earshot Schwartz pleaded that Reilly had asked a similar question and gotten away with it. But before he could continue, the judge laced into him. "Every time you begin to make a speech in front of the jury, I am going to start pounding on you," she said. "I don't want to do that."

"I think you *have* been, Your Honor," Schwartz said.

"No, I have not," the judge replied defiantly. "If you have something you want to show me, just call my attention to page so-and-so, so-and-so, without a speech, and I'll rule."

"Your Honor, since the jury is not here, I think I should say this: I have been practicing in the courts of this state for thirty-plus years . . . "

"So have I," the judge interjected.

" . . . and I have never been pounded upon by a judge before to the extent that I have been here."

"If you ask proper questions, I will not sustain objections," the judge declared. "But if you persist in leading, I will sustain objections."

Schwartz came up with a precedent: On April 11, Reilly had asked one of his witnesses whether she'd ever observed Basia speaking to Seward "in an affectionate tone of voice." Christ had objected, and was overruled. But the judge, unpersuaded, offered her novel notion of an acceptably nonleading inquiry: "What did you see with reference to any signs of affection?"

Reilly, meantime, spotted a chance to skewer Schwartz and defend Lambert simultaneously. "I think he made a comment about the Court that in his thirty-odd years' experience he never had this kind of commentary directed to him," Reilly began. "Well, I think I have been practicing as long as Mr. Schwartz, perhaps a lot longer. In all that time I have never seen any lawyer, on my side or the other side, ask questions so persistently and improperly leading a witness." Reilly said he was "dumbfounded" by Schwartz's ineptitude.

"Mr. Reilly, you know, you could talk about that on summation," the judge kibitzed.

"I plan to devote part of my summation to that," Reilly said obligingly.

Court resumed. "Mrs. Fanfani, did you ever see any affection between Mr. and Mrs. Johnson? Yes or no?" the indomitable Schwartz asked.

"Yes."

"What did you see?"

"Hands on the hands, arm around the shoulder sometimes, and smile, always smiling," she said.

Schwartz wasn't going to do any better than that with this witness, this adversary, this judge. "I have no further questions," he said as the befuddled *signora* stepped down. "I think Italy is going to declare war on the United States," Ted Rogers of S&C remarked afterward.

Fanfani was one of several rebuttal witnesses to incur Lambert's wrath. Another was Michael Loyack, an administrator at the Princeton Medical Center who'd seen Seward often during his illnesses—hospital executives tend to take unusual interest in the ailments of millionaires— and who'd handled the donation Seward had made for a CAT scanner. Reilly grilled Loyack on cross-examination, suggesting he'd come to court simply to butter up Basia. How much more money was he looking for? Reilly asked. Twenty million? Fifty? Loyack confessed that he'd like at least $500,000, but wouldn't mind more. How much more? A couple million more? Maybe an even ten? He wouldn't want to say anything to jeopardize such a donation, would he? It was a question Loyack had been told to expect, one to which the only response was that he was there to tell the truth. Instead, the flustered witness, whom the judge had treated contemptuously from the moment he'd set foot in court, blew it. "No," he said. Afterward, Loyack didn't hold anything against Reilly, who was, after all, just doing his job. There were no such excuses for Lambert. "I don't like to say this very often," Loyack said at the end of the day, as he walked down the steps of Surrogate's Court, "but that woman is a cunt."

Throughout the trial Lambert shared her feelings about the case generously with friends, fellow judges, and journalists. Over pasta and wine at Forlini's, a politicos' watering hole not far from the courthouse, a fellow judge heard her denounce the lawyers in the case as ineffectual leeches, unable to function without five bag carriers nearby, unable to ask decent questions, interested only in running up their meters. If it weren't for her, she insisted, the whole trial would have degenerated into farce. She was particularly critical of Nina Zagat. "She definitely considered her the heavy in the case," the judge's dining companion later recalled. Lambert felt equally at ease with the press. After court one day she approached a reporter and a friend. "Have you ever seen a jury that's so bored?" she asked. S&C, she went on, was producing two types of witnesses: big shots who barely knew Basia, and people who'd either worked for her or had gotten money from her. Then Lambert offered her unsolicited thoughts on Basia herself. "She knew from the very beginning what she was going to do," Lambert said. "Have you ever met a young woman who *really* likes old men? I don't even like old men. The men my age are too old for me. They're not vigorous or intelligent enough. Have you ever cared for someone who was sick? Let me tell you, my husband was a very handsome man and I loved the ground he walked on, and yet there were times when I wanted to hit him, even though he had a mental disorder and it wasn't his fault. This woman set up the scenarios from the beginning. Every time she wanted something, she would be nice. I noticed that she was massaging his feet shortly before the executors' fees were raised." She then turned to the reporter. "Do you have a girlfriend?" she asked. "Has anyone ever massaged *your* feet?"

The ruminations continued, turning to the idyllic photographs of Basia and Seward that had been introduced into evidence. They hadn't fooled Lambert. "Let me show you *my* pictures," she said, beckoning her visitors to enter her chambers and directing their attention to rows of smiling faces on the wall. "Look at this picture!" she said emphatically, pointing to a photograph of herself with Geraldine Ferraro. "I happen to like Gerry, but of course I'm smiling." Then she turned to another, in which she stood next to Judge Louis Fusco of the Bronx. "I hate Judge Fusco, but I'm smiling with him too. Someone takes a picture, you smile. Everyone smiles in all of my pictures. Do you see a single face that's not smiling?"

One evening after court the judge had a similar chat with Basia and Nina. For what must have been an hour, she urged Basia to settle the case. What difference could all that money make? she asked. How much of it could Basia possibly need? Don't look at what you're giving away, look at what you're keeping! How many cars can you drive? How many dinners can you eat? The judge also talked about her own financial situation—how her niece didn't have enough money to go to college, how Lambert couldn't leave her son as much as she would like. To Nina, it was an odd conversation for a judge to have; to Basia, it was an oblique request for money.

Their suspicions were further inflamed in mid-May when Nina received a strange phone call at her apartment. The caller, who would not identify himself, said he had information that, were she to mention it to Marie Lambert, could win the trial for her. The caller was willing to sell his secrets to the highest bidder; the bids started at $2 million. Nina stalled. She got the man to agree to call her again, then informed Schwartz, who contacted Rudolph Giuliani, then the United States attorney in Manhattan. One of Giuliani's deputies, Benito Romano, called Nina and arranged to have two FBI agents come to her office. When the caller next contacted her at her home, Nina had taping equipment by her bed and federal agents nearby. In that and several subsequent conversations she kept the man on the line as long as she could, pumping him for details. The very meticulousness that made her so tedious as a witness proved valuable here; over time, he told her how, in a case involving his family, his stepmother's lawyer had allegedly bought favors from Lambert for fifty thousand dollars in Krugerrands. In the meantime the FBI closed in, tracing the call to a Long Island phone booth, where it arrested the man. But despite an extensive investigation, federal agents could never substantiate his charges against Lambert. Indeed, they concluded that he was, as one of them later put it, "a total whack job, without a kernel of sanity."

Throughout the trial Ed Reilly's days began around six-thirty, when he'd wake up at the apartment he'd rented at UN Plaza, run until ten or eleven, when he'd drop off Charles Berry to his wife and newly born twins at Twentieth Street, and return to his empty hotel room. But no matter how tiring or lonely the routine, Reilly always sprang to life in court. There, in his own world, he was oblivious to everything except judge, jury, witness, adversary, and the occasional beautiful woman in the gallery. He was inhumanly frigid to anyone he considered hostile, not just opposing counsel but reporters he deemed unsympathetic to his clients. Truth be told, even his clients occasionally got under his skin. The biggest bother was Junior, who was constantly offering him advice, calling him at midnight, passing him notes with proposed questions that Reilly routinely crumpled up. Junior quickly learned that when he wanted his hand held, Forger was the man to see.

Reilly's cross-examinations were compact, confident, devastating. Some witnesses he bypassed altogether, and with those he questioned, he seldom wasted words. He kept them on the stand long enough only to underline how little they knew, what they stood to gain from their testimony, or how remote their ties to the Johnsons had been. He drew blood quickly, like a doctor with a lancet, jumping on inconsistencies, making witnesses sound ridiculous, dishonest, unreliable, or exploitative. "Four hundred thousand dollars just for the marble?" Reilly asked Maurizio Bufalini, the man supplying the stone for Jasna Polana's chapel, in feigned astonishment ("Is a very good price, for your information," Bufalini coolly replied). There were some leitmotivs. Anyone attesting to Seward's rationality was asked whether he'd ever heard the old man fantasizing about war with Russia or Nazi submarines. Anyone describing the lovingness of the Johnsons' marriage was asked whether she'd ever heard Basia call Seward "stupid" or "senile" or "ga-ga." Anyone alluding to a tirade was asked to elaborate; this was how the jury first heard the sad saga about Count Krasinski and the painted grass.

Reilly knew his facts intimately. There were times, though, when he seemed positively omniscient—for instance, when he caught the doctor who'd treated Seward at the Princeton Medical Center misreading Seward's CAT scan. Reilly was on the kind of high one feels in battle. He seemed invincible and fearless. Around the time that American planes bombed Libya, Lambert dropped a reference to the "Mad Dog." "Is that Qaddafi?" Reilly asked one of the S&C lawyers. "No," his counterpart replied. "That's you when you're cross-examining a witness."

Only Toni Rossi, a dark, lithe beauty who had once been Seward's masseuse, came close to disarming him. Like most attractive women, she knew when someone was flirting with her, and as she awaited Reilly's cross-examination on May 14, she detected a certain light in his eye. This lawyer, whose barbed questions she'd been warned about, was letting her know he wanted her. As Reilly lobbed a few softballs her way, Delahunty scratched out a note to Nina. "Do you suppose we can get her to practice some undue influence on Reilly?" he wrote. Had all the proponents' witnesses been as pretty, they would not have been in such a predicament. "I just wanted to get her phone number and make an appointment," Reilly joked with the other lawyers afterward.

More often than not, Reilly destroyed his adversaries surgically, without splattering any blood on himself. There were times, though, when his fervor clouded his judgment, and it was then that the true tawdriness of his case came out. One such moment came in cross-examining Jerome Wiesner, president emeritus of the Massachusetts Institute of Technology. Wiesner had met Seward in the early 1960s and stayed in touch thereafter, hoping he'd throw some funds M.I.T.'s way. Once, fishing for funds to build an art and media technology building, Wiesner had gone to Fort Pierce. He netted nothing ("I made the suggestion that he might consider taking it out of capital, and he seemed shocked by that," Wiesner recalled. "I said it seemed to me that he had a sufficiently large capital base so that a few million dollars would hardly be noticed; he said he didn't like to do that") except, now, entanglement in this sordid mess. He could only hope Basia would remember M.I.T. once she got her money.

In his direct examination the professor, like several witnesses, contradicted Milbank's claim that Basia had banished Seward to bed early during Jasna Polana's opening party, the better to engage in some heavy-duty philandering with the pimply, porcine Polish musician. Attempting to undo Wiesner's testimony, Reilly asked him at what time he and his wife had left that night. Around eleven, replied Wiesner, who clearly viewed the proceedings with a "what fools these mortals be" mixture of bemusement and contempt.

"Were you present when Barbara Johnson said to Seward Johnson, 'Go to bed! Go up to your room!'?" Reilly asked.

"I did not hear that," replied Wiesner.

"You didn't hear that? You didn't hear Mr. Johnson respond, 'No, I don't want to go to bed! It's not late enough!'?"

"No."

"You didn't observe that incident?"

"No," Wiesner replied calmly. "He saw me to the door, as a matter of fact, when I left."

At this point, with an eminent scientist, the onetime adviser to John F. Kennedy, contradicting the disgruntled bodyguard upon whom Milbank had relied, and on the sleaziest imaginable topic, Reilly should have dropped the subject. But he wouldn't. Or couldn't.

"Were you present when one of the musicians was communicating with Mrs. Johnson?" he asked.

"I don't know," Wiesner replied.

"Were you present when you observed a musician grab Mrs. Johnson by her breasts?"

Schwartz rose to his feet, this time without bumping Reilly. "Objection, Your Honor," he said. "That is not in the record, I'm told."

"Counsel is a little bit tardy to be making these objections," Reilly said acerbically. "You should have come earlier."

"The word 'grabbed' is not in the record," Schwartz added helpfully.

But Reilly was not about to stop. "Were you present when a musician touched Mrs. Johnson's breasts?" A wave of discomfort swept across the room. And a strange expression, half-disgusted, half-amused, came across Wiesner's sleepy face. "No," he said.

"Were you present when a musician on that same evening touched her buttocks?"

"No," he reiterated. "At least, I didn't observe it." With that, Wiesner completed his testimony, and prepared to head back to Massachusetts. In the hall Basia kissed him and thanked him for his testimony. "Everything I said was the truth," Wiesner replied as he walked away. "But it's also true that you've never given us the money."

Lambert greeted P. James Roosevelt, an Oyster Bay investment counselor who testified for S&C on May 14, with uncharacteristic friendliness, probably because a portrait of Franklin D. Roosevelt, a fifth cousin once removed in two ways of the man in the witness box, had probably once hung in Nicola Macri's barbershop in Brooklyn. "You look very much like your father," Lambert told him. In fact Roosevelt, a small man with a thin, lined face, thick glasses, and a belt buckle that read FLOW WITH GOD, bore no discernible resemblance either to Franklin or Theodore (a first cousin twice removed in two ways) or Eleanor (a second cousin once removed in two ways). He had another distinction, however; technically, he had known Seward longer than just about anyone outside the Johnson family. He'd first met Seward during Cousin Franklin's first term, when Seward was a renowned sailor and P. James but five years old. Unfortunately, some time was to pass before their next encounter: forty-seven years, to be precise. In the fall of 1982 Roosevelt, by now the official historian of the Seawanhaka Corinthian Yacht Club of Oyster Bay, spent five hours at Jasna Polana talking with Seward about his sailing exploits.

Truth be told, Roosevelt was actually a Milbank client, and was testifying under subpoena. But he knew Milbank's depiction of Seward was absurd; when he'd seen the old man, whatever ailed him had yet to reach his brain. Seward had stood straight, spoken with a strong voice, displayed a photographic memory. "If I'm in the same shape when I'm eighty-seven, I'll consider myself fortunate," Roosevelt testified. There was only one problem: He'd seen Seward six months before he'd signed his last will.

As evidence of Seward's acuteness, Sullivan & Cromwell produced several witnesses to talk about Seward's late-in-life obsession with solar energy. But all the talk about solar water-heating systems, swimming-pool blankets, reversible-pitch propellers, and other assorted gizmos was itself extremely energy-inefficient. "I mean, we've been through this solar system till it comes out of our ears!" Lambert exclaimed at one point. Still, the proponents' case on competence, which seemed increasingly to be the issue upon which the case would be decided, gradually emerged. Esther Senter, the housekeeper in Fort Pierce, described Seward as a "very determined man, strong-willed, very forceful, not easily intimidated." Toni Rossi, the masseuse who tamed Reilly, said Seward was "much stronger mentally" than most of her clients, even though he was one of her oldest. A Harbor Branch engineer named Oscar Heil recalled how Seward talked about propellers and rudders in late January, could convert horsepower and British thermal units into megawatts in late February, discussed air-conditioning in late March and solar steam-generation in late April. Asked whether Seward's acts appeared rational, Wiesner, a man who knew from empirical evidence, replied, "They certainly appeared rational to me."

The rebuttal version of Seward had been assertive enough to boss around the very Mrs. Fanfani who bossed around her husband; optimistic enough to resubscribe to the Audubon Society and Smithsonian magazines at the age of eighty-seven; pro-Polish enough to support Solidarity but prescient enough to know it was seeking too much too soon; smart enough to discuss the effects on marine life of dumping garbage into the ocean; cantankerous enough to insist on ordering his own food in the hospital; serious enough to watch the news but lively enough to like *I Love Lucy*; and libidinous enough to covet women well into his ninth decade. Four months before he died, he rented "*Last Tango in Paris*" and watched most of it before instructing his nurse to send it back to the video store labeled "Porn."

To counter stories about how much Seward hated Jasna Polana, Arthur Louis James Charles Chaplin, a British-born butler of the Arthur Treacher school, told of meeting an enthusiastic Seward once on the construction site, blueprints in hand. Wiesner recalled the guided tour of the place Seward had proudly given him. There was ample testimony about Seward's familiarity with (and access to) guns, including how he had kept a Colt .38 revolver in a hollowed-out book on his bedside table. There were romantic scenes from Fort Pierce—where Seward would fill the house with orchids when Basia was due to return—and Princeton, where they kissed and blessed one another on their last Christmas together. S&C collected an inventory of kisses, caresses, pats, hugs, and rubs. Bufalini talked about how much Seward loved Basia's hair. Other witnesses disclosed that at least through the late 1970s, Seward and Basia still slept together. Once, when Esther Senter was asked to elaborate, Reilly rose to object. "I don't think that is necessary, Your Honor," he said. But sex, particularly the insatiable sexual appetite of the octogenarian Johnson, was something that interested Lambert, enough even for her to overrule Reilly. "They're all big boys and girls," she declared. Alas, the account offered by Senter, who devoted much of her spare time to evangelizing, was more "G" than "X" or even "R." "Holding hands, affectionate hugging, kissing, just sitting together quietly, just very affectionate," she said. Squeamish, priggish, unimaginative S&C didn't go any further than that. There was no stronger evidence of Seward's passion for Basia than his anguish, at the age of eighty-five, over his impotence, and his interest in a penile prosthesis. But those facts remained buried in the medical records; the jury learned nothing about them.

Wisely, the S&C lawyers were no longer portraying Basia as a junior

Sister Mary Louise Flowers. The lawyers not only acknowledged but embraced the Johnsons' marital spats, at least those in which Seward had fought back. Halina Rodzinski, wife of the former conductor of the New York Philharmonic, who knew Basia through New York's Polish community, recalled how, during her trip to the Bahamas with the Johnsons in 1981, she'd seen Seward, fearing that sharks were in the area, forbid Basia from scuba diving. "You see, I cannot do anything!" Basia complained to her. A nurse described how Seward once stormed out of the room during one of Basia's fits. Senter testified how Seward would either say nothing or tell Basia to "shut up" when she flew off the handle. It was true, she said, that from time to time Basia called Seward "stupid," but she offered an explanation. "She was mad," she recalled. "She had a disadvantage when she got angry. Her arguments were in English. That was not her normal language. And when she could not find the English word, she would resort to the first word that she remembered, which sometimes would be 'stupid.' She would get louder as she got frustrated." The answer, predictably enough, was stricken, but the point was made.

As the nuances of the Johnsons' marriage emerged for everyone else, Reilly's view became more simplistic; as people came to view Basia a bit more benevolently, he bared his fangs. On May 16 Maurizio Bufalini, the marble man, was describing some amorous scene between Basia and Seward when Reilly hit him head-on. "Do you know whether she was expressing affection for Mr. Johnson because of her real feelings about him or her feelings about his money?" Reilly asked. Bufalini, like many of the other witnesses, had felt Basia's lash and was well aware of her shortcomings. "She will never be a lady," he once told a friend. But he defended her now. "Just because she loved him. There was no question about it," he replied.

"I'm not asking you about whether she did or did not love him," Reilly went on. "I'm asking you whether, in your view, she loved him because of his personal qualities as a human being or because he was going to leave her about half a billion dollars?"

"He was such a man, you couldn't stop loving him," Bufalini said deftly. "I'm sure she was not the only one."

"You don't think that influenced her opinion of him, that he was leaving her about half a billion dollars?"

"Absolutely not."

"You don't think that prompted her perhaps to be a little more tender toward him and perhaps hold his hand now and then?"

"Not..."

"No?"

"They were good feeling "

"That had nothing to do with it?"

"Yes," Bufalini replied. "Nothing to do."

XLVIII

B ufalini had hoped to recount how he'd once seen Seward affectionately pat Basia's rear end, but so badly had Lambert flustered him that he forgot. For the same reason Halina Rodzinski had neglected to mention how she'd once heard Mary Lea Richards praise Basia for bringing the Johnsons together. But to at least two of the proponents' witnesses, Marie Lambert was uncharacteristically deferential: Seward's sons.

Fearful, perhaps, of self-inflicted wounds, Milbank had not called either Junior or Jimmy Johnson to the stand. S&C was not so reluctant, at least partly because, were he to testify truthfully, Junior, who had spoken with Seward often toward the end, could be among its stronger witnesses. The monosyllabic Jimmy, who appeared first, had far less to say.

As he took the stand on May 14, James Loring Johnson looked like a slimmed-down, more youthful version of Mr. Mum, the cartoon character who said nothing and found himself immersed in a perpetually baffling world. Spending his quiet days on his father's old farm, painting his watercolors, insulated from undesired conversations or other annoying aspects of life on earth, he'd never wanted to challenge the will in the first place. His trust fund was the largest of any of the children; he didn't need more, particularly if it meant appearing or speaking publicly to get it. In midtrial he'd fled briefly to the South Pacific; for the most part, he could be seen sitting, in pained and befuddled silence, alongside his more gregarious wife. On the stand, his military academy–model glasses in place, he looked still more forlorn. During a break in his second day of testimony he begged a reporter not to write about him. The reporter had the sad task of saying that a story about him, complete with a photograph, had appeared on the front page of his newspaper that very morning. "But don't worry, Jimmy," the scribe said soothingly. "It's an old picture."

All that Christ, who was examining the family members, could hope to accomplish with such a witness was to underline a few points, chip

away at his credibility, and pump him for evidence of his father's competence. He got Jimmy to admit that, as Seward had said in his will,
he'd made his children financially independent. By now, Lambert had
agreed to let the jury know just how rich the Johnsons were, and Christ
asked Jimmy his net worth. Though the youngest Johnson had majored
in mathematics, he hadn't much of a mind for figures. "Sixty million
dollars, roughly," he replied. Christ handed him a document. "Does
reviewing that change your testimony?" he asked gently. "I don't want
to retract what I said, but it shows that it is different than what I
thought it was," Jimmy replied. Indeed it was. Jimmy's figure was $36
million too low.

Jimmy backed off from even the mild praise he'd given Basia at his
deposition, admitting now only that she'd taken better care of Seward
than his own seventy-six-year-old mother could have. Seemingly out
to spare Jimmy any undue embarrassment, Lambert refused to admit
into evidence the note Seward had written to Larry Hopp (the man
who'd helped spare Jimmy from the Vietnam-era draft) the day after
he'd signed his last will ("If you want to bring the Vietnam War into
this case, fine, I'll let him express his opinion on the Vietnam War!"
she told Christ. "This is ridiculous! We are going to try the Vietnam
War here? Come on!"). And Christ could not very well use Jimmy to
establish Seward's capacity, considering the kinds of conversations the
two had had. Jimmy recounted one of their typically scintillating talks.
"I think we were sitting in front of the house in Fort Pierce, alone,
once," he recalled. "I would say, 'It's really a nice spot here. I've always
been very fond of it.' He would say, 'Yes, it is,' or something like that."

Once upon a time, Junior's appearance on the stand might have
been one of the high points of the case. But when it finally came to
pass it was a bit anticlimactic. Christ questioned him with all the zest
of a customs official going through luggage, but even if he had chosen
to be confrontational, he probably would have found Lambert blocking
his way. No one needed less help under oath than Junior, by now
among the most frequently interrogated men in the history of American
litigation. But when he took the stand, Lambert suddenly turned sympathetic, jocular, motherly. Christ's questions droned on—"Why is it
you ask questions so slowly you can eat a sandwich between them?"
the judge asked him during one break—but this time, there was a
method to his monotony. The best way to elicit information from the
loquacious Junior was not to antagonize him but to set him at ease, to
play casual, to pretend this was just a cozy conversation between friends.
Besides, Junior was not like the others in his family, particularly his

brothers-in-law Wold and Richards. As much as he craved Seward's money, he craved Seward's love, even his posthumous love, still more.

Christ marched Junior through his last six months of encounters with his father, and Junior obligingly rambled on, reciting the stories he'd told so often in depositions past. Most notably, there was his affectionate account of his nightlong talkathon with Seward in late February, at least a month after Milbank's own expert had said Seward couldn't possibly have been competent. "Would you describe your conversation as 'intense'?" Christ asked him, invoking one of the words Junior himself had chosen in his Merck testimony.

"Yes," Junior replied.

"Would you describe it as 'wonderful'?"

"Yes."

"And 'memorable'?"

"Yes."

Christ and Junior went forward from there, with every conversational fragment between the Seward Johnsons not just fortifying Junior's relationship with his father, but Basia's case for competence. (Standing outside the courtroom during a break, Keith Wold was fuming about his brother-in-law's testimony. Here we all came close to perjuring ourselves, only to have him turn around and do *this*? he complained.) Junior recalled his meeting in March with Seward and David Clare of J&J, and how, during the same trip, he had told his skeptical father about those magic mollusks that could produce stainless steel biologically. Attempting, as it were, to demonstrate Seward's competence and Junior's incompetence simultaneously, Christ, who'd brought a small bottled mollusk to court, asked how Seward had reacted to the proposal.

"He shook his head," Junior said. "I think he misunderstood me. He thought that I was planning to go out and reap these off of the reefs, and he thought that we would have to get tons and tons of them to produce a little bit of steel."

"He didn't think that was a very good idea?"

"No. I wouldn't have, either."

Christ got in a few more questions—about the size of the average mollusk's tooth and whether he had shown a specimen to his father—before Reilly finally spoiled the party. "I object to this," he complained. Lambert seconded him. "Mr. Christ, maybe you are trying to put me to sleep," she said.

Christ led Junior through his second momentous discussion with his hospitalized father—the one of March 30, when he'd pressed Seward, his arm attached to an intravenous line, to resign from Harbor Branch. The jury heard how, only two weeks before the will was signed, Junior asked Seward to sign a document whose validity he had never disputed. But while Reilly's rendition of events leading up to April 14 was crisp, Christ's was a block of formless prose, without periods or exclamation points or italics. Indeed, what the jury was most likely to take away from Junior's testimony was not how functional Seward, Sr., had been in April 1983, but what a nice guy Seward, Jr., was in May 1986. And what a fun sculptor. Lambert, who'd severely limited the number of pictures showing Basia and Seward together she would allow into evidence, permitted the jury to peruse an entire album of Junior's sculptures, including the one of King Lear. "When you told your father the story of King Lear, did you tell him that after the king had divided his empire among his children, that they turned on their father and destroyed him?" Christ asked. It was an unusually daring and imaginative question for him, one he'd plotted out laboriously with Delahunty and Bauman beforehand. Still, it came out wrong—he had overlooked the faithful daughter, Cordelia, in his rendition of the plot—and Reilly objected. "Counsel is misstating the story of King Lear," he said. Christ tried again, and again, but with each attempt the allusion lost more of its sting. From his reply, it was clear that if anything, Junior's understanding of the play was even flimsier than Christ's. Even so, he stepped down from the stand to the collective congratulations of his family and lawyers, while Christ stepped into a meat grinder. Immediately, Basia began pillorying him for his inept examination, calling him a "piece of soap," "mashed potatoes," and "a knucklehead." Schwartz finally shut her up; the jury, he cautioned, might overhear what she was saying.

Having failed to enlist any of the most crucial nurses, Sullivan & Cromwell produced some lesser lights. S&C read into the record the testimony of Lorene Chavis, the nurse who'd heard Seward's hallucination about war with Russia that Reilly had harped on so; in it she said Seward had been rational seven eighths of the time that day. S&C's first live nurse, Luella Johnson, came next. Johnson, who'd worked in Fort Pierce from late April until the end and now lived in a remote area of Michigan's Upper Peninsula, came to court reluctantly; Basia had branded her a "stupid American" a few times too often. Moreover, she'd been on duty when Basia summoned the priest for last rites, and as a deeply pious woman herself, she'd been offended by such religious heavy-handedness. Only after a personal appeal from Sheryl Michael-son—the lawyer Basia had pegged as Reilly's mole—had she agreed to come.

This Mrs. Johnson had little in common with the Mrs. Johnson in the gallery, the one everyone was really hoping to hear. This Mrs. Johnson was a plain, heavyset woman in a plain black skirt with a plain white coat over a plain print blouse. She spoke with a flat northern midwestern accent, the kind in which "day" rhymes with "me," and seemed plucked from the choir of a rural evangelical church. For all his afflictions, she testified, Seward had remained cheerful, talkative, and rational. He didn't just stare at his newspaper, he read it; she'd even learned how to fold *The New York Times* for him. Nor was this, as Milbank's Reisberg had theorized, all an elaborate ploy to look func-tional; she'd turned to the wrong page once, and he'd corrected her. Graham asked the unassuming woman whether she and Seward had ever discussed their shared surname. "No, except we talked about John-son & Johnson products," she said quietly, only to pause. "I don't know if you want to hear it."

"What did he say about that?" Graham pressed.

"Well, I was giving him his morning bath, and I says, 'You know, I had six children, and I never thought I would be taking care of the master of Johnson and Johnson after using all of his products all these years,' and he says, 'Well, they are good products.' I says, 'Well, nat-urally, that's why I used them.' "

Luella Johnson had been on duty the morning of the arc-striking ceremony, and she recalled how Seward had complained about the bugs, watched rapturously as the event proceeded, then requested cham-pagne for himself and her afterward. That was only four days before Seward's death, but as things turned out, it was not their last conver-sation. When Graham asked her to describe their final encounter, though, she looked up at him beseechingly. "Do I have to go into that?" she asked.

"Try, briefly," Graham replied gently. "I'm sorry."

In the affidavit she'd given Osgood two years earlier, Luella Johnson had alluded to some "meaningful" talks she'd had with Seward in his final days, but until meeting with Michaelson, she'd never shared them with anyone else. She braced herself now, then related what she and her dying patient had said to one another on Seward's last afternoon of life, almost exactly three years earlier. Normally, the nurse knew, she was not supposed to discuss religious matters with a patient. But sensing as she did that Seward's sands were quickly running out, this was one time, she believed, for making an exception. A few years earlier her own faith had been tried and deepened, when a gas tank had exploded in her son's face, blowing half of it away. Confounding everyone's predictions, he had survived—in part, she was convinced, because parishioners from five different churches in her hometown had prayed for him. If she could find such solace in God, so, too, she thought, might Seward.

She began describing their conversation, only to falter momentarily. "I'm not much on composure," she explained before pressing on. "I could see he was . . . it was as if he was struggling or very uncomfortable, and I asked him, I asked him if he was afraid of dying. He said . . . he looked up at me and he said, 'Well, no. I have tried to be good to everyone that has been good to me,' and I said, 'Well, I think the harder test in life is being good to people who aren't good to you,' and he says, 'That's right. That is hard.' And I said, 'Well, don't be afraid of dying.' " She paused once more to collect herself, as everyone in the courtroom who was ever going to die listened raptly. "I said, 'When you have been on the ocean and it has gotten rough, wasn't it easier to ride the waves sometimes than to fight them?' And he says, 'Yes,' and I said, 'Well, dying can be the same. Go in with the waves, and your Lord will be waiting for you.' And he said, 'Thank you,' and he kissed my cheek." The nurse looked down toward her lap, then rubbed her face with the crumpled Kleenex she had been holding in her hand.

"No further questions," Graham said. It was a quarter to one. Concerned for his fragile witness, hoping to leave her magic spell hanging over the courtroom, Graham asked Lambert to break fifteen minutes early for lunch. Reilly agreed. Now was not the time to cross-examine this woman.

But the judge was clearly put out by what she had just witnessed. Maybe it was that a woman of indisputable honesty and sincerity had offered testimony indicating that Seward had been competent only hours before his death. Or maybe it was that for Marie Lambert, former lioness of the trial bar, tears had generally been tactical weapons. Whatever it was, she turned angrily toward the nurse and hit her with a barrage of indignation.

"Can I ask you what time you were on, what shift, on May 22?" she snapped.

"I was on the day shift from seven," the nurse replied timidly.

"What time did you start?" the judge repeated, even more sharply.

"At seven, and I left at three-fifteen," she said.

"Tell us what time this conversation that you had with Mr. Johnson was at!"

"I don't remember," the nurse responded uneasily. "It was around . . . I think it was just about . . . between . . . sometime within the hour before I left."

"Did you put anything into your notes about that conversation?"

"No," the witness whimpered. "I felt it was personal."

"No, no!" the judge cried out. "Did—you—have—a—notation—in—there—about—your—conversation?" There were long pauses between her words, as if she were addressing a simpleton.

"No, I don't think I did."

The judge had shown no comparable indignation when Patricia Reid had parlayed what appeared in her contemporaneous notes as two fleeting moments of confusion into a whole shift's worth. Similarly, when another of Milbank's nurses told of an episode she had failed to record contemporaneously, the judge had proven forgiving. "Did you write *everything* in your notes, every single word that was said?" she'd asked the nurse. "There is no way I could, no, ma'am," the nurse replied, as the judge nodded her head approvingly.

But now, with an opposing nurse on the stand, the rules had changed. Convinced Luella Johnson was lying, Lambert ordered the nurse to read aloud everything she'd written that shift: every notation for every dose of medicine she'd administered, every drop of urine urinated, every change of Chux. The nurse was aghast, not for herself but for her patient: This amounted to disrobing a dead man in public, robbing him of his dignity. But read she did, partly because she had to, partly because she thought the stunt would backfire on a biased judge. That done, and after a cursory cross-examination, the court finally broke for lunch. Moments later in the Titanic Room, an incredulous Marvin Schwartz poured himself a drink. "This judge is a *beast*," he declared.

The next witness, Judy Smith, seemed even more certain to arouse Lambert. Here was the nurse whose hospital bills Basia had covered, and, Milbank charged, whose testimony Basia had thereby bought. Smith, it was true, had described Seward shortly before his death as "disoriented" in the first account, "exhausted" in the second. Moreover, the confusion she'd noted at the time she downplayed somewhat in her deposition. Reilly argued that these changes—clarifications, really—came only after Basia had given Smith twenty-three thousand dollars, nearly three times her total income in 1983. The charge was flimsy, particularly since it related to events a month after the will-signing.

But it was the best Reilly had, and he was certain to exploit it.

Smith, a thin woman with long, straight gray hair, had an air of innocence about her, a childlike quality that led Bonnie Weisser to describe her once as "a rather Pollyanna-ish happy-type person." Hers was the credulous happiness of someone who had almost entered a convent, a believer in a benevolent God; even now, she wore two rings said to have touched all of the places Jesus visited—among them Bethlehem, the Garden of Gethsemane, and Calvary—and with which she touched all her patients, Seward included. Her faith, like Luella Johnson's, had been tested and tempered by pain. After her car accident, in which her niece had been killed, her doctor told her she would never walk again. But she did, and she felt she had God and Basia to thank. Her innocence or her faith, and maybe they were one and the same, served her well in her toils. Once, during Seward's endgame, after he'd defecated while she washed his back, he'd asked her, out of embarrassment and disgust and amazement and gratitude, how she could stand such work. "Mr. Johnson, this could very easily be me in that bed, and you up here," she'd replied.

Much of what Smith had to say was, to put it in lawyers' lingo, "cumulative." There was more testimony about Basia's tender loving care and attentiveness. Whenever Seward summoned her, Basia came "like a flash." And when she walked into his room, a peaceful, easy expression came over Seward's face; he would purr "Basiahhhhh," close his eyes, and relax. Smith worked nights—what she would have called, with her thick Rhode Island accent, the "lawbsta shift"—and she'd been on duty during the early morning hours of April 14, before Patricia Reid punched in. Though she'd seen some instances of confusion a few days earlier, she'd detected none that shift. She recalled how, one time, Seward had shown her a picture of him and Basia kissing. "Oh, boy, what a picture!" Smith exclaimed. "Oh, boy, what a woman!" Seward responded. Only at the very end, she said, when Seward was "really going downhill," had his confusion reappeared.

Mindful of the onslaught to come, Graham tried broaching the subject of Basia's hospital payments preemptively, only to run into Lambert. "You aren't going to whitewash your own witness!" she said at the bench. So when Reilly rose to question Smith on the afternoon of May 21, there was the sense of an impending execution. "Fasten your seat belt," someone whispered. But if calling Smith posed risks for the proponents, cross-examining the fragile, ingenuous nurse, particularly with Lambert lending a helping hand, posed risks for Reilly, too.

Before Smith took the stand, Sister Mary Louise Flowers warned her that Lambert was evil and would prevent her from telling her story. Smith asked the nun to pray for her. But any prayers had clearly gone for naught. In a strange town, testifying for the first time, over her head intellectually and emotionally, Smith was an exasperating witness. Rather than help, Lambert badgered, bullied, and belittled her. "How far did you go in school? How far did you go in school?" she snapped once. The judge's behavior, which reminded Smith of her days caring for disturbed children, worried even Reilly, and prompted some of the jurors to throw Smith some encouraging glances. "I felt that to be human, we had to smile at her," one of them later recalled. As day's end approached, Reilly finally reached the subject of Smith's accident, and the help Basia had extended to her. To demonstrate that gratitude could corrupt as easily as greed, Reilly asked to read to the jury the two "thank you" notes Smith had sent Basia afterward. The decision dumbfounded the Sullivan & Cromwell lawyers; it seemed that once more Reilly's zeal had bested his judgment.

" 'Dear Mrs. Johnson,' " Reilly read in his booming basso profundo. "'My Mom and I hope you are well and that you had a very nice Easter. Your loving kindness and generosity has so deeply touched us. How can I ever thank you for your help? I would have had to spend the rest of my life trying to pay my debts as they gathered interest. How blessed I am. I thank you for the great comfort you have brought to my Mom and me and I thank God for bringing you into my life. As I walk, your beautiful voice is with me saying "Fly, Judy, fly!" I can take a few steps alone. I plan to walk into the doctor's office on May 17th carrying my crutches. Right now with therapy, I am fighting to get a good bend in my right leg. We are going to get it soon. My Mom and I pray for your comfort and happiness and I will remember in my special prayer for you to the Blessed Mother to hold your hand tight. Bless you and thank you again from the bottom of my heart.'" It was signed, "Love, Judy."

Reilly paused for a moment, picked up a second piece of cheap stationery, and resumed reading. " 'Dear Mrs. Johnson,' " he began. " 'My mother and I hope you are able to enjoy the rest of the summer and all is well. How we hope you can feel the love, joy, and peace that you give to others. Those are the gifts that the baby Jesus brought to us that you share, and you give them with endless kindness. Your deep concern and caring has changed what my life would have been like, as I collect my first paycheck this week. It would have taken a lifetime of penny-pinching to attempt to pay my debts. This is a great weight off my shoulders. Take care of yourself. You remain with us always in our hearts and prayers.' " It was signed the same way.

Like Luella Johnson's testimony a day earlier, the letters had a moving, unsettling effect. Clearly, Reilly believed they showed Smith would stop at nothing, even perjury, to repay Basia. But to most listeners, the letters made the nurse seem more sympathetic and incorruptible, and Basia, more generous and compassionate. On that odd note, court adjourned, and Judy Smith hobbled off the stand. But the following day, only seconds after bidding Smith his stiff "Good morning," Reilly attacked. Hadn't she thought it improper for her, a potential witness in the case, to accept such a payment? "I never intended to be a witness," she replied. "I had no idea I'd be sitting in this courtroom at all, ever. I just never dreamed I'd be in this courtroom, never."

"That's not the question before you, Miss Smith!" the judge broke in. "Don't volunteer! Just answer the question!"

For most of the trial, as their witnesses were bloodied from the bench, the S&C lawyers had sat on their hands. Graham did not. "Your Honor, I don't think she was volunteering," he said. "She didn't understand the question."

"She certainly was volunteering!" the judge snapped back. "There was no question before her as to whether she was going to be in this courtroom; and she's now tried to volunteer three times that she never dreamed she was going to be in this courtroom."

The lawyers then moved up to the bench. "This witness has a high school education," Graham pleaded quietly. "She's untrained. She's never been in a courtroom before. She's doing her best. I don't think that scolding her in front of the jury is the proper approach, and I respectfully ask that it not be done again."

The judge interpreted this politest of requests as a challenge to her authority. "The fact that you keep saying I scolded her doesn't mean I scolded her!" she snapped. "I have a right to run my courtroom! That's what I'm doing! I'm going to run my courtroom, and nobody is going to ride roughshod over me!"

"I'm not trying to ride roughshod over you," Graham said.

"No, the witness is trying to ride roughshod!" she replied.

The inquisition resumed. Had anyone ever told her to testify in a certain way? "No, I'm sorry," Smith replied. "Nobody said to me how to testify." Had anyone ever asked her to say that "confusion" actually meant "exhaustion," or that "disorientation" really meant "fatigue?" No one had, she said. Reilly was getting nowhere. So the judge took over.

When she'd described Mr. Johnson as "confused" on May 19, had she really meant "just plain exhausted?" Smith breathed a prayer, as

568   D A V I D   M A R G O L I C K

she did repeatedly whenever she felt Reilly or Lambert zeroing in on her. She then attempted to say she'd simply tried to clarify one isolated observation, not change her account of anything. But before she could, Lambert cut her off. Three more times, she accusingly asked Smith whether "confused" meant "exhausted." Finally, Smith conceded she'd been wrong to describe Seward as "disoriented" on the night of May 19. Reilly then reentered the ring. "When did you find out you were wrong?" he asked. "After you received the twenty-three thousand dollars from Barbara Johnson?" The pathetic Smith only fumbled an answer. She'd endured lawyers in the aftermath of her accident, but this was worse. Reilly scored his point, for whatever little it was worth.

In his redirect examination Graham seemed more intent upon generating sympathy for the witness than on rehabilitating her. And the best way to do that, he reasoned, was to ask her to explain the events leading to Basia's largess.

"You were injured in the accident?" he asked her.

"Yes," she replied.

"Were there any fatalities?"

Instantly, Reilly was on his feet, objecting. He was promptly and predictably sustained, but not before Smith answered Graham's question.

"Yes," she said softly. It was only the latest of many blurts in the case—in the most outrageous one, Izabella Poterwicz had blurted out that she'd lost her baby after Basia fired her—none of which had especially exercised the judge. This time, though, she ordered the jury to ignore the answer, kicked them out of the courtroom, and promptly called both Graham and his witness onto the carpet.

"Who is to blame for the answer, Mr. Graham, the witness or you?"

"I'm not sure what Your Honor means by that," Graham replied. "It was a proper question." Graham then tried defending a decision both S&S and S&C warned Basia would come back to haunt her. Milbank, he said, had charged that Basia had bribed Smith. To understand Basia's real motivation, one had to understand the tragedy Smith had just endured.

Lambert was not listening. "And this is not the only payment that's been made, from the evidence of this case!" she declared.

"Your Honor, that has nothing to do with my question," Graham said.

"It has a lot to do with your question," Reilly replied.

"It has to do with a lot of things!" the judge said ominously.

The lawyers kept arguing. If Basia felt charitable, Reilly said, she could have given the money to someone else, or waited until the case was over, or sent her the money anonymously. As they spoke, Smith suffered silently in the witness box. When Graham uttered the word "fatality," she began sobbing, then reached into her purse for a handkerchief. The judge, unmoved by what she undoubtedly thought was more stage-managed lachrymosity, continued hectoring Graham. Meantime the weeping nurse was belatedly allowed to step down and retreat to the corridor. For the next several minutes she sobbed quietly by herself, pacing up and down the hallway on her gimpy leg. Finally, an onlooker approached and offered to fetch her some tissues; the judge, he explained, kept some on the bench. Smith thankfully agreed, only to quickly change her mind. No, she explained, she didn't want any of this judge's anything. Instead, she asked a court officer to bring her some more abrasive paper towels from the bathroom.

At that moment Junior Johnson ambled by. "You don't smoke, do you?" he cheerfully asked the sobbing Smith. "I'm looking for a match."

XLIX

S&C may have spurned a Peach. But now, as its medical case began, it was counting on a Plum.

On May 22, a distinguished-looking man with wavy gray hair took the stand. In the starkest possible contrast to Judy Smith, he had an unruffled, almost military manner about him. "Give your name and address to the jury," the judge said to him. "I am Dr. Fred Plum," he replied. "My working address is the New York Hospital, Five-twenty-five East Sixty-eighth Street."

Plum, neurologist in chief at the hospital and chairman of the department of neurology at Cornell Medical School—what he called "the ultimate, I suppose, 'the-buck-stops-here' position" there—proceeded to list his credentials. Quickly, it became clear he was not just more experienced than Milbank's medical experts but one step further along medical academia's ego chain, having reached the point where one is not so much boastful of one's accomplishments as bored by them. Asked if he belonged to any honorary societies, he named three, then stopped. "The list is a little long," he said. "I won't burden you with it." He mentioned receiving a prize given only four times over the past century, but asked when he had won it, he wasn't sure. "Oh, I think three years ago, if I'm not mistaken," he said. Asked how many books he'd written, he replied, "Directly, I think, four; with revisions and so forth I think eight or nine, perhaps more. I don't remember." Asked whether his résumé contained a complete bibliography, he replied, "Oh, I think not. Everything doesn't get in. My secretary is sometimes too busy."

Had there been any neurologists in the house, even this truncated recitation would have been unnecessary. In their world, Fred Plum was a legend. With Jerome Posner (who had seen Seward in February 1982 and had testified unmemorably a few days earlier), Plum had written a revolutionary book, one whose title could just as easily have referred to the medical testimony of the Johnson case: *Stupor and Coma.* He'd treated Agnes de Mille after her stroke, collaborating on the book she wrote about her illness, and appeared with her once on *The Tonight*

Show. ("Nothing whatever escaped him," de Mille wrote. "He was interested in everything and his word was a command. The hospital staff simply fell away when he appeared.") When Ann Landers needed a neurologist—for instance, when a reader asked whether cats could be left- or right-pawed—it was to Fred Plum that she turned. Plum was the man who'd coined the phrase "persistent vegetative state" to describe a comatose patient; when the parents of Karen Ann Quinlan sought to remove her from her respirator, he'd been among those called to court to describe how bleak her prospects were.

Plum had trained an entire generation of doctors, who acknowledged he was a great teacher. But they often did so begrudgingly, because he was so distasteful a person—cold, arrogant, snobbish even by the standards of his snooty institution. Plum stories were legion. Many involved bloody squash games, including one in which he'd refused to quit despite developing a lemon-sized hematoma on his ankle. Others concerned his rigorous training regimen. But with all of his responsibilities, Plum was spread extremely thin, and, on rounds or in classes, some felt he did only what was necessary to get by. Many thought he was coasting on his reputation, although even when he was wrong, few dared correct him. He was, in a way, neurology's answer to Marvin Schwartz.

Given Plum's eminence, it was not surprising that both sets of lawyers had courted him. But it was altogether fitting that Sullivan & Cromwell had landed him, for in a will defense long on costly credentials but short on common sense—that, after all, was how S&C itself had been selected—Plum was the perfect witness. Just as Milbank had found doctors cast in their own image—scrappy, industrious, committed—so, too, had S&C: overpriced, cocky, complacent.

Plum deemed trials annoyances and did his best to avoid them. After all, even the glitziest were, medically speaking, humdrum. It was an attitude that Graham quickly diagnosed. Like everyone else (except, perhaps, Ann Landers) Graham found he had to schedule appointments with Plum far in advance, and even when they met, he was afraid to ask the doctor to review everything he needed to know. It is not a good thing for a lawyer to be intimidated by his own witness. When the two men began preparating for court, Graham could not help but feel Plum had not done his homework.

But once he took the stand, Plum performed with aplomb. He endorsed a far more modest variety of the mental-status examination than the third degree Besdine and Samuels had posited; a doctor could learn much about a patient's condition simply while establishing rapport, he said, particularly when their relationship was long-standing. He told the court that the conversational fragments that had come up thus far—Seward's comments about steel, boats, investments—revealed he had good memory, normal language function, a knowledge of prospective events, a considerable capacity for abstract judgment, and an excellent ability to recall names, even of persons beyond his immediate family.

Graham took Plum down Milbank's list of Seward's ailments, asking whether each would have affected Seward's cognitive functioning. Always, the answer was essentially "no." (For dramatic effect, Graham tried to cross off each item on Milbank's; poster with a Magic Marker, but the judge refused to let him.) Similarly, Plum said none of the drugs Seward was taking would have impaired his reasoning. While his hematocrit was below normal—placing him, on the Milbank chart, in the yellow area of "anemia"—it never was so low as to thrust him into the navy-blue region of confusion.

Seward's only potential problem, according to Plum, had been his electrolytic imbalance. Twice—on April 5 and 25—his count approached the point where symptoms of confusion could have appeared. But each time, that deficiency had quickly been remedied. Had Seward been continually confused during the first two weeks of April? "No evidence for that," Plum replied firmly. On the afternoon of April 14, did Seward possess the three requisite elements of testamentary capacity? "I think he had that capacity," Plum declared. Shot by shot, the most eminent doctor in his field had calmly blown holes in the children's case. Fred Plum had resurrected Seward Johnson. Graham yielded to Reilly.

The respite was brief. Milbank's experts were credible because, quite apart from their expertise, they were so familiar with the facts and cast. Samuels needed no crib sheet to know the names of the hospitals to which Seward had been admitted; names like "Schilling" and "Link," "Wold" and "Wideroff" came tripping off his tongue. For all of his cockiness, Plum's grasp was more tentative. Besdine and Samuels were "the two gentlemen from Harvard," Reid and Weisser were "the two nurses," the Princeton Medical Center was some undefined hospital somewhere in New Jersey. Many answers he prefaced with "If I'm not mistaken . . . " Plum said he'd spent fifteen to twenty hours preparing to testify. Samuels had spent seventy.

Reilly quickly perceived, and exploited, Plum's ignorance. Had he read the testimony of John Peach or Mary Banks? Plum admitted he had not. Had he gone over the testimony of Martin Richards? No, Plum replied; who was Mr. Richards? How about Keith Wold? "I don't believe so, no. I don't remember the name, sir." Had he read Schilling's deposition? "No." Why not? It hadn't been provided to him. Hadn't he felt a responsibility, as a distinguished doctor, to be certain he knew all the relevant facts and let the chips fall where they may? "In the sense that you use it, no." In only one respect had Plum outdone his rivals: his fees. He said he charged five hundred dollars an hour for work outside the courtroom, eight hundred dollars in it. The gallery buzzed, as if the Dow Jones Industrial Average had just reached some previously unimaginable height. Besdine's hourly rate was two hundred dollars; Samuels charged three hundred dollars. "Eight hundred dollars an hour?" Reilly repeated with his finely honed brand of spontaneous amazement. "Yes, sir," the unperturbed Plum replied. "I do everything I can not to be in court."

Reilly asked the doctor if he'd seen Seward's last will, and the doctor admitted he had not. Then how, Reilly snarled, could he have surmised that Seward had understood it? Plum replied that he had inferred it from his general familiarity with other aspects of his life.

"You just assumed that?" Reilly asked.

"Of course," Plum replied.

"Is that what you came down here for at eight hundred dollars an hour, to make assumptions of this kind?" asked Reilly, addressing Plum with an irreverence that would have thrilled generations of medical residents. "Don't you think your opinion as to Mr. Johnson's comprehension of his will might be affected somewhat by whether it is a relatively simple, reasonably brief will, or whether it is very complex and complicated?"

"In the special instances of this case, I would have expected it to be complicated," Plum replied.

The interrogation resumed the next morning. It was May 23—the third anniversary of Seward's death, an occasion Basia marked by wearing black (and a gesture Junior mocked by handing out Kleenexes). Now, Reilly confronted Plum with some of the more disconcerting evidence, mostly the highly dubious observations of Keith Wold and Marty Richards from April 10, that S&C, characteristically, had neglected to discuss with Plum in his direct examination. Had he studied it, Plum, more than anyone else, could have said their descriptions clashed with those of trained nurses and doctors and should be discounted. Instead, he had to admit that if they were true, Seward could not have been of sound mind and memory at the moments they described. Reilly then turned to Reid's observations of confusion on the morning of the fourteenth, which Graham had also omitted in his questions. This, Plum said, he had read—"rapidly." He admitted that based on Reid's notes, Seward might not have been of sound mind and memory that morning. Reilly was closing in. He asked the doctor if the confusion might have extended beyond that.

"My view is that these are fluctuating states, and at the moment of maximal fluctuation he would have been regarded as confused," Plum said. "That does not mean that he was that way later in the day, nor that, as the nurse said, he was continuously that way that morning."

Reilly reminded Plum of Reid's assertion that Seward had had "several bouts of confusion" that had lasted throughout her shift. "Do you know what time her shift ended?" he asked.

"Noon, if I'm not mistaken."

"No, you are mistaken!" Reilly declared triumphantly. "It ended at three P.M."

Graham listened with a mixture of anger and nausea. He'd gone over the timing of the nurse's shifts repeatedly with Plum, and the doctor had forgotten anyway. "I see," Plum offered lamely.

"You are learning that now for the first time?"

Plum bobbed. "No. I just . . . it wasn't . . . "

"It was a mistake?"

"It was a mistake."

"Wouldn't it also be true, Dr. Plum, that he was not of sound mind and memory right up to three P.M. on April fourteenth? Isn't that your opinion?"

"If that was the only testimony available."

"I'm asking you to accept this testimony as being truthful."

"Episodically, as she says, he was not sound."

"Up to three P.M.?"

"Up till three P.M."

The will was signed at four. Plum, it turned out, was a lemon.

After its sorry experience with Plum, Sullivan & Cromwell might have dispensed with more doctors. Instead, Graham found himself scrambling for reinforcements. In a rare dose of realpolitik, the proponents con-sidered calling a psychiatrist whose chief qualification was his friendship with the judge. A gerontologist agreed to come, but Graham concluded that the restless jury could neither stand nor sit still for yet another expert. Graham weighed calling Seward's longtime ophthalmologist to say that the old man's watery eyes stemmed from malfunctioning tear ducts rather than a bad marriage, as well as an expert on battered spouses. Instead, Graham concluded that the thrust of Milbank's undue-influence case wasn't husband-beating so much as brainwashing. That was what needed to be addressed, and countered.

Dr. Herbert Spiegel, a member of the faculty of Columbia University's College of Physicians and Surgeons, took the stand on the afternoon of May 23. Spiegel's first love was hypnosis, and he'd become an authority on susceptibility to coercion and persuasion of any kind. He was also an expert on combat stress. He'd often testified in court, including one extremely unpleasant appearance before Lambert (his diagnosis of her: "an arrogant, controlling bitch, a small mind with a weak ego who was utterly intoxicated with her own power"). Before her once again now, he marveled at her primitiveness, particularly at how overtly she was trying to curry favor with the jury.

Susceptibility to coercion varied, Spiegel testified. Those who were most hypnotizable, who could disassociate most freely, tended to be emotional and intuitive. On the other end of the spectrum were more cerebral types, like Seward. Seward, he said, used his great wealth to build himself a secure, well-organized life, one he kept under his own tight control. He spent his life defining and protecting his turf, whether it was his estate, his homes, or at the very end, the paraphernalia on his bedside table. Such territoriality was a sign of life, an indication that for all of Seward's problems, some stubbornness and resolve remained.

Throughout his life, Spiegel told Graham, Seward tended personally to those things that mattered to him most: his money, his business affairs, his boats, his oceanography, his marriages. Everything else he delegated to others, often to his wives. Because they did not threaten his "main core domain," Spiegel said, Basia's screams would not have affected him much. "Much of this was like water off a duck's back," he said. "To be accused in emotional language that he was either 'senile' or 'stupid' didn't mean a thing to him. He was secure about who he was." He paused for a second. "The other side of that story is that these kinds of noises, although they may sound like noises to other people, can sound like music to a man who knows that there is somebody so close to him. She conveys the feeling of being concerned even though it's in this awkward, emotional manner. He accepted the fact that she was a peppery, effervescent, emotional, volatile person, and I suspect that he found that very attractive. That's probably one of the reasons he liked to have her around." Besides, he said, Seward knew how to cope when Basia lost her temper. He would either ignore her, escape from her, or defy her.

Like many men his age, Spiegel, who was in his sixties, had been molded by his experiences during World War II—he'd taken part in the invasion of North Africa and been wounded in Tunisia—and, to elaborate on his point, he used a military metaphor. "It's very similar to trying to identify the noise of an artillery blast," he said. "When men in combat hear that artillery blast and they hear the whistle going over them, going toward the enemy as they are moving forward, that's like the sound of music."

It was a nice image, but in the context of a cursed case, it proved to be his Waterloo. To be sure, Spiegel brought his own peculiar liabilities into court. Bald and empathetic, he seemed too archetypally the New York shrink, the sort who'd nod solemnly while listening to Virgil Starkwell, Fielding Melish, or some other character out of early Woody Allen. There was also his association with hypnosis (which had led the diet-conscious Tim Zagat, among others, to consult him). But in fairness to him, he was also the victim of what had by now become the richly justified belief that anyone the proponents produced had to be ridiculous. This jury had grown too jaded to buy whatever Spiegel was selling, no matter how high-quality it might be. When he described Basia as "peppery," two of the jurors turned to one another and laughed. When the talk turned to artillery blasts, waves of derisive mirth swept across the courtroom. Reilly was on his feet, poised to object, but only after making sure that the ridicule had run its course.

"Your Honor, I am reluctant to interrupt. . . . " he began, with a broad smile on his face, the confident smile of one who knew his point of view had utterly and completely prevailed.

"I sustain the objection, and I will strike the artillery blast also," the judge responded, without even waiting for Reilly to explain himself. "I think most of the people on this jury, thank God, haven't been subjected to artillery blasts. And there is no evidence in this case about artillery blasts. Doctor, please. Come on, Mr. Graham."

By this point, after putting in seventy hours of work over the previous four days, chasing down witnesses, preparing testimony, fighting a belligerent judge, Graham was feeling some of the battle fatigue Spiegel had spoken about. In a few hours Plum had fallen, and now Spiegel was wounded. But Graham carried on gamely. He listed for Spiegel all of the episodes that Milbank had dredged up—the aborted barbecue, the Crockpot episode, and others. "Peripheral stuff," Spiegel said. He was then asked about the physical abuse Maffatone had allegedly seen. "That stands out like a sore thumb, because no other data . . . " At this point Reilly objected, and the judge abruptly cut the doctor off. It was another crucial point in the testimony, and, once again, Lambert in sisted that whatever the doctor had to say on the subject be filtered first through her, out of the jury's earshot.

"It stands out like a sore thumb, because it is so atypical of the record that I read about her conduct with him," Spiegel explained at the bench. "Had this been part of a pattern, I would have taken it very seriously. I simply assume that his response to that was one of surprise and, since it was not repeated, it was dismissed as something transient."

The response apparently satisfied Reilly, perhaps because Spiegel had stopped short of calling Maffatone a liar. "That's okay. Just read it that way," he said.

"You will read that answer," the judge directed Nat Weiss, the court reporter.

"Can't the jury hear the witness say it?" Graham pleaded, well aware that anything read in Weiss's professional monotone had no impact at all. "No," Lambert replied. "The stenographer will read the answer, because I don't want any changes in it."

As Spiegel described them, Basia and Seward were a loving, complementary couple. She offered him an "emotional coloring" that had heretofore been lacking in his married life; he gave her financial and social security, as long as she steered clear of his terrain. It was Seward, not Basia, who called the shots; he could have pulled the plug on her whenever he wished. Conversely, it was Basia's impotence, and not her power, that accounted for her behavior. There was no evidence whatever, Spiegel said, that when Seward signed his will anyone else "in any way influenced him away from his own private understanding and commitment about what he wanted to do." That he was physically dependent on Basia changed nothing.

Spiegel had regained his balance, but not for long. When the witness had first appeared in court, Reilly had immediately called Reisberg for the lowdown on the man. Now, a few moments into his cross-examination, Reilly asked Spiegel if he had a private practice. Spiegel said he had. The Milbank lawyer then leaned over the lectern and peered contemptuously at him. "And isn't it a fact," he began, "that your private practice is devoted almost exclusively to administering hypnosis in order to assist people in quitting smoking?"

The disclosure did not surprise Sullivan & Cromwell, least of all Schwartz, who had availed himself of Spiegel's services a few years earlier. (During a break Schwartz was asked whether the hypnosis had worked. In response, he sheepishly held up a lit Camel.) When Spiegel had begun such work years earlier, it was trailblazing, newsworthy stuff. But by 1986 quit-smoking remedies had become a fixture of late-night television and matchbook-cover culture. With one question, Reilly had made Spiegel look like a quack.

Spiegel betrayed some of the same sloppiness as Plum, calling Wideroff "Widemeyer" and "Weisen-something" and Schilling "Sherman." More damaging, he admitted he hadn't listened to the entire Poterewicz tape. "You still say that being yelled at like that might sound like music to his ears?" Reilly asked him caustically. "Some of it," Spiegel replied. Asked whether a slap in the face would have had a devastating effect on Seward, Spiegel again stuck to his guns. "He was a strong, powerful man," he said. "If he felt it that way, he would have done something about it."

Reilly might have neutralized much of what Spiegel had said. But one point he could not touch. Graham asked the doctor if there had been any occasion when Seward's "core" interests *had* been intruded upon. Yes, Spiegel replied, there had been one, but the intruder had not been Basia. It happened on March 31, 1983, when Junior had pushed his father to relinquish control of Harbor Branch. "I think he was hurt and insulted and experienced this as a kind of disappointment that a father has when his son shows such little respect for him, that he would dare to do that knowing full well that he didn't have long to live," Spiegel replied. No one laughed at this portion of Spiegel's testimony. Indeed, in the rear of the courtroom Junior's wife, Joyce, began to weep. In her, at least, Spiegel had struck a nerve. As for Junior, it was hard to know what he thought. Protected throughout the trial by a zealous lawyer, a solicitous judge, and inept opposition, this would have been his only moment of real discomfiture. But he was nowhere to be seen. In all likelihood he was taking a cigarette break in the corridor.

Stripped of its colorful imagery, Spiegel's views were probably closer to the mark than anyone's. But by this late stage in the case, even the sensible sounded silly, particularly about Basia ("QUESTION: What is the difference between an alligator and Basia Johnson?" went the riddle circulating in the jury room. "ANSWER: An alligator doesn't speak Polish"). No doctor, even Albert Schweitzer, could have cured Basia's sullied image. By now, it seemed that only one person could save Basia, and that was Basia herself.

L

Milbank was ready for Basia Johnson. Everything it needed could be found in the black binder on Paul Shoemaker's shelf. Inside were 150 pages of questions, neatly divided into thirty different categories. And it was a looseleaf, instantly and infinitely expandable should anyone think of anything else.

The areas of inquiry ranged from the April 14 letter to Basia's treatment of Seward to Seward's courtship to the courtroom uprising to prior and current boyfriends, fiancés, and husbands in Europe and the United States. Some questions, like "Did you ever spend a night with——prior to Mr. Johnson's death?" had endless possible permutations. Other categories included "Excessive Spending," "Nina Zagat," "Harbor Branch: JSJ's Devotion, BPJ's Disloyalty," "Discharge of Perree, Myers, and Kelsey," "The Age Difference and BPJ's Knowledge of JSJ's Background," "Diving," and "BPJ's Improper Involvement in JSJ's Treatment." Under "Jasna Polana, Art and Other Extravagances" were questions concerning the orchid and dog houses, the chapel, the monumental staircase. How many fur coats did she own? Where did she store them? Had she ever bought out the entire contents of an antique store? Milbank was prepared to ask Basia everything everyone had ever wanted to ask her, and this time, Reilly would do the asking. He estimated his cross-examination alone could last a week. That sounded conservative.

S&C flip-flopped on whether Basia should testify. On one side of the ledger, the jury wanted, expected, and needed to hear her, certainly if the proponents hoped to salvage something from the case. But the other side of the ledger was longer. Many of the most important things she had to say would be barred by the Dead Man's Statute. Basia might blow up under Reilly's examination, even if it fell during the proper time of the month or phase of the moon. There would be the usual language problems. And aside from how she would say things was what she would say. Basia's own lawyers found chunks of her story extremely hard to swallow. They choked on the first few chapters, especially her description of Seward's patient, platonic courtship, and her position with his fledgling art collection. "Mrs. Johnson, if you testify about this 'curator' stuff, you'll be the laughingstock of the city," Bauman warned. The lawyers' skepticism grew as relations with her deteriorated. Basia's reminiscences, they believed, were saturated with wishful thinking. Her stories about even the simplest things kept changing. Some claims just didn't ring true—for instance, her protestations of innocence in the courtroom uprising. "Who in his right mind would have thought that that estate manager, who never went to the can without consulting someone, would take all of the cars and come to the courthouse on his own?" an S&C lawyer later asked.

Schwartz, whose task it was to prepare Basia to testify, vetted her stories scrupulously; whenever Basia recalled her wartime experiences, for instance, he had an encyclopedia, some maps of Poland, and some historically trained associates at the ready. Shoemaker surmised there was one chance in fifty that Basia's testimony could turn the case around. By the time he'd finished preparing her to testify, Schwartz put it at one in a hundred. He saw a better way out: to settle.

There had been little activity on that front since the first tape had been played, six weeks earlier, and Basia had called a halt to all negotiations. "To the end!" she told the troops, clenching her fist and thrusting it into the air. Her name had been besmirched, and she refused to quit until she told her side of the story, or at least had her surrogates tell it for her.

By now, that had happened, however sputteringly, and Bauman, among others, was urging settlement. "Mrs. Johnson, you're fifty years old," he told her, and so she would soon be. "The next ten years should be the most crucial period of your life. Do you want to spend them all fighting in court?" Costs were mounting; Sullivan & Cromwell had submitted bills for $750,000 in February and for another $900,000 in April. Though it seemed unlikely, were the children to prove undue influence, Lambert could replace Basia and Nina as executors with one of her own hacks: Basia would no longer control the funds for court, or for that matter, for anything else. Even at Jasna Polana, battle fatigue was setting in. At one point Basia's nephew, eleven-year-old Seward Piasecki, forlornly approached one of his aunt's bodyguards. For young Piasecki, all the attention and security were proving too much; his classmates, he complained, were taunting him about how rich he'd be one day. "When I grow up, I'm going to get a little apartment on a little street and live like everyone else," he told the guard sadly.

It was also clear that the children had peaked—or, to put it another way, had no more mud to sling. Reilly had raised the settlement ante dramatically but could probably elevate it no further. A favorable verdict seemed more certain than ever but just as unsatisfactory: The decision would surely be appealed and quite possibly reversed, and even were it not, there were still all those prior wills to overturn.

The lawyers, too, generally favored settlement. S&C wanted to spare itself a humiliating defeat, Shearman & Sterling the embarrassment of having one of the most important wills it ever drafted invalidated. S&S now warned Basia that the children's claim to half the estate, the claim Christ had once said was worth less than his necktie, had a 30 to 50 percent chance of succeeding, and that it alone could cost $57 million to settle. Both firms wanted their fees; Shearman & Sterling hadn't been paid anything since February. And for all her talk of sacrifice— "I don't need anything to live on," she would say, "I live simply. I can close Jasna Polana and move into my New York apartment. I can get a job; I know how to work"—Basia was running out of money. Already, she had gone through more than half her war chest. As for Milbank, it knew it could probably secure larger fees in a settlement—fees determined by Lambert and paid for by Basia—than it ever could by adding up all of the billable hours. Corn, too, wanted to settle. The flames that threatened to engulf Marie Lambert might still singe him.

At least three things blocked any deal: Basia's ego, the children's appetite, and Reilly's will to win. By Basia's lights, any settlement would give the children money they did not deserve. But here Lambert could help, offering Basia the sweetener she had previously dangled before Christ: She could collapse the trusts and give Basia her fortune outright, thereby, as she put it, "getting Nina Zagat off Basia's back." Weeks earlier, when Christ had relayed Lambert's proposal to her, Basia had reacted indignantly. "That's not what Seward wanted!" she said. "Who does she think she is?" But as Basia grew depressed about the case, disenchanted with Nina, and enamored of Fox, her resistance waned. The arrangement would cost Nina $900,000 annually, money Basia could presumably provide her in other ways. Three years into the case, in some ways Seward Johnson remained a mystery. ("We didn't get a good picture of this guy," Harvey Corn said afterward. "We know he liked oatmeal.") But two things, at least, were clear: He wanted Basia to inherit his fortune, and he wanted Nina watching over it. By countermanding half of Seward's wishes, however, Lambert could buy herself out of the mess she'd made. Nina was too bloodied, or loyal to Basia, or benumbed, to complain. And with their fee from Basia on the line, the folks at Shearman & Sterling were not about to stick up for the wishes of their late client. "He's dead and we're alive," was how Henry Ziegler put it.

The case was entering its death throes. To settle or not to settle; to testify or not to testify; to collapse the trusts or not to collapse the trusts; with all of these questions before her, Basia—with Fox's encouragement—again felt the need for a second legal opinion, one with no ties to Nina or S&C or S&S. Fox promptly came up with some all-star nominees: David Boies, Arthur Liman, Harold Tyler, Harvey Myerson, John Martin, Peter Fleming. All practiced in New York, though, and Basia reasoned from bitter experience that they might be reluctant to take on a local judge. Fox then proposed Frederick Lacey, a former federal prosecutor and judge in New Jersey who'd recently opened a Newark office for New York's LeBoeuf, Lamb, Leiby & McRae. "Basia, there are two kinds of fighters in this town: the Irish and the Jews, O'Connor and Koch," Fox told her. "What better way to fight Reilly than with another Irishman?" Lacey had more going for him than ethnicity. He had a reputation for fearlessness and rectitude. The stars, too, were favorable. Basia's fortune teller, who'd already warned her to beware of lawyers whose last names began with C and had foreseen that a younger man would come along and give her wise counsel, encouraged her to hire Lacey, too.

On May 13, the Zagats, along with Basia, Bauman, and Maria Pia Fanfani, dined together at the Quilted Giraffe. There was plenty of grumbling about the case—Bauman once more speculated that Lambert had to be fixed, while Fanfani harrumphed that the humiliation she'd just endured could never have happened in Italy—but there were no signs of an impending rupture between the proponents. The next night, however, Fox and Basia met Lacey at his firm's New York office. For three hours Basia bad-mouthed her current lawyers. Once, she lamented, they told her she couldn't lose; now, they were saying she couldn't win. Lacey agreed to assess the situation. The next morning, after he'd heard the news, Bauman worried aloud that Basia was getting ready to sue both Shearman & Sterling and Sullivan & Cromwell for malpractice.

Lacey soon met with Schwartz and Osgood, who filled him in on the case and client. Then, along with other LeBoeuf lawyers, he pored over the trial record. Quickly, he seconded Bauman's insistence that Basia testify, a question on which Basia herself still flip-flopped. In the end the counsel she heeded came not from LeBoeuf Lamb nor Shearman & Sterling nor Sullivan & Cromwell, but Anderson & O'Brien—that is, her bodyguards, Bob Anderson and Marty O'Brien. Oftentimes during their long rides back to Jasna Polana after court, leaning forward from her backseat to cut down on the very distance from the help her limousine was built to provide, Basia confided in the two; now, they urged her to spare herself the aggravation of testifying. Let her lawyers fight for her, they urged; with Reilly and Lambert arrayed against her, O'Brien predicted, "it would be a slaughter." That sounded about right to her.

On another trip along the New Jersey Turnpike, the topic turned to Nina. With Lacey and Fox now on top and Nina's influence and stock waning, the bodyguards figured they were finally free to unburden themselves of years of accumulated resentment over Nina and her high-handedness. If it weren't for Nina, they told Basia, she wouldn't be in court to begin with, fighting for what was rightly hers. Nina was lazy, had Shearman & Sterling's and her own interests at heart, and hadn't done her anything but harm "We really heaped the shit on her. We buried her," recalled O'Brien, who also told Lacey that Nina had "stunk" on the stand. Basia didn't defend her friend. In fact, she told her bodyguards they were right.

Nina had built her career around the Johnsons, and had stood to profit handsomely from it. But with Seward gone and Basia going, everything was fast crumbling around her. Suddenly, she could be made to bear a disproportionate share of any settlement, and no one—not Basia, not Lambert, not S&C, nor Shearman & Sterling, nor any lawyer of her own—would raise any voice in opposition. Already, her trustees' fees stood to be eliminated, with only Basia's promise that they'd be restored once the case was over as compensation. Now, ostensibly to sweeten things for the children—she thought they might be more willing to drop the case if some of what had been earmarked for Nina came their way instead—Basia proposed slashing Nina's executor's commission from $8 million to $1.8 million. Once more, Nina was powerless to object; once more, Basia assured her she would be made whole once the trial was over. Nina knew Basia's nature, though, and knew, too, that there was no way she could count on anything.

As the trial wound down, settlement talks heated up. By the time Judy Smith took the stand, S&C was offering the children $4 million each tax-free—roughly half of what Forger was demanding. Under both arrangements Junior would get twice as much as the others, to make up for his forsaken fees; Harbor Branch would get $20 million, and Uncle Sam would get much more than that. How much more depended upon how various tax laws were construed; the two sides negotiated over not only the gap, but who would bear the risks of various tax decisions. As Memorial Day approached, the parties began drafting an agreement. With five different sets of lawyers—from S&C, S&S, Milbank, Dewey, and LeBoeuf—around to raise every imaginable contingency, it was slow going. What if Basia had money squirreled away in some Swiss bank account? What if she upped and left the country, absconding with her fortune? What if, having settled with her stepchildren, she was sued by her stepgrandchildren instead? If certain trusts remained intact only until Basia's death, would someone have an incentive to murder her?

Tensions ebbed and flowed. S&S's Arthur Field grated on the Milbank lawyers, who viewed him as pedantic, condescending, and niggling. So did Lacey. After fifteen minutes in the case, one complained, he'd come "breezing in like Loretta Young, pretending to know everything." Forger and Brinck riled up Shearman & Sterling; Schwartz continued to annoy Lambert. Meanwhile, shuttling between the parties, hammering out details, tending to frayed feelings, Corn and Lambert worked overtime. Months after it really mattered, Lambert was finally living up to her advance billing, finally "knocking heads." While the tax lawyers—whom the litigators dubbed "the undertakers"—crunched numbers, Reilly and Christ paced anxiously on the sidelines, praying things would fall through. Christ remained convinced that S&C would win if the case ever reached the jury, and he found support from an unexpected source: his wife's astrologer. Nina was sitting in the *Titanic* Room one afternoon when the phone rang; an excited Iris Christ was on the line. If the case went to the jury over the next four days, Iris told Nina, "it's a go for Donald." Alas, the signs were conflicting: In the midst of settlement talks, Jasna Polana's white squirrel, the one whose appearance was supposed to have brought Basia good luck, was electrocuted.

In late May, sandwiched in amid the negotiations, S&C called its final witnesses, Scott and Joyce MacLeod. Christ had inexplicably saved the best for last. More than anyone else, the MacLeods had watched Seward's third marriage evolve. Moreover, in a case filled with alien aliens, they were perfect all-Americans. As Seward's onetime flame, Joyce could attest better than anyone to the void that had been Basia's to fill, and how well she filled it. So could Scott, a former navy fighter pilot and test astronaut who'd been Walter Cronkite's color man on various space shots.

The appearance gave Lacey his first chance to watch Christ in action, and as he saw the S&C lawyer reading questions off his script he understood Basia's frustration. He could also see how, between Reilly's objections and Lambert's rulings, the proponents' best evidence had been hacked to death by the time it reached the jury. At one point Joyce MacLeod tried to recount a conversation she'd had with Seward, in which he lamented how little he and Essie had in common. "In the sixteenth week of trial, we are not trying Mr. Johnson's second wife," Lambert interjected. "By next week we'll get to his first wife—I don't know what her name is—and then maybe we'll get to his mother and father." Joyce recalled another time when Seward told her he'd like more contact with his children, but that they felt differently. "They don't need me," he'd said. "I'm not leaving them anything. I set them up with trust funds, and they're all very wealthy in their own right." It was crucial testimony, but this, too, was blocked.

Joyce MacLeod was a hearty, seemingly unsentimental woman, who retained the fresh athleticism that had so attracted Seward years earlier. But when Christ asked her about the brief visit she and her husband made to Fort Pierce two and a half weeks before Seward's death, her breeziness disappeared. When they'd arrived, she recalled, Seward was sitting up in his bed, a newspaper on his lap. They'd had lunch with him, then gone outside for tea. "His voice was very weak, so I really had to bend close to talk to him," she recalled. "But, yes, he was talking about the vessel *Seward Johnson* getting under way, and he was very pleased—that maybe we could go cruising next year on it." Christ asked what else she remembered about that encounter. Biting her lip between words, she added, ". . . that his legs were hurting and he was very disturbed that it was hard for him to move and he couldn't walk anymore," she said. When Christ pumped her still more, she began to weep. "Excuse me," she managed to say between sobs, looking down at her lap. "I'm sorry."

Lambert did not accept her apology. Tears, like so many other exhibits S&C had tried to get into evidence during this cursed trial, were inadmissible in her courtroom, at least when proferred by the proponents. First, they were barred by the statute of limitations. There came a time, Lambert had apparently decreed, when the crying had to stop; for those who'd loved Seward, dead three years now, that time had already passed. Moreover, Joyce MacLeod lacked standing: She wasn't even a member of the family. To Lambert, these weren't tears of grief but of envy: Someone else had married the old goat and ended up with all his loot. "Don't do that!" she barked at the witness. "Not in this room!" Once again, she kicked the jurors into the corridor and summoned the lawyers to the bench. "I don't want to hear 'you're sorry'!" the judge snapped at MacLeod. "I know a faker when I see one! You deliberately faced the jury when you cried. You could have faced this way. This man has been dead for over three years. To have this kind of display in the courtroom with the last witness! Maybe we should get the children up here to cry!"

"I agree, Your Honor," Reilly said.

As the tongue-lashing continued, Scott MacLeod began to rise to his wife's defense, but Rogers restrained him. It would do more harm than good, Rogers said.

When testimony resumed, Christ asked Joyce to describe how the two Johnsons spoke to each other. "She often called him pet names and he would call her pet names, and they'd chuck each other under the chin and use baby talk," she said. "She'd call him a 'Romeo' and her 'Sewardo' and kind of babbly things like 'oochy poochy poochy.' " But they'd also argue, she said, and what she saw then were "two very strong-willed people butting heads." A year or so before he died, she recalled, Seward told her Basia was "the best girl he'd ever known."

On that note her testimony, and the testimony in the case, concluded. It was 11:10 on the morning of Thursday, May 29. Already, the courtroom had the air of a circus after the tent had been struck. "Hallelujah!" the judge declared. She directed the jury to return by two-thirty for summations. She would charge them the next morning, she said, then send them off to deliberate. It would never happen.

The parties continued to close in on a deal. The night before, they'd summoned the judge from an Italian restaurant, and around eleven o'clock the lawyers (including Dewey's Warren, who had to be dragged out of bed) converged on the courthouse. Two hours passed, and with no agreement in sight, a frustrated Forger tried staging a dramatic exit. "Come on, we're getting out of here!" he said to his partners, only to be told by Corn that the front door was locked, and that Corn himself had the only key. The parties talked on for another hour and a half.

By Friday the parties had settled on some figures. Each of the children would receive approximately $6 million tax-free, with Junior collecting an additional $7 million to make up for most of his lost commissions. It was less than they sought, but Basia, not they, would be liable for any unexpected tax rulings. Harbor Branch would get its $20 million, minus the $1 million in fees racked up by Dewey Ballantine. In exchange, the children would drop their challenge to the April 14 will and the claims proceeding. The lawyers projected taxes of $90 million or so. But that could change; indeed, there remained the chance that despite all of Shearman & Sterling's precautions, the New Jersey tax authorities would still insist Seward resided in Princeton, setting off a chain reaction of adverse tax consequences that could consume much of the estate.

S&S's Arthur Field had always said the key to any settlement lay not just in buying off the children but Milbank, too, and Milbank made out handsomely in the proposed deal: Its fees would total $10 million, all payable out of Basia's share of the estate. While every other figure on Forger's ledger—including the amount his clients would collect—was open to discussion, the fee Milbank was demanding, roughly twice what it had earned on a hourly basis, was absolutely unnegotiable. Having been lacerated by Reilly & Company, Basia would now be fleeced by them as well. (Never, Corn told one participant, had he seen a firm so greedy for its fee.) This, of course, would come on top of what Basia would owe Sullivan & Cromwell and Shearman & Sterling. All told, the case would cost Basia in legal fees what Jasna Polana cost Seward: $25 million, and without even an air-conditioned doghouse to show for it.

Until the last minute, each side kept introducing additional complications. Schwartz tried and failed to extract two pledges, one from Milbank to withdraw its accusations against Osgood, one from Basia that she would not sue S&C. Forger proposed several new and costly items, prompting an angry outburst from Corn. "Stop playing with yourself!" he told Forger. As the parties moved toward settlement, an S&C lawyer spotted Reilly sitting in the courtroom. His eyes were dilated, and he was staring dead ahead, like a racehorse champing at his bit. He seemed to be mumbling something—perhaps, the S&C lawyer speculated, the closing argument he still hoped to deliver. It contained an impassioned denunciation of Basia, a woman who, he would say, had broken Seward's spirits if not his bones, who'd made him a pauper for all his millions. He would harp on Basia's failure to testify, attack Nina, and remind the jury of the powerful message it could send to lawyers and doctors alike: Don't mess with the elderly.

Before he could convince any jury, though, Reilly had to convince his own clients to carry on. For more than an hour—as the children, their spouses, and the chief dealmaker, Forger, sat listening—Reilly implored them not to quit. They were on the brink of winning, he said; with Basia evidently not testifying, victory was more certain still. He urged them to reject the easy money, money they didn't need anyway, and stand up for the lofty principles for which they'd said they'd brought their case, principles for which witnesses like

Izabella Poterewicz and Edmund Sulikowski had risked their lives, principles for which, though he would never have said it, he had worked all but three days over the previous eight months. Even if they lost the verdict, he noted, they still had the claims proceeding. Reilly's plea upset some of those urging a deal. The Johnson children, Gretchen Johnson complained, had no real will of their own; with a settlement within reach, why allow Reilly to confuse them anew? Lambert was also not pleased. Here she'd labored over a deal, spending one night on Tom Ford's office couch, only to have Reilly attempting to upset everything. "Ask him if he'll put his fees on the line if he loses the case!" she told Junior.

She need not have worried. Reilly and the Johnsons had never really been fighting for the same thing anyway, and now, with cash on the barrelhead, the schism was becoming visible. Reilly's clients, aided and abetted by Reilly's partners, were about to sell Reilly down the river. For the Firestones and Richardses, there were debts to pay. For the Wolds and Jennifer Johnson, there were easy millions. For Jimmy, there was an end to a case he'd never wanted to begin. For the Junior Johnsons, there was a fortune to replenish. Publicly, Junior said he settled in part because he couldn't trust the jury: Perhaps, he hinted darkly, Basia had gotten to it. To one of his lawyers, he was far more candid. "We weren't born to earn our livings, and our children weren't born to earn theirs, either," he said. "Whatever they have, they'll get by inheritance. Who am I to put their birthright at risk?" By two-fifteen that afternoon, the children had decided to settle.

Reilly was disconsolate. When approached in the corridor, he turned and faced the wall. He was still mumbling, though now, one observer thought, he was saying his rosary. "I feel as if I've been running a race, and I was about to win, and someone tripped me just as I was getting to the finish line," he said bitterly. A friend, alarmed at his despondency and concerned he might actually hurt himself, took him to a Mexican restaurant that night just to watch over him. For months to come he gave Forger and Brinck the brush-off. Christ took the settlement more philosophically. "I want to go home and see my dog, Beaver," he told one reporter. "Also, some of my clients think I've died." He paused. "Perhaps I have."

By nine that night the lawyers had hammered out a six-page agreement. By ten Basia and Nina were ready to leave the building, though not together. Only at the entrance to the courthouse did the two run into one another. They talked for a few minutes, silhouetted by the lights of the Woolworth Building behind them. When it came time to leave one another, Nina moved haltingly, as if she weren't quite sure where she now stood with her old confrere. Appearing uncertain as to whether to kiss Basia or shake her hand, Nina compromised, and kissed her unconvincingly. Then they went their separate ways.

LI

On Monday, June 2, Basia Johnson came to court dressed to settle, but to settle triumphantly. She wore a cheerful white dress with polka dots on it and white gloves on her hands— her way of telling the world that none of the filth that had been hurled her way had stuck. There were yet more last-minute snags. To everyone's amazement, Schwartz suddenly had second thoughts about a settlement. An adverse verdict was not preordained, he argued; if one came, the firm would handle an appeal for free. But neither Basia nor anyone else had the stomach to continue.

When the children came to Shearman & Sterling to sign the agreement, Forger was his affable public self, heartily greeting the woman he'd attacked so ferociously in his famous affidavit. "You must be Nina Zagat!" he said cheerfully. "I think it's time we met each other." Nina looked at him briefly, then walked away. Meantime the S&C litigators gathered for the final time in the Titanic Room. The last lunch: jumbo shrimp on a skewer. Someone opened a bottle of wine, which turned out to be sour. "It must be Polish wine," Iris Christ muttered.

By a quarter to four the lawyers—six from Milbank, three each from S&C and S&S, two each from Dewey and LeBoeuf—gathered in the judge's chambers. Representatives of New York State attorney general Robert Abrams, conspicuously absent for most of the case, also put in the most token of appearances. Four of the children, with Keith Wold and Marty Richards substituting for their ailing wives, were sworn in, and Lambert, addressing each by his first name, asked them whether the settlement was acceptable to them. It was. The children then departed, and Basia and Nina were summoned. The judge, referring to them as "Mrs. Johnson" and "Mrs. Zagat," respectively, asked the same question and got the same answer. After Basia left, Lambert cornered Nina for a moment. "I just want you to know I only worked so hard on the settlement because of you," she said. "I didn't want to see a lawyer go before the jury." She stood expectantly in front of Nina, as if anticipating an embrace. Instead, Nina simply shook her hand po-

litely, thanked her, then left. The proceedings moved into the courtroom, where the jury was seated and the gallery filled. For the last time
the court officer rapped his fist on the mahogany door. "Honorable
Marie M. Lambert, Surrogate!" he barked.

Lambert strode in, removed her oversized glasses, and began reading
in the wooden singsong with which she declaimed anything canned. If
the timbre was uncharacteristic, the sentiments—self-congratulatory,
self-pitying—were not. Once, she'd told a reporter that "a poor settlement was better than a trial." In *Johnson* v. *Johnson,* she'd managed to
have both. For seventeen weeks the world had witnessed an outlandish
spectacle, one that left Seward Johnson stripped bare and his testamentary wishes in tatters. "Any resemblance to Seward Johnson's actual
last will seemed purely coincidental," William Zabel, a prominent New
York probate lawyer, was to write. "Mr. Johnson should be a veritable
whirling dervish in his grave, because all of his expressed intentions
were flouted." Zabel left out one important point: Seward was the fellow
picking up the tab for the entire debacle. But Lambert's only regret,
she joked to one reporter, was that she never got a chance to put Seward
Johnson's millions into hundred-dollar bills, just to see what all that
money looked like.

"Good afternoon," she began. "I hope you had a good weekend. If
you did, you did better than I did. We have sat here together for
seventeen weeks. During this trial the third anniversary of Mr. Johnson's
death passed. In the almost three years before the trial started, over
sixty pretrial motions were made, thousands of pages of examinations
before trial were taken, and hundreds of hours of court time were spent
deciding motions and conferences. During the trial approximately ten
more motions were made, and many conferences were held. You heard
testimony from some of the richest and most powerful people in the
world and from others who came from diverse walks of life. You heard
testimony from nurses and professional people, and even from a nun.
You and the Court were subjected to a demonstration during the course
of the trial. You will never know the personal courage it took for me
to continue to sit in this case, and to withstand the threats of physical
violence that were made to me.

"Finally, after marathon negotiations a settlement was hammered
out. It could not have happened without the aid of all the lawyers,
who refused to drop the settlement ball when they spotted the goal
line, and my fantastic law secretary, Harvey Corn, whose patience,
loyalty, integrity, and intelligence are beyond belief. This agreement
was finally accepted somewhere about eleven-fifteen A.M. this morning

and was put on the record and signed by everyone a few minutes ago.

"Notwithstanding the efforts of everyone who worked on the settlement, you, the jury, were the real catalyst which induced the settlement. Your presence has saved the state and the litigants millions of dollars and the Court hours of future untold anguish. This case has again reaffirmed my faith in the jury system and all that it stands for. Only in the United States could we have achieved such a result, and only a jury such as you could bring it about. I know that you are disappointed that you did not get to render a verdict, but you can take pride in the role you played in bringing peace to the parties and conferring a measure of sanity and security to this Court."

It was vintage Lambert. So, too, in their own ways, were the remarks that followed from each of the lawyers. Christ, thanking the jurors for their patience, attention, "and above all, for their sense of humor," was characteristically terse, low-key, and sardonic. Reilly was stiff, somber, visibly reluctant to let go. Hirth, like his case, was brief, polite, and largely redundant, though Dewey's Bill Warren was more voluble, going so far as to invite the jurors to stop by Harbor Branch were they ever "down Fort Pierce way." Schwartz, who'd been eclipsed during the settlement talks, was brief. Then Forger rose. He spoke the longest of anyone, perhaps because he had the most thanks to give.

"Your Honor, on behalf of the Johnson children, I, too, would like to express my deep appreciation for the presence of the jury and its work," he said in his rich baritone. "As one of the negotiators—and maybe that translates into 'frustrators'—we apologize for having prevented you from that last step. Your presence there was very much felt." Forger then turned his gaze slightly counterclockwise, toward the bench. He and Marie Lambert had come a long way from that time, nearly a decade earlier, when she'd listed him among those patronage-taking lawyers who profited from death, and he had stood in principled opposition to her. "I couldn't close without making reference to a very superb judge, whom we had the pleasure of being involved with," he said with a big grin. "She is a very unique person in the life of this Surrogate's Court. She really turned the heat up. I think maybe you heard her say, 'Come on! Let's go!' which was heard frequently by those among the negotiating team. It was in large measure through her persistent and sensitive efforts that we were able to resolve the issues—and also with the help of Harvey." Lambert smiled broadly.

But Forger wasn't done. He still had his partner to placate and his clients to flatter. "One of the great joys is to be a part of this process and of course to watch the experts at work here," he continued. "All of them made a major contribution. Indeed, I think my good colleague and friend Ed Reilly was superb. And of course, without super clients, the Johnson family, we couldn't be here. Thank you."

Lambert the beneficent announced she'd arranged for the jury to receive double pay—twenty-four dollars a day—for the time they'd worked beyond their regular tour of duty, as well as a special certificate of commendation, the kind of document, suitable for lamination, she would surely have hung on her chambers walls were she to have received one, and were there still some room. "Thank you very, very much from the bottom of my heart for all the help that you have been in this case," she said. "It is people like you that are responsible for our wonderful system of government and for what we have in these United States. And it's very precious. We are not about to give it up."

Christ turned to his associates, Ted Rogers, Sheryl Michaelson, Basil Zirinis, and Robert Delahunty, and shook their hands. Their ordeal was over. At her invitation, the jurors met for half an hour with Lambert (and some of the Johnson children) in her chambers. Then they headed out to the corridor and a press corps ravenous for their thoughts. Reilly's case on competency had clearly reached them. "I don't think that on that day, April 14, 1983, Mr. Johnson was of sound mind," the most gregarious of the group, Jeffrey Schwab, said. "I frankly don't believe that he knew what he was doing." José Santana said he felt Seward had been "out of it" when he'd signed his will. Milbank's undue-influence claim was more problematical. "I think they had a terrible relationship, but I really am not prepared to say he was forced to do what he did," said Debra Califia, the widowed juror on whom S&C had pinned its hopes.

The children and their spouses made their way downstairs, with Forger, as one Dewey lawyer later put it sourly, "leading the flock like Il Duce." There, as reporters and cameramen gathered beneath them, they took their places on the monumental stairway and struggled to explain precisely what, apart from enriching themselves, they had accomplished in the case. "We had a commitment to do, we had a job, we did the job, and I think we made the points that we wished to make: that you don't take advantage of a man in his... who's finishing his life, who's elderly and weak," Junior said. He grew indignant when someone referred to the case as "bickering." "I don't conceive this as 'bickering'!" he shot back. "I conceive this as unearthing some very basic human... ah... that applies to everyone... ah... problems that go on in life and I think that it it has it has all come out and and and been washed and and I think it's been a service to do this and . . . "

"To whom?" a skeptical reporter interjected.

" . . . and that we . . . A public service! Because who can afford to do this but someone with money?"

"The widow says that she hopes to be friends with the children some day," another reporter chimed in. "Do you think that's possible?" To the laughter of his last crowd, Junior rolled his eyes. "I don't know exactly what we would have to talk about," he finally said.

Characteristically enough, it was Marty Richards, the Jewish boy from the Bronx, who did much of the talking for the family. Putting his arm around Junior, he declared, "Miss Johnson, Mrs. Johnson, Basia Johnson, found out one thing: She has always said that the Johnsons were weak. She found out that they were *strong*, and that's terrific!"

"Good for you, Marty!" a beaming Junior gushed.

Quietly, unceremoniously, Christ slipped out of the Surrogate's Court, his reputation as a trial lawyer tarnished but his dignity intact. He had stayed with his case and his client uncomplainingly until the end. He did tell someone, however, that it would be nice to leave litigation behind and return to trusts and estates, where one could deal with people rather than with lawyers. A few days later the Christs held a quiet party at Wuff Woods, where each member of the S&C team was given a framed sketch of a courtroom scene, which had been bought in bulk from one of the television illustrators. There were awards and toasts, including one from Iris Christ in which she said how proud she was of her husband and Sullivan & Cromwell, "the best law firm in the world."

The Johnsons having cleared out of the lobby, Basia took her position. On one side of her was Nina, on the other, Schwartz, the same Schwartz who had recently concluded she was too unreliable ever to take the stand. But now was no time for him or anyone else at S&C to antagonize Basia Johnson; after all, she still owed the firm millions in fees. "I won!" Basia beamed. "I am the winner because I feel wonderful and I'm now free to do what I want to do, to carry on our plans, our dreams—my late husband's and mine." Asked why, after vowing not to give the children "the dust off half a penny," she'd bestowed over four billion pennies on them, she replied, "I changed my mind. Intelligent people always change their mind. I think that peace is more important than prolonged litigation." Was she angry at her stepchildren? "Not at all," she replied, but her magnanimity was fleeting. "I feel sad that they brought that contest. They ridiculed their father."

The press conference complete, Basia left the building, a somber and silent Nina at her side. Anyone who'd sat through the trial knew of the shellacking Basia had taken inside the Surrogate's Court. But now, with a single ingenious gesture, Basia became the winner everywhere else. As she prepared to enter her limousine, she remembered what Franco Zeffirelli, an old hand at stagecraft, had told her over the telephone the night before: that whoever acted like a victor was, *ipso facto*, victorious. Taking his cue, Basia held her gloved hand high and, as the photographers snapped away, flashed a "V for Victory." The proponents went back to Shearman & Sterling, where they drank sherry, munched on Dove Bars, and watched themselves on television. Zeffirelli proved prophetic. Though some of the papers saw the settlement as a victory for the children—"$159M SALVES J&J HEIRS," the *Daily News* declared—the more enduring image was the one that landed on the front page of the *New York Post*, of Basia striking her Churchillian pose. "THE $340M WOMAN," the tabloid called her. Similar stories appeared in Poland. "MILLIONS OF DOLLARS IN THE HANDS OF OUR PATRIOT," one paper declared.

As Basia held court downstairs, Junior Johnson began rounding up the jurors, whom he had invited while in Lambert's chambers to a victory party. Some hopped in the Johnsons' limousines and headed toward Broadway, while others joined the Milbank lawyers and press corps on foot. The groups converged on a hip TriBeCa eatery called the Odeon, only to learn that the restaurant couldn't seat so many people. Reilly opened up his briefcase, took out his *Zagat Restaurant Survey*, and selected Le Zinc, a cozy bistro around the corner on Duane Street, a few blocks west of the now-sunken Titanic Room. Quickly, three tables filled up with Johnsons, Johnson spouses, Johnson lawyers, Johnson journalists, Johnson jurors, and, oddly enough, the Johnson judge. Corn, with characteristic shrewdness, had begged off, pleading exhaustion. But Marie Lambert was raring to go and went.

The waiters took drink orders, all of which would go on Reilly's American Express tab. At one table some jurors joked with Reilly about starring roles in the inevitable movie on the case. For the part of the Milbank lawyer, one admiring juror nominated Gregory Peck, who had portrayed another lawyer-hero, Atticus Finch, in *To Kill a Mockingbird*. Another quickly dissented. No, he insisted: Only Mr. Reilly could play Mr. Reilly. Nearby, Marie Lambert ordered a club soda and settled in at the table farthest from the door. At one point Junior came over and kissed her, just as he had kissed her in chambers, and mentioned making a sculpture of her and donating it to the Surrogate's Court. Would that be allowed? someone asked. "Sure! Don't worry about it!" she replied. A juror told the judge he wasn't sure how he and his colleagues would have ruled on undue influence. "You wouldn't have had any doubts after I'd finished with my charge!" she replied.

Lambert then explained her take on the case. Seward Johnson, she told the folks at her table, was a bit like her late husband: a gentleman, but a pushover. Basia and Nina took advantage of the man and his nature. The jury saw what Basia did to him; she totally controlled his environment. She wouldn't let him leave the property without permission, she surrounded him with strangers, she wouldn't even let him have a barbecue when he wanted one. And what does she feed him instead? Eggplant! No wonder the jurors were all laughing! You know what pureed eggplant looks like? *It looks like shit! It looks like shit!* Lambert, at least dimly aware that what she was saying was quite inappropriate, appended an "off the record" to her remarks. If any of this got out, she said, she would deny having ever said it.

A few nights later the Sullivan & Cromwell lawyers treated the jurors, sans Marie Lambert, to something far fancier: dinner at Primavera, the very restaurant where Basia and Nina had taken their legal team, under very different circumstances, only a few months before. It was a casual, wine-filled evening, filled with tales of the case. Zirinis recounted how, minutes after commenting on Basia's foul mouth, Reilly had told him to fuck off; Schwartz explained that he'd not called Basia to the stand because he'd considered her a liar; Christ was asked whether he respected Reilly as a litigator ("Not particularly," he replied), and Osgood finally resurfaced in public. "We missed you!" a juror told him. "What happened?" He and Basia had had a disagreement, Osgood explained. "In other words," the juror said, "you disappeared like some of the servants did!"

After dinner the group repaired to Schwartz's pied-à-terre on Sutton Place South, just a few doors down from where Basia and Seward had first lived together sixteen years earlier. The conversation turned abusive, with derisive cracks about the personal histories and sexual proclivities of Junior, Marty Richards, and Mervyn Nelson. A still-fuming Schwartz vowed that as long as he had anything to say about it, Reilly would never be admitted into the American College of Trial Lawyers, the organization of self-designated elite litigators to which Schwartz himself belonged. Shaking his fist vehemently, Robert Delahunty spoke of justice. "It's more important than you or me or the judge," he said, "and it was not done in this case."

Later, Delahunty, along with Zirinis and an S&C paralegal named

Richard Trostle, walked over to P. J. Clarke's for a nightcap. Delahunty did much of the talking, and as he did, it became clear that what he had witnessed in Lambert's courtroom had precipitated for him a crisis of faith every bit as shattering as the one he'd experienced years earlier under that flowering tree in Brooklyn. Delahunty did not attend the party at the Christs' the following night, and by Monday he had quit the firm. Before departing, he approached a reporter with a brief request. "Write a just book," he said simply. To Christ he inscribed a copy of his own book on Spinoza. *"Sed quis custodiet ipsos Custodes?"* he'd written, quoting from the Roman poet Juvenal. "Who is to guard the guards themselves?" He then left Sullivan & Cromwell for a new post— appropriately enough, in the United States Department of Justice.

So concerned was Marie Lambert upon learning of the dinner that she telephoned the most talkative juror, Jeffrey Schwab, with an unusual request—something, she explained, that would remain "just between you and me." She then elaborated. "I'd like you to prepare a memo- randum for me, and write down any of the comments Sullivan and Cromwell had to say about me, any questions they asked the jurors about me, whether I was biased." Unsure how to react to so extraor- dinary a request, Schwab said he'd think about it. By now, Schwab was used to unusual ex parte contacts. In the waning days of the case, while the jury remained sequestered, Tracy Hudson, the perky S&C paralegal who'd developed a crush on him, paid him an impromptu visit at his apartment building. "I wanted to see what you looked like in the flesh," she explained.

On *Good Morning America* Jimmy Breslin offered his own postmortem on the case. "Can you imagine," he asked, "going to college, fighting to get your LSATs to get into a prominent law school, and you join Sullivan & Cromwell, and here is what you do with your life: You fight a case involving the upstairs maid and the old man who went a little ga-ga and the children over a hundred million dollars. This is what you have done with your life." The whole spectacle, he said, was "disgusting."

On June 4 Basia staged a grand press tour of Jasna Polana, the one she hadn't had when it might have mattered. At long last she could testify, but on her own terms and turf, without Reilly cross-examining, or Lambert interrupting, her. Jack Raymond distributed a revised bi- ography for the occasion; it painted Basia in heroic hues, noting how she'd been born but a stone's throw from the birthplace of another Polish hero, Kościuszko, to a family of wealthy, aristocratic landowners, "among the oldest in Poland." Basia's family was now filled with "academics, engineers, writers and clergy." Oddly, though, it was minus one of her brothers, Piotr, who after a brief stay at Jasna Polana had fled to Florida, where he took a job as a gardener for another prominent Polish-American heiress, Blanca Rosenstiel. Though Raymond's biographical sketch mentioned Basia's eldest brother, Roch, Piotr had been airbrushed out.

"I was a prisoner for three years in this house," Basia told the voyeuristic throng. "Now, I have my freedom. I have invited you here to celebrate in my freedom." Together, the reporters and cameramen traipsed through the house, over carpets that once belonged to Louis XIV, by furniture that had belonged to Louis XVI. They passed by the sites of many of the episodes they'd heard about in court, including the Anthony Maffatone memorial terrace and the breakfast room/doghouse. "Papaya juice will be served!" a reporter chimed in. "Oatmeal!" added another. As Basia introduced her dogs, one reporter remarked that Jasna Polana's doghouse was larger than his apartment. "If you have dogs, you have to take care of them," she said. Basia's brother Gregory, who remained on the estate, gave a tour of the as-yet uncompleted chapel/bomb shelter, on which work would soon resume. By now, it included, at Basia's suggestion, three sixty-thousand-dollar periscopes, installed, it seemed, so that its inhabitants could tell when the Russians had departed and the coast was clear.

As Basia pointed out her artworks to the press, she used another line from Zeffirelli's script. "This is to show you the quality—not the quantity but the quality—of my money," she said. "When you put it in the bank, you can't share it with anyone." As the press stood on the monumental staircase, Bob Anderson went to fetch the recently acquired Raphael. "I used to have modern art, but I got rid of it," Basia said. "I changed my mind. As I said before about my husband's will, intelligent people do change their minds." A light lunch was served: poached-salmon sandwiches, white wine, strawberries. Then Basia, with Schwartz acting as chaperon and censor, held an impromptu press conference in the garden. "The whole thing was envy," she said of the case. "Envy causes hate; hate causes war, and that's what I wanted to avoid. I think I was very generous in the settlement," she continued. "The children have their own problems. Let them be. They are the children of my beloved husband. They're always welcome here." Finally, it was time to bid her guests good-bye. "As you can see, you cannot have everything. But my dreams, they came true."

The next morning, page one of *Newsday* featured a triumphant Basia—AMERICA'S MOST ELIGIBLE WOMAN—in living color, standing in front of Jasna Polana. Here, too, she exuberantly flashed victory signs, this time with both of her gloveless hands. But the keenest observation came from Hal Davis of the *New York Post*. Beneath the headline WALKING ON HEIR, he neatly summarized the state in which "America's most eligible woman" found herself. "Surrounded by beauty and guns," he wrote, "Barbara Johnson says she is a free woman now."

EPILOGUE

One day shortly after the trial was over, Basia and some guests were sitting around a table in Jasna Polana's dining room when the butler said something softly to her in Polish. Basia then told the group they were about to have a most unlikely visitor: a daughter-in-law of Mary Lea Richards. Soon, a tall, striking woman of about thirty, the first posttrial emissary from the other side, was ushered into the room. After several moments of awkward chitchat she was asked why she had come. Her eyes began to water, and her voice grew thick and shaky. "You have no idea how many times we wanted to pick up a pen and write you," she told Basia. "We wanted you to know how ashamed we were of what the family was doing to you."

❄

Financially and personally, Marty Richards had been among the biggest winners of *Johnson v. Johnson.* Within days of the settlement, a grateful Mary Lea bestowed $1 million of her winnings on him. He'd also won a reputation for gallantry before a wider and more appreciative audience than ever before. "Marty Richards sounds like a prince," *New York* magazine's Rhoda Koenig wrote. "If there are two of him, I want the other one." But his triumph came at a cost: He soon learned he had been kicked out of the Knights of Malta, for denigrating his father-in-law and fellow chevalier during the trial. Richards blamed Basia for the expulsion, and threatened to sue the order. Basia, who'd had nothing to do with the move, flirted with announcing the excommunication in *The New York Times.*

❄

In late 1986 a young lawyer arrived for a job interview at Shearman & Sterling. The partner urged him to ask something probing about the firm. The applicant asked what had been the firm's biggest fiasco ever. The partner then fulminated about the Johnson case, and how, had S&S done its job, it would never have reached court. The young man never got the job, but the firm, anxious to avoid another public relations debacle, hired its first "director of communications" (i.e. publicist).

※

Relations between Milbank and Sullivan & Cromwell remained frosty. When Forger was introduced at a bar function shortly after the trial concluded, a hiss emanated from the S&C table. "Come on!" a partner scolded the associate sitting next to him, who had worked on the Johnson case. "You're not hissing loud enough!"

※

A few weeks after the settlement Donald Christ told a friend he was "still pulling the pieces of glass out of my ass." In January 1987 he bought a cow, named it "Basia," then had it slaughtered and ground up into patties. The resulting "Basia burgers," he reported, were tough and sinewy. Christ continued at S&C, but not for long; in 1992 he semiretired, and followed his wife to "Llama Woods Farm" in Bend, Oregon. "With a commitment to excellence and a true love for llamas, Iris and Donald Christ are building one of the premier llama herds in North America," a promotional brochure stated. Inside was a picture of Christ, sporting a cowboy hat. Meantime, as the disciplinary probe into his activities languished (he eventually was given a private reprimand, the mildest possible sanction), Bob Osgood moved on to his next debacle: the presidential campaign of Joseph Biden. After that, he was reassigned—or, some thought, banished—to S&C's London office.

※

"Why don't you go to Tahiti and get laid for three months?" a Milbank partner advised Reilly once the trial concluded. But Reilly wouldn't, or couldn't, leave. Instead, he began specializing in bloody family feuds, including one involving the estate of Armand Hammer. Reilly married again briefly, then divorced. Later, disgusted by changes at the firm and disillusioned with his old friend Forger—as the economy turned sour, Milbank fired dozens of lawyers, including many partners, with Forger the man handing out the pink slips—Reilly made plans to leave. As for Forger, in 1992, shortly after Milbank axed seven more partners and he'd won the "Good Scout Award" from the Greater New York Council of Boy Scouts of America, he stepped down as head of the firm.

❋

In the weeks following the trial, Marie Lambert continued to bask in
the glow cast by the case. To one interviewer, she took stock of her
judicial career, and of her critics. "I didn't care what they thought of
me," she said. "I thought I was going to be a great judge. And in
retrospect, I was right." While at the Waldorf-Astoria Hotel to deliver
a luncheon speech on her recent triumph, Lambert spotted Nina Zagat
and approached her with some collegial advice. "Nina," she said, "just
remember, all clients are . . . "—and here she made quotation marks
in the air—". . . it begins with a *w* and ends with an *s*." Nina looked
at her uncomprehendingly. "Whores!" the judge whispered. "They
take, take, take, and never give."

During the trial Marvin Schwartz had vowed revenge against Lambert
for her egregious conduct. But good sense—good business sense—prevailed, and S&C never filed any complaint. Her appearance at Le Zinc
caught the attention of her old friends at the Commission on Judicial
Conduct, however, who pressed her for an explanation. She offered
the panel a smorgasbord of red herrings: Marty Richards had assured
her the feed was bipartisan; she stayed for only forty-five minutes; she
ate nothing and drank only club soda; Basia had invited her to Jasna
Polana, so things were even. The matter was quietly dropped.

But as Lambert's mandatory retirement neared in 1990, federal prosecutors began closing in on her favored few flunkies. Vincent Catalfo,
the once-suspended lawyer to whom she'd doled out $750,000 in pa-
tronage, received five years in prison for tax evasion and for robbing a
man with Down's syndrome of his $45,000 bequest. Then Melvyn
Altman, who'd received $390,000 in court-awarded business from Lam-
bert, was indicted for stealing nearly three times that from the very
people she had appointed him to protect. On January 1, 1991, Marie
Lambert left office just as she had entered it: under an ethical cloud.
This time, though, she was alone. Sensing she was trouble, the fancy
lawyers reverted to their old, standoffish ways. The testimonials to her
were few, muted, sparsely attended.

❋

On July 2, 1986, checks for $5,903,930.39 went out to each of the six
Johnsons, with Junior pocketing an additional $7 million for his forgone
fees as executor and trustee. The extra funds helped Jennifer and Jimmy
crack the *Forbes* 400 in 1992, by which time each was worth an estimated $300 million. But they did not spare Bert Firestone's real estate

company from filing for bankruptcy in 1991. Mary Lea went through hers even more quickly; by the end of 1986, John Lindsay regretfully informed her trustees, the money had already been spent.

All the recent attention proved addictive to the Richardses. They poured out their innards to Barbara Goldsmith, the self-described "social historian" writing a book on the case. It was they, presumably, who "revealed" both that Seward had been dyslexic and that his sexual initiation came at the age of fourteen, when he'd been held prisoner by one of his mother's friends—stories the elderly Evangeline, Seward's sister, considered rubbish. "I don't believe a word of it," she said. They also told Goldsmith the tale Marty had been peddling privately, the one Mary Lea's friends and children had heard, and dismissed, before: that between the ages of nine and fifteen, Mary Lea had been the victim of Seward's incest. So it was that Seward, whose memory the children had supposedly just championed, now found himself posthumously trashed by one of his own children and described by a manipulable media as a "worm," a "monster," a "bully," and a "villain." "Where I come from, they'd hang you for what he did," Chevalier Marty Richards now said. Soon Goldsmith was traipsing a doddering Mary Lea around the talk-show circuit to decry child abuse and, incidentally, to help her hawk her book.

Characteristically, Seward's other children said nothing publicly in defense of their father. Only Junior expressed some private doubts, attributing Mary Lea's claim to what he called her "need to be dramatic." Basia made her feelings on the subject known when Liza Minnelli wrote her soliciting funds for Brake the Cycle, an organization fighting child abuse. "I suggest you contact your friend, Mary Lee [sic] Richards, and her 'famous' husband, Marty," Basia replied. "Another suggestion would be to contact Barbara Goldsmith, who made so much money from her false accusations that my husband was a child abuser. He was as much a child abuser as I am Liza Minnelli." Basia nonetheless abandoned plans to name her new center on Central European studies after Seward. This hardly mattered, for the institute itself never got off the ground.

In late 1987 five of Mary Lea's six children took her to court. Their ostensible object was to block her trustees from forgiving the $7 million Mary Lea had borrowed from her trust; in reality, it was another Johnson will contest, with all of the usual props—mud, venom, talk of undue influence and incompetence, a wicked stepparent with "an insatiable desire for material wealth," disinherited children—everything, in fact, but a corpse. "I do not wish to see or hear from any of you again,"

Mary Lea wrote her children after they'd filed suit. "Understand that this is the last pain and humiliation I will allow you to inflict upon me. I have all intentions of cutting you out of my life both on a financial and personal level." Short of cash for legal fees, the Ryans turned to an unlikely angel: Basia. "We are outraged about our mother's vilifying your husband in her reprehensible quest for public attention," they wrote her. "We find her vicious attacks on our grandfather both irrational and utterly unbelievable." Basia never replied.

Over the ensuing months, Mary Lea accused her children of spreading rumors she had AIDS, was addicted to drugs or alcohol, had lost her mind, and was being manipulated by her husband. She also catalogued her own children's problems with brutal exactitude, describing Seward Ryan's drug addiction, Hillary Ryan's purported tendency to torture animals, and Quentin Ryan's wish to assassinate Marty Richards. The Ryans sought to have Mary Lea examined by a court-appointed psychiatrist. Meantime, two of Mary Lea's daughters-in-law shopped around *their* proposed book on the Johnsons, or, as they put it, on "the hideous reality of the descendants of the founder of Johnson & Johnson" and "the insanity and dysfunctionality" of the family they'd married into.

Mary Lea's much-abused body finally began to fail. In her own flurry of last-minute testamentary activity, she agreed to leave each of her estranged children at least $2 million once they promised not to contest her last will, which she signed from her hospital bed in Pittsburgh on April 17, 1990. Her hand was even shakier than Seward's; there was no indication that the witnesses, Alex Forger and Jeffrey Brinck, administered a mental-status examination before attesting to her competence. The document left Marty Richards half of her $86 million estate, as well as the homes in Southampton and Manhattan. On May 3, 1990, after a failed liver transplant, Mary Lea died. Marty gave her a send-off like their marriage: lavish, filled with an odd but poignant kind of love, paid for with her own money but a hell of a show anyway. While his private life remained brisk, Richards went through a long, public mourning. When, in 1991, the Producer Circle won a Tony, he saluted her on national television. Later that year, Mervyn Nelson, more estranged from Marty than ever, died of cancer. "The money destroyed him," Nelson lamented shortly before he passed on. Marty gave Nelson as grand a good-bye as Mary Lea, then threatened to sue Nelson's half-sister unless she handed over his ashes.

❋

Basia did not spend the aftermath of the trial in deep, self-critical introspection. "I didn't learn anything about myself," she told a reporter. "I was and I am and I will be the same person." She made *Spy* magazine's list of "12 Spooky People"; joined Ivan Boesky, Sydney Biddle Barrows, and Claus von Bülow as a guest of choice at wicked eighties-era dinner parties; and also made her debut in the *Forbes* 400. Estate managers, architects, accountants, lawyers, and friends came into and went out of her life in their normal way. Basia maintained a list of potential "fiancés," but there were few who fit her requirements: The lucky man had to be ten times richer than she. ("The first time you marry for love, the second for money," she explained.) Much of her time was spent in restless wanderings along the Continental social circuit. At a Save Venice fund-raiser, reported *European Travel & Life* magazine, the question on everyone's mind was "What *will* Basia Johnson wear next? It was hard to see because the widow of John Seward Johnson traveled with an entourage consisting of her English decorator-cum-art adviser and a bevy of hungry young men snapping at her heels like Venetian puppies."

John Fox consolidated his hold over Basia's affairs. And as his influence grew, Nina's waned—as did her prospects of ever collecting the moneys she'd forgone as part of the settlement. When the Zagats spent a day at Jasna Polana in July 1986, listening to Basia complain about the United States and how Americans failed to appreciate her properly, they could not have known it would be their last visit. By August Basia was attempting to sever all ties to Nina. But one night, in a brief burst of sentimentality over Bloody Marys at the Princeton Club, a choked-up Basia told Fox of a conversation she'd once had with Seward that, for whatever reason, she'd neglected to mention to her lawyers. In it, Seward had told her he'd always considered most lawyers to be self-interested, high-class crooks, and that he'd selected Nina not because she was the best lawyer available but because she was young and impressionable enough to develop loyalties to him. He'd provided for her so handsomely, he continued, because he wanted Nina to protect Basia once he was gone—something she would do properly, he was convinced, only were she totally beyond temptation herself.

Before long, Fox, too, had fallen from grace. Convinced he was trying to run her life, by early 1987, Basia had hired investigators to scour through his background; by June, she was accusing him of mismanagement, embezzlement, and membership in the KGB; by August she had fired him; and by November (assisted by her new chief of staff, one John Peach), she sued him. Fox promptly countersued and, in the end, collected $150,000 in damages. "I have had to wonder if with your wild swings of temper, suspicion and accusation, something in you is not almost determined to make an enemy out of me and so many others," Fox wrote her before all ties were cut. "You many times told me that you can be your own worst enemy. Having tried honestly, honorably and faithfully to work with you, I have come to feel the chilling truth of your wisdom."

Once the trial was over, S&C demanded an additional $5 million in fees, on top of the $5 million it had already collected. The second installment was based on the forty-five thousand additional billable hours that seventeen of its partners and eighty-seven other employees had poured into the case. By tradition, S&C had never sent itemized bills, favoring instead what John Foster Dulles quaintly called "suggestions embodying our own estimate of what is a fair charge." Basia demanded one anyway, and when it did not come, she refused to pay. In September Christ asked Marie Lambert for help collecting the money. By one count his motion to her contained eight references to how great a settlement S&C had procured for Basia, sixteen to how hard its lawyers had worked, seven to what a terrific job they had done, five to all the other business the firm turned away, three to how sterling S&C's reputation was, two to how much larger its tab could have been, and one to how the now-resolved claims proceeding, the one Christ had once said was "worth less than my necktie," had actually "posed a serious challenge" to her. If Milbank earned $10 million for collecting a measly $42 million for its clients, S&C all but said, surely it was entitled to at least that much for netting Basia ten times more.

Basia quite rightly called Christ's claims "absurd." The matter seemed headed for court before cooler heads at S&C and LeBoeuf Lamb, Basia's new counsel, prevailed. In the end, Basia gave S&C another $2.3 million, plus—at least as important—a pledge not to sue them for malpractice. But the ink on the agreement had barely dried before Basia grew disenchanted with it. So humiliating was her subsequent treatment of the LeBoeuf Lamb lawyers that they soon quit on her.

Having settled one account, however unhappily, Basia turned to another: Shearman & Sterling. In listing Basia among the world's wealthiest women, *Forbes* magazine had gone to press a bit hastily. During settlement negotiations, no one had bothered telling Basia one important fact: Most of her money would remain off-limits to her until the federal and state tax authorities signed off on the deal. As co-executors, Basia and Nina were personally liable for any additional taxes; and with Basia threatening to move back to Europe, Nina feared she alone would be left holding the bag. As far as Basia was concerned, however, the fortune was already hers, with no strings attached; Nina, she was con-vinced, was guarding the money solely to control her. She began pres-suring Shearman & Sterling to pressure Nina to hand over everything immediately.

Now was Shearman & Sterling's turn for a conflict of interest. As counsel for the executors of the Johnson estate, it represented both Nina and Basia. Basia still owed the firm $4 million and, worse, could sue for malpractice. But Nina, from Shearman & Sterling's point of view, had essentially outlived her usefulness. Henry Ziegler, who'd succeeded Tom Ford as head of Nina's department, had never had much use for her. A distant man to begin with, he distanced himself still further from her as her trial travails intensified. Now, as he might have put it, Nina was no longer "keeping the Johnsons happy." Moreover, since Nina was an employee as well as a client, S&S had leverage over her. Ziegler proposed what he called an "elegant solution" to the prob-lem: Nina should resign as Seward's co-executor, leaving Basia, as sole remaining executor, to pay out everything in Seward's estate to herself. On the advice of her own counsel, Robert Sisk of Hughes, Hubbard & Reed, Nina refused. Resigning, Sisk said, would violate her legal duties and still leave her liable for any taxes due. Then Shearman & Sterling played its trump card: It informed Nina that unless she could placate Basia, she would be fired. To underline its seriousness, it showed her a draft letter to that effect, awaiting only the signature of Robert Car-swell, the firm's managing partner.

Nina gave Basia some funds to tide her over—$35 million or so. She also tried keeping in touch, calling, writing, inviting her for dinner, sending her the latest *Zagat Restaurant Survey*. But by October 1986, Basia was sending Nina hate mail by Federal Express. "You fit fully the description which Seward once wrote to his daughter—'You are a trou-ble-maker beyond imagination,'" she wrote. "When I was settling the case I understood that you would be out of my life forever because you never did fit in and you never will." Between bad legal and financial advice, she charged, Nina had caused her to lose more than half of Seward's estate, and she remained a stumbling block now. "I will not take that easily," she concluded. "I warn you for the last time, get out of my life."

Basia hired a Miami lawyer named James Whisenand, gave him a $3 million war chest, and told him to build a case against Shearman & Sterling. For much of 1987, that was what he did. In April, five years to the day after Seward signed his last will, Basia sued Shearman

& Sterling, all of its partners, and Nina Zagat for $115 million. Hoping to get the case away from Marie Lambert and what Basia had come to consider New York's incestuous legal community, she filed suit in Florida. "Band-Aid heiress Barbara Johnson can't stay out of court," the *Daily News* reported. "Poor Babs. It's so hard to get by on $340-odd million nowadays."

Artificially and temporarily reunited by Basia's assault, Shearman & Sterling and Nina each retained counsel and filed counterclaims before Marie Lambert: Nina for the $1.8 million (plus $400,000 interest) to which she was entitled under the settlement as co-executor, Shearman & Sterling for its $4 million fee. As shabbily as Lambert had treated them, they concluded, she was certain to favor Nina over Basia and local lawyers over interlopers from Florida. But taking no chances, Shearman & Sterling hired a veteran friend-of-Marie: Thomas McGrath of Simpson, Thacher & Bartlett. Nina retained Arthur Liman of Paul, Weiss, Rifkind, Wharton & Garrison, who delegated the courtroom work to another professional Lambert friend: his partner, Bernard Greene, veteran of the Kimmelman case. Basia hired her own Lambert loyalist: Maurice Nessen, who'd represented the judge years earlier before the Judicial Conduct commissars.

For the next year the parties battled, publicly and privately. At one point, Shearman & Sterling learned that Basia's lawyers were seeking someone to plant wiretaps in their offices, and had the firm's phones—plus the home phones of some partners—swept for bugs. "When she won her $350 million, she gave everyone a V-for-Victory sign," Simpson, Thacher's William Manning told the *Times*. "Now that Shearman & Sterling wants to be paid, she has changed her mind." Soon Basia, who even without the millions more still coming her way was wealthy enough to be anywhere in the world she wished, found herself back in Marie Lambert's dreary courtroom, once more under attack. "The primary characteristic of this widow is an absolute lack of loyalty," Greene said, standing where the ghosts of Christ and Reilly still lingered. Whisenand and Nessen proved no more successful defending Basia than had Christ, lending credence to Arnold Bauman's thesis that in Lambert's courtroom Jesus H. Christ couldn't have represented Basia successfully.

This time, though, Basia took the stand. "I am fed up with the New York lawyers," she said at one point to explain her decision to sue in Florida. "They took me as a target because I am rich, so they can run their meters as much as they can. They let me down, Shearman and Sterling, and they [are] supposed to be the best firm in the country."

Whenever she could, she took potshots at Nina, recalling how, in a private conversation during settlement talks, Lambert opposed even the reduced fee Nina had agreed to accept. "You said 'shouldn't get anything. Should get zero,' " Basia recalled, looking fraternally at her old tormentor behind the bench. She denied complicity in the courtroom uprising ("It came as a complete surprise") or even that she'd ever shrieked so loudly at Izabella Poterewicz. ("The volume of the voice can be as high as the volume you put.") The first trial could not have gone worse for Basia if she had taken the stand. But with all its gaps and inconsistencies, her testimony at the second trial reminded everyone that it might not have gone much better, either.

By May, Basia was growing bored, and soon she capitulated once more, agreeing to pay Nina and Shearman & Sterling what she owed them, along with the legal fees. Once more, New York's great law firms had a feeding frenzy, with Basia, or Seward, picking up the tab. Oddly enough, the only parties unhappy at the outcome were the Johnson children. By signing the decree the parties had fashioned for her, Marie Lambert now ruled that Seward had been competent when he signed his will, and had not been the victim of undue influence. Once more, yet again, Seward's children marched into Surrogate's Court, Milbank at their side. "The Johnson children are rightly offended by this ex parte rewriting of history," Forger huffed. But this time, at least, Milbank lost. Lambert's remained the last judicial word on the case.

Though she had been so rudely treated there already, Nina remained at Shearman & Sterling two more years before quietly and unceremoniously departing for the more hospitable precincts of the *Zagat Restaurant Survey*. As for Basia, with no old associates left to sue, she was finally free to turn her gaze upward and eastward. Basia's raging disenchantment with America now extended to American causes. "Let the Rockefellers or other Americans give money to American charities!" she sneered to one supplicant. "A Polish maid does not have to give."

Within days of leaving Lambert's courtroom she journeyed to Gdańsk, where she took her place alongside Lech Wałęsa in the annual Corpus Christi procession. It was then, in what had been a casual conversation, that she pledged to save the Lenin Shipyard and strike a blow for the battered Polish economy. What she had in mind would dwarf the substantial contribution she had already made to Solidarity.

So excited was Wałęsa, Basia later recalled, that he started to hug and kiss her uncontrollably. He said, "'I won't sleep all night! I am saved! I am saved!'" she recalled. " 'I've met presidents, kings, queens, heads of state, the most important people in the world, but never someone as wonderful as you. From now on, when I see the world, I want to have you always at my side.' " By June 1, 1989, Basia signed a formal document with shipyard officials, pledging to spend up to $100 million of her money to purchase a 55 percent interest in the yard, "subject to the organization's books and cash flow being in shape." The parties had until January 1, 1990, to complete the deal.

Before she laid out a złoty, Basia basked. She appeared alongside Wałęsa, on the cover of *The New York Times Magazine*. In *Parade* magazine, her friend and traveling companion Iris Love called her "the Angel of Gdańsk" and "the Joan of Arc of Poland"; a French publication referred to her as "Notre Dame de Gdańsk." The Polish press described this wealthy but seemingly simple woman with near-religious awe. Priests praised her from the pulpit. "Let the Communists close the Lenin Shipyard," Father Henryk Jankowski, Solidarity's favorite priest, defiantly told his flock. "We will re-open the 'Gdańsk Piasecka-Johnson Yard.' " Along the ancient, dusty streets of Gdańsk, women pelted her with flowers, surrounded her limousine, clamored for her autograph. Color photographs of her (five hundred złotys for large, four hundred for wallet-sized) went on sale at the souvenir stand outside the shipyard gate. "God is helping her," Jankowski said. "Obviously, God wanted it this way."

Wałęsa flirted with her publicly—"What's a delicate woman like you doing in a shipyard with cranes and rusting metal?" he asked her. "You belong in a garden of flowers, or in a coffee shop, with me." Or, as he told a reporter, "I didn't think she'd be so first-rate, with such personal charm and courage. I thought that with all her money, she would walk around with a lot of cats and dogs and men carrying her bags. Instead, I found a simple, pretty girl—quiet, composed, unpretentious, and at the same time, quite great. In short: grand in her simplicity.

"I like Pani Basia as a woman, not only for her money," he continued. "I like to kiss her and I am quite happy that she still lets me. And I'm quite interested to see how long she lets me." The interpreter cautioned Wałęsa, the father of seven, that what he said could appear in *The New York Times*. "That's all right," he replied. "My wife doesn't read English."

From her suite on a high floor of Gdańsk's Hotel Hevelius, Basia overlooked her future domain. When some American senators visited in August, she asked them whether they'd seen "her" shipyard yet. Wearing a helmet with her name and the Solidarity logo on it, she took frequent walking tours of the premises, posing for photographs with workers. From the European Parliament in Strasbourg, to the

Polish-American Congress in Chicago, she carried her new gospel, preaching how her homeland, awakening after forty years of Communist slumber, was a "gold mine" for Western capitalists.

Amid the euphoria there were skeptics. Shipping experts doubted even the largest infusion of cash could make an antiquated facility competitive. Economists warned that the interests of Basia and of Solidarity, like capital and labor anywhere, were inherently antagonistic. Cynics likened her proposed investment to the kind of glorious but doomed gesture to which, Balzac once wrote, the Poles are peculiarly prone. And old associates believed Basia was too impulsive, too mercurial, too capricious, ever to follow through. As she watched Jane Pauley interview her on the *Today* show, Nina couldn't help but think that Basia already looked ambivalent. What the shipyard deal really demonstrated, Nina believed, was why Seward had wanted Basia to inherit his fortune in trust.

Sure enough, as romantic impulsiveness yielded to hardheaded number-crunching between Polish officials and the swarms of consultants Basia brought in, the giddiness quickly gave way to impatience, misunderstanding, and bitterness. Polish leaders accused Basia of trying to buy the facility for nothing; Polish workers feared a ban on strikes, massive layoffs, and pay cuts as their purported savior streamlined operations. Basia accused the government of dragging its feet, misrepresenting the terms of the deal, and sabotaging her efforts through leaks to the press. The January 1 deadline came and went. Within days, the picture of Basia with Pope John Paul II posted by the shipyard gate disappeared.

Under the headline MIRAGE BOUGHT WITH GREEN, one Polish newspaper related how even Wałęsa had grown disillusioned with her. "How can you do business with a dame?" he asked. After spending $7 million on the talks, Basia abruptly aborted the deal. "I was a pioneer, and pioneers are sometimes misunderstood," she later said. In fact, it appeared she simply lost interest in the whole thing and was looking for a fig leaf. Nonetheless, the episode left Basia a celebrity, if not necessarily a heroine, in her native land. In a poll, high school students were asked to name the most famous Polish woman in history. Ten percent of them named Madame Curie. Eighty percent named Basia.

Basia remained active in Europe. She began collecting homes there the way she had once bought Old Master paintings, purchasing properties in Cracow, Vienna, Monte Carlo, and Rome. She bought more furniture to fit in them, including the 1726 Badminton Cabinet for $15.2 million. In April 1990 she mounted an exhibition of her religious paintings—with some of her newly found pretentiousness she entitled the display "*Opus Sacrum*"—in the Warsaw National Museum. But even the finest arts could not rehabilitate a reputation left in tatters by the Gdańsk shipyard fiasco. In an essay appearing in 1992, a Polish writer depicted Basia as a megalomaniac, and warned any young Polish women tempted to emulate her that Basia personified the dangers of marrying money. Basia promptly sued his publisher for libel.

In the meantime Basia's life in America continued to atrophy. One of her few friends, the art dealer Harry Bailey, died of AIDS. His illness led her in turn to sever her ties to the ever-faithful Jan Waligura. She had grown furious with him for failing to warn her Bailey had AIDS, then letting her kiss him on the cheek, and banished Waligura from her life. Finally, even Peach was canned. Twenty-two years after she arrived in America, Basia had returned to what she had been the moment she got off the plane from Rome: completely and utterly alone.

In March 1990 a Princeton township official visited Jasna Polana's bomb shelter and came back awestruck by its two 50,000-pound doors, its crematorium, its periscopes, and maids' quarters. "It's a marvelous, marvelous thing," the official said. But as time passed, it seemed increasingly unlikely it would ever be occupied, and not just because the Cold War was coming to a close. Around Princeton, word spread that Jasna Polana was on the market. Rumors abounded that it would soon be sold to a Japanese businessman or a Kuwaiti prince, or converted into an executive retreat, conference center, or golf course—one that would surely have the world's largest and fanciest clubhouse. With Seward still squirreled away at the Hillcrest Memorial Gardens, with no signs that he would ever be moved north, suddenly it seemed poor Princey would soon have Jasna Polana all to himself. As for Basia, who could say where she would eventually land, or whether she would find happiness or serenity along the way?

INDEX